Current Psychotherapies

EDITORS

Raymond J. Corsini

Danny Wedding

CURRENT PSYCHOTHERAPIES

Fifth Edition

F.E. Peacock Publishers, Inc.
Itasca, Illinois

Cover Image: Robert Kristofik/The Image Bank

Copyright © 1995
F.E. Peacock Publishers, Inc.
All rights reserved.
Printed in the U.S.A.
Library of Congress Catalog Card No. 94-74615
ISBN 0-87581-392-5
Printing 10 9 8 7 6 5
Year 00 99 98 97

To My Teachers

Rudolf Dreikurs, J. L. Moreno, Carl Rogers

—RJC—

Outline of Book

Contents

Contributors

Jacob A. Arlow, M.D.
Clinical Professor of Psychiatry,
New York University College of Medicine,
New York, New York

Aaron T. Beck, M.D.
Professor of Psychiatry, University of
Pennsylvania, Philadelphia, Pennsylvania

Adam Blatner, M.D.
Private Practice, Austin, Texas

Raymond J. Corsini, Ph.D.
Affiliate, Graduate faculty, University of
Hawaii, Honolulu, Hawaii

Claire Douglas, Ph.D.
Private Practice, Malibu, California

Albert Ellis, Ph.D.
Institute for Rational-Emotive Therapy,
New York, New York

William Glasser, M.D.
Private Practice, Canoga Park, California

Herbert Goldenberg, Ph.D.
Emeritus Professor, California State University,
Los Angeles, California

Irene Goldenberg, Ed.D.
Professor of Psychiatry, University of
California—Los Angeles, Los Angeles,
California

Arnold A. Lazarus, Ph.D.
Distinguished Professor, Graduate School of
Applied and Professional Psychology, Rutgers
University, Piscataway, New Jersey

Alexander Lowen, M.D.
Director, International Institute for
Bioenergetic Analysis, New York, New York

Rollo May, Ph.D.
Deceased

Harold H. Mosak, Ph.D.
Private Practice, Chicago, Illinois

Nathaniel J. Raskin, Ph.D.
Professor of Psychiatry and Behavioral
Sciences, Northwestern University Medical
School, Chicago, Illinois

Carl R. Rogers, Ph.D.
Deceased

Roger Walsh, M.D., Ph.D.
Professor of Psychiatry, Social Sciences, and
Philosophy, University of California, Irvine,
California

Danny Wedding, Ph.D.
Director, Missouri Institute of Mental Health,
St. Louis, Missouri

Marjorie E. Weishaar, Ph.D.
Private Practice, Providence, Rhode Island

G. Terence Wilson, Ph.D.
Oscar K. Buros Professor of Psychology,
Rutgers University, Piscataway, New Jersey

Robert Wubbolding, Ed.D.
Professor, Counseling, Xavier University,
Cincinnati, Ohio

Irvin Yalom, M.D.
Professor of Psychiatry and Behavioral
Sciences, Stanford University School of
Medicine, Stanford, California

Acknowledgments

At the end of every edition, we ask colleagues as well as all professors known to be using *Current Psychotherapies* as a text to give us suggestions for the next edition. The people listed below have in various ways made worthwhile suggestions, and we thank them for their contributions.

Mary Ballou
Northeastern University

Bernie Beitman
University of Missouri–Columbia

Stephen F. Bono
University of Maryland

John L. Carew
Cambridge College

Carolyn Dillon
Boston University

Glen Eskedal
Suffolk University

Richard F. Heath
Ramapo College

Barry Farber
Columbia University

Bruce Forgus
University of Idaho

Brenda Freeman
University of Wyoming

William Frey
Middlebury College

Bagher Ghobary
University of Teheran

Glenn E. Good
University of Missouri

David Harder
Tufts University

James Hennessy
Fordham University

Ishu Ishiyama
University of British Columbia

William King
City University of New York

Wayne Klug
University of Massachusetts

John R. Korte
University of Dayton

Arthur Lerner
Los Angeles City College

Mary Livingstone
Louisiana Technical School

Mildred Malick
Hunter College

Margaret McCluskey
St. Louis University

John McKinnon
Connecticut College

Robert Roth
Keane College

Rodney Skager
University of California–Los Angeles

Adaline Tryon
Salisbury State University

Nancy Webb
Fordham University

Michael Wogan
Rutgers University

Preface

This fifth edition of *Current Psychotherapies* is its most extensive revision so far. Two new chapters have been added: Reality Therapy and Current Issues in Psychotherapy. Psychoanalysis, Analytic Psychotherapy, and Family Therapy have new authors. Rational-Emotive Therapy is now relabeled Rational Emotive Behavior Therapy, and it has been completely rewritten. Behavior Therapy has been extensively revised, and all chapters retained from prior editions have been updated.

From its beginning, *Current Psychotherapies* has been based on a number of principles that have made it the most successful text of its kind:

Chapters selected represent the most important systems in the current practice of psychotherapy. Since psychotherapy is in constant change, deciding what to put in new editions and what to take out calls for a great deal of research. The opinions of professors were central in determining changes. Professors who have taught from this book at least two years are asked at the end of each edition what they would want in the next edition and what they no longer want in the current one. Their diverse opinions helped us decide what changes to make.

The most competent available authors are recruited. Newly established systems are described by their founders; older systems are covered by those best qualified to describe their systems.

This book is highly disciplined Each author follows an outline in which the various sections are limited in length and structure. The purpose of this feature is to make the systems as comparable to one another as possible, so that one can read the book "horizontally" (from section to section across the various systems) as well as in the usual "vertical" manner (chapter to chapter). Those who want to understand psychotherapy in depth should read the book twice: first vertically and then horizontally.

Current Psychotherapies is carefully edited. Every section is examined to make certain its contents are appropriate and clear. In the twenty-five-year history of this text, only one chapter was ever accepted in its first draft. Some chapters have been returned to their original authors up to four times before finally being accepted.

Chapters are as concise as they can possibly be and still cover the systems completely. In the prior edition, Dr. Judith MacMahon went over the entire manuscript to see if she could find anything to cut; in this edition, Dr. Barbara Cubic repeated the same process. Suggested changes were approved by Dr. Wedding and me, then by the authors. In response to a demand that the chapters be shorter, the section on Management was dropped. This is a topic of special interest only to professionals; some of the material in that section that might be of interest to students has been retained in the section on Treatment.

The glossary has been expanded. A good way to begin any chapter would be to first read relevant entries in the glossary, thereby generating a mind-set that will facilitate understanding the systems. Personality theorists tend to invent new words when no existing word suffices. This clarifies their ideas, but it also makes understanding their chapters more difficult. A careful study of the glossary will reward the reader.

Thanks to many who have assisted. In Honolulu, Kristine Altwies was helpful in various ways; in St. Louis, Vicki Eichthorn assisted Dr. Wedding. Linda Sage helped revise Chapter 14, and Janet Tilden reviewed the whole book, striving for linguistic perfection. As always our wives, Kleona (Corsini) and Cynthia (Wedding) were of help in various ways, and they seldom complained about the hundreds of hours we spent on this edition.

Our authors deserve special thanks, particularly those in this edition for the first time. They were patient and forgiving when their manuscripts were returned, often mutilated, with requests sometimes for dozens of changes. Our recommendations almost always had to do with clarifying language. In all cases, authors complied when we explained this edition would be read by more than one hundred thousand students.

Dr. Wedding has read and approved every new chapter and every change, and consequently this edition represents our combined editorial judgments, but since I am the responsible editor for this edition, any errors can be attributed to me.

Raymond Corsini
Honolulu, Hawaii

1 Introduction

Raymond J. Corsini

Psychotherapy cannot be defined with any precision. A definition might go as follows:

> Psychotherapy is a formal process of interaction between two parties, each party usually consisting of one person but with the possibility that there may be two or more people in each party, for the purpose of amelioration of distress in one of the two parties relative to any or all of the following areas of disability or malfunction: cognitive functions (disorders of thinking), affective functions (suffering or emotional discomforts), or behavioral functions (inadequacy of behavior), with the therapist having some theory of personality's origins, development, maintenance and change along with some method of treatment logically related to the theory and professional and legal approval to act as a therapist.

The definition may appear rather comprehensive. Nevertheless, some modes of therapy will not fit it.

Would the system of psychotherapy that Sigmund Freud underwent, about which Karen Horney (1942) wrote a book, and which Theodore Reik (1948) claimed to be the best of all therapies fit this definition? The system is *self-therapy*. In self-therapy there is only one party; there is no formality and no professional or legal approval, and yet it certainly is therapy.

If we examine various theories and procedures in psychotherapy, we find a bewildering set of ideas and behaviors. There have been systems of therapy that had no therapist (Schmidhoffer, 1952); systems in which the therapist says and does nothing (Bion, (1948); systems in which patients are asked to scream or to strike out (Bach & Goldberg, 1975; Janov, 1970); methods in which the therapist makes fun of the patient, treating him or her with apparent disrespect (Farrelly & Brasma, 1974), and methods that treat the patient or client with utmost respect (Losoncy, 1981); methods in which patients are treated as children (Painter & Vernon, 1981); methods that stress religion (Lair & Lair, 1973; van Kaam, 1976); and methods that are conglomerates of a wide variety of procedures (Gazda, 1981; Shostrom & Montgomery, 1978).

What one authority considers to be psychotherapy may be completely different from how other authorities see the process.

Counseling and psychotherapy are the same qualitatively; they differ only quantitatively. There is nothing that a psychotherapist does that a counselor does not do. Table 1.1 illustrates this basic point.

No definition can be made that will include all psychotherapies and exclude all counseling methods. Various attempts to separate the psychotherapies and exclude all counseling methods have failed. The concept that psychotherapy goes into depth, while counseling does not, is gainsaid by procedures such as behavior modification that operate at the level of symptom removal (Wolpe, 1958). Behavior modifiers could hardly be called counselors, because they do not counsel. Also, when we have a term such as *nondirective counseling,* we have a semantic absurdity.

❖ COUNSELING AND PSYCHOTHERAPY

The terms *counseling* and *psychotherapy* probably seem interchangeable to many people, but they tend to have different meanings for people in the helping professions. Generally, counseling is understood by helping professionals to be a relatively short process, often occurring in one session and rarely comprising more than five sessions, whereas psychotherapy usually runs for many sessions and can even continue for years. Counseling is usually seen as problem-oriented, while psychotherapy is person-oriented. As Table 1.1 indicates, the actual processes that occur in counseling and psychotherapy are identical, but they do differ relative to the time spent, and thus quantity affects quality.

TABLE 1.1 ❖ **Estimate of Percent of Time Spent by "Counselors" and "Psychotherapists" in Professional Activities***

Process	Counseling	Psychotherapy
Listening	20	60
Questioning	15	10
Evaluating	5	5
Interpreting	1	3
Supporting	5	10
Explaining	15	5
Informing	20	3
Advising	10	3
Ordering	9	1

*Based on R. J. Corsini, "Counseling and Psychotherapy" in E. F. Borgatta and W. W. Lambert (Eds.), *Handbook of Personality Theory and Research* (Chicago: Rand McNally, 1968).

Essentially, counseling stresses the giving of information, advice, and orders by someone considered to be an expert in a particular area of human behavior, while psychotherapy is a process of helping people discover why they think, feel, and act in unsatisfactory ways. A counselor is primarily a teacher, while a psychotherapist is essentially a detective.

A simple example will help illustrate the difference between counseling and psychotherapy. Say that a married couple comes to a professional helper (a psychiatrist, psychologist, social worker, nurse practitioner, etc.) for help in their marriage. The helper puts on her counseling hat, listens as they tell their stories, asks questions and finally gives information, advice, and "orders" (that is to say, she may insist that the couple must follow her suggestions if they are to achieve their goals). After all, if they came to her for counseling, they must be prepared to make suggested changes.

Let us assume the counselor gives the couple the following information: Many marriages are unhappy because of little things, but if a couple can communicate their dissatisfactions to each other and agree by means of a mutual contract to change their behavior, the marriage may change from being unhappy to happy. She then advises them to establish a new contract within their marriage. Let us assume the couple agrees to establish a mutual contract. The husband states that he wants his wife to stop smoking, and the wife wants her husband to put away his clothes and belongings rather than scattering them all over the house (two common complaints in marriages).

Consequently, the helper, working as a counselor, helps the couple establish a contract relative to the wife's smoking and the husband's sloppiness in the house.

Now, let us assume that both partners live up to their agreements and that thereby marital harmony is established. The counseling has been successful.

Now let us assume a different scenario. The couple returns to report that they are still unhappy. The wife has stopped smoking, but the husband is still leaving his possessions all over the house. As the result of further discussions, the helper suggests that the husband may need psychotherapy to try to discover why, even though he has agreed to stop this behavior, he continues it. Say that the husband accepts the suggestion and decides to have psychotherapy.

The professional now puts on her psychotherapy hat. From now on, she no longer views herself as an expert on marriage who can give information, advice, and orders but instead sees herself as a facilitator, helping the husband to understand himself in general, and specifically to find out why he was not able to keep to his agreement to be neat in the house.

The helper may give no information, advice, or orders, but may act in any of a variety of unusual ways. For example, if she is a follower of Carl Rogers she will not ask or answer questions, and she will be unwilling to give advice or suggestions. In this book we discuss more than a dozen ways of thinking and acting in therapy. The helper may have her own eclectic theory, and her methods of operating may be quite diverse.

Let us say that the therapy is successful, that the reason for the husband's resistance is uncovered, and that a favorable change in his behavior then occurs and the marriage is happy.

Successful therapy may result regardless of theory and the method used. But what is important to recognize here is that in acting as a psychotherapist the helper did not presume to be an expert on marriage but rather served as a kind of detective relative to the husband's inability or unwillingness to conform to his own agreement. The helper as the therapist was a partner or collaborator with the husband to achieve a new state of being.

Consequently, counselors are generally people who have considerable knowledge and expertise in specific areas of behavior. There are marriage and family counselors, educational and vocational counselors, counselors for people who abuse substances such as alcohol, for people who are handicapped in particular ways or have special problems such as chronic or contagious illnesses. Counselors depend on their specialized knowledge and their common sense. On the other hand, psychotherapists are generalists who tend to have any of a variety of unusual theories or combinations of theories and who may use one or more procedures to try to achieve desired results.

❖ PATIENT OR CLIENT

In the first four editions of this book, in the Adlerian chapter, Dr. Harold Mosak used the term *patient*; in this edition he changed this term to *client*. Some of our authors use one or the other of the two terms, and some use both.

Psychotherapists who come out of a medical orientation tend to see those they work with as patients, while those who come from other orientations tend to see them as clients. So, it is possible for two therapists to see the same person at the same time in multiple therapy, with one viewing that person as a patient and the other therapist seeing that same person as a client.

Neither term is really satisfactory. *Patient* implies illness, and *client* implies a business relationship. Someday, someone may coin a term that more exactly describes the role of the person who is undergoing psychotherapy. Meanwhile, in this book, every author uses whatever term he or she feels most comfortable with.

All modes of trying to help people improve themselves via symbolic methods can be called *psychotherapy*, just as all methods to help improve psychological functioning through medications, surgery, electric shock, and other somatic procedures may be called *psychiatry*. Consequently, the interview, hypnosis, role-playing, projective techniques, and the like that we shall take up in this book can be considered procedures in counseling/psychotherapy, but it is best, in my judgment, to call them all processes of psychotherapy. Therefore, when Carl Rogers repeats what you have said, using his own terminology (as he did with me when I was in therapy with him), *this is psychotherapy*; and when Rudolph Dreikurs, an Adlerian, points out basic life-style errors (as he did for me when I was in therapy with him), *this is psychotherapy*; and when Albert Ellis contradicts your point of view (as he often has with me), *this is psychotherapy*; and when J.L. Moreno has people play different roles in front of a group (as I did when working with him) then *this is psychotherapy*.

A number of years ago, in Paris, I met with a French colleague, and during the course of our conversation I mentioned psychotherapy. "Ah," she said, "*Psychothérapie comme ça—ou comme ça?*" (Psychotherapy like this—or like this?) At the first *ça* she put the palms of her hands about an inch apart, and at the second *ça* she moved her hands out as far as she could, with the palms still facing each other. She was asking me whether I had a narrow conception of psychotherapy or a wide one. We can do the same thing with the hands vertically and ask about the depth of psychotherapy. Essentially, depth is a function of time spent in therapy rather than a matter of technique, and two people with the same theory and technique will vary with respect to depth, depending primarily on the time spent with the client. (I call the subjects of psychotherapy *clients* if I see them in a private office and *patients* if they are in a hospital or institution.)

❖ AN UNUSUAL EXAMPLE OF PSYCHOTHERAPY

About fifty years ago, when I was working as a psychologist at Auburn Prison in New York, I participated in what I believe was the most successful and elegant psychotherapy I have ever done. One day an inmate, who had made an appointment, came into my office. He was a fairly attractive man in his early 30s. I pointed to a chair, he sat down, and I waited to find out what he wanted. The conversation went somewhat as follows:

> Prisoner: I am leaving on parole Thursday.
> Corsini: Yes?
> P: I did not want to leave until I thanked you for what you had done for me.
> C: What was that?
> P: When I left your office about two years ago, I felt like I was walking on air. When I went into the prison yard, everything looked different, even the air smelled different. I was a new person. Instead of going over to the group I usually hung out with—they were a bunch of thieves—I went over to another group of square Johns [prison jargon for noncriminal types]. I changed from a cushy job in the kitchen to the machine shop, where I could learn a trade. I started going to the prison high school and I now have a high school diploma. I took a correspondence course in drafting and I have a drafting job when I leave Thursday. I started back to church even though I had given up my religion many years ago. I started writing to my family and they have come up to see me and they remember you in their prayers. I now have hope. I know who and what I am. I know I will succeed in life. I plan to go to college. You have freed me. I used to think you bug doctors [prison slang for psychologists and psychiatrists] were for the birds, but now I know better. Thanks for changing my life.

I listened to this tale in wonderment, because to the best of my knowledge I had never spoken with him. I looked at his folder and the only notation there was that I had given him an IQ test about two years before.

"Are you sure it was me?" I finally said. "I am not a psychotherapist, and I have no memory of ever having spoken to you. What you are reporting is the sort of personality and behavior change that takes many years to accomplish—and I certainly haven't done anything of the kind."

"It was you, all right," he replied with great conviction, "and I will never forget what you said to me. It changed my life."

"What was that?" I asked.

"You told me I had a high IQ," he replied.

With one sentence of five words I had (inadvertently) changed this person's life.

Let us try to understand this event. If you are clever enough to understand why this man changed so drastically as a result of hearing these five words "You have a high IQ," my guess is that you have the capacity to be a good therapist.

I asked him why this sentence about his IQ had such a profound effect, and I learned that up to the time that he heard these five words he had always thought of himself as "stupid" and "crazy"—terms that had been applied to him many times by his family, teachers, and friends. In school, he had always gotten poor grades, which confirmed his belief in his mental subnormality. His friends did not approve of the way he thought and called him crazy. And so he was convinced that he was both an ament (low intelligence) and a dement (insane). But when I said, "You have a high IQ," he had an "aha!" experience that explained everything. In a flash, he understood why he could solve crossword puzzles better than any of his friends. He now knew why he read long novels rather than comic books, why he preferred to play chess rather than checkers, why he liked symphonies rather than jazz. With great and sudden intensity he realized through my five words that he was really normal and bright and not crazy or stupid. No wonder he had felt as if he were walking on air when he left my office two years before!

His interpretation of my five words generated a complete change of self-concept—and consequently a change in both his behavior and his feelings about himself and others.

In short, I had performed psychotherapy in a completely innocent and informal way. Even though what happened in no way accords to the definition given earlier, even though there was no agreement between us, no theory, no intention of changing him—the five-word comment had a most pronounced effect, and so it *was* psychotherapy.

I have had two clients—each seen for more than ten years—and in neither case did I do much for them, as far as I can tell.

❖ COMPARISONS OF THEORIES

Karl Popper (1968), the philosopher of science who wrote *Conjectures and Refutations*, makes the astute observation that Marxists, Freudians, and Adlerians are all able to find evidence of the validity of their theories in any aspect of human behavior. In this book he states:

> During the summer of 1919...I began to feel more and more dissatisfied with these theories...and I began to feel dubious about their claim to scientific status... Why are they so different from Newton's theory and especially from the theory of relativity?...It was not my doubting the truth of these theories which bothered me...what worried me was...that these...theories, though posing as sciences, had in fact more in common with primitive myths than with science: that they resembled astrology more than astronomy. (p. 34)

Popper goes on to say that he at the time had no reason to believe that Einstein's theory was correct, but Eddington's observation that light did not travel in a straight line but was bent by the sun due to gravitational attraction gave proof of the incorrectness of previous theories (such as Newton's) and so established Einstein's theory as superior to Newton's theory. Popper concluded: (1) it is easy to find confirmation of the validity of theories, (2) confirmation should only be considered if it results from a *risky prediction*, (3) the more a theory "forbids," the better it is, (4) a theory that is not possibly refutable is a poor theory, (5) genuine tests of theories are attempts to refute them, and (6) the only good evidence is negative evidence—i.e., an unsuccessful attempt to refute a particular theory.

Unfortunately, if we accept Popper's contention that the scientific status of any theory rests on its potential for falsification, no theory of psychotherapy qualifies as scientific.

❖ MODES OF PSYCHOTHERAPY

All psychotherapies are methods of learning. All psychotherapies are intended to change people: to make them think differently (cognition), to make them feel differently (affection), and to make them act differently (behavior). Psychotherapy is learning: it may be learning something new or relearning something one has forgotten; it may be learning how to learn or it may be unlearning; paradoxically, it may even be learning what one already knows.

Cognition

There are two general ways we learn: directly by experience, or indirectly by symbols.

To give a simple example: A child about three years old sees the toast shooting up from a toaster and goes to touch the shiny gadget. The child has no idea that the toaster is hot. Now, how can the child learn that a toaster can be hot and can hurt? One way would be for the child to touch the toaster, thus learning by direct experience. Another way is by symbols (words), by being told: "When we use the toaster, it gets hot, and if you touch it you will be burned."

In both cases, the child learns—in one case, actively (through experience) and in another case, passively (through information).

Some therapists tend to use "active" methods, and their clients essentially learn on their own, while some therapists tend to make their clients passive learners. Two strongly contrasting learning styles are represented by the methodologies of Carl Rogers and Albert Ellis. In psychoanalysis, both modes occur. For example, while free associating, the patient may be said to be learning actively. Let us show this by a hypothetical example:

> Patient: "And I really think my mother liked my brother more than she liked me. I can't understand why. I tried so hard to win her affection, but somehow I never was able to make her really like me. But recently when I spoke about this with my brother, he told me he always thought that I was Mother's favorite. How could this be? Could I have misinterpreted my mother? He thought I was the favorite and I thought he was. Who was? Maybe no one? Maybe Mamma liked us both equally, or as equally as possible. How did we come to have opposite conclusions? I think we are just both pessimists, that's what it is! I am sure of it, both of us misinterpreted Mother...."

This is an example of someone talking to himself, conducting a self-analysis, engaged in active learning.

An example of passive learning follows:

> C: I had the funniest dream. I was being chased by a rooster, and I was running for my life, and I knew if I got to Lokonner Bay that I would be safe.
> T: How do you spell that?
> C: I don't know. It is pronounced LOKONNER BAY.
> T: And you don't know any such place?
> C: No.
> T: Can you figure out what Lokonner means?
> C: I have been thinking all day about it. It makes no sense to me.
> T: Should I tell you what I think it means?
> C: Please. I have absolutely no idea.
> T: Well, dreams are all symbols. The rooster that is chasing you is a symbol of the male sexual organ, so you are running away from sex. But you believe you will be safe if you can get to Lokonner Bay.
> C: But what does Lokonner Bay mean? I have never heard of such a place.
> T: Lokonner is probably a contraction for "Love, honor, and obey." What you are saying in your dream is this: Some man is pressuring you to have sex and you want him to marry you. You are afraid to have sex, but if you can get him to marry you (love, honor, and obey), you will be safe.

The examples illustrate two general ways of learning in psychotherapy: actively through self-analysis and passively through being helped to understand the meaning of a dream.

Behavior

Learning can also occur through action. For example, during World War I, Ernst Simmel was a German army psychiatrist, concerned with curing German soldiers who were suffering from what was then called shell shock (Simmel, 1949). Believing that their condition was caused by repressed hatred of their officers, he gave these men bayoneted rifles and had them attack straw-filled dummies dressed as German officers.

The modality of treatment was physical action, what Eugene Landry (1994) calls disjunctive therapy. Plain physical exercise is believed to be psychotherapeutic by some people. Action is used in a number of psychotherapies.

One argument for body therapies is the assertion that there is no mind. If we can affect the body, that is all that is needed: the body learns, the body is real, all else is an illusion. A contrary argument for body therapies is that the mind does exist, that conditions of the body affect the mind, and that if we work from the outside in, by changing the body we can change the mind. An example might be plastic surgery. Changing someone's looks can affect how that person views himself or herself.

Other examples of physical behavior as psychotherapy would include complex physical activities, such as role-playing, or doing therapeutic "homework," that is, doing under direction things one would not ordinarily do, such as asking for a date or looking for a job. As in the case of cognitive therapies, behavioral work in therapy can range from active to passive. In examining the various systems in this book, the reader may want to consider how much physical behavior is called for in the particular therapy.

Affection

A third modality in psychotherapy is affection, known more popularly as emotions or feelings. The therapist may believe that this modality will be most effective with a particular client or patient, and so will do things to stir up the person: to raise the individual's emotional state through attempts to make him or her fearful, anxious, angry, hopeful, and so on. We cannot really work directly with the emotions and must reach them indirectly through the intellect or the body.

Emotions are an important part of human psychology. However, we cannot manipulate emotions in the sense that we can manipulate thinking or behaving. Some systems of psychotherapy are intended to reduce or negate emotions, seeing them as hindering the therapeutic process. Adlerian psychotherapy, for example, is essentially a cognitive therapy, and Adlerians usually see emotions as sabotaging efforts in the therapeutic process. However, in psychodrama, for example, both the words that the therapist will employ and the behavior directed by the other actors are intended to generate strong emotions.

Some people see emotions as epiphenomena accompanying but not affecting therapeutic change, others see emotions as powerful agents leading to change, and still others see emotions as evidence of change. The whole issue of the relationship of emotions to psychotherapy is unsettled. The reader would do well to attempt to see the place of emotions in the various systems described.

All therapies are essentially combinations of all three of these modalities. While some are rather pure in that they attempt to deal only with the body, the intellect, or the emotions, elements of each apply in most cases. Thus, for example, in rational emotive behavior therapy, even though rational thinking is utilized for the most part in dealing with the patient, the therapist may give the client direct orders to do certain things (homework). In cognitive therapy, emotionally upsetting situations will develop.

A therapist may think that improvement is a function of one element, but the curative process may actually be something else. It may not be a message that generates a change, but rather the interpretation that the client gives to it. Were exactly the same treatment to be done by a robot, it might not have any beneficial psychological effect. Change may well result from the interpretation, "Someone cares for me enough to do this to me."

One final common pathway for all therapies is a new way of seeing life, a reevaluation of self and others. If so, then all therapies are essentially cognitive. Still another way of considering psychotherapy is to see it as a process of "selling"—of trying to help a person to accept a new view of self and of others. From this point of view, the psychotherapist is a persuader or a facilitator attempting to change opinions.

A clear-cut example of persuasion would be attempting to do psychotherapy with someone with a fixed paranoid delusion. A more common example is dealing with a person with incapacitating feelings of inferiority by trying "to sell him" on the notion that he is really OK. Another common example would be dealing with someone with mistaken ideas about marriage or parenting. In all these cases, the therapist is, in a real sense, a salesperson attempting to sell new ideas, new concepts, and new behaviors.

❖ MECHANISMS OF THERAPY

One of the most exciting meetings I ever attended included a major presentation by Carl Rogers on the necessary and sufficient conditions for psychotherapy. It was a most logical and impressive speech and it deeply affected me. However, the next speaker was Albert Ellis, who had been asked to comment on Rogers's paper. Ellis stated that in 25 years of clinical experience he had had many successful cases but none of Rogers's criteria seemed to him to be either necessary or sufficient.

There was not then and there is not now any consensus about what constitutes the basis for change in psychotherapy. Each contributor to this volume uses a section titled *Mechanisms of Psychotherapy* to discuss what makes psychotherapy work. However, I have my own ideas that I would like to share with readers at this point.

Some forty years ago, with a psychiatrist colleague, Dr. Bina Rosenberg, I searched through over 300 articles to identify the critical elements necessary for changing people (Corsini & Rosenberg, 1955). We found 220 statements such as "People change when they think that others believe in them" and "The realization that they are not alone makes the difference." We eliminated redundant items and performed a "clinical factor analysis" and identified nine factors.

Cognitive Factors

Universalization. Clients improve when they realize that they are not alone, that others have similar problems, and that human suffering is universal.

Insight. Growth occurs as clients increasingly come to understand themselves and others and gain different perspectives on their own motives and behaviors.

Modeling. People benefit from watching other people. A client may model himself or herself on the therapist.

Affective Factors

Acceptance. This factor reflects the sense of getting unconditional positive regard, especially from the therapist.

Altruism. Change can result from the recognition that one is the recipient of the love and care of the therapist or other members of the group or from being the one who provides love and care to others as well as feeling he is helping others.

Transference. This factor identifies the emotional bond that occurs between the therapist and the client or between clients in a group setting.

Behavioral Factors

Reality testing. Change becomes possible when clients experiment with new behaviors in the safety of the therapy hour, receiving support and feedback from the therapist and other group members.

Ventilation. This factor encompasses those statements attesting to the value of "blowing off steam" through shouting, crying, or displaying anger in a context in which one could still feel accepted.

Interaction. Clients improve when they are able to openly admit to the group that there is something wrong with themselves or their behavior.

I believe these nine factors encapsulate the basic mechanisms of therapeutic change. Close examination of this model reveals that the cognitive factors imply "Know yourself," the affective factors tell us "Love your neighbor," and the behavioral factors essentially suggest "Do good works." Perhaps there is nothing new under the sun, for this is what philosophers have told us for millennia: know thyself, love thy neighbor, and do good works.

❖ THE CURRENT SITUATION IN PSYCHOTHERAPY

Corsini (1981) listed 250 different systems of psychotherapy, but as of 1994 there are probably more than 400 such systems. Just as there are some religions that are well known and well accepted, so too, some psychotherapies are well known and well accepted. And just as there are religions viewed as unorthodox and absurd, there are systems of psychotherapy that exist on the fringe of traditional approaches.

I was originally trained as a Rogerian therapist (which I believe is probably the best way for a would-be therapist to start training—and for some people, the best way to remain). After ten years' experience with this mode of therapy, I applied for a job at a prestigious institute, and while being interviewed I was asked how I dealt with the problem of transference. I think I could not have shocked my learned colleagues more had I slapped them on the face when I replied, "To the best of my knowledge, none of my clients ever formed a transference relationship with me." They held their mouths open, staring first at me and then at each other, unable to believe what they had heard me say. For this particular group, transference was a necessary factor in psychotherapy, and for someone who claimed to be a psychotherapist to deny transference was unthinkable.

In psychotherapy, ideological enclaves are found. Some enclaves consist of people who believe that they have the right, the final, the complete, and the only answer—and that all other systems are incomplete, tentative, weak, or simply mistaken.

People within these enclaves (known as schools of therapy) tend to communicate mostly with others they meet at conventions. They read each other's writings, and they tend over time to develop specialized vocabularies. They reinforce one another by recounting their successes with the former clients of therapists of different persuasions, "proving" to one another the superiority of their way of thinking and acting. As time goes on, within any particular method of psychotherapy, alternative positions tend to develop, schismatic groups begin to form, and then these groups are either expelled from the original enclave or take off on their own. This has happened many times in the case of people originally trained as Freudian psychoanalysts.

I believe this situation is changing and these ideological boundaries are becoming more permeable. Garfield and Bergin state: "A decisive shift in opinion has quietly occurred; and it has created an irreversible change in professional attitudes about psychotherapy and behavior change. The new view is that the long-term dominance of the major theories is over and that an eclectic position has taken precedence" (1986, p. 7).

I would go even further and state that all good therapists are eclectic. This does not mean that they do not follow a particular theory or use specific methods associated with particular approaches to therapy; it does mean that technique and method are always secondary to the clinician's sense of what is the right thing to do with a given client at a given moment in time, irrespective of theory. Put more simply, psychotherapy remains an art. So if formal eclecticism is on the rise, this is all to the good: it shows the maturing of psychotherapy.

Why then, a book such as this? In order to be effectively eclectic, one needs to know as many different theories and systems as possible, from which one can develop a personal theory, a personal system, and an integrated approach. Initially, the neophyte therapist is best served by operating as strictly as possible within the limits of a given system, with close supervision by a skilled practitioner of that system. Later, and with experience, one can begin to develop one's own individual style of therapy.

The Whohowwhom Factor

I have come to believe that what counts in psychotherapy is who does it and how and to whom it is done: the whohowwhom factor. This belief developed from my experiences in a small group practice in which all the therapists had the same basic theoretical and operational concepts. We consulted on each other's cases, worked together in co-therapy, met weekly to discuss cases we were handling, and came to know each other quite well over the six-year period that I was with this group. However, although we all shared the same theoretical position and generally operated in the same manner, any new clients who came to our clinic were likely to get different kinds of therapy due to the *whohowwhom* factor. One therapist liked to tell stories to make various points. Another liked to ask Socratic questions. Still another would frequently interrupt to demonstrate errors in the client's thinking and behavior. One played the role of the loving father, while another was quite sarcastic. Some were friendly, while others were distant. Some saw clients as equals, while others saw clients as students who needed to be taught more effective ways to operate. So even in this particular group with a shared theory and methodology, there were wide variations in therapy practice and style. The senior therapist, who had trained the others, was in a good position to decide which new client was to go which therapist. For example, I tended to be assigned difficult adult clients but no adolescents.

Sometimes the *how* variable will be of less importance than the match between *who* and *whom*, because differences in actual technique may be relatively small for some systems. However, at times an apparently circumscribed method, such as the person-centered approach, may achieve superior results for some people when other more complex methods will fail. I am reminded of the fable of the cat and the fox. The fox bragged about how he had so many ways of escaping from dogs. The cat had only one: to climb a tree. Both the cat and the fox were chased by dogs. The cat went up the tree and remained there until the dogs went away. The fox used all his tricks but eventually was caught. So too, sometimes something simple is superior to something complex, and even in psychotherapy, less can be more.

Research

Many people in the recent history of psychotherapy have wondered about the effectiveness of counseling and psychotherapy. At one time, Dr. Wedding wanted to include a section in every chapter of this book examining relevant research findings for each system, but practically every contributor was against the idea. Nonetheless, the sentiment expressed by Strupp and Bergin (1969, p. 20) is very much on the minds of people:

> The problem of psychotherapy research in its most general terms should be reformulated as a standard scientific question: What specific therapeutic interventions produce specific changes in specific patients under specific conditions?

Perhaps the best and most complete answer to the issue of such research was given by C.H. Patterson (1987, p. 247):

> Before this model (relative to research) could be implemented we would need (1) a taxonomy of client problems or psychological disorders…;(2) a taxonomy of client personalities; (3) a taxonomy of therapeutic techniques…; (4) a taxonomy of therapists; and (5) a taxonomy of circumstances.… If we did have such systems of classification, the practical problems would be insurmountable. Assuming five classes of variables, each with ten classifications,… a research design would require $10 \times 10 \times 10 \times 10 \times 10$ or 100,000 cells.… So, I conclude we don't need complex multivariate analyses and should abandon any attempt to do the crucial, perfect study of psychotherapy. It simply is not possible.

It is difficult for me or anyone else brought up with nomothetic approaches, imbued with Edward Lee Thorndike's concept that anything that exists can be measured, to accept this pessimistic point of view, but I contend that Patterson, who has studied this issue intensively and written widely on the problems of research in counseling and psychotherapy, is essentially correct.

Psychotherapy is an art based on science, and as is true for any art, there can be no simple measures of so complex an activity.

❖ CORRECTION OF A HISTORICAL ERROR

In many historical accounts found in textbooks, an essentially incorrect view of the early years of psychotherapy is recounted. The story given generally goes as follows: In the beginning Sigmund Freud started a brand new system of psychotherapy called psychoanalysis. A number of other people learned about it and became his students. In later years, for a variety of reasons, they decided to separate from him and went on to start their own systems of thought.

In reality, numerous people preceded Freud, doing psychotherapy in a variety of ways. We may start with the Swiss physician Paul Dubois (1848–1918), one of the first psychotherapists in the modern sense of the term, because his method of treating psychotics was to talk with them in a reasonable manner. Still another person to be considered is Pierre Janet (1859–1947), referred to by Ellenberger as "the first person to found a new system of dynamic psychiatry aimed at replacing those of the nineteenth century" (1970, p. 331). Janet, at about the time that Sigmund Freud began his work, was the best-known and most respected psychotherapist of his time.

There was a great deal of interest and activity in psychotherapy prior to Freud, and there were already the conflicts, schisms, claims, and jealousies that were also to be found later. The whole history of psychotherapy is replete with personality clashes and other signs of struggles for superiority.

In 1902, Sigmund Freud invited several colleagues to meet with him to discuss personality theory. The group was later to be called the Wednesday Psychological Society. Some of the members were independent thinkers, each with his own position; Freud, the oldest, the best known, and the most published, was the host. It is important to understand that some members of this group were *psycho-analysts* and not *psychoanalysts*. Hyphenated, this word meant that these people were interested in the analysis of the psyche; spelled as one word it meant that they were followers of Sigmund Freud.

Three members of this Wednesday night group are the subjects of the next three chapters: Sigmund Freud, Alfred Adler, and Carl Jung. From the beginning, these three moved in quite different directions. Freud was a mechanistic, deterministic thinker who developed a system of psychology with essentially biological/hydraulic elements: a system of stresses and strains, conflicts and tensions, with a dynamic interaction between biological instinctive drives and social demands. Adler was essentially a commonsense thinker with a shrewd understanding of people's motivations. Jung was an internalized person, mystical, religious, creative.

Freud was the ideal German scientist, a keen student of minutiae, a pedant; Adler was a man of the people, socially oriented and concerned; Jung was an introverted, distant but friendly person. Their theories of personality and their psychotherapeutic systems can be seen as direct extensions of their manifest personalities.

Since the deaths of Freud in 1939, Adler in 1937, and Jung in 1961, the theories of the latter two have remained more or less constant. On the other hand, the theory of Freud has divided into a number of different approaches, some quite different from Freud's original thinking. There are now a variety of psychoanalytic groups with varying orientations. To make a religious analogy, psychoanalysis may be likened to Christianity, with various groups using the same ultimate authority (the Bible) but having different interpretations of these basic writings.

During the period from 1910 to about 1939, these big three dominated psychotherapy in Europe and the United States. However, a number of other points of view existed at that time, most of which have either disappeared or have been incorporated into eclectic thinking, including the theories of such people as Pierre Janet, Jules Déjèrine, Trigant Burrow, Albert Korzybski, Otto Rank, and Wilhelm Reich. However, a number of theories and methodologies considered to be deviations from pure Freudian psychoanalysis, such as the therapies of Harry Stack Sullivan, Karen Horney, and Theodore Reik, are still very much alive.

Since 1940, when Carl Rogers gave his historic Psi Chi paper in Minnesota, a considerable number of alternative systems of psychotherapy have begun. It is difficult to establish the dates of their beginnings because there is generally a considerable lapse of time between when a system starts and when publications about it first appear. But it might not be too far off to say that from about 1900 to 1939 there were three major points of view and about a dozen minor ones in psychotherapy and that during the next 60 years there were a dozen major points of view (including the original three) and perhaps two dozen others of consequence.

This situation leads to the speculation that as time goes on there may continue to be an expanding universe of major and minor system of psychotherapy. If psychotherapy is essentially a matter of philosophy, then ultimately there will be multiple systems; if it is essentially a matter of science, then ultimately there will be one eclectic system.

❖ PSYCHOTHERAPY AND PSYCHOTHERAPIST

There appears to be a concordance between the personality of a psychotherapy innovator and the system he or she has developed. In an article called "Freud, Rogers and Moreno" (Corsini, 1956), I made a comparison between the manifest personalities of these three men and their systems of psychotherapy. I never met Freud, but there is a good deal of biographical information about him, and there seems to be no question that his personality and his method of psychoanalysis were congruent. Freud was a rather shy person, uncomfortable with people, a pedantic bookish type, an intellectual. His methodology—having people lie down, with him sitting behind them and out of sight while he listened intently to what they said—fits exactly his manifest personality. The system and the man seem identical.

I got to know Carol Rogers quite well. As a graduate student at the University of Chicago (1953–55), I was in contact with him both as a client and as a student. In later years I met him on many occasions socially and at professional meetings. Rogers, whether in his social life, as a teacher, or as a therapist, was exactly the same. He and his system were identical.

I also got to know J.L. Moreno, the founder of psychodrama, quite well. I listened to him lecture many times, I was often on the psychodrama stage with him, and we had a social relationship. There was no question at all about the congruence of Moreno's unique personality and his methodology. Again, the system and the man were identical.

What is the implication of these similarities for the reader? I believe that if one is to go into the fields of counseling and psychotherapy, then the best theory and methodology to use have to be one's own! The reader will not be either successful or happy using a method not suited to his or her own personality. The really successful therapist adopts or develops a theory and methodology congruent with his or her own personality. [See Corsini (1991) for examples.]

In reading these accounts, in addition to attempting to determine which school of psychotherapy seems most sensible, the reader should also attempt to find one that fits his or her philosophy of life, one that seems most right in terms of its theory, and one with a method of operation that appears most appealing in use.

A final value of this book lies in the greater self-understanding that may be gained by close reading. This book about psychotherapies may be psychotherapeutic for the reader. Close reading vertically (chapter by chapter) and then horizontally (section by section) may well lead to personal growth as well as better understanding of the current psychotherapies.

❖ REFERENCES

Bach, G.R., & Goldberg, H. (1975). *Creative aggression*. Garden City, NY: Doubleday.

Bion, J. (Ed.). (1948). *Therapeutic social clubs*. London: Lewis.

Corsini, R. J. (1991) *Five therapists and one client*. Itasca, IL F.E. Peacock.

Corsini, R. J. (1968). Counseling and psychotherapy. In E. F. Borgotta & W. W. Lambert (Eds.), *Handbook of personality theory and research*. Chicago, IL: Rand McNally.

Corsini, R. J. (1956). Freud, Rogers and Moreno. *Group Psychotherapy, 9*, 274-281.

Corsini R. J. (Ed.) (1981). *Handbook of innovative psychotherapies*. New York: Wiley.

Corsini, R. J., & Rosenberg, B. (1955). Mechanisms of group psychotherapy. *Journal of Abnormal and Social Psychology, 51*, 406-411.

Ellenberger, H. (1970). *The discovery of the unconscious*. New York: Basic Books.

Farrelly, F., & Brasma, J. (1974) *Provocative therapy*. Cupertino, CA: Meta.

Garfield, S. L., & Bergin, A. E. (1986). *Handbook of psychotherapy and behavior change*. New York: Wiley.

Gazda, G.M. (1981). Multiple impact training. In R. J. Corsini (Ed.), *Handbook of innovative psychotherapies*. New York: Wiley.

Horney, K. (1942). *Self-analysis*. New York: Norton.

Janov, A. (1970). *The primal scream*. New York: Vintage Books.

Lair, J., & Lair, J. C. (1973). *Hey, God, what should I do now?* New York: Doubleday.

Landry, E. E. (1994). Disjunctive therapies. In R. J. Corsini, *Encyclopedia of psychology* (2nd ed.) New York: Wiley.

Losoncy, L. (1981). *Encouragement therapy*. Englewood Cliffs, NJ: Prentice-Hall.

Painter, G., & Vernon, S. (1981). Primary relationship therapy. In R. J. Corsini (Ed.), *Handbook of innovative psychotherapies*. New York: Wiley.

Patterson, C. H. (1987). Comments. *Person-Centered Review, 1*, 246-248.

Popper, K. R. (1968). *Conjectures and refutations*. Oxford: Oxford University Press.

Reik, T. (1948). *Listening with the third ear*. New York: Farrar and Strauss.

Schmidhoffer, E. (1952). Mechanical group therapy. *Science, 115*, 120-123.

Shostrom, E. L., & Montgomery, D. (1978). *Healing love*. Nashville: Abington.

Simmel, E. (1949). War neuroses. In S. Lorand (Ed.), *Psychoanalysis today*. New York: International Universities Press.

Struppp, H. H., & Bergin, A. E. (1969). Some empirical and conceptual bases for coordinated research in psychotherapy. *International Journal of Psychiatry, 1*, 18-90.

van Kaam, A. (1976). *The dynamics of spiritual self-direction*. Denville, NY: Dimension Books.

Wolpe, J. (1958). *Psychotherapy by reciprocal inhibition*. Stanford, CA: Stanford University Press.

Sigmund Freud, 1856–1939

2   Psychoanalysis

Jacob A. Arlow

❖ OVERVIEW

Psychoanalysis is a system of psychology derived from the discoveries of Sigmund Freud. Originating as a method for treating psychoneurotic disorders, psychoanalysis has come to serve as the foundation for a general theory of psychology. Knowledge derived from the treatment of individual patients has led to insights into art, religion, social organization, child development, and education. In addition, by elucidating the influence of unconscious wishes on the physiology of the body, psychoanalysis has made it possible to understand and treat many psychosomatic illnesses.

Basic Concepts

According to Ernst Kris (1950), psychoanalysis may be defined as human nature seen from the vantage point of conflict. Psychoanalysis views the mind as the expression of conflicting forces. Some of these forces are conscious; others, perhaps the major ones, are unconscious. Psychoanalysis emphasizes the importance of unconscious forces in mental life.

Conflict is an inexorable dimension of the human condition. It reflects the contradiction inherent in humans as biological animals and social beings. Each human infant has to be civilized and acculturated to incorporate and integrate the ideals and values, the inhibitions and the taboos, of society. The primary instrument in this process is the family. Later, the more formalized institutions of society take over much of the responsibility for acculturating the individual. In this development, frustration, anger, disappointment, and conflict are inevitable.

The functioning of the mind is related to events in the body. The body is the substrate of all psychology, including psychoanalysis. Basic responses to stimuli are part of man's biological inheritance. These responses, phylogenetically determined, undoubtedly were of evolutionary significance in the struggle of the species to survive. A fundamental principle of psychoanalytic theory is that human psychology is governed by a tendency to seek pleasure and to avoid pain: the *pleasure principle* (Freud, 1911). Although this principle is operative throughout life, it is patently and overwhelmingly dominant in the first few years of existence. The earliest experiences of pleasure and pain play a crucial role in shaping each individual's psychological structure. The impact of the earliest experiences is intensified in the case of the human infant, because in contrast to animals, the human has a much longer period of dependence upon adults. Without their care and solicitude, he could not survive. This fact of biology eventuates in an early and abiding attachment to others.

Freud's revolutionary perceptions represent a fusion of the most advanced humanistic and scientific ideas of the late nineteenth and early twentieth centuries. In psychoanalysis, he combined the liberal ideal of respect for the integrity of each individual with a rigorous attempt to establish a scientific method for studying the individual as a living, social entity. He emphasized clinical observation. Theory for Freud was a superstructure erected on clinical observation that could be altered by new findings. Accordingly, it was essential to establish an objective method by which reliable observations could be made. This prerequisite Freud met in his formulation of the psychoanalytic situation, which is at the same time a form of therapy and a method of investigation.

Psychoanalysis is the most extensive, inclusive, and comprehensive system of psychology. It encompasses humans' inner experiences and outer behavior, their biological nature and social roles, how they function individually and how they function in groups.

Essentially, psychoanalysis continues the rationalist spirit of Greek philosophy, to "know thyself." Knowing one's self, however, is understood in quite a different way. It is not to be found in the pursuit of formal, logical analysis of thinking. As far as the individual is concerned, the sources of his neurotic suffering are by their very nature "unknowable." They reside outside the realm of consciousness, barred from awareness by virtue of their painful, unacceptable quality. By enabling the patient to understand how neurotic symptoms and behavior represent derivatives of unconscious conflicts, psychoanalysis permits the patient to make rational choices instead of responding automatically. Self-knowledge of a very special kind strengthens the individual's ability to make choices and seek fulfillment. For the successfully analyzed individual, freedom from neurotic inhibition and suffering is often experienced as a liberating, self-fulfilling transformation, which promotes not only self-actualization but also the ability to contribute to the advancement and happiness of others. Knowing oneself may have far-reaching social implications. It is important to bear this in mind, because even under the best of circumstances, only a relatively small number of people can or will be analyzed.

Other Systems

Almost every form of modern psychotherapy owes some debt to psychoanalysis. As Leo Rangell (1973) has shown, most forms of psychotherapy now widely practiced are based on some element of psychoanalytic theory or technique. Usually some procedure or a particular concept is borrowed from psychoanalysis and used as the rationale for a par-

ticular treatment. This is not to imply that other forms of therapy are invalid or ineffectual. Quite the contrary. Although there are many ways to treat neuroses, there is but
one way to understand them—psychoanalysis (Fenichel, 1945). It has been stated in
many quarters that psychoanalysts believe their method is the only worthwhile form of
treatment. This is not true. There are many situations where a nonanalytic treatment is
preferable to an analytic one. For many forms of mental illness, psychoanalysis is inadvisable or contraindicated.

Historically, the line of descent of *Jungian analysis* and *Adlerian therapy* from
psychoanalysis is clear. Both Carl Jung and Alfred Adler broke with Freud early in the
history of the psychoanalytic movement. Jung had serious differences with Freud concerning the nature of drives. His approach places less emphasis on maturational and developmental processes. Jung emphasized the significance of culturally determined, unconsciously transmitted symbolic representations of the principal themes of human
existence. Behind the transformations of individual experience, Jung and his followers see
the constant recurrence of mythic themes common to all humanity. Jung's concept of the
transmission of unconscious fantasies through a collective unconscious has been criticized as being too mystical. In some respects, Jung's views on the collective unconscious
correspond to the Freudians' concept of primitive universal fantasy, but the latter regard
these only as vehicles for derivatives of the instinctual drives of childhood rather than original determinants of behavior. They are secondary rather than primary factors in shaping
personality. Some of Jung's concepts are particularly useful in elucidating the more regressed manifestations seen in schizophrenic patients (Jung, 1909).

Adler (Ansbacher & Ansbacher, 1956) believed the role of social and political pressures was underestimated by Freudian psychoanalysts. There was considerable validity to
this criticism, analysts having concentrated primarily on the transformation of the derivatives of the energy of the sexual drive, the *libido*. To Adler, the cause of conflicts was determined by factors such as inferiority over social status, inadequate physical endowment,
sexual weakness, and discrimination. Many of his concepts presaged later psychoanalytic
contributions concerning the role of self-esteem, particularly in relation to the so-called
narcissistic personality disorders.

Recent years have seen the burgeoning of many forms of therapy in which the central
aspect of the treatment consists of self-expression, releasing emotion, overcoming inhibitions, and articulating in speech and behavior the fantasies or impulses previously suppressed. The *encounter movement* (Burton, 1969; Schultz, 1967) represented one such
school. *Primal scream therapy* was another. These forms of treatment were exaggerations
and caricatures of the principle of emotional catharsis that Freud advanced in his early
studies of hysteria (Freud, 1895). At that time, he thought that discharge of pent-up emotion could have a beneficial therapeutic effect. Subsequent experience with the treatment
of neurotic patients, however, convinced Freud that his method was limited and, in the
long run, ineffectual, since it did not give sufficient weight to the needs of self-punishment and the various defenses the ego uses to ward off anxiety. In the expressive forms of
treatment, the group experience plays an enormous role in mitigating anxiety. Expressing in the presence of others what is ordinarily inexpressible can go far in ameliorating a
sense of guilt. The burden of guilt, furthermore, is lightened by the knowledge that other
members of the group admit to the same or similar feelings and impulses. Everyone's guilt
is no one's guilt (Sachs, 1942). The effect of such treatment, however, depends to a large
extent on the continuity of contact with the group experience. Since no essential insight or
psychological restructuring has taken place, the tendency for relapse once the group experience is discontinued is very strong. Furthermore, there are cases in which the individ-

ual perceives the temptation and the opportunity to express derivatives of forbidden impulses as so overwhelming a danger that he is unable to cope with it and in some instances may suffer a psychotic break.

Mitigating the influence of the superego on the total psychological equilibrium seems to be the essential feature of the *rational-emotive system* of Albert Ellis (1970). Ellis attempts to get the patient to change his values, particularly in regard to sexuality, helping relieve the patient of irrational guilt that may have inhibited many aspects of his life and behavior. When this treatment is effective, it can be understood in terms of the patient's having made an identification with the therapist's personality and values. The therapist comes to serve as an auxiliary superego that may replace or alter the patient's patterns of judgment, self-evaluation, and ideal aspirations. This is similar to what one observes in cases where individuals are "cured" of their difficulties through religious conversion, usually as the result of an attachment to some charismatic religious (sometimes political) figure.

As part of the psychoanalytic situation, the analyst listens patiently, sympathetically, uncritically, and receptively. This aspect of psychoanalytic technique forms the core of the nondirective listening of Carl R. Rogers (1951). In other forms of treatment, sympathetic listening may be combined with counseling, trying to guide the patient in a rational manner through the real and imaginary pitfalls of living. Otto Fenichel (1945) pointed out that verbalization of vaguely felt anxieties may bring relief because the individual can face concretized, verbalized ideas better than unclear, emotional sensations. Transference also plays a role. The fact that a therapist spends time and shows interest and sympathy reawakens echoes of previous situations of having been helped by friends or relatives. For lonely people it can be a substantial relief to have someone to talk with. When the patient can see some connection between his worries and other patterns of behavior, he feels an accession of strength in relation to the deeper unconscious forces within his personality.

All the foregoing forms of therapy make use of one or more of the fundamental features of psychoanalytic therapy, namely, a setting in which the patient can express thoughts and feelings spontaneously and freely to an uncritical, receptive observer; the achievement of insight through interpretation; and finally, and perhaps most important, an awareness of the power of the transference relationship.

Other forms of therapy, such as *reality therapy* (Glasser, 1967) and *behavior therapy* (Wolpe, 1958), illustrate the principles just mentioned. Essentially, the therapist is unconsciously cast in the role of a model or the transference instrument in an effort either to deny or to project the effects of internal conflicts. The therapist unconsciously joins the patient in a pattern of playing out some derivative of the patient's childhood fantasies. Accordingly, such forms of therapy play into patients' tendency to try to act out expressions of their unconscious conflicts. For this reason, one can expect that such forms of therapy can have only limited usefulness and short-term effectiveness.

❖ HISTORY

Precursors

Psychoanalysis, as originated by Sigmund Freud (1856-1939), represented an integration of the major European intellectual movements of his time. This was a period of unprecedented advance in the physical and biological sciences. A new liberal humanism was abroad, a humanism based on materialist philosophy and the free exercise of thought. The crucial issue of the day was Darwin's theory of evolution. A group of young biologists, deeply influenced by the teachings of Hermann Helmholtz (Berenfeld, 1944), took it as a matter of principle to explain biological phenomena solely in terms of physics and chemistry. One member of that group was Ernst Brücke (Jones, 1953), later chief of the biological research laboratories at the University of Vienna, where Freud went to pursue a career as a research biologist. Models borrowed from physics, chemistry, and the theory of evolution recur regularly throughout Freud's writings, but most strikingly in his early psychological works.

Freud came to psychoanalysis by way of neurology. During his formative years, great strides were being made in neurophysiology and neuropathology. Freud himself contributed to the advancement of the science with original work on the evolution of the elements of the central nervous system, on aphasia, on cerebral palsy, and on the physiological functions of cocaine. In *The Interpretation of Dreams*, he offered a model of the human mind based on the physiology of the reflex arc.

This was also the time when psychology separated from philosophy and began to emerge as an independent science. Freud was interested in both fields. He knew the works of the "association" school of psychologists (J. F. Herbart, Alexander von Humboldt, and Wilhelm Wundt), and he had been impressed by the way Gustav Fechner (Freud, 1894) applied concepts of physics to problems of psychological research. Ernest Jones (1953) has suggested that the idea of using free association as a therapeutic technique may be traced to the influence of Herbart. In the mid-nineteenth century, there was great interest in states of split consciousness (Zilboorg & Henry, 1941). The French neuropsychiatrists had taken the lead in studying conditions such as somnambulism, multiple personalities, fugue states, and hysteria. Hypnotism was one of the principal methods used in studying these conditions. The leading figures in this field of investigation were Jean Charcot, Pierre Janet, Hippolyte Bernheim, and Ambrose Liebault. Freud had the opportunity to work with several of them and was particularly influenced by Charcot.

Beginnings

Freud wrote two essays on the history of psychoanalysis: *The History of the Psychoanalytic Movement* (1914a) and *An Autobiographical Study* (1925). Both works are concerned primarily with how Freud's theories evolved. In what follows, this evolution is traced by organizing developments around Freud's major works:

1. *Studies on Hysteria*
2. *The Interpretation of Dreams*
3. *On Narcissism*
4. Papers on Metapsychology
5. Dual Instinct Theory
6. Structural Theory

Studies on Hysteria (1895)

The history of psychoanalysis proper begins when Josef Breuer, a Viennese physician with research interests, told Freud about a remarkable experience he was having with a patient (Anna O.) who seemed to be curing herself of the symptoms of hysteria by means of talking. Breuer had observed that when he placed his patient into a hypnotic trance and had her relate what was oppressing her mind, she would tell of some highly emotional fantasy or event in her life. If the telling of this material was accompanied by a massive outburst of emotion, the patient would be relieved of her symptoms. Once awake, the patient was totally unaware of the "traumatic event" she had related or of its connection to her disability. Freud tried the same procedure on other patients and was able to confirm Breuer's findings. They summarized their findings in a publication entitled *Studies on Hysteria* (1895), in which they reasoned that the symptoms of hysteria were the result of an undischarged quantity of emotion, connected with a very painful memory. These memories have been split off from their connection with the rest of the mind, but they continue to exert a dynamic, intrusive effect in the form of symptoms. The task of therapy was to bring about recollection of the forgotten event together with a cathartic abreaction of the undischarged emotion. Working independently, Freud came to the conclusion that the traumatic events involved in causing hysteria took place in childhood and were regularly of a sexual nature. Because at the time it was generally believed that children before the age of puberty had no sexual drives, Freud was led to the conclusion that the patients he observed had all been seduced by an older person. Further investigation demonstrated that this was not always true. Freud unknowingly had come upon the data that were to serve as the basis for the discovery of childhood sexuality.

The Interpretation of Dreams (1900)

The second phase of Freud's discoveries concerned a solution to the riddle of the dream. The idea that dreams could be understood occurred to Freud when he observed how regularly they appeared in the associations of his neurotic patients. *Dreams* and *symptoms*, he came to realize, had a similar structure. They were both the end product of a compromise between two sets of conflicting forces in the mind, between unconscious childhood sexual wishes seeking discharge and the repressive activity of the rest of the mind. In effecting this compromise, an inner censor disguised and distorted the representation of the unconscious sexual wishes from childhood. This process makes dreams and symptoms unintelligible. The kind of wishes that entered into the formation of dreams were connected with the pleasurable sensations that children get from stimulating the mouth, anus, skin, and genitals, and resembled the various forms of overt sexual activity typical for the perversions.

The Interpretation of Dreams was at the same time a partial record of Freud's own self-analysis. In it Freud first described the Oedipus complex, perhaps the most striking of his many ideas. In the concluding chapter of this work, Freud attempted to elaborate a theory of the human mind that would encompass dreaming, psychopathology, and normal functioning. The central principle of this theory is that mental life represents an unrelenting conflict between the conscious and unconscious parts of the mind. The unconscious parts of the mind contain the biological, instinctual sexual drives, impulsively pressing for discharge. Opposed to these elements are forces that are conscious or readily available to consciousness, functioning at a logical, realistic, and adaptive level. Because the fundamental principle of this conceptualization of mental functioning concerned the depth or "layer" of an idea in relationship to consciousness, this theory was called the *topographic theory*.

In the years that followed the publication of *The Interpretation of Dreams*, Freud used the concepts of unconscious conflict, infantile sexuality, and the Oedipus complex to attain new insights into the psychology of religion, art, character formation, mythology, and literature. These ideas were published in a group of major contributions: *The Psychopathology of Everyday Life* (1901), *Jokes and Their Relationship to the Unconscious* (1905a), *Three Essays on Sexuality* (1905b), and somewhat later, *Totem and Taboo* (1913).

On Narcissism (1914)

The next phase in the development of Freud's concepts came when he attempted to apply methods of psychoanalysis to understand the psychoses. Up to this point, Freud saw the major conflict in mental life as a struggle between the energy of the sexual drive (*libido*), which was directed towards preserving the species, and the *ego*, the self-preservative drives. This frame of reference did not seem adequate to elucidate the symptoms of psychosis. These phenomena, Freud felt, could be better understood in terms of a conflict between libidinal energies vested in the self and libidinal energies vested in the representation of objects of the external world. The concept of *narcissism* proved useful, in addition, in explaining such phenomena as falling in love and pride in one's own children (Freud, 1914a, 1914b, 1921).

Papers on Metapsychology (1915)

From his clinical observations, Freud came to recognize certain inconsistencies in his topographical model of the mind. He noted, for example, that many unconscious mental contents were, in fact, anti-instinctual and self-punitive; clearly, a strict qualitative differentiation of mental phenomena according to the single criterion of accessibility to consciousness was no longer tenable. In several papers, notably *Repression* (1915a) and *The Unconscious* (1915b), Freud tried to synthesize his psychological concepts under the heading of *metapsychology*. By this term he meant "describing a mental process in all of its aspects—dynamic, topographic, and economic." The papers written during this period represent a transitional phase in Freud's thinking before he embarked upon a major revision of his theory.

Dual Instinct Theory (1920)

The role of aggression in mental life convinced Freud that he had to revise his theory of drives. He observed how self-directed aggression operated in depression, masochism, and, generally, in the many ways people punish themselves. Individuals wrecked by success, persons who commit crimes out of a sense of guilt in the hope of being punished, and patients in therapy who respond negatively to the insight they achieve during treatment are typical of this category. In 1920, in his essay *Beyond the Pleasure Principle*, Freud extended his dualistic concept by putting forward the notion of two instincts, libido and aggression, both derived in turn from broader, all-pervading biological principles—an instinct of love (*Eros*) and an instinct towards death and self-destruction (*Thanatos*).

Structural Theory (1923)

Having recognized that in the course of psychic conflict, conscience may operate at both conscious and/or unconscious levels, and having perceived that even the methods by which the mind protects itself from anxiety may be unconscious, Freud reformulated his theory in terms of a structural organization of the mind. Mental functions were grouped according to the role they played in conflict. The three major subdivisions of the psychic apparatus he called the ego, the id, and the superego. The *ego* comprises a group of functions that orient the individual toward the external world and mediate between it and the inner world. It acts, in effect, as an executant for the drives and correlates these demands with a proper regard for conscience and the world of reality. The *id* represents the organization of the sum total of the instinctual pressures on the mind, basically the sexual and aggressive impulses. The *superego* is a split-off portion of the ego, a residue of the early history of the individual's moral training and a precipitate of the most important childhood identifications and ideal aspirations. Under ordinary circumstances, there is no sharp demarcation among these three major components of the mind. Intrapsychic conflict, however, makes the differences and the demarcations stand out clearly.

One of the major functions of the ego is to protect the mind from internal dangers, from the threat of a breakthrough into consciousness of conflict-laden impulses. The difference between mental health and illness depends upon how well the ego can succeed in this responsibility. In his monograph *Inhibitions, Symptoms and Anxiety* (1926), Freud detailed that the key to the problem is the appearance of the unpleasant affective state of anxiety, perhaps the most common symptom of psychoneurosis. Anxiety serves as a warning signal alerting the ego to the danger of overwhelming anxiety or panic that may supervene if a repressed, unconscious wish emerges into consciousness. Once warned, the ego may undertake any of a wide array of defenses. This new view had far-reaching implications for both theory and practice.

Current Status

Since Freud, developments in psychoanalysis have been many and varied. Under the leadership of Melanie Klein (1932), the English school of psychoanalysis has emerged. It emphasizes the importance of primitive fantasies of loss (the *depressive* position) and persecution (the *paranoid* position) in the pathogenesis of mental illness. This school is particularly influential in Europe and South America.

When Nazi persecution forced many of the outstanding European analysts to migrate to this country, the United States became the world center for psychoanalysis. The leading figures in this movement were Heinz Hartmann, Ernst Kris, and Rudolph Loewenstein. These three collaborators (1946, 1949) tried to establish psychoanalysis as a general psychology. They did so by extending Hartmann's concepts of the adaptive function of the ego (Hartmann, 1939) and clarifying fundamental working hypotheses concerning drives and development of the psychic apparatus. Their theories integrated the invaluable contributions of Anna Freud (1936, 1951) derived from studies of long-term child development. In the course of these investigations, several questions concerning the sense of self were posed. How and when does the sense of self develop and what are the consequences to the individual if the process miscarries? Edith Jacobson (1954), D.W. Winnicott (1953), and John Bowlby (1958) were among those who contributed to the clarification of the problem. The most cogent studies in the field, however, come from the meticulous clinical and developmental observations conducted by Margaret Mahler (1975) and her coworkers. All of these studies underline the importance of the early attachment to the mother and the vicissitudes of the processes of separation and individuation.

These early experiences seem to play a crucial role in the development of self-esteem. Considerations of self-esteem are central in the psychology of narcissistic character disorders and borderline personalities. Clinical and theoretical illumination of these conditions were offered in the writings of Annie Reich (1973) and have been extended in an original way by Heinz Kohut (1971) and Otto Kernberg (1968).

More recent developments in the field are too numerous to describe. David Rapaport (1951) and several of his students have integrated psychoanalytic theories with broad psychological principles and findings. Jacob Arlow and Charles Brenner (1964) have attempted to synthesize newer clinical findings into the framework of the structural theory. Other authors, critical of some of the propositions of psychoanalysis, are attempting to reformulate psychoanalytic theory in terms of communications theory (Peterfreund, 1971; Schafer, 1976) and neurophysiology (Rubenstein, 1967). Some authors have emphasized the importance of interpersonal relationships (Sullivan, 1953) and the role of identification and the transformations of the personality during the life cycle (Erikson, 1968). Karen Horney (1940) and Erich Fromm (1955) have stressed the social, political, and cultural factors in the development of the individual.

The American Psychoanalytic Association is the largest and most prestigious of psychoanalytic societies in the United States. It consists of almost 2,500 members and affiliates. It comprises 33 affiliate societies and conducts centers for the professional training of psychoanalysts in 26 institutes in the United States. With the exception of some recent changes, admission to training in affiliate institutes and to membership in the American Psychoanalytic Association is restricted to members of the medical profession. (This condition does not hold in the other affiliate societies of the International Psychoanalytical Association.) Standards for training in psychoanalysis are set by the Board on Professional Standards of the American Psychoanalytic Association. In addition to the requirement of an M.D. degree, a candidate must have had residency training in psychiatry. The course of study is from four to eight or more years and consists of three parts: (1) the training analysis, (2) formal courses in the literature and technique of psychoanalysis, and (3) the treatment of at least three or four patients under the supervision of a training analyst.

There are many other psychoanalytic organizations in the United States. The American Academy of Psychoanalysis is a scientific organization that has not in the past conducted programs of training. Although many of its members belong to the American Psychoanalytic Association, membership in the academy is not restricted to physicians. There are, in addition, several societies composed of physicians, psychologists, social workers, and other professionals who have received training at either the William Alanson White Institute or other centers for training in the United States. Perhaps the largest of these is the National Psychological Association for Psychoanalysis.

Recent years have witnessed a rich burgeoning of the psychoanalytic literature. In addition to the long-standing major publications in the field, such as the *American Psychoanalytic Association Journal*, the *International Journal of Psychoanalysis*, the *Psychoanalytic Quarterly*, the *Psychoanalytic Study of the Child*, the *Psychoanalytic Review*, and *Psychiatry*, many new journals have appeared, such as the *International Psychoanalytic Review*, the *Chicago Annual of Psychoanalysis*, the *International Journal of Psychoanalytic Psychotherapy*, *Psychoanalysis and Contemporary Science*, and *Psychological Issues*.

The 24-volume *Standard Edition of the Complete Works of Sigmund Freud* is the basic source for theory and instruction in psychoanalysis. In 1945 Fenichel wrote *The Psychoanalytic Theory of Neurosis*, the closest work to a textbook in psychoanalysis. Unfortunately, this valuable source book has not been brought up to date. The 3-volume biography of Freud by Ernest Jones (1953–57) contains a comprehensive overview of Freud's contributions. The most concise, accurate, and readable statement of current psychoanalytic theory is to be found in Charles Brenner's (1973) *An Elementary Textbook of Psychoanalysis*. Alexander Grinstein (1971) edited *The Index of Psychoanalytic Writings*. Consisting of 14 volumes, it covers all the psychoanalytic literature up to and including the year 1969.

❖ PERSONALITY

Theory of Personality

The psychoanalytic theory of personality is based on a number of fundamental principles. The first and foremost is *determinism*. Psychoanalytic theory assumes that mental events are not random, haphazard, accidental, unrelated phenomena. Thoughts, feelings, and impulses are events in a chain of causally related phenomena. They result from antecedent experiences in the life of the individual. Through appropriate methods of investigation, the connection between current mental experience and past events can be established. Many of these connections are unconscious.

The second principle is the *topographic* viewpoint. Every mental element is judged according to its accessibility to consciousness. The process by which certain mental contents are barred from consciousness is called *repression*, an active effort to keep certain thoughts out of awareness to avoid pain or unpleasantness. Psychoanalytic investigation of normal and pathological phenomena has demonstrated the important role unconscious forces play in the behavior of the individual. Some of the most important decisions in one's life may be determined by unconscious motives.

The third basic approach is the *dynamic* viewpoint. This pertains to the interaction of libidinal and aggressive impulses. Because of their biological roots, these impulses have been loosely and inaccurately referred to as *instincts*. The correct term in psychoanalytic theory, translated from the German *Treib*, is *drives*. Because this has become common usage, *instinct* and *drive* will be used interchangeably in the rest of this chapter.

It is important to distinguish drives in humans from instinctive behavior in animals. *Instinct* in animals is a stereotyped response, usually with clear survival value, evoked by specific stimuli in particular settings. As used in psychoanalysis, *drive* is a state of central excitation in response to stimuli. This sense of central excitation impels the mind to activity, with the ultimate aim of bringing about the cessation of tension, a sense of gratification. Drives in humans are capable of a wide variety of complex transformations. Drive theory in psychoanalysis is intended to account for the psychological findings gathered in the clinical setting. Biology supports many of the formulations regarding the libidinal drive. This is not so in the case of the aggressive drive, a concept founded almost exclusively on psychological data (Brenner, 1971).

The fourth approach to personality theory has been called the *genetic* viewpoint, tracing the origins of later conflicts, character traits, neurotic symptoms, and psychological structure to the crucial events and wishes of childhood and the fantasies they generated. The genetic approach is not a theory; it is an empirical finding confirmed in every psychoanalysis. In effect, it states that in many ways, we never get over our childhood. We do not have a complete answer to the questions of why we fail to do so. One factor undoubtedly resides in the long period of biological dependence characteristic of the human infant. There seems to be a broad tendency in the higher forms of life for the earliest experiences to have a persistent and crucial effect on later development. Freud's observations about the crucial role of events in early childhood in shaping later behavior have been confirmed by ethologists in their studies of other forms of life (Lorenz, 1952; Tinbergern, 1951).

Personality evolves out of the interaction between inherent biological factors and the vicissitudes of experience. For any individual, given an average expectable environment, one may anticipate a more or less predictable sequence of events constituting the steps in the maturation of the drives and the other components of the psychic apparatus. Whatever happens to the individual—illness, accidents, deprivation, abuse, seduction, abandonment—in some way will alter the native endowment and will contribute towards determining the ultimate personality structure.

The terminology used for describing the development of the drives originally applied only to the libidinal drives. Freud had conceptualized them first and did not postulate an independent aggressive drive until later. The early phases of the libidinal drives are quite distinct and clearly relate to specific zones of the body. The somatic substrate of aggression is not so clearly defined.

Variety of Concepts

Oral Phase

The earliest phase of instinctual life is *oral*. This phase extends from birth to approximately 18 months. The chief source of libidinal gratification centers around feeding and the organs connected with that function—the mouth, the lips, and the tongue. Gratification of oral needs in the form of satiety brings about a state of freedom from tension and induces sleep. Many disturbances of sleep seem to be connected with unconscious fantasies of an oral libidinal nature (Lewis, 1946, 1949). Biting and sucking serve both to gratify oral drives and to "explore" the world. During the oral phase, the basic orientation of the psychic apparatus is to take in what is pleasurable and to expel what is unpleasant. According to Karl Abraham (1924), people whose early oral needs have been excessively frustrated turn out to be pessimists. On the other hand, individuals whose oral needs have been gratified tend to have a more optimistic view of the world.

Anal Phase

Between the ages of 18 months and 3 years, the main source of pleasure and libidinal gratification comes from retaining and passing feces. The fundamental instinctual orientation concerns what is to be retained and is therefore valuable, and what is to be expelled and ultimately becomes worthless. During the *anal* phase, interest in the bodily processes, in smelling, touching, and playing with feces, is paramount. Regarded for a while as an extruded portion of one's self, the feces are considered a particularly valuable and highly prized possession. The disgust that those who train the child evince and the shame the child is made to feel may contribute toward a lowered sense of self-esteem. In reaction, the child may respond by stubborn assertiveness, contrary rebelliousness, and the determination to be in control of whatever happens to him. Through *reaction formation* the child may overcome the impulse to soil by becoming meticulously clean, excessively punctual, and quite parsimonious in handling possessions (Freud, 1917).

Phallic Phase

After the third year, the main area of libidinal gratification shifts to the genitals. For both boys and girls, the penis becomes the principal object of interest in the *phallic phase*. At this time the clitoris, embryologically an analogue of the penis, begins to be appreciated for the pleasurable sensations evoked by stimulation. Some awareness of the pleasure potential of the vagina is present at this phase in many little girls (Greenacre, 1967). Also prominent in the phallic phase are exhibitionistic and voyeuristic wishes.

By the time children have reached the phallic phase, they have made marked advances in the complexity of their psychological structure. The basic orientation during this phase is therefore much more subtle and complicated. Although children remain basically self-centered, their relations with others in the environment take on a rich texture. They love and want to possess those who give them pleasure; they hate and want to annihilate those who stand in their way and frustrate them. They become curious about sexual differences and the origin of life, and in a primitive childlike way they fashion their own answers to these important questions. They want to love and to be loved, to be admired and to be like those they admire. They may overidealize themselves or share a sense of power by feeling at one with those they idealize. During this time, children may entertain intensely hostile wishes, with the penis serving as an instrument for aggression. This gives rise to intense fears of retaliation, usually directed against the penis. It is also the era of the discovery of the anatomical distinction between the sexes, a phase from which the fear of female genitalia and envy of male genitalia originate.

Three salient features in the development of the drives must be mentioned here. First is the concept of *autoerotism*. When gratification of a particular instinctual urge is not forthcoming, it is always possible for children to gratify themselves by stimulating the appropriate zones of their bodies, combining such activities with appropriate fantasies. This evolves into the more common forms of childhood masturbation. Second, as the individual passes from one libidinal phase to another, the interest in the gratification of the preceding phase is not completely surrendered. It is only partially superseded by the succeeding libidinal gratification. When there is a particularly strong and persistent attachment to libidinal gratification from a particular object of infancy, one speaks of *fixation*. Fixations are usually unconscious and often serve as a focus for symptom formation later in life. A third feature of libidinal development is the potentiality for *regression*, the reactivation of or the return to an earlier mode of libidinal gratification. Regressive reactivation of earlier modes of mental functioning is common and not necessarily pathological. Usually the regression reactivates some childhood libidinal impulse that had been involved in the process of fixation.

For each of the aforementioned phases of development, there is a characteristic danger. During the oral phase, the greatest danger is that the mother will not be available. This is usually referred to as the danger of *loss of the* (need-satisfying) *object*. During the anal phase, after the concept of the mother as an independent entity has crystallized, *losing the mother's love* constitutes the danger. Typical of the phallic phase is fear of retaliation or punishment for forbidden sexual and aggressive wishes. The kind of punishment usually fantasied by both boys and girls takes the form of injury to the body, specifically to the genitals. For this reason, the danger characteristic of the phallic phase is referred to as the *fear of castration*. Later in life, after external prohibitions and threats of punishment have been internalized into the personality in the form of the superego, *fear of conscience* takes its place among the danger situations. Each one of these situations evokes anxiety as a signal alerting the ego to set in motion various mental maneuvers to eliminate or minimize the danger. These maneuvers Anna Freud (1936) called the *mechanisms of defense*, because they protect the rest of the personality from the unpleasant affect of anxiety.

The combined influence on the mind of the libidinal and aggressive wishes constitutes the id. The other components of the mind are the ego and the superego. It will be possible to present only a few observations on the development of these psychological structures. The earliest psychological experience of the infant is most likely one of global sensory impingement (Spitz, 1955). The infant makes no differentiation between self and the rest of the world, between what is in the body and what is outside of it. The inherent capacities to perceive, to move, and later, to speak, mature gradually. The concept of the self as an independent entity develops over a period of two to three years (Jacobson, 1954; Mahler et al., 1975). There is evidence that for a certain period during the first year of life, the child is unable to distinguish between himself and the person who cares for him. An object in the external world, such as a blanket or a stuffed animal toy, may be experienced at times as being part of the self and at other times as part of the external world (Winnicott, 1953).

At first the instinctual drives center mainly on the self—a state called *narcissism*. As other people come to be appreciated as sources of sustenance, protection, and gratification, some of the energy of the libidinal drive settles (is vested) on mental representations of others. Technically, these others are referred to as *love objects*, or *objects* for short. At its core, the human personality retains a considerable complement of childish self-centeredness. The capacity to need others, to love, to want to please, and to want to become like others is one of the most significant indicators of psychological maturity. In addition to constitutional factors, the quality of experience with objects during the early years is decisive in shaping the all-important capacity to love and identify with others. Disturbances in this process because of traumatic experiences or poor object relations contribute to the severe forms of pathology known as narcissistic character disorders, borderline states, and the psychoses.

Needing, wanting, and identifying with valued persons are fraught with the dangers of frustration, disappointment, and, inevitably, conflict. The imperious wishes of childhood can never be gratified in full. Inexorably, relations with the important objects become a mixture of love and hatred. Such feelings come to a climactic crisis with the oedipal longings of the phallic phase. As a rule between the ages of three and six, the child develops intense erotic longings for the parent of the opposite sex and a hostile competitive orientation toward the parent of the same sex. Circumstances may induce enormous variations in this basic pattern, including a total inversion of the choice of sexual object. It is the responsibility of the ego to deal with these conflicts. Under favorable circumstances, oedipal wishes are given up, repressed. They become unconscious. They are, however, not totally obliterated but continue as a potential source of instinctual pressure in the form of unconscious fantasies. Disguised versions of these fantasies may persist in consciousness as the familiar daydreams of childhood. They continue to exert an important influence on nearly every aspect of mental life: on the forms and objects of adult sexuality; on creative, artistic, vocational, and other sublimated activity; on character formation; and on whatever neurotic symptoms the individual may develop later (Brenner, 1973).

Under favorable circumstances, the child relinquishes most of the hostile and neurotic impulses of the Oedipus complex and identifies with the parent of the same sex, especially with his or her moral standards and prohibitions. This is the matrix of the moral part of the personality called the superego. This agency observes the self and judges its thoughts and actions in terms of what it considers right and wrong. It may prescribe punishment, reparation, or repentance for wrong-doing or may reward the self with heightened esteem and affection for virtuous thought and action. The superego is the seed of the conscience and the source of guilt. Under certain conditions, its functioning may be as impulsive and demanding as any primitive instinctual wish of the id. This is particularly true in states of depression.

Latency Period

With the passing of the Oedipus complex and the consolidation of the superego, a relatively quiescent phase ensues, called the *latency period*. Children now can be socialized and can direct their interests to the larger world, where the process of education becomes a more formalized experience. This state prevails until the onset of *puberty and adolescence*. The transformations that take place during this period are crucial in establishing the adult identity. As a result of the physiological and psychological changes involved in assuming the adult role, the conflicts of childhood are evoked anew. Variations of fantasies that originally served as vehicles for the drives during childhood become the conscious concomitants of adolescent masturbation. Guilt over masturbation derives primarily from the unconscious wishes that find substitute expression in the masturbation fantasies. During adolescence, a second attempt is made to master the conflicts arising from childhood wishes. (Through the successful resolution of these conflicts, individuals consolidate their adult identity about their sexual role, more responsibility, and choice of work or profession.)

Conflicts stemming from some phase of life are part of normal human development. Uncontrolled expression of certain instinctual impulses could have calamitous consequences for the individual. Free expression of drives represents a major confrontation with one's morality and could, under certain circumstances, provoke a severe superego response in the form of guilt or self-punishment. It falls upon the ego to mediate the demands made upon it by the id and the superego with due consideration for the exigent needs of reality. All of mental life represents a shifting balance, a tenuously stable equilibrium between the pressures of the id, the superego, and reality. Presumably, the most effective way to deal with a conflict would be to bar the impulse permanently from consciousness. When this occurs, one may speak of successful repression. In most instances, however, the victory is by no means one-sided. By their very nature, unconscious wishes remain dynamic and from time to time threaten to overcome the repression instituted to constrain them. Such intrusion may precipitate attacks of panic or, in lesser form, anxiety. Under such circumstances, the ego undertakes fresh measures to ward off the unpleasant affect of anxiety. If successful repression cannot be maintained, various compromises have to be effected by calling into play the different mechanisms of defense, which may become permanent features of the individual's character.

Unsuccessful resolution of intrapsychic conflicts eventuates in neurotic illness and neurotic character traits, inhibitions, sexual perversions, and patterns of behavior of a neurotic or self-defeating nature.

❧ PSYCHOTHERAPY

Theory of Psychotherapy

The principles and techniques of psychoanalysis as therapy are based upon the psychoanalytic theory of neurosis. As the theory of neurosis changed, so did the technique of therapy. Originally, Freud felt that neurotic symptoms were the result of pent-up, undischarged emotional tension connected with the repressed memory of a traumatic childhood sexual experience. At first, he used hypnosis to bring about emotional catharsis and abreaction of the trauma. Because many of his patients could not be hypnotized, he dropped hypnosis in favor of forced suggestion, a technique of recollection fostered by the insistent demanding pressure of the therapist. Among other things, this technique produced artifacts in the form of sexual fantasies about childhood, which the patient offered the therapist as if they were recollections of actual events. Taking advantage of his new operational concepts of the dynamic unconscious and the principle of strict psychic determinism, Freud reduced the element of suggestion to a minimum by a new technical procedure in which he asked his patients to report freely and without criticism whatever came into their minds. Thus, the technique of *free association* evolved.

During the period when the topographic model of the psychic apparatus was paramount in Freud's mind, the principal technical goal was to make the contents of the unconscious conscious. The patient's productions were interpreted according to principles very similar to those used in *The Interpretation of Dreams*. The most striking discovery Freud made during this period was that of *transference*, a highly emotional attitude the patient develops towards the analyst which represents a repetition of the individual's fantasy wishes concerning objects of the past, foisted onto the analyst. The discovery that the anti-instinctual forces of the mind, such as the defense mechanisms, guilt, and self-punishment, could operate at an unconscious level contributed to the elaboration of the structural theory. The structural theory pointed to the need to analyze the functioning of the defense mechanisms and the self-punitive trends. Elucidating the nature of the unconscious danger and the quality of the anxiety attendant upon its appearance have since become central points of analytic technique.

In later years, in an attempt to apply psychoanalytic therapy to types of cases that have heretofore been refractory to treatment, newer techniques were suggested. Franz Alexander (1932) felt that because most patients had been traumatized by parental mismanagement during childhood, it was necessary for the analyst to arrange "a corrective emotional experience" to counteract the effects of the original trauma. A more recent elaboration of these ideas has been proposed by E. R. Zetzel (1970) and Ralph Greenson (1967), who emphasized particular measures required to instill confidence and create a proper alliance between therapist and patient. Greenson emphasizes the importance of the real personality of the analyst. Some analysts, influenced by Melanie Klein, see in the analyst's emotional reaction a mirror of what the patient is experiencing consciously or unconsciously (Racker, 1953; Weigert, 1970). Heinz Kohut (1971) has suggested strengthening the self-esteem of patients with narcissistic personality disorders.

Recent years have seen the development of major innovations and changes in the psychoanalytic theory of pathology and treatment. The teachings of Kohut have become the basis for a school known as self psychology. According to this approach, the regulation of self-esteem and the vicissitudes of what is called the "self state" are perhaps the primary factors in pathology and dictate in many ways the analyst's approach to the treatment of the patient. Very early dissonance in a mother/child interaction creates the basis for narcissistic vulnerability, the untoward effects of which have to be compensated for during treatment. Another major development may be seen in the theories concerning object relations. These theories, as well as those of Kohut, developed out of experience with so-called borderline and narcissistic personality disorders. A preeminent spokesman for the object relations school is Kernberg, who emphasizes in his writings how the relations with the earliest significant objects in the individual's life leave a residue of internalized relationship concepts that may continue throughout the individual's life. In addition, the combination of psychoanalysis with other modalities of treatment, such as drugs, group therapy, and family interaction, has been advanced.

Onset of Neurosis

In the genesis of neurotic disorders, the conflicts of childhood are of critical importance. By far the most common and most significant conflicts involve the wishes of the oedipal phase. All children have conflicts, and most of them develop some kind of childhood neurosis. Usually *childhood neurosis* assumes the form of general apprehensiveness, nightmares, phobias, tics, mannerisms, or ritualistic practices. Most primary behavior disorders of children represent disguised forms of neurosis from which the element of manifest fear has disappeared. Phobia is probably the most frequent symptom of childhood neurosis. In most cases, with the passage of the oedipal phase, the disturbances caused by instinctual conflicts have been sufficiently ameliorated to permit the child to progress normally. In some cases, a childhood neurosis continues with relatively little change into adult life.

Neurosis in adults may develop anew when the balance between the pressures of the drives and the defensive forces of the ego is upset. There are three typical situations in which this may occur.

1.   An individual may be unable to cope with the additional psychological burden of normal development. The unconscious significance of becoming an adult and undertaking the competitive and aggressive challenges of maturity may prove too much for the ego.

2.   Disappointment, defeat, loss of love, physical illness, or some other consequence of the human condition may lead an individual to turn away from current reality and unconsciously seek gratification in the world of fantasy. This usually involves a reactivation (regression) of the fantasy wishes of the oedipal phase. As these wishes are regressively reactivated, the conflicts and anxieties of childhood are revived and the process of symptom formation begins. The fantasy wishes that are regressively reactivated are the ones that earlier had been the subject of fixation.

3.   By a combination of circumstances, an individual may find himself in adult life in a situation that corresponds in its essential features to some childhood trauma or conflict-laden fantasy. Current reality is then misperceived in terms of the childhood conflict, and the individual responds as he did in childhood, by forming symptoms.

Process of Psychotherapy

The standard technical procedure of psychoanalysis for studying the functioning of the mind is known as the *psychoanalytic situation*. The patient is asked to assume a recumbent position on the couch, looking away from the analyst. The patient is asked to express in words whatever thoughts, images, or feelings come to mind, and to express these elements without distortion, censorship, suppression, or prejudgment concerning the significance or insignificance of any particular idea. Seated behind the couch, the analyst listens in an uncritical, non-judgmental fashion, maintaining an attitude of benign curiosity. The analyst's values and judgments are strictly excluded from the therapeutic interaction.

From time to time the analyst interrupts the patient's associations. In doing so, he momentarily interferes with the patient's role as passive reporter and makes him observe and reflect upon the significance and possible connections among his associations. The analyst's interventions momentarily change the patient's role from passive reporter to active observer and, at times, interpreter. The principle of free association is somewhat modified in connection with the interpretation of dreams. In this instance, the analyst may ask the patient to tell him whatever comes to mind in connection with this or that particular image of the dream.

The practical conditions of the treatment are also strictly regulated. A fixed schedule of fees and appointments is maintained. Any attempt by the patient to deviate from the basic understanding of the analytic situation calls for investigation and analysis. Changes in the basic conditions of the treatment are inadvisable and when necessary are effected by mutual consent between the patient and the analyst after the problem has been analyzed.

The patient's thoughts and associations should come primarily from persistent dynamic internal pressure of the drives as organized in unconscious fantasies. Thoughts and associations should not represent responses to external manipulation, exhortation, stimulation, or education. This is what is uniquely psychoanalytic in the therapeutic interaction. Under the conditions of the analytic situation, the influence of inner mental forces can be more easily and clearly observed than in more usual situations. It becomes possible for the material hitherto suppressed or repressed to be verbalized and examined. This presupposes the strictest adherence to professional principles on the part of the analyst. Everything done must be in the interest of advancing the patient's insight through the process of analysis. There is no greater responsibility in the analytic situation than strict preservation of the patient's confidentiality. Communication of any material of the analysis to any source is contrary to the spirit of the analytic situation, even when the patient believes a breach of confidentiality is in his own best interests.

Psychoanalysis involves a commitment to change through critical self-examination. To maintain continuity of the analytic process, at least four sessions a week are indicated.

Each session lasts at least 45 minutes. The course of treatment may run for several years. Undertaking psychoanalytic treatment involves considerable sacrifice in time, effort, and money. These are not conditions into which one may enter lightly.

The psychoanalytic situation has been structured in this manner with the intention of making it possible to accomplish the goal of psychoanalytic therapy, namely, to help the patient achieve a resolution of intrapsychic conflict through understanding conflicts and dealing with them in a more mature manner. Because the analytic situation is relatively uncontaminated by the intrusion of ordinary interpersonal relationships, the interaction of the three components of the mind—the ego, the id, and the super-ego—may be studied in a more objective way, making it possible to demonstrate to the patient what parts of thought and behavior are determined by inner wishes, conflicts, and fantasies and what parts represent a mature response to objective reality.

Mechanisms of Psychotherapy

The treatment process may be divided into four phases:

1. Opening phase
2. Development of transference
3. Working through
4. Resolution of transference

The Opening Phase

Psychoanalytic observation begins with the very first contact. Everything the patient says and does is noted for possible significance and use later in the treatment. The initial set of interviews is part of the opening phase. During these interviews, the nature of the patient's difficulty is ascertained and a decision is reached concerning whether analysis is indicated. To determine this, it is necessary for the analyst to learn as much as possible about the patient; for example, his current life situation and difficulties, what he has accomplished, how he relates to others, and the history of his family background and childhood development. Formalized history taking, following a prescribed outline, is not encouraged. Priorities in the subjects to be discussed should be left to the patient's intuition. Much is learned from how the patient approaches the practical task of making his problems known to the therapist and how he responds to the delineation of the analytic contract. The understanding of the analytical situation must be clearly defined from the very beginning and the respective responsibilities of both parties explicitly stated.

After a few sessions of face-to-face interviews, the second part of the opening phase begins when the patient assumes the couch. No two patients begin treatment in the same way. Some find it difficult to lie on the couch and say whatever comes to mind; others take readily to this new set of conditions. Everything the patient says and does—the position assumed on the couch, the clothes worn, characteristic phrases, what the patient chooses to present as the opening statement of the session, and punctuality—are all clues to unconscious mental processes.

During the opening phase, the analyst learns more about the patient's history and development. He gets to understand in broad outline the nature of the patient's unconscious conflicts and has an opportunity to study the characteristic ways by which the patient resists revealing himself or becoming aware of repudiated thoughts and feelings. Gradually the analyst is able to detect a continuous thread of themes that follow relatively uniform sequences and repeat themselves in a variety of meaningful configurations. These productions can be understood in terms of the persistent, unconscious fantasy representing wishes from childhood, dynamically active in the patient's current life in disguised and distorted ways. In the early phases, the analyst deals almost exclusively with the superficial aspects of the patient's material. He tries to demonstrate to the patient significant correlations in the material presented but restricts himself primarily to those elements that are readily accessible to consciousness and that are not too close to the patient's basic conflicts. In ordinary cases, the initial phase of the treatment lasts from three to six months.

The Development of Transference

The next two phases of treatment, the transference and working through, constitute the major portion of the therapeutic work and actually overlap. At a certain stage in the treatment, when it appears the patient is just about ready to relate his current difficulties to unconscious conflicts from childhood concerning wishes over some important person or persons in his life, a new and interesting phenomenon emerges. Emotionally, the analyst assumes major significance in the life of the patient. The patient's perceptions of and demands upon the analyst become inappropriate, out of keeping with reality. The professional relationship becomes distorted as he tries to introduce personal instead of professional considerations into their interaction. Understanding transference was one of Freud's greatest discoveries. He perceived that in the transference, the patient was unconsciously reenacting a latter-day version of forgotten childhood memories and repressed unconscious fantasies. *Transference*, therefore, could be understood as a form of memory in which repetition in action replaces recollection of events.

Analysis of the transference is one of the cornerstones of psychoanalytic technique. It helps the patient distinguish fantasy from reality, past from present, and it makes real to the patient the force of the persistent unconscious fantasy wishes of childhood. Analysis of transference helps the patient understand how one misperceives, misinterprets, and relates to the present in terms of the past. In place of the automatic, uncontrolled, stereotyped ways through which the patient unconsciously responds to unconscious fantasies, the patient is able to evaluate the unrealistic nature of impulses and anxieties and to make appropriate decisions on a mature and realistic level. In this way, analysis helps the patient achieve a major realignment in the dynamic equilibrium between impulse and conflict that ultimately leads to a satisfactory resolution of the pathogenic conflict once the patient comes to understand not only the nature of the fears that motivate his defenses, but self-punitive trends as well. For the most part, these are also unconscious.

Working Through

This phase of the treatment coincides with and continues the analysis of transference. One or two experiences of insight into the nature of one's conflicts are not sufficient to bring about change. Analysis of the transference has to be continued many times and in many different ways. The patient's insight into problems by way of the transference is constantly deepened and consolidated by working through, a process that consists of repetition, elaboration, and amplification. Working through acts as a kind of catalyst between analysis of transference and the overcoming of the amnesia for crucial childhood experiences (Greenacre, 1956). Usually the experience of successful analysis of a transference phenomenon is followed by the emergence into memory of some important event or fantasy from the patient's past. Analysis of the transference facilitates recall. Recall illuminates the nature of the transference. This reciprocal interplay between understanding the transference and recollecting the past consolidates the patient's insight into conflicts and strengthens his conviction concerning the interpretive reconstructions made in the course of treatment.

Resolution of Transference

The resolution of transference is the termination phase of treatment. When the patient and the analyst are satisfied that the major goals of the analysis have been accomplished and the transference is well understood, a date is set for ending treatment. Technically, the analyst's aim is to resolve the patient's unconscious neurotic attachment to him. There are a number of striking features typical of this phase of treatment. Most characteristic and dramatic is a sudden and intense aggravation of the very symptoms for which the patient sought treatment. It seems as if all the analytic work had been done in vain. Upon further analysis, this turn of events can be understood as a last-ditch effort on the part of the patient to convince the analyst that he is not yet ready to leave treatment and that he should be permitted to continue the relationship indefinitely. There are many motives for this unconscious attitude. In part, the patient is unwilling to surrender so gratifying and helpful a relationship. In part, it constitutes a continuation of some passive, dependent orientation from childhood. But most of all, it represents a last-chance endeavor to get the analyst to fulfill the very unconscious, infantile fantasy wishes that were the source of the patient's conflicts to begin with.

Another interesting thing that happens during the termination phase of treatment is the emergence of hitherto repressed memories that confirm or elaborate the reconstructions and interpretations made earlier in the treatment. It is as if the patient presents new insight or findings to the analyst as a parting gift of gratitude. Unconsciously, it often has the significance of presenting the analyst with a child, a gift of new life, as a form of thanks for the new life that analysis has made possible for the patient.

Finally, during the closing phase of treatment, the patient may reveal a hitherto concealed group of wishes amounting to a desire to be magically transformed into some omnipotent or omniscient figure, a striving kept secret throughout the analysis but that the patient had quietly hoped would be fulfilled by the time the treatment was over. It is important during this phase to analyze all the fantasies the patient has about how things will be after the analysis is over (Schmidcberg, 1938). If one fails to deal with all the problems mentioned above, the possibilities of relapse remain high.

❖ APPLICATIONS

Problems

From the description of psychoanalysis as therapy, it should be clear that any potential patient must be able to fulfill certain objective as well as personal requirements. Essentially, patients must be strongly motivated to overcome their difficulties by honest self-scrutiny. Because it is difficult at the beginning to predict how long treatment will last, individuals must be in a position to commit a considerable period in advance for the purpose of carrying the analysis through to successful termination. In addition, psychoanalysis patients must accept the discipline of the conditions proposed by the psychoanalytic contract. The psychoanalytic dialogue is an unusual form of communication, inevitably entailing frustration of transference wishes. Patients must be able to accept such frustration and to express thoughts and feelings in words rather than action. Impulsive, willful, self-centered, and highly narcissistic individuals may not be able to accommodate themselves to such structures. People who are basically dishonest, psychopathic, or pathological liars obviously will not be equal to the task of complete and unrelenting self-revelation. Furthermore, because cooperation with the analyst in an enterprise of self-exploration requires some degree of objectivity and reality testing, functions severely impaired in the psychoses, psychoanalysis can rarely be used in the treatment of such conditions except under very special circumstances.

Because psychoanalysis is a time-consuming, expensive, and arduous form of treatment, it is not indicated when difficulties are minor. Genuine suffering and pain are the most reliable allies of the analytic process. Through insight, psychoanalysis hopes to enable the patient to overcome inner conflicts. This can be helpful only insofar as such insights can be put to constructive use in altering one's life situation. If the person's objective situation is so bad that there is nothing one can do about it, psychoanalysis will be of no avail. This can be seen, for example, where the analyst recognizes how the story the patient presents reflects a lifelong struggle against murderous, destructive, and self-destructive impulses, the psychological consequences of severe congenital deformity or crippling disease early in childhood. No psychological insight can compensate for the injustices of fate.

Because so much of psychoanalytic technique depends on analysis of the transference, psychoanalysis is best suited for conditions in which transference attachments tend to be strong. This is true in the classical psychoneurotic entities—hysteria, anxiety hysteria, obsessive-compulsive neurosis, and a variety of states characterized by anxiety. In actual practice, the symptomatologies of the psychoneuroses tend to overlap. The diagnostic label attached to a particular condition usually reflects the major mechanism of defense characteristically employed to ward off anxiety. In hysteria, for example, by a process called *conversion*, the energy of a sexual wish that the ego was unable to repress successfully may be transformed into alterations of body functions, such as paralysis, absence of sensation, and abnormal sensations. An unconscious fantasy of sucking on a penis or swallowing it may manifest itself consciously in the feeling that there is an abnormal lump in the throat that cannot be swallowed—the classical globus hystericus. A symptom is compromise formation. Unconsciously, it gratifies the wish and the need for punishment at the same time.

Phobias are typical of anxiety hysteria. The phobic patient wards off anxiety by treating some other external object or situation as the representative of the unconscious impulse. In one form of *agoraphobia*, a patient may become anxious whenever she goes out on the street, the street representing the place where it is possible to realize her unconscious wish to be a prostitute. The mechanism of defense is a double one. The internal (sexual) danger is projected onto the street, an external situation. By avoiding the external object, the patient controls an internal danger. The mechanisms of defense represent a combination of projection and avoidance.

Psychoanalysis is also applicable for character disorders that represent substitutes for psychoneurotic symptoms. For a person whose unconscious fantasies lead him unconsciously to misconstrue dancing as indulgence in dangerous sexual activity, it may prove much more acceptable just to avoid dancing than to experience blushing, palpitations, and sweating whenever he attempts it. Such a person may be diagnosed as suffering from phobic character disorders. There are many forms of character disorders of this type—hysterical, obsessive, compulsive, depressive, and so on. Arlow (1972) has demonstrated how certain character traits may represent transformations from what originally had been transient perversions. Petty liars, hoaxers, and unrealistic personalities may be said to be suffering from character perversions.

Sexual difficulties and psychoneurotic depressions are ordinarily quite amenable to psychoanalytic treatment. More generalized patterns of behavior that interfere with the patient's conscious goals for happiness and success can be traced to unconscious conflicts and treated psychoanalytically. Some men, for example, repeatedly fall in love with and marry the same kind of woman, although they know from previous experience that the marriage will end disastrously. Similarly, certain women seem incapable of choosing men other than those who will hurt, abuse, and humiliate them. Other people will unconsciously arrange their lives so any success is followed by an even greater failure. In these cases, their normal way of life or choice of love object or self-engineered fate is the equivalent of a psychoneurotic disorder.

In recent years, many patients seeking psychoanalytic treatment seem to be suffering from masochistic character disorders or from narcissistic neuroses. Into this latter category fall those paradoxical combinations of low self-esteem and heightened grandiosity. Mood swings, depression, tendencies toward drug dependence, compulsive strivings for recognition and success, and patterns of promiscuous sexuality are not uncommon. Such patients often complain of inner emptiness, lack of goals, hypochondriasis, and an inability to make lasting attachments or love relationships. Because of new contributions to the technical management of these problems, the prognosis of their treatment by psychoanalysis seems much better today than in previous years.

A number of conditions may be helped by psychoanalysis under specially favorable conditions. Among these are some cases of drug addiction, perversions, borderline personalities, and, on rare occasions, psychoses. Pioneering work applying psychoanalytic principles, if not the complete technique, to the treatment of psychotics has been done by Paul Federn (1952), Frieda Fromm-Reichmann (1950), H. Rosenfeld (1954), and H. F. Searles (1965).

Evaluation

Unfortunately, there exists no adequate study evaluating the results of psychoanalytic therapy. In a general way, this is true of almost all forms of psychotherapy. There are just too many variables to be taken into account to make it possible to establish a controlled, statistically valid study of the outcome of the therapy. Several attempts have been made in this direction beginning with Otto Fenichel (1930), including studies by Fred Feldman (1968), H. J. Eysenck (1965), Julian Meltzoff and Melvin Kornreich (1970), R. S. Wallerstein and N. J. Smelser (1969), and A. Z. Pfeffer (1963), as well as several studies by the American Psychoanalytic Association. None of the findings of these studies has proven definitive and irrefutable. By and large, the number of "cures" range from 30 to 60 percent, depending on the studies and the criteria employed.

In any individual case, evaluation of the outcome of treatment has to be judged in a global fashion. Comparisons are made between the situation at the beginning of treatment and the alteration in the patient's life and symptoms at termination. The patient may have been cured of more conditions than initially complained about; previously unforeseen possibilities of self-fulfillment may have been realized. On the other hand, unrecognized complicating difficulties and intercurrent events may have changed the total configuration of the patient's life. In the face of objective reality, the claims of psychoanalysis must be modest. At best, psychoanalysis tries to help the patient effect the best possible solution of difficulties that circumstances will allow. It seeks to achieve the most stable equilibrium possible between the various forces at conflict in the mind. How well that equilibrium is sustained will also depend on how favorably life treats the patient during and after treatment. Freud himself was quite modest about the therapeutic claims of psychoanalysis (Freud, 1937). The validity of what psychoanalysis has discovered concerning human nature and the functioning of the human mind are not necessarily related to the effectiveness of psychoanalysis as treatment. Nonetheless, the fact remains that when properly applied to the appropriate condition, psychoanalysis remains the most effective mode of therapy yet devised.

Treatment

Freud compared writing about psychoanalysis to explaining the game of chess. It is easy to formulate the rules of the game, to describe the opening phases, and to discuss what has to be done to bring a chess game to a close. What happens in between is subject to infinite variation. The same is true of psychoanalysis. The analytic contract, the opening phase, and the tasks of termination can be described definitively. The analysis of the transference and the process of working through consist of countless bits of analytic work. Rudolf Loewenstein (1958) approached the problem by distinguishing between tactical and strategic goals in psychoanalytic technique. *Tactical* concerns involve the analysis of the immediate presenting material in terms of some conflict, usually involving the analyst. The *strategic* goal is to elucidate the nature of the unconscious childhood fantasy and to demonstrate the many ways in which it affects the patient's current life.

How this appears in actual practice may be demonstrated in the following illustration. The patient was a middle-aged businessman whose marriage had been marked by repeated strife and quarrels. His sexual potency had been tenuous. At times he suffered from premature ejaculation. At the beginning of one session, he began to complain about having to return to treatment after a long holiday weekend. He said, "I'm not so sure I'm glad to be back in treatment even though I didn't enjoy my visit to my parents. I feel I just have to be free." He then continued with a description of his visit home, which he said had been depressing. His mother was bossy, aggressive, manipulative, as always. He felt sorry for his father. At least in the summertime, the father could retreat to the garden and work with the flowers, but the mother watched over him like a hawk. "She has such a sharp tongue and a cruel mouth. Each time I see my father he seems to be getting smaller and smaller; pretty soon he will disappear and there will be nothing left of him. She does that to people. I always feel that she is hovering over me ready to swoop down on me. She has me intimidated just like my wife."

The patient continued, "I was furious this morning. When I came to get my car, I found that someone had parked in a way that hemmed it in. It took a long time and lots of work to get my car out. During the time I realized how anxious I was; the perspiration was pouring down the back of my neck.

"I feel restrained by the city. I need the open fresh air; I have to stretch my legs. I'm sorry I gave up the house I had in the country. I have to get away from this city. I really can't afford to buy another house now, but at least I'll feel better if I look for one."

"If only business were better, I could maneuver more easily. I hate the feeling of being stuck in an office from nine until five. My friend Bob had the right idea—he arranged for retirement. Now he's free to come and go as he pleases. He travels, he has no boss, no board of directors to answer to. I love my work but it imposes too many restrictions on me. I can't help it, I'm ambitious. What can I do?"

At this point, the therapist called to the patient's attention the fact that throughout the material, in many different ways, the patient was describing how he feared confinement, that he had a sense of being trapped.

The patient responded, "I do get symptoms of claustrophobia from time to time. They're mild, just a slight anxiety. I begin to feel perspiration at the back of my neck, and I have a sense of restlessness. The hair seems to stand up on the back of my neck. It happens when the elevator stops between floors or when a train gets stuck between stations. I begin to worry about how I'll get out."

The fact that he suffered from claustrophobia was a new finding in the analysis. The analyst noted to himself that the patient felt claustrophobic about the analysis. The conditions of the analytic situation imposed by the analyst were experienced by the patient as confining. In addition, the analyst noted, again to himself, these ideas were coupled with the idea of being threatened and controlled by his mother.

The patient continue, "You know, I have the same feeling about starting an affair with Mrs. X. She wants to and I guess I want to also. Getting involved is easy. It's getting uninvolved that concerns me. How do you get out of an affair once you're in it?"

In this material, the patient associates being trapped in a confined space with being trapped in the analysis and with being trapped in an affair with a woman.

The patient continued, "I'm really chicken. It's a wonder I was ever able to have relations at all and to get married. No wonder I didn't have intercourse until I was in my twenties. My mother was always after me, 'Be careful about getting involved with girls; they'll get you into trouble. They'll be after you for your money. If you have sex with them, you can pick up a disease. Be careful when you go to public toilets; you can get an infection, etc., etc., etc.' She made it all sound dangerous. You can get hurt from this, you can get hurt from that. It reminds me of the time I saw two dogs having intercourse. They were stuck together and couldn't separate the male dog was yelping and screaming in pain. I don't even know how old I was then, maybe five or six or perhaps seven, but I was definitely a child and I was frightened."

At this point, the analyst is able to tell the patient that his fear of being trapped in an enclosed space is the conscious derivative of an unconscious fantasy in which he imagines that if he enters the woman's body with his penis, it will get stuck; he will not be able to extricate it; he may lose it. The criteria used in making this interpretation are clear: they consist of the sequential arrangement of the material, the contiguity of related themes, the repetition of the same or analogous themes, and the convergence of the different elements into one common hypothesis that encompasses all the data, namely, an unconscious fantasy of danger to the penis once it enters a woman's body. This is the tactical goal that can be achieved on the basis of this material. In this instance, it constitutes an important step toward the strategic goal, which, in this case, would consist of making the patient aware of childhood sexual strivings toward the mother, of a wish to have relations with her, and of a concomitant fear growing out of the threatening nature of her personality, that, like a hawk, she would swoop down upon him and devour him. These interpretations would give him insight into the causes of his impotence and his stormy relations with women, particularly his wife. The material also demonstrates how a neurotic person misperceives, misinterprets, and responds inappropriately to current experience in terms of his unconscious fantasy. To this patient, having to keep a definite set of appointments with the analyst, having his car hemmed in between two other cars, being responsible to authorities, and getting stuck in elevators or in trains were all experienced as dangerous situations that evoked the symptoms of anxiety. Consciously, he experienced restrictions by rules and confinement within certain spaces. Unconsciously, he was thinking in terms of experiencing his penis inextricably trapped inside a woman's body.

This is the essence of the neurotic process—the persistent unconscious fantasies of childhood serve to create a mental set according to which the individual in a selective and idiosyncratic way interprets everything that happens to him. Therefore, neurotic conflicts do not represent conflicts with reality. They are intrapsychic conflicts (Arlow, 1963).

The material of any one analytic session is by no means always so dramatic. Yet one must be careful not to prejudge the significance and possible ramifications of any event or session, no matter how trivial it may appear at first. A seemingly insignificant interaction between the patient and the analyst may lead to very important discoveries illuminating the origins and the meaning of the neurosis. For the most part, however, the major portion of the analytic work is directed toward understanding the patient's defenses and overcoming resistances. It is not always easy to distinguish between mechanisms of defense and resistances. Typically, the *mechanisms of defense* are repetitive, stereotyped, automatic means used by the ego to ward off anxiety. A *resistance* is any one of a wide range of phenomena distracting the patient from pursuing the requirements of the analytic situation.

It may seem strange that a patient who has made so serious a commitment to self-understanding should not follow the course of action in treatment that is intended to bring relief. However, this is not at all unexpected. Because the mind characteristically turns away from or tries to repress unpleasant feelings and thoughts and because the neurotic process develops when it is has been unable to accomplish this end successfully, it should come as no surprise that the endeavor to both fulfill and control forbidden impulses should continue into analytic experience. Herman Nunberg (1926) showed how the patient unconsciously brings into the analysis a wish to preserve intact the same infantile strivings that caused his difficulties in the first place.

The analysis of defenses and resistances is slow, piecemeal work. Nevertheless, much can be learned from it about how the patient's character was shaped in response to the critical events and object relations of childhood. A particularly difficult resistance to overcome during treatment comes from the use of the mechanism known as *isolation*. This is the tendency for the patient to deal with his thoughts as if they were empty of feeling or unrelated to other ideas or to his behavior. A patient may begin a session, for example, by mentioning in two or three short sentences an incident that took place on his way to the session. He had passed a man on the street who suddenly, without cause or warning, extended his arm in such a way that he almost struck the patient. This reminded the patient of an incident some years earlier when he saw someone actually being hit in this very same manner. On this occasion, as in the past, the patient, not a native New Yorker, shrugged the incident off with the reassuring judgment, "Well, that's New York for you. It's a good thing he didn't have a knife." All of this was stated in an even, flat, unemotional tone.

With no transition, the patient turned to matters of closer concern to him. He described at great length, and again in an even-tempered way, how his boss had criticized his work in front of his colleagues. Many of the criticisms, he felt, were unjustified, but mindful of his position, he had maintained a calm, respectful demeanor. Even when recounting the incident, in the session, he showed little sign of anger. When this was called to his attention, he admitted that indeed he had been angry and was surprised that he had not transmitted that feeling to the therapist. At this point, the therapist made the connection for the patient between his opening report of a near-assault on the street and the experience with his boss. Actually, the patient had been saying, "There are dangerous people abroad. If one is not careful, they may strike you, even kill you. They have murderous impulses." The incident in the street served as a convenient locus onto which the patient projected his own murderous wishes to retaliate against the boss. He dealt with these impulses in an isolated way, an intellectual judgment he made about someone else's motives.

At this stage of the treatment, he could grasp only intellectually, by inference, the intensity of his vengeful wishes. Much could be learned from the analysis of this experience beyond illustrating how the patient manages to control and to suppress his feelings. This patient was particularly vulnerable to any assault on his pride, any humiliation of his narcissism, especially if it occurred as part of a public spectacle. Later in the analysis, it was possible to demonstrate the connection between these components of the patient's character and the feelings of defeat, insignificance, and humiliation he experienced during the oedipal phase while watching his parents having intercourse in the bedroom he shared with them.

It would be impossible to catalogue all the forms that resistance can take. Some of the more usual ones may be noted here. The most direct and unequivocal form of resistance occurs when the patient finds he has nothing to say. The patient may remain silent on the couch for minutes on end. Even a trivial lateness of a few minutes may carry some hidden meaning. Often a patient may miss sessions, forget them, or oversleep. He may be tardy in paying the bill for treatment, giving very realistic explanations to account for the tardiness. Sometimes patients will talk endlessly about trivial day-to-day events, revealing little or nothing that can be used to understand their problems. A patient may introduce a dream at the beginning of a session and make no reference to it for the rest of the analytic hour. On the other hand, the patient may fill the entire session with dreams, making it impossible to learn more than the facade of what had been recorded of the night's experience. Some patients report how they have become ardent advocates of psychoanalysis, proselytizing their friends and relatives, urging all of them to enter into treatment, at the very time when they themselves are making little effort or progress in the analytic work.

The important principle governing all manifestations of resistance is that they must be analyzed like everything else that happens in the course of analysis. What must be understood is why the patient is behaving the way he is at a particular moment. What is the motive behind his unconscious wish to break off the analytic work? What conflict is he trying to evade? Exhortation, suggestion, encouragement, prohibitions—any of a number of educational procedures that in other forms of therapy may be introduced at such a time—must be carefully avoided. No matter how provocative, frustrating, or irritating the patient's behavior may be, the analyst never departs from the responsibility to make the patient understand his behavior. His attitude must remain at all times analytic.

How the analyst works can best be understood by examining three aspects of treatment: *empathy, intuition,* and *introspection.* An analyst must be capable of empathizing with his patient. *Empathy* is a form of "emotional knowing," the experiencing of another's feelings. It is a special mode of perceiving. It presupposes an ability on the analyst's part to identify with the patient and to share the patient's experience affectively as well as cognitively. The empathic process is central to the psychotherapeutic relationship and is also a basic element in all human interaction. It finds its highest social expression in the aesthetic experience of the artist as well as in religion and other group phenomena. It is based upon the dynamic effect of unconscious fantasies shared in common (Beres & Arlow, 1974). Two features characterize empathy. First, the identification with the patient is only transient. Second, the therapist preserves separateness from the object (the person being analyzed). The analyst's empathy makes it possible to receive and perceive both the conscious and unconscious processes operating in the patient.

It is impossible for the analyst at any one time to keep in the foreground of his thinking everything the patient has shared. How then does he arrive at an understanding of the patient? This is done *intuitively.* The myriad data communicated by the patient are organized in the analyst's mind into meaningful configurations outside the scope of consciousness. What the analyst perceives as his understanding of the patient is actually the end product of a series of mental operations carried out unconsciously. He becomes aware of this by the process of *introspection* when the interpretation comes to his mind in the form of a free association. Not everything that comes to the analyst's mind in the course of a session is necessarily the correct interpretation. If he is working properly, it is usually some commentary on the patient's material. After introspection presents to the analyst's consciousness the result of his intuitive work, he does not necessarily impart this information to the patient immediately. He checks his idea with what he has learned from the patient and judges its validity in terms of contiguity, repetition, coherence, consistency, and convergence of theme, as outlined earlier. Intuition gives way to *cognitive elaboration*. In the long run, the validity of the interpretation is confirmed by the dynamic impact it has upon the patient's productions, that is, how it affects the equilibrium between impulse and defense in the patient's mind.

There is much disagreement in analytic literature about the analyst's emotional response to the patient. Sometimes this is referred to as *countertransference*, the counterpart of the patient's transference onto the analyst.

Neurotic countertransference to the patient on the part of the analyst can constitute a real problem. Ordinarily the analyst will try to analyze the problem for himself. If this is ineffective, he may seek a consultation with a colleague. When the analyst finds that he cannot control his countertransference responses, he discusses the issues honestly and frankly with the patient and arranges for transfer to another analyst.

❖ CASE EXAMPLE

It is impossible to capture in any condensed presentation the essence of the psychoanalytic experience. The course of an analysis proceeds unevenly. Seemingly fragmented material, arduously assembled over long periods, incompletely comprehended, suddenly may be brilliantly illuminated in a few dramatic sessions, when thousands of disparate threads organize themselves into a tapestry of meaning. Accordingly, any effort to describe in an overall way the course of psychoanalysis inevitably must sound oversimplified and slick. For practical purposes, only the main trends and conclusions can be described. The taxing day-to-day struggle with resistances and defenses has to be inserted by one's imagination. With these warnings in mind, let us proceed to the description of a relatively uncomplicated case.

The patient, whom we will call Tom, was a junior faculty member in a prominent eastern university. At age 30 he was still unmarried, although recently he had begun to live with a woman who had studied under him when she was a graduate student. Although Tom was a popular and successful teacher, much admired and appreciated by his students, he was unable to advance professionally because he could not fulfill the requirements for the Ph.D. degree. He had passed the requisite courses and had completed his doctoral thesis except for a few notes and bibliographical references. The next step was to defend his thesis before the committee, but he could not do so as long as he had not put the final touches on his thesis. This he seemed unable to do. Several years had gone by and he was afraid that all the work he had done might have been in vain.

Tom had another problem that concerned his difficulties with women. He did not seem to be able to maintain a long-term relationship with any woman. For almost a year, he had been genuinely fond of a woman, whom we will call Anita, and at her urging, had finally decided to let her live with him. That was four months ago, and since that time, he had become increasingly irritable and found himself quarreling with Anita, criticizing many of the things she did around the house. He would have liked her to move out but he was not quite sure how to tell her. Since she had moved in with him, his sexual performance had deteriorated. Whereas previously he had suffered from premature ejaculation after entry, in the past few months he had had difficulty getting and maintaining an erection. The only times he had been able to perform well sexually were with women he knew to be frigid.

Tom's father, a practical and industrious man, operated a small business. Through judicious and conservative investments, he was able to acquire a comfortable fortune. Although he was proud of Tom, he was unable to share his son's intellectual interests. Tom's mother was a delicate, sensitive, somewhat hypochondriacal woman. As a child, she had had rheumatic fever, which had left her with a mild case of mitral stenosis. Her doctors had advised her not to have any children. But her wish for a child overrode her doctor's admonition, and after a rather difficult labor, which left her exhausted for several months, she gave birth to Tom. When Tom was five years old, she had a miscarriage. She was much concerned with Tom's development. She saw to it that he was well fed and clean. He was toilet trained by 18 months and seemed to thrive in all ways.

During the preliminary interviews, Tom stated that he was not aware of any neurotic problems he may have had in childhood. He recalled no phobias or nightmares but had been told that at the age of five he was something of a behavior problem. He had become contrary and disobedient toward his mother and had refused to let her kiss him good night. Once when his mother was out of the kitchen for a while, he had emptied the contents of the refrigerator on the kitchen floor. However, after a few months, he seemed to change. He reverted to the obedient child he had been before but became a finicky eater and remained so.

Tom was not happy about starting school. Because his mother was ill, a favorite aunt accompanied him on the first day. He was quite shy and fearful of the other children. Once he learned how to read, however, things began to change. He was clearly the best student in the class and was well liked because he generously helped slower students with their work. Through various activities, he soon became the most popular student in each class. He could keep his classmates amused by inventing funny stories. At lunchtime, he would readily share his sandwiches with his friends. In spite of this, he was quite fearful of the other children. He avoided contact sports and never got involved in a fistfight. He welcomed the frequent absences from school occasioned by repeated respiratory infections. He could stay in bed, munch crackers, and eat to his heart's delight.

Tom's academic progress was not as good as his teachers and parents had expected. Being naturally gifted, it was easy for him in the lower grades to be outstanding without exerting any real effort. In high school and college, he refused to be "a greasy grind." No one was going to accuse him of putting in extra effort just to get good marks. Repeatedly, his teachers informed him and his parents that he was not working up to his potential. When he had to recite in class, his heart would pound and his face would flush even though he knew the answers to the questions posed by the teacher. On two occasions in college, on crucial examinations, he made gross blunders in interpreting the questions. Ordinarily, he should have failed, but his teachers, cognizant of his abilities, after discussing the matter with him, gave him passing grades. In the Ph.D. program, he fulfilled the requirements at a satisfactory level. It was when he had to work independently that his performance faltered.

Although he liked girls, he never seemed to get along well with them. When he was 5½ years old, he pinched the infant sister of a friend when no one was looking. When she began to cry, he disclaimed any knowledge of why she might be doing so. When he was 12 or 13, he recalled having a crush on a lovely girl who lived next door, but he never did anything about it. At 14 he was extremely disappointed when a girl he took to a party spent most of the evening in the company of his best friend. He never dated the girl again, but, surprisingly, his relationship with his friend remained unchanged. He felt a definite antagonism toward attractive girls, thinking they were all vain and self-centered. With those girls he did date, he maintained a haughty, condescending air. He would rupture the relationship through some seemingly inadvertent act that hurt the girl's feelings. He came to realize on his own that there was something malicious about his gaucherie. On several occasions, while talking to one girl, he would address her with the name of another, a slip of the tongue hardly flattering to the girl involved.

From the very beginning, Tom was a "good patient." He followed the rules of the analytic situation and was agreeable and deferential. He soon began to display the vast fund of knowledge he had on a great variety of subjects. In the course of some observation, I made a comment indicating some familiarity with one of the subjects Tom was discussing. This proved very upsetting to him. For a few days, he became anxious and depressed. Intellectually, he was convinced he was superior to everyone else, at least in the areas of his expertise. He believed the only reason it was not generally acknowledged was that he did not try hard enough. He realized that he wanted me, as his analyst, to admire him, but he had not realized that behind his deferential facade, he was intensely competitive. A few days later, he reported a recurrent fantasy. He imagined what would happen if a holdup man confronted him with a gun. He would tell the villain, "My life is too important to me. Money doesn't mean anything to me—just don't hurt me," and he would passively hand over his wallet.

In the clothes closet, Tom noted a fur coat belonging to the patient who preceded him. He left the door of the waiting room open a fraction and placed his chair in a position where he could see the patient as she left the consulting room. She was an attractive woman with blonde ringlets, just the type he despised. In the sessions, he began to make disparaging comments concerning her. "How easy it is to be a woman. You just have to be attractive and everything is taken care of for you." He was certain that I was more interested in her and that I would be taken in by her self-centered complacency and smugness. It would be impossible for him to compete with her for my attention. She had the inside track. He began to realize some of the reasons for his antagonism towards such women. He felt that a woman so attractive would never pay any attention to him.

Tom began one session in a state of almost uncontrollable fury. I had begun his session seven minutes later than usual. Although this was due to my lateness in arriving at the office, he was certain that I had done so because I was too fascinated with what my previous patient was telling me to let her go on time. He began the session by saying that while he was in the clothes closet, he had had the impulse to take the coat belonging to the previous patient and throw it on the floor. On the way to his appointment that morning, the bus was very crowded and he had become quite anxious. People jostled him and he felt he could not breathe. He became so uncomfortable that he left the bus and walked the rest of the way to the office. He thought the city was getting overcrowded, with too many people on the relief rolls who had to be supported by hard-working citizens like himself. They were all parasites like my previous patient, who probably lived luxuriously on her husband's hard-earned income.

In the ensuring weeks, he began to talk about his relationship with Anita. Her presence in his house had been intrusive. She did not contribute sufficiently to the maintenance of the household. At night, after they had had intercourse, he would want to get as far away from her as possible. In fact, it would have been better if he could have told her to leave the bed completely. Several times he had a fantasy of choking her. He recalled a definite sense of pleasure when he saw her leaving the house. The thing that seemed to irritate him most, however, was how careless Anita was with food. She would take a portion of meat larger than she could eat, so much had to be thrown out. In addition, she left the refrigerator door open for long periods. He then had to dispose of the milk that had gone sour. He did make the observation, "After all, I'm an only child. It never was easy for me to share." He remembered that when he was six years old, a friend of his and his friend's sister had received a play house for Christmas and the two had fought over who should occupy the house. He then remembered reading in the Bible years later how Jacob and Esau had fought with each other inside their mother's womb.

During this phase of the analysis, he began to have nightmares. The following dream is typical. The patient reported, "I was swimming in the lake, the water was dark and murky. Suddenly, I was surrounded by a school of small fish, the kind I used to raise when I was a kid. They seemed prepared to lunge at me as if to bite me. I woke up gasping for breath."

Tom learned to swim late. He was most comfortable in a pool. In an ocean, he feared being bitten by a large fish or being stung by an eel. Worst of all was swimming in a lake, where the reeds growing from the muddy bottom could tangle him, draw him down, and drown him. Between the ages of 8 and 12, he raised tropical fish. He was always careful to be present when the baby fish were hatched to remove them from the tank so the other fish would not eat them.

Shortly before he was five, his mother told him that he might be getting a baby sister or brother. She explained that his father had introduced something like an egg into her that had hatched, and a future baby was swimming around in a special fluid inside her body. Clearly this news did not please Tom, for the story goes that he pointed his ray gun at his mother's abdomen. During the same period he emptied the contents of the refrigerator onto the kitchen floor. The pregnancy did not come to term. A few months later his mother began to bleed and she was taken to the hospital. Tom saw some of the blood on the bathroom floor. From the behavior of the grown-ups, Tom could conclude that something terrible was happening. His mother did not come home from the hospital with a baby. Tom was relieved that he had his mother back again and that he did not have to share her and the food with a younger sibling. But unconsciously, he imagined that he was responsible for the baby's death. He fantasized that when he was inside his mother's body, he had destroyed the potential sibling, lacerating it with his teeth. About this time, he developed an aversion to eating eggs or fish, a characteristic that persisted into his adult life. Unconsciously, he feared that these representatives of siblings whom he had destroyed within his mother's body would retaliate by destroying him from within his own body. The attractive patient in the consultation room, the grimy welfare recipients in the bus, and the sloppy Anita in his apartment all represented potential siblings he wanted to oust and destroy because they threatened to invade his territory and rob him of his mother's love and food. He feared they in turn would do to him exactly what he intended to do to them, namely, destroy them with his mouth. As he overcame these fears, he became more giving with Anita. He invited her to share his apartment again. Sexually, his potency began to improve.

His former rival, the attractive blonde with the fur coat, began to intrigue him. What kind of sexual life did she lead? Through the partially open doorway of the waiting room he observed her comings and goings. Perhaps the analyst was interested in her sexually. She seemed the type to go for older men.

Before his session one day, Tom went to the bathroom and forgot to lock the door. As he was standing urinating, the blonde patient entered. Surprised and embarrassed, she withdrew in great confusion. Somehow Tom found the incident amusing and gratifying.

A short time later, he had the following dream, "I get up at night and to go the bathroom. I sit on the toilet and masturbate, looking at the pictures in some porno girlie magazine. Suddenly I notice that there are two sets of large french windows. They swing open, people are passing by on what seems to be a boardwalk. I'm angry and embarrassed because they're all looking in on me. In the background I hear the sounds of a choo-choo train going by."

Immediately, he related the dream to the experience with the previous patient. From the french windows, he could place the setting of the dream exactly. There were such windows in a room he and his parents had occupied in a rooming house at the Jersey shore, where they had gone for a two-week vacation. He was four and a half years old at the time and he was much intrigued by what was going on in the adjoining room at the rooming house. Two young women shared the room. It had a sliding door that did not close completely. Through the half-inch-wide space, little Tom tried to watch the girls getting undressed, and he was especially curious when their boyfriends came to visit them over the weekend.

There had been a wreck on the Asbury Park railroad just before he and his parents had arrived at the seashore. Several people had been killed and the derailed cars had not yet been removed. He recalled for the first time that as a child he had had frequent nightmares in which he heard the huffing and puffing of a locomotive train, the volume and pitch of the noise increasing in unbearable intensity until he awoke in great anxiety. As it turned out, the room he used to occupy at home was next to his parents' bedroom and from time to time he had been aware of strange noises coming from their room.

Going to the bathroom in the dream reminded him of a number of "dirty habits" he had. After his bowels moved, he was not too meticulous about wiping himself, so frequently there were stains on his underwear. His mother used to scold him about this. When he undressed at night, he would let his dirty clothes pile up on the floor for his mother to pick up in the morning. Later when he began to masturbate, he would ejaculate onto the bedsheet, leaving a stain that his mother would have to notice when she changed the bedding. He did something similar when he began to entertain girlfriends in his bedroom. In no way did he try to conceal from his parents, who often were home, what was going on in his bedroom, and if any doubt lingered in their minds, he left unambiguous evidence in the form of a rumpled bed and a stained sheet, making clear to them exactly what had been taking place. He defended his life-long pattern of masturbating. "To begin with," he said, "I'm completely in control. No girl can disappoint me; I have all the satisfaction I want and I get it by myself."

Working through the themes suggested in this material was very rewarding. It was clear that the patient had witnessed his parents having intercourse during that summer vacation. His response was as complex as it was long-lasting. He felt left out, betrayed, and humiliated. In his mind, his mother became a whore who did dirty things and who preferred his father because he was more powerful and had a bigger penis, while he was so small and insignificant. In his subsequent nightmares of the sounds of the locomotive, he feared his own wishes that his parents would die during the act as the people had perished in the railroad accident. He no longer trusted his mother, and this affected his attitude toward all women, especially after his sweetheart had turned her affections to his best friend when he was 12 years old. He became convinced that no woman would be interested in him, and he decided "to show them." He would grow up, become outstanding and famous, and show that he had no use for them. He would take his vengeance by doing to his mother (and women in general) what she had done to him. He would flaunt before her the signs of his own dirty sexual activity and he would leave her and other women embarrassed, angered, and confused, as he had left the blonde patient who had come into the bathroom while he was urinating. After some of these conflicts had been worked through, the blonde patient no longer seemed so haughty, and if Anita did not close the door to the refrigerator promptly, it no longer seemed catastrophic.

Tom's interests now turned to his professional work, which for a long time he had been treating lightly. He became more demanding of his students and less deferential to the chairman of his department. In fact, he realized how often he had thought of becoming the chairman himself. Behind his "good-guy" affability, he could see how competitive and ambitious he really was. He decided that he was being underpaid, that he needed more money, and that the thing to do was to get on with his work and earn the Ph.D. degree. Without the Ph.D., he felt like a boy. It was time to become a man.

No sooner had he begun to work on his thesis than the old inhibition returned. He blocked on using key references from important authorities in the field. He thought that I would accuse him of being a plagiarist, stealing his teacher's ideas. Guilt over stealing was not a new theme in his life. During his latency years, for a few months, in the company of a friend, he went on a stealing spree. He took some of the small change his father had left on the dresser and went to his mother's pocketbook looking for bills he knew his father had put there. From the most popular boy in his class, a born leader, he stole a fountain pen, which he hid under his shirt. From a cousin whom he admired for his strong physique and athletic ability, he stole a textbook of an advanced grade. As he put it, "I devoured the book voraciously."

From childhood on, stealing was prominent in his fantasy life. His favorite story was "Jack and the Beanstalk." "I loved to hear again and again how Jack ran off with the giant's money." His favorite movie was *The Thief of Baghdad*. The most exciting part was where the thief, Ali, goes to the mountains, climbs the great statue of the god, and steals from his forehead the largest jewel in the world, one that bestows on its owner magic, knowledge, and wealth. It reminded him of the myth of Prometheus, who stole knowledge from the gods, and of his own Promethean wish for omniscience. In this connection, he remembered that he had forgotten to return some books he had borrowed from the university library several years back. He recalled going with his father, at the age of four, to a turkish bath. He was awed by the gigantic size of his father's penis and wanted to reach up and touch it.

Coming a bit late for his session one day, he saw the blonde patient walking toward him on the street. He nodded to her and she acknowledged his greeting with a friendly smile. He felt he should have stopped to talk with her; perhaps he could have arranged for a date that ultimately could lead to an affair. As he entered the lobby of the building, he found himself caught up in a fantasy of a violent quarrel with me because I was forbidding him to have anything to do with the patient. Going up, he thought the elevator man seemed ominously threatening. This material led to the theme that I was standing in the way of his sexual freedom and of his achieving manhood, just as earlier in life, he had felt his father had stood in the way.

On two occasions, he lost the bill for the previous month's analysis and brought in a check for several sessions fewer than he was actually supposed to pay. He came to realize that he wanted to steal from me not just my money, but also my profession and my powers. He developed a craving for food before he came to the sessions; he was particularly fond of hot dogs and chocolate bars. For a while, he thought it would be a good idea to become an analyst himself. He could do as well, if not better. During this time, he became increasingly irritable and anxious, and the work he had undertaken to complete his Ph.D. thesis came to a complete standstill.

The anxiety that appeared during this phase of the analysis was connected to three types of dreams or fantasies. They were (1) dreams in which there was a danger of being devoured by sharks, dogs, or lions roaming in the jungle; (2) fantasies of a confrontation with a holdup man (only now Tom would often see himself fighting back); and (3) fantasies and dreams of struggle with an adversary in an enclosed space: the lobby of my building, a tunnel, or the basement of his childhood home. He had several dreams in which he saw himself perched at the window of his basement with a gun, ready to defend the house against assault by intruders.

From his associations, it became clear in time that the feared adversary who threatened to mutilate him physically represented at different times myself, his father, the chief of his department, and the man who was to serve as chairman of the oral examining board for the Ph.D. examination. An examination represented to him a bloody, competitive struggle in which one either kills or is killed. It also had the unconscious significance of a trial where one is pronounced innocent or guilty. To pass the examination was to be permitted to enter the council of elders, to have the rights to be sexual, to have a woman, and to become a father. He told Anita that until he got the Ph.D., he could not think of marrying her, but would do so as soon as he passed. Unconsciously he felt he could not become a husband or father as long as he was in analysis, which meant to him as long as his father was alive. Accordingly, successful termination of treatment had the unconscious significance of killing his father. Fear of retaliation for his murderous wishes against authority figures intensified. His impotence grew more severe; unconsciously he imagined that within the woman's vagina was the adversary who would kill or mutilate him. During this period, he recapitulated the events and fantasies of his childhood in which he competed with his father for his mother's attention. The experiences between the ages of four and five proved to be the crucial ones. They centered around the boy's hostility and envy of the father due to having slept in the same room with his parents at the Jersey coast. He recollected and reexperienced surges of tender loving feelings for his mother, who risked her life giving birth to him. He felt he had to repay her in kind. If only he could restore her heart to its original condition. As a child, he would fantasize about giving her new life in the form of a child.

After many months of working through the anxieties of these unconscious fantasies of childhood, the patient began to make progress in his work and he became potent again. He was well prepared for his Ph.D. oral exam. The day before he took the examination, confident that he would pass, while giving a talk before a large audience in a lecture hall, he had the following fantasy: his eye had fastened on the elaborate chandelier that hung from the ceiling. He imagined himself reaching up with one hand and tearing the chandelier out of the ceiling. He recalled how as a child he had been greatly impressed when he saw his father, seemingly gigantic, standing on a ladder reaching up to the ceiling to change an electric bulb. His Promethean wish was about to be fulfilled. Indeed, he did succeed.

Tom married Anita after he got the Ph.D. Five years after finishing the analysis, he reported that he was doing well in his work. He had been promoted and would soon be eligible for tenure. He was the proud father of a daughter, and his wife was expecting a second child. Anita continued to forget to close the refrigerator door.

❖ SUMMARY

As a system of thought and a technique for dealing with mental illness, psychoanalysis has been developing and changing over the years. What seemed at first a monolithic theory is now being examined critically from many different points of view. Technical innovations and reformulations of theoretical concepts are appearing in ever-increasing numbers. In addition, the literature of psychoanalysis has expanded enormously and there are special volumes dedicated to psychoanalysis and sociology, anthropology, history of childhood, aesthetics, developmental psychology, religion, and biography. Clinical investigation in the therapeutic setting according to the rules of the psychoanalytic situation remains the fundamental base of psychoanalytic knowledge and will clearly continue to be so in the future. Many alternative forms of psychotherapy appear from time to time on the horizon, draw great attention to themselves, but soon fade from the scene. Psychoanalysis has remained a steady, reliable, and growing discipline.

Two points have to be borne in mind about the position of psychoanalysis as therapy and as a system of thought. Not all forms of mental disturbance can or should be treated by psychoanalysis. Paradoxically, the demands of psychoanalysis require the cooperation of a patient with a fairly healthy ego who is well motivated to change and capable of facing himself honestly. For properly selected patients, psychoanalysis can offer the promise of help in attaining the best possible solution that can be realized from overcoming inner conflicts. It does not pretend to create perfectly balanced superhumans, in harmony with themselves and the universe.

The second point to be emphasized is that the reliability of the conclusions of psychoanalytic investigation diminishes the further one gets away from the clinical base of the psychoanalytic situation. Whenever psychoanalytic knowledge and insights are applied outside the analytic situation, one must take into consideration the possibility of innumerable alternative hypotheses and influences.

Because of the changing nature of the psychopathology of our time, notably the great increase in patients suffering from narcissistic, neurotic, and character disorders, and from mild perversions and addictions, one can anticipate new discoveries, fresh observations, original theoretical formulations, and innovative technical procedures.

❖ ANNOTATED BIBLIOGRAPHY

The following books are recommended for those who want to attain deeper knowledge of psychoanalysis as theory and practice:

Brenner, C. (1973). *An elementary textbook of psychoanalysis.* New York: International Universities Press.

There is no better presentation of current psychoanalytic theory than this volume, which has become a worldwide introduction to psychoanalysis and has been translated into nine languages. It is the most comprehensive, systematic, and intelligible presentation of the subject, a worthy companion piece to Anna Freud's *The Ego and the Mechanisms of Defense.* The theoretical development flows smoothly, logically, and cautiously. In addition to the basic theory of psychoanalysis, the book describes the part played by unconscious forces in day-to-day living and surveys the remarkable contribution of psychoanalysis to human knowledge. Current trends in the field are assessed, and problems still requiring exploration are examined.

Freud, A. (1966). *The ego and the mechanisms of defense. The writings of Anna Freud (Vol. 2).* New York: International Universities Press. (Originally published in 1936).

Perhaps the finest and clearest writing style in psychoanalysis belongs to Anna Freud. *The Ego and* *the Mechanisms of Defense* is an established classic for its lucidity in portraying the theoretical implications of the structural theory and its application to problems of technique. In a relatively small volume, the author offers a definitive presentation of the psychoanalytic concept of conflict, the functioning of the anxiety signal, and the many ways in which the ego attempts to establish a stable homeostasis between impulse and defense. The sections on the origin of the superego, identity, and the transformations in adolescence afford the best picture of how the postoedipal child becomes an adult.

Freud, S. (1915-1917). *Introductory lectures on psychoanalysis.* London: Hogarth Press.

These lectures make up Volumes 15 and 16 of *The Complete Psychological Works of Sigmund Freud.* The books constitute a set of lectures Freud gave at the University of Vienna. His lectures are a model of lucidity, clarity, and organization. Introducing a new and complicated field of knowledge, Freud develops his thesis step by step, beginning with simple, acceptable, commonsense concepts, and advancing his argument consistently until the new and startling ideas that he was to place before his audience seem like the inevitable and logical consequences of each individual's own reflection. *Introductory Lectures on Psychoanalysis* provide the easiest and most direct approach to the understanding of psychoanalysis.

Hartmann, H. (1964). *Essays on ego psychology.* New York: International Universities Press.

For the advanced reader who is interested in the broadest theoretical applications of psychoanalysis to psychology, science, and sociology, there is no more authoritative exposition than this book of essays by the outstanding American psychoanalytic theoretician of the twentieth century. Hartmann discusses the concept of health, rational and irrational action, and the application of psychoanalytic concepts to social science and developmental psychology. This is not an easy set of essays to read, but the meticulous student who wants to be ex-posed to the broadest and highest level of analytic theory will be well rewarded for his or her efforts.

Jones, E. (1953–1975). *The life and work of Sigmund Freud.* New York: Basic Books.

This three-volume biography of Freud is one of the great biographies of our time. It captures the intellectual and spiritual ambience of Freud's period in history. It is a remarkable portrayal of the personality and thought of a genius. In addition, this book contains an accurate and readable summary of almost all of Freud's important contributions. It traces the history and leading personalities of the psychoanalytic movement to the death of Freud in 1939.

❖ CASE READINGS

Arlow, J. A. (1976). Communication and character: A clinical study of a man raised by deaf-mute parents. *Psychoanalytic Study of the Child,* 31, 139–163.

The adaptive capacities of the individual, even under difficult environmental circumstances, are illustrated in this well-documented case of someone raised by deaf-mute parents. In many respects, overcoming real hardships and conquering shame contributed to the character development of this person. In addition, one can observe how more than adequate mothering was possible on the part of a woman handicapped by deafness, as well as being educationally deprived.

Boyer, L. B. (1977). Working with a borderline patient. *The Psychoanalytic Quarterly,* 46, 389–420. [Reprinted in D. Wedding and R.J. Corsini (Eds.) (1995). *Case studies in psychotherapy.* Itasca, IL: F. E. Peacock.]

This is a teaching case that illustrates the application of psychoanalytic techniques in the treatment of a patient with a severe character disorder. Dr. Boyer describes his long relationship with this patient with considerable humor and sensitivity. The case provides vivid examples of many of the issues discussed in the current chapter.

Bornstein, B. (1949). The analysis of the phobic child, some problems of theory and technique in child analysis. *Psychoanalytic Study of the Child,* 4, 181–226.

This case represents an illustration of the classical technique of child analysis, as practiced by one of Anna Freud's principle collaborators and pupils. The relationship between theory and clinical technique is clearly expounded.

Freud, S. (1963). The rat man. In S. Freud, *Three case histories.* New York: Crowell-Collier. [Reported in D. Wedding and R. J. Corsini (Eds.) (1979). *Great cases in psychotherapy.* Itasca, IL: F. E. Peacock.]

The case of the "rat man" was a landmark in Freud's developing theory of psychoanalysis. In precise, clinical reporting, Freud outlined the role of the primary process, magical thinking, ambivalence and anal fixation in the structure of the obsessive-compulsive neurosis. Although in his later writings Freud expanded his clinical theory and metapsychology, this case report represents a prime example of how Freud utilized the data of his observation to elucidate new findings and to shed light on problems hitherto obscure.

Winnicott, D.W. (1972). Fragment of an analysis. In P. L. Giovacchini, *Tactics and technique in psychoanalytic therapy* (pp. 455–493). New York: Science House.

Winnicott's approach to psychoanalytic theory and practice represented an important turning point in psychoanalysis. This case report demonstrates his special approach to problems of pathogenesis and treatment, an approach which emphasizes the influence of interpersonal interactions and feelings. Winnicott's technical precepts have had a strong and lasting effect on psychoanalytic practice.

❖ REFERENCES

Abraham, K. (1924). The influence of oral eroticism on character formation. *Selected papers of Karl Abraham* (Vol.1, pp. 393–496). London: Hogarth Press.

Alexander, F. (1932). *The medical value of psychoanalysis.* New York: Norton.

Ansbacher, H., & Ansbacher, R. (Eds.) (1956). *The individual psychology of Alfred Adler.* New York: Basic Books.

Arlow, J. A. (1963). Conflict, regression and symptom formation. *International Journal of Psychoanalysis* 44, 12–22.

Arlow, J. A. (1972). Character perversion. In I. M. Marcus (Ed.), *Currents in psychoanalysis.* (pp. 317–336). New York: International Universities Press.

Arlow, J. A., & Brenner, C. (1964). *Psychoanalytic concepts in the structural theory.* New York: International Universities Press.

Berenfeld, S. (1944). Freud's earliest theories and the school of Helmholtz. *Psychoanalytic Quarterly*, 13, 341–362.

Beres, D., & Arlow, J.A. (1974). Fantasy and identification in empathy. *Psychoanalytic Quarterly*, 43, 4–25.

Bowlby, J. (1958). The nature of the child's ties to the mother. *International Journal of Psychoanalysis*, 39, 350–373.

Brenner, C. (1971). The psychoanalytic concept of aggression. *International Journal of Psychoanalysis*, 52, 137–144.

Brenner, C. (1973). *An elementary textbook of psychoanalysis.* New York: International Universities Press.

Breuer, J., & Freud, S. (1895). *Studies on hysteria. Standard edition of the complete psychological works of Freud* (Vol. 2). London: Hogarth Press.

Burton, A. (Ed.). (1969). *Encounter.* San Francisco: Jossey-Bass.

Ellis, A. (1970). *Reason and emotion in psychotherapy.* New York: Lyle Stuart.

Erikson, E. (1968). *Identity, youth and crisis.* New York: Norton.

Eysenck, H .J. (1965). The effects of psychotherapy. *International Journal of Psychiatry*, 1, 99–142.

Federn, P. (1952). *Ego psychology and the psychoses.* New York: Basic Books.

Feldman, F. (1968). Results of psychoanalysis in clinic case assignments. *Journal of the American Psychoanalytic Association*, 16, 274–300.

Fenichel, O. (1930). *Zehn Jahre Berliner psychoanalytischer Institut.* Vienna: International Psychoanalytischer Verlag.

Fenichel, O. (1945). *The psychoanalytic theory of neurosis.* New York: Norton.

Freud, A. (1936). *The ego and mechanisms of defense.* New York: International Universities Press.

Freud, A. (1951). Observations on child development. *Psychoanalytic Study of the Child*, 6, 18–30.

Freud, S. (1894).[1] *The neuropsychoses of defense. (Standard Edition* Vol. 3).

Freud, S. (1895). *Studies on hysteria. (Standard Edition* Vol. 2).

Freud, S. (1900). *The interpretation of dreams. (Standard Edition* Vol. 4).

Freud, S. (1901). *The psychopathology of everyday life. (Standard Edition* Vol. 6).

Freud, S. (1905a). *Jokes and their relationship to the unconscious. (Standard Edition* Vol. 8).

Freud, S. (1905b). *Three essays on sexuality. (Standard Edition* Vol. 7).

Freud, S. (1911). *Formulations regarding the two principles of mental functioning. (Standard Edition* Vol. 12).

Freud, S. (1913). *Totem and taboo. (Standard Edition* Vol. 13).

Freud, S. (1914a). *The history of the psychoanalytic movement. (Standard Edition* Vol. 14).

Freud, S. (1914b). *On narcissism: An introduction. (Standard Edition* Vol. 14).

Freud, S. (1915a). *Repression. (Standard Edition* Vol. 14).

Freud, S. (1915b). *The unconscious. (Standard Edition* Vol. 14).

Freud, S. (1917). *On transformations of instinct as exemplified in anal eroticism. (Standard Edition* Vol. 17).

Freud, S. (1920). *Beyond the pleasure principle. (Standard Edition* Vol. 18).

Freud, S. (1921). *Group psychology and the analysis of the ego. (Standard Edition* Vol. 18).

Freud, S. (1923). *The ego and the id. (Standard Edition* Vol. 19).

Freud, S. (1925). *An autobiographical study. (Standard Edition* Vol. 20).

Freud, S. (1926). *Inhibitions, symptoms and anxiety. (Standard Edition* Vol. 20).

Freud, S. (1937). *Analysis terminable and interminable. (Standard Edition* Vol. 23).

Fromm, E. (1955). *The sane society.* New York: Holt, Rinehart and Winston.

Fromm-Reichmann, F. (1950). *Principles of intensive psychotherapy.* Chicago: University of Chicago Press.

Glasser, W. (1967). *Reality therapy.* New York: Julian Press.

Greenacre, P. (1956). Re-evaluation of the process of working through. *International Journal of Psychoanalysis*, 37, 439–444.

---

[1]All references to Sigmund Freud are from the *Complete Psychological Works of Sigmund Freud*, edited by James Strachey and published by Hogarth Press, London.

Greenacre, P. (1967). The influence of infantile trauma on genetic pattern. *Emotional Growth, 1,* 216–299.

Greenson, R. (1967). *The technique and practice of psychoanalysis.* New York: International Universities Press.

Grinstein, A. (Ed.) (1971). *The index of psychoanalytic writings.* New York: International Universities Press.

Hartmann, H. (1939). *Ego psychology and the problem of adaptation.* New York: International Universities Press.

Hartmann, H., & Kris, E. (1945). The genetic approach to psychoanalysis. *Psychoanalytic Study of the Child, 1,* 11–30.

Hartmann, H., Kris, E., & Loewenstein, R. N. (1946). Comments on the formation of psychic structure. *Psychoanalytic Study of the Child, 2,* 11–38.

Hartmann, H., Kris, E., & Loewenstein, R. N. (1949). Notes on the theory of aggression. *Psychoanalytic Study of the Child, 4,* 9–36.

Horney, K. (1940). *New ways in psychoanalysis.* New York: Norton.

Jacobson, E. (1954). The self and the object world: Vicissitudes of their infantile cathexes and their influence on ideational and affective development. *Psychoanalytic Study of the Child, 9,* 75–127.

Jones, E. (1953). *The life and work of Sigmund Freud.* New York: Basic Books.

Jung, C. (1909). *The psychology of dementia praecox.* New York & Washington: Nervous and Mental Disease.

Kernberg, O. (1968). The therapy of patients with borderline personality organization. *International Journal of Psychoanalysis, 49,* 600–619.

Klein, M. (1932). *The psychoanalysis of children.* London: Hogarth Press.

Kohut, H. (1971). The analysis of the self. *Monograph Series of the Psychoanalytic Study of the Child (No. 4).* New York: International Universities Press.

Kris, E. (1950). Preconscious mental processes. *Psychoanalytic Quarterly, 19,* 540–560.

Lewin, B. D. (1946). Sleep, the mouth and the dream screens. *Psychoanalytic Quarterly, 15,* 419–434.

Lewin, B. D. (1949). Mania and sleep. *Psychoanalytic Quarterly, 18,* 419–433.

Loewenstein, R. (1958). Remarks on some variations in psychoanalytic technique. *International Journal of Psychoanalysis, 39,* 202–210.

Lorenz, C. (1952). *King Solomon's ring.* New York: Crowell.

Mahler, M., Pine, F., & Bergman, A. (1975). *The psychological birth of the human infant.* New York: Basic Books.

Meltzoff, J., & Kornreich, M. (1970). *Research in psychotherapy.* New York: Atherton Press.

Nunberg, H. (1926). The will to recovery. *International Journal of Psychoanalysis, 7,* 64–78.

Peterfreund, E. (1971). Information systems and psychoanalysis. *Psychological Issues Monograph (Nos. 25–26).* New York: International Universities Press.

Pfeffer, A. Z. (1963). The meaning of the analyst after analysis: A contribution to the theory of therapeutic results. *Journal of the American Psychoanalytic Association, 11,* 229–244.

Racker, E. (1953). A contribution to the problem of countertransference. *International Journal of Psychoanalysis, 34,* 313–324.

Rangell, L. (1973). On the cacophony of human relations. *Psychoanalytic Quarterly, 42,* 325–348.

Rapaport, D. (1951). *The organization and pathology of thought.* New York: Columbia University Press.

Reich, A. (1973). *Psychoanalytic contributions.* New York: International Universities Press.

Rogers, C. (1951). *Client-centered therapy.* New York: Houghton Mifflin.

Rosenfeld, H. (1954). Consideration concerning the psychoanalytic approach to acute and chronic schizophrenia. *International Journal of Psychoanalysis, 35,* 135–140.

Rubenstein, B. B. (1967). Explanation and mere description: A metascientific examination of certain aspects of the psychoanalytic theory of motivation in motives and thought. Psychoanalytic essays in honor of David Rapaport. *Psychological Issues Monograph (Nos. 18–19).* New York: International Universities Press.

Sachs, H. (1942). *The creative unconscious.* Cambridge, MA: Sci-Art Publishers.

Schafer, R. (1976). *A new language of psychoanalysis.* New Haven & London: Yale University Press.

Schmideberg, M. (1938). After the analysis. *Psychoanalytic Quarterly, 7,* 122–142.

Schultz, W. C. (1967). *Joy.* New York: Grove Press.

Searles, H. F. (1965). *Collected papers on schizophrenia and related subjects.* New York: International Universities Press.

Spitz, R. (1955). The primal cavity: A contribution to the genesis of perception and its role in psychoanalytic theory. *Psychoanalytic Study of the Child, 10,* 215–240.

Sullivan, H. S. (1953). *The interpersonal theory of psychiatry.* New York: Norton.

Tinbergern, N. (1951). *The study of instinct.* London: Oxford University Press.

Wallerstein, R. S., & Smelser, N. J. (1969). Articulations and applications. *International Journal of Psychoanalysis, 50,* 693–710.

Weigert, E. (1970). *The courage to love.* New Haven: Yale University Press.

Winnicott, D. W. (1953). Transitional objects and transitional phenomena: A study of the first not-me possession. *International Journal of Psychoanalysis, 34,* 89–97.

Wolpe, J. (1958). *Psychotherapy by reciprocal inhibition.* Stanford, CA: Stanford University Press.

Zetzel, E. R. (1970). *The capacity for emotional growth: Theoretical and clinical contributions to psychoanalysis.* New York: International Universities Press.

Zilboorg, G., & Henry, G.W. (1941). *A history of medical psychology.* New York: Norton.

Alfred Adler, 1870–1937

3 Adlerian Psychotherapy

Harold H. Mosak

❖ OVERVIEW

Adlerian psychology (Individual Psychology), developed by Alfred Adler, views the person holistically as a creative, responsible, "becoming" individual moving toward fictional goals within his or her phenomenal field. It holds that one's life-style is sometimes self-defeating because of inferiority feelings. The individual with "psychopathology" is discouraged rather than sick, and the therapeutic task is to encourage the person to activate his or her social interest and to develop a new life-style through relationship, analysis, and action methods.

Basic Concepts

Adlerian psychology is predicated upon assumptions that differ in significant ways from the Freudian "womb" from which it emerged. Adler throughout his lifetime credited Freud with primacy in the development of a dynamic psychology. He consistently gave credit to Freud for explicating the purposefulness of symptoms and for discovering that dreams were meaningful. The influence of early childhood experiences in personality development constitutes still another point of agreement. Freud emphasized the role of psychosexual development and the Oedipus complex, and Adler focused upon the effects of children's perceptions of their family constellation and their struggle to find a place of significance within it.

Adlerian basic assumptions can be expressed as follows:

1. All behavior occurs in a social context. Humans are born into an environment with which they must engage in reciprocal relations. The oft-quoted statement by the Gestalt psychologist Kurt Lewin that "behavior is a function of person and environment" bears a striking parallel to Adler's contention that people cannot be studied in isolation (1929).

2. Individual Psychology (Adler's term) is an interpersonal psychology. How individuals interact with the others sharing "this crust of earth" (Adler, 1958, p. 6) is paramount. Transcending interpersonal transactions is the development of the feeling of being a part of a larger social whole that Adler (1964b) incorporated under the heading of *Gemeinschaftsgefühl,* or social interest.

3. Adlerian psychology rejects reductionism in favor of holism. The Adlerian demotes part-functions from the central investigative focus in favor of studying the whole person and how he or she moves through life. This renders the polarities of *conscious* and *unconscious, mind* and *body, approach* and *avoidance, ambivalence* and *conflict* meaningless except as subjective experiences of the whole person. That is, people behave *as if* the conscious mind moves in one direction while the unconscious mind moves in another. From the external observer's viewpoint, all part-functions are subordinate functions of the individual's goals and style of life.

4. *Conscious* and *unconscious* are both in the service of the individual, who uses them to further personal goals. Adler (1963a) treats *unconscious* as an adjective rather than a noun. That which is unconscious is the non-understood. Like Otto Rank, Adler felt that humans know more than they understand. *Conflict,* defined as intrapersonal by others, is defined as a "one step forward and one step backward movement," the net effect being to maintain the individual at a point "dead center." Although people experience themselves in the throes of a conflict, unable to move, in reality they *create* these antagonistic feelings, ideas, and values because they are unwilling to move in the direction of solving their problems (Mosak & LeFevre, 1976).

5. Understanding the individual requires understanding his or her *cognitive organization* and life-style. The latter concept refers to the convictions individuals develop early in life to help them organize experience, to understand it, to predict it, and to control it. *Convictions* are conclusions derived from the individual's apperceptions, and they constitute a biased mode of apperception. Consequently, a *life-style* is neither right nor wrong, normal nor abnormal, but merely the "spectacles" through which people view themselves in relationship to the way in which they perceive life. Subjectivity rather than so-called objective evaluation becomes the major tool for understanding the person. As Adler wrote, "We must be able to see with his eyes and listen with his ears" (1958, p. 72).

6. Behavior may change throughout a person's lifespan in accordance with both the immediate demands of the situation and the long-range goals inherent in the life-style. The life-style remains relatively constant through life unless the convictions change through the mediation of psychotherapy. Although the definition of *psychotherapy* customarily refers to what transpires within a consulting room, a broader view of psychotherapy would include the fact that life in itself may often be psychotherapeutic.

7. According to the Adlerian conception, people are not pushed by causes; that is, they are not determined by heredity and environment. "Both are giving only the frame and the influences which are answered by the individual in regard to the styled creative power" (Ansbacher & Ansbacher, 1956). People move toward self-selected goals that they feel will give them a place in the world, will provide them with security, and will preserve their self-

esteem. Life is a dynamic striving. "The life of the human soul is not a 'being' but a 'becoming'" (Adler, 1963a, p. ix).

8. The central striving of human beings has been variously described as completion (Adler, 1958), perfection (Adler, 1964a), superiority (Adler, 1972), self-realization (Horney, 1951), self-actualization (Goldstein, 1939), competence (White, 1957), and mastery (Adler, 1926). Adler distinguishes among such strivings in terms of the direction a striving takes. If strivings are solely for the individual's greater glory, he considers them socially useless and, in extreme conditions, characteristic of mental problems. On the other hand, if the strivings are for the purpose of overcoming life's problems, the individual is engaged in the striving for self-realization, in contribution to humanity, and in making the world a better place to live.

9. Moving through life, the individual is confronted with alternatives. Because Adlerians are either non-determinists or soft determinists, the conceptualization of humans as creative, choosing, self-determined decision makers permits them to choose the goals they want to pursue. Individuals may select socially useful goals or they may devote themselves to the useless side of life. They may choose to be task-oriented or they may, as does the neurotic, concern themselves with their own superiority.

10. The freedom to choose (McArthur, 1958) introduces the concepts of *value* and *meaning* into psychology. These were unpopular concepts at the time (1931) that Adler wrote *What Life Should Mean to You*. The greatest value for the Adlerian is *Gemeinschaftsgefühl*, or social interest (Ansbacher, 1968). Although Adler contends that it is an innate feature of human beings, at least as potential, acceptance of this criterion is not absolutely necessary. People possess the capacity for coexisting and interrelating with others. Indeed, the "iron logic of social living" (Adler, 1959) demands that we do so. Even in severe psychopathology, total extinction of social interest does not occur. Even the psychotic retains some commonality with "normal" people.

As Rabbi Akiva noted two millennia ago, "The greatest principle of living is to love one's neighbor as oneself." If we regard ourselves as fellow human beings with fellow feeling, we are socially contributive people interested in the common welfare and, by Adler's pragmatic definition of *normality*, mentally healthy (Dreikurs, 1969; Shoben, 1957).

If my feeling derives from my observation and conviction that life and people are hostile and I am inferior, I may divorce myself from the direct solution of life's problems and strive for personal superiority through over-compensation, wearing a mask, withdrawal, attempting only safe tasks where the outcome promises to be successful, and other devices for protecting my self-esteem. Adler said the neurotic in terms of movement displayed a "hesitating attitude" toward life (1964a). Also, the neurotic was described as a "yes-but" personality (Adler, 1934); at still other times, the neurotic was described as an "if only…" personality (Adler, 1964a): "If only I didn't have these symptoms, I'd…." The latter provided the rationale for "The Question," a device Adler used for differential diagnosis as well as for understanding the individual's task avoidance.

11. Because Adlerians are concerned with process, little diagnosis is done in terms of nomenclature. Differential diagnosis between functional and organic disorder does often present a problem. Because all behavior is purposeful, a *psychogenic* symptom will have a psychological or social purpose and an *organic* symptom will have a somatic purpose. An Adlerian would ask "The Question" (Adler, 1964a; Dreikurs, 1958, 1962), "If I had a magic wand or a magic pill that would eliminate your symptom immediately, what would be different in your life?" If the patient answers, "I'd go out more often socially" or "I'd write my book," the symptom would most likely be psychogenic. If the patient responds, "I wouldn't have this excruciating pain," the symptom would most likely be organic.

12. Life presents challenges in the form of life tasks. Adler named three of these explicitly but referred to two others without specifically naming them (Dreikurs & Mosak, 1966). The original three tasks were those of *society, work,* and *sex*. The first has already been alluded to. Because no person can claim self-sufficiency, we are all interdependent. Not only do we need social recognition, each of us also is dependent upon the labor of other people and they, in turn, are dependent upon our contribution. Work thus becomes essential for human survival. The cooperative individual assumes this role willingly. In the sexual realm, because two different sexes exist, we must also learn how to relate to that fact. We must define our sex roles, partly on the basis of cultural definitions and stereotypes, and train ourselves to relate to the *other*, not the *opposite*, sex. Other people, of either sex, do not represent the enemy. They are our fellows, with whom we must learn to cooperate.

Fourth (Dreikurs & Mosak, 1967) and fifth tasks (Mosak & Dreikurs, 1967) have been described. Although Adler alluded to the *spiritual*, he never specifically named it (Jahn & Adler, 1964). But each of us must deal with the problem of defining the nature of the universe, the existence and nature of God, and how to relate to these concepts. Finally, we must address the task of *coping with ourselves*. William James (1890) made the distinction between the self as subject and the self as object, and it is as imperative, for the sake of mental health, that good relations exist between the "I" and the "me" as between the "I" and other people.

13. Because life constantly provides challenges, living demands courage (Neuer, 1936). Courage is not an *ability* one either possesses or lacks. Nor is courage synonymous with bravery, such as falling on a grenade to save one's buddies from injury or death. *Courage* refers to the *willingness* to engage in risk-taking behavior when one either does not know the consequences or when the consequences might be adverse. We are all *capable* of courageous behavior provided that we are *willing*. Our willingness will depend upon many variables, internal and external, such as our life-style convictions, our degree of social interest, the extent of risk as we appraise it, and whether we are task-oriented or prestige-oriented. Given that life offers few guarantees, all living requires risk taking. It would require very little courage to live if we were perfect, omniscient, or omnipotent. The question we must each answer is whether we have the courage to live despite the knowledge of our imperfections (Lazarsfeld, 1966).

14. Life has no intrinsic meaning. We give meaning to life, each of us in our own fashion. We declare it to be meaningful, meaningless, an absurdity, a prison sentence (cf., the adolescent's justification for doing as he pleases—"I didn't ask to be born"), a vale of tears, a preparation for the next world, and so on. Dreikurs (1957, 1971) maintained that the meaning of life resided in doing for others and in contributing to social life and social change. Viktor Frankl (1963) believed the meaning of life lay in love. The meaning we attribute to life will "determine" our behavior. We will behave *as if* life were really in accord with our perceptions, and, therefore, certain meanings will have greater practical utility than others. Optimists will live an optimistic life, take chances, and not be discouraged by failure and adversity. They will be able to distinguish between failing and being a failure. Pessimists will refuse to be engaged with life, refuse to try, sabotage their efforts if they do make an attempt, and, through their methods of operation, endeavor to confirm their pre-existing pessimistic anticipations (Krausz, 1935).

Other Systems

Students often have asked, "Do you Adlerians believe in sex too?" The question is not always asked facetiously. Freud accorded sex the status of the master motive in behavior.

Adler merely categorized sex as one of several tasks the individual was required to solve. Freud employed esoteric jargon and Adler favored common-sense language. One story has it that a psychiatrist took Adler to task after a lecture, denigrating his approach with the criticism, "You're only talking common sense," to which Adler replied, "I wish more psychiatrists did." We can place other differences between these two men in columnar form, as shown in Table 3.1.

A more extended comparison of Freud's and Adler's concepts of humankind may be found in articles by H.W. von Sassen (1967) and Otto Hinrichsen (1913).

Adler and the Neo-Freudians

Adler once proclaimed that he was more concerned that his theories survived than that people remembered to associate his theories with his name. His wish apparently was granted. In discussing Adler's influence upon contemporary psychological theory and practice, Henri Ellenberger commented, "It would not be easy to find another author from which so much has been borrowed from all sides without acknowledgment than Adler" (1970, p. 645). Many neo-Freudians have credited Adler with contributing to and influencing their work. In her last book, Karen Horney wrote of "neurotic ambition," "the need for perfection," and "the category of power." "All drives for glory have in common the reaching out for greater knowledge, wisdom, virtue or powers than are given to human beings; they all aim at the *absolute*, the unlimited, the infinite" (1951, pp. 34–35). Those familiar with Adler's writings on the neurotic's perfectionistic, godlike striving will immediately be struck with the similarity in viewpoint.

Horney (1951) rejected Freud's pessimism, "his disbelief in human goodness and human growth," in favor of the Adlerian view that a person could grow and could "become a decent human being."

Others have also remarked upon the resemblance between the theories of Horney and Adler; the reviewer of one Horney book wrote that Karen Horney had just written a new book by Alfred Adler (Farau, 1953).

Erich Fromm also expresses views similar to those of Adler. According to Fromm, people make choices. The attitude of the mother in child rearing is of paramount importance. Life fosters feelings of powerlessness and anxiety. Patrick Mullahy (1955) indicates that

> The only adequate solution, according to Fromm, is a relationship with man and nature, chiefly by love and productive work, which strengthens the total personality, sustains the person in his sense of uniqueness, and at the same time gives him a feeling of belonging, a sense of unity and common destiny with mankind. (pp. 251–252)

Although Harry Sullivan places greater emphasis upon developmental child psychology than does Adler, Sullivan's "person" moves through life in much the same manner as does Adler's. Thus, Sullivan (1954) speaks of the "security operation" of the individual, a direct translation of Adler's and Lene Credner's (1930) *Sicherungen*. His "good me" and "bad me" dichotomy, in expression if not in manner of development, is essentially the same as that described by Adlerians.

So many similarities between Adler and the neo-Freudians have been noted that Gardner Murphy concluded, "If this way of reasoning is correct, neurosis should be the general characteristic of man under industrialism, a point suspected by many Freudians and, in particular, by that branch of the Freudian school (Horney and her associates) that has learned most from Adler" (1947, p. 569). A summary of such resemblances appears in Heinz and Rowena Ansbacher's *Individual Psychology of Alfred Adler* (1956) as well as in

TABLE 3.1 Comparison of Freud's and Adler's Concepts

Freud	*Adler*
1. Objective	1. Subjective
2. Physiological substratum for theory	2. A social psychology
3. Emphasized causality	3. Emphasized teleology
4. Reductionistic. The individual was divided into "parts" that were antagonistic toward each other: e.g., id-ego-superego, Eros vs. Thanatos, conscious vs. unconscious.	4. Holistic. The individual is indivisible. He or she is a unity, and all "parts" (memory, emotions, behavior) are in the service of the whole individual.
5. The study of the individual centers about the intrapersonal, the intrapsychic.	5. People can only be understood interpersonally and as social beings moving through and interacting with their environment.
6. The establishment of intrapsychic harmony constitutes the ideal goal of psychotherapy. "Where id was, there shall ego be."	6. The expansion of the individual, self-realization, and the enhancement of social interest represent the ideal goals for the individual.
7. People are basically "bad." Civilization attempts to domesticate them, for which they pay a heavy price. Through therapy the instinctual demands may be sublimated but not eliminated.	7. People are neither "good" nor "bad," but as creative, choosing human beings, they may choose to be "good" or "bad" or both, depending upon their life-styles and their appraisal of the immediate situation and its payoffs. Through the medium of therapy people can choose to actualize themselves.
8. People are victims of both instinctual life and civilization.	8. People, as choosers, can shape both their internal and their external environments. Although they cannot always choose what will happen to them, they can always choose the posture they will adopt toward life's stimuli.
9. Description of child development was postdictive and not based upon direct observation of children but upon the free associations of adults.	9. Children were studied directly in families, in schools, and in family education centers.
10. Emphasis upon the Oedipus situation and its resolution	10. Emphasis upon the family constellation
11. People are enemies. Others are our competitors, and we must protect ourselves from them. Theodore Reik quotes Nestroy, "If chance brings two wolves together,… neither feels the least uneasy because the other is a wolf; two human beings, however, can never meet in the forest, but one must think: That fellow may be a robber" (1948, p. 477).	11. Other people are *mitmenschen*, fellow human beings. They are our equals, our collaborators, our cooperators in life.
12. Women feel inferior because they envy men their penises. Women are inferior. "Anatomy is destiny."	12. Women feel inferior because in our cultural milieu women are undervalued. Men have privileges, rights, preferred status, although in the current cultural ferment, these roles are being reevaluated.
13. Neurosis has a sexual etiology.	13. Neurosis is a failure of learning, a product of distorted perceptions.
14. Neurosis is the price we pay for civilization.	14. Neurosis is the price we pay for our lack of civilization.

an article by Walter James (1947). Fritz Wittels (1939) has proposed that the neo-Freudians should more properly be called "neo-Adlerians," and a study by Heinz Ansbacher (1952) suggests that many traditional Freudians would concur.

Adler and Rogers

Although the therapies of Adler and Carl Rogers are diametrically opposed, their theories share many commonalities. Both are phenomenological, goal-directed, and holistic. Each views people as self-consistent, creative, and capable of change. To illustrate, Rogers (1951) postulates the following:

1. The organism reacts as an organized whole to the phenomenal field (p. 486).
2. The best vantage point for understanding behavior is from the internal frame of reference of the individual himself (p. 494).
3. The organism reacts to the field as it is experienced and perceived (p.484–85).
4. The organism has one basic tendency and striving—to actualize, maintain, and enhance the experiencing organism (p. 487).

Much of the early research on nondirective and client-centered therapy measured the discrepancy between *self-concept* and *self-ideal*. The Adlerian would describe the extent of discrepancy as a measure of inferiority feelings.

Adler and Ellis

The theories of Adler and Ellis exhibit many points of convergence. Albert Ellis (1970, 1971) finds his rational-emotive psychology to parallel that of Adler. What Adler calls basic mistakes, Albert Ellis refers to as irrational beliefs or attitudes. Both accept the notion that emotions are actually a form of thinking and that people create or control their emotions by controlling their thinking. They agree that we are not victims of our emotions but their creators. In psychotherapy, they (1) adopt similar stances with respect to unconscious motivation, (2) confront patients with their irrational ideas (basic mistakes or internalized sentences), (3) counterpropagandize the patient, (4) insist upon action, and (5) constantly *encourage* patients to assume responsibility for the direction of their lives in more positive channels. The last phrase seems to reflect the major disagreement between Adler and Ellis, namely, what is "positive." Ellis argues,

> Where Adler writes, therefore, that "All my efforts are devoted towards increasing the social interest of the patient," the rational therapist would prefer to say, "Most of my efforts are devoted towards increasing the self-interest of the patient." He assumes that if the individual possesses rational self interest he will, on both biological and logical grounds, almost invariably tend to have a high degree of social interest as well. (1957, p. 43)

Adler and Other Systems

The many points of convergence and divergence between Adler and several of the existentialist thinkers have been noted by many writers (Birnbaum, 1961; Farau, 1964; Frankl, 1970). Phyllis Bottome had written in 1939 that "Adler was the first founder of an existence psychology" (p. 199). Given that existential psychology is not a school but a viewpoint, it is difficult to make comparisons, but interested readers may discover for themselves in an editorial by Ansbacher (1959) the lines of continuity between Adler and current existential thought.

The recognition of Adler as one of the earliest humanistic psychologists is clear. Ellis pays homage to Adler as "one of the first humanistic psychologists" (1970, p. 32). Abraham Maslow (1962, 1970) published five papers in Adlerian journals over a period of 35 years.

As we have already observed, many of Adler's ideas have been incorporated by the humanistic psychologists with little awareness of Adler's contributions. "The model of man as a composite of part functions" that James Bugental (1963) questioned has been repudiated by Adlerians for more than half a century. Adlerian psychology is a value psychology (Adler wrote *What Life Should Mean to You* in 1931), as Viktor Frankl and Rollo May, among others, acknowledge in their debt to Adler. Frankl wrote:

> What he [Adler]…achieved and accomplished was no less than a Copernican switch…. Beyond this, Alfred Adler may well be regarded as an existential thinker and as a forerunner of the existential-psychiatric movement. (1970, p. 38)

May expresses his debt as follows:

> I appreciate Adler more and more…. Adler's thoughts as I learned them in studying with him in Vienna in the summers of 1932 and 1933 led me indirectly into psychology, and were very influential in the later work in this country of Sullivan and William Alanson White, etc. (1970, p. 39)

Abraham Maslow wrote:

> For me Alfred Adler becomes more and more correct year by year. As the facts come in, they give stronger and stronger support to his image of man. I should say that in one respect especially the times have not yet caught up with him. I refer to his holistic emphasis. (1970, p. 39)

❖ HISTORY

Precursors

Adler's insistence that people cannot be studied in isolation but only in their social context was previously expressed by Aristotle, who referred to the human being as a *zoon politikon*, a political animal (Adler, 1959). Adler exhibits his affinity with the philosophy of stoicism, as both Ellenberger (1970) and H. N. Simpson (1966) point out. Other commentators have noted the resemblance of Adler's writings to Kant's philosophy, especially with respect to the categorical imperative, private logic, and overcoming. Adler and Nietzsche have often been compared, and much has been made of their common usage of the concept of the *will to power*. Adler spoke of it in terms of the normal strivings for competence, however, while Nietzsche's references to this concept involved what Adler would call the "useless side of life." Nietzsche stressed the *Übermensch* (Superman) and Adler spoke of equality. Adler further stressed *social feeling*, a concept totally alien to the Nietzschian philosophy.

Throughout history, philosophers have struggled with the mind-body problem. Psychology experienced a renaissance when psychologists and psychiatrists began to address themselves to the study of psychosomatic syndromes. Psychosomatic and somatopsychic hypotheses were advanced to explain how emotions could influence the production of symptoms and how bodily states might create emotional or mental illness. Adler rejected such divisions. Like Kurt Lewin (1935), he rejected categorization and dichotomies. Like Jan Smuts (1961), he was a holist; *Individual Psychology* was not meant to describe the psychology of the individual. It referred rather to Adler's holistic stance, that a person could be understood only as a whole, an indivisible unity. To study people atomistically was to not capture fully the nature of humanity. For Adler, the question was neither "How does mind affect body?" nor "How does body affect mind?" but rather "How does the individual use body and mind in the pursuit of goals?" Although Adler's *Study of Organ Inferiority and Its Psychical Compensation* (1917) might seem to contradict such statements by expressing a causalistic viewpoint, this highly original theory was formulated when Adler was a member of the Freudian circle. Later Adler added the subjective factor:

> It might be suggested, therefore, that in order to find out where a child's interest lies, we need only to ascertain which organ is defective. But things do not work out quite so simply. The child does not experience the fact of organ inferiority in the way that an external observer sees it, but as modified by his own scheme of apperception. (1969)

Perhaps the greatest influence upon Adler was Hans Vaihinger's (1965) "philosophy of 'as if.'" According to Vaihinger, a fiction is "a mere piece of imagination" that deviates from reality but that is nevertheless utilitarian for the individual. Both the concept of the world and the concept of the self are subjective, that is, fictional, and therefore in error. *Truth* is "only the most expedient error, that is, the system of ideas which enables us to act and to deal with things most rapidly, neatly, and safely, and with the minimum of irrational elements" (p. 108).

Finally, Adler's psychology has a religious tone (Adler, 1958; Jahn & Adler, 1964; Mosak, 1987c). His placement of social interest at the pinnacle of his value theory is in the tradition of those religions that stress people's responsibility for each other. Indeed, Adler maintained that "Individual Psychology makes good religion if you are unfortunate enough not to have another" (Rasey, 1956, p. 254).

Beginnings

Adler was born near Vienna on February 7, 1870, and he died while on a lecture tour in Aberdeen, Scotland, on May 27, 1937. After graduating from the University of Vienna in 1895, Adler entered private practice as an ophthalmologist in 1898. He later switched to general practice and then to neurology. During this period, Adler gave portents of his later social orientation by writing a book on the health of tailors (1898). In this respect, he may be regarded as the progenitor of industrial medicine.

In 1902, Adler, at Freud's invitation, joined in the latter's Wednesday evening discussion circle. Biographers agree that Adler wrote two defenses of Freud's theories that may have gained him the invitation. Although textbooks frequently refer to Adler as a student of Freud, Adler was actually a colleague (Ansbacher, 1962; Ellenberger, 1970; Federn, 1963; Maslow, 1962). Through the next decade, Adler had one foot in and one foot out of the Freudian circle. Although his *Study of Organ Inferiority* won Freud's unqualified endorsement, Adler's introduction of the aggression instinct in 1908 met with Freud's disapproval. Not until 1923, long after Adler had discarded instinct theory, did Freud incorporate the aggressive instinct into psychoanalysis (Sicher & Mosak, 1967), at which time Adler declared, "I enriched psychoanalysis by the aggressive drive. I gladly make them a present of it!" (Bottome, 1939, p. 63).

Adler's increasing divergence from Freud's viewpoint led to discomfort and disillusion in the Vienna Society. Adler criticized Freud's sexual stance; Freud condemned Adler's ego psychology. They disagreed on (1) the unity of neuroses, (2) penis envy (sexual) versus the masculine protest (social), (3) the defensive role of the ego in neuroses, and (4) the role of the unconscious. Freud did not think Adler had discovered anything new but had merely reinterpreted what psychoanalysis had already said. He believed that what Adler discovered was "trivial," and that it was "methodologically deplorable and condemns his whole work to sterility" (Colby, 1951). After a series of meetings where these issues were discussed in an atmosphere of fencing, heckling, and vitriol (Brome, 1968), Adler in 1911 resigned as president of the Vienna Psychoanalytic Society. Later that year, Freud forced the choice between Adler and himself. Several members of the circle expressed their sympathy for Adler by resigning and forming the Society for Free Psychoanalytic Research.

During the next decade, with the exception of the war period, Adler and his co-workers developed the social view of the neuroses. Their focus was primarily clinical, although Adler (1914) as early as 1908 had demonstrated an interest in children and in education. In 1922 Adler initiated what was perhaps the first community-outreach program, child-guidance centers within the community. These centers were located in public schools and were directed by psychologists who served without pay. The method, for which Adler drew much criticism, was that of public family education, a method still used in Adlerian family education centers. Twenty-eight such centers existed in Vienna until 1934, when an unfriendly government closed them. This form of center was transported to the United States by Rudolf Dreikurs and his students (Dreikurs, Corsini, Lowe & Sonstegard, 1959). The success of these centers motivated the Vienna School authorities to invite several Adlerians to plan a school along Adlerian lines, and from this invitation emerged the school described in Oskar Spiel's *Discipline Without Punishment* (1962). The school emphasized encouragement, class discussions, democratic principles, and the responsibility of children for themselves and for each other—educational methods that are still in use today.

The social orientation of Adler's Individual Psychology inevitably led to interest in group methods and Adler's introduction of family therapy (1922). Dreikurs (1959) is credited with the first use of group psychotherapy in private practice.

Between World Wars I and II, Adlerian groups existed in 20 European countries and in the United States. In 1926 Adler was invited to the United States to lecture and until 1934, when fascism took hold in Austria, he divided his time between the United States, where he was on the medical faculty of the Long Island College of Medicine, and abroad. Two of his children, Alexandra and Kurt, now practice psychiatry in New York City. With the march of Nazism, many Adlerians were forced to flee their European homelands and made the United States the center of their activities. Today Individual Psychology societies exist in the United States, England, Canada, France, Denmark, Switzerland, Germany, Austria, the Netherlands, Greece, Italy, Israel, and Australia.

Current Status

The resurgence of the Adlerian school after the dispersion from Europe was an uphill effort. Personal hardships of refugee Adlerians were compounded by the existing psychological climate in this country. The economic depression still prevailed. The Freudian school held a near monopoly, both in the treatment area and with respect to appointments in medical schools. Some Adlerians defected; others became crypto-Adlerians. However, others persevered in retaining their identity and their optimism. Local societies were founded, and 1952 saw the formation of the American Society of Adlerian Psychology (now the North American Society of Adlerian Psychology). Several journals appeared; the major American one is *Individual Psychology*, formerly called the *Journal of Individual Psychology*, which itself was the successor to the *Individual Psychology Bulletin*, of which Dreikurs was for many years the editor. The International Association of Individual Psychology also publishes the *Individual Psychology Newsletter*.

Training institutes that offer certificates in psychotherapy, counseling, and child guidance are found in New York, Chicago, Minneapolis, Berkeley, San Francisco, St. Louis, Fort Wayne, Vancouver, Montreal, and Toronto. Individual courses and programs of study are offered at many universities, such as Oregon, Arizona, West Virginia, Vermont, Governors State, Southern Illinois and Georgia State. Masters degrees based on an Adlerian curriculum are offered by Bowie State College and by the Adler School of Professional Psychology in Chicago. The latter has been accredited to offer a doctoral program in clinical psychology.

Although Adlerian psychology was once dismissed as moribund, superficial (i.e., an "ego psychology"), and suitable mainly for children, it is today considered a viable psychology.

Today's Adlerian may operate as a traditional clinician but remains innovative. Joshua Bierer has been a pioneer in social psychiatry (1969) and a leader in the day-hospital movement (1951). Therapeutic social clubs have been in operation at the Alfred Adler Mental Hygiene Clinic in New York and at Saint Joseph Hospital in Chicago. Dreikurs originated multiple psychotherapy (1950), and he, Harold Mosak, and Bernard Shulman have contributed to its development (1952a, 1952b, 1982). Rudolf Dreikurs, Asya Kadis, Helene Papanek, and Bernard Shulman have made extensive contributions to group therapy. Because they prefer the goal of prevention to that of healing, Adlerians function extensively in the area of education. Manford Sonstegard, Raymond Lowe, Bronia Grunwald, Oscar Christensen, Raymond Corsini, and Loren Grey are among those responsible for applying Adlerian principles in the schools. All of these have been students of Dreikurs, who transported the tradition from Vienna, and who himself made a great contribution in this area. In the Adlerian social tradition, Adlerians may be involved in community outreach programs or dedicating their efforts to the study of subjects such as drugs, aging, delinquency, religion, and poverty.

The contemporary Adlerian finds the growth model of personality infinitely more congenial than the sickness model. The Adlerian is not interested in curing sick individuals or a sick society, but in reeducating individuals and in reshaping society.

❖ PERSONALITY

Theory of Personality

Adlerian psychology is a psychology of use rather than of possession. This assumption decreases the importance of the question, "How do heredity and environment shape the individual?" The functionalist, holistic Adlerian asks instead, "How does the individual use heredity and environment?"

For Adler, the family constellation constitutes the primary social environment. Every child searches for significance in this environment and competes for position within the family constellation. One sibling becomes the "best" child, another the "worst" one. Being favored, being one of the favored sex within the family, adopting the family values, or identifying or allying oneself with a parent or sibling may provide the grounds for the feeling of having a place. Handicaps, organ inferiorities, or being an orphan are other "position makers" for some children.

Of supreme importance is the child's position in the family constellation. Thus, it would appear that the first child usually is a conservative and the second is often a rebel. The baby is ordinarily either everyone's darling or one who stands on tiptoes to see above the preceding siblings. If these general characteristics possess any validity, at best they exist as statistical probabilities and not as defining traits. Considering the family constellation in terms of birth order or ordinal position creates the problem of characterizing, let us say, the fifth child in the family. Although the fifth child is often encountered in the therapy situation, he or she never receives any attention in the literature. Birth order, per se, also ignores the gender position of the child. The children in two-sibling families in which the possible configurations are boy-boy, girl-girl, boy-girl, and girl-boy do not possess similar characteristics based upon ordinal position alone (Shulman & Mosak, 1977).

The Adlerian prefers to study the family constellation in terms of the *psychological* position. A simple example illustrates this point of view. Take two siblings separated in age by 10 years. In birth order research, these would be treated as a first child and a second child. From the Adlerian point of view the psychological position of each would *most likely* be that of an only child with *perhaps* the older child functioning as an additional parent figure for the younger. The italicized terms *most likely* and *perhaps* are used expressly to indicate that: (1) Adlerians do not recognize a causalistic, one-to-one relationship between family position and sibling traits; and (2) whatever relationship exists can only be understood in context, that is, when one knows the family climate and the total configuration of factors in the family constellation. Adler, whenever he generalized or ventured a prediction, was fond of reminding his students, "Everything could also be quite different."

The search for significance and the consequent sibling competition reflect the values of the competitive society in which we live. We are encouraged to be first, to excel, to be popular, to be athletic, to be a "real" man, to "never say die," to recall that "practice makes perfect," and to "dream the impossible dream." Consequently, each child must stake out a piece of "territory" that includes the attributes or abilities that are hoped will give a feeling of worth. If through their evaluations of their own potency (abilities, courage, and confidence) children are convinced that they can achieve this place through useful endeavor, they will pursue "the useful side of life." Should children feel that they cannot attain the goal of having a "place" in this fashion, they will become discouraged and engage in disturbed or disturbing behavior in their efforts to find a place. For the Adlerian the "maladjusted" child is not a "sick" child. He or she is a "discouraged" child. Dreikurs (1948, 1949) classifies the goals of the discouraged child into four groups—attention getting, power seeking, revenge taking, and declaring deficiency or defeat. Dreikurs is speaking of immediate rather than long-range goals. These are the goals of children's "misbehavior," not of all children's behavior (Mosak & Mosak, 1975).

In the process of becoming socialized human beings, children form conclusions on the basis of their subjective experiences. Because judgment and logical processes are not highly developed in young children, many of their growing convictions contain errors or only partial "truths." Nevertheless, they accept these conclusions about themselves and others *as if* they were true. They are subjective evaluations, biased apperceptions of themselves and of the world, rather than objective "reality." Thus, one can be truly inferior without feeling inferior. Conversely, one can feel inferior without being inferior.

The child creates a cognitive map or life-style that will assist "little me" in coping with the "big" world. The life-style includes the aspirations, the long-range goals, and a "statement" of the conditions, personal or social, that are requisite for the individual's "security." The latter are also fictions and are stated in therapy as "If only…, then I…." Mosak (1954) divided life-style convictions into four groups:

1. The *self-concept*—the convictions I have about who I am.

2. The *self-ideal* (Adler coined this phrase in 1912)—the convictions of what I should be or am obliged to be to have a place.

3. The *Weltbild*, or "picture of the world"—convictions about the not-self (world, people, nature, and so on) and what the world demands of me.

4. The *ethical convictions*—the personal "right-wrong" code.

When there is a discrepancy between self and ideal-self convictions ("I am short; I should be tall"), *inferiority feelings* ensue. Although an infinite variety of inferiority feelings exist, one should be mentioned that Adler discussed while he was still in the Freudian Society, which eventuated in the rift between himself and Freud. It assumes monumental importance in some circles today—the masculine protest. In a culture that places a premium on masculinity, some women feel inferior because they have not been accorded the prerogatives or privileges of men. ("I am woman; I should be equal to man"). But men also suffered from the masculine protest because being a man is not sufficient to provide a "place" for some men ("I am a man; but I should be a *real* man"). Because Adler believed in the equality of the sexes, he could not accept these fictions (Mosak & Schneider, 1977).

Lack of congruence between convictions in the self-concept and those in the *Weltbild* ("I am weak and helpless; life is dangerous") also results in inferiority feelings. Discrepancies between self-concept and ethical convictions ("One should always tell the truth; I lie") lead to inferiority feelings in the moral realm. Thus, the guilt feeling is merely a variant of the inferiority feeling (Mosak, 1987b).

These variations of inferiority feelings in and of themselves are not "abnormal." It would be difficult to quarrel with Adler's observations that to live is to *feel* inferior. It is only when individuals act *as if* they were inferior, develop symptoms, or behave as "sick" that we see evidences of what in the medical model would be called *pathology* and what Adlerians call *discouragement* or the *inferiority complex*. To oversimplify, the *inferiority feeling* is universal and "normal"; the *inferiority complex* reflects the discouragement of a limited segment of our society and is usually "abnormal." The former may be masked or hidden from the view of others; the latter is an open demonstration of inadequacy, or "sickness."

Using their "maps," people facilitate their movements through life. This permits them to evaluate, understand, experience, predict, and control experience. Lawrence Frank writes in this connection:

> The personality process might be regarded as a sort of rubber stamp which the individual imposes upon every situation by which he gives it the configuration that he, as an individual, requires; in so doing he necessarily ignores or subordinates many aspects of the situation that for him are irrelevant and meaningless and selectively reacts to those aspects that are personally significant. (1939, p. 392)

Although the life-style is the instrument for coping with experience, it is very largely nonconscious. The life-style comprises the cognitive organization of the individual rather than the behavioral organization. As an illustration, the conviction "I require excitement" may lead to the vocational choices of actor, racing car driver, explorer, or to "acting out" behavior. Such a conviction may further lead to getting into jams or exciting situations, or engaging in creative acts, or discovery.

Within the same life-style, one can behave usefully or uselessly. The above distinction permits Adlerians (e.g., Dreikurs, 1961; Nikelly, 1971a) to distinguish between *psychotherapy* and *counseling*. The former, they maintain, has as its aim the change of life-style; the latter has as its goal the change of behavior within the existing life-style.

Because the Adlerian literature discusses the life tasks of occupation, society, and love so extensively, these tasks of life will not be elaborated upon here, except for some brief comments. Lewis Way points out that "The problems they pose can never be solved once and for all, but demand from the individual a continuous and creative movement toward adaptation" (1962, pp. 179–80).

Love, as an emotion, like other emotions is cognitively based. People are not "victims" of their emotions. They create emotions to assist them in the attainment of their goals. Love is the conjunctive emotion we create when we want to move toward people.

Although the life tasks of love, occupation, and society demand solution, it is possible to avoid or postpone them if one can compensate in other areas. "Even successful persons fall into neurosis because they are not more successful" (Way, 1962, p. 206). The *neurotic symptom* is an expression of "I *can't* because I'm sick"; the person's movement betrays the "I *won't* because my self-esteem might get hurt" (Krausz, 1959, p. 112). Although neurotics' movements are consonant with their "private logic" (Nikelly, 1971b), they still cling to "common sense." They know what they should do or feel, but they "can't." Adler referred to them as "yes-but" personalities. Eric Berne (1964) has graphically described their interpersonal maneuvers in the "Why don't you—Yes, but" game. The genesis of neurosis lies in discouragement. People avoid and postpone or take circuitous routes to solutions so they can "save face." Even when they expect or arrange to fail, they try to salvage some self-esteem. Students, fearful of failing examinations, will refrain from studying. In the event they do fail, they merely have to hold that they were lazy or neglectful but not stupid.

The *psychotic's* goal of superiority is often loftier than that which can be achieved by mere humans. "Individual Psychology has shown that the goal of superiority can only be fixed at such attitudes when the individual has, by losing interest in others, also lost interest in his own reason and understanding…common sense has become useless to him" (Adler, 1964a, pp. 128–29). Adler used "common sense" in much the same manner that Sullivan spoke of "consensual validation." In the pseudo work area, the psychotic becomes superintendent of the mental hospital. In the pseudo social area, the hypomanic patient resembles the cheerful extrovert and the more acutely manic patient becomes a "name dropper" and "swallows up" people (Shulman, 1962). The paranoid patient pictures people as threatening and manifests a "search for glory," to use Karen Horney's (1951) phrase, by the persecutory delusion that *they* are conspiring to do something to *me*. The delusions of grandeur of the psychotic depressive patients ("I'm the *worst* sinner of all time") and of the schizophrenic who claims to be Christ are some other "solutions" to the spiritual pseudo tasks. The reifying hallucinations of talking with the devil fall in this category (Adler, 1963b; Mosak & Fletcher, 1973).

The *psychologically healthy* or *normal* individual has developed social interest and is willing to commit to life and the life tasks without evasion, excuse, or "side shows" (Wolfe, 1932). This person proceeds with confidence and optimism about meeting life's challenges. There is a sense of belonging and contributing, the "courage to be imperfect," and the serene knowledge that one can be acceptable to others, although imperfect. Above all, this person rejects the faulty values that culture projects and attempts to substitute for them values more consonant with the "ironclad logic of social living." Such a person does not exist, nor will psychotherapy produce such a person. Yet this is the Adlerian ideal, and because Adler's intent was to substitute small errors for larger errors, many of these goals can be approximated in psychotherapy. Many fortunate people have the courage (Adler, 1928) and social interest to do this for themselves without therapeutic assistance.

Variety of Concepts

The simplicity of Adlerian vocabulary renders definition and interpretation generally unnecessary. Yet some differences of opinion and emphasis about Adlerian concepts remain unresolved. In terms of *life-style*, Adlerians disagree with respect to what it describes—behavioral or cognitive organization. *Social interest* (Bickhard & Ford, 1976; Crandall, 1981; Edgar, 1975; Kazan, 1978; Mosak, 1991) apparently is not a unitary concept but a cluster of feelings and behaviors (Ansbacher, 1968). Although social interest is often described as "innate," many Adlerians wonder what makes it so, given that it appears to be neither genetic nor constitutional. As one looks at the theories of Adler, Freud, and Jung, one is struck with the effort on the part of all three to "biologize" their theories. Perhaps it was the temper of the times. Perhaps it was because all three were physicians. Perhaps it resulted from the need to make their theories respectable during a period when psychoanalysis was held in low esteem. None of these theories would incur any great damage if "instincts," "social interest," and "racial unconscious" were treated as psychological constructs rather than as biological processes. Adler, having introduced the concept of *organ inferiority* with its consequent compensation, actually had proposed a biopsychological theory, but it must be recalled that this transpired during his "Freudian period." Later he substituted the *social inferiority feeling* for actual organ inferiority, and with the exception of one important article (Shulman & Klapman, 1968), Adlerians have published little on organ inferiority. Although people undoubtedly do compensate for organ inferiority, the latter is no longer the cornerstone of the Adlerian edifice.

Gardner Murphy (1947) took issue with Adler's use of compensation as the only defense mechanism. Literally, Adler's writings do read that way. On the other hand, if one reads more closely, compensation becomes an umbrella to cover all coping mechanisms. Thus, Adler speaks of safeguards, excuses, projection, the depreciation tendency, creating distance, and identification. Although a Freudian might view these as defense mechanisms, the Adlerian prefers to view them as problem-solving devices to person uses to protect self-esteem, reputation, and physical self. Because Adlerians do not accept the concept of *the* unconscious, such mechanisms as repression and sublimation become irrelevant. Adlerian theory has no room for instincts, drives, libido, and other alleged movers.

Because of their mutual emphasis on behavior (movement), Adlerian psychology and behavior-modification theory have been equated. This is an error. Adlerians, although interested in changing behavior, have as their major goal not behavior modification but *motivation* modification. Dreikurs writes: "We do not attempt primarily to change behavior patterns or remove symptoms. If a patient improves his behavior because he finds it profitable at the time, without changing his basic premises, then we do not consider that as a therapeutic success. We are trying to change goals, concepts, and notions" (1963, p. 79).

❖ PSYCHOTHERAPY

Theory of Psychotherapy

All scientific schools of psychotherapy have their shares of successes and failures. A considerable number of therapies based upon nonscientific foundations probably reach equal success levels. In any event, regardless of its validity or endurance, any theory must be implemented within the context of the therapist-patient relationship. As Fred Fiedler (1950) has shown, therapeutic success is a function of the expertness of the therapist rather than of the therapist's orientation.

Given that the underlying psychodynamic theory is not the crucial factor in therapy, perhaps it is the special techniques that contribute to therapeutic effectiveness. This would certainly seem to have been Rogers's early position before nondirective therapy became person-centered therapy. For the early nondirective school, the creation of a warm, permissive, nonjudgmental atmosphere; reflection of feeling; and avoidance of interpretation, advice, persuasion, and suggestion were paramount in the therapeutic situation.

The Freudian assigns central importance to transference, but behavior modification therapists ignore it. To many directive therapists, content and manner of interpretation are crucial. The Adlerian emphasizes interpretation of the patient's life-style and movement.

Criteria for "getting well" correspond to the particular therapeutic emphasis. Some therapists propose depth of therapy as the decisive factor. For most Adlerians, depth of therapy does not constitute a major concern. In this connection, therapy is neither deep nor superficial except as the patient experiences it as such.

If neither theory nor the use of prescribed techniques is decisive, is it the transference relationship that makes cure possible? Or the egalitarian relationship? Or the warm, permissive atmosphere with the nonjudgmental therapist accepting the patient as is? Because all of these relationships are involved in various forms of both effective and noneffective therapy, we must hypothesize either that therapeutic effectiveness is a matter of matching certain therapeutic relationships to certain patients or that all therapeutic relationships possess common factors. These factors—variations on the Christian virtues of faith, hope, and love—appear to be necessary, but not sufficient, conditions of effective therapy.

Faith

D. Rosenthal and Jerome D. Frank (1956) discuss the implications of faith in the therapeutic process. Franz Alexander and Thomas French state:

> As a general rule, the patient who comes for help voluntarily has this confidence, this expectation that the therapist is both able and willing to help him, before he comes to treatment; if not, if the patient is forced into treatment, the therapist must build up this feeling of rapport before any therapeutic change can be effected. (1946, p. 173)

Many therapeutic mechanisms may enhance the patient's faith. A simple explanation clarifies matters for some patients, a complex interpretation for others. The therapist's own faith in him- or herself, therapist's appearance of wisdom, strength, and assurance, and the therapist's willingness to listen without criticism may all be used by patients to strengthen their faith.

Hope

Patients seek treatment with varying degrees of hope, running the gamut from complete hopelessness to hope for (and expectation of) everything, including a miracle. Because of the efficacy of the self-fulfilling prophecy, people *tend* to move in the direction of making their anticipations come true. Therefore, the therapist must keep the patient's hope elevated.

Because the Adlerian holds that the patient suffers from discouragement, a primary therapeutic technique lies in encouragement. Expression of faith in the patient, noncondemnation, and avoidance of being overly demanding may give the patient hope. The patient may also derive hope from feeling understood. Accordingly, the construction of therapy as a "we" experience where patients do not feel they stand alone, where they feel security in the strength and competency of their therapist, and where they feel some symptom alleviation may all prove helpful. They may also gain hope from attempting some course of action they feared or did not know was available to them. Humor assists in the retention of hope (Mosak, 1987a). Lewis Way comments, "Humor such as Adler possessed in such abundance, is an invaluable asset, since, if one can occasionally joke, things cannot be so bad" (1962, p. 267). Each therapist has faith in his methods for encouraging and sustaining hope. They are put to the most severe test in patients who are depressed or suicidal.

Love

In its broadest sense, the patient must feel that the therapist cares (Adler, 1963a, 1964a). The mere act of treating the patient may furnish such evidence by employing empathic listening, "working through" together, or having two therapists in multiple psychotherapy offering interest in the patient. Transfer of a patient to another therapist or from individual to group therapy may have a contrary effect unless it is "worked through."

But the therapist must avoid pitfalls such as infantilizing, oversupporting, or becoming a victim of the patient when the patient accuses the therapist of not caring enough. In Adlerian group therapy, the group is conceptualized as a "reexperiencing of the family constellation" (Kadis, 1956). Thus, the therapist may be accused of playing favorites, of caring too much for one or too little for another patient.

The Adlerian theory of psychotherapy rests on the notion that psychotherapy is a co-operative educational enterprise involving one or more therapists and one or more patients. The goal of therapy is to develop the patient's social interest. To accomplish this, therapy involves changing faulty social values (Dreikurs, 1957). The subject matter of this course in reeducation is the patient—the life-style and the relationship to the life tasks. Learning the "basic mistakes" in the cognitive map, the patient has the opportunity to decide whether to continue in the old ways or move in other directions. "The consultee must under all circumstances get the conviction in relation to treatment that he is absolutely free. He can do, or not do, as he pleases" (Ansbacher & Ansbacher, 1956, p. 341). The patient can choose between self-interest and social interest. The educational process has the following goals:

1. The fostering of social interest.
2. The decrease of inferiority feelings, the overcoming of discouragement, and the recognition and utilization of one's resources.
3. Changes in the person's life-style, that is, perceptions and goals. The therapeutic goal, as has been mentioned, involves transforming big errors into little ones (as with automobiles, some need a "tune-up" and others require a "major overhaul").
4. Changing faulty motivation that underlies even acceptable behavior, or changing values.
5. Encouraging the individual to recognize equality among people (Dreikurs, 1971).
6. Helping the person to become a contributing human being.

"Students" who reach these educational objectives will feel a sense of belonging and display acceptance of themselves and others. They will feel that they can arrange, within life's limits, their own destinies. Such patients eventually come to feel encouraged, optimistic, confident, courageous, secure—and asymptomatic.

Process of Psychotherapy

The process of psychotherapy, as practiced by Adlerians, has four aims: (1) establishing and maintaining a "good" relationship; (2) uncovering the dynamics of the patient, including life-style and goals, and assessing how they affect life movement; (3) interpretation culminating in insight; and (4) reorientation.

Relationship

A "good" therapeutic relationship is a friendly one between equals. Both the Adlerian therapist and the patient sit facing each other, their chairs at the same level. Many Adlerians prefer to work without a desk because distancing and separation may engender undesirable psychological sets. Having abandoned the medical model, the Adlerian looks with disfavor upon casting the doctor in the role of the actor (omnipotent, omniscient, and mysterious) and the patient in the role of the acted-upon. Therapy is structured to inform the patient that creative human beings play a role in creating their problems, that one is responsible (not in the sense of blame) for one's actions, and that one's problems are based upon faulty perceptions and inadequate or faulty learning, especially of faulty values (Dreikurs, 1957). If this is so, one can assume responsibility for change. What has not been learned can be learned. What has been learned "poorly" can be replaced by better learning. Faulty perception and values can be altered and modified. From the initiation of treatment, the patient's efforts to remain passive are discouraged. The patient has an active role in the therapy. Although assuming the role of student, the patient is still an active learner responsible for contributing to his or her own education.

Therapy requires cooperation, which means alignment of goals. Noncoincidence of goals may not permit the therapy to get off the ground, as, for example, when the patient denies the need for therapy. The initial interview(s) must not, therefore, omit the consideration of initial goals and expectations. The patient may wish to overpower the therapist or to make the therapist powerful and responsible. The therapist's goal must be to avoid these traps. The patient may want to relinquish symptoms but not underlying convictions, and may be looking for a miracle. In each case, at least a temporary agreement upon goals must be arrived at before the therapy can proceed. Way cautions:

> A refusal to be caught in this way [succumbing to the patient's appeals to the therapist's vanity or bids for sympathy] gives the patient little opportunity for developing serious resistances and transferences, and is indeed the doctor's only defence against a reversal of roles and against finding that he is being treated by the patient. The cure must always be a cooperation and never a fight. It is a hard test for the doctor's own balance and is likely to succeed only if he himself is free from neurosis. (1962, p. 265)

Adler (1963a) offers similar warnings against role reversal.

Because the problems of resistance and transference are defined in terms of patient-therapist goal discrepancies, throughout therapy the goals will diverge and the common task will consist of realigning the goals so patient and therapist move in the same direction.

The patient, in bringing a life-style to therapy, expects from the therapist the kind of response expected from all others. The patient may feel misunderstood, unfairly treated, or unloved and may anticipate that the therapist will behave accordingly. Often the patient unconsciously creates situations to invite the therapist to behave in this manner. For this reason, the therapist must be alert to what Adlerians call "scripts," and Eric Berne (1964) calls "games," and foil the patient's expectations. A patient, for example, will declare, "Have you ever seen a patient like me before?" to establish uniqueness and to challenge the therapist's competence. The therapist's response may just be a straightforward, but nonsarcastic, "Not since the last hour," followed by a discussion of uniqueness. Because assessment begins with the first moment of contact, the patient is generally given some interpretation, usually phrased as a guess, during the first interview. This gives the patient something to think about until the next interview. The therapist will soon find it possible to assess how the patient will respond to interpretation, to therapy, and to the therapist, and will gain some glimpse of the life-style framework. The therapist does not play the patient's game because at that game the patient is the professional, having played it successfully since childhood (although often in self-defeating fashion), whereas the therapist is a relative amateur. The therapist does not have to *win* the game but merely does not play it. Only one side wins in a tug-of-war. However, in this case, one side (the therapist) is uninterested in victories or defeats and merely does not pick up the end of the rope. This renders the "opponent's" game ineffective, and the two can proceed to play more productive, cooperative games.

The whole relationship process increases the education of the patient. For some patients, it is their first experience of a good interpersonal relationship involving cooperation, mutual respect, and trust. Despite occasional bad feelings, the relationship can endure and survive. The patient learns that good and bad relationships do not merely happen—they are products of people's efforts—and that poor interpersonal relationships are products of misperceptions, inaccurate conclusions, and unwarranted anticipations incorporated in the life-style.

Analysis

Investigation of a patient's dynamics is divided into two parts. First, the therapist wants to understand the patient's life-style and, second, aims to understand how the life-style affects current function with respect to the life tasks. Not all suffering stems from the patient's life-style. Many patients with adequate life-styles develop problems or symptoms in the face of intolerable or extreme situations from which they cannot extricate themselves.

Analytic investigation begins with the first moment. The way a patient enters the room, posture, and choice of seating (especially important in family therapy) all provide important clues. What the patient says and how it is said expand the therapist's understanding, especially when the therapist interprets the patient's communications in interpersonal terms, or "scripts," rather than in descriptive terms. Thus, the Adlerian translates the descriptive statement, "I am confused" into the admonition, "Don't pin me down." "It's a habit," conveys the declaration, "And that's another thing you're not going to get me to change" (Mosak & Gushurst, 1971). As therapy progresses, the therapist assesses, follows up, and juxtaposes clues in patterns, accepting some hypotheses and rejecting others in an effort to understand the patient. As therapy progresses, the patient offers information one way or another, and the therapist pieces it together bit by bit like a jigsaw puzzle.

The Life-style Investigation

In formal assessment procedures, the patient's family constellation is explored. We obtain glimpses of what position the child found in the family and how he or she went about finding a place within the family, in school, and among peers. The second portion of the assessment consists of interpreting the patient's early recollections. An *early recollection* occurs in the period before continuous memory and may be inaccurate or a complete fiction. It represents a single event ("One day I remember…") rather than a group of events ("We used to…"). Adlerians refer to the latter as a *report* rather than a recollection. Recollections are treated as a projective technique (Mosak, 1958). If one understands the early recollections, one understands the patient's "Story of My Life" (Adler, 1931), because people selectively recollect from their past incidents consonant with their life-styles. The following recollection of Adler (1947) may serve to illustrate the consonance between his earliest recollection and his later psychological views:

> One of my earliest recollections is of sitting on a bench, bandaged up on account of rickets, with my healthy elder brother sitting opposite me. He could run, jump, and move about quite effortlessly, while for me movement of any sort was a strain and an effort. Everyone went to great pains to help me, and my mother and father did all that was in their power to do. At the time of this recollection I must have been about two years old. (p. 9)

In a single recollection, Adler refers to organ inferiority, the inferiority feeling, the emphasis upon "my desire to move freely—to see all psychic manifestations in terms of movements" (p. 10), and social feeling (Mosak & Kopp, 1973).

The summary of early recollections, the story of the patient's life, permits the derivation of the patient's "basic mistakes." The life-style can be conceived as a personal mythology. The individual will behave *as if* the myths were true because, for him or her, they are true. So there are "truths" or partial "truths" in myths and there are myths we confuse with truth. The latter are *basic mistakes*.

Basic mistakes may be classified as follows:

1. *Overgeneralizations.* "People are hostile." "Life is dangerous."

2. *False or impossible goals of "security."* "One false step and you're dead." "I have to please everybody."

3. *Misperceptions of life and life's demands.* Typical convictions might be "Life never gives me any breaks" and "Life is so hard."

4. *Minimization or denial of one's worth.* "I'm stupid" and "I'm undeserving" or "I'm just a housewife."

5. *Faulty values.* "Be first even if you have to climb over others."

Finally, the therapist is interested in how the patient perceives his or her assets.

The following sample life-style summary is not intended to be a complete personality description, but it does offer patient and therapist initial hypotheses.

Summary of Family Constellation

John is the younger of two children, the only boy, who grew up fatherless after age nine. His sister was so precocious that John became discouraged. Because he felt he would never become famous, he decided perhaps he could at least be notorious, and through negative behavior brought himself to the attention of others. He acquired the reputation of a "holy terror." He was going to do everything his way, and nobody was going to stop him. He followed the guiding lines of a strong, masculine father from whom he learned that the toughest man wins. Because notoriety came with doing the disapproved, John early became interested in and engaged in sex. This also reinforced his feelings of masculinity. Because both parents were handicapped and yet still "made it," John apparently decided that without any physical handicaps, the sky would be the limit for him.

Summary of Early Recollections

"I run scared in life, and even when people tell me there's nothing to be scared of, I'm still scared. Women give men a hard time. They betray them, they punish them, and they interfere with what men want to do. A real man takes no crap from anybody. Somebody always interferes. I am not going to do what others want me to do. Others call that bad and want to punish me for it, but I don't see it that way. Doing what I want is merely part of being a man."

"Basic Mistakes"

1. John exaggerates the significance of masculinity and equates it with doing what he pleases.
2. He is not on the same wavelength as women. They see his behavior as "bad"; he sees it as only "natural" for a man.
3. He is too ready to fight, many times just to preserve his sense of masculinity.
4. He perceives women as the enemy, even though he looks to them for comfort.
5. Victory is snatched from him at the last moment.

Assets

1. He is a driver. When he puts his mind to things, he makes them work.
2. He engages in creative problem solving.
3. He knows how to get what he wants.
4. He knows how to ask a woman "nicely."

During the course of the treatment, other forms of analysis will occur. Because the therapist views the life-style as consistent, it will express itself in all of the patient's behavior—physical behavior, language and speech, fantasy productions, dreams, and interpersonal relationships, past and present. Because of this consistency, the patient may choose to express self in any or all of these media because they all express life-style. The therapist observes behavior, speech, and language closely during each interview. Sometimes, the dialogue will center on the present, sometimes on the past, often on the future. Free association and chitchat, except when the latter serves a therapeutic purpose, are mostly discouraged. Although dream analysis is an integral part of psychotherapy, the patient who speaks only of dreams receives gentle dissuasion (Alexandra Adler, 1943). The analysis proceeds with an examination of the interplay between life-style and the life tasks—how the life-style affects the person's function and dysfunction vis-à-vis the life tasks.

Dreams

Adler saw the dream as a problem-solving activity with a future orientation, in contrast to Freud's view that it was an attempt to solve an old problem. The *dream* is seen by Adlerians as a rehearsal of possible future courses of action. If we want to postpone action, we forget the dream. If we want to dissuade ourselves from some action, we frighten ourselves with a nightmare.

The dream, Adler said, was the "factory of emotions." In it we create moods that move us toward or away from the next day's activities. Commonly, people say, "I don't know why but I woke up in a lousy mood today." The day before Adler died, he told friends, "I woke smiling…so I knew my dreams were good although I had forgotten them" (Bottome, 1939, p. 240). Just as early recollections reflect long-range goals, the dream experiments with possible answers to immediate problems. In accord with the view of the individual's uniqueness, Adlerians reject the theory of fixed symbolism. One cannot understand a dream without knowing the dreamer, although Adler (1936) and Erwin Wexberg (1929) do address themselves to some frequently encountered dream themes. Way admonishes:

> One is reminded again of two boys, instanced by Adler [1964a, p. 150], each of whom wished to be a horse, one because he would have to bear the responsibility for his family, the other to outstrip all the others. This should be a salutary warning against making dictionary interpretations. (1962, pp. 282–284)

The interpretation of the dream does not terminate with the analysis of the content but must include the purposive function. Dreams serve as weathervanes for treatment, bringing problems to the surface and pointing to the patient's movement. Dreikurs describes a patient who related recurrent dreams that were short and actionless, reflecting his life-style of figuring out "the best way of getting out of a problem, mostly without doing anything.…When his dreams started to move and become active he started to move in his life, too" (1944, p. 26).

Reorientation

Reorientation in all therapies proceeds from persuading the patient, gently or forcefully, that change is in his or her best interest. The patient's present manner of living accords "safety" but not happiness. Because neither therapy nor life offers *guarantees*, one must risk some "safety" for the possibility of greater happiness and self-fulfillment. This dilemma is not easily solved. Like Hamlet, the patient wonders whether it is better to "bear those ills we have than fly to others that we know not of."

Insight

Analytic psychotherapists frequently assign central importance to insight, upon the assumption that "basic change" cannot occur in its absence. The conviction that insight must precede behavioral change often results in extended treatment, in encouraging some patients to become "sicker" to avoid or postpone change, and in increasing their self-absorption rather than their self-awareness. Meanwhile, patients relieve themselves from the responsibility of living life until they have achieved insight.

A second assumption, treasured by therapists and patients alike, distinguishes between *intellectual* and *emotional* insight (Ellis, 1963; H. Papanek, 1959), a dualism the holistic Adlerian experiences difficulty in accepting. This and other dualisms, such as conscious versus unconscious, undeniably exist in the patient's subjective experience. But these antagonistic forces are creations of the patient that delay action. Simultaneously the patient can maintain a good conscience because he or she is the victim of conflicting forces or an emotional block. Solving problems is relegated to the future while the patient pursues insight. *Insight*, as the Adlerian defines it, is understanding translated into constructive action. It reflects the patient's understanding of the purposive nature of behavior and mistaken apperceptions as well as an understanding of the role both play in life movement. So-called intellectual insight merely reflects the patient's desire to play the game of therapy rather than the game of life.

Interpretation

The Adlerian therapist facilitates insight mainly by interpretation of ordinary communications, dreams, fantasies, behavior, symptoms, the patient-therapist transactions, and the patient's interpersonal transactions. The emphasis in interpretation is on purpose rather than cause, on movement rather than description, on use rather than possession. Through interpretation, the therapist holds up a mirror for the patient.

The therapist relates past to present only to indicate the continuity of the maladaptive life-style, not to demonstrate a causal connection. The therapist may also use humor or illustrate with fables (Pancner, 1978), anecdotes, and biography. Irony may prove effective but it must be handled with care. The therapist may "spit in the patient's soup," a crude expression for exposing the patient's intentions in such a way as to make them unpalatable. The therapist may offer the interpretation directly or in the form of "Could it be that...?" or may invite the patient to make interpretations. Although timing, exaggeration, understatement, and accuracy are technical concerns of any therapist, they are not too important for the Adlerian therapist, who does not view the patient as fragile.

Other Verbal Techniques

Advice is often frowned upon by therapists. Hans Strupp relates, "It has been said that Freud, following his own recommendations, never gave advice to an analysand on the couch but did not stint with the commodity from the couch to the door" (1972, p. 40). Wexberg (1970) frowned on giving advice to a patient, but the Adlerian therapist freely gives advice, as did Freud, taking care, however, not to encourage dependency. In practice, the therapist may merely outline the alternatives and let the patient make the decision. This invitation develops faith in self rather than faith in the therapist. On the other hand, the therapist may offer direct advice, taking care to encourage the patient's self-directiveness and willingness to stand alone.

Given that Adlerians consider the patient discouraged rather than sick, it is no surprise that they make extensive use of encouragement. Enhancing the patient's faith in self, "accentuating the positive and eliminating the negative," and keeping up the patient's hope all contribute to counteracting discouragement. The patient who "walks and falls" learns it is not fatal and can get up and walk again. Therapy also counteracts the patient's social values, thus altering his or her view of life and helping give meaning to it. Moralizing is avoided, although therapists must not deceive themselves into believing their system has no value orientation. The dialogue concerns "useful" and "useless," rather than "good" or "bad" behavior.

The therapist avoids rational argument and trying to "out-logic" the patient. These tactics are easily defeated by the patient who operates according to the rules of *psychologic* (private) logic rather than formal logic. Catharsis, abreaction, and confession may afford the patient relief by freeing him or her from carrying the burden of "unfinished business," but as has been noted (Alexander & French, 1946), these may also be a test of whether the patient can place trust in the therapist.

Action Techniques

Adlerians regularly use role-playing, talking to an empty chair (Shoobs, 1964), the Midas technique (Shulman, 1962), the behind-the-back technique (Corsini, 1953), and other action procedures to assist the patient in reorientation. The extent of use is a function of the therapist's preference, training, and readiness to experiment with the novel.

Mechanisms of Psychotherapy

The Therapist as Model

The therapist represents values the patient may attempt to imitate. Adlerian therapists represent themselves as "being for real," fallible, able to laugh at themselves, caring—models for social interest. If the therapist can possess these characteristics, perhaps the patient can, too, and many patients emulate their therapists, whom they use as referents for normality (Mosak, 1967).

Change

There comes a time in psychotherapy when analysis must be abandoned and the patient must be encouraged to move forward. Insight has to give way to decisive action.

Some of the techniques Adlerians use to elicit change are described below. They are not panaceas, nor are they used indiscriminately. The creative therapist will improvise techniques to meet the needs of the therapeutic moment, and remember, above all, that people are more important than techniques and strategies. Losing sight of these cautions, the therapist is a technician who does all the "right" things but is never engaged in a human encounter with another human being.

Acting "as if"

A common patient refrain in treatment is "If only I could…" (Adler, 1963a). We often request that for the next week the patient act "as if." The patient may protest that it would only be an act and therefore phony. We explain that all acting is not phony pretense, that one can try on a role as one might try on a suit. It does not change the person wearing the suit, but sometimes with a handsome suit of clothes, one may feel differently and perhaps behave differently, thus becoming a different person.

Task Setting

Adler (1964a) gave us the prototype for task setting in his treatment of depressives, writing:

> To return to the indirect method of treatment: I recommend it especially in melancholia. After establishing a sympathetic relation I give suggestions for a change of conduct in two stages. In the first stage my suggestion is "Only do what is agreeable to you." The patient usually answers, "Nothing is agreeable." "Then at least," I respond, "do not exert yourself to do what is disagreeable." The patient, who has usually been exhorted to do various uncongenial things to remedy this condition, finds a rather flattering novelty in my advice, and may improve in behavior. Later I insinuate the second rule of conduct, saying that "it is much more difficult and I do not know if you can follow it." After saying this I am silent, and look doubtfully at the patient. In this way I excite his curiosity and ensure his attention, and then proceed, "If you could follow this second rule you would be cured in fourteen days. It is—to consider from time to time how you can give another person pleasure. It would very soon enable you to sleep and would chase away all your sad thoughts. You would feel yourself to be useful and worthwhile."
>
> I receive various replies to my suggestion, but every patient thinks it is too difficult to act upon. If the answer is, "How can I give pleasure to others when I have none myself?" I relieve the prospect by saying, "Then you will need four weeks." The more transparent response, "Who gives *me* pleasure?" I counter with what is probably the strongest move in the game, by saying, "Perhaps you had better train yourself a little thus: do not actually DO anything to please anyone else, but just think out how you COULD do it!" (pp. 25–26)

The tasks are relatively simple and are set at a level at which patients can sabotage the task, but they cannot fail and then scold the therapist.

> The patient must understand that not the physician but life itself is inexorable. He must understand that ultimately [he will have] to transfer to practical life that which has been theoretically recognized....But from the physician he hears no word of reproach or of impatience, at most an occasional kindly, harmless, ironical remark. (p. 101)

A 50-year-old man who professed "genuine" intention to get married but simultaneously avoided women was instructed to seek one meaningful contact with a woman (how to do so was up to him) every day. After raising many objections, he complained, "But it's so hard! I'll get so tired out I won't be able to function." The therapist good-humoredly relented and informed him, "Since God rested on the seventh day, I can't ask you to do more than God. So you need carry out the task only six days a week."

One form of task setting Adler introduced is called *antisuggestion* by Wexberg (1929) and *paradoxical intention* by Frankl (1963). This method used nonclinically by Knight Dunlap (1933) was labeled *negative practice*. The symptomatic patient unwittingly reinforces symptoms by fighting them, by saying, "Why did this have to happen to *me*? The insomniac keeps one eye open to observe whether the other is falling asleep and then wonders at the difficulty in falling asleep. To halt this fight, the patient is instructed to intend and even increase that which he or she is fighting against.

Creating Images

Adler was fond of describing patients with a simple phrase, for example, "The beggar as king." Other Adlerians give patients similar shorthand images that confirm the adage that "one picture is worth a thousand words." Remembering this image, the patient can remember goals, and in later stages, can learn to use the image to laugh at self. One over-ambitious patient, labeled "Superman," one day began to unbutton his shirt. When the therapist made inquiry, the patient laughingly replied, "So you can see my blue shirt with the big 'S' on it." Another patient, fearing sexual impotence, concurred with the therapist's observation that he had never seen an impotent dog. The patient advanced as explanation, "The dog just does what he's supposed to do without worrying about whether he'll be able to perform." The therapist suggested that at his next attempt at sexual intercourse, before he made any advances, he should smile and say inwardly, "Bow wow." The following week he informed the members of his group, "I bow wowed."

Catching Oneself

When patients understand personal goals and want to change, they are instructed to catch themselves "with their hand in the cookie jar." Patients may catch themselves in the midst of their old behavior but still feel incapable of doing anything about it at the moment. With additional practice, they learn to anticipate situations before their occurrence.

The Push-Button Technique

This method, effective with people who feel they are victims of their disjunctive emotions, involves requesting patients to close their eyes, recreate a pleasant incident from past experience, and to note the feeling that accompanies this image. Then they are asked to recreate an unpleasant incident of hurt, humiliation, failure, or anger and to note the accompanying feeling. Following this the patient recreates the first scene again. The lesson Adlerians try to teach clients is that they can create whatever feeling they wish merely by deciding what they will think about. One is the creator, not the victim, of emotions. To be depressed, for example, requires *choosing* to be depressed. We try to impress the patient with their power for self-determination. This method, devised for clinical use by Mosak (1985), has been the subject of experimental investigation by Brewer (1976), who found it an effective technique in treating state depression.

The "Aha" Experience

The patient who gains awareness in treatment and increases participation in life recurrently has "aha" or "eureka" experiences. With this greater understanding, the patient generates self-confidence and optimism, resulting in increased encouragement and willingness to confront life's problems with commitment, compassion, and empathy.

Post-therapy

After therapy is over, the patient can implement newly acquired learning. Operationally, the goal of therapy may be defined as that of making the therapist superfluous. If therapist and patient have both done their jobs well, the goal will have been achieved.

❖ APPLICATIONS

Problems

Although Adler, like the other *Nervenärzte* ("nerve doctors") of his era, conducted one-to-one psychotherapy, his own social outlook moved him out of the consulting room and into the community. Although he never relinquished his clinical interests, he concurrently was an educator and a social reformer. Joost Meerloo, a Freudian, eulogizes Adler with his confession:

> As a matter of fact, the whole body of psychoanalysis and psychiatry is imbued with Adler's ideas, although few want to acknowledge this fact. We are all plagiarists, though we hate to

confess it....The whole body of social psychiatry would have been impossible without Adler's pioneering zest. (1970, p. 40)

Clinical

All the early pioneers in psychotherapy treated neurotics. Psychotics were considered not amenable to psychotherapy because they could not enter into a transference relationship. Adlerians, unencumbered by the concept of transference, treated psychotics regularly. Henri Ellenberger (1970) suggests that "among the great pioneers of dynamic psychiatry, Janet and Adler are the only ones who had personal clinical experience with criminals, and Adler was the only one who wrote something on the subject from his direct experience." An Adlerian, Ernst Papanek (1971), of whom Claude Brown (1965) wrote so glowingly in his *Manchild in the Promised Land*, was director of Wiltwyck School (a reform school), and Mosak set up a group therapy program at Cook County Jail in Chicago employing paraprofessionals as therapists (O'Reilly, Cizon, Flanagan & Pflanczer, 1965). The growth model implicit in Adlerian theory has prompted Adlerians to see human problems in terms of people's realizing themselves and becoming fellow human beings. Much "treatment" then is of "normal" people with "normal" problems. A therapy that does not provide the client with a philosophy of life, whatever else it may accomplish in the way of symptom eradication or alleviation, behavior modification, or insight, is an incomplete therapy. Hence, the Adlerian is concerned with the client's problems of living and existence. Deficiency, suffering, and illness do not constitute the price of admission to Adlerian therapy. One may enter therapy to learn about oneself, to grow, and to actualize oneself.

Social

Adler's interests were rather catholic. In the area of education, he believed in prevention rather than cure and founded family education centers. Dreikurs and his students (Dreikurs et al., 1959) have founded family education centers throughout the world. Offshoots of these centers include hundreds of parent study groups (Soltz, 1967). In addition, professional therapists have used a variety of methods for teaching child-rearing practices (Allred, 1976; Beecher & Beecher, 1966; Corsini & Painter, 1975; Dreikurs, 1948; Dreikurs & Soltz, 1964; Painter & Corsini, 1989).

Adler himself wrote on social issues and problems such as crime, war, religion, group psychology, Bolshevism, leadership, and nationalism. Among contemporary Adlerians (Angers, 1960; Clark, 1965, 1967a, 1967b; Elam, 1969a, 1969b; Gottesfeld, 1966; Hemming, 1956; La Porte, 1966; Lombardi, 1969; and Nikelly, 1971c) the "newer" social problems of protest, race, drugs, social conditions, and the "newer" views of religion (Mosak, 1987b) have been added to the Adlerians' previous interests.

Evaluation

Until very recently, little research had emerged from the Adlerian group. As was the case with most European clinicians, European Adlerians were suspicious of research based upon statistical methods. A complicating factor was the *idiographic* (case method) approach upon which Adlerians relied. Even now statisticians have not developed appropriate sophisticated methods for idiographic studies. The research methods lent themselves well to studies of "causal" factors, but the Adlerian rejected causalism, feeling that causes can only be imputed (and therefore disputed) in retrospective fashion but that they contributed little to the understanding of humans.

The most often-cited studies involving Adlerian psychology were conducted by non-Adlerians. Fred Fiedler (1950) compared therapeutic relationships in psychoanalytic, nondirective, and Adlerian therapy. He found there was greater similarity between therapeutic relationships developed by experts of the three schools than between expert and less expert therapists within the same school. Crandall (1981) presented the first large-scale investigation of an Adlerian construct. Using his Social Interest Scale, Crandall found positive correlations between social interest and optimism about human nature, altruism, trustworthiness, being liked, and several measures of adjustment and well-being. Because of the number of ways social interest has been defined (Bickhard & Ford, 1976; Crandall, 1981; Edgar, 1975; Kazan, 1978; Mosak, 1991), his study represents a valuable contribution to the understanding of this concept.

A joint research study conducted by the (Rogerian) Counseling Center of the University of Chicago and the Alfred Adler Institute of Chicago examined the effects of time limits in psychotherapy (Shlien, Mosak, & Dreikurs, 1962). Patients of both groups of therapists were given 20 interviews, and the groups were compared with each other and with two control groups. The investigators reported changes in self-ideal correlations. These correlations improved significantly and, according to this measure, suggest that time-limited therapy "may be said to be not only *effective*, but also twice as *efficient* as time-unlimited therapy." Follow-up of these patients in both experimental groups indicated that the gains were retained one year later.

Much of the research in family constellation has also been done by non-Adlerians. Charles Miley (1969) and Lucille Forer (1977) have compiled bibliographies of this literature. The results reported are contradictory probably because non-Adlerians treat birth order as a matter of ordinal position and Adlerians consider birth order in terms of psychological position (Mosak, 1972). Walter Toman (1970) recognized this distinction in his many studies of the family constellation.

Ansbacher (1946) and Mosak (1958) have also distinguished between Freudian and Adlerian approaches to the interpretation of early recollections. Robin Gushurst (1971) provides a manual for interpreting and scoring one class of recollections. His reliability studies demonstrate that judges can interpret early recollection data with high interjudge reliability. He also conducted three validity studies to investigate the hypothesis that life goals may be identified from early recollections data and found that he could do this with two of his three experimental groups. While Fiedler compared therapists of different orientations, Heine (1953) compared patients' reports of their experiences in Adlerian, Freudian, and Rogerian therapy.

Adlerian psychology would undoubtedly benefit from more research. With the shift in locus from Europe to the United States, with the accelerated growth of the Adlerian school in recent years, with the introduction of more American-trained Adlerians into academic settings, and with the development of new research strategies suitable for idiographic data, there is increasing integration of Adlerians into research activities. A summary of these activities appears in two articles by Watkins (1982, 1983).

Treatment

One can hardly identify a mode of treatment in which some Adlerian is not engaged. From a historical viewpoint the initial Adlerian modality was one-to-one psychotherapy. Many Adlerians still regard individual psychotherapy as the treatment of choice. Adlerians have demonstrated willingness to undertake treatment with any who sought their services.

Dreikurs, Mosak, and Shulman (1952a, 1952b, 1982) introduced *multiple psychotherapy*, a format in which several therapists treat a single patient. It offers constant consultation between therapists, prevents the emotional attachment of a patient to a single therapist, and obviates or dissolves impasses. Countertransference reactions are minimized. Flexibility in the number of therapist roles and models is increased. Patients are more impressed or reassured when two therapists independently agree. The patient also may benefit from the experience of observing disagreement between therapists and learn that people can disagree without loss of face.

Multiple therapy creates an atmosphere that facilitates learning. Therapeutic impasses and problems of dependency are resolved more easily. These include the responsibility for self, absence of the therapist-transference reactions, and termination. In the event that therapist and patient do not hit it off, the patient does not become a therapeutic casualty and is merely transferred to the second therapist.

Dreikurs (1959) in the mid-1920s initiated group therapy in private practice. This application was a natural evolution from the Adlerian axiom that people's problems were always social problems. Group therapy finds considerable adherents among Adlerians. Some Adlerian therapists regard group therapy as the method of choice either on practical grounds (e.g., fees, large numbers of patients to be treated, etc.) or because they believe that human problems are most effectively handled in the group social situation. Others use group therapy as a preface to individual therapy or to taper patients off from intensive individual psychotherapy. A number of therapists combine individual and group psychotherapy in the conviction that this combination maximizes therapeutic effect (H. Papanek, 1954, 1956). Still other therapists visualize the group as assisting in the solution of certain selected problems or with certain types of populations. Co-therapist groups are very common among Adlerians.

An offshoot of group treatment is the therapeutic social club in a mental hospital as initiated by the British Adlerian, Joshua Bierer. Although these clubs possess superficial similarities to Abraham Low's recovery groups (Low, 1952) and to halfway houses in that all attempt to facilitate the patient's reentrance into society, the therapeutic social club emphasizes the "social" rather than the "therapeutic" aspects of life, taking the "healthy" rather than the "sick" model. Psychodrama has been used by Adlerians, sometimes as separate therapy, sometimes in conjunction with another therapeutic modality (Starr, 1977).

Marriage counseling has figured prominently in Adlerian activities. Adlerians defied the trend of the times and preferred to treat the couple as a unit rather than as separate individuals. To "treat" merely one mate may be compared to having only half the dialogue of a play. Seeing the couple together suggests that they have a joint relationship problem rather than individual problems and invites joint effort in the solution of these problems. The counselor can observe and describe their interaction (Mozdzierz & Lottman, 1973; Pew & Pew, 1972). Married couples group therapy (Deutsch, 1967) and married couples study groups constitute two more settings for conducting marriage counseling. Phillips and Corsini (1982) have written a self-help book to be used by married people who are experiencing trouble in their marriage.

In the early 1920s, Adler persuaded the Viennese school administration to establish child-guidance centers. The social group was the primary vehicle for treatment (Adler, 1963a; Alexandra Adler, 1951; Seidler & Zilahi, 1949). Dreikurs wrote several popular books and many articles (Dreikurs, 1948; Dreikurs & Grey, 1968; Dreikurs & Soltz, 1964) to disseminate this information to parents and teachers, and currently thousands of parents are enrolled in study groups where they obtain supplementary information on child rearing.

Adler's preventive methods in schools were adopted by educators and school counselors who used them in individual classes, schools, and in one instance in an entire school system (Mosak, 1971a). The methods were originally applied in the Individual Psychological Experimental School in Vienna (Birnbaum, 1935; Spiel, 1962) and have been elaborated upon in this country (Corsini, 1977, 1979; Dinkmeyer & Dreikurs, 1963; Dreikurs, 1968, 1972; Dreikurs, Grunwald & Pepper, 1982; Grunwald, 1954).

With respect to broader social problems, Dreikurs devoted the last part of his life to the problem of interindividual and intergroup conflict resolution. Much of this work was performed in Israel and has not been reported. Kenneth Clark, a former president of the American Psychological Association, has devoted much of his career to studying and providing recommendations for solutions for problems of black people, as have Harry Elam (1969a, 1969b) and Jacqueline Brown (1976).

The Setting

Adlerians function in every imaginable setting: the private-practice office, hospitals, day hospitals, jails, schools, and community programs. Offices do not need any special furnishings, but reflect either the therapist's aesthetic preferences or the condition of the institution's budget. No special equipment is used, except perhaps for special projects. Although voice recordings are a matter of individual choice, they are sometimes maintained as the patient's file.

In the initial interviews, the therapist generally obtains the following kinds of information (in addition to demographic information):

1. Was the patient self-referred?
2. Is the patient negative about treatment? If the patient is reluctant, "conversion" is necessary if therapy is to proceed.
3. What does the patient come for? Is it treatment to alleviate suffering? If so, suffering from what?

    Some new patients are "supermarket shoppers" who announce the number of therapists who have helped them already. Their secret goal is to be perfect. Unless such a patient's fictional goal is disclosed, today's therapist may be the latest of many therapists about whom the patient will be telling the next therapist.
4. What are the patient's expectations about treatment?
5. What are the patient's expectations about outcome? Perfection? Failure? A solution for a specific problem without any major personality alterations? Immediate cure?
6. What are the patient's goals in psychotherapy? We must distinguish between stated goals—to get well, to learn about self, to be a better spouse and parent, to gain a new philosophy of life—and nonverbalized goals—to remain sick, to punish others, to defeat the therapist and sabotage therapy, to maintain good intentions without changing.

The patient may also resist in order to depreciate or defeat the therapist because the patient lacks the courage to live on the useful side of life and fears that the therapist might nudge him or her in that direction. The intensification of such escape methods may become most pronounced during the termination phase of treatment, when the patient realizes he or she must soon face the realistic tasks of life without the therapist's support.

Tests

Routine physical examinations are not required by Adlerians in view of the therapy's educational orientation. Nevertheless, many patients do have physiological problems, and Adlerians are trained to be sensitive to the presence of these problems. The therapist who suspects such problems will make referrals for physical examination.

Adlerians are divided on the issue of psychological testing. Most Adlerians avoid noso-logical diagnosis, except for nontherapeutic purposes such as filling out insurance forms. Labels are static descriptions and ignore the *movement* of the individual. They describe what the individual *has*, but not how he or she moves through life.

Regine Seidler placed more faith in projective testing than in so-called objective tests, maintaining that the latter are actually subjective tests because "the *subjective attitude* of each and every individual toward any given test necessarily renders the test non-objec-tive" (1967, p. 4). Objective tests were more useful to her as measures of test-taking atti-tude than of what the test was purportedly measuring.

Early recollections serve as a test for Adlerians, assisting them in the life-style assess-ment. Younger Adlerians employ many conventional tests and some nonconventional ones for diagnostic purposes as well as in the treatment of the patient.

The Therapist

The Adlerian therapist ideally is an authentically sharing, caring person. Helene and Ernst Papanek write: "The therapist participates actively. Without playing any sharply defined 'role,' he shows warmth toward and a genuine interest in the patient and encourages es-pecially his desire for change and betterment. The relationship itself has a purpose: to help the patient help himself" (1961, p. 117).

Adlerian therapists remain free to have feelings and opinions and to express them. Such expression in a spontaneous way permits patients to view therapists as human beings. If therapists err, they err—but then the patient may learn the courage to be imperfect from this experience (Lazarsfeld, 1966). The experience may also facilitate therapy.

Therapists must not inject evaluation of their worth into the therapy; rather, they must do their therapeutic job without concern for prestige, not reveling in successes or becom-ing discouraged by failures. Otherwise, they may bounce like a rubber ball from therapy hour to therapy hour or perhaps even within the same hour. The therapist's worth does not depend upon external factors but rather on what lies within the self. The therapist is task-oriented rather than self-oriented.

Therapists reveal themselves as persons. The concept of the *anonymous therapist* is foreign to Adlerian psychology. Such a role would increase social distance between ther-apist and patient, interfering with the establishment of an egalitarian, human relation-ship. The "anonymous therapist" role was created to facilitate the establishment of a transference relationship, and because the Adlerian rejects the transference concept as Freud formulated it, the maintenance of such a posture is considered irrelevant, if not harmful, to the relationship. Dreikurs (1961) deplored the prevalent attitude among therapists of not coming too close to patients because it might affect the therapeutic re-lationship adversely. Shulman (Wexberg, 1929/1970, p. 88) defines the role of the ther-apist as that of "a helping friend." Self-revelation can only occur when therapists feel secure, at home with others, unafraid to be human and fallible, and thus unafraid of their patients' evaluations, criticism, or hostility (cf. Rogers's "congruence"). For these and other reasons, Adlerian training institutes customarily require a "didactic analysis" of their candidates.

Is the Adlerian therapist judgmental? In a sense all therapists are judgmental in that therapy rests upon some value orientation: a belief that certain behavior is better than other behavior, that certain goals are better than other goals, that one organiza-tion of personality is superior to another form of organization. Given that two cardinal principles of the Adlerian intervention are caring and encouragement, a critical or judg-mental stance is best avoided.

Patient Problems

If the therapist does not like the patient, it raises problems for a therapist of any persuasion (Fromm-Reichman, 1949). Some therapists merely do not accept such patients. Still others feel they ought not to have or ought to overcome such negative feelings and accept the patient for treatment, leading to both participants' "suffering." It appears difficult to possess "unconditional positive regard" for a patient you dislike. Adlerians meet this situation in the same manner other therapists do.

Seduction problems are treated as any other patient problem. The secure therapist will not frighten, panic, or succumb. If the patient's activities nevertheless prevent the therapy from continuing, the patient may be referred to another therapist. Flattery problems are in some ways similar and have been discussed elsewhere (Berne, 1964; Mosak & Gushurst, 1971).

Suicide threats are always taken seriously (Ansbacher, 1961, 1969). Alfred Adler warned, however, that our goal is "to knock the weapon out of his hand" so the patient cannot make us vulnerable and intimidate us at will with his threats. As an example, he narrates, "A patient once asked me, smiling, 'Has anyone ever taken his life while being treated by you?' I answered him, 'Not yet, but I am prepared for this to happen at any time'" (Ansbacher & Ansbacher, 1956, pp. 338-39).

Kurt Adler postulates "an underlying rage against people" in suicide threats and believes that this goal of vengefulness must be uncovered. He "knocks the weapon out of the patient's hand" as follows:

> Patients have tested me with the question of how would I feel if I were to read of their suicide in the newspaper. I answer that it is possible that some reporter hungry for news would pick up such an item from a police blotter. But, the next day, the paper will already be old, and only a dog perhaps may honor their suicide notice by lifting a leg over it in some corner. (1961, p. 66)

Alexandra Adler (1943), Lazarsfeld (1952) and Oscar Pelzman (1952) discuss problems beyond the scope of this chapter.

❖ CASE EXAMPLE

Background

The patient was a 53-year-old, Viennese-born man, in treatment almost continuously with Freudian psychoanalysts, here and abroad, since he was 17. With the advent of tranquilizers, he had transferred his allegiances to psychiatrists who treated him with a combination of drugs and psychotherapy and finally with drugs alone. When he entered Adlerian treatment, he was being maintained by his previous therapist on an opium derivative and Thorazine. He failed to tell his previous therapist of his decision to see us and also failed to inform us that he was still obtaining medication from his previous therapist.

The treatment process was atypical in the sense that the patient's "illness" hampered us from following our customary procedure. Having over the years become therapy-wise, he invested his creativity in efforts to run the therapy. Cooperative effort was virtually impossible. In conventional terms, the co-therapists, Drs. A and B, had their hands full dealing with the patient's resistances and "transference."

Problem

When the patient entered treatment, he had taken to bed and spent almost all his time there because he felt too weak to get up. His wife had to be constantly at his side or he would panic. Once she was encouraged by a friend to attend the opera alone. The patient wished her a good time and then told her, "When you return, I shall be dead." His secretary was forced into conducting his successful business. Everyone was forced into "the emperor's service." The price he paid for this service was intense suffering in the form of depression, obsessive-compulsive behavior, phobic behavior, especially agoraphobia, divorce from the social world, somatic symptoms, and invalidism.

Treatment

The patient was seen in multiple psychotherapy by Drs. A and B, but both therapists were not present at each interview. We dispensed with the life-style assessment because the patient had other immediate goals. It seemed to us from the patient's behavior that he probably had been raised as a pampered child and that he was using "illness" to tyrannize the world and to gain exemption from the life tasks. If these guesses were correct, we anticipated he would attempt to remain "sick," would resist giving up drugs, and would demand special attention from his therapists. As part of the treatment strategy, the therapists decided to wean him from medication, to give him no special attention, and not to be manipulated by him. Given that he had undergone analysis over a period of more than three decades, the therapists thought he could probably produce a better analysis of his problems than they could. For this reason, interpretation was kept at a minimum. The treatment plan envisaged a tactical and strategic, rather than interpretive, approach. Some excerpts from the early part of treatment are reproduced on the following pages.

March 8

Dr. B wanted to collect life-style information but the patient immediately complained that he wanted to terminate. He said his previous therapist, Dr. C, had treated him differently. Therapist B was too impersonal. "You won't even give me your home phone number. You aren't impressed by my illness. Your treatment is well meaning but it won't help. Nothing helps. I'm going back to Dr. C and ask him to put me in the hospital. He gave me advice and you are so cruel by not telling me what to do."

March 19

Relatively calm. Compares B with Dr. C. Later compares B with A. Favors B over Dr. C because he respects former's strength. Favors B over A because he can succeed in ruffling latter but not former. Talk centers about his use of weakness to overpower others.

March 22

Telephones to say he must be hospitalized. Wife left him [untrue] and secretary left him [it turns out she went to lunch]. Would B come to his office to see him? B asks him to keep appointment in B's office. Patient races about office upset. "I'm sweating water and blood." When B remains calm, patient takes out bottle of Thorazine and threatens to take all. Next he climbs up on radiator, opens window (17th floor), jumps back, and says, "No, it's too high."

"You don't help me. Why can't I have an injection?" Then he informs B that B is a soothing influence. "I wish I could spend the whole day with you." B speaks softly to patient and patient speaks quietly. Patient asks for advice about what to do this weekend. B gives antisuggestion and tells him to try to worry as much as he can. He is surprised, and dismisses it as "bad advice."

March 29

B was sick on March 26, so patient saw A. "It was useless." No longer worried about state hospital. Thinks he will now wind up as bum because he got drunk last week. His secretary gave him notice but he hopes to keep her "by taking abuse. No one treats a boss like she treats me." Got out of bed and worked last week. Went out selling but "everyone rejected me." When B indicates that he seems to be better, he insists he's deteriorating. When B inquired how, he replies paradoxically, "I beat out my competitors this week."

April 2

Has habit of sticking finger down throat to induce vomiting. Threatens to do so when enters office today. B tells patients about the logical consequences of his act—he will have to mop up. Patient withdraws finger. "If you would leave me alone, I'd fall asleep so fast." B leaves him alone. Patient angrily declaims, "Why do you let me sleep?"

April 9

Too weak even to telephone therapist. If wife goes on vacation, he will kill himself. How can he survive with no one to tell him to eat, to go to bed, to get up? "All I do is vomit and sleep." B suggests that he tyrannizes his wife as he did his mother and sister. He opens window and inquires, "Shall I jump?" B recognizes this as an attempt to intimidate rather than a serious threat and responds, "Suit yourself." Patient closes window and accuses, "You don't care either." Asks whether he can see A next time and before receiving answer, says, "I don't want him anyway." Follows this with, "I want to go to the state hospital. Can you get me a private room?" At end of interview falls to knees and sobs, "Help me! Help me to be a human being."

April 12

Enters, falls to knees, encircles therapist's knees, whimpers, "Help me!" So depressed. If only he could end it all. B gives him Adler's suggestion to do one thing each day that would give someone pleasure. Patient admits behaving better. Stopped annoying secretary and let her go home early because of bad weather. Agitation stops.

April 15

Didn't do anything this weekend to give pleasure. However, he did play cards with wife. Took her for drive. Sex with wife for "first time in a long time." B gives encouragement and then repeats "pleasure" suggestion. He can't do it. Calm whole hour. Says his wife has told him to discontinue treatment. Upon inquiry, he says she didn't say exactly that but had said, "I leave it up to you."

April 19

Wants B to accompany him back to his office because he forgot something. Wants shorter hour this week and longer one next week. "Dr. C let me do that." When B declines, he complains, "Doctor, I don't know what to do with you anymore."

April 23

Wouldn't consider suicide. "Perhaps I have a masochistic desire to live." B suggests he must be angry with life. He responds that he wants to be an infant and have all his needs gratified. The world should be a big breast and he should be able to drink without having to suck [probably an interpretation he had received in psychoanalysis]. Yesterday he had fantasy of destroying the whole city.

This weekend he helped his wife work in the garden. He asks for suggestions for weekend. B and patient play "yes-but." B does so deliberately to point out game (cf. Berne's "Why don't you…? Yes but" [1964]) to patient. Patient then volunteers possibility of clay modeling. B indicates this may be good choice in that patient can mold, manipulate, and "be violent."

April 29

Had birthday last week and resolved to turn over new leaf for new year but didn't. Cries, "Help me, help me." Depreciates B. "How much would you charge me to come to my summer home? I'm so sick, I vomited blood." When B tells him if he's that sick, hospitalization might be advisable, he smiles and says, "For money, you'd come out." B and patient speak of attitude toward B and attitude toward his father. Patient depreciates both, possibly because he could not dominate either.

May 1

Didn't think he could make it today because he was afraid to walk on street. Didn't sleep all night. So excited, so upset [he seems calm]. Perhaps he should be put in hospital, but then what will happen to his business?

"We could sit here forever and all you would tell me is to get clay. Why don't you give me medicine or advice?" B points out that the patient is much stronger than any medication, as evidenced by number of therapists and treatments he has defeated.

He says he is out of step with world. B repeats an earlier interpretation by A that the patient wants the world to conform to him and follows with statement about his desire to be omnipotent, a desire that makes him feel weak and simultaneously compensates for his feelings of weakness. He confirms with "All Chicago should stand still so I could have a holiday. The police should stop at gunpoint anyone who wants to go to work. But I don't want to. I don't want to do anything anymore. I want a paycheck but I don't want to work." B remarks on shift from "I can't" to "I don't want to." Patient admits and says, "I don't want to get well. Should I make another appointment?" B refers decision back to him. He makes appointment.

May 6

"I'm at the end, dying with fear [enumerates symptoms]. Since 5 this morning I'm murdering — — — and — — —. Such nice people and I'm murdering them and I'm electrocuted. And my secretary and wife can't stand it anymore. Take me to a state hospital. I don't want to go. Take me. I'm getting crazy and you don't help me. Help me, *Lieber Doktor*! I went to the ladies' room twice today to get my secretary and the girls complained to the building office. I'm not above the rules. I knew I violated them. My zipper was down again [he frequently "forgets"] and I just pulled it up before you came in today." B agrees that state hospital might be appropriate if he is becoming "crazier." "Then my wife will divorce me. It's terrible. They have bars there. I won't go. I'm not that bad yet. Why, last week I went out and made a big sale!" B suggests he "practice" his fears and obsessions.

May 8

Seen by A and B, who did summary of his family constellation. It was done very tentatively because of the meager information elicited.

May 13

Complains about symptoms. He had taken his wife to the movie but "was too upset to watch it." He had helped with the raking. Returns to symptoms and begging for Thorazine. "How will I live without Thorazine?" B suggests they ought to talk about how to live. He yells, "With your quiet voice, you'll drive me crazy." B asks, "Would you like me to yell at you like your father did?" "I won't talk to you anymore."

"*Lieber Gott*, liberate me from the evil within me." Prays to everyone for help. B counters with, "Have you ever solicited your own help?" Patient replies, "I have no strength, I could cry. I could shout. I don't have strength. Let me vomit."

May 15

Demands Thorazine or he will have heart attack. B requests a future autobiography. Responds "I don't anticipate anything" and returns to Thorazine question. B points out his real achievement in staying off Thorazine. Patient mentions price in suffering. B points out that this makes it an even greater achievement. Patient accepts idea reluctantly. B points out that they are at cross-purposes because patient wants to continue suffering but have pills; B's goal is to have him stop his suffering. "I want pills." B offers clay. "Shit on your clay."

May 20

Must have Thorazine. Has murderous and self-castrating fantasies. Tells A that A doesn't know anything about medicine. Dr. C did. Whey don't we let him go back to Dr. C? A leaves room with patient following. After three to four minutes patient returns and complains, "You call this treatment?" Dr. A points out demand of patient to have own way. He is a little boy who wants to be big but doesn't think he can make it. He is a pampered tyrant. A also refers to patient's favorite childhood game of lying in bed with sister and playing "Emperor and Empress."

Patient points out innate badness in himself. A points out he creates it. Patient talks of hostility and murder. A interprets look on his face as taking pride in his bad behavior. Patient picks up letter opener, trembles, then grasps hand with other hand but continues to tremble. A tells him that this is a spurious fight between good and evil, that he can decide how he will behave.

He kneaded clay a little while this weekend.

May 22

Last weekend he mowed lawn, tried to read but "I'm nervous. I'm talking to you like a human being but I'm not really a human being." Raw throat. Fears might have throat cancer. Stopped sticking finger down throat to vomit as consequence. Discussion of previously expressed ideas of "like a human being." Fantasy of riding a boat through a storm. Fantasy of A being acclaimed by crowd and patient in fantasy asking B, "Are you used to A getting all the attention?"

Complains about wife and secretary, neither of whom will any longer permit tyrannization.

June 3

Relates fantasy of being magician and performing unbelievable feats at the White House. He asked the President whether he was happily married and then produced the President's ring. Nice weekend. Made love to wife at his initiative. Grudgingly admits enjoying it.

June 10

"Ignored my wife this week." Yet he took initiative and they had sex again. Both enjoyed it but he was afraid because he read in a magazine that sex is a drain on the heart. At work secretary is angry. After she checks things, he rechecks. Pledged his God today he wouldn't do it anymore. He'll only check one time more. Outlines several plans for improving business "but I don't have the strength." Wants to cut down to one interview per week because he doesn't get well and can't afford to pay. B suggests that perhaps he is improving if he wants to reduce the number of sessions. Patient rejects and agrees to two sessions weekly.

June 24

Talks about fears. B tells him he will go on vacation next week. He accepts it calmly although he had previously claimed to be unendurably upset. Patient tells B that he has given up vomiting and masturbation, saying, "You have enormous influence on me." B encourages by saying patient made the decision by himself.

Sept. 4

[Patient was not seen during August because he went on a "wonderful" vacation.] Stopped all medication except for occasional use of a mild tranquilizer his family physician prescribed. Able to read and concentrate again. Has surrendered his obsessive ruminations. He and his secretary get along without fighting although she doesn't like him. He is punctual at the office. He and wife get along well. He is more considerate of her. Both are sexually satisfied.

B and patient plan for treatment. Patient expresses reluctance, feeling that he has gone as far as he can. After all, one psychoanalyst said that he was hopeless and had recommended a lobotomy, so this was marked improvement. B agreed, telling patient that if he had considered the patient hopeless, he would not have undertaken treatment, nor would he now be recommending continuation. "What kind of treatment?" B tells him that no external agent (e.g., medicine, lobotomy) will do it, that his salvation will come from within, that he can choose to live life destructively (and self-destructively) or constructively. He proposes to come weekly for four weeks and then bi-weekly. B does not accept the offer.

Sept. 17

Since yesterday his symptoms have returned. Heart palpitations.

Sept. 25

Took wife to dinner last night. Very pleasant. Business is slow and his obligations are heavy but he is working. He has to exert effort not to backslide. B schedules double interview. Patient doesn't want to see A. It will upset him. He doesn't see any sense in seeing B either but since B insists…Heart palpitations disappeared after last interview. Expresses realistic concerns today and has dropped usual frantic manner. Wants biweekly interviews. B wants weekly. Patient accepts without protest.

As therapy continued, the patient's discussion of symptoms was superseded by discussion of realistic concerns. Resistance waned. When he entered treatment, he perceived himself as a good person who behaved badly because he was "sick." During therapy, he saw through his pretenses and settled for being "a bad guy." However, once he understood his tyranny and was able to accept it, he had the opportunity to ask himself how he preferred to live his life—usefully or uselessly. Because the therapists used the monolithic approach (Alexander & French, 1946; Mosak & Shulman, 1963), after resolving the issue of his tyranny, therapy moved on to his other "basic mistakes," one at a time. The frequency of interviews was decreased and termination was by mutual agreement.

Follow-up

The patient improved, remaining off medication. When he devoted himself to his business, it prospered to the point where he could retire early. He moved to a university town, where he studied archaeology, the activity he liked best in life. The relationship with his wife improved and they traveled abroad. Because of the geographical distance between them, the therapists and the patient had no further contact.

❧ SUMMARY

Adlerian theory may be described as follows:

1. Its approach is social, teleological, phenomenological, holistic, idiographic, and humanistic.

2. Its underlying assumptions are (a) the individual is unique, (b) the individual is self-consistent, (c) the individual is responsible, (d) the person is creative, an actor, a chooser, and (e) people in a soft-deterministic way can direct their own behavior and control their destinies.

3. Its personality theory takes as its central construct the life-style, a system of subjective convictions held by the individual that contains his self-view and world view. From these convictions, other convictions, methods of operation, and goals are derived. The person behaves *as if* these convictions were true and uses his life-style as a cognitive map with which he explores, comprehends, prejudges, predicts, and controls the environment (the life tasks). Because the person cannot be understood *in vacuo* but only in his social context, the interaction between the individual and his life tasks is indispensable for the purpose of fully comprehending the individual.

4. "Psychopathology," "mental illness," and similar nomenclature are reifications and perpetuate the nominal fallacy, "the tendency to confuse naming with explaining" (Beach, 1955). The "psychopathological" individual is a discouraged person. Such people either have never developed or have lost their courage with respect to meeting the

life tasks. With their pessimistic anticipations, they create "arrangements,"—evasions, excuses, sideshows, symptoms—to protect their self-esteem, or they may "cop out" completely.

5.   Because people's difficulties emanate from faulty perceptions, learnings, values, and goals that have resulted in discouragement, therapy consists of an educative or reeducative endeavor in which two equals cooperatively tackle the educational task. Many of the traditional analytic methods have been retained, although they are understood, and sometimes used, differently by the Adlerian. The focus of therapy is the encouragement of the individual. The individual learns to have faith in self, to trust, and to love. The ultimate, *ideal* goal of psychotherapy is to release people's social interest so they may become fellow human beings, cooperators, contributors to the creation of a better society. Such patients can be said to have actualized themselves. Because therapy is learning, everyone can change. On the entrance door of the Guidance Clinic for Juvenile Delinquency in Vienna was the inscription, "IT IS NEVER TOO LATE" (Kramer, 1947).

Adlerian psychology has become a viable, flourishing system. Neglected for several decades, it has in recent years acquired respectability. Training institutes, professional societies, family-education centers, and study groups continue to proliferate. With Adlerians being trained in universities rather than solely in institutes, they are writing more and doing research. Non-Adlerians are also engaged in Adlerian research. The previously rare Adlerian dissertation has become more commonplace. Currently Adlerians are moving into society to renew their attention to the social issues Adler raised 50 years ago—poverty, war, conflict resolution, aggression, religion, substance abuse, and social cooperation. As Way apprises, "We shall need not only, as Adler says, more cooperative individuals, but a society better fitted to fulfill the needs of human beings" (1962, p. 360).

Complementing the Adlerians' endeavors are individuals and groups who have borrowed heavily from Adler, often without acknowledgment or awareness. Keith Sward, for example, reviewed Alexander and French's *Psychoanalytic Therapy* (1946), writing:

> The Chicago group would seem to be Adlerian through and through....The Chicago Institute for Psychoanalysis is not alone in this seeming rediscovery of Rank and Adler. Psychiatry and psychology as a whole seem to be drifting in the same direction. Adler has come to life in other vigorous circles, notably in the publications of the "Horney" school. (1947, p. 601)

We observe glimpses of Adler in the Freudian ego-psychologists, neo-Freudians, existential systems, humanistic psychologies, client-centered theory, rational-emotive therapy, integrity therapy, transactional analysis, and reality therapy. This is not an augury of the eventual disappearance of Adlerian psychology through absorption into other schools of psychology, for, as the motto of the Rockford, Illinois, Teacher Development Center claims, "Education is like a flame....You can give it away without diminishing the one from whom it came." As Joseph Wilder writes in his introduction to *Essays in Individual Psychology* (Adler & Deutsch, 1959), "most observations and ideas of Alfred Adler have subtly and quietly permeated modern psychological thinking to such a degree that the proper question is not whether one is Adlerian but how much of an Adlerian one is" (p. xv).

❖ ANNOTATED BIBLIOGRAPHY

Ansbacher, H. L., & Ansbacher, R. (Eds.) (1964). *The individual psychology of Alfred Adler*. New York: Harper Torchbooks.

An almost encyclopedic collection of Adler's writings, this volume displays both the great variety of topics that commanded his attention and the evolution of his thinking. Because of the nature of the construction of this book, it is imperative that the reader read the preface.

Manaster, G. J., & Corsini, R. J. (1982). *Individual psychology*. Itasca, IL: F. E. Peacock.

This is the first textbook of Adlerian psychology written in English by two students of Rudolf Dreikurs. Corsini was the former editor of the *Journal of Individual Psychology* and Manaster succeeded him. Written in a much simpler style than the Ansbacher and Ansbacher text (1956), this book covers more or less the same materials. Two features make it unique: it contains the single most complete Adlerian psychotherapy case summary published to date, and there is a section abstracting the more important research studies published in the field of Adlerian psychology.

❖ CASE READINGS

Adler, A. (1929). *The Case of Miss R. The interpretation of a life study*. New York: Greenberg.

Adler does an interlinear interpretation of the case study of a patient who in his time would have been labeled "psychoasthenic." The patient is also agoraphobic. Since Adler did not treat this patient, the course of therapy is unknown. However, we can observe how Adler constructs a life-style as well as his understanding of the patient's approach to the life tasks.

Adler, A. (1964). *The case of Mrs. A.: The diagnosis of a life style*. In H. L. Ansbacher & R. R. Ansbacher (Eds.), *Superiority and social interest* (pp.159–190). Evanston, IL: Northwestern University Press (1969). Chicago: Alfred Adler Institute. Reprinted in D. Wedding & R. J. Corsini (Eds.) (1979) *Great cases in psychotherapy*. Itasca, IL: F. E. Peacock. (Original work published in 1931.)

This publication is similar to the above and interprets the case study of an obsessive compulsive woman who fears that she will kill her children.

Ansbacher, H. L. (1966). Lee Harvey Oswald: An Adlerian interpretation. *Psychoanalytic Review*, 53, 379–390.

The psychodynamics of John F. Kennedy's assassin are presented from the Adlerian point of view.

Dreikurs, R. (1959). A record of family counseling sessions. In R. Dreikurs, R. Lowe, M. Sonstegard, & R. J. Corsini (Eds.), *Adlerian family counseling* (pp. 109–152). Eugene, OR: University of Oregon Press.

Two sessions of family counseling conducted by Rudolf Dreikurs and Stefanie Necheles are presented. The identified patient, a nine-year-old boy, is described by his parents as an angry child.

Frank, I. (1981). My flight toward a new life. *Journal of Individual Psychology*, 37(1), 15–30.

A young anorexic woman describes the course of her eating problem as well as the various treatments, Adlerian and non-Adlerian, which she underwent until the problem was resolved.

Manaster, G. J., & Corsini, R. J. (1982). *Individual Psychology*. Itasca, IL: F. E. Peacock

Chapter 17 offers verbatim excerpts of a course of therapy of a man who in dualistic fashion perceives himself in conflict, ambivalent, and self-contradictory.

Mosak, H. H. (1972) Life style assessment: A demonstration based on family constellation. *Individual Psychology*, 28, 232–247.

A verbatim description of a life-style assessment done in public demonstration is presented. The subject is a teenage girl who feels that she is the sole "non-very" person in a "very" family.

Mosak, H. H., & Maniacci, M. (1991). The case of Roger. In D. Wedding & R. J. Corsini (Eds.), *Case studies in psychotherapy*. Itasca, IL: F. E. Peacock.

This case history was specifically written to complement the current chapter and it illustrates many of the methods, techniques, and principles of Adlerian psychotherapy. Careful reading of the case should help the student more fully appreciate how the Adlerian actually proceeds in therapy.

❖ REFERENCES

Adler, Alexandra (1943). Problems in psychotherapy. *American Journal of Individual Psychology*, 3, 1-5.

Adler, Alexandra (1951). Alfred Adler's viewpoint in child guidance. In E. Harms (Ed.), *Handbook of child guidance*. New York: Child Care Publications.

Adler, A. (1898). *Gesundheitsbuch für das Schneidergewerbe*. Berlin: C. Heymanns.

Adler, A. (1914). *Das Zärtlichkeitsbedürfnis des Kindes*. In A. Adler & C. Furtmüller (Eds.), *Heilen und Bilden*. München: Reinhardt.

Adler, A. (1917). *Study of organ inferiority and its psychical compensation*. New York: Nervous & Mental Disease Publishing Co.

Adler, A. (1922). *Erziehungsberatungsstellen*. In A. Adler & C. Furtmüller (Eds.), *Heilen und Bilden*. München: Bergmann.

Adler, A. (1926; reprinted 1972). *The neurotic constitution*. Freeport, NY: Books for Libraries Press.

Adler, A. (1928). On teaching courage. *Survey Graphic*, 61, 241–242.

Adler, A. (1929). Position in family influences lifestyle. *International Journal of Individual Psychology*, 3, 211–227.

Adler, A. (1931; reprinted 1958). *What life should mean to you*. New York: Capricorn Books.

Adler, A. (1934). Lecture to the Medical Society of Individual Psychology, London. *Individual Psychology Pamphlets*, 13, 11–24.

Adler, A. (1935/1982). The fundamental views of Individual Psychology. *Individual Psychology*, 38 (1) 3–6. (Reprinted from *International Journal of Individual Psychology*, 1935, 1(1), 5–8.)

Adler A. (1947). How I chose my career. *Individual Psychology Bulletin*, 6, 9–11.

Adler, A. (1959). *Understanding human nature*. New York: Premier Books.

Adler, A. (1963a). *The practice and theory of individual psychology*. Paterson, NJ: Littlefield, Adams.

Adler, A. (1964a). *Problems of neurosis*. New York: Harper & Row.

Adler, A. (1964b). *Social interest: A challenge to mankind*. New York: Capricorn Books.

Adler, A. (1969). *The science of living*. New York: Doubleday Anchor Books.

Adler, K. A. (1961). Depression in the light of individual psychology. *Journal of Individual Psychology*, 17, 56–67.

Adler, K. A., & Deutsch, D. (Eds.) (1959). *Essays in individual psychology*. New York: Grove Press.

Alexander, F., & French, T. M. (1946). *Psychoanalytic therapy*. New York: Ronald Press.

Allred, G. H. (1976). *How to strengthen your marriage and family*. Provo, UT: Brigham Young University Press.

Angers, W.P. (1960). Clarifications toward the rapprochement between religion and psychology. *Journal of Individual Psychology*, 16, 73–76.

Ansbacher, H. L. (1946). Adler's place today in the psychology of memory. *Journal of Personality*, 15, 197–207.

Ansbacher, H. L. (1952). "Neo-Freudian" or "Neo-Adlerian"? *American Journal of Individual Psychology*, 10, 87–88. (Also in *American Psychologist* (1953), 8, 165–166.)

Ansbacher, H. L. (1959). A key to existence. *Journal of Individual Psychology*, 15, 141–142.

Ansbacher, H. L. (1961). Suicide: Adlerian point of view. In N. L. Farberow & E. S. Schneidman (Eds.), *The cry for help*. New York: McGraw-Hill.

Ansbacher, H. L. (1962). Was Adler a disciple of Freud? A reply. *Journal of Individual Psychology*, 18, 126–135.

Ansbacher, H. L. (1968). The concept of social interest. *Journal of Individual Psychology*, 24, 131–141.

Ansbacher, H. L. (1969). Suicide as communication: Adler's concept and current applications. *Journal of Individual Psychology*, 25, 174–180.

Ansbacher, H. L., & Ansbacher, R. (Eds.). (1956). *The individual psychology of Alfred Adler*. New York: Basic Books.

Beach, F. A. (1955). The descent of instinct. *Psychological Review*, 62, 401–410.

Beecher, W., & Beecher, M. (1966). *Parents on the run*. New York: Agora Press.

Berne, E. (1964). *Games people play*. New York: Grove Press.

Bickhard, M. H., & Ford, B. L. (1976). Adler's concept of social interest. *Journal of Individual Psychology*, 32, 27–49.

Bierer, J. (1951). *The day hospital, an experiment in social psychiatry and synthoanalytic psychotherapy*. London: H.K. Lewis.

Bierer, J., & Evans, R. I. (1969). *Innovations in social psychiatry*. London: Avenue Publishing.

Birnbaum, F. (1935). The Individual Psychological Experimental School in Vienna. *International Journal of Individual Psychology*, 1, 118–124.

Birnbaum, F. (1961). Frankl's existential psychology from the viewpoint of Individual Psychology. *Journal of Individual Psychology*, 17, 162–166.

Bottome, P. (1939). *Alfred Adler: A biography*. New York: Putnam.

Brewer, D. H. (1976). *The induction and alteration of state depression: A comparative study*. Unpublished doctoral dissertation. University of Houston.

Brome, V. (1968). *Freud and his early circle*. New York: William Morrow.

Brown, C. (1965). *Manchild in the promised land*. New York: Signet Books.

Brown, J. F. (1976). Parallels between Adlerian psychology and the Afro-American value system. *Individual Psychologist*, 13, 29–33.

Bugental, J. F. T. (1963). Humanistic psychology: A new breakthrough. *American Psychologist, 18*, 563–67.

Clark, K. B. (1965). Problems of power and social change: Toward a relevant social psychology. *Journal of Social Issues, 21*, 4–20.

Clark, K. B. (1967a). *Dark ghetto.* New York: Harper Torchbooks.

Clark, K. B. (1967b). Implications of Adlerian theory for understanding of civil rights problems and action. *Journal of Individual Psychology, 23*, 181–190.

Colby, K. M. (1951). On the disagreement between Freud and Adler. *American Image, 8*, 229–238.

Corsini, R. J. (1953). The behind-the-back technique in group psychotherapy. *Group Psychotherapy, 6*, 102–109.

Corsini, R. J. (1967). Let's invent a first-aid kit for marriage problems. *Consultant* (Smith, Kline & French Laboratories), 7, 40.

Corsini, R. J. (1977). Individual education. *Journal of Individual Psychology, 33*, 295–349.

Corsini, R. J. (1979). Individual education. In E. Ignas & R. J. Corsini (Eds.), *Alternative educational systems* (pp. 200–256). Itasca, IL: F.E. Peacock.

Corsini, R. J., & Painter, G. (1975). *The practical parent.* New York: Harper & Row.

Crandall, J. E. (1981). *Theory and measurement of social interest.* New York: Columbia University Press.

Credner, L. (1930). Sicherungen. *Internationale Zeitschrift für Individual-psychologie, 8*, 87–92. (Translated as Safeguards (1936). *International Journal of Individual Psychology, 2*, 95–102.)

Deutsch, D. (1967). Group therapy with married couples. *Individual Psychologist, 4*, 56–62.

Dinkmeyer, D., & Dreikurs, R. (1963). *Encouraging children to learn: The encouragement process.* Englewood Cliffs, NJ: Prentice-Hall.

Dreikurs, R. (1948). *The challenge of parenthood.* New York: Duell, Sloan & Pearch.

Dreikurs, R. (1949). The four goals of children's misbehavior. *Nervous Child, 6*, 3–11.

Dreikurs, R. (1950). Techniques and dynamics of multiple psychotherapy. *Psychiatric Quarterly, 24*, 788–799.

Dreikurs, R. (1957). Psychotherapy as correction of faulty social values. *Journal of Individual Psychology, 13*, 150–158.

Dreikurs, R. (1958). A reliable different diagnosis of psychological or somatic disturbances. *International Record of Medicine, 171*, 238–242.

Dreikurs, R. (1959). Early experiments with group psychotherapy. *American Journal of Psychotherapy, 13*, 882–891.

Dreikurs, R. (1961). The Adlerian approach to therapy. In Morris I. Stein (Ed.), *Contemporary psychotherapies* (pp. 80–94). Glencoe, IL: The Free Press.

Dreikurs, R. (1962). Can you be sure the disease is functional? *Consultant* (Smith, Kline & French Laboratories).

Dreikurs, R. (1963). Psychodynamic diagnosis in psychiatry. *American Journal of Psychiatry, 119*, 1045–1048.

Dreikurs, R. (1968). *Psychology in the classroom.* New York: Harper & Row.

Dreikurs, R. (1969). Social interest: The basis of normalcy. *The Counseling Psychologist, 1*, 45–48.

Dreikurs, R. (1971). *Social equality: The challenge of today.* Chicago: Henry Regnery.

Dreikurs, R. (1972). Technology of conflict resolution. *Journal of Individual Psychology, 28*, 203–206.

Dreikurs, R., Corsini, R. J., Lowe, R., & Sonstegard, M. (1959) *Adlerian family counseling.* Eugene, OR: University of Oregon Press.

Dreikurs, R., & Grey, L. (1968). *Logical consequences.* New York: Meredith.

Dreikurs, R., Grunwald, B., & Pepper, F. C. (1982). *Maintaining sanity in the classroom* (2nd ed.). New York: Harper & Row.

Dreikurs, R., & Mosak, H. H. (1966). The tasks of life. I. Adler's three tasks. *Individual Psychologist, 4*, 18–22.

Dreikurs, R., & Mosak, H. H. (1967). the tasks of life. II. The fourth life task. *Individual Psychologist, 4*, 51–55.

Dreikurs, R., Shulman, B. H., & Mosak, H. H. (1952a). Patient-therapist relationship in multiple psychotherapy. I. Its advantages to the therapist. *Psychiatric Quarterly, 26*, 219–227.

Dreikurs, R., Mosak, H. H., & Shulman, B. H. (1952b). Patient-therapist relationship in multiple psychotherapy. II. Its advantages for the patient. *Psychiatric Quarterly, 26*, 590–596.

Dreikurs, R., Shulman, B. H., & Mosak, H. H. (1982). *Multiple psychotherapy.* Chicago: Alfred Adler Institute.

Dreikurs, R., & Soltz, V. (1964). *Children: The challenge.* New York: Duell, Sloan & Pearce.

Dunlap, K. (1933). *Habits: Their making and unmaking.* New York: Liveright.

Edgar, T. (1975). Social interest—another view. *Individual Psychologist, 12*, 16–24.

Elam, H. (1969a). Cooperation between African and Afro-American, cultural highlights. *Journal of the National Medical Association, 61*, 30–35.

Elam, H. (1969b). Malignant cultural deprivation, its evolution. *Pediatrics, 44*, 319–326.

Ellenberger, H. F. (1970). *The discovery of the unconscious.* New York: Basic Books.

Ellis, A. (1957). Rational psychotherapy and Individual Psychology. *Journal of Individual Psychology, 13*, 38–44.

Ellis, A. (1963). Toward a more precise definition of "emotional" and "intellectual" insight. *Psychological Reports, 13*, 125–126.

Ellis, A. (1970). Humanism, values, rationality. *Journal of Individual Psychology, 26*, 37–38.

Ellis, A. (1971). Reason and emotion in the Individual Psychology of Adler. *Journal of Individual Psychology, 27*, 50–64.

Farau, A. (1953). The influence of Alfred Adler on current psychology. *American Journal of Individual Psychology, 10,* 59–76.

Farau, A. (1964). Individual psychology and existentialism. *Individual Psychologist, 2,* 1–8.

Federn, E., (1963). Was Adler a disciple of Freud? A Freudian view. *Journal of Individual Psychology, 19,* 80–81.

Fiedler, F. E. (1950). A comparison of therapeutic relationships in psychoanalytic, non-directive and Adlerian therapy. *Journal of Consulting Psychology, 14,* 436–445.

Forer, L. K. (1977). Bibliography of birth order literature of the 1970s. *Journal of Individual Psychology, 33,* 122–141.

Frank, L. K. (1939). Projective methods for the study of personality. *Journal of Personality, 8,* 389–413.

Frankl, V. E. (1963). *Man's search for meaning.* New York: Washington Square Press.

Frankl, V. E. (1970). Forerunner of existential psychiatry. *Journal of Individual Psychology, 26,* 38.

Fromm-Reichman, F. (1949). Notes on personal and professional requirements of a psychotherapist. *Psychiatry, 12,* 361–378.

Goldstein, K. (1939). *The organism.* New York: American Book Co.

Gottesfeld, H. (1966). Changes in feelings of powerlessness in a community action program. *Psychological Reports, 19,* 978.

Grunwald, B. (1954). The application of Adlerian principles in a classroom. *American Journal of Individual Psychology, 11,* 131–141.

Gushurst, R. S. (1971). The reliability and concurrent validity of an idiographic approach to the interpretation of early recollections. Unpublished doctoral dissertation. University of Chicago.

Heine, R. W. (1953). A comparison of patients' reports on psychotherapeutic experience with psychoanalytic, nondirective, and Adlerian therapists. *American Journal of Psychotherapy, 7,* 16–23.

Hemming, J. (1956). *Mankind against the killers.* London: Longmans, Green.

Hinrichsen, O. (1913). Unser Verstehen der seelischen Zusammenhänge in der Neurose und Freud's und Adler's Theorien. *Zentralblätter für Psychoanalyse, 3,* 369–393.

Horney, K. (1951). *Neurosis and human growth.* London: Routledge & Kegan Paul.

Jahn, E., & Adler, A. (1964). Religion and Individual Psychology. In H. L. Ansbacher & R. Ansbacher (Eds.), *Superiority and social interest.* Evanston, IL: Northwestern University Press. [Adler's essay is reprinted in *Individual Psychology,* 1987, 43(4), 522–526.]

James, W. T. (1947). Karen Horney and Erich Fromm in relation to Alfred Adler. *Individual Psychology Bulletin, 6,* 105–116.

James, W. (1890). *Principles of psychology.* New York: Holt.

Kadis, A. L. (1956). Re-experiencing the family constellation in group psychotherapy. *American Journal of Individual Psychology, 12,* 63–68.

Kazan, S. (1978). *Gemeinschaftsgefühl* means caring. *Journal of Individual Psychology, 34,* 3–10.

Kramer, H. D. (1947). Preventive psychiatry. *Individual Psychology Bulletin, 7,* 12–18.

Krausz, E. O. (1935). The pessimistic attitude. *International Journal of Individual Psychology, 1,* 86–99.

Krausz, E. O. (1959). The commonest neurosis. In K. A. Adler & D. Deutsch (Eds.), *Essays in individual psychology* (pp. 108–118). New York: Grove Press.

La Porte, G. H. (1966). Social interest in action: A report on one attempt to implement Adler's concept. *Individual Psychologist, 4,* 22–26.

Lazarsfeld, S. (1952). Pitfalls in psychotherapy. *American Journal of Individual Psychology, 10,* 20–26.

Lazarsfeld, S. (1966). The courage for imperfection. *Journal of Individual Psychology, 22,* 163–165.

Lewin, K. (1935). *A dynamic theory of personality.* New York: McGraw-Hill.

Lombardi, D. M. (1969). The special language of the addict. *Pastoral Psychology, 20,* 51–52.

Low, A. A. (1952). *Mental health through will training.* Boston: Christopher.

Maslow, A. H. (1962). Was Adler a disciple of Freud? A note. *Journal of Individual Psychology, 18,* 125.

Maslow, A. H. (1970). Holistic emphasis. *Journal of Individual Psychology, 26,* 39.

May, R. (1970). Myth and guiding fiction. *Journal of Individual Psychology, 26,* 39.

McArthur, H. (1958). The necessity of choice. *Journal of Individual Psychology, 14,* 153–157.

Meerloo, J. A. M. (1970). Pervasiveness of terms and concepts. *Journal of Individual Psychology, 26,* 40.

Miley, C. H. (1969). Birth-order research, 1963–1967: Bibliography and index. *Journal of Individual Psychology, 25,* 64–70.

Mosak, H. H. (1954). The psychological attitude in rehabilitation. *American Archives of Rehabilitation Therapy, 2,* 9–10.

Mosak, H. H. (1958). Early recollections as a projective technique. *Journal of Projective Techniques, 22,* 302–311. [Also in G. Lindzey & C.S. Hall (Eds.) (1965). *Theories of Personality: Primary sources and research.* New York: Wiley.]

Mosak, H. H. (1967). Subjective criteria of normality. *Psychotherapy, 4,* 159–161.

Mosak, H. H. (1971a). Strategies for behavior change in schools: Consultation strategies. *Counseling Psychologist, 3,* 58–62.

Mosak, H. H. (1972). Life style assessment: A demonstration based on family constellation. *Journal of Individual Psychology, 28,* 232–247.

Mosak, H. H. (1985). Interrupting a depression: The pushbutton technique. *Individual Psychology, 41(2),* 210–214.

Mosak, H. H. (1987a). *Ha Ha and Aha: The role of humor in psychotherapy*. Muncie, IN: Accelerated Development.

Mosak, H. H. (1987b). Guilt, guilt feelings, regret and repentance. *Individual Psychology, 43(3)*, 288–295.

Mosak, H. H. (1987c). Religious allusions in psychotherapy. *Individual Psychology, 43(4)*, 496–501.

Mosak, H. H. (1991). "I don't have social interest": Social interest as construct. *Individual Psychology, 47*, 309–320.

Mosak, H. H., & Dreikurs, R. (1967). The life tasks. III. The fifth life task. *Individual Psychologist, 5*, 16–22.

Mosak, H. H., & Fletcher, S. J. (1973). Purposes of delusions and hallucinations. *Journal of Individual Psychology, 29*, 176–181.

Mosak, H. H., & Gushurst, R. S. (1971). What patients say and what they mean. *American Journal of Psychotherapy, 3*, 428–436.

Mosak, H. H., & Kopp, R. (1973). The early recollections of Adler, Freud, and Jung. *Journal of Individual Psychology, 29*, 157–166.

Mosak, H. H., & LaFevre, C. (1976). The resolution of "intrapersonal conflict." *Journal of Individual Psychology, 32*, 19–26.

Mosak, H. H., & Mosak, B. (1975). *A bibliography for Adlerian psychology*. Washington, DC: Hemisphere.

Mosak, H. H., & Mosak, B. (1975). Dreikurs' four goals: The clarification of some misconceptions. *Individual Psychologist, 12(2)*, 14–16.

Mosak, H. H., & Schneider, S. (1977). Masculine protest, penis envy, women's liberation and sexual equality. *Journal of Individual Psychology, 33*, 193–201.

Mozdzierz, G. J., & Lottman, T. J. (1973). Games married couples play: Adlerian view. *Journal of Individual Psychology, 29*, 182–194.

Mullahy, P. (1955). *Oedipus: Myth and complex*. New York: Evergreen.

Murphy, G. (1947). *Personality: A biosocial approach to origins and structure*. New York: Harper.

Neuer, A. (1936). Courage and discouragement. *International Journal of Individual Psychology, 2*, 30–50.

Nikelly, A. G. (1971a). Basic processes in psychotherapy. In A. G. Nikelly (Ed.), *Techniques for behavior change* (pp. 27–32). Springfield, IL: Charles C. Thomas.

Nikelly, A. G. (1971b). Developing social feeling in psychotherapy. In A.G. Nikelly (Ed.), *Techniques for behavior change* (pp. 91–95). Springfield, IL: Charles C. Thomas.

Nikelly, A. G. (1971c). The protesting student. In A.G. Nikelly (Ed.), *Techniques for behavior change*. Springfield, IL: Charles C. Thomas.

O'Reilly, C., Cizon, F., Flanagan, J., & Pflanczer, S. (1965). *Men in jail*. Chicago: Loyola University.

Painter, G., & Corsini, R. J. (1989). *Effective discipline in the home and the school*. Muncie, IN: Accelerated Development.

Pancner, K. R. (1978). The use of parables and fables in Adlerian psychotherapy. *Individual Psychologist, 15*, 19–29.

Papanek, E. (1971). Delinquency. In A.G. Nikelly (Ed.), *Techniques for behavior change* (pp. 177–183). Springfield, IL: Charles C. Thomas.

Papanek, H. (1954). Combined group and individual therapy in private practice. *American Journal of Psychotherapy, 8*, 679–686.

Papanek, H. (1956). Combined group and individual therapy in the light of Adlerian psychology. *International Journal of Group Psychotherapy, 6*, 135–146.

Papanek, H. (1959). Emotion and intellect in psychotherapy. *American Journal of Psychotherapy, 13*, 150–173.

Papanek, H., & Papanek, E. (1961). Individual Psychology today. *American Journal of Psychotherapy, 15*, 4–26.

Pelzman, O. (1952). Some problems in the use of psychotherapy. *Psychiatric Quarterly Supplement, 26*, 55–58.

Pew, M. L., & Pew, W. (1972). Adlerian marriage counseling. *Journal of Individual Psychology, 28*, 192–202.

Phillips, C. E., & Corsini, R. J. (1982). *Give in or give up*. Chicago: Nelson-Hall.

Rasey, M. I. (1956). Toward the end. In C. E. Moustakas (Ed.), *The self: Explorations in personal growth* (pp. 247–260). New York: Harper.

Reik, T. (1948). *Listening with the third ear*. New York: Farrar, Straus & Cudahy.

Rogers, C. R. (1951). *Client-centered therapy*. Boston: Houghton Mifflin.

Rosenthal, D., & Frank, J. D. (1956). Psychotherapy and the placebo effect. *Psychological Bulletin, 53*, 294–302.

Seidler, R. (1967). The individual psychologist looks at testing. *Individual Psychologist, 5*, 3–6.

Seidler, R., & Zilahi, L. (1949). The Vienna child guidance clinics. In A. Adler & Associates, *Guiding the child* (pp. 9–27). London: Allen & Unwin.

Shlien, J. M., Mosak, H. H., & Dreikurs, R. (1962). Effect of time limits: A comparison of two psychotherapies. *Journal of Counseling Psychology, 9*, 31–34.

Shoben, E. J., Jr. (1957). Toward a concept of normal personality. *American Psychologist, 12*, 183–189.

Shoobs, N. E. (1964). Role-playing in the individual psychotherapy interview. *Journal of Individual Psychology, 20*, 84–89.

Shulman, B. H. (1962). The meaning of people to the schizophrenic and the manic-depressive. *Journal of Individual Psychology, 18*, 151–156.

Shulman, B. H., & Mosak, H. H. (1977). Birth order and ordinal position. *Journal of Individual Psychology, 33*, 114–121.

Shulman, B. H., & Klapman, H. (1968). Organ inferiority and psychiatric disorders in childhood. In E. Harms (Ed.), *Pathogenesis of nervous and mental diseases* (pp. 49–62). New York: Libra.

Sicher, L., & Mosak, H. H. (1967). Aggression as a secondary phenomenon. *Journal of Individual Psychology, 23*, 232–235.

Simpson, H. N. (1966). *Stoic apologetics.* Oak Park, IL: Author.

Smuts, J. C. (1961). *Holism and evolution.* New York: Viking Press.

Soltz, V. (1967). *Study group leader's manual.* Chicago: Alfred Adler Institute.

Speil, O. (1962). *Discipline without punishment.* London: Faber & Faber.

Starr, A. (1977). *Psychodrama.* Chicago: Nelson-Hall.

Strupp, H. H. (1972). Freudian analysis today. *Psychology Today, 6*, 33–40.

Sullivan, H. S. (1954). *The psychiatric interview.* New York: Norton.

Sward, K. (1947). Review (Review of *Our inner conflicts*). *Science,* December 1, 600–601.

Toman, W. (1970). Never mind your horoscope, birth order rules all. *Psychology Today, 4*, 45–48, 68–69.

Vaihinger, H. (1965). *The philosophy of "as if."* London: Routledge & Kegan Paul.

Von Sassen, H. W. (1967). Adler's and Freud's concepts of man: A phenomenological comparison. *Journal of Individual Psychology, 23*, 3–10.

Watkins, C. E., Jr. (1982). A decade of research in support of Adlerian psychological theory. *Individual Psychology, 38*(1), 90–99.

Watkins, C. E., Jr. (1983). Some characteristics of research on Adlerian theory, 1970–1981. *Individual Psychology, 39*(1), 99–110.

Way, L. (1962). *Adler's place in psychology.* New York: Collier Books.

Wexberg, E. (1929). *Individual Psychology.* London: Allen & Unwin.

Wexberg, E. (1970). *Individual psychological treatment.* Chicago: Alfred Adler Institute. (Originally published in 1929.)

White, R. W. (1957). Adler and the future of ego psychology. *Journal of Individual Psychology, 13*, 112–124.

Wittels, F. (1939). The neo-Adlerians. *American Journal of Sociology, 45*, 433–445.

Wolfe, W. B. (1932). *How to be happy though human.* London: Routledge & Kegan Paul.

Carl G. Jung, 1875–1961

4 Analytical Psychotherapy

Claire Douglas

❖ OVERVIEW

Analytical psychology, the psychodynamic system and personality theory created by Carl Gustav Jung, builds upon Freud's and Adler's perspectives, offering an expanded view of humanity's personal and collective realities. Analytical psychotherapy offers a map of the human psyche that encompasses conscious and unconscious elements, including both a transpersonal (archetypal) and personal layer in the unconscious. The goals of psychotherapy are reintegration, self-knowledge, and individuation, with a heartfelt awareness of the human condition, individual responsibility, and a connection to the transcendent replacing a wounded, one-sided, rationalistic, and limited sense of self. Therapy taps into the healing and self-regulating potential of the psyche by means of a profound encounter between the interacting personalities of patient and therapist.

Basic Concepts

The cornerstone of Jung's psychological system is his concept of the psyche, the inner realm of personality that balances the outer reality of material objects. Jung defined psyche as a combination of spirit, soul, and idea; he viewed psychic reality as the sum of conscious and unconscious inner processes. According to Jung, this inner world influences biochemical processes in the body, affects the instincts, and determines one's perception of outer reality. Jung proposed that physical matter can only be known through a person's psychic images of outside reality; thus, what people perceive is in large part determined by who they are.

The reality of the psyche was Jung's working hypothesis, confirmed through material he gathered from fantasy, myth, image, and the behavior of individual people. Jung mapped the psyche in terms of a whole made up of balancing and compensatory opposites. Key aspects of his map of the psyche are a personal and collective unconscious as well as a personal and collective consciousness.

Jung's description of the personal unconscious is similar to, but more extensive than, Freud's. In Jungian theory, an individual's personal unconscious contains not only material unacceptable to one's ego and superego and therefore repressed, but also material unimportant to the psyche, temporarily or permanently dropped from consciousness. It also contains undeveloped parts of one's personality not yet ready for or admitted to consciousness, as well as elements rising from the collective unconscious.

The *collective unconscious* is Jung's term for the vast, hidden psychic resource shared by all human beings. Jung discovered the collective unconscious through his patients' disclosures, his own self-analysis, and cross-cultural studies. He found the same basic motifs expressed in fantasies, dreams, symbols, or myths. Images that emerge out of the collective unconscious are shared by all people but modified by their personal experiences. Jung called these motifs *archetypal images* and depicted the collective unconscious as organized in underlying patterns.

An *archetype* is an organizing principle, a system of readiness, and a dynamic nucleus of energy. As an organizing principle, an archetype is analogous to the circuitry pattern in the brain that orders and structures reality; as a system of readiness, it parallels animals' instincts; as a dynamic nucleus of energy, it propels a person's actions and reactions in a patterned way. Jung believed that humans have an inherited predisposition to form their personalities and to view reality according to universal inner patterns.

Archetypes can be seen as pathways along whose course energy flows from the collective unconscious into consciousness and action. Jung wrote that there were as many archetypal images in the collective unconscious as there were typical situations in life, and that they have appeared in individual experience from time immemorial and will reappear in the future whenever analogous situations arise. Some archetypal patterns that became a major focus of Jung's work and a fertile source for popular psychology are the Heroic Quest; the Night Sea Journey; the Inner Child (often seen as the childlike part of one's own personality) and Divine Child; the Maiden, Mother, and Goddess; the Wise Old Man; and the Wild Man.

While the collective unconscious reveals itself to a person by means of such archetypal images, the personal unconscious makes itself known through *complexes*. Archetypal images flow from the collective unconscious into the personal unconscious by means of a *complex* (a sensitive, energy-filled cluster of emotions, such as an attitude toward one's father or anyone resembling him). Jung's idea of the complex came from his research on the Word Association Test (1904–7). Jung would read a list of words aloud, asking subjects to respond with the first word that came to their minds; he then repeated the list, with the subjects attempting to recall their initial responses. Jung noticed pauses, failures to respond or remember, and bodily reactions, and he believed that such variations revealed sensitive, hidden areas. Jung named these reactions complexes—emotionally charged associations of ideas and feelings that act as magnets to draw a net of imagery, memories, and ideas into their orbit.

Jung believed the complex to be so important that when he broke from Freud and looked for a name for his form of psychoanalysis, his first choice was Complex Psychology. Though Freud and Adler adopted Jung's terminology of the complex, Jung's formulation was far richer than those of his colleagues. Jung believed that though a complex may have restricting, upsetting, or other disturbing consequences in some instances, it can also be positive, serving to bring matters of importance to consciousness. Complexes demand personal confrontation and response that can promote a person's development and growth. One can relate to a complex positively by meeting its demand, but this takes hard psychological work. Many people try to manage a complex by projecting its contents: a man with a negative mother complex, for instance, may see all women in an exaggeratedly negative light. (Projection means attributing to another person something that really belongs to one's own personality.) Another way a person may try to avoid a complex is by repression. Thus, a woman with a negative mother complex may cut herself off from all that she considers feminine so as not to resemble her mother in any way. Another woman with a mother complex might perceive herself as an all-good, "earth mother" type of woman. In more extreme cases, a complex may overpower an individual so that the person loses touch with reality, becoming psychotic; a psychotic woman who has a mother complex may believe she *is* Mother Nature and the mother of everything and everybody on earth.

Rather than seeing the unconscious as something needing to be cleaned out and made conscious, Jung felt that individuals grow toward wholeness when both conscious and unconscious parts of the mind work in harmony. Because of this natural movement toward balance and self-healing, Jung concluded that neurosis contained the seeds for its own cure and had the energy to bring about growth and healing. The Jungian analyst serves as a catalyst to promote balance, growth, and integration.

Other Systems

Jung's theories have influenced contemporary religious, cultural, and sociological thought, as well as art, literature, and drama. Nevertheless, psychology in general, and modern psychotherapeutic systems in particular, frequently overlook or ignore Jung's influence. There are many reasons for this, including the difficulty of Jung's writing style and the bitter parochialism of some early psychoanalysts. The situation is compounded by the tendency of psychologists to believe what they have *heard* about Jung rather than reading what he wrote. Today's psychologists receive a rigorously scientific education that often leads them to fear "soft" science and to avoid a system that they have been told is mystical. In reality, the pragmatism of Jung's practical and inclusive approach to psychotherapy has contributed much to the general field of psychology. To ignore one of the three great early psychodynamic theoreticians of this century is to travel with an incomplete map of the human psyche.

Jung started to develop his own form of psychoanalysis and to treat patients before he met Freud. However, his debt to Freud is great. Perhaps most important to Jung was Freud's exploration of the unconscious through free association, his focus on the significance of dreams, and his stress on the role of early childhood experiences in the formation of personality (Ellenberger, 1970). Jung constructed a map of these areas that became broader and more inclusive than Freud's.

Jung focused on the complex as the royal road to the unconscious, while Freud emphasized the importance of dreams. Yet dreams play a more significant role in Jung's system than in Freud's, since Jung saw dreams as more meaningful than simple wish-fulfillments, requiring a more thorough and well-rounded technique of dream analysis. For Jung, Freud's Oedipus complex was only one of many possible complexes and not necessarily the most important one. Sexuality and aggression, rather than being the sole channels for the expression of libido, were only two of its many possible routes. Neurosis had many causes, including, but not limited to, sexual problems. Perhaps the most salient difference between Freud and Jung resulted from Jung's belief that the quest for meaning was as strong a need as the sex drive.

Jung believed that certain people would profit most from a Freudian analysis, others from an Adlerian analysis, and still others from a Jungian analysis. He viewed Adler's theory of dreams as similar to his own. Both theories held that dreams could reveal what an individual wanted not to recognize in himself or herself (what Jung called the *shadow* aspects of the personality). Both Jung and Adler believed that dreams reveal the underlying pattern of the way an individual relates to the world. Adler and Jung also stressed the importance of first memories, and of fulfilling life tasks and one's duties to society. Jung taught that unless these tasks were met, neurosis would result. They both met the individual patient on a more equal footing than Freud. Freud had his patients lie on a couch and free associate, but Jung and Adler sat face-to-face with their patients. Finally, both Adler and Jung believed that psychotherapy should look to the future as well as to the past. Jung's ideas of life-goals and forward-looking (teleological) energy are similar to Adler's views.

Lifespan psychologists owe much to Jung. Erik Erickson's life stages, as well as Lawrence Kohlberg's stages of moral development and Carol Gilligan's reevaluation and redefinition of Kohlberg's work to reflect women's development, all express Jung's ideas of individuation over the life span. Jung's theories inspired Henry A. Murray's Needs-Press theory of Personology, and Jung's encouragement of fantasies inspired the Thematic Apperception Test (Christiana Morgan, its first author, and Murray were analyzed by Jung). Gestalt Therapy can be seen as an extension of Jung's method of dream interpretation. Modern Jungians, such as E. C. Whitmont and Sylvia Perera (1989), use a combination of gestalt enactment and active imagination (a conscious exploration of one's fantasies) as core analytic tools. J. L. Moreno's psychodrama reflects Jung's encouragement of patients' enacting their dreams and fantasies; Moreno's ideas of role and of surplus reality mirror Jung's belief in a pluralistic psyche composed of many archetypal images and possible roles.

Harry Stack Sullivan's *good me* and *bad me* reflect Jung's concepts of positive and negative *shadow* (the rejected or unrecognized parts of one's personality). Alexander Lowen's bioenergetic theory follows Jung's theory of typology, and Jung's four functions of *thinking*, *feeling*, *sensation*, and *intuition* loosely parallel Lowen's hierarchy of personality functions. Holistic therapies of all varieties, from the Adlerian to the most modern, share with Jung the idea of a person made up of many parts in service to the whole, with the individual having a normal urge toward growth and healing. Self-actualizing theories, such as those derived from Abraham Maslow's work, stress the forward-looking and optimistic parts of Jung's psychology, while the person-centered psychology of Carl Rogers echoes Jung's human interest and personal devotion to his patients. Jung (1935a) insisted on the human quality in analysis, emphasizing the integrity of the patient who "inasmuch as he is an individual…can only become what he is and always was…the best thing the doctor can do is lay aside his whole apparatus of methods and theory" (p. 10) in order to be with the patient as a fellow human being.

Neo-Freudian ego psychology, such as Melanie Klein's and Erich Fromm's theories, share so much with Jungian thought that they cross-fertilize each other and may produce a vigorous hybrid. Jungians have pointed out the similarity of their constructs to Jung's original formulations in realms such as the description of infancy and its tasks, the internalization of parts of others' personalities, projections, and the death instinct (e.g., Maduro and Wheelwright, 1977).

Jung's emphasis on the value of being as well as doing, and his deep trust in religious or mystical feelings, are similar to many Asian psychotherapies. Jung's method for incubating fantasies in active imagination is a directed meditation. Jung lectured widely on Asian systems of thought, comparing them to his own theories; perhaps his most cogent lecture was on yoga in relation to the analysis of one of his patients (Douglas, 1993).

❖ HISTORY

Precursors

Carl Gustav Jung (1875–1961), the eldest son of a clergyman, grew up in the German-speaking part of Switzerland during the final quarter of the nineteenth century. His mother came from a family of theologians; his father's father, a physician, had also been a renowned poet, philosopher, and classical scholar. Jung received a thorough education embedded not only in the Protestant theological tradition but also in classical Greek and Latin literature. He was influenced especially by the pre-Socratic philosopher Heraclitus, the mystic Jacob Boehme, by Romantic philosophy and psychiatry, and by Asian philosophy. During an era that marked the rise of scientific positivism, Jung's teachers emphasized a rational, optimistic, and progressive view of human nature. Nevertheless, Jung was drawn instead to Romanticism, which valued the irrational, the occult, the mysterious, and the unconscious. Romanticism had a more pessimistic view of human nature than positivism did. According to Romantic philosophy, humans were divided and polarized; they yearned for a unity and wholeness that had been lost. This yearning manifested itself through the desire to plumb the depths of the natural world as well as the individual soul (Douglas, 1990).

Romantic philosophy underlay nineteenth-century anthropology, linguistics, and archaeology, as well as research on sexuality and the inner worlds of the mentally ill—all topics that interested Jung. Romanticism also manifested itself in the exploration of parapsychological phenomena and the occult.

Tracing the specific sources of Jung's ideas would require many chapters. Perhaps the best brief coverage is by Henri Ellenberger (1970), who stresses Jung's debt to Romantic philosophy and psychiatry. The theories of Goethe, Kant, Schiller, and Nietzsche were influential in forming Jung's style of thinking in terms of opposites.

Jung's fellow townsman, Johann Bachofen, was interested in the religious and philosophical importance of myths and the meaning of symbols. Nietzsche had borrowed Bachofen's concept of a Dionysian-Apollonian duality, which Jung, in turn, also adopted. (Dionysius stood for the sensual side of life, while Apollo represented the rational.) Nietzsche shared with Jung a sense of the tragic ambiguity of life and the presence of good and evil in every human interaction. Nietzsche's ideas about the origin of civilization, humanity's moral conscience, and the importance of dreams, together with his concern about evil, influenced Jung. Nietzsche's description of the Shadow, the Persona, the Superman, and the Wise Old Man were taken up by Jung as specific archetypal images.

Carl Gustav Carus and Arthur Schopenhauer also influenced Jung. Carus had written about the creative and healing functions of the unconscious fifty years before Freud or Jung. Carus outlined a tripartite model of the unconscious that prefigured Jung's concepts of the archetypal, collective, and personal unconscious. Schopenhauer possessed a view of life that attracted Jung. Both wrote about the irrational in human psychology, as well as the role played by human will, repression, and the power of the instincts. Schopenhauer and Neitzsche inspired Jung's theory of archetypes; also influential was Schopenhauer's emphasis on imagination, the role of the unconscious, the reality of evil, and the importance of dreams. Both Schopenhauer and Jung were interested in moral issues and in Eastern philosophy, and both shared a belief in the possibility of personal wholeness.

Ellenberger (1970) traces Jung's psychotherapeutic emphasis on transference and countertransference (*transference* refers to feelings the patient projects onto the analyst and *countertransference* to the ways in which the analyst is influenced by patients' projections) to a chain of thought that originates in the exorcism of devils, winds through Anton Mesmer's theory of animal magnetism, and lead to the early nineteenth-century use of hypnosis by Pierre Janet to cure mental illness. Janet also influenced Jung through his classifications of mental diseases and his interest in multiple personality and fixed ideas. For Janet, as for Jung, the dedication of the doctor and the personal harmony between doctor and patient were major elements in cures.

Beginnings

Jung wrote, "Our way of looking at things is conditioned by what we are" (1929/1933/1961, p. 335). He believed all psychological theories were subjective, reflecting the personal history of their founders. Jung's parents had been raised in prosperous city families and were well educated; their mutual discontent with their life in the poor rural parish of Kesswil, where Jung's father served as a country pastor, affected Jung's childhood. Jung described his youth as lonely. Until he went to high school, his companions were mostly peasants. His early experience with peasants brought out a practical and earthy side of Jung that balanced his tendency toward introspection (Jung, 1965).

Jung was close to his mother. He experienced her as having two sides. One side was intuitive, with an interest in parapsychology that he feared; the other side was warm and maternal, which comforted him. In his mind, Jung split her into a daytime/nighttime, good/bad person. Jung's later efforts to integrate these contrasting aspects of his mother found form in his emphasis on the importance of the Hero's quest to free himself from the Terrible Mother, as well as his depiction of powerful feminine archetypal images. Jung's unsatisfactory relationship with his father may have led to his later problems with men, especially male mentors and other authority figures.

Throughout his life, Jung was interested in and attracted to women. He married a woman with an earthy side similar to his mother's, but he remained captivated by intuitive women whom he described as his lost feminine half. In his autobiography, Jung remembered a nursemaid who took care of him when his mother was hospitalized for several months. This nurse became the prototype for a series of women who were to fascinate and inspire him. The parapsychological experiments of Jung's cousin, Helene Preiswerk, became the subject of his medical school dissertation. Her influence was seminal to the development of Jung's theories.

Much of Jung's reading during his university and medical school years concerned multiple personality, trance states, hysteria, and hypnosis. He brought this interest to his coursework and to his lectures to fellow students, as well as to his dissertation. His fascination with these subjects, and his reading of Richard von Krafft-Ebing's study of sexual psychopathology, propelled Jung into psychiatry (Jung, 1965). Soon after Jung finished his dissertation, he started work under Eugen Bleuler at the Burgholzli Psychiatric Hospital, then a famous center for research on mental illness. Jung lived at the Burgholzli Hospital from 1902 to 1909, intimately involved with the daily lives of mentally disturbed patients. Their inner worlds intrigued him, and his exploration of the symbolic universe of one of his schizophrenic patients, Babette, was a major source of Jung's study on schizophrenia, *The Psychology of Dementia Praecox* (1907). At the Burgholzli, Jung developed and administered a number of psychological tests. His Word Association Test studies (1904–7) gained him renown. These studies were the first demonstration of the reality of the unconscious. This work led Jung to begin a correspondence with Sigmund Freud.

Freud appreciated Jung's contributions to psychoanalytic theory and accepted Jung as his heir apparent. He appointed Jung president of the International Psychoanalytic Association and editor of the *Jahrbuch*, the first psychoanalytic journal. The two men traveled together to the United States in 1909 to lecture on their respective views of psychoanalysis at Clark University. Jung considered himself Freud's collaborator, not his disciple. Divergent perceptions, as well as their conflicting personalities, caused them to sever their alliance. Jung announced his break with Freud in *The Psychology of the Unconscious* (1911, revised in 1956 as *Symbols of Transformation*). In this book, Jung set forth his own form of psychoanalysis, in which myth, cultural history, and personal psychology were interwoven; he also redefined *libido* more comprehensively than had Freud. During this period, Jung married and then left the Burgholzli for private practice. He began to train his followers in his own method, and his wife, Emma Jung, became one of the first analytical psychotherapists.

After his break with Freud, Jung suffered a period of extreme introversion that Ellenberger (1970) called a creative illness. At this time, a third in the series of women who inspired him, his former patient and a future analyst, Toni Wolff, served as Jung's guide for his descent into the unconscious. Jung acknowledged his debt to her, as well as to the women who were the subjects of his first three books, and to his female patients when he wrote: "What this psychology owes to the direct influence of women...is a theme that would fill a large volume. I am speaking here not only of analytical psychology but of the beginnings of psychopathology in general" (Jung, 1927/1970, p. 124). He added that "I have had mainly women patients, who often entered into the work with extraordinary conscientiousness, understanding and intelligence. It was essentially because of them that I was able to strike out on new paths in therapy" (Jung, 1965, p. 145).

Jung's emergence from his period of creative introversion was signaled by the 1921 publication of his *Psychological Types*. Its inspiration came from Jung's long pondering over the destructive antagonism among Freud, Adler, and himself. Jung made his private peace with them through creating a system of typology that allowed for and explained the different ways each experienced and reacted to the world.

Current Status

Interest in Jungian psychology is growing as the incompleteness of positivistic science becomes more apparent and the world becomes increasingly complex. In spite of the dismissal of analytical psychology by some pragmatic psychologists, the fact that analytical psychology answers a strong need for many people can be seen in the growing number of Jungian professional training Institutes and analysts. As of 1994, thirty-one professional societies were affiliated with the International Association for Analytical Psychology (thirteen in the United States), as well as more than 1800 certified analysts. There are Jungian study groups and analytical psychology clubs in cities that have professional societies and in many places not large enough to have Institutes, and there are increasing numbers of people who call themselves Jungian-oriented therapists but have not gone through an Institute's rigorous training. Professional journals are associated with specific Institutes; among the more important ones are the British *Journal of Analytical Psychology*; the *San Francisco Jung Institute Library Journal*; the Los Angeles Institute's *Psychological Perspectives*; New York's *Quadrant*; Chicago's series of *Chiron* monographs on clinical practice; and the post-Jungian journal of archetypal studies, *Spring*. Important non-English journals include the *Cahiers de Psychologie Jungienne* from Paris, the *Zeitschrift fur Analytische Psychologie* from Berlin, and Rome's *La Rivista di Psicologia Analitica*.

Training varies from Institute to Institute and country to country. Though Jung accepted lay analysts, the trend toward increasing professionalism grows. In the United States, Institutes most often accept physicians, clinical psychologists, and social workers for training. Jung was the first psychoanalyst to insist that an analyst be personally analyzed. The cornerstone of Jungian training remains a thorough analysis over many years and often with two different analysts. Six or more years of controlled case supervision comes next in importance. Coursework in the United States commonly takes four years and involves seminars that provide a thorough grounding in clinical theory and practice (from both a Jungian and neo-Freudian perspective), dream analysis, and archetypal psychology. Extensive personal reviews, oral and written examinations, and a clinical dissertation are generally required for professional certification as a Jungian analyst. The average length of training is from six to eight years.

There is an exciting ferment within Jungian studies at this time. Interest in child analysis, group work, body work, and art therapy is increasing, as is a concomitant interest in a hybrid of Jungian psychology and Melanie Klein's object relations theory, which focuses on the analysis of early childhood development and early childhood wounds (Maduro and Wheelwright, 1977). *Object relations* is an unfortunate term for the way people relate to other people. This hybrid is becoming increasingly popular with a number of analysts in the United States. Others are revising or discarding the more time- or culture-bound aspects of Jung's theory. Two examples are a Jungian psychology of women that fits the reality of contemporary women and a reformulation of Jung's anima-animus concept. *Anima* is a feminine archetypal image most often represented through the feminine part of a man; *animus* is a masculine archetypal image most often represented through the masculine part of a woman. Jungians are currently reassessing what were once held to be traditionally "masculine" and "feminine" characteristics and are reappraising Jungian typological theory. There is also an extension of archetypal theory to images relevant to contemporary life, both in scholarly works and in popular works that reach a wide and receptive audience. There has been a gradual easing of the bad feelings and jealousy that divided the various schools of depth psychology since Freud, Adler, and Jung parted ways. Thus, for example, the National Accreditation Association for Psychoanalysis includes depth psychologists and Institutes from many different, and formerly opposing, schools.

❖ PERSONALITY

Theory of Personality

Jung's theory of personality rests on the concept of a dynamic unity of all parts of a person. The psyche is made up of conscious and unconscious components with connections to the *collective unconscious* (underlying patterns of images, thoughts, behaviors, and experiences). According to Jungian theory, our conscious understanding of who we are comes from two sources: the first derives from encounters with social reality, such as the things people tell us about ourselves, the second from what we deduce from our observations of others. If others seem to agree with our self-assessment, we tend to think we are normal; if they disagree, we tend to see ourselves, or to be seen by others, as abnormal.

In addition, each individual has a personal unconscious. This is an area of personality that cannot be understood directly but can only be approached indirectly, through dreams and through analysis. The personal unconscious is affected by what Jung called the collective unconscious, an inherited human factor that expresses itself in the personal unconscious by means of archetypal images and complexes.

So, in effect, there are two aspects to the human psyche: one is an accessible side referred to as consciousness, comprising one's senses, intellect, emotions, and desires, and the other is an inaccessible side—the personal unconscious, containing elements of personal experience we have forgotten or denied—as well as elements of the collective unconscious that can be discerned through archetypal images and complexes.

Jung defined the Self as archetypal energy that orders and integrates the personality, an encompassing wholeness out of which personality evolves. The Self is the goal of personal development. The infant starts in a state of initial wholeness, as a unitary Self that soon fragments into subsystems. Through this fragmentation, mind and consciousness develop; over the course of a lifetime, the healthy personality then reintegrates at a higher level of development.

The most important fragment of the Self, the *ego*, appears first as the young child gains some sense of identity as an independent being. The ego in early life is like an island of consciousness set in an ocean of personal and unconscious material. The island grows in size and definition as it gathers and digests the deposits from the sea around it. This ego becomes the "I" — an entity comprising everything a person believes himself or herself to be, including thoughts, feelings, wants, and bodily sensations. The ego, as the center of consciousness, mediates between the unconscious realm and the outer world. Part of human psychological development consists of creating a strong and resilient ego that can filter stimuli from each of these domains without identifying or being overcome by either side.

The *personal shadow* balances the ego in the personal unconscious. The shadow contains everything that could or should be part of the ego but that the ego denies or refuses to develop. The personal shadow can contain both positive and negative aspects. Shadow elements often appear in dreams in attacking or frightening forms of the same gender as the dreamer; they also erupt into consciousness through projection onto hated or envied individuals or groups. The personal shadow tends to be the vehicle through which archetypal images of evil emerge out of the collective unconscious, as when, for instance, a mob gets carried away in mindless acts of violence. Confronting shadow material, making it and one's response to it conscious, can reclaim important parts of the personality to consciousness; these are essential tasks for the mature personality.

Jung believed in the reality of evil and viewed it as an increasing problem in the world. Jung felt that humans could confront evil by becoming conscious of it and aware of archetypal, inherited images of absolute evil. He thought that responsibly facing human evil meant becoming conscious of what is in one's own shadow, confronting archetypal images of evil instead of being overwhelmed by them, and taking personal responsibility for one's own evil propensities and actions rather than projecting shadow material and complexes onto others.

The *persona* is the public "face" of an individual in society. Jung named the persona for the Greek theatrical mask that hid the actor's face and indicated the part he chose to play. The persona shields the ego and reveals appropriate aspects of it, smoothing the individual's interactions with society. The development of an adequate persona allows for the privacy of thoughts, feelings, ideas, and perceptions, as well as for modulation in the way they are revealed. Just as people can identify with their egos, they can identify with their persona, believing they really *are* the role they have chosen to play.

Jung believed that the task of the first part of life was strengthening the ego, taking one's place in the world in relationships with others, and fulfilling one's duty to society. The task of the second half of life was to reclaim undeveloped parts of oneself, fulfilling these aspects of personality more completely. He called this process *individuation* and felt this life task drew many of his older patients into analysis. By individuation, Jung did not mean perfection; the idea refers to completion and wholeness, including acceptance of the more negative parts of one's personality and adoption of an ethical, though individual, response to them. Fordham (1969) and many other contemporary Jungians believe that individuation does not have to wait until middle age. Jung's emphasis on individuation as the task of the second half of life further differentiated his personality theory from Freud's because it allowed for growth and transformation throughout the life cycle. The mid-life crisis, looked at in this way, becomes a challenging opportunity for further development.

Part of the process of individuation concerns not only assimilation of personal shadow material but also awareness and integration of the contrasexual elements in the psyche— what Jung called the *anima* (an archetypal image of the feminine) and *animus* (an archetypal image of the masculine), which serve as bridges to the unconscious. The form and character of the archetypal images of anima and animus are highly individual, based on a person's experience of the opposite sex, cultural assumptions, and the archetype of the feminine or masculine. Since so much about gender and gender roles is in flux today, current images no longer match those of Jung's time and are changing as culture and experience change (Douglas, 1990). Contemporary reevaluation of this concept holds much promise for a reappraisal of homosexuality as a natural occurrence.

Typology is one of the most important and best known contributions Jung made to personality theory. In *Psychological Types* (1921/1971), Jung describes varying ways individuals habitually respond to the world. Two basic responses are *introversion* and *extraversion.* Jung saw introversion as natural and basic. Energy for the introvert flows predominantly inward, with reality being the introvert's reaction to an event, object, or person. Introverts need solitude to develop and maintain their rich inner worlds; they value friendship, having few but deep relationships with others. The extravert's reality, on the other hand, consists of objective facts or incidents. The extravert connects with reality mainly through external objects. While the introvert adapts outer reality to inner psychology, the extravert adapts himself or herself to the environment and to people. Extraverts usually communicate well, make friends easily, and have a great deal of libido for interactions with other people. Jung described nations as well as people as being either predominantly introverted or extraverted. For instance, he saw Switzerland as basically introverted and the United States not only as being primarily extraverted but also as tending to look on introversion as unhealthy.

In his theory of typology, Jung went on to differentiate personality into functional types, based on people's tendency to perceive reality primarily through one of four mental functions: *thinking, feeling, sensation,* and *intuition.* Each of these four functions can be experienced in an extraverted or an introverted way. According to Jung,

> For complete orientation all four functions should contribute equally: thinking should facilitate cognition and judgment, feeling should tell us how and to what extent a thing is important or unimportant for us, sensation should convey concrete reality to us through seeing, hearing, tasting, sensing, etc., and intuition should enable us to divine the hidden possibilities in the background, since these too belong to the complete picture of a given situation. (1921/1971, p. 518).

According to Jung, a thinker finds rules, assigns names, makes classifications, and develops theories; a feeling person puts a value on reality, often by liking or disliking something; a sensing type uses the five senses to grasp inner or outer reality; and an intuitive person has hunches that seem to penetrate into past and future reality, as well as an ability to pick up accurate information from the unconscious of another person.

Most people seem to be born with one of these four primary functions dominant. The dominant function is used more and is developed more fully than the others. Often a secondary function will develop as the person matures, then a third, but the weakest function—such as feeling for the thinker, or sensation for the intuitive person—remains shadowy and undeveloped. Jung stressed the importance of the least developed function. Largely unconscious, it is often seen first in shadow and animus/anima subpersonalities. This undeveloped function causes trouble when it breaks into consciousness, but it can also bring creativity and freshness, appearing when the mature personality feels lifeless and spent.

People tend to develop one primary attitude and function and then rely on these, sometimes inappropriately. For instance, a predominantly thinking type tends always to consider the facts of the case when it may be better simply to understand that something is right or wrong, good or bad, worthy of acceptance or rejection.

Everyone has access to all four functions as well as to introversion and extraversion. Part of personality development, according to Jungians, consists of first refining one's predominant type and then cultivating one's less evolved functions. In lifespan development, the secondary function matures after the first and is followed by the third; the blooming of the least-developed function comes last and can be a source of great creativity in the latter part of life. It is important to stress that typological theory is a blueprint or map far clearer than the terrain of the personality itself, which is full of individual differences.

Variety of Concepts

Opposites

Jung (1976) wrote, "Opposites are the ineradicable and indispensable preconditions for all psychic life" (p. 169). In line with the dualistic theories of his day, Jung saw the world in terms of paired opposites such as good and evil, light and dark, positive and negative. He designed his personality theory with *consciousness* opposing the *unconscious*, *masculine* opposing *feminine*, *good aspects* of an archetypal image opposing the *bad* (e.g., the *Nourishing* opposing the *Devouring* Mother), *ego* opposing *shadow*, and so on. These opposites engage in active struggle; personality development takes place through the tension this conflict produces in the psyche. For instance, a woman's conscious sexuality may war with her animus figure, who may appear in her dreams as a negative and judgmental male cleric. Caught in the conflict, she may go from one pole to the other and may develop neurotic symptoms from the split. Through bringing the fight between her eroticism and her spirituality into awareness, attentively following it, and allowing both sides their voice in fantasies and therapy, the woman may increase her consciousness and thus integrate the opposing sides of her sexuality and her religious feelings at a higher level of awareness.

Enantiodromia

This word refers to Heraclitus' law that everything sooner or later turns into its opposite. To illustrate enantiodromia, Jung liked to tell the story of the man who laughed on the way up a precipitous mountain path and cried on the easy way down. While climbing, he remembered the effortless descent, but while ambling down, he remembered the difficult ascent he had made. Jung believed enantiodromia governed the cycles of human history as well as personal development. He thought that one could escape such cycles only through consciousness. Jung's belief in Heraclitus's law underlies his theory of compensation.

Compensation

Jung not only divided the world into paired opposites but formed a theory built on the idea that just as the opposites lay in dynamic balance, so everything in the personality balanced or supplemented its opposite in a self-regulatory way. Jung referred to this tendency as compensation. Thus, the personal unconscious balances an individual's consciousness, giving rise in dreams, fantasies, or somatic symptoms to its opposite; the more rigidly one holds the conscious position, the more strongly will its opposite appear in images or symbols and break through into consciousness. Thus, someone who consciously identifies with a harshly judgmental spirituality may have a prostitute figure active in his or her unconscious who, if further repressed, may induce a scandalous alliance in the outer world.

The Transcendent Function

Jung called reconciling symbols, or images that form bridges between opposites, compensatory or transcendent functions. These symbols synthesize two opposing attitudes or conditions in the psyche by means of third forces different from both but uniting the two. Jung used the word *transcendent* because the image or symbol went beyond, as well as mediated between, the two opposites, allowing a new attitude or relationship between them. Bringing the opposites of one's conscious ego and the personal unconscious together generates a conflict in the personality that is highly charged and full of energy. The specific image that appears at the height of a seemingly unsolvable conflict between two opposites seems both unexpected and inevitable, holding an energy-filled charge capable of uniting and reconciling the opposing sides. The woman whose animus male cleric warred with her womanly sexuality had a fantasy in which she was crowned with grape leaves and led a snake to the foot of an altar; the snake slithered up the cross and wrapped itself about it (Douglas, 1993). The grape leaves were emblems of sensuality, while the snake on the cross (connected with feminine energy in many myths, the most familiar being Eve and the Garden of Eden) reconciled the woman's opposing sides in a surprising new form of union.

Mandala

Jung defined the mandala as a symbol of wholeness and of the center of the personality. The word *mandala* comes from the Sanskrit word for a geometric figure in which a circle and square lie within each other, and each is further subdivided. The mandala usually had religious significance. A mandala often appears in dreams, both as a symbol of wholeness and as a compensatory image during times of stress. An example of a mandala is shown below.

Preoedipal Development

In contrast to Freud's stress on the Oedipal phase of personality development, Jung focused on *preoedipal experience*. He was one of the first psychoanalysts to stress the importance of early mother-child interactions. The initial relationship between mother and child affects personality development at its most basic and profound level. Jung paid far more attention to this stage and its problems than to the father-son complications of the Oedipus complex. He placed the archetypal image of the Good and Bad Mother at the center of an infant's experience.

Development of Consciousness

Jungian theory holds that the infant follows the pattern of the development of consciousness in general, first experiencing total merger with the mother in a state of primordial fusion, then partially splitting off from her through perceiving her as sometimes all good and sometimes all bad. The child follows humanity's general historical development, emerging into self-awareness in a patriarchal stage where the father and male values are paramount. This stage affects girls as well as boys and is considered a stumbling block to women's development. When the ego is firmly in place, however, a person can integrate the mother world and father world, uniting both energies to become a more complete personality (Jung, 1934a/1970; Whitmont, 1980).

Psychopathology

Psychopathology derives in large part from problems and conflicts that arise in early mother-child relationships but is made worse by other stresses. The psyche directs attention to such disharmony and calls out for a response. Since the psyche is a self-regulating system, pathological symptoms derive from the frustrated urge toward wholeness and often contain within themselves the clue to their own healing. Thus, for instance, extreme switches between love and hate for the same person typify an individual with borderline personality disorder calling attention to faulty infantile development.

Defense Mechanisms

Defense mechanisms are seen as attempts of the psyche to survive the onslaught of complexes. They can represent normal as well as destructive modes of protection. Jung felt that any rigidly held defense caused an imbalance and would become increasingly pathological if its calls for attention were ignored. *Regression*, for example, is a defense that becomes pathological only when a person remains stuck in it. Jung felt that regression was often a natural and necessary period of consolidation and regeneration that could herald an individual's subsequent personality growth.

❖ PSYCHOTHERAPY

Theory of Psychotherapy

To Sigmund Freud's predominantly analytic, reductive system, Carl Jung added a synthesis that included the psyche's purposiveness. According to Jung, the personality not only has the capacity to heal itself but also becomes enlarged through experience. Jung (1934b/1966) built his system of psychotherapy on four tenets: (a) the psyche is a self-regulating system, (b) the unconscious has a creative and compensatory component,

(c) the doctor-patient relationship plays a major role in facilitating self-awareness and healing, and (d) personality growth takes place at many stages over the life span.

Jung found that neurosis tends to appear when a person slights or shrinks back from some important worldly or developmental task. A neurosis is a symptom of disturbance in the personality's equilibrium; thus, the whole personality has to be considered, not only the symptom of distress. Rather than concentrating on isolated symptoms, the psychotherapist looks for an underlying complex. The symptom and the complex are important clues that both hide and reveal "the patient's secret, the rock against which he is shattered" (Jung, 1965, p. 117). Jung stated that when therapists discover their patients' secret, they have the key to treatment.

Overt symptoms, dreams, and fantasies can reveal to the analyst a complex hidden from the patient's consciousness. Analytical psychotherapists deal with secrets, complexes, and neuroses by tracking their roots to past events and traumas, by seeing how they manifest themselves in the relationship between doctor and patient, and by recognizing the archetypal patterns that emerge into consciousness through the action of complexes.

Analytical psychotherapy also deals with "the mental and moral conflicts of normal people" (Jung, 1948/1980, p. 606). Jung differentiated normal from pathological conflicts according to the degree of consciousness a person has of the conflict and the amount of power exerted by the underlying complex. The level of dissociation between conscious and unconscious content reflects the intensity of the disturbance and the amount of pathology. Jung lectured frequently on his psychotherapeutic theory; yet he also declared that the practice of psychotherapy "does not involve intellectual factors only, but also feeling values and above all the important question of *human relationship*" (Jung, 1948/1980, p. 609). The dialogue and partnership between patient and analyst probably play the most essential roles in therapy. Jung himself was a notably effective therapist who followed the tenets of his theory, adapting it to the needs of each of his cases. This interaction between theory and the personal equation gives creative energy to analytical psychology as a whole and particularly to its practice of psychotherapy.

Analytical psychotherapy is, in essence, a dialogue between two people undertaken to facilitate growth, healing, and a new synthesis of the patient's personality at a higher level of functioning. By means of the analytic relationship, one works through personal problems and gains greater understanding of one's inner and outer worlds. Because of the importance of this relationship, the therapist's character, training, development, and individuation is crucial to the healing process. Jung insisted not only on the training analysis of the analyst but also on constant self-examination by the analyst. Next, and equal in importance, he valued the therapist's respect for patients, care for their values, and "supreme tact and…artistic sensitiveness" toward psychic material (Jung, 1934b/1966, p. 169). Jung wrote of the therapist's need to consider the patient from many angles, including a sociocultural one: "Psychic modes of behavior are, indeed, of an eminently historical nature. The psychotherapist has to acquaint himself not only with the personal biography of his patient, but also with the mental and spiritual assumptions prevalent in his milieu, both present and past, where traditional and cultural influences play a part and often a decisive one" (Jung, 1957, pp. vii-viii).

Through his emphasis on the mutual influence of the two people in therapy, Jung was one of the first psychoanalysts to focus on both transference and countertransference phenomena. Rather than viewing therapy as something done by one person to another, Jung acknowledged that the therapist needs to be affected before transformation can occur in the patient. Jung emphasized the influence of the patient's unconscious on the analyst as well as the need for the analyst to be open to this power. The therapist's own analysis and continued self-examination are essential if the therapist is going to maintain a beneficial role.

The psychotherapeutic process can (and often should) stop when specific goals are reached or specific problems are overcome. Nevertheless, analytical psychotherapy in its most complete form has the goal of self-actualization—helping patients discover and live up to their full potential. Thus, Jungian psychotherapy goes beyond the resolution of complexes, the strengthening of the conscious mind, and ego development, to include a larger comprehension of the psyche. Through this process, patients achieve greater personal self-knowledge and the capacity for improved relationships with themselves, with others, and with the world at large.

Michael Fordham (1990) has enriched Jung's basic theory of psychotherapy by carefully observing young children's behavior and by analyzing children and childhood, focusing on the primary infantile wounds behind complexes. A growing number of Jungians stress the analysis of early childhood experiences, including the analysis of fantasy material. They also stress the value of verbal interpretation and explanations of present behavior. This approach has resulted in a synthesis of Jungian psychotherapy with neo-Freudian psychoanalysis.

Another major movement in Jungian psychotherapy questions the value of verbal interpretation as the primary mode of analysis. Instead, the patient's affect, feelings, and body awareness are emphasized, and therapists are more likely to use the traditionally feminine realm of subjective and shared experience (Whitmont, 1982). Hillman (1992) finds emotion to be the core subject matter in a therapeutic setting where patient and therapist meet as equals. Sullivan (1989), Siegelman (1990), Carotenuto (1992), and Beebe (1992) focus on the importance of subjective feelings. They emphasize the analyst's empathy, free-floating or hovering attention, and shared metaphoric images. They also provide a theoretical base for what has been a neglected but important aspect of analytical psychotherapy.

John Beebe stresses "active passivity," in which the analyst opens himself or herself to the wide range of stimuli emitted by the patient. Beebe points out that infringements of a person's privacy inevitably occur in psychotherapy, since its subject matter concerns sensitive secrets about which one is often ashamed. These secrets, when sensitively examined, may lead to the recall and healing of early infringements of bodily or psychological space. Because of sensitive subject matter, therapists need to adhere to an ethical code that honors and respects the integrity of their patients' boundaries. Beebe suggests that ethical principles in psychotherapy derive from the necessity of protecting patients' self-esteem while also protecting the integrity of the therapeutic setting and the beliefs that are essential for progress in analytical psychotherapy.

These views remain faithful to Jung's ideas of the primacy of patients and also preserve Jung's belief that the principle aim of psychotherapy is ultimately neither curing nor alleviating patients' unhappiness but increasing patients' self-respect and self-knowledge. A sense of peace and a greater capacity for both suffering and joy can accompany this expanded sense of self, and patients are more likely to take personal responsibility for their behavior.

Process of Psychotherapy

Psychotherapy takes place among fallible equals; however, Andrew Samuels's (1985) term *asymmetrical mutuality* may be preferred to *equals* insofar as it acknowledges the differing roles and responsibilities of patients and analysts. Jung (1933/1966) delineated four stages in the process of psychotherapy: *confession, elucidation, education,* and *transformation.*

Confession

The first stage, confession, is a cathartic recounting of personal history. During this stage, the patient shares conscious and unconscious secrets with the therapist, who serves as a nonjudgmental, empathic listener. Jung found that confession brought the basic material of psychotherapy to the surface. Confession makes people feel less like outcasts, restoring them to their place in the human community. The analyst facilitates this process through an accepting attitude that drains the poison of guilt at the same time that it releases emotions long held hostage. The process of confession does, however, tend to bind the patient to the therapist through transference.

Elucidation

During elucidation, the therapist draws attention to the transference relationship as well as to dreams and fantasies in order to connect the transference to its infantile origins. The goal of this stage is insight on both affective and intellectual levels. Jung describes the successful outcome of this procedure as leading to a person's "normal adaptation and forbearance with his own shortcomings: these will be his guiding moral principles, together with freedom from sentimentality and illusion" (Jung, 1933/1966, p. 65).

Education

The third stage, education, moves the patient into the realm of the individual as an adapted social being. Confession and elucidation primarily involve exploring the personal unconscious, while education is concerned with persona and ego tasks. At this stage the therapist encourages the patient to develop an active and health-promoting role in everyday life. Insight, previously mostly intellectual, is now translated into responsible action.

Transformation

Many people stop therapy at the completion of the first three stages, but Jung noted that some clients seemed impelled to go further, especially people in the second half of life. The transference does not go away for these patients, even though its infantile origins have been thoroughly explored. These people feel a desire for greater knowledge and insight leading them toward the final stage—*transformation*. Jung described this as a period of self-actualization; the person in this stage values unconscious as well as conscious experience. The archetypal image of the Self appears in the transference as well as in dream and fantasy; this archetypal image of wholeness inspires the patient to become a uniquely individual self, encompassing all that he or she can be, yet without losing a sense of responsible integrity.

In this most Jungian of stages, the transference-countertransference becomes even more profound, and what happens to the patient "must now happen to the doctor, so that his personality shall not react unfavorably on the patient. The doctor can no longer evade his own difficulty by treating the difficulties of others" (Jung, 1933/1966, p. 74). The analyst often has to face a challenge in his or her own life before something changes in the patient. Jung gave an example when he was becoming quite famous and was treating a woman patient who worshipped him. Nothing changed until he realized that he had become too removed from his patients and was starting to feel superior to this one especially; he then dreamed he was kneeling before her as if she were a female divinity. With this, he was brought back to himself, and the analysis started to progress again.

Jung spent the latter part of his career explaining this stage through a series of analogies to alchemy. He found that the symbols and processes of medieval alchemy were comparable to those of the psychotherapeutic process in that alchemists most often worked in pairs and left records showing that they were examining their own psyches while trying to transform some base material, through a series of stages, into gold. Jung's inclusion of self-realization as part of the process broadened the scope of psychology immeasurably, bringing analytical psychotherapy into the area of human potential, consciousness study, and field theory.

Jung became increasingly interested in the transformative stage and gathered much of the material in his case studies from it. He found the transference and dream symbols went from the personal to the archetypal during this stage. Jung illustrated the process with the case study of a patient who projected a personal father image onto Jung in the first three stages of her therapy. When she got to the transformative stage, however, her dreams of him as her good father changed. Now she dreamed of a giant father figure towering over a field of ripe wheat; as she nestled in the palm of this giant's hand, he rocked her in rhythm with the blowing wind. Jung interpreted this as an archetypal image of the Great Father in the form of a vegetation god and declared that it, along with the ripeness of the wheat, signaled that the patient was entering the final stage of analysis (Jung, 1935b/1966).

Jung noted that each stage of the analytical process seems to be accompanied by a sense of finality, as if it were a goal in itself. Though each can be a temporary goal or the endpoint of a partial analysis, all four belong in a complete analysis. The stages overlap and can be concurrent, with no stage excluding the others because neither their order nor duration is fixed.

Mechanisms of Psychotherapy

The Analysis of the Transference

Jungian psychotherapists agree with all practitioners of depth psychology that transference plays a crucial role throughout therapy; however, the idea takes on a different resonance and complexity in Jungian theory. In his Tavistock Lectures (Jung, 1935c/1980), Jung described four stages of analysis of the transference itself. In the first stage, transference projections onto the therapist mirror the personal history of the patient. Patients, in working through each of their earlier relationships, relate to the analyst as if he or she were the problematic person. This is an invaluable aid to therapy, as it brings the past into the consulting room. The three goals at this stage are to have one's patients realize that the projections belong to themselves and not to others, withdraw the projections from the analyst, and integrate them as conscious parts of the patient's own personalities. Jung, writing about this first stage, said "to establish a really mature attitude, [the patient] has to see the *subjective value* of all these images which seem to create trouble for him. He has to assimilate them into his own psychology; he has to find out in what way they are part of himself" (Jung, 1933/1966, p. 160).

Jung expanded the scope of transference by considering its sociocultural and archetypal components. These impersonal aspects also get projected onto the therapist. During the second stage of the analysis of the transference, patients learn to discriminate between the personal and the impersonal contents they project onto the therapist; they determine what belongs to their own psyches and what belongs to the collective realms of culture and archetype. The impersonal cannot be assimilated, but the act of projecting it can be stopped. In the case of the woman who dreamed of the Giant Vegetation God, Jung helped her see that this image was a transpersonal one reflecting a need for her personal connection to her image. When she had seen the difference between what belonged to her, to Jung, and to the impersonal archetypal image of the Great Father, she could establish a more healing relationship with the image's power.

In the third stage of analyzing the transference, the personal reality of the analyst becomes differentiated from the image assigned the healer by the patient. At this stage, the patient can begin to relate to the therapist as a normal human being, and the personality of the therapist plays a pivotal role. As the transference is resolved and greater self-knowledge and self-realization take place, a truer evaluation of the therapist emerges, along with a more straightforward and empathic connection between patient and therapist.

Active Imagination

To help his patients get in touch with unconscious material, Jung taught a form of meditative imagery based on his own self-analysis. This came to be known as active imagination. The process calls for clearing the mind and concentrating intensely, so that inner images can be activated. The patient watches these, always returning his or her mind to them until movement is observed, upon which the patient enters into the scene, becoming part of the picture or action. Patients are instructed to pay relaxed meditative attention to what is going on. After the images stop, patients are to write, draw, paint, or even dance the story (Douglas, 1993). The starting point for the exercise of active imagination can be a mood, a complex, an obsessive thought or feeling, or an image from a dream (Hannah, 1981). Active imagination allows unconscious images to reveal themselves with little conscious intervention, yet it is more focused than dreams because of the presence of a witnessing consciousness. Therapists today emphasize that a patient must have a strong ego if unconscious images are to be dealt with in this way. Until then, the personal daily reality of the patient is the main focus of therapy; archetypal images or fantasies, if they appear, need to be grounded in a more objective, down-to-earth, and personal way than through active imagination.

Dream Analysis

Not all people remember their dreams, nor do all people who enter Jungian therapy discuss their dreams. The perspective offered by a dream does, however, often compensate for one-sidedness of the waking ego. Dreams, according to Jung, don't necessarily conceal, as in the traditional Freudian view, nor do they always denote unfulfilled wishes, nor can they be interpreted according to a standard symbology. They are accurate renderings of something to which one may need to pay attention and take as seriously as a conscious event. Dreams may represent wishes and fears; they often express impulses the dreamer either represses or finds impossible to voice; they can also point to solutions to both exterior and interior problems. They arc of great value in exposing a patient's hidden inner life, and through their evolving symbolic imagery, they reveal changes occurring in the patient's psyche. For example, at the start of therapy, a woman may dream of hostile men breaking into her house. As she deals with past traumas and begins to explore and integrate her own masculine energy, these malevolent male figures slowly change. In the latter part of a long dream series, the figures often turn into friends, helpers, and guides. Their positive and helpful behavior markedly contrasts with their earlier threatening demeanor. By watching the archetypal images of the unconscious through dreams, the personality is able to regulate itself.

An analytical psychotherapist looks for the role a dream may play in relation to the patient's conscious attitude. The therapist often explores the dream first on the objective level, considering in what ways it accurately portrays an actual person or situation. A dream is also probed for what it reveals about the patient's own behavior and character. Jung gave the example of a young man who dreamed of a headstrong father smashing a car. Jung first investigated the objective reality but found little that resonated with his patient. On the subjective level, however, the dream compensated for the boy's tendency to over-idealize his father and any other man in a position of authority as well as to ignore the heedless part of himself (Jung, 1934c/1966). In treating this patient, a Jungian therapist would ascertain if something akin to the image might be shadowing the therapy; for instance, if either the therapist or the patient were recklessly endangering the analysis by their attitudes or actions. In dream analysis, the unconscious and the dream are relied on far more than the therapist's interpretation. Jung believed that if the interpretation was not accurate, another dream would inevitably correct the faulty understanding.

Types of Dreams

The initial dream, recurrent dreams, dreams containing shadow material, and dreams about the therapist or therapy are especially useful to the therapist. The initial dream at or near the start of therapy may indicate the path that a particular therapy may take and the type of transference that may occur. For instance, a short and unsuccessful therapy was predicted by an initial dream in which a female patient dreamed her therapist neither looked at nor listened to her but admired a beautiful jade figurine instead. She switched to a different analyst and then dreamed she was a baby lion being roughly groomed by the mother lion. This initial dream boded well for the course of the new therapy. Though the patient experienced some pain from what she felt was the therapist's fierce mothering, over the course of the therapy the patient regained a connection to her instinctual nature and discovered her own feminine power.

Recurrent dreams, especially those from early childhood, suggest problematic complexes and/or a repressed traumatic event. In trauma, the dream remains a photographic replay. Over the course of the therapy the dreams change from flashback accuracy to less realistic and more neutral imagery and finally include scenarios in which the patient exerts some control (Wilmer, 1986). Dreams that contain rage, violence, or immoral conduct provide a clearer illustration of the patient's shadow than the therapist's own observations. This is because the material comes from the patient, with the unconscious part of the personality commenting on another part. Dreams about the therapist, the setting, or the therapy itself bring to light transference feelings of which the patient is either unaware or fearful. They provide symbols and language for both the patient and the analyst.

Dreams can block therapy as well as advance it. This happens when patients bring in a flood of dream material and use it to fill up the therapy hour; when they prefer to remain in their dream worlds rather than confront life; or when they distance themselves from the dream by refusing to engage their emotions or feelings (Dieckmann, 1991; Whitmont & Perera, 1989). The therapist can observe this for a while and then, at an appropriate moment, bring the situation to the patient's attention and explore the reasons for these defensive maneuvers.

❖ APPLICATIONS

Problems

There is wide latitude in the type of patients Jungians see and the form of therapy they employ. Jungian therapists treat people of all ages, at all levels of functioning. Analytical therapy is suitable for people facing the common problems of life and accompanying symptoms of stress, anxiety, depression, and low self-esteem. It is also useful in dealing with people who have severe personality disorders or psychoses. The problems an analytical psychotherapist chooses to treat are dependent on that analyst's personality, ability, and training. Specific types of therapists seem to attract specific patients, yet each patient creates a different situation. The therapist's technique must be flexible enough to adapt to the particular patient and situation, and firm enough that the therapist works within his or her limits of expertise.

Some of the most interesting applications of analytical psychotherapy involve people with severe personality disorders; hospital and followup care of psychotics; treatment of post-traumatic stress, disturbed children, the aging, the sick, and those gravely ill, dying, or preparing for death. Some Jungian therapists specialize in short-term psychodynamic psychotherapy, treating substance abusers, battered women, or the sexually abused. Some analysts integrate feminism with Jungian theory, often attracting patients who are reevaluating traditional gender roles or who are dealing with sexual trauma. Innovative work is also being done with people who have creative, religious, relationship, or sexual problems.

People who have undergone other depth analyses are increasingly undergoing a Jungian analysis because they feel their earlier analysis did not touch a dimension of their psyche. So, too, some Jungians, especially those who were more archetypally analyzed, seek some type of other therapy to fill gaps in their own self-knowledge.

Patients who adapt well to talking cures are those who have an ability for introspection and are able to regress and yet maintain a working alliance with the therapist. Analytical psychotherapists working with people who have less intact egos, such as borderline personalities, adapt their technique to focus on supportive ego building. Other patients may need to remain in any one of the first three stages of therapy—*confession, elucidation*, and *education*—so that they can learn to live more easily in the human community, have better relationships with others, and establish and maintain themselves through meaningful work.

Analytical psychotherapy is singularly beneficial for those people undergoing a mid-life crisis and concerned with the problems of the second half of life. Dieckmann (1991) mentions three types of people who are drawn toward the process of individuation at midlife: those who find deep meaning within themselves and want to further explore their inner worlds; those who realize they have failed to reach the goals of their youth, or who find these goals are insufficient or no longer compelling; and finally, those who have reached their goals and are confronting problems that came with worldly success. Because the scope of Jung's theory is so wide and concerns final causes as well as the status quo, many are also drawn to analytical psychotherapy who look for some profounder meaning in their lives and are concerned with people's impact on each other and on the world's survival.

Evaluation

Evaluation of the Therapist

A Jungian analyst undergoes a rigorous training program during which he or she is evaluated in classes, in case seminars, in individual supervision, and through appearances before various committees that closely monitor the quality of candidates' patient care as well as their self-knowledge. A combination of clinical and theoretical exams and a written case study and/or thesis round out training based on the depth of the candidate's own analysis. Participation in monthly meetings of individual analytic societies, regional yearly meetings, and international meetings is combined with reading or writing articles in various Jungian clinical journals. Each society of Jungian analysts has education and ethics committees that monitor and review the quality of care therapists deliver.

Evaluation of Therapy

The most convincing and conclusive studies evaluating particular forms of psychodynamic psychotherapy conclude that therapy is more beneficial than no therapy, but that the type of therapy is less important than the quality of the person who delivers it and the match, and/or empathic bond between patient and therapist (e.g., Hunt, 1987). Thus, followers of a specific modality can make only modest claims for their theory's value, even though therapists' and patients' *belief* in that theory enhances positive outcomes.

The evaluation of the success of analytical psychotherapy comes from clinical observation, mainly through single case studies. In them as well as in patients' reports, the patient's quality of life usually improves slowly over the course of the therapy. Dreams can be evaluated by the evolution of the type of images and by changes in their affective content over the course of the analysis. For example, nightmares usually cease, and their terrifying images or threatening figures slowly change into more benign or friendly ones. A specific dream may indicate that the time for the termination of therapy has arrived; this could be as graphic as a dream in which the patient bids good-bye to the therapist before a positive move or journey, or as subtle as one in which the patient not only acquires a piece of beautiful fabric she once dreamed her therapist owned but is now weaving her own material as well.

Subjectively, the improving patient reports symptom relief, looks more alive, has more energy, and often can release and experience blocked or untapped channels of creativity. Relationships with other people improve markedly. The process of growth becomes in dependent of the therapist when patients start to do their own work between sessions, master new and enriching habits of introspection and self-examination, pay attention to their dreams and fantasies, and deal with themselves and others with integrity. An analytical psychotherapist would agree with Freud that learning to love and to work is the key to measuring the outcome of a successful analysis. Jungians would also want to see their patients develop more complete knowledge of, relationship with, and responsibility for all aspects of their psyche. This development often leads patients to grapple with philosophical and religious questions about the meaning of existence, including their personal responsibility to the world in which they find themselves and which they will pass on to others.

Evaluation of Theory

Both qualitative and quantative studies have examined Jung's theory of typology. These types, or personality dimensions, consist of the two basic attitudes of introversion and extraversion and the four functions of thinking, feeling, intuition, and sensation. We all have these qualities to different degrees, but we often prefer one mode over the others. The Myers-Briggs and the Grey-Wheelwright typology tests ascertain a person's predominant attitude and function as well as the relative amounts of each attitude and function in an individual's personality (Quenk, 1993). Both tests are questionnaires that follow Jung's original formulations, determining a person's predominance of introversion and extraversion as well as his or her relative preference for the thinking, feeling, sensing, and intuitive modes of experiencing reality. The tests give a more rounded view of character than does simply looking at a single function or attitude. The Myers-Briggs adds questions to determine whether one perceives things first (as Jung wrote of sensates and intuitives) or judges them first (as both feelers and thinkers do). It yields sixteen different personality types. Many analysts find these typology tests especially beneficial when working with couples. By indicating differences in the way people of differing types tend to interpret their environment, they provide an objective explanation for many problems in communication.

Jung used statistics in his Word Association Tests to display evidence of his theory of complexes. Some analysts make use of these association tests to uncover material in patients who have difficulties in self-exploration. Projective tests such as the Rorschach and the Thematic Apperception Test, which are based on Jung's theories of complex and projection, are also used. Contemporary studies of the validity of projective tests have been less persuasive, but the tests themselves still prove clinically useful.

Treatment

Jung was open to a wide variety of modalities, settings, and styles in his treatment of patients. Today, analytical psychotherapy most often takes place at a regular time and place, for a set fee. The encounter is often face-to-face, with therapist and patient both seated, though many analysts use a couch from time to time or as a matter of course.

Jungian analysts also work with body movement, dramatization, art, sand trays, or an eclectic mixture of these methods. Just as the primary mode of therapy varies among analysts, so too does the timing. Most often sessions in the United States are for fifty minutes once or twice per week, though three times is not uncommon. The timing varies and often includes more frequent and shorter visits for hospitalized clients, disturbed children, and the ill or severely impaired.

Group Therapy

Often as an adjunct to and amplification of individual therapy, individuals will meet in groups of approximately six to ten people. Members are usually patients of the analyst who runs the group, although some analysts will accept referrals. The meetings customarily take place once a week and run for about ninety minutes. The group is usually carefully selected to create a balance of gender, typology, age, and type of problem. Some therapists run single-issue or single-gender groups, though an eclectic mixture of patients is more usual. Undergoing group therapy is often suggested or required of an analyst in training. Patients need adequate ego strength because the situation is apt to be confrontive as well as supportive. Group therapy has been found to be particularly suitable for introverts drawn to Jungian psychotherapy. It is also recommended for patients who tend to intellectualize or aestheticize their analysis or otherwise defend themselves from their feelings and for those who have been unable to translate what they have learned in private therapy into real life.

Group work focuses on therapeutic issues through discussions, dream analysis, active imagination, psychodrama, gestalt, and bioenergetic modalities. The group is most effective, however, when complexes become active and particular issues come to life through the various clashes, alliances, and confrontations between and among members of the group. Participating in group therapy allows individuals to experience themselves interacting with others, experiencing their shared humanity as they reality test, reveal themselves, and give clarifying feedback. Within the group, patients must agree to confidentiality. Whether patients socialize between meetings is up to the group and the particular therapist.

During the course of the meetings, the individual tends to project his or her own shadow (that part of the personality people cannot acknowledge in themselves) onto the group, while the group inevitably picks up on parts of the personality that the individual conceals. Resistances are often more visible in a group than in private therapy and can be dealt with more easily. The group reconstellates the family, so issues of family dynamics arise, including a recreation of sibling rivalries or problems of an individual's position within the family. Each member of the group, therefore, is able to work on family issues in a way not possible in individual therapy. Transference issues with the analyst can be transferred to the group and worked on in this arena as well. An analyst's shadow can also be seen more clearly in the group. Patients who have felt the analyst to be too powerful in individual therapy may be able to express feelings toward the therapist in group work. Patients who have gone through group therapy remark on the difficulty of the process as well as on the depth of feeling engendered through the group's acceptance of their most vulnerable or wounded sides. They report a greater feeling of resiliency, more ease in social settings, and more acceptance of themselves after group work.

Family and Marital Therapy

Bradway and Wheelwright (1978) found that 73 percent of Jungian analysts use or refer their patients to some mode of analytical family therapy. Analysts will see the couple or family sometimes as a unit and sometimes separately or will do conjoint family work. The use of Jungian terminology, especially the concepts of *typology, anima* and *animus, shadow,* and *projection* form a language through which the family or couple can discern and reflect on their own dynamics.

Therapists often administer a typology test to the couple or family members. Through its interpretations, family members realize that one source of their differences may be a typology problem. Dissimilarities can be accepted and worked with more easily when interpreted as a typological clash, while knowledge of each family member's various mixture of attitude and function types — introversion and extraversion, thinking, feeling, sensation, and intuition — can lead to improved family communication. Individual family members often have different typological ways of perceiving reality, and people often tend to choose partners with a typology opposite to their own.

Analysts working with families and couples emphasize family dynamics caused by members' shadow and animus/anima projections onto other family members. Fights arise when a family member projects these, believing the other person is behaving in ways that really belong to the accuser's own shadow or anima/animus. Thus, a predominantly thinking type man might fall prey to inferior feelings and fight his wife through moods while accusing her of his own sulkiness, and she, if she is predominantly a feeling type, might defend herself with theoretical arguments and blame her husband for her own judgmentalism. An argument of this sort is doomed to failure. Scapegoating of a specific individual frequently takes place when the scapegoated person is typologically different from the rest of the family or when the scapegoated person reminds the mother or father of a disliked parent or sibling.

Body/Movement Therapy

Jung encouraged patients to engage in active imagination through body movement or dance. Jung found that by using his own body to mirror the gestures of his psychotic and withdrawn patients at the Burgholzli, he could better understand feelings they were trying to communicate. He found that the body stores, holds, experiences, and communicates psychological and emotional experience as much as, if not more than, words. Joan Chodorow (1982) has described movement as a type of active imagination that, in therapy, accompanies and is followed by discussion. She found that the transference as well as trauma, early or crisis experiences, grief, dreams, fantasies, feelings, and moods can be embodied and expressed in movement. As the patient moves, the therapist observes or serves as a mirror moving along with the patient.

Art Therapy

Jung often suggested that a patient draw or paint an image from a dream or from active imagination. During his own self-analysis, Jung painted his dream and fantasy images; he perceived therapeutic value in doing this, in playing with stones like a child, and later, in sculpting in stone and carving at his retreat in Bollingen. Jung encouraged his patients to do the same in their own analysis through painting, sculpting, and other form-giving methods that provided a feeling and image through which the contents of the unconscious could find expression. He felt this was especially valuable for people who were out of touch with their feelings or who tried to deal with their experience solely through logic.

Analytical psychotherapy encourages art in therapy as a conscious way to express elements of the unconscious. Art therapy is especially useful in working through and integrating traumatic material when isolated images and feeling states tend to explode into consciousness. The expression of these images or feeling states through art releases their archetypal power and domesticates them in a way that gives the survivor a sense of control. Art therapy is useful, as well, in overcoming mental blocks or side-stepping an overly one-sided consciousness. The point of the therapy is not to produce a finished or aesthetically pleasing object but to allow an active dialogue with the unconscious.

Sand Tray Therapy

This method was inspired by Jung's construction of stone "villages" during his self-analysis and then further developed by Dora Kalff, who combined Jung's ideas with Margaret Lowenfeld's World Technique. In Kalff's adaptation, a rectangular box measuring approximately 30 x 20 x 3 inches is filled with sand and becomes a miniature world that a child or adult can shape and form, meanwhile arranging any of the hundreds of figurines the analyst provides. In therapy, the sand tray becomes a world through which complexes, pain, trauma, moods, emotions, and feelings are given expression. Use of the sand tary, like other forms of active imagination, provides a bridge to the unconscious; during the process the child or adult can also recover undeveloped elements of his or her character. Sandplay studies document the efficacy of the procedure (C.G. Jung Institute of San Francisco, 1989). Over the course of therapy, the trays show a progressive change from a primitive and disorganized state, through images representative of vegetation, animals, the shadow and the human, toward more order, peacefulness, and integration. Symbols appearing toward the end of therapy often have a mandala form and tend to evoke a holy feeling. Sand tray therapy with children is useful as a structured and healing form of free play that promotes the child's ego development and unblocks hidden feelings; in adults, it returns the patient to a world of childhood play where lost parts of the personality can again come alive and contribute to self-healing.

Child Analysis

Children pick up and reflect what is going on in their surroundings. This happens to such a degree that Jung once analyzed a parent through the dreams and nightmares of his son. Training in child analysis is required at a growing number of Jungian Institutes and is based on core work by the Jungian analysts Frances Wickes, Erich Neumann, Dora Kalff, and Edith Sullwold. Treatment is based on the theory that children have within themselves what they need for a natural process of growth and self-healing to occur. The process works by providing a safe environment in which the therapist serves as witness, participant, and ally, who not only treats the child but intervenes appropriately so that the child's family and life situation can be improved. During therapy, the child slowly learns to integrate and humanize potentially overwhelming archetypal images. While children's therapy is similar to adults' analytical psychotherapy, it uses a wide variety of tactile and nonverbal modalities. A child finds expression for dreams, fantasies, and fears through sand tray, arts and crafts, clay modeling, musical instruments, and body movement as well as through stories and myths. The therapist provides boundaries and a safe space so that the child can work out problems, strengthen ego and resilience, and become more self-accepting, independent, and better functioning.

Post-Traumatic Stress

In 1934, in a letter to a Dr. Birnie, Jung wrote of the profound biological (as well as psychological) changes that can follow the experience of an overwhelming trauma. He went on to write about repetitive dreams and the way the unconscious keeps bringing the trauma up as if to search for its healing through repetition. Modern research on post-traumatic stress disorder (PTSD) supports Jung's observations and documents similar physical and psychological changes in survivors of wars, abuse, torture, and other overwhelming situations. Werner Engel (1986) has described his work with Nazi concentration camp survivors and their long-lasting feelings of guilt. He states that the power of Jungian psychotherapy lies in the curative value of patient and therapist listening together to a patient's horrors, combined with a belief in self-healing and the application of archetypal theory.

Henry Wilmer (1986) studied 103 patients suffering from PTSD subsequent to their Vietnam service, focusing on their repetitive nightmares. He felt such photographic repetition must have a psychological and/or biological purpose. He shared the pain of one PTSD patient as expressed through his dreams and experience. Accompanying the patient in a receptive, non-interpretive way, Wilmer watched as the patient's nightmares finally began to change. The patient started to wake up, not caught in the frozen repetition of a flashback, but in tears. Healing took place when the patient mourned what had happened, found meaning in his experience, and finally saw his role in the dream shift into one in which he could actively change the outcome.

The Treatment of Psychosis

Jung as a psychiatrist treated a full range of severe mental problems. He discerned a pattern and internal logic in the psychotic utterances and fantasies of patients he treated and concluded that the personality of the patient in a psychosis is dominated by a complex split from reality and/or is overwhelmed by (and identifies with) archetypal images that belong to the collective unconscious. Jung believed that the psychotic's upheaval led to distinct psychosomatic changes as well as chemical changes in the brain. He also speculated that some bodily toxin could produce the psychosis. Today, analytical treatment of psychosis includes listening for the meaning or metaphor behind the symptom so that psychotics' mental worlds and imagery can be used in their healing. Group work, a safe living environment, and art therapy are valuable adjuncts to psychotherapy, as is medication. All help build an environment in which patients can emerge from their chaotic and mythic worlds and prepare for a more regular life. A minority of analytical therapists believe that medication blunts the regression of a psychotic person and prevents the individual from working through the psychosis. Some therapists have run types of home-based therapy, where patients and therapists interact in a home-like setting throughout the day. They report the successful treatment of a schizophrenic episode without the use of drugs and with no relapse; however, no long-range study of this form of therapy has been done.

❖ CASE EXAMPLE

Rochelle, a divorced white woman in her mid-thirties, taught at a community college. Her self-consciousness and anxiety brought her into analysis, as did the nightmares that had plagued her since childhood. She was drawn to Jungian psychotherapy because of a lifelong interest in dreams and a love of myths and fairy tales. She had been in therapy before; it had started off well but ended in disappointment, and she wondered if working with a female analyst this time would make a difference.

During the initial stages of therapy, Rochelle settled into twice-weekly sessions. The following facts emerged during the first months of treatment, often in association with dream material. She remembered little about her childhood except having had an active fantasy and dream life and having been happiest alone, outdoors, or daydreaming. Her family life had been chaotic. For several years while she was in grade school and partly because of her father's illness, Rochelle was sent by her mother to live with a series of relatives. Later she was dispatched to a girls' boarding school where she did well. She was a good student who was active in student government. Rochelle had earned her own living since she was eighteen, putting herself through college with a scholarship and a series of part-time jobs.

She reported being close to neither parent but having more negative feelings toward her mother, blaming her for neglect. Rochelle had a form of negative mother complex expressed in her determination to do everything opposite from the way the mother did things. Rochelle kept clear of her mother psychically through the development of her thinking function, especially in academic work in which she excelled. She typified Jung's further description of this type of unmothered daughter as being awkward, lacking body awareness, and suffering from a variety of uterine problems; in Rochelle's case a hysterectomy had been suggested.

Though Rochelle most often appeared to be dryly rationalistic, there was also a charged emotional component in her personality that revealed itself in the outbursts of tears that accompanied early therapy sessions. Her therapist gave Rochelle typology tests. Rochelle was found to be markedly introverted, with thinking as her primary function followed by intuition; sensation and feeling were conspicuously low. Rochelle gained comfort from reading about these types and learning that she behaved fairly typically for a person with an undeveloped and primitive feeling function.

In the initial stages of therapy, Rochelle exhibited a strong idealizing transference and worked hard during the hour, though she felt to her therapist as if she were encased in ice. (The therapist was primarily an introverted sensation type and so tended to experience things first as inner images or sensations rather than as ideas or emotions.) However, Rochelle took great pleasure in having someone listen to the story of her life and take her dreams seriously. Her therapist kept interpretations to a minimum and directed attention as much as possible to Rochelle's daily life. Rochelle could not accept anything that seemed like criticism from her analyst, but flourished under the analyst's empathic reflection of Rochelle's feelings; gradually she started to look more relaxed and attractive as she felt herself valued and cared for.

Rochelle had one or two women friends but had trouble relating to men. She tended to fall in love rapidly, idealize the man and often negate her own interests to meet his and to help him with his career. Overidealization and a romantic belief in living happily ever after, however, soon turned into hypercriticism and rejection, withdrawal, and flight. Some of these dynamics in her personal life started to appear in the consulting room. Though compliance and admiration marked Rochelle's conscious relationship to her therapist, she seemed to be always on guard. The therapist's countertransference was a strong bodily feeling of distance, at times as if her patient were miles away across the room or vanishing. There was something almost desperate behind the exaggeratedly "Jungian" quality and quantity of the material Rochelle brought to her therapy hour. It was as if Rochelle was trying very hard to produce what she thought her therapist would want, without noticing her therapist's efforts to focus on Rochelle's anxiety symptoms and her outer life. The therapist used the dream material sparingly, primarily as a doorway into the reality of Rochelle's experience. Rochelle concealed from herself her contempt for her analyst's continued emphasis on the here and now and for her focus on Rochelle's physical and psychological condition. When this was brought to Rochelle's attention, she responded with a fierce burst of anger that brought the pain of her negative mother complex to the surface. There ensued a number of months of transference in which Rochelle attacked the analyst as the negative mother while the analyst subjectively felt the misery Rochelle had felt under her mother's care.

Despite the negative transference, however, Rochelle kept turning up for sessions. In response to the therapist's support of Rochelle's sensation function and her need for autonomy, she went for a second opinion concerning her hysterectomy and found that it was not indicated. Rochelle also started to pay attention to her body. About nine months after her decision not to undergo the operation, she enrolled in a dance class upon learning from an acquaintance that her analyst liked to dance.

The analyst did not interpret her behavior but held it in the back of her mind. She continued to pay a hovering, almost free-floating attention to Rochelle's behavior and words as well as to the images and sensations they brought up in her own mind. She noticed that the feeling quality in the room was growing warmer but still contained chilling voids that seemed to parallel Rochelle's own recollection of her past. The therapist felt a sense of foreboding building up with each visit as if Rochelle was accompanied by some chaotic and unspecific feeling of violence.

Rochelle attended a weekend dance/movement seminar at the local Jungian Institute; at the following session as she started to describe a nightmare, her nose started to bleed. A look of horror came over Rochelle's face as she experienced the first of a series of flashbacks accompanied by recurrent nightmares. They concerned the rape and other sexual attacks she had endured as a child after she had been sent to live with a relative who was an elder in their church. He had coerced her into secrecy under the threat of God's wrath, and he explained the blood on the child's bedclothes to the housekeeper as the result of a nose bleed.

The slow recall of discrete images and memories marked a critical point in therapy. Rochelle fell into a depression and entered a needy and fearful regression during which her sessions were increased to four times a week. At this time, Rochelle made considerable use of the clay, art materials, and sand tray that her analyst kept in her office. Most of the history of her trauma came first through her hands, and only later could it be put into words. It took many more months before the gaps in Rochelle's memory were slowly filled in and the story of her early life emerged in a linear way. Rochelle now looked to her therapist as a positive mother figure and felt entirely safe only in the therapy room and its boundaries, though she lashed out at her therapist for causing the return of her memories and for taking away the lovely dreams into which she had escaped.

In her regression, Rochelle found weekends and holidays intolerable but got through them by borrowing a small figure from the sand tray. Her analyst felt great tenderness for her patient as she witnessed Rochelle's experience and shared her pain. She allied herself with her patient's efforts to recall secrets that had long been repressed. She let them unfold in their own order and time, without questioning or probing. Sometimes the therapist felt drained by the quantity of pain that was now flooding the room, and struggled with herself to neither block it nor silence Rochelle. For both analyst and patient, these were difficult times in the analysis, as both allowed the surfacing of the agony that Rochelle had not been able to permit herself to feel before. The therapist found herself increasingly inclined to comfort Rochelle and found herself tempted to break her own boundary rules by extending the hour or letting Rochelle stay on for a cup of tea. She considered how much of her feelings were countertransference and how much something she needed to process further in herself. The analyst knew how crucial it was for her to symbolically hold the transference in this charged arena and not act it out; she also knew that part of the force field generated by Rochelle's initial trauma came from the dangerous pull toward repetition that Rochelle and all incest survivors experience. In order to check that she completely understood her own countertransference issues, the analyst went into supervision with a senior analyst. Through weeks of self-confrontive work, the analyst gained a deeper understanding of the powerfully destructive pull to reenactment that makes incest survivors all too often fall victim to reinjury. Both Rochelle and her therapist succeeded in maintaining their boundaries without cutting off the current between them. [See Zabriskie (1982) and Rutter (1989) for a further discussion of this important subject from a Jungian standpoint.]

Shortly after her therapist had completed her own self-examination, Rochelle emerged from her depression and started intensive work on the transference on a different level. This was accompanied by Rochelle's reading about goddesses and images of powerful female archetypes. At this point, work on the archetypal image of incest started to accompany the personal work. Rochelle came into the session one day with an Irish myth she said both terrified and fascinated her. For a time, its analogies with her own trauma became the focus of much of Rochelle's interest, as she and the therapist began to use the myth as a common metaphor. This caused renewed work on Rochelle's childhood abuse at a deeper but also more universal level.

The myth was about a girl named Saeve, whose relative, a Druid named Dark, pursued her. Unable to escape his advances, she turned herself into a deer and vanished into the woods. Three years later a hero, Fionn, found her and led her to his castle, where she turned back into a beautiful young woman. They lived completely enraptured with each other until Fionn had to leave for battle. Soon after Fionn's departure, Saeve thought she saw him returning; she raced out of the castle to meet him but realized too late that it was the Druid disguised as Fionn. He tapped her with his hazel rod and turned her back into a deer, and they vanished.

Rochelle used this fairy tale to picture her own neurotic patterns of behavior. Through the story, she could start to view them objectively, without shame. The myth gave form and an image to the damage she had experienced from too potent and too early experience of an invasive other. Rochelle gained a feeling for her own horrors through her feelings for Saeve; she also began to understand her defense of splitting off from reality (becoming a deer) when scared and vanishing into daydreams. The story also helped Rochelle comprehend why she seemed incapable of maintaining a relationship, turning every lover from a Fionn into a Druid. Eventually she even recognized that she had internalized the church elder into an inner negative animus who kept judgmentally assaulting her.

As Rochelle's therapy progressed, she stopped turning against the childlike parts of herself that needed to idealize someone as all-good, and she started to forgive herself for what had happened to her. She also started to understand the protective value of splitting off from an intolerable reality and assuming a deer-like disguise. As she did this, that particular defense started to drop away. Rochelle also grew to understand her desire for a savior: what she had experienced was so vile (the touch of the Druid), that what she longed for became impossibly pure (Fionn). She also better understood her self-consciousness and fear of people as well as her feelings of loneliness; she felt she had lived much of her life alone as a deer in the woods hiding in disguise, flight, and illusion instead of being able to maintain a relationship with a man.

Her therapist's accompanying Rochelle on this voyage of discovery allowed her the time to look at the world by means of the separation and division of opposites: the blackest of villains versus the noblest of heroes. Rochelle realized that she was repeatedly searching for Fionn, the hero, protector, and savior, whom she inevitably scanned for the slightest defect, and, just as inevitably, looked upon him, when he showed a failing or two, as an all-evil Druid. She then escaped in deer disguise and in a split-off little-girl vulnerability, yet behind her meltingly doe-like softness lay a self-destructive, self-hating, abuser, rapist animus tearing at her sad child's soul. On the other side, her inner hero tended to become icily rational or heady; he drove Rochelle into unmercifully heroic activity and disdained the dark, the sensual, and unmaidenly feminine inside her. The Druid animus brutalized her inner child-maiden and the deer, while the virtuous animus punished her for the very brutalization she experienced.

At this point Rochelle became kinder to herself. She stopped ricocheting from one opposite to the other and stopped mistaking the dark for the light or turning someone she had thought good into bad as soon as he made a mistake. Her impaired relations with others started to heal as she allowed her therapist to be neither all-light nor all-dark but intermingled. Through confronting and fighting with her analyst, Rochelle started to regain some of her own darkly potent female energy. Now she also started to be able to claim her own needs in a relationship rather than disguise herself as an all-giving woman.

Assimilation of her shadow, not identification with it, grounded Rochelle. Her nightmares lessened in intensity after a watchful and self-contained black cat, whom Rochelle associated with her therapist, started to appear in her dreams sitting on a round rug and silently witnessing the dream's turmoil. Rochelle felt that the female cat figure symbolized something old and complex, as if it held attributes of both a Wise Woman and a Terrible Mother in its centered witnessing. From this center and with the continued empathic witnessing support of her therapist, Rochelle's inner and outer life gradually changed as she mulled over her now-remembered life history and her powerfully archetypal myth and dream material. It was not enough for her to experience something of this intensity in the consulting room; she needed to see what the images meant in her own life. As Rochelle slowly reclaimed and integrated the cat as well as the animus figures and finally the good-enough mother analyst in herself, the black cat figure in her dreams assumed a human form. Rochelle decided to leave an analysis that had taken three and a half years; there followed a newly creative turn in her work, and she also risked loving a quiet and fallible man. Over the next few years, Rochelle returned to her therapy now and then as her complexes occasionally reappeared, but she generally could rely on her own inner therapist for recentering herself.

❖ SUMMARY

Jung pioneered an approach to the psyche that attracts a growing number of people through its breadth of vision and its deep respect for the individual. Rather than pathologizing, Jung looked for the meaning behind symptoms, believing that symptoms held the key to their own cure. Jung discovered methods and techniques for tapping into the self-healing potential in human beings and taught a process that engages therapist and patient alike in a profound and growth-promoting experience. Jung's purpose was to assist psychological development and healing by involving all aspects of the personality.

Analytical personality theory provides a map of the psyche that values the unconscious as much as consciousness, seeing each complementing the other. In the personal realm, the personal conscious (the ego or I) and persona (the social mask) are matched with the personal unconscious. The personal unconscious contains things repressed, forgotten, or at the verge of consciousness as well as the personal shadow (what the ego does not accept in itself), and the animus and anima (ego-alien contrasexual elements). The impersonal or collective unconscious can never be known, but can be pictured as a vast deposit that flows into the personal unconscious and consciousness by means of archetypal images: propensities, motifs, and forms common to all humanity. The interface between the collective and personal unconscious may represent the most archaic and least mapped layer of the psyche.

Complexes grow in this interface. Complexes are energy-filled constellations of psychic elements that have an archetypal core and erupt into consciousness, often in an autonomous way. They are both personal and impersonal. The personal unconscious is created by the individual and ultimately is his or her personal responsibility. Since the collective unconscious is innate and impersonal, it would be an error for the individual to claim its powers or in any way identify with its contents. The unconscious itself is completely neutral and only becomes dangerous to the degree that the ego has a wrong relationship to it or represses it. The impersonal realm is home also to the collective consciousness, the giant matrix of the outer world in which an individual lives his or her life.

The archetype of the Self encompasses the personal unconscious and conscious and a bit of the other realms as they impinge on or seep into the personal. A newborn infant is immersed in the self; it soon splits (or deintegrates) into fragments of ego, consciousness, and unconscious. The task of psychotherapy is to consolidate the ego and let the psyche heal and responsibly enlarge itself so that all the parts of the self can develop, reintegrate, and maintain a more balanced and less egocentric relationship with each other. In analytical psychotherapy it is not enough to understand these concepts and their activity; they must be experientially *felt* by the individual in relation to the past and as they come into play in the therapy room through transference and countertransference. The new understanding then needs to be lived so that the individual can participate in life with integrity. To this end, experiential methods of analytical psychotherapy are especially valuable, as is the therapist's inclusion of the feminine dimension of receptive empathy, groundedness, nurturing, and ability to hold the personality as it develops. This generative approach allows growth and healing to take place alongside what can be gained from insight and interpretation.

Analytical psychotherapy stresses the patient-therapist encounter as one that involves empathy, trust, openness, and risk. Through the interaction of the two personalities and the quality of this relationship, the self-regulating and healing potential of the personality can come into play, repairing old wounds while allowing the individual to grow in self-knowledge. This is why analytical psychotherapy stresses the quality, training, analysis, and continuing self-analysis of therapists.

Depth psychotherapy, as it is understood today, is less than a century old. Jung often wrote of psychology being in its infancy; he believed no one map of its realm could be complete. Depth-oriented psychotherapeutic systems of all types contain more similarities than differences. The systems reflect the language and style of their creator and attract those of like mind. It is as if the founders of the varied schools have each drawn slightly different maps of the same terrain—the human psyche. Though the particular style of these maps varies, those that are still useful have more and more in common as original rivalries are forgotten and each is freer to borrow what it needs from the others. At the same time, a specifically Jungian map may be best for one person, while someone else may need an Adlerian, a Rogerian, a neo-Freudian or some other map.

Jungian psychology is especially inclusive, as its four stages of therapy cover essential elements of the others' theories while adding a particular emphasis on wholeness, completion, and individuation. Analytical psychotherapy allows room for the depths of the collective unconscious and the width of humanity's collective history, art, and culture while grounding itself solidly in the particular individual at a particular time and moment. It is a rich and diverse system that rests on a theory whose practice undergoes constant transformation as the experience and needs of the individual and society both change.

❖ ANNOTATED BIBLIOGRAPHY

Primary Sources

Jung, C.G. (1954–1991). *The collected works of C.G. Jung.* (22 Volumes). Princeton: Princeton University Press. See especially the following:

Jung, C.G. (1957). *The practice of psychotherapy. Collected works*, Vol. 16.

This collection of Jung's essays and lectures includes both basic and in-depth discussions of Jung's methods and techniques of psychotherapy. Part One concerns general problems in psychotherapy and clearly differentiates Jung's theory and practice from that of Freud and Adler. Part Two examines specific topics such as abreaction, Jungian dream analysis, and transference. Most of the book is highly suitable for general study; however, the article on the transference is steeped in Jung's alchemical studies and is somewhat arcane.

Jung, C.G. (1935/1956). *Two essays on analytical psychology. Collected works*, Vol. 17.

A clear, succinct portrayal of the basic concepts of analytical psychology, this book also gives a good account of the early history of depth psychology. Part One sets out Jung's ideas on the psychology of the unconscious, clearly differentiating the personal from the impersonal unconscious. Part Two deals with the ego and its relationship to the personal and collective unconscious and to the task of integration and individuation.

Secondary Sources

Dieckmann, H. (1991). *Methods in analytical psychology.* Wilmette, IL: Chiron.

This is a good introductory primer on the essentials of individual analysis that covers the major problems that present themselves to a therapist. Written by a noted German analyst, it emphasizes traditional Jungian technique as well as the engagement of the whole personality of the therapist and the importance of individual differences. Within this context, the book deals with the problems, methods and technique of analytical psychotherapy in detail, including discussion of the initial interview, frequency, setting, format of the hour, fees, age groups, methods of dream interpretation, transference and countertransference, active imagination, and typology.

Stein, M. (Ed.). (1982). *Jungian analysis.* La Salle, IL: Open Court.

A basic, clear, and tough-minded review of Jungian history, method, techniques, and training by analysts practicing in the United States, this book is an excellent survey of the field (though it omits discussion of the London inspired, Jungian-Kleinian approach). Part One covers history, practice, aims and goals. Part Two explores the structure and dynamics of therapy, including transference and countertransference. Part Three, on methods of analysis, is especially valuable for its wide range, covering dreams, typology, active imagination, movement therapy, sandplay therapy, and group work. Part Four extends Part Three, focusing on analysis with children, the aged, and psychotics; it also looks at gender issues in therapy and at new trends in analytic technique. Part Five is on training.

Sullivan, B. S. (1989) *Psychotherapy grounded in the feminine principle.* Wilmette, IL: Chiron.

This pioneering book synthesizes all aspects of analytical theory while demonstrating the key role that a nurturing, receptive, accommodating stance plays in the therapeutic relationship. Sullivan examines the bias against these more feminine modes in both theory and process; she argues not only for the integration of the feminine dimension, but also sees it as a particularly healing aspect of therapy.

❖ CASE READINGS

Jung, C. G. (1968). An analysis of a patient's dream. *Analytical psychology: Its theory and practice*. New York: Pantheon.

This analysis of a patient's dream is taken from one of Jung's speeches. It demonstrates the ways in which dreams can be used to support clinical inferences.

Klein, B. C. (1986). A piece of the world. Some thoughts about Ruth. *Women and Therapy, 5,* 33–40.

This is the case of an alcoholic woman suffering from post-traumatic stress disorder (PTSD) as a result of her experiences as a nurse in Vietnam.

Lockart, R. A. (1975). Mary's dog is an ear mother: Listening to the voices of psychosis. *Psychological Perspectives, 6,* (2), 144–160.

This case presents a Jungian analysis of a 19-year-old male with auditory hallucinations that are found to have meaning and purpose when examined closely.

Savitz, C. (1986). Healing and wounding. *Journal of Analytical Psychology, 31* (4), 319–340.

Case study of a three-year-old boy with a narcissistic injury. It provides a fascinating account of the way mythology, literature, and archetypal theory enrich therapy.

Spielvogel, A. (1988). The case of Chris. *Journal of Transpersonal Psychology, 20,* 21–28.

This case describes a young man with a highly developed intellectual side and an underdeveloped and neglected emotional side. The case includes good examples of dream analysis.

Sullivan, B. S. (1989). Christina. In *Psychotherapy grounded in the feminine principle* (pp. 164–172). Wilmette, IL: Chiron. [Reprinted in D. Wedding & R. J. Corsini (Eds.) (1995), *Case studies in psychotherapy*. Itasca: F.E. Peacock.]

This case deals with the therapy of a woman plagued with guilt over her decision to leave her husband and children to pursue her own psychological growth. The case is especially useful in highlighting issues of transference and countertransference.

❖ REFERENCES

Beebe, J. (1992). *Integrity in depth*. College Station, TX: Texas A&M Press.

Bradway, K., & Wheelwright, J. B. (1978). The psychological type of the analyst in relation to analytical practice. *Journal of Analytical Psychology, 23* (3), 211–225.

C. G. Jung Institute of San Francisco. (Eds.) (1989). *Sandplay studies: Origins, theory, practice*. Boston: Sigo.

Carotenuto, A. (1992). *The difficult art: A critical discourse on psychotherapy*. Wilmette, IL: Chiron.

Chodorow, J. (1982). Dance/movement and body experience in analysis. In Murray Stein (Ed.), *Jungian analysis* (pp. 192–203). La Salle, IL: Open Court.

Dieckmann, H. (1991). *Methods in analytical psychology*. Wilmette, IL: Chiron.

Douglas, C. (1990). *The woman in the mirror*. Boston: Sigo.

Douglas, C. (1993). *Translate this darkness: The life of Christiana Morgan*. New York: Simon & Schuster.

Ellenberger, H. (1970). *The discovery of the unconscious*. New York: Basic Books.

Engel, W. H. (1986). Postscript. *Quadrant, 19* (1), 62.

Fordham, M. (1969) *Children as individuals*. New York: G. Putnam's Sons.

Fordham, M. (1990). *Jungian psychotherapy*. London: Karnac.

Hannah, B. (1981). *Encounters with the soul: Active imagination as developed by C.G. Jung*. Santa Monica: Sigo.

Hillman, J. (1992). *Emotion: A comprehensive phenomenology of theories and their meanings for therapy*. Evanston, IL: Northwestern University Press.

Hunt, M. (1987, August 30). Navigating the therapy maze. In *The New York Times Magazine*.

Jung, C. G. (1904-7, 1973). Studies in word association. In *Experimental researches. Collected works*, Vol. 2 (pp. 3–482). Princeton: Princeton University Press.

Jung, C. G. (1907/1960). Psychology of dementia praecox. In *The psychogenesis of mental disease. Collected works*, Vol. 3 (pp. 1–151). Princeton: Princeton University Press.

Jung, C. G. (1911/1956). *The psychology of the unconscious*. Revised as *Symbols of transformation. Collected works*, Vol. 5. Princeton: Princeton University Press.

Jung, C. G. (1921/1971). *Psychological types. Collected works*, Vol. 6. Princeton: Princeton University Press.

Jung, C. G. (1927/1970). Woman in Europe. In *Civilization in transition. Collected works*, Vol 10 (pp. 113–133). Princeton: Princeton University Press.

Jung, C. G. (1928–30/1984). *Dream analysis: Notes of the seminar given 1928–1930.* W. McGuire (Ed.) Princeton: Princeton University Press.

Jung, C. G. (1929/1933/1961). Freud and Jung: Contrasts. In *Freud and psychoanalysis. Collected works*, Vol. 4 (pp. 333–340). Princeton: Princeton University Press.

Jung, C. G. (1933/1966). Problems of modern psychotherapy. In *The practice of psychotherapy. Collected works*, Vol. 16. (pp. 53–75). Princeton: Princeton University Press.

Jung, C. G. (1934a/1970). *The development of personality. Collected works*, Vol. 17. Princeton: Princeton University Press.

Jung, C. G. (1934b/1966). The state of psychotherapy today. In *The practice of psychotherapy. Collected works*, Vol. 16 (pp. 157–173). Princeton: Princeton University Press.

Jung, C. G. (1934c/1966). The practical use of dream analysis. In *The practice of psychotherapy. Collected works*, Vol. 16 (pp. 139–161). Princeton: Princeton University Press.

Jung, C. G. (1935a/1966). Principles of practical psychotherapy. In *The practice of psychotherapy. Collected works*, Vol. 16 (pp. 3–20). Princeton: Princeton University Press.

Jung, C. G. (1935b/1966). The relations between the ego and the unconscious. In *Two essays on analytical psychology. Collected works*, Vol. 7 (pp. 132–134). Princeton: Princeton University Press.

Jung, C. G. (1935c/1980). The Tavistock lectures. In *Symbolic life: Miscellaneous writings. Collected works*, Vol. 18 (pp. 1–182). Princeton: Princeton University Press.

Jung, C. G. (1948/1980). Techniques of attitude change conducive to world peace. In *The symbolic life. Collected works*, Vol. 18 (pp. 606–613). Princeton: Princeton University Press.

Jung, C. G. (1957). *The practice of psychotherapy. Collected works*, Vol. 16. Princeton: Princeton University Press.

Jung, C. G. (1965). *Memories, dreams, reflections.* New York: Vintage

Jung, C. G. (1976). *Mysterium Coniunctionis. Collected works*, Vol. 14. Princeton: Princeton University Press.

Maduro, R., & Wheelwright, J. B. (1977). Analytical psychology. In R. Corsini (Ed.), *Current personality theories* (pp. 83–124). Itasca: Peacock.

Quenk, N. L. (1993). *Beside ourselves.* Palo Alto: CPP Books.

Rutter, P. (1989). *Sex in the forbidden zone: When men in power—therapists, doctors, clergy, teachers, and others—betray women's trust.* Los Angeles: Jeremy Tarcher.

Samuels, A. (1985). *Jung and the post-Jungians.* Boston: Routledge & Kegan Paul.

Samuels, A. (Ed.). (1991). *Psychopathology: Contemporary Jungian perspectives.* New York: Guilford Press.

Siegelman, E. Y. (1990). *Metaphor and meaning in psychotherapy.* New York: Guilford Press.

Sullivan, B. S. (1989). *Psychotherapy grounded in the feminine principle.* Wilmette, Illinois: Chiron.

Whitmont, E. C. (1980). Reassessing femininity and masculinity. *Quadrant*, 16 (2), 109–122.

Whitmont, E. C. (1982). Recent influences on the practice of Jungian analysts. In Murray Stein (Ed.), *Jungian analysis* (pp. 335–364). La Salle, IL: Open Court.

Whitmont, E. C., & Perera, S. (1989). *Dreams, a portal to the source.* New York: Routledge.

Wilmer, H. A. (1986). The healing nightmare: A study of the war dreams of Vietnam combat veterans. *Quadrant*, 19 (1), 47–61.

Zabriskie, B. (1982). Incest and myrrh: Father-daughter sex in therapy. *Quadrant*, 15, 4–24.

Carl R. Rogers, 1902–1987

5　Person-Centered Therapy

Nathaniel J. Raskin and
Carl R. Rogers

❖ OVERVIEW

Person-centered therapy is an approach to helping individuals and groups in conflict. Its essentials were formulated by psychologist Carl R. Rogers in 1940. A clearly stated theory, accompanied by the introduction of verbatim transcriptions of psychotherapy, stimulated a vast amount of research on a revolutionary hypothesis: that a self-directed growth process would follow the provision and reception of a particular kind of relationship characterized by genuineness, nonjudgmental caring, and empathy. This hypothesis has been tested over decades in situations involving teachers and students, administrators and staff, facilitators and participants in cross-cultural groups, as well as psychotherapists and clients.

Basic Concepts

Perhaps the most fundamental and pervasive concept in person-centered therapy is trust. The foundation of Rogers's approach is an *actualizing tendency* present in every living organism—in human beings, movement toward the realization of an individual's full potential. Rogers (1980) described this actualizing force as part of a *formative tendency*, observable in the movement toward greater order, complexity, and interrelatedness that can be observed in stars, crystals, and microorganisms, as well as in human beings.

On a practical level, the person-centered approach is built on trust that individuals and groups can set their own goals and monitor their progress toward these goals. This has special meaning in relation to children, students, and workers, who are often viewed as requiring detailed and constant guidance and supervision. In the context of psychotherapy, a person-centered approach assumes that clients can be trusted to select their own therapists, to choose the frequency and length of their therapy, to talk or to be silent, to decide what needs to be explored, to achieve their own insights, and to be the architects of their own lives. Groups are believed to be capable of developing the processes that are right for them, and of resolving conflicts within the group.

One particular person-centered application of trust involves the therapist or facilitator. In the early days of the movement, the focus was entirely on the client. The therapist provided continuous and consistent empathy for the client's perceptions, meanings, and feelings. With experience came growing recognition that it was important for the therapist to be appreciated as a person in the relationship and to be regarded with trust, as is the client.

Eugene Streich formulated one of the earliest statements of this trust:

> When the therapist's capacity for awareness is thus functioning freely and fully without limitations imposed by theoretical formulations of his role, we find that we have, not an individual who may do harm, not a person who must follow certain procedures, but a person able to achieve, through the remarkable integrative capacity of his central nervous system, a balanced, therapeutic, self-growing, other-growth facilitating behavior as a result of all these elements of awareness. To put it another way, when the therapist is less than fully himself—when he denies to awareness various aspects of his experience—then indeed we have all too often to be concerned about his effectiveness, as our failure cases would testify. But when he is most fully himself, when he is his most complete organism, when awareness of experience is most fully operating, then he is to be trusted, then his behavior is constructive. (1951, pp. 8–9)

Some thirty years later Rogers, in more intuitive and spiritual language, expressed such trust in the therapist or group facilitator, referring to it as "one more characteristic" of a growth-promoting relationship, supplementing the classical conditions of congruence, unconditional positive regard, and empathy:

> When I am at my best, as a group facilitator or a therapist, I discover another characteristic. I find that when I am closest to my inner, intuitive self, when I am somehow in touch with the unknown in me, when perhaps I am in a slightly altered state of consciousness in the relationship, then whatever I do seems to be full of healing. Then simply my presence is releasing and helpful. (1986a, p. 198)

Congruence, *unconditional positive regard*, and *empathy* represent basic concepts of person-centered therapy. These are qualities the therapist provides. While distinguishable, these three concepts are intimately related (Rogers, 1957). Congruence refers to the correspondence between the thoughts and the behavior of the therapist; thus, genuineness describes this characteristic. The therapist does not put up a professional front or personal facade.

The therapist also possesses *unconditional positive regard* for the client. The client may be reserved or talkative, address any issue of choice, and come to whatever insights and resolutions are personally meaningful. The therapist's regard for the client will not be affected by these particular choices, characteristics, or outcomes.

The therapist expresses this quality of genuine regard through empathy. Being empathic reflects an attitude of profound interest in the client's world of meanings and feelings. The therapist receives these communications and conveys appreciation and understanding, assisting the client to go further or deeper. The notion that this involves nothing more than a repetition of the client's last words is erroneous. Instead, an interaction occurs in which one person is a warm, sensitive, respectful companion in the typically difficult exploration of another's emotional world. The therapist's manner of responding should be individual, natural, and unaffected. When empathy is at its best, the two individuals are participating in a process comparable to that of a couple dancing, with the client leading and the therapist following.

Basic concepts on the client side of the process include *self-concept, locus-of-evaluation,* and *experiencing.* In focusing on what is important to the person seeking help, client-centered therapists soon discovered that the person's perceptions and feelings about self were of central concern (Raimy, 1948).

A major component of self-concept is self-regard. Clients typically lacked self-esteem. Some of the earliest psychotherapy research projects showed that when clients were rated as successful in therapy, their attitudes toward self became significantly more positive (Sheerer, 1949).

Successful clients were also found to progress along a related dimension, *locus-of-evaluation.* At the same time that they gained in self-esteem, they tended to shift the basis for their standards and values from other people to themselves. People commonly began therapy overly concerned with what others thought of them—their locus-of-evaluation was external. With success in therapy, their attitudes toward others, as toward themselves, became more positive, and they were less dependent on others for their values and standards (Raskin, 1952).

A third central concept in person-centered therapy is *experiencing,* a dimension along which successful clients improved (Rogers, Gendlin, Kiesler, & Truax, 1967), shifting from a rigid mode of experiencing self and world to an attitude of openness and flexibility.

The three therapist qualities and the three client constructs described in this section have been carefully defined, measured, and studied in scores of research projects relating therapist practice to the outcome of psychotherapy. There is considerable evidence that when clients receive congruence, unconditional positive regard, and empathy, their self-concepts become more positive and realistic, they become more self-expressive and self-directed, they become more open and free in their experiencing, their behavior is rated as more mature, and they deal better with stress (Rogers, 1986a).

Other Systems

Person-centered therapy evolved predominantly out of Rogers's own experience. There are both important differences and conceptual similarities between the person-centered approach and other personality theories.

Self-actualization, a concept central to person-centered theory, was advanced most forcefully by Kurt Goldstein. His holistic theory of personality emphasizes that individuals must be understood as totalities and that they strive to actualize themselves (Goldstein, 1959). Goldstein's work and ideas preceded those of Abraham Maslow, a founder of humanistic psychology, who was opposed to the Freudian and behavioral interpretations of human nature.

Heinz Ansbacher, a leading proponent of Adlerian theory, joined Maslow (1968) and Floyd Matson (1969) in recognizing a host of theories and therapists "united by six basic premises of humanistic psychology":

1.   People's creative power is a crucial force, in addition to heredity and environment.

2.   An anthropomorphic model of humankind is superior to a mechanomorphic model.

3.   Purpose, rather than cause, is the decisive dynamic.

4. The holistic approach is more adequate than an elementaristic one.

5. It is necessary to take humans' subjectivity, their opinions and viewpoints, and their conscious and unconscious fully into account.

6. Psychotherapy is essentially based on a good human relationship (Ansbacher, 1977, p. 51).

Among those subscribing to such beliefs were Alfred Adler, William Stern, Gordon Allport, the Gestalt psychologists (Max Wertheimer, Wolfgang Kohler, and Kurt Koffka), the neo-Freudians (Franz Alexander, Erich Fromm, Karen Horney, and Harry Stack Sullivan), post-Freudians, such as Judd Marmor and Thomas Szasz, phenomenological and existential psychologists, such as Rollo May, the cognitive theorist George A. Kelly, and of course, Carl Rogers (Ansbacher, 1977).

While some fundamental person-centered concepts and values are consonant with the proponents of other systems, Rogers and Sanford (1985) have listed a number of distinctive characteristics of client-centered therapy:

1. The hypothesis that certain attitudes in therapists constitute the necessary and sufficient conditions of therapeutic effectiveness;

2. The concept of therapists being immediately present and accessible to clients, relying on moment-to-moment experiencing in each relationship;

3. The intensive and continuing focus on the phenomenological world of the client (hence the term "client-centered");

4. A developing theory that the therapeutic process is marked by a change in the client's manner and immediacy of experiencing, with increasing ability to live more fully in the moment;

5. A concern with the process of personality change, rather than with the structure of personality;

6. Emphasis on the need for continuing research to learn more about psychotherapy;

7. The hypothesis that the same principles of psychotherapy apply to all persons, whether they are categorized as psychotic, neurotic, or normal;

8. A view of psychotherapy as one specialized example of all constructive interpersonal relationships…;

9. A determination to build all theoretical formulations out of the soil of experience, rather than twisting experience to fit a preformed theory;

10. A concern with the philosophical issues that derive from the practice of psychotherapy.

Meador and Rogers (1984) distinguished person-centered therapy from psychoanalysis and from behavior modification in these terms:

> In psychoanalysis the analyst aims to interpret connections between the past and the present for the patient. In person-centered therapy, the therapist facilitates the client's discoveries of the meanings of his or her own current inner experiencing. The psychoanalyst takes the role of a teacher in interpreting insights to the patient and encouraging the development of a transference relationship, a relationship based on the neurosis of the patient. The person-centered therapist presents him- or herself as honestly and transparently as possible and attempts to establish a relationship in which he or she is authentically caring and listening.
>
> In person-centered therapy, transference relationships may begin, but they do not become full-blown. Rogers has postulated that transference relationships develop in an evaluative at-

mosphere in which the client feels the therapist knows more about the client than the client knows about him- or herself, and therefore the client becomes dependent. Person-centered therapists tend to avoid evaluation. They do not interpret for clients, do not question in a probing manner, and do not reassure or criticize clients. Person-centered therapists have not found the transference relationship, central to psychoanalysis, a necessary part of a client's growth or change.

In behavior therapy, *behavior change* comes about through external control of associations to stimuli and the consequences of various responses. In practice, if not in theory, behavior therapy *does* pay attention to the therapy relationship; however, its major emphasis is on specific changes in specific behaviors. In contrast, person-centered therapists believe behavior change evolves from within the individual. Behavior therapy's goal is symptom removal. It is not particularly concerned with the relationship of inner experiencing to the symptom under consideration, or with the relationship between the therapist and the client, or with the climate of their relationship. It seeks to eliminate the symptom as efficiently as possible using the principles of learning theory. Obviously, this point of view is quite contrary to person-centered therapy, which maintains that fully functioning people rely on inner experiencing to direct their behavior. (1984, p. 146)

Raskin (1974), in a comparison of Rogers's practice with those of leaders of five other orientations, found that client-centered therapy was distinctive in providing empathy and unconditional positive regard. Psychoanalytically oriented and eclectic psychotherapists agreed with client-centered theory on the desirability of empathy, warmth, and unconditional positive regard, but examples of rational-emotive, psychoanalytically oriented, and Jungian interviews were ranked low on these qualities.

This study provided a direct comparison of audiotaped samples of therapy done by Rogers and by Albert Ellis, the founder of rational-emotive therapy (RET). Among 12 therapist variables rated by 83 therapist-judges, the only one on which Rogers and Ellis were alike was Self-Confident. The therapy sample by Rogers received high ratings on the following dimensions: Empathy, Unconditional Positive Regard, Congruence, and Ability to Inspire Confidence. The interview by Ellis was rated high on the Cognitive and Therapist-Directed dimensions. Rogers was rated low on Therapist-Directed, while Ellis received a low rating on Unconditional Positive Regard.

This research lends support to the following differences between person-centered therapy and rational-emotive therapy.

1. Unlike RET, the person-centered approach greatly values the therapeutic relationship.

2. Rational-emotive therapists provide much direction, while the person-centered approach encourages the client to determine direction.

3. Rational-emotive therapists work hard to point out deficiencies in their clients' thought processes; person-centered therapists accept and respect their clients' ways of thinking and perceiving.

4. Person-centered therapy characteristically leads to actions chosen by the client; rational-emotive methods include "homework" assignments by the therapist.

5. The person-centered therapist will relate to the client on a feeling level and in a respectful and accepting way; the rational-emotive therapist will be inclined to interrupt this affective process to point out the irrational harm that the client may be doing to self and interpersonal relationships.

While Rogers and Ellis have very different philosophies and methods of trying to help people, they share some very important beliefs and values:

1. A great optimism that people can change, even when they are deeply disturbed;

2. A perception that individuals are often unnecessarily self-critical, and that negative self-attitudes can become positive;

3. A willingness to put forth great effort to try to help people, both through individual therapy and through professional therapy and non-technical writing;

4. A willingness to demonstrate their methods publicly;

5. A respect for science and research.

Similar differences and commonalities will be found when Rogers is compared to other cognitive therapists, such as Aaron Beck.

❖ HISTORY

Precursors

One of the most powerful influences on Carl Rogers was learning that traditional child-guidance methods in which he had been trained did not work very well. At Columbia University's Teachers College he had been taught testing, measurement, diagnostic interviewing, and interpretive treatment. This was followed by an internship at the psychoanalytically oriented Institute for Child Guidance, where he learned to take exhaustive case histories and do projective personality testing. It is important to note that Rogers originally went to a Rochester child-guidance agency believing in this diagnostic, prescriptive, professionally impersonal approach, and it was only after actual experience that he concluded that it was not effective. As an alternative, he tried listening and following the client's lead rather than assuming the role of the expert. This worked better, and he discovered some theoretical and applied support for this alternative approach in the work of Otto Rank and his followers at the University of Pennsylvania School of Social Work and the Philadelphia Child Guidance Clinic. One particularly important event was a three-day seminar in Rochester with Rank (Rogers & Haigh, 1983). Another was his association with a Rankian-trained social worker, Elizabeth Davis, from whom "I first got the notion of responding almost entirely to the feelings being expressed. What later came to be called the reflection of feeling sprang from my contact with her" (Rogers & Haigh, 1983, p. 7).

Rogers's methodology and, later, his theory, grew out of the soil of his own experience. At the same time, a number of links to Otto Rank are apparent in Rogers's early work.

The following elements of Rankian theory bore a close relationship to principles of nondirective therapy:

1. The individual seeking help is not simply a battleground of impersonal forces such as id and superego, but has personal creative powers.

2. The aim of therapy is acceptance by the individual of self as unique and self-reliant.

3. In order to achieve this goal, the client rather than the therapist must become the central figure in the therapeutic process.

4. The therapist can be neither an instrument of love, which would make the patient more dependent, nor an instrument of education, which attempts to alter the individual.

5. The goals of therapy are achieved by the patient not through an explanation of the past, which the client would resist if interpreted, and which, even if accepted, would

lessen responsibility for present adjustment, but rather through experiencing the present in the therapeutic situation (Raskin, 1948, pp. 95–96).

Rank explicitly, eloquently, and repeatedly rejected therapy by technique and interpretation, stating:

> Every single case, yes every individual hour of the same case, is different, because it is derived momentarily from the play of forces given in the situation and immediately applied. My technique consists essentially in having no technique, but in utilizing as much as possible experience and understanding that are constantly converted into skill but never crystallized into technical rules which would be applicable ideologically. There is a technique only in an ideological therapy where technique is identical with theory and the chief task of the analyst is interpretation (ideological), not the bringing to pass and granting of experience. (1945, p. 105)

Rank is obscure about his actual practice of psychotherapy, particularly the amount and nature of his activity during the treatment hour. Unsystematic references in *Will Therapy* (1945) reveal that, despite his criticism of educational and interpretive techniques and his expressed value of the patient being his or her own therapist, he assumed a position of undisputed power in the relationship.

Beginnings

Carl Ransom Rogers was born in Oak Park, Illinois, on January 8, 1902. Rogers's parents believed in hard work, responsibility, and religious fundamentalism and frowned on activities such as drinking, dancing, and card playing. The family was characterized by closeness and devotion but did not openly display affection. While in high school, Carl worked on the family farm, and he became interested in experimentation and the scientific aspect of agriculture. He entered the University of Wisconsin, following his parents and older siblings, as an agriculture major. Rogers also carried on his family's religious tradition. He was active in the campus YMCA and was chosen to be one of ten American youth delegates to the World Student Christian Federation's Conference in Peking, China, in 1922. At that time he switched his major from agriculture to history, which he thought would better prepare him for a career as a minister. After graduating from Wisconsin in 1924 and marrying Helen Elliott, a childhood friend, he entered the Union Theological Seminary. Two years later, and in part as a result of taking several psychology courses, Rogers moved "across Broadway" to Teachers College, Columbia University, where he was exposed to what he later described as "a contradictory mixture of Freudian, scientific, and progressive education thinking" (Rogers & Sanford, 1985, p. 1374).

After Teachers College, Rogers worked for twelve years at a child-guidance center in Rochester, New York, where he soon became an administrator as well as a practicing psychologist. He began writing articles and became active at a national level. His book, *The Clinical Treatment of the Problem Child*, was published in 1939, and he was offered a professorship in psychology at Ohio State University.

Once at Ohio State, Rogers began to teach newer ways of helping problem children and their parents.

In 1940, Rogers was teaching an enlightened distillation of child-guidance practices described in *The Clinical Treatment of the Problem Child*. From his point of view, this approach represented a consensual direction in which the field was moving and was evolutionary rather than revolutionary. The clinical process began with an assessment, including testing of children and interviewing of parents, and the results of assessment provided the basis for a treatment plan. In treatment, nondirective principles were followed.

Rogers's views became more radical. His presentation at the University of Minnesota, on December 11, 1940, entitled "Some Newer Concepts in Psychotherapy," is the single event most often identified with the birth of client-centered therapy.

Rogers decided to expand this talk into a book titled *Counseling and Psychotherapy* (1942). The book, which included an electronically recorded eight-interview case, described the generalized process in which a client begins with a conflict situation and a predominance of negative attitudes and moves toward insight, independence, and positive attitudes. Rogers hypothesized that the counselor promoted such a process by avoiding advice and interpretation and by consistently recognizing and accepting the client's feelings. Research corroborating this new approach to counseling and psychotherapy was offered, including the first (Porter, 1943) of what soon became a series of pioneering doctoral dissertations on the process and outcomes of psychotherapy. In a very short time, an entirely new approach to psychotherapy was born, as was the field of psychotherapy research. This approach and its accompanying research led to the eventual acceptance of psychotherapy as a primary professional function of clinical psychologists.

After serving as Director of Counseling Services for the United Service Organizations during World War II, Rogers was appointed Professor of Psychology at the University of Chicago and became head of the university's counseling center. The twelve years during which Rogers remained at Chicago were a period of tremendous growth in client-centered theory, philosophy, practice, research, applications, and implications. In 1957, Rogers published a classic "necessary and sufficient conditions" paper in which congruence and unconditional positive regard were added to empathy as three essential therapist-offered conditions of therapeutic personality change. This was followed by a comprehensive and rigorous theory of therapy, personality, and interpersonal relationships (Rogers, 1959b). Rogers's philosophy of the "exquisitely rational" nature of the behavior and growth of human beings was further articulated and related to the thinking of Sören Kierkegaard, Abraham Maslow, and others. The practice of client-centered therapy deepened and broadened. The therapist was also more fully appreciated as a person in the therapeutic relationship. Psychotherapy research, which had begun so auspiciously at Ohio State, continued with investigations by Godfrey T. Barrett-Lennard (1962), John Butler and Gerard Haigh (1954), Desmond Cartwright (1957), Eugene Gendlin (1961), Nathaniel Raskin (1952), Julius Seeman (1959), John Shlien (1964), and Stanley Standal (1954), among others.

At Ohio State, there was a sense that client-centered principles had implications beyond the counseling office. At Chicago, this was made most explicit by the empowerment of students and the counseling center staff. About half of Rogers's *Client-Centered Therapy* (1951) was devoted to applications of client-centered therapy, with additional chapters on play therapy, group therapy, and leadership and administration.

In 1957, Rogers accepted a professorship in psychology and psychiatry at the University of Wisconsin. With the collaboration of associates and graduate students, a massive research project was mounted, based on the hypothesis that hospitalized schizophrenics would respond to a client-centered approach (Rogers, Gendlin, Kiesler & Truax, 1967). Two relatively clear conclusions emerged from a complex maze of results: (1) the most successful patients were those who had experienced the highest degree of accurate empathy, and (2) it was the client's, rather than the therapist's, judgment of the therapy relationship that correlated more highly with success or failure.

Current Status

Rogers left the University of Wisconsin and full-time academia and began living in La Jolla, California, in 1964. He was a resident fellow for four years at the Western Behavioral

Sciences Institute and then, starting in 1968, at the Center for Studies of the Person. In more than two decades in California, Rogers wrote books on a person-centered approach to teaching and educational administration, on encounter groups, on marriage and other forms of partnership, and on the "quiet revolution" that he believed would emerge with a new type of "self-empowered person." Rogers believed this revolution had the potential to change "the very nature of psychotherapy, marriage, education, administration, and politics" (Rogers, 1977). These books were based on observations and interpretations of hundreds of individual and group experiences.

A special interest of Rogers and his associates was the application of a person-centered approach to international conflict resolution. This resulted in trips to South Africa, Eastern Europe, and the Soviet Union, as well as in meetings with Irish Catholics and Protestants and with representatives of nations involved in Central American conflicts (Rogers & Ryback, 1984). In addition to Rogers's books, a number of valuable films and videotapes have provided data for research on the basic person-centered hypothesis that individuals and groups who have experienced empathy, congruence, and unconditional positive regard will go through a constructive process of self-directed change.

Since 1982, there have been biennial international forums on the Person-Centered Approach, meeting in Mexico, England, the United States, Brazil, the Netherlands, and Greece. Alternating with these meetings have been international conferences on Client-Centered and Experiential Psychotherapy in Belgium, Scotland, and Austria.

The *Person-Centered Review*, "an international journal of research, theory, and application," was initiated by David Cain in 1986 with a worldwide editorial board. The *Review* was succeeded, in 1992, by *The Person-Centered Journal*, co-edited by Jerold Bozarth and Fred Zimring. Zimring and Raskin (1992), in a volume on the history of psychotherapy during the first hundred years of the American Psychological Association, wrote:

> The *Review* has published articles about many aspects of client-centered therapy. In addition, *Client-Centered and Experiential Psychotherapy in the Nineties* (Lietaer, Rombauts, & Van Balen, 1990) contains many papers about ...the use of the approach with various populations... children and child therapy...family and couples therapy...disturbed clients...and clients who are working with fears of death and dying.

❖ PERSONALITY

Theory of Personality

Rogers moved from a disinterest in psychological theory to the development of a rigorous nineteen-proposition "theory of therapy, personality, and interpersonal relationships" (Rogers, 1959b). On one level, this signified a change in Rogers's respect for theory. On another, this comprehensive formulation can be understood as a logical evolution. His belief in the important of the child's conscious attitudes toward self and self-ideal was central to the test of personality adjustment he devised for children (Rogers, 1931). The portrayal of the client's growing through a process of reduced defensiveness and of self-directed expansion of self-awareness was described in a paper on the processes of therapy (Rogers, 1940). Rogers wrote here of a gradual recognition and admission of a real self with its childish, aggressive, and ambivalent aspects as well as more mature components. As data on personality changes in psychotherapy started to accumulate rapidly, with the objective analyses of verbatim interviews, Rogers found support for his belief that the facts are always friendly, despite some results at variance with his hypotheses.

As outgoing president of the American Psychological Association, Rogers summed up this perspective:

> Client-centered therapy has led us to try to adopt the client's perceptual field as the basis for genuine understanding. In trying to enter this internal world of perception…we find ourselves in a new vantage point for understanding personality dynamics.…We find that behavior seems to be better understood as a reaction to this reality-as-perceived. We discover that the way in which the person sees himself, and the perceptions he dares not take as belonging to himself, seem to have an important relationship to the inner peace which constitutes adjustment. We discover…a capacity for the restructuring and reorganization of self, and consequently the re-organization of behavior, which has profound social implications. We see these observations, and the theoretical formulations which they inspire, as a fruitful new approach for study and research in various fields of psychology. (1947, p. 368)

Rogers expanded his observations into a theory of personality and behavior that he described in *Client-Centered Therapy* (1951). This theory is based on nineteen basic propositions:

1. Every individual exists in a continually changing world of experience of which he is the center.

2. The organism reacts to the field as it is experienced and perceived. This perceptual field is, for the individual, "reality."

3. The organism reacts as an organized whole to this phenomenal field.

4. The organism has one basic tendency and striving—to actualize, maintain, and enhance the experiencing organism.

5. Behavior is basically the goal-directed attempt of the organism to satisfy its needs as experienced, in the field as perceived.

6. Emotion accompanies and in general facilitates such goal-directed behavior, the kind of emotion being related to the seeking versus the consummatory aspects of the behavior, and the intensity of the emotion being related to the perceived significance of the behavior for the maintenance and enhancement of the organism.

7. The best vantage point for understanding behavior is from the internal frame of reference of the individual himself.

8. A portion of the total perceptual field gradually becomes differentiated as the self.

9. As a result of interaction with the environment, and particularly as a result of evaluational interaction with others, the structure of self is formed—an organized, fluid, but consistent conceptual pattern of perceptions of characteristics and relationships of the "I" or the "me," together with values attached to these concepts.

10. The values attached to experiences, and the values which are a part of the self structure, in some instances are values experienced directly by the organism, and in some instances are values introjected or taken over from others, but perceived in distorted fashion, as if they had been experienced directly.

11. As experiences occur in the life of the individual, they are either (a) symbolized, perceived, and organized into some relationship to the self, (b) ignored because there is no perceived relationship to the self-structure, or (c) denied symbolization or given a distorted symbolization because the experience is inconsistent with the structure of the self.

12. Most of the ways of behaving which are adopted by the organism are those which are consistent with the concept of self.

13. Behavior may, in some instances, be brought about by organic experiences and needs which have not been symbolized. Such behavior may be inconsistent with the structure of the self, but in such instances the behavior is not "owned" by the individual.

14. Psychological maladjustment exists when the organism denies to awareness significant sensory and visceral experiences, which consequently are not symbolized and organized into the gestalt of the self-structure. When this situation exists, there is a basis for potential psychological tension.

15. Psychological adjustment exists when the concept of the self is such that all the sensory and visceral experiences of the organism are, or may be, assimilated on a symbolic level into a consistent relationship with the concept of self.

16. Any experience which is inconsistent with the organization or structure of self may be perceived as a threat, and the more of these perceptions there are, the more rigidly the self-structure is organized to maintain itself.

17. Under certain conditions, involving primarily complete absence of any threat to the self-structure, experiences which are inconsistent with it may be perceived and examined, and the structure of self revised to assimilate and include such experiences.

18. When the individual perceives and accepts into one consistent and integrated system all his sensory and visceral experiences, then he is necessarily more understanding of others and is more accepting of others as separate individuals.

19. As the individual perceives and accepts into his self-structure more of his organic experiences, he finds that he is replacing his present value system—based so largely upon introjections which have been distortedly symbolized—with a continuing organismic valuing process. (pp. 481–533)

Rogers comments that

> This theory is basically phenomenological in character, and relies heavily upon the concept of the self as an explanatory construct. It pictures the end-point of personality development as being a basic congruence between the phenomenal field of experience and the conceptual structure of the self—a situation which, if achieved, would represent freedom from internal strain and anxiety, and freedom from potential strain; which would represent the maximum in realistically oriented adaptation; which would mean the establishment of an individualized value system having considerable identity with the value system of any other equally well-adjusted member of the human race. (p. 532)

Further investigations of these propositions were conducted at the University of Chicago Counseling Center in the early 1950s in carefully designed and controlled studies. Stephenson's (1953) Q-technique was used to measure changes in self-concept and self-ideal during and following therapy and in a no-therapy control period. Many results confirmed Rogers's hypotheses, e.g., a significant increase in congruence between self and ideal occurred during therapy, and changes in the perceived self were toward better psychological adjustment (Rogers & Dymond, 1954).

Rogers's personality theory has been described as growth-oriented rather than developmental. While this is accurate, it does not acknowledge Rogers's sensitivity to the attitudes with which children are confronted, beginning in infancy:

> While I have been fascinated by the horizontal spread of the person-centered approach into so many areas of our life, others have been more interested in the vertical direction and are discovering the profound value of treating the *infant*, during the whole birth process, as a person who should be understood, whose communications should be treated with respect, who should

be dealt with empathically. This is the new and stimulating contribution of Frederick Leboyer, a French obstetrician who...has assisted in the delivery of at least a thousand infants in what can only be called a person-centered way. (Rogers, 1977, p. 31)

Rogers goes on to describe the infant's extreme sensitivity to light and sound, the rawness of the skin, the fragility of the head, the struggle to breathe, etc., and the specific ways in which Leboyer has taught parents and professionals to provide a beginning life experience that is caring, loving, and respectful.

This sensitivity to children was further expressed in Rogers's explanation of his fourth proposition *(The organism has one basic tendency and striving—to actualize, maintain, and enhance the experiencing organism)*:

> The whole process (of self-enhancement and growth) may be symbolized and illustrated by the child's learning to walk. The first steps involve struggle, and usually pain. Often it is true that the immediate reward involved in taking a few steps is in no way commensurate with the pain of falls and bumps. The child may, because of the pain, revert to crawling for a time. Yet the forward direction of growth is more powerful than the satisfactions of remaining infantile. Children will actualize themselves, in spite of the painful experiences of so doing. In the same way, they will become independent, responsible, self-governing, and socialized, in spite of the pain which is often involved in these steps. Even where they do not, because of a variety of circumstances, exhibit the growth, the tendency is still present. Given the opportunity for clear-cut choice between forward-moving and regressive behavior, the tendency will operate. (Rogers, 1951, pp. 490–491)

One of Rogers's hypotheses about personality (Proposition 8) was that a part of the developing infant's private world becomes recognized as "me," "I," or "myself." Rogers described infants, in the course of interacting with the environment, as building up concepts about themselves, about the environment, and about themselves in relation to the environment.

Rogers's next suppositions are crucial to his theory of how development may proceed either soundly or in the direction of maladjustment. He assumes that very young infants are involved in "direct organismic valuing," with very little or no uncertainty. They have experiences such as "I am cold, and I don't like it," or "I like being cuddled," which may occur even though they lack descriptive words or symbols for these examples. The principle in this natural process is that the infant positively values those experiences that are perceived as self-enhancing and places a negative value on those that threaten or do not maintain or enhance the self.

This situation changes once children begin to be evaluated by others (Holdstock & Rogers, 1983). The love they are given and the symbolization of themselves as lovable children become dependent on behavior. To hit or to hate a baby sibling may result in the child's being told that he or she is bad and unlovable. The child, to preserve a positive self-concept, may distort experience.

> It is in this way...that parental attitudes are not only introjected, but...are experienced...in distorted fashion, *as if* based on the evidence of one's own sensory and visceral equipment. Thus, through distorted symbolization, expression of anger comes to be "experienced" as bad, even though the more accurate symbolization would be that the expression of anger is often experienced as satisfying or enhancing.... The "self" which is formed on this basis of distorting the sensory and visceral evidence to fit the already present structure acquires an organization and integration which the individual endeavors to preserve. (Rogers, 1951, pp. 500–501)

This type of interaction may sow the seeds of confusion about self, self-doubt, and disapproval of self, and reliance upon the evaluation of others. Rogers indicated that these consequences may be avoided if the parent can accept the child's negative feelings and the child as a whole while refusing to permit certain behaviors such as hitting the baby.

Variety of Concepts

Various terms and concepts appear in the presentation of Rogers's theory of personality and behavior that often have a unique and distinctive meaning in this orientation.

Experience

Experience refers to the private world of the individual. At any moment, some of this is conscious; for example, we feel the pressure of the pen against our fingers as we write. Some of it may be difficult to bring into awareness, such as the idea, "I am an aggressive person." While people's actual awareness of their total experiential field may be limited, each individual is the only one who can know it completely.

Reality

For psychological purposes, reality is basically the private world of individual perceptions, though for social purposes reality consists of those perceptions that have a high degree of communality among various individuals. Two people will agree on the reality that a particular person is a politician. One sees her as a good woman who wants to help people and, based on this reality, votes for her. The other person's reality is that the politician appropriates money to win favor, and therefore this person votes against her. In therapy, changes in feelings and perceptions and, therefore, reality may occur.

The Organism Reacting as an Organized Whole

A person may be hungry, but because of a report to complete, will skip lunch. In psychotherapy, clients often become more clear about what is more important to them, resulting in behavioral changes directed toward the clarified goals. A politician may decide not to run for office because he decides that his family life is more important.

The Organism's Actualizing Tendency

This is a central tenet in the writings of Kurt Goldstein, Hobart Mowrer, Harry Stack Sullivan, Karen Horney, and Andras Angyal, to name just a few. The child's painful struggle to learn to walk is an example. It is Rogers's belief and the belief of most other personality theorists that, given a free choice and in the absence of external force, individuals prefer to be healthy rather than sick, to be independent rather than dependent, and in general to further the optimal development of the total organism.

The Internal Frame of Reference

This is the perceptual field of the individual. It is the way the world appears and the meanings attached to experience and feelings. From the person-centered point of view, this internal frame of reference provides the fullest understanding of why people behave as they do. It is to be distinguished from external judgments of behavior, attitudes, and personality.

The Self, Concept of Self, Self-structure

"These terms refer to the organized, consistent, conceptual Gestalt composed of perceptions of the characteristics of the 'I' or 'me' and the perceptions of the relationships of the 'I' or 'me' to others and to various aspects of life, together with the values attached to these perceptions. It is a Gestalt available to awareness although not necessarily in awareness. It is a fluid and changing process, but at any given moment it…is at least partially definable in operational terms" (Meador & Rogers, 1984, p. 158).

Symbolization

This is the process by which the individual becomes aware or conscious of an experience. There is a tendency to deny symbolization to experiences at variance with the concept of self—e.g., people who think of themselves as truthful will tend to resist the symbolization of an act of lying. Ambiguous experiences tend to be symbolized in ways that are consistent with self-concept. A speaker lacking in self-confidence may symbolize a silent audience as unimpressed; one who is confident may symbolize such a group as attentive and interested.

Psychological Adjustment or Maladjustment

This refers to the consistency, or lack of consistency, between an individual's sensory and visceral experiences and the concept of self. A self-concept that includes elements of weakness and imperfection facilitates the symbolization of failure experiences. The need to deny or distort such experiences does not exist and therefore fosters a condition of psychological adjustment.

Organismic Valuing Process

This is an ongoing process in which individuals freely rely on the evidence of their own senses for making value judgments. This is in distinction to a fixed system of introjected values characterized by "oughts" and "shoulds" and by what is supposed to be right or wrong. The organismic valuing process is consistent with the person-centered hypothesis of confidence in the individual and, even though established by each individual, makes for a highly responsible socialized system of values and behavior. The responsibility derives from people making choices on the basis of their direct, organic processing of situations, in contrast to acting out of fear of what others may think of them or what others have taught them is the way to think and act.

The Fully Functioning Person

Rogers defined those who rely on organismic valuing processes as fully functioning people, able to experience all of their feelings, afraid of none of them, allowing awareness to flow freely in and through their experiences. Seeman (1984) has been involved in a 25-year research program to clarify and describe the qualities of such optimally functioning individuals. These empirical studies highlight the possession of a positive self-concept, greater physiological responsiveness, and an efficient use of the environment.

❖ PSYCHOTHERAPY

Theory of Psychotherapy

The basic theory of person-centered therapy is that if the therapist is successful in convey-
ing genuineness, unconditional positive regard, and empathy, then the client will respond
with constructive changes in personality organization. Research has demonstrated that
these qualities can be made real in a relationship and can be conveyed and appreciated in
a short time. Changes in self-acceptance, immediacy of experiencing, directness of relating, and movement toward an internal locus-of-evaluation may occur in short-term intensive workshops or even in single interviews.

After a four-day workshop of psychologists, educators, and other professionals conducted by Rogers and R. C. Sanford in Moscow, participants reported their reactions. The
following is a typical response:

> This is just two days after the experience and I am still a participant. I am a psychologist, not a
> psychotherapist. I have known Rogers's theory but this was a process in which we were person-
> ally involved. I didn't realize how it applied. I want to give several impressions. First was the ef-
> fectiveness of this approach. It was a kind of process in which we all learned. Second, this
> process was moving, without a motor. Nobody had to lead it or guide it. It was a self-evolving
> process. It was like the Chekhov story where they were expectantly awaiting the piano player
> and the piano started playing itself. Third, I was impressed by the manner of Carl and Ruth. At
> first I felt they were passive. Then I realized it was the silence of understanding. Fourth, I want
> to mention the penetration of this process into my inner world. At first I was an observer, but
> then the approach disappeared altogether. I was not simply surrounded by this process, I was ab-
> sorbed into it! It was a revelation to me. We started moving. I wasn't simply seeing people I had
> known for years, but their feelings. My fifth realization was my inability to control the flow of
> feelings, the flow of the process. My feelings tried to put on the clothes of my words. Sometimes
> people exploded; some even cried. It was a reconstruction of the system of perception. Finally,
> I want to remark on the high skill of Carl and Ruth [Sanford], of their silences, their voices,
> their glances. It was always some response and they were responded to. It was a great phenom-
> enon, a great experience. (Rogers, 1987, pp. 298–299)

This kind of experience speaks against the perception of the person-centered approach as safe, harmless, innocuous, and superficial. It is intended to be safe, but clearly it
can also be powerful.

Empathy

Empathy, in person-centered therapy, is an active, immediate, continuous process. The
counselor makes a maximum effort to get within and to *live* the attitudes expressed instead
of observing them, diagnosing them, or thinking of ways to make the process go faster.
Such understanding must be acquired through intense, continuous and active attention to
the feelings of others, to the exclusion of any other type of attention (Rogers, 1951).

The accuracy of the therapist's empathic understanding has often been emphasized,
but more important is the therapist's interest in appreciating the world of the client and offering such understanding with the willingness to be corrected. This creates a process in
which the therapist gets closer and closer to the client's meanings and feelings, developing
an ever-deepening relationship based on respect for and understanding of the other person.

Person-centered therapists vary in their views of the empathic understanding process.
Some aim to convey an understanding of just what the client wishes to communicate.
For Rogers, it felt right not only to clarify meanings of which the client was aware, but also

those just below the level of awareness. Rogers was especially passionate about empathy's not being exemplified by a technique such as "reflection of feeling," but by the therapist's sensitive immersion in the client's world of experience.

Unconditional Positive Regard

Other terms for this condition are *warmth, acceptance, nonpossessive caring,* and *prizing.*

> When the therapist is experiencing a positive, nonjudgmental, acceptant attitude toward whatever the client *is* at that moment, therapeutic movement or change is more likely. It involves the therapist's willingness for the client to *be* whatever immediate feeling is going on — confusion, resentment, fear, anger, courage, love, or pride....When the therapist prizes the client in a total rather than a conditional way, forward movement is likely. (Rogers, 1986a, p. 198)

Congruence

Rogers regarded congruence as

> the most basic of the attitudinal conditions that foster therapeutic growth....[it] does not mean that the therapist burdens the client with all of his or her problems or feelings. It does not mean that the therapist blurts out impulsively any attitudes that come to mind. It does mean, however, that the therapist does not deny to himself or herself the feelings being experienced and that the therapist is willing to express and to be open about any persistent feelings that exist in the relationship. It means avoiding the temptation to hide behind a mask of professionalism. (Rogers & Sanford, 1985, p. 1379)

Correspondingly, an effective way of dealing with the common occurrence of therapist fatigue is to express it. This strengthens the relationship because the therapist is not trying to cover up a real feeling. It may also reduce or eliminate the fatigue and restore the therapist to a fully attending and empathic state.

Implied Therapeutic Conditions

There are three other conditions in addition to the "therapist-offered" conditions of empathy, congruence, and unconditional positive regard (Rogers, 1957):

1. The client and therapist must be in psychological contact.
2. The client must be experiencing some anxiety, vulnerability, or incongruence.
3. The client must receive or experience the conditions offered by the therapist.

Rogers described the first two as preconditions for therapy. The third, the reception by the client of the conditions offered by the therapist, sometimes overlooked, is essential. Research relating therapeutic outcome to empathy, congruence, and unconditional positive regard based on external judgments of these variables is moderately supportive of the person-centered hypothesis. If the ratings are done by clients themselves, the relationship to outcome is much stronger. Orlinsky and Howard (1978) reviewed 15 studies relating client perception of empathy to outcome and found that 12 supported the critical importance of perceived empathy.

Process of Psychotherapy

The practice of person-centered therapy dramatizes its differences from most other orientations. Therapy begins immediately, with the therapist trying to understand the client's world in whatever way the client wishes to share it. The first interview is not used to take a history, to arrive at a diagnosis, to determine if the client is treatable, or to establish the length of treatment.

The therapist immediately shows respect for clients, allowing them to proceed in whatever way is comfortable for them. She listens without prejudice. She does not have her own agenda. She is open to either positive or negative feelings, speech or silence. The first hour may be the first of hundreds or it may be the only one; this is for the client to determine. If the client has questions, the therapist tries to recognize and to respond to whatever feelings are implicit in the questions. "How am I going to get out of this mess?" may be the expression of the feeling, *My situation seems hopeless.* The therapist will convey recognition and acceptance of this attitude. If this question is actually a plea for suggestions, the therapist may reply that she does not have the answers, but hopes she can help the client find the ones that are right for him. There is a willingness to stay with the client in moments of confusion and despair. There is a realization that reassurance and easy answers are not helpful and show a lack of respect for the client.

The therapist looks to the client for decisions about the timing and frequency of therapy. The therapist must respect her own availability, but is guided as much as possible by scheduling that feels right to the client. Person-centered therapists commonly share with their clients the responsibility for fee setting and manner of payment. In a money-oriented society, this is an opportune area for showing respect for the client.

Regard is also demonstrated through discussion of options such as group therapy and family therapy, in contrast to therapists of other orientations who "put" the client in a group or make therapy conditional on involvement of the whole family. This is not to be interpreted as meaning that the client is allowed to dictate the circumstances of therapy, but to make clear that the client is a vital partner in determining these conditions. On many issues, the client is regarded as the expert.

An Interview Illustrating the Process of Therapy

It has always been characteristic of the person-centered approach to illustrate its principles with verbatim accounts. This has the advantage of depicting the interaction between therapist and client more exactly and gives readers the opportunity to agree or to differ with the interpretation of the data.

The following is a demonstration interview carried out by Carl Rogers in 1983. Because of space limitations, the middle third of the interview has been omitted. Asterisks indicate words that could not be made out in the transcription.

> Therapist 1: OK, I think I'm ready. And you…ready?
> Client 1: Yes.
> T-2: I don't know what you might want to talk about, but I'm very ready to hear. We have half an hour, and I hope that in that half an hour we can get to know each other as deeply as possible, but we don't need to strive for anything. I guess that's my feeling. Do you want to tell me whatever is on your mind?
> C-2: I'm having a lot of problems dealing with my daughter. She's 20 years old; she's in college; I'm having a lot of trouble letting her go…. And I have a lot of guilt feelings about her; I have a real need to hang on to her.
> T-3: A need to hang on so you can kind of make up for the things you feel guilty about—is that part of it?
> C-3: There's a lot of that…Also, she's been a real friend to me, and filled my life…And it's very hard***a lot of empty places now that she's not with me.
> T-4: The old vacuum, sort of, when she's not there.

C-4: Yes. Yes. I also would like to be the kind of mother that could be strong and say, you know, "Go and have a good life," and this is really hard for me to do that.

T-5: It's very hard to give up something that's been so precious in your life, but also something that I guess has caused you pain when you mentioned guilt.

C-5: Yeah, and I'm aware that I have some anger toward her that I don't always get what I want. I have needs that are not met. And, uh, I don't feel I have a right to those needs. You know…She a daughter; she's not my mother—though sometimes I feel as if I'd like her to mother me…It's very difficult for me to ask for that and have a right to it.

T-6: So it may be unreasonable, but still, when she doesn't meet your needs, its makes you mad.

C-6: Yeah, I get very angry, very angry with her.

PAUSE

T-7: You're also feeling a little tension at this point, I guess.

C-7: Yeah. Yeah. A lot of conflict…

T-8: Umm-hmm…

C-8: A lot of pain.

T-9: A lot of pain. Can you say anything more what that's about?

C-9: [Sigh.] I reach out for her, and she moves away from me. And she steps back and pulls back…And then I feel like a really bad person. Like some kind of monster, that she doesn't want me to touch her and hold her like I did when she was a little girl…

T-10: It sounds like a very double feeling there. Part of it is, "Damn it, I want you close." The other part of it is, "Oh my God, what a monster I am to not let you go."

C-10: Umm-hum. Yeah. I should be stronger. I should be a grown woman and allow this to happen.

T-11: But instead, sometimes you feel like her daughter.

C-11: Umm-hmm Yeah. Sometimes when I cuddle her, I feel I'm being cuddled.

T-12: Umm-hmm.

PAUSE

But you place a lot of expectations on yourself: "I should be different."

C-12: Yeah. I should be more mature. I should have my needs met so that I don't have to get anything from her.

T-13: You should find other ways and other sources to meet your needs, but somehow that doesn't seem to be happening?

C-13: Well, I feel I get a lot of my needs met, but the need from her is very strong—it's the need from a woman really, I think…It doesn't quite make up the needs I get from men******…

T-14: Thee are some things that you just want from her.

C-14: Umm-hmm. Yeah. Just from her. [Sigh.]

T-15: When she pulls back, that's a very painful experience.

C-15: Yeah, that really hurts. That really hurts. [Big sigh.]

PAUSE

T-16: It looks like you're feeling some of that hurt right now.

C-16: Yeah, I can really feel her stepping back.

T-17: Umm-hmm. Umm-hmm.

PAUSE

T-18: Pulling away from you.

C-17: Yeah…Going away.

T-19: ***you feel her sort of slipping away, and you…and it hurts…and—

C-18: Yeah. I'm just sort of sitting here alone. I guess like, you know, I can feel her gone and I'm just left here.

T-20: Umm-hmm. You're experiencing it right now: that she's leaving and here you are all alone.

C-19: Yeah. Yeah. Yeah. I feel really lonely. [Cries.]

T-21: Umm-hmm. Umm-hmm. If I understand right, not lonely in every respect, but lonely for her.

C-20: Lonely for her. Yeah. Yeah. [Cries.]

T-22: I'm not a good therapist—I forgot a box of Kleenex, but…I think I've got… [Laughs.]

C-21: Thank you. [Laughs.] I feel like I could cry a million tears about that. [Laughs.]

T-23: Umm-hmm. It feels as if the tears could just flow and flow on that score.

C-22: Yeah. Never stop.

T-24: That just to have her leave, have her pull away is just more than you can take.

C-23: Yeah. Yeah. It's really hard to go on without her. [Cries.]

T-25: It sounds as though that is almost the center of your life.

C-24: It's very close to that, you know. My husband, my children, my home…My work is important too, but there's something about the heart that's connected to her. [Sigh.]

T-26: And there's a real ache in your heart with her leaving.

C-25: Yeah. Yeah. [Cries.]

PAUSE

C-26: Oh…I just don't want her to go.

T-27: I want to keep her as my daughter, as my little girl, as the one I can cuddle…

C-27: Yeah, yeah. The one I can cuddle. She likes to cuddle too.

T-28: Umm-hmm. Umm-hmm.

C-28: [Cries.] And you know, I'm also scared for her. I'm scared for her out in the world. I'm scared for her to have to go through all the things that I did and how painful that is. I'd like to save her from that.

T-29: You'd like to protect her from that life out there and all the pain that you went through…

C-29: Yeah, yeah. And all the new stuff that all the young people are going through…It's very hard. She's struggling.

T-30: It's a hard world…

C-30: Yeah, very hard…

T-31: And you'd like to cushion it for her…

C-31: Yeah, make it perfect…

[Middle third of interview omitted]

T-73: Does that mean that you feel no one cares, no one accepts?

C-73: No. I feel like now that there are people who do, who care and accept and hear and value me. But there's that little—

T-74: So that the person who can't care and accept and value you is you.

C-74: Umm-hmm. Yeah. It's mostly me.

T-75: The person who sees those things as unforgivable is you.

C-75: Yeah. Yeah. Nobody else is that hard on me.

T-76: Umm-hmm. Nobody could be that cruel to you, or make such awful judgment.

C-76: [Sigh.]

T-77: Or hate you so.

C-77: Or hate me so. Yeah.

T-78: Sounds like you're the judge, the jury, and the executioner.

C-78: Yeah, my own worst enemy.

T-79. You pass a pretty tough sentence on yourself.

C-79: Yeah. Yeah, I do. Not a very good friend to me.

T-80: No.

C-80: *** —

T-81: You're not a very good friend to yourself. Umm-hmm.

C-81: Umm-hmm.

T-82: And you wouldn't think of doing to a friend what you do to yourself.

C-82: That's right. I would feel terrible if I treated anyone the way I treat me.

T-83: Umm-hmm. Umm-hmm. Umm-hmm.

PAUSE

T-84: Because to you, your self is just unlovable.

C-84: Well, there's a part of me that's lovable…

T-85: OK. OK.

C-85: Yeah.

T-86: OK. So in some respects you do love yourself.

C-86: Yeah. I love and appreciate the little child part of me—

T-87: Umm-hmm—

C-87: That's really struggled and come through—

T-88: Umm-hmm—

C-88: And survived—

T-89: Umm-hmm—

C-89: An awful lot.

T-90: Umm-hmm. That's a damned nice little girl.

C-90: Yeah. She's really special—

T-91: Umm-hmm.

C-91: She's like my daughter.

T-92: Uh-huh.

C-92: [Sigh.]

T-93: And she's a daughter you can hold on to.

C-93: Yeah. Yeah. I can still cuddle her. And tell her she's beautiful. And love her.

T-94: And she's a survivor, and she's strong, and she's been through a lot, but she's OK

C-94: Yeah. Yeah, she is. She's real special.

PAUSE

T-95: It must be nice to have such a special person in your life.

C-95: Yeah. It is. That is nice. Yeah. She's very nice.

T-96: Can she care for the other parts of you?

C-96: She's starting to*** —

T-97: She's staring to.

C-97: Yeah.

T-98: Umm-hmm.

C-98: Just beginning.

T-99: Umm-hmm. She's not as hard on you as the adult you.

C-99: No. That's right.

T-100: Umm-hmm.

C-100: She's much more understanding.

T-101: Umm-hmm.

C-101: And compassionate.

T-102: Umm-hmm

C-102: [Sigh.]

PAUSE

T-103: Sounds like she loves you.

C-103: Yeah. She gives me all that unconditional love that I didn't feel like I got.

T-104: Umm-hmm. Umm-hmm. Umm-hmm. And she loves all of you.

C-104: Yeah. Yeah. She loves all of me.

T-105: To her, none of it is unforgivable.

C-105: No. It's all OK.

T-106: All OK.

C-106: Yeah. [Sigh.]

PAUSE

T-107: I like her.

C-107: I like her too. [Sigh.] She's going to save me.

T-108: Hmm?

C-108: She's going to save me.

T-109: She's going to save you.

C-109: [Laughs.] From hurting myself anymore.

T-110: Umm-hmm… She may really be able to keep you from being so hard on yourself. Really save you.

C-110: Yeah. I think she will; I think she will; I just have to give her a little help too.
T-111: Umm-hmm. Umm-hmm.
C-111: Like we'll work together…***save me.
T-112: She's a good companion to have, isn't she?
C-112: Yeah, she is. [Sigh.] It's good to have a friend.
T-113: Yeah. Umm-hmm. To have that kind of a friend inside really touches you.
C-113: Yeah. It really does. It'll never go away.
T-114: Umm-hmm.
C-114: It'll always be there for me.
T-115: Umm-hmm. She's not going to pull away and—
C-115: Go out into the world and do her thing. Laughs.***gonna stay home with Mama.
T-116: Umm-hmm. Umm-hmm. And be a mother to Mama too, huh?
C-116: Yeah. Yeah.
PAUSE
[Sigh.]
T-117: What's that smile?
C-117: It's your eyes are twinkling. [Both laugh.]
T-118: Yours twinkle too.
[Laugh.]
[Sigh.]
Tape Over.[1]

Commentary

The interview illustrates, in concrete form, many principles of the process of person-centered therapy:

In T-2, Rogers makes it clear that he is leaving it up to the client to talk about what she wishes. He indicates that this can be a deep exchange but that it does not have to be.

T-1 and T-2 signify that Rogers is ready to enter immediately into a person-to-person exchange in which he will be "very ready to hear" whatever the client chooses to bring up.

After this, his responses are consistent attempts to understand the client and to communicate, or check out, his understanding of her feelings. They show that he is open to whatever kinds of feelings the client verbalizes. In T-6, he recognizes a negative feeling, anger; in T-10, he responds to a mixture of feelings; in T-23, he accepts her feeling that her tears are endless; in T-85 and T-86 and many succeeding responses, he conveys his recognition of positive self-attitudes.

The therapist's last two statements (T-117 and T-118) reveal a mutuality in the relationship implicit throughout the interview but often not obvious on the printed page.

The client's tears and frequent expressions of self-depreciation could provide a stimulus for reassurance. However, Rogers consistently does not do this; he is a reliable, understanding partner who stays with the client as she lives with her various negative feelings and accompanies her as she finds the strength to rise above them.

Mechanisms of Psychotherapy

The interview just quoted reveals many examples of the way in which change and growth are fostered in the person-centered approach. Rogers's straightforward statements in open-

---

[1]From a previously unpublished article by Carl Rogers given to me for this chapter. N.J.R.

ing the interview (T-1 and T-2) allow the client to begin with a statement of the problem of concern to her and to initiate dialogue at a level comfortable for her.

Just as he does not reassure, Rogers does not ask questions. In response to C-2, he does not ask the myriad questions that could construct a logical background and case history for dealing with the presenting problem. Rogers does not see himself as responsible for arriving at a solution to the problem as presented, or determining whether *this* is the problem that will be focused on in therapy, or changing the client's attitudes. The therapist sees the client as having these responsibilities and respects her capacity to fulfill them.

In this excerpt from a person-centered interview are numerous examples of the client's expanding her view of the problem after the therapist recognized her stated percept, accepted it unconditionally, and communicated his understanding to her:

1. Rogers's recognition of the client's stated need to hang on to her daughter (T-3) is followed by the client's recognition that her daughter has been "a real friend to me" (C-3).

2. The therapist's appreciation of the difficulty the client has in letting go of her daughter (T-5) is followed by the revelation of anger felt toward her daughter because "I don't always get what I want" (C-5). The therapist's acceptance of the anger as stated (T-6) helps the client to bring out the extent of the emotion (T-6).

3. The therapist's continued recognition of the client's feelings (T-7 and T-8) helps her to express and share the extreme pain she feels (C-8).

Another result worth nothing is the experiencing of emotion in the moment, as distinguished from the recounting of the emotion. This comes out in the exchange (T-15, C-15) and continues into the tears that begin in C-20.

In the final third of the interview, we see another result of the therapist's empathic way of being with the client. She has now shifted from her daughter to herself as the agent of bad self-treatment: "That's right. I would feel terrible if I treated anyone the way I treat me" (C-82).

The mechanism of therapist acceptance leading to change of self-attitude is shown operating powerfully in T-84, C-84: "Because to you, your self is just unlovable." "Well, there's a part of me that's lovable..." The client goes on to define that part as "the little child part of me" (C-86), "She's really special" (C-90), relates that part of herself to her daughter (C-91), and sees that she herself can provide all the caring feelings she has been seeking unsuccessfully from her daughter (C-93). The remainder of the interview clarifies a reciprocal relationship in which she sees that a part of herself that she prizes and loves is also a part she can depend on as a permanent source of support.

The interview exemplifies empathy backed by genuineness and unconditional positive regard. It helps the client to (1) examine her problems in a way that shifts responsibility from others to herself, (2) experience emotions in the immediacy of the therapy encounter, (3) accept aspects of self formerly denied to awareness, and (4) raise her general level of self-regard.

Therapeutic change involves both cognitive and affective elements. The integration of intellect and feelings is occurring in the therapist and in his relationship with the client. He is grasping her perceptions of her external and internal worlds, doing so with warmth and genuine caring. The client is also looking at some of the most troubling aspects of her life, changing the way she looks at others and self, and experiencing anger, pain, loneliness, tearfulness, nurturance, disgust, tenderness, and compassion. The resolution that she introduces toward the end of the interview (C-114), "It'll always be there for me" [the part of herself that will never let her down], may be seen as the therapeutic blending of conation, cognition, and affect.

An Early Formulation

In a paper given at the first meeting of the American Academy of Psychotherapists in 1956, Rogers (1959a) presented "a client-centered view" of "the essence of psychotherapy." He conceptualized a "molecule" of personality change, hypothesizing "therapy is made up of a series of such molecules, sometimes strung rather closely together, sometimes occurring at long intervals, always with periods of preparatory experiences in between" (p. 52). Rogers attributed four qualities to such a "moment of movement":

> (1) It is something which occurs in this existential moment. It is not a *thinking* about something, it is an *experience* of something at this instant, in the relationship. (2) It is an experiencing which is without barriers, or inhibitions, or holding back. She is consciously *feeling* as sorry for herself as she *is* sorry for herself. (3) This is…an experience which has been repeated many times in her past, but which has never been completely experienced. In the past she has felt it at some physiological level, but has "covered it up." This is the first time that it has been experienced completely. (4) This experience has the quality of being acceptable. It is…not "I feel sorry for myself, and that is reprehensible." It is instead an experience of "My feeling is one of sorrow for myself, and this is an acceptable part of me" (pp. 52–53).

This mechanism of psychotherapy described by Rogers in 1956 closely matches the experience of the client just discussed: She has a full, emotional experience of a part of herself, a lovable child, of which she has been aware but also covered up; she now experiences that part of herself, and accepts the child completely as part of a newly integrated self. Her laughter and twinkling eyes express the great emotional gratification that accompanies this reorganization.

❖ APPLICATIONS

Problems

Person-centered therapists offer the same basic conditions to all prospective clients. These conditions do not include psychological tests, history taking, or other assessment procedures leading to diagnoses and treatment plans. Diagnostic labels take away from the person of the client; assuming a professional posture takes away from the person of the therapist. The therapist's task is uncluttered by the need to be an expert. Rogers clearly stated his position on this issue:

> We have come to recognize that if we can provide understanding of the way the client seems to himself at this moment, he can do the rest. The therapist must lay aside his preoccupation with diagnosis and his diagnostic shrewdness, must discard his tendency to make professional evaluations, must cease his endeavors to formulate an accurate prognosis, must give up the temptation to subtly guide the individual, and must concentrate on one purpose only: that of providing deep understanding and acceptance of the attitudes consciously held at this moment by the client as he explores step-by-step into the dangerous areas which he has been denying to consciousness. (1946, p. 420)

A consequence of this position is that the person-centered approach has been used with individuals diagnosed by others as psychotic or retarded, as well as with people simply seeking a personal growth experience.

"James" was one of the patients in the Wisconsin study (Rogers et al., 1967). In the course of a detailed description of two interviews with this patient, a "moment in change" is described in which the patient's hard shell is broken by this perception of the therapist's warmth and caring, and he pours out his hurt and sorrow in anguished sobs. This followed an intense effort by Rogers, in two interviews a week for the better part of a year, to reach this 28-year-old man, whose sessions were filled with prolonged silences. Rogers stated, "We were relating as two…genuine persons. In the moments of real encounter the differences in education, in status, in degree of psychological disturbance, had no importance—we were two persons in a relationship" (Rogers et al., 1967, p. 411). Eight years later, this patient telephoned Rogers and reported continued success on his job and general stability in his living situation, and he expressed appreciation for the therapeutic relationship with Rogers (Meador & Rogers, 1984).

This clinical vignette emphasizes the person-centered rather than problem-centered nature of this approach. All people have feelings, like to be understood, and have issues of self-concept maintenance and enhancement. The person-centered approach respects the various ways people use to deal with these issues. In this regard, it may work particularly well with people who are "different."

This nonconcern with a person's "category" can be seen in person-centered cross-cultural and international conflict resolution. Empathy is provided in equal measure for Catholics and Protestants in Northern Ireland (Rogers & Ryback, 1984) and for oppressed blacks and troubled whites in South Africa (Rogers, 1986c). Conflict resolution is fostered when the facilitator appreciates the attitudes and feelings of opposing parties, and then the stereotyping of one side by the other is broken down by the protagonists' achievement of empathy.

Evaluation

The heart of evaluation in person-centered therapy is the evaluative process in the client. The client evaluates whether therapy is useful and the specific ways in which he or she can use it. The client decides what to bring up, how much to explore any particular issue, the level of emotional intensity, and so on. The natural extension of this client-centered responsibility is that the client decides when it is time to terminate therapy.

Because the theory of personality development in person-centered therapy is based on how clients experience change, there is a smooth transition from clients' descriptions of change and those of therapists or external judges. Victor Raimy's (1948) pioneering dissertation on self-concept at Ohio State University was based on self-references in counseling interviews and on simple quantitative analysis of changes in self-approval in 14 complete series of counseling interviews. He defined a *self-reference* as "a group of words spoken by the client which directly or indirectly described him as he appears in his own eyes." Self-ratings of this type were used extensively in the "parallel studies" project analyzing the first 10 completely recorded cases at the University of Chicago Counseling Center (Rogers & Raskin, 1949). Rogers described his experience involving clients' perceptions of the importance of self:

> In my early days as a therapist, I tended to scorn any thinking about the self…[it] seemed so ephemeral…Another problem was that it had very different meanings for different people.
> But my clients kept pushing me toward its consideration. It cropped up so frequently in therapeutic interviews. "I can't be my real self;" "I think that underneath I have a solid self, if I could get to it;" "I don't understand my self;" "With my mother, I never show my true self;" "I'm always afraid that if I uncover the real me, I'll find there is nothing there." Clearly, it was important to find a way of defining, of thinking about, the *self*. But how? (1986d, p.1)

Rogers eventually found an answer in William Stephenson's Q-sort technique. It was possible to study "the self as perceived by the individual," with items such as "I am assertive," "I feel inadequate," or "I am a responsible person." One hundred such items were sorted by the client into nine piles in a continuum from "most like me" to "least like me." This method allowed for quantified descriptions of self-concept and correlations between perceived self before and after therapy, between perceived self and ideal self, and so on.

After the formulation of "the necessary and sufficient conditions of constructive personality change" (Rogers, 1957), considerable research was generated on the measurement of empathy, congruence, and unconditional positive regard and their effects on the outcome of psychotherapy. In the early 1970s, the relationship of outcome to the provision of person-centered conditions was generally regarded as impressive (Bergin & Garfield, 1971). By the late 1970s, some psychotherapy researchers concluded that the "potency and generalizability" of the earlier evidence were "not as great as once thought" (Mitchell, Bozarth, & Krauft, 1977). More recently, Patterson (1984), Raskin (1985), and Stubbs and Bozarth (1994) have challenged the basis for questioning the strength of the original conclusions.

Through all of these assessments, a consistent finding has been that when the measurement of the therapist-offered conditions is based on client perception rather than external judgement, the relationship to outcome is stronger. Most of this research has utilized the *Relationship Inventory* (Barrett-Lennard, 1986.)

Treatment

The process of the person-centered approach has been described particularly in the context of individual psychotherapy with adults, its original arena. The broadening of the "client-centered" designation to "person-centered" stemmed from the generalizability of client-centered principles to other areas of human relations.

Play Therapy

Rogers deeply admired Jessie Taft's play therapy with children at the Philadelphia Child Guidance Clinic and was specifically impressed by her ability to accept the negative feelings verbalized or acted out by the child, which led to positive attitudes in the child.

One of Rogers's graduate student associates, Virginia Axline, formulated play therapy as a comprehensive system of treatment for children. Axline shared Rogers's deep conviction about self-direction and self-actualization and, in addition, was passionate in her interest in helping fearful, inhibited, sometimes abused children to develop the courage to express long-buried emotions and to experience the exhilaration of being themselves. She used play when children could not overcome the obstacles to self-realization by words alone.

Axline made major contributions to research on play therapy, group therapy with children, schoolroom applications, and parent-teacher as well as teacher-administrator relationships. She also demonstrated the value of play therapy for poor readers, for clarifying the diagnosis of mental retardation in children, and for dealing with race conflicts in young children (Axline, 1947; Rogers, 1951)

Ellinwood and Raskin (1993) offer a comprehensive chapter on client-centered play therapy that starts with the principles formulated by Axline and shows how they have evolved into practice with parents and children in the 1990s. Empathy with children and adults, respect for their capacity for self-directed change, and the congruence of the therapist are emphasized and illustrated.

Client-Centered Group Process

Beginning as a one-to-one method of counseling in the 1940s, client-centered principles were being employed in group therapy, classroom teaching, workshops, organizational development, and concepts of leadership less than ten years later. Teaching, intensive groups, and peace and conflict resolution exemplify the spread of the principles that originated in counseling and psychotherapy.

Classroom Teaching

In Columbus, while Rogers was beginning to espouse the nondirective approach, he accepted the role of the expert who structured classes and graded students. At Chicago, he began to practice a new philosophy, which he later articulated in *Freedom to Learn*:

> I ceased to be a teacher. It wasn't easy. It happened rather gradually, but as I began to trust students, I found they did incredible things in their communication with each other, in their learning of content material in the course, in blossoming out as growing human beings. Most of all they gave me courage to be myself more freely, and this led to profound interaction. They told me their feelings, they raised questions I had never thought about. I began to sparkle with emerging ideas that were new and exciting to me, but also, I found, to them. I believe I passed some sort of crucial divide when I was able to begin a course with a statement something like this: "This course has the title 'Personality Theory' (or whatever). But what we do with this course is up to *us*. We can build it around the goals we want to achieve, within that very general area. We can conduct it the way *we* want to. We can decide mutually how we wish to handle these bugaboos of exams and grades. I have many resources on tap, and I can help you find others. I believe I am one of the resources, and I am available to you to the extent that you wish. But this is our class. So what do we want to make of it?" This kind of statement said in effect, "We are *free* to learn *what* we wish, *as* we wish." It made the whole climate of the classroom completely different. Though at the time I had never thought of phrasing it this way, I changed at that point from being a *teacher* and *evaluator*, to being a *facilitator of learning*—a very different occupation. (1983, p. 26)

The change was not easy for Rogers. Nor was it easy for students who were used to being led and experienced the self-evaluation method of grading as strange and unwelcome.

The Intensive Group

The early 1960s witnessed another important development, the intensive group. Rogers's move to California in 1964 spurred his interest in intensive groups, and in 1970, he published a 15-step formulation of the development of the basic encounter group.

Rogers visualized the core of the process, the "basic encounter," as occurring when an individual in the group responds with undivided empathy to another in the group who is sharing and also not holding back

Rogers conceptualized the leader or facilitator's role in the group as exemplifying the same basic qualities as the individual therapist; in addition, he thought it important to accept and respect the group as a whole, as well as the individual members. An outstanding example of the basic encounter group can be seen in the film *Journey into Self*, which shows very clearly the genuineness, spontaneity, caring, and empathic behavior of co-facilitators Rogers and Richard Farson (McGaw, Farson, & Rogers, 1968).

Peace and Conflict Resolution

Searching for peaceful ways to resolve conflict between larger groups became the cutting edge of the person-centered movement in the 1980s. The scope of the person-centered movement's interest in this arena extends all the way to conflicts between nations. In some instances opposing groups have met in an intensive format with person-centered leadership. This has occurred with parties from Northern Ireland, South Africa, and Central America. A meeting in Austria on the "Central American Challenge" included a significant number of diplomats and other government officials (Rogers, 1986e). A major goal accomplished at this meeting was to provide a model for person-centered experiences for diplomats in the hope that they would be strengthened in future international meetings by an increased capacity to be empathic. Rogers (1987) and his associates also conducted workshops on the Person-Centered Approach in Eastern Europe and the Soviet Union.

Rogers offered a person-centered interpretation of the Camp David accord and a proposal for avoiding nuclear disaster (Rogers & Ryback, 1984). One notion is central to all these attempts at peaceful conflict resolution: When a group in conflict can receive and operate under conditions of empathy, genuineness, and caring, negative stereotypes of the opposition weaken and are replaced by personal, human feelings of relatedness (Raskin & Zucconi, 1984).

❖ CASE EXAMPLE[2]

Introduction

In 1964 Carl Rogers was filmed in a half-hour interview with a woman client for a film series, *Three Approaches to Psychotherapy* (Rogers, 1965). That interview contains many of the elements of person-centered therapy discussed in this chapter and is a typical example of the person-centered way of working.

Rogers had never seen the woman before the interview and knew his contact with her would be limited to a half-hour. In his introduction to the interview, he describes the way he will hope to be with her. He says he will, if he is fortunate, first of all, be real, try to be aware of his own inner feelings and to express them in ways that will not impose these feelings on her. Second, he hopes he will be caring of her, prizing her as an individual and accepting her. Third, he will try to understand her inner world from the inside; he will try to understand not just the surface meanings, but the meanings just below the surface. Rogers says if he is successful in holding these three attitudes, he expects certain things to happen to the client. He expects she will move from a remoteness from her inner experiencing to a more immediate awareness and expression of it; from disapproving of parts of her self to greater self-acceptance; from a fear of relating to relating to him more directly; from holding rigid, black-and-white constructs of reality to holding more tentative constructs; and from seeing the locus-of-evaluation outside herself to finding the locus-of-evaluation in her own inner experiencing.

The fact that the interview lasted for only half an hour and the client was seen by the therapist only one time emphasizes that the person-centered approach depends on the here-and-now attitudes of the therapist, attitudes as valid and constant in a brief interaction as over a long period.

The Interview

The interview is with a young woman, Gloria, a 30-year-old divorcée. The first portion of the interview concerns the problem Gloria presents initially, that she has not been honest with her 9-year-old daughter Pammy about the fact that she has had sexual relationships

---

[2]This example is borrowed from Meador & Rogers, 1984, pp. 187–192.

with men since her divorce. Gloria has always been honest with her children and is feeling great conflict over having lied to Pammy. She wants to know whether telling Pammy the truth about her sexual relationships would affect Pammy adversely.

At the very beginning Gloria tells Rogers, "I almost want an answer from you. I want you to tell me if it would affect her wrong if I told her the truth, or what." Later, on two occasions, she asks again for a direct answer to her question. Clearly, she wants an "authority" to tell her what to do. Rogers's responses assure her that he understands her dilemma and guide her to her own resources for answering. After each time that she asks the question and hears the response, Gloria explores her own feelings a little more deeply.

To her first request, Rogers replies, "And it's this concern about her (Pammy) and the fact that you really aren't —that this open relationship that has existed between you, now you feel it's kind of vanished?" After Gloria's reply, he says, "I sure wish I could give you the answer as to what you should tell her." "I was afraid you were going to say that," she says. Rogers replies, "Because what you really want is an answer."

Gloria begins to explore her relationship with Pammy and concludes that she feels real uncertainty about whether or not Pammy would accept her "devilish" or "shady" side. Gloria finds she is not certain she accepts that part of herself. Again she asks Rogers for an answer: "You're just going to sit there and let me stew in it and I want more." Rogers replies, "No, I don't want to let you just stew in your feelings, but on the other hand, I also feel this is the kind of very private thing that I couldn't possibly answer for you. But I sure as anything will try to help you work toward your own answer. I don't know whether that makes any sense to you, but I mean it." Gloria says she can tell he really does mean it and again begins to explore her feelings, this time focusing more on the conflict she herself feels between her actions and her inner standards. Shortly, she again says, "I want you very much to give me a direct answer."

Rogers replies:

I guess, I am sure this will sound evasive to you, but it seems to me that perhaps the person you are not being fully honest with is you, because I was very much struck by the fact that you were saying, 'If I feel all right about what I have done, whether it's going to bed with a man or what, if I really feel all right about it, then I do not have any concern about what I would tell Pam or my relationship with her.'

To this Gloria answers:

Right. All right. Now I hear what you are saying . Then all right, then I want to work on accepting *me* then. I want to work on feeling all right about it. That makes sense Then that will come natural and then I won't have to worry about Pammy....

This statement indicates that Gloria has assimilated a real insight, an understanding that the solution to her problem is in herself rather than in an authoritative opinion on how knowledge of her sex life will affect Pammy.

From this point in the interview she focuses on her inner conflict. She tells Rogers what she "wishes he would tell her" and then says she can't quite take the risk of being the way she wants to be with her children "unless an authority tells me that." Rogers says with obvious feeling, "I guess one thing that I feel very keenly is that it's an awfully risky thing to *live.* You'd be taking a chance on your relationship with her and taking a chance on letting her know who you are, really." Gloria says she wishes very strongly that she could take *more risks,* that she could act on her own feelings of rightness without always needing encouragement from others. Again she says what she'd like to do in the situation with

Pammy, and then adds, "Now I feel like 'Now that's solved'—and I didn't even solve a thing; but I feel relieved."

> *Gloria:* I do feel like you have been saying to me—you are not giving me advice, but I do feel like you are saying, "You know what pattern you want to follow, Gloria, and go ahead and follow it." I sort of feel a backing up from you.
>
> *Rogers:* I guess the way I sense it, you've been telling me that you know what you want to do, and yes, I do believe in backing up people in what they want to do. It's a little different slant than the way it seems to you.

Gloria's expressing the feeling, "Now that's solved—and I didn't even solve a thing; but I feel relieved," exemplifies an awareness of inner experiencing, a felt meaning she has not yet put into words. She "feels relieved," as though her problem is solved. Therapeutic movement has occurred in her inner self before she understands its explicit meaning. It is interesting that she says in the same speech, "I feel a backing up from you." She *feels* the support of Rogers's empathic understanding and acceptance of her. From the person-centered point of view there is a relationship between her feeling understood and valued and her movement from seeking the locus-of-evaluation outside herself to depending on her own inner feeling of "rightness" for a solution to her problem.

The next portion of the interview involves Gloria's experience of her own inner valuing processes and the conflicts she sometimes feels. She explains her use of the word *utopia*, which refers to times she is able to follow her inner feelings: "When I do follow a feeling and I feel this good feeling inside of me, that's sort of utopia. That's what I mean. that's the way I like to feel whether it's a bad thing or a good thing. But I feel right about me." Rogers's response that in those moments she must feel "all in one piece" brings tears to Gloria's eyes, for those moments are all too few. In the midst of her weeping, she continues speaking.

> *Gloria:* You know what else I was just thinking? I...a dumb thing...that all of a sudden while I was talking to you, I thought, "Gee, how nice I can talk to you and I want you to approve of me and I respect you, but I miss that my father couldn't talk to me like you are." I mean, I'd like to say, "Gee, I'd like you for my father." I don't even know why that came to me.
>
> *Rogers:* You look to me like a pretty nice daughter. But you really do miss that fact that you couldn't be open with your own Dad.

Gloria is now quite close to her inner experiencing, allowing her tears to flow as she thinks of her rare moments of "utopia" and then expressing a feeling that comes into awareness of positive affection for Rogers. She then explores her relationship with her father, as she says, "You know, when I talk about it, it feels more flip. If I just sit still a minute, it feels like a great big hurt down there."

Gloria looks at and feels her deep inner hurt over her relationship to her father. She has moved significantly from seeking a solution outside herself to a problem with her children to looking inward at a painful hurt. She says she tries to soothe the hurt through relationships with fatherly men, pretending they are her father, as she is doing with Rogers.

> *Rogers:* I don't feel that's pretending.
>
> *Gloria:* Well, you're not really my father.
>
> *Rogers:* No. I meant about the real close business.
>
> *Gloria:* Well, see, I sort of feel that's pretending too, because I can't expect you to feel very close to me. You don't know me that well.
>
> *Rogers:* All I can know is what I am feeling, and that is I feel close to you in this moment.

Here Rogers presents himself as he really is, offering Gloria the experience of genuine caring, an experience she missed in her relationship with her father. Shortly after this exchange, the interview ends.

Evaluation

It is clear that the therapist's empathy, genuineness, and caring come through and are received by the client throughout the course of the interview. His acceptance helps her make important progress. For instance, she begins the interview looking for an authority to tell her what to do, and by its end has much greater faith in her own ability to make decisions. She moves from trying to keep some distance from her emotions to letting them be expressed without inhibition, going so far as to focus directly on the great hurt she feels about her relationship with her father. She also starts off not accepting part of herself, and then sees greater self-acceptance as an important task for future work. Her self-concept becomes more complete, her experiencing becomes less rigid, her locus-of-evaluation moves from external to more internal, and her self-regard increases. All the important qualities of the therapist and client are revealed in this brief interview.

The intensity of Rogers's genuineness and presence in the relationship is readily apparent from watching the film. The strength of his feelings comes through when he says, "It's an awfully risky thing to live," and when he clearly expresses his inner self, "All I can know is what I am feeling, and that is I feel close to you in this moment."

The therapeutic movement the client makes follows the direction and manner that Rogers initially predicted. First, he says she will move from a remoteness from her feelings to an immediate awareness and expression of them. She does in fact begin the interview wanting an answer to a troubling question and does move to a a point toward the end where her feelings are flowing into awareness and she is expressing them as they occur. At one point she says, concerning her wanting a father like Rogers, "I don't even know why that came to me." She is allowing her feelings to come into expression without censoring, questioning, or even knowing where they are coming from.

Rogers also predicts Gloria will move from disapproving of herself toward self-acceptance. In the beginning, Gloria says she is not sure she accepts her "shady" or "devilish" side. Later, she very explicitly asks to work on accepting herself and spends much of the remaining time exploring the nuances of her self-acceptance.

Initially, Gloria believes there is a true answer that will solve her problem. She construes reality in this black-and-white fashion. Later, she tentatively considers relying on her own inner experiencing for solutions as she says, "I wish I could take more risks." Finally, she describes the utopian experience of feeling so sure of herself that whatever she does comes out of her inner experience and feels "right." This same example demonstrates the therapeutic process of moving from finding the locus-of-evaluation outside oneself to finding it in one's inner self.

The quality of this interview is like a piece of music that begins on a thin persistent note and gradually adds dimension and levels until the whole orchestra is playing. The intuitive interaction and response of the therapist are not unlike the interplay in a creative improvisation. Whatever wisdom science can bring to how the instruments are made and which combinations make for harmony and growth will greatly enrich the players, but we must never lose sight of the primacy of the creative human beings making the music.

As a result of countless inquiries about Gloria from people who had viewed his interview with her, Rogers (1984) published a historical note in which he stated that for about 10 years after the interview, Gloria wrote to him approximately once or twice a year.

Her last letter was written "shortly before her untimely death" 15 years following the interview. He also described her reactions at a weekend conference led by him a year or more after the interview, during which her interviews with Rogers and with Fritz Perls and Albert Ellis were shown. She expressed much anger about the fact that she had done all the things Perls had asked her to do and that she had given over her power to him. Having seen the interview at this point, she did not like it, which contrasted with her positive reaction soon after the interview.

Rogers also described Gloria's request, at the end of a luncheon with him and his wife Helen, during the same weekend, that they allow her to think of them as "parents in spirit," parents she would have liked to have had. "We each replied that we would be pleased and honored to have that status in her life. Her warm feelings for us were reciprocated.... In the ensuing years she wrote me about many things in her life....There were very good times, and there were tragic times...and she showed sensitivity, wisdom, and courage in meeting the different aspects of her experience." Rogers concludes, "I am awed by the fact that this fifteen-year association grew out of the quality of the relationship we formed in one thirty-minute period in which we truly met as persons. It is good to know that even one half-hour can make a difference in a life" (pp. 423–425).

❖ SUMMARY

The central hypothesis of the person-centered approach is that individuals have within themselves vast resources for self-understanding and for altering their self-concepts, behavior, and attitudes toward others. These resources will become operative in a definable, facilitative, psychological climate. Such a climate is created by a psychotherapist who is empathic, caring, and genuine.

Empathy, as practiced in the person-centered approach, refers to a consistent, unflagging appreciation of the experience of the client. It involves a continuous process of checking with the client to see if understanding is complete and accurate. It is carried out in a manner that is personal, natural, and free-flowing; it is not a mechanical kind of reflection or mirroring. *Caring* is characterized by a profound respect for the individuality of the client and by unconditional, nonpossessive regard. *Genuineness* is marked by congruence between what the therapist feels and says, and by the therapist's willingness to relate on a person-to-person basis rather than through a professionally distant role.

The impetus given to psychotherapy research by the person-centered approach has resulted in substantial evidence demonstrating that changes in personality and behavior occur when a therapeutic climate is provided. Two frequent results of successful person-centered therapy are increased self-esteem and greater openness to experience.

Trust in the perceptions and the self-directive capacities of clients expanded client-centered therapy into a person-centered approach to education, group process, organizational development, and conflict resolution.

The world in the last decade of the twentieth century is characterized by forces of enormous magnitude that threaten life on earth and, at the same time, the significance of the individual. In psychotherapy, the client and the practitioner are being increasingly hemmed in by externally managed care. These magnify the power of institutions and regulations and reduce the importance of individuals, feelings, and experience. In one sense this weakens the person-centered approach; in another it ensures its continued existence and growth as a scientifically based system prizing individual worth.

❧ ANNOTATED BIBLIOGRAPHY

Rogers, C. R. (1942). *Counseling and psychotherapy.* Boston: Houghton Mifflin.

This was the first book-length presentation of an approach to therapy relying entirely on the client's capacity to construct his or her own personality change. Chapter 2 is a slightly revised version of the talk given by Rogers at the University of Minnesota on December 11, 1940, which is regarded as the beginning of client-centered therapy.

Rogers, C. R. (1951). *Client-centered therapy.* Boston: Houghton Mifflin.

This book describes the orientation of the therapist, the therapeutic relationship as experienced by the client, and the process of therapy. It expands and develops the ideas expressed in the earlier book *Counseling and Psychotherapy.*

Rogers, C. R. (1961). *On becoming a person.* Boston: Houghton Mifflin.

Perhaps Rogers's best-known work, this book helped to make his personal style and positive philosophy known globally. The book includes an autobiographical chapter and sections on the helping relationship; the ways in which people grow in therapy; the fully functioning person; the place of research; the implications of client-centered principles for education, family life, communication, and creativity; and the impact on the individual of the growing power of the behavioral sciences.

Rogers, C. R. (1980) *A way of being.* Boston: Houghton Mifflin.

As the book jacket states, this volume "encompasses the changes that have occurred in Dr. Rogers's life and thought during the decade of the seventies in much the same way *On Becoming a Person* covered an earlier period of his life. The style is direct, personal, clear—the style that attracted so many readers to the earlier book." There is a large personal section, including chapters on what it means to Rogers to listen and to be heard and one on his experience of growing as he becomes older (he was 78 when the book came out), as well as important theoretical chapters. An appendix contains a chronological bibliography of Rogers's publications from 1930 to 1980.

Rogers, C. R. (1983). *Freedom to learn for the 80s.* Columbus, Ohio: Charles E. Merrill.

This is a substantial revision of *Freedom to Learn*, published in 1969. It was Rogers's last full-length book. One of the areas about which Rogers felt most passionately was learning. He was aware of the contrast between the marvelous capacity of children and adults to learn and to grow and the stultifying influence of most educational institutions. This book describes some of his own experiences in facilitating classroom learning and the experiments of others in promoting "responsible freedom."

❧ CASE READINGS

Rogers, C. R. (1942). The case of Herbert Bryan. In C. R. Rogers, *Counseling and psychotherapy* (pp. 261–437). Boston: Houghton Mifflin.

This may be the first publication of a completely recorded and transcribed case of individual psychotherapy that illustrates the new nondirective approach. Rogers provides a summary of the client's feelings after each interview and additional commentary.

Rogers, C. R. (1954). The case of Mrs. Oak. In C. R. Rogers & R. F. Dymond (Eds.), *Psychotherapy and personality change.* Chicago: University of Chicago Press. [Also found in abridged form in C. R. Rogers (1961). *On becoming a person.* Boston: Houghton Mifflin. Also in D. Wedding & R. J. Corsini (Eds.) (1989). *Case studies in psychotherapy.* Itasca, IL: F. E. Peacock.]

This is a classic case illustrating therapist empathy and client change in terms of Rogers's self-theory.

Rogers, C. R. (1977). A person-centered workshop: Its planning and fruition. In C. R. Rogers, *Carl Rogers on personal power* (pp. 149–185). New York: Dell.

This is an account of a 16-day intensive workshop in the person-centered approach. It is included because so much of the person-centered approach has been expressed in a group context and because it was so meaningful to Rogers, who said, "Of all the ventures in which I have ever been involved, this was the most thoroughly person-centered...it has been, for me, a thoroughgoing test of the value of person-centeredness."

Rogers, C. R. (1967). A silent young man. In C. R. Rogers, G. T. Gendlin, D. V. Kiesler, & C. Truax (Eds.), *The therapeutic relationship and its impact: A study of psychotherapy with schizophrenics* (pp. 401–406) Madison, WI: University of Wisconsin Press.

This case consists of two transcribed interviews that were conducted by Rogers as part of a year-long treatment of a very withdrawn hospitalized schizophrenic patient who was part of a client-centered research project on client-centered therapy with a schizophrenic population.

Rogers, C. R. (1986). The dilemmas of a South African white. *Person-Centered Review*, 1, 15–35.
This article includes the transcription of a 30-minute demonstration interview conducted by

Rogers. It is followed by the client's and therapist's reactions, a presentation of the themes of the interview, and two follow-up statements from the client, the second one coming three years after the interview.

❖ REFERENCES

Ansbacher, H. L. (1977). Individual psychology. In R. J. Corsini (Ed.), *Current psychotherapies*. Itasca, IL: F. E. Peacock.

Axline, V. M. (1947). *Play therapy*. Boston: Houghton Mifflin.

Barrett-Lennard, G. T. (1962). Dimensions of therapist response as causal factors in therapeutic change. *Psychological Monographs*, 76 (43, Whole No. 562).

Barrett-Lennard, G. T. (1986). The relationship inventory now: Issues and advances in theory, method, and use. In L. S. Greenberg & W. M. Pinsof (Eds.), *The psychotherapeutic process: A research handbook* (pp. 439–476). New York: Guilford.

Bergin, A. E., & Garfield, S. L. (Eds.). (1971). *Handbook of psychotherapy and behavior change: An empirical analysis*. New York: Wiley.

Butler, J. M., & Haigh, G. V. (1954). Changes in the relation between self-concepts and ideal concepts consequent upon client-centered counseling. In C. R. Rogers & R. F. Dymond (Eds.), *Psychotherapy and personality change* (pp. 55–75). Chicago: University of Chicago Press.

Cartwright, D. S. (1957). Annotated bibliography of research and theory construction in client-centered therapy. *Journal of Counseling Psychology*, 4, 82–100.

Ellinwood, C. G. , & Raskin, N. J. (1993), Client-centered/humanistic psychotherapy. In T. R. Kratochwill & R. J. Morris (Eds.) *Handbook of psychotherapy with children and adolescents* (pp. 258–287). Boston: Allyn & Bacon.

Gendlin, E. T. (1961). Experiencing: A variable in the process of therapeutic change. *American Journal of Psychotherapy*, 15, 233–245

Goldstein, K. (1959). *The organism: A holistic approach to biology derived from psychological data in man*. New York: American Book (Originally published 1934).

Holdstock, T. L., & Rogers, C. R. (1983). Person-centered theory. In R. J. Corsini & A. J. Marsella (Eds.), *Personality theories, research and assessment*. Itasca, IL: F. E. Peacock.

Lietaer, G., Rombauts, J., & Van Balen, R. (1990). *Client-centered and experiential psychotherapy in the nineties*. Leuven, Belgium: Leuven University Press.

Maslow, A. H. (1968). *Toward a psychology of being* (2nd ed.). Princeton, NJ: Van Nostrand.

Matson, F. W. (1969). Whatever became of the Third Force? *American Association of Humanistic Psychology Newsletter*, 6 (1), 1 & 14–15.

McGaw, W. H., Farson, R. E., & Rogers, C. R. (Producers) (1968). *Journey into self* [Film]. Berkeley: University of California Extension Media Center.

Meador, B. D., & Rogers, C. R. (1984). Person-centered therapy. In R. J. Corsini (Ed.), *Current Psychotherapies* (3rd ed.) (pp. 142–195). Itasca, IL: F. E. Peacock.

Mitchell, K. M., Bozarth, J. D., & Krauft, C. C. (1977). A reappraisal of the therapeutic effectiveness of accurate empathy, non-possessive warmth, and genuineness. In A. S. Gurman & A. M. Razin (Eds.), *Effective psychotherapy: A handbook of research* (pp. 482–502). New York: Pergamon Press.

Orlinsky, D. E. & Howard, K. L. (1978). The relation of process to outcome in psychotherapy. In S. L. Garfield & A. E. Bergin (Eds.), *Handbook of psychotherapy and behavior change: An empirical analysis* (2nd ed.) (pp. 283–329). New York: Wiley.

Patterson, C. H. (1984). Empathy, warmth, and genuineness in psychotherapy: A review of reviews. *Psychotherapy*, 21, 431–438.

Porter, E. H., Jr. (1943). The development and evaluation of a measure of counseling interview procedures. *Educational and Psychological Measurement*, 3, 105–126, 215–238.

Raimy, V. C. (1948). Self-reference in counseling interviews. *Journal of Consulting Psychology*, 12, 153–163.

Rank, O. (1945). *Will therapy, truth and reality*. New York: Knopf.

Raskin, N. J. (1948). The development of nondirective therapy. *Journal of Consulting Psychology*, 12, 92–110.

Raskin, N. J. (1952). An objective study of the locus-of-evaluation factor in psychotherapy. In W. Wolfe & J. A. Pecker (Eds.), *Success in psychotherapy* (pp. 143–162). New York: Grune & Stratton.

Raskin, N. J. (1974). Studies of psychotherapeutic orientation: Ideology and practice. *Research Monograph No. 1*. Orlando, FL: American Academy of Psychotherapists.

Raskin, N. J. (1985). Client-centered therapy. In S. J. Lynn and J. P. Garske (Eds.), *Contemporary psychotherapies: Models and methods* (pp. 155–190). Columbus, OH: Charles F. Merrill.

Raskin, N. J., & Zucconi, A. (1984). Peace, conflict resolution, and the person-centered approach. Program presented at the annual convention of the American Psychological Association, Toronto.

Rogers, C. R. (1931). *Measuring personality adjustment in children nine to thirteen.* New York: Teachers College, Columbia University, Bureau of Publications.

Rogers, C. R. (1939). *The clinical treatment of the problem child.* Boston: Houghton Mifflin.

Rogers, C. R. (1940). The process of therapy. *Journal of Consulting Psychology, 4,* 161–164.

Rogers, C. R. (1942). *Counseling and psychotherapy.* Boston: Houghton Mifflin.

Rogers, C. R. (1946). Significant aspects of client-centered therapy. *American Psychologist, 1,* 415–422.

Rogers, C. R. (1947). Some observations on the organization of personality. *American Psychologist, 2,* 358–368.

Rogers, C. R. (1951). *Client-centered therapy.* Boston: Houghton Mifflin.

Rogers, C. R. (1957). The necessary and sufficient conditions of therapeutic personality change. *Journal of Consulting Psychology, 21,* 95–103.

Rogers, C. R. (1959a). The essence of psychotherapy: A client-centered view. *Annals of Psychotherapy, 1,* 51–57.

Rogers, C. R. (1959b). A theory of therapy, personality and interpersonal relationships as developed in the client-centered framework. In S. Koch (Ed.), *Psychology: A study of science: Formulations of the person and the social context* (pp. 184–256). New York: McGraw-Hill.

Rogers, C. R. (1965). Client-centered therapy. Part I. In E. Shostrom (Ed.), *Three approaches to psychotherapy.* Santa Ana, CA: Psychological Films.

Rogers, C. R. (1977). *Carl Rogers on personal power.* New York: Delacorte Press.

Rogers, C. R. (1980). *A way of being.* Boston: Houghton Mifflin.

Rogers, C. R. (1983). *Freedom to learn for the 80s.* Columbus, OH: Charles E. Merrill.

Rogers, C. R. (1984). A historical note—Gloria. In R. F. Levant & J. M. Shlien (Eds.), *Client-centered therapy and the person-centered approach* (pp. 423–425). New York: Praeger.

Rogers, C. R. (1986a). Client-centered therapy. In I. L. Kutash & A. Wolf (Eds.), *Psychotherapist's casebook: Therapy and technique in practice* (pp. 197–208). San Francisco: Jossey-Bass.

Rogers, C. R. (1986b). A comment from Carl Rogers. *Person-Centered Review, 1,* 3–5.

Rogers, C. R. (1986c). The dilemmas of a South African white. *Person-Centered Review, 1,* 15–35.

Rogers, C. R. (1986d). Measuring the self and its changes: A forward step in research. *Archives of Humanistic Psychology,* 1–13.

Rogers, C. R. (1986e). The Rust workshop: A personal overview. *Journal of Humanistic Psychology, 26,* 23–45.

Rogers, C. R. (1987). *Inside the world of the Soviet professional. Journal of Humanistic Psychology, 27,* 277–304.

Rogers, C. R., & Dymond, R. F. (Eds.), (1954). *Psychotherapy and personality change.* Chicago: University of Chicago Press.

Rogers, C. R., Gendlin, G. T., Keisler, D. V., & Truax, C. (Eds.) (1967). *The therapeutic relationship and its impact: A study of psychotherapy with schizophrenics.* Madison: University of Wisconsin Press.

Rogers, C. R., & Haigh, G. (1983). I walk softly through life. *Voices: The Art and Science of Psychotherapy, 18,* 6–14.

Rogers, C. R., Raskin, N. J., et al. (1949). A coordinated research in psychotherapy. *Journal of Consulting Psychology, 13,* 149–220.

Rogers, C. R., & Ryback, D. (1984). One alternative to nuclear planetary suicide. In R. F. Levant & J. M. Shlien (Eds.), *Client-centered therapy and the person-centered approach: New directions in theory, research, and practice* (pp. 400–422). New York: Praeger.

Rogers, C. R., & Sanford, R. C. (1985). Client-centered psychotherapy. In H. I. Kaplan, B. J. Sadock, & A. M. Friedman (Eds.), *Comprehensive textbook of psychiatry* (4th ed.) (pp. 1374–1388). Baltimore: William & Wilkins.

Seeman, J. (1959). Toward a concept of personality integration. *American Psychologist, 14,* 794–797.

Seeman, J. (1984). The fully functioning person: Theory and research. In R. R. Levant & J. M. Shlien (Eds.), *Client-centered therapy and the person-centered approach: New directions in theory, research, and practice* (pp. 131–152). New York: Praeger.

Sheerer, E. T. (1949). An analysis of the relationship between acceptance of and respect for others in ten counseling cases. *Journal of Consulting Psychology, 13,* 169–175.

Shlien, J. M. (1964). Comparison of results with different forms of psychotherapy. *American Journal of Psychotherapy, 28,* 15–22.

Standal, S. (1954). *The need for positive regard: A contribution to client-centered theory.* Unpublished Ph.D. dissertation, University of Chicago.

Stephenson, W. V. (1953). *The study of behavior.* Chicago: University of Chicago Press.

Streich, E. R. (1951). The self-experience of the client-centered therapist. Unpublished paper. Chicago: The University of Chicago Counseling Center.

Stubbs, J. P., & Bozarth, J. D. (1994). The dodo bird revisited: A qualitative study of psychotherapy efficacy research. *Journal of Applied and Preventive Psychology, 3,* 109–120.

Zimring, F. M., & Raskin, N. J. (1992). Carl Rogers and client/person-centered therapy. In D. K. Freedheim (Ed.), *History of psychotherapy: A century of change* (pp. 629–656). Washington, D.C.: American Psychological Association.

Albert Ellis

6 Rational Emotive Behavior Therapy

Albert Ellis

❖ OVERVIEW

Rational emotive behavior therapy (REBT), a theory of personality and a method of psychotherapy developed in the 1950s by Albert Ellis, a clinical psychologist, holds that when a highly charged emotional consequence (C) follows a significant activating event (A), A may seem to, but actually does not, cause C. Instead, emotional consequences are largely created by B—the individual's *belief system*. When an undesirable emotional consequence occurs, such as severe anxiety, this can usually be traced to the person's irrational beliefs, and when these beliefs are effectively disputed (at point D), by challenging them rationally and behaviorally, the disturbed consequences are reduced. From its inception, REBT has viewed cognition and emotion integratively, with thought, feeling, desires, and action interacting with each other. It is therefore a comprehensive cognitive-affective behavioral theory and practice of psychotherapy (Ellis, 1962, 1991c).

Formerly known as rational-emotive therapy (RET), this approach is more accurately referred to as rational emotive behavior therapy (REBT). From the beginning, REBT considered the importance of both mind and body, or of thinking/feeling/wanting (contents of the mind according to psychology) and of behavior (the operations of the body). It has stressed that personality change can occur in both directions: therapists can talk with people and attempt to change their minds so that they will behave differently, or they can do what Eugene Landry (1994) calls "disjunctive therapy"—get clients to change their behavior and thus modify their thinking. An example of this is Corsini's (1979) concept of betting clients that if they actually do what he asks them to do, they will change. He says, "Do this and your thoughts and feelings will change." They reply, "No, this will not happen." He says, "I'll bet you two dollars. Do it, and if I am wrong, I will pay you and you will be the judge." Corsini claims he has never lost one of these bets.

As stated in several early writings on REBT, especially in "The Rational-Emotive Approach to Sex Therapy" (Ellis, 1975, p. 20), RET theory states that humans rarely change and keep operating according to a profound self-defeating belief unless they *act* against it. So RET has really always been REBT, and it is about time to call it by its right name!

Basic Concepts

The main propositions of REBT can be described as follows:

1. People are born with a potential to be rational (self-constructive) as well as irrational (self-defeating). They have predispositions to be self-preserving, to think about their thinking, to be creative, to be sensuous, to be interested in their fellows, to learn by mistakes, and to actualize their potentials for life and growth. They also tend to be self-destructive, to be short-range hedonists, to avoid thinking things through, to procrastinate, to repeat the same mistakes, to be superstitious, to be intolerant, to be perfectionistic and grandiose, and to avoid actualizing their potentials for growth.

2. People's tendency to irrational thinking, self-damaging habituations, wishful thinking, and intolerance is frequently exacerbated by their culture and their family group. Their suggestibility (or conditionability) is greatest during their early years, because they are then highly influenced by family and social pressures.

3. Humans perceive, think, emote, and behave simultaneously. They are, therefore, at once and the same time cognitive, conative, and motoric. They rarely act without thinking. Their sensations and actions are viewed in a framework of prior experiences, memories, and conclusions. People seldom emote without thinking, because their feelings include, and are usually triggered by, an appraisal of a given situations and its importance. People rarely act without perceiving, thinking, and emoting, because these processes provide reasons for acting. Just as "normal" human behavior is a function of perceiving, thinking, emoting, and acting, so, too, is disturbed behavior. To help change malfunctioning, it is usually desirable to use a variety of perceptual-cognitive, emotive-evocative, and behavioristic-reeducative methods (Bernard & Wolfe, 1993; Ellis, 1962, 1985, 1988, 1991c; Walen, DiGiuseppe, & Dryden, 1992).

4. Although all the major psychotherapies employ a variety of cognitive, emotive, and behavioral techniques, and although all (including unscientific methods such as witch doctoring) may help individuals who have faith in them, they are probably not equally effective or efficient. Highly cognitive, active-directive, homework-assigning, and discipline-oriented therapies such as REBT are likely to be more effective, usually in briefer periods, and with fewer sessions.

5. Rational-emotive therapists do not believe a warm relationship between counselee and counselor is a necessary or a sufficient condition for effective personality change, though it is often desirable. They stress unconditional acceptance of and close collaboration with clients but also clearly point out the deficiencies of their *behavior*. REBT therapists accept clients as fallible humans. They may use a variety of impersonal therapeutic methods, including didactic discussion, behavior modification, bibliotherapy, audiovisual

aids, and activity-oriented homework assignments. To keep clients from becoming and remaining unduly dependent, they often use hardheaded methods of convincing them that they had better damned well resort to self-discipline and work hard at therapy.

6.   Rational-emotive therapies use role-playing, assertion training, desensitization, humor, operant conditioning, suggestion, support, and a whole bag of other "tricks." As A. A. Lazarus points out in his "multimodal" therapy, such wide-ranging methods are effective in helping clients achieve deep-seated cognitive change. REBT is not just oriented toward symptom removal, except when it seems that this is the only kind of change likely to be accomplished. It is designed to help people examine and change some of their basic values—particularly those that keep them disturbed. If clients seriously fear failing on the job, REBT does not merely help them to give up this particular symptom, but also tries to show them how to minimize their basic "awfulizing" tendencies. The usual goal of REBT is to help people reduce their underlying symptom-creating propensities. There are two basic forms of rational emotive behavior therapy: (a) general REBT, which is almost synonymous with cognitive-behavior therapy; and (b) preferential REBT, which includes general REBT but which also emphasizes a profound philosophic change. General REBT tends to teach clients rational or appropriate behaviors. Preferential REBT teaches them how to dispute irrational ideas and inappropriate behaviors and to become more creative, scientific, and skeptical thinkers.

7.   REBT holds that most neurotic problems involve magical, empirically unvalidatable thinking and that if disturbance-creating ideas are vigorously disputed by logico-empirical thinking they can be recognized as false and minimized. No matter how defective people's heredity may be, and no matter what trauma they may have experienced, the *main* reason they now overreact or underreact to obnoxious stimuli (at point A) is that they *now* have some dogmatic, irrational, unexamined beliefs (at point B). Because these beliefs are unrealistic, they will not withstand objective scrutiny. They are often deifications or devil-ifications of themselves and others, and tend to wane when empirically checked, logically disputed, and shown to be as destructive as they are. Thus, a woman with severe emotional difficulties does not merely believe it is *undesirable* if her lover rejects her. She tends to believe, also, that (a) it is *awful*; (b) she *cannot stand* it; (c) she *should* not, *must* not be rejected; (d) she will *never* be accepted by a desirable partner; (e) she is a *worthless person* because one lover has rejected her; and (f) she *deserves to be rejected* for being so worthless. Such common covert hypotheses are illogical and unrealistic. They can be elicited and demolished by any scientist worth his or her salt, and the rational-emotive therapist is partly that: an exposing and skeptical scientist.

8.   Rational-emotive psychology asserts that insights often do not lead to major personality change. It is not the activating events (A) of people's lives that "cause" dysfunctional emotional consequences (C); it is the fact that people interpret these events unrealistically and therefore have self-defeating beliefs (B) about them. The "real" cause of upsets, therefore, mainly lies in people and not in *what happens* to them (even though gruesome experiences obviously have considerable influence over what people think and feel).

In REBT, insight number 1—namely, that the person's self-defeating behavior is related to antecedent and understandable causes—is duly stressed, but clients are shown that these antecedents have power largely in terms of their own presently maintained beliefs and not just in terms of past or present activating events.

Insight number 2 is the understanding that although they became emotionally disturbed (or, more accurately *made* themselves disturbed) in the past, they are *now* upset because they *keep indoctrinating themselves* with similar constructed beliefs. These beliefs do not continue because people were once "conditioned" and so now hold them "automatically." No! People still, here and now, *actively reinforce them*, and their present active *self-propagandizations* and *constructions* keep them alive. Unless they fully admit and face their own responsibilities for the continuation of these dysfunctional beliefs, it is unlikely they will uproot them.

Insight number 3 acknowledges that *only hard work and practice* will correct irrational beliefs—and keep them corrected. Insights 1 and 2 are not enough! Only repeated rethinking of irrational beliefs and repeated actions designed to undo them are likely to extinguish or minimize them.

9. Historically, psychology was considered to be an S-R science, with the S meaning stimulus and R meaning Response. Later, it became evident that similar stimuli produced different responses in different people. This meant that there presumably was something between the S and the R that was responsible for variations.

Let us make an analogy. If you hit the same billiard ball from the same spot with exactly the same force and let it bounce off the side of the billiard table, that ball will always come back to exactly the same spot. Otherwise, no one would play billiards. So, hitting the billiard ball is the S (Stimulus), and the movement of the second ball is the R (Response). However, let us suppose that inside a billiard ball was a little person who could control to some degree the direction and the force of the ball after it was hit. Then it could move in different directions because the ball could be directed to different locations.

Exactly this concept came into scrutiny in psychology in the later 1800s as a result of the conceptualization of James McKeen Cattell, an American psychologist studying with Wilhelm Wundt in Leipzig, Germany. In so doing he started an entirely different kind of psychology known as *idiographic psychology*, whereas the prior psychology that Wundt and his students were working on is known as *nomothetic psychology*.

The German scientists were looking for average behavior, or SR behavior, and were discounting individual variations. The truth was, according to them, the average. Cattell disagreed, and he started a new kind of psychology known as *individual differences*. As a result, the S-R concept changed to S-O-R. The O stood for organism, but what it really meant was that the ball (or the person) had a mind of its own, and it did not go precisely where a ball that had no mind of its own would go, because O had independence.

REBT has precisely the same concept. The RE represents the contents of the mind: Rationality and Emotions; and it is these that REBT therapists attempt to reach, to change people's thinking and feelings (let us call the combination the *philosophy* of a person), with the final intention of permitting them to change their behavior through having a new understanding and a new set of feelings about self and others. By showing their clients how to combine thinking and feeling, REBT therapists have given the little man in the "billiard ball" the ability to change directions. So when the ball is hit again (an event that previously would have generated a particular reaction), the ball no longer goes where it used to go.

Now, this analogy is a weak comparison of a person to a billiard ball, but the basic notion is there: In REBT, we want to empower individuals, by changing their thinking and feelings, to act differently—in a manner desired by the client, by the therapist, and by society. At the same time, REBT encourages people to act differently—this is where the B (for Behavior) comes in—and thereby to think and feel differently. The interaction goes both ways!

Other Systems

REBT differs from most other schools of psychotherapy by eschewing free association, compulsive gathering of material about the client's past history, and dream analysis. It is not concerned with the presumed sexual origins of disturbance or with the Oedipus complex. When transference does occur in therapy, the rational therapist is likely to attack it, showing clients that transference phenomena tend to arise from the irrational belief that they must be loved by the therapist (and others). Although REBT practitioners are much closer to modern neoanalytic schools, such as those of Karen Horney, Erich Fromm, Harry Stack Sullivan, and Franz Alexander, than to the Freudian school, they employ considerably more persuasion, philosophical analysis, homework activity assignments, and other directive techniques than practitioners of these schools use.

REBT overlaps significantly with Adlerian theory, but departs from the Adlerian practices of stressing early childhood memories and insisting that social interest is the heart of therapeutic effectiveness. REBT is more specific than Adler's Individual Psychology in disclosing, analyzing, and disputing clients' concrete internalized beliefs and is closer in this respect to general semantic theory and philosophical analysis than to Individual Psychology.

Adler contended that people have basic fictional premises and goals and that they generally proceed quite logically on the basis of these false hypotheses. REBT, on the other hand, holds that people, when disturbed, may have both irrational premises and illogical deductions from these premises. Thus, in Individual Psychology, a male who has the unrealistic premise that he *should* be the king of the universe, but actually has only mediocre abilities, is shown that he is "logically" concluding that he is an utterly inferior person. But in REBT this same individual, with the same irrational premise, is shown that in addition to this "logical" deduction he may also be making several other illogical conclusions, for example, (a) he should be king of the universe because he was once king of his own family; (b) his parents will be impressed by him only if he is outstandingly achieving and *therefore* he must achieve outstandingly; (c) if he cannot be king of the universe, he might as well do nothing and get nowhere in life; and (d) he deserves to suffer for not being the noble king that he *should be*.

REBT has much in common with parts of the Jungian therapeutic outlook, especially in that it views clients holistically, holds that the goal of therapy should include growth and achievement of potential as well as relief of disturbed symptoms, and emphasizes individuality. REBT deviates radically from Jungian treatment because Jungians are preoccupied with dreams, fantasies, symbol productions, and the mythological or archetypal contents of their clients' thinking—most of which the REBT practitioner deems a waste of time.

REBT is in close agreement with person-centered or relationship therapy in some ways: They both emphasize what Stanley Standal and Carl Rogers call unconditional positive regard and what in rational-emotive psychology is called *full acceptance* or *tolerance*. Rational therapists differ from Rogerian therapists in that they actively *teach* (a) that blaming is the core of much emotional disturbance; (b) that it leads to dreadful results; (c) that it is possible, although difficult, for humans to learn to avoid rating themselves even while continuing to rate their performances; and (d) that they can give up self-rating by challenging their grandiose (*must*urbatory), self-evaluating assumptions and by deliberately risking (through homework activity assignments) possible failures and rejections. The rational-emotive practitioner is more persuading, more didactic, and more information-giving than the person-centered practitioner (Ellis, 1962, 1973, 1988; Hauck, 1992).

REBT is in many respects an existential, phenomenologically oriented therapy because its goals overlap with the usual existentialist goals of helping clients to define their own freedom, cultivate individuality, live in dialogue with others, accept their experiencing as highly important, be fully present in the immediacy of the moment, and learn to accept limits in life (Ellis, 1973). Many who call themselves existential therapists, however, are rather anti-intellectual, prejudiced against the technology of therapy, and confusingly nondirective, while REBT makes much use of incisive logical analysis, clear-cut techniques (including behavior modification procedures), and directiveness and teaching by the therapist.

REBT has much in common with behavior modification. Many behavior therapists, however, are mainly concerned with symptom removal and ignore the cognitive aspects of conditioning and deconditioning. REBT is therefore closer to multimodal behavior modifiers—such as Aaron Beck, Arnold Lazarus, and Donald Meichenbaum.

❖ HISTORY

Precursors

The philosophical origins of rational emotive behavior therapy go back to some of the Asian philosophers, such as Confucius, Lao-Tse, and Buddha, and especially to the Stoic philosophers, particularly Epictetus and Marcus Aurelius. Although most early Stoic writings have been lost, their gist has come down to us through Epictetus, who in the first century A.D. wrote in *The Enchiridion*, "People are disturbed not by things, but by the view which they take of them."

The modern psychotherapist who was the main precursor of RET was Alfred Adler. "I am convinced," he stated, "that *a person's behavior springs from his ideas*" (1964, italics in original). According to Adler (1964),

> The individual...does not relate himself to the outside world in a predetermined manner, as is often assumed. He relates himself always according to his own interpretation of himself and of his present problem...It is his attitude toward life which determines his relationship to the outside world.

Adler (1931) put the A-B-C or S-O-R (Stimulus-Organism-Response) theory of human disturbance neatly: No experience is a cause of success of failure. We do not suffer from the shock of our experiences—the so-called *trauma*—but we make out of them just what suits our purposes. We are self-determined by the meaning we give to our experiences; and there is probably something of a mistake always involved when we take particular experiences as the basis of our future life. Meanings are not determined by situations, but we determine ourselves by the meanings we give to situations. In his first book on individual psychology, Adler's motto was *Omnia ex opinione suspensa sunt* (Everything depends on opinion).

An important precursor of the rational-emotive approach was Paul Dubois, who used persuasive forms of psychotherapy. Alexander Herzberg was one of the inventors of homework assignments. Hippolyte Bernheim, Andrew Salter, and a host of other therapists have employed hypnosis and suggestion in a highly active-directive manner. Frederick Thorne created what he called directive therapy. Franz Alexander, Thomas French, John Dollard, Neal Miller, Wilhelm Stekel, and Lewis Wolberg all practiced forms of psychoanalytic psychotherapy that diverged so far from the Freudian theory that they more properly can be classified in the active-directive therapy column and can in many ways be identified with REBT.

In addition, a large number of individuals during the early 1950s, when REBT was first being formulated, independently began to arrive at some theories and methodologies that significantly overlap with the methods outlined by Ellis (1962). These include Eric

Berne, Jerome Frank, George Kelly, Abraham Low, E. Lakin Phillips, Julian Rotter, and Joseph Wolpe.

Beginnings

After practicing psychoanalysis for several years during the late 1940s and early 1950s, Ellis discovered that no matter how much insight his clients gained or how well they seemed to understand the events of their early childhoods, they rarely lost their symptoms and still retained tendencies to create new ones. He realized that this was because they were not merely indoctrinated with irrational, mistaken ideas of their own worthlessness when they were young, but that they also *constructed* dysfunctional demands on themselves and others and kept *reindoctrinating* themselves with these commands (Ellis, 1962, 1991c).

Ellis also discovered that as he pressed his clients to surrender their basic irrational premises, they often tended to resist giving up these ideas. This was not, as the Freudians hypothesized, because they hated the therapist, or wanted to destroy themselves, or were still resisting parent images, but because they *naturally*, one might say *normally*, tended to *mus*turbate, to demand (a) that they do well and win others' approval, (b) that other people always act considerately and fairly, and (c) that environmental conditions be unfrustrating and gratifying. Ellis concluded that humans are *self-talking, self-evaluating,* and *self-construing*. They frequently take strong preferences, such as desires for love, approval, success, and pleasure, and misleadingly *define* them as needs. They thereby create "emotional" difficulties.

People are not exclusively the products of social learning. Their so-called pathological symptoms are the result of *bio*social learning. *Because they are human*, they tend to have strong, irrational, empirically unvalidatable ideas; and as long as they hold on to these ideas they tend to be what is commonly called "neurotic." These main irrational ideologies are not infinitely varied or hard to discover. They can be listed under a few major headings and, once understood, quickly uncovered by REBT analysis.

Ellis also discovered that these irrational assumptions were so biosocially deep-rooted that weak methods were unlikely to budge them. Passive, nondirective methodologies (such as reflection of feeling and free association) rarely changed them. Warmth and support often helped clients live more "happily" with unrealistic notions. Suggestion or "positive thinking" sometimes enabled them to cover up and live more "successfully" with underlying negative self-evaluations. Abreaction and catharsis frequently helped them to feel better but tended to reinforce rather than eliminate their demands. Classic desensitizing sometimes relieved clients of anxieties and phobias but did not undermine their anxiety-arousing, phobia-creating fundamental meanings and philosophies.

What would work effectively, Ellis found, was an active-directive, cognitive-emotive-behavioristic attack on major self-defeating musts and commands. The essence of effective psychotherapy according to REBT is full tolerance of oneself and of others as *persons*, combined with a campaign against clients' self-defeating *ideas, traits,* and *performances*.

As Ellis abandoned his previous psychoanalytic approaches, he obtained better results (Ellis, 1962). Other therapists who began to employ REBT also found that when they switched to rational-emotive procedures, more progress was made in a few weeks than had been made in months or years of prior treatment (Ellis, 1985, 1988; Lyons & Woods, 1991; Walen, DiGiuseppe & Dryden, 1992).

Current Status

The Institute for Rational-Emotive Therapy, Inc., a nonprofit scientific and educational organization, was founded in 1959 to teach the principles of rational living. With headquarters in New York City and affiliates in several cities in the United States and other countries, it disseminates the rational emotive behavioral approach through (1) adult education courses and workshops in the principles of rational living, (2) postgraduate training programs, (3) moderately priced clinics for individual or group therapy, (4) special workshops, seminars, and training practica for professionals, and (5) the publication of books, monographs, pamphlets, audiovisual materials, and the *Journal of Rational-Emotive and Cognitive-Behavior Therapy*, in which the latest developments in REBT are published.

The Institute has a register of hundreds of psychotherapists who have received training in REBT. In addition, thousands of other therapists primarily follow REBT principles, and a still greater number use some major aspects of REBT in their work. Cognitive restructuring, employed by almost all cognitive-behavior therapists today, stems mainly from REBT. But REBT also includes many other emotive and behavioral methods.

Research Studies

Many researchers have tested the main hypotheses of RET, and the majority of their findings support central RET contentions. For example, (a) clients tend to receive more effective help from a highly active-directive approach than from a more passive one, (b) efficient therapy includes activity-oriented homework assignments; (c) people largely choose to disturb themselves and can choose to surrender these disturbances; (d) helping clients modify their beliefs helps them to make significant changes; and (e) many effective methods of cognitive therapy exist, including modeling, role-playing, skill training, and problem solving.

In addition, hundreds of clinical and research papers present empirical evidence supporting REBT's main theories of personality. Many of these studies are reviewed in Ellis and Whitely (1979). These studies tend to substantiate the following hypotheses:

(a) Human thinking and emotion do not constitute two disparate or different processes, but significantly overlap.

(b) Although activating events (A) significantly contribute to emotional and behavioral consequences (C), people's beliefs (B) about A more importantly and more directly "cause" C.

(c) The kinds of things people say to themselves, as well as the form in which they say these things, affect their emotions and behavior and often disturb them.

(d) Humans not only think, and think about their thinking, but also think about thinking about their thinking. Whenever they have strong feelings at C (consequence) after something has happened in their lives at A (activating events), they tend to make C into a new A—to perceive and think about their emotions (and emotional disturbances) and thereby escalate, diminish, or otherwise modify these emotions and create new ones.

(e) People not only think about what happens to them in words, phrases, and sentences but also by images, fantasies, and dreams. Nonverbal cognitions contribute to their emotions and behaviors and can be used to change such behaviors.

(f) Just as cognitions contribute to emotions and actions, emotions also contribute to or "cause" cognitions and actions, and actions contribute to or "cause" cognitions and emotions. When people change one of these three modalities of behaving, they concomitantly tend to change the other two (Ellis, 1991c; Ellis & Dryden, 1987).

❖ PERSONALITY

Theory of Personality

Physiological Basis of Personality

REBT emphasizes the biological aspects of human personality. Obliquely, some other systems do this, too, saying something like this: "Humans are easily influenced by their parents during early childhood and thereafter remain similarly influenced for the rest of their lives, unless some intervention, such as years of psychotherapy, occurs to enable them to give up this early influenceability and to start thinking much more independently." These psychotherapeutic systems implicitly state an "environmentalist's" position, which is really physiologically and genetically based, because only a *special, innately predisposed* kind of person would be so prone to be "environmentally determined."

Although REBT holds that people have considerable untapped resources for growth and that they are in many important ways able to change their social and personal destinies, it also holds that they have powerful innate tendencies to think irrationally and to harm themselves (Ellis, 1976).

Most such human tendencies may be summarized by stating that humans are born with a tendency to want, to "need," and to condemn (1) themselves, (2) others, and (3) the world when they do not immediately get what they supposedly "need." They consequently think "childishly" (or "humanly") all their lives and are able only with enormous difficulty to achieve and maintain "mature" or realistic behavior. This is not to deny, as Abraham Maslow and Carl Rogers have pointed out, that humans have impressive self-actualizing capacities. They do, and these are strong inborn propensities, too. But, alas, they frequently defeat themselves by their inborn and acquired self-sabotaging ways.

There is a great deal of evidence that people's basic personality or temperament has strong biological, as well as environmental, influences. People are born, as well as reared, with greater or lesser degrees of demandingness, and therefore they can only change from demanding to *desiring* with great difficulty. If their demandingness is largely acquired rather than innate, they still seem to have great difficulty in ameliorating this tendency toward disturbance, and the REBT theory of psychotherapy seems to be relevant and accurate in helping people change.

Social Aspects of Personality

Humans are reared in social groups and spend much of their lives trying to impress, live up to the expectations of, and outdo the performances of other people. On the surface, they are "ego-oriented," "identity seeking," or "self-centered." Even more importantly, however, they usually define their "selves" as "good" or "worthwhile" when they believe that others accept and approve of them. It is realistic and sensible for people to find or fulfill "themselves" in their interpersonal relations and to have a good amount of what Adler calls "social interest." For, as John Donne beautifully expressed it, no one is an island unto himself or herself. The healthy individual finds it enjoyable to love and be loved by significant others and to relate to almost everyone he or she encounters. In fact, the better one's interpersonal relations are, the happier one is likely to be.

However, what is called *emotional disturbance* is frequently associated with caring *too much* about what others think. This stems from people's belief that they can accept themselves *only* if others think well of them. When disturbed, they escalate their desire for others' approval, and the practical advantages that normally go with such approval, into an absolutistic *dire need* to be liked, and in so doing they become anxious and prone to depression (Bernard, 1991; Ellis, 1962, 1988; Ellis & Dryden, 1987; Ellis & Harper, 1975). Given that we have our being-in-the-world, as the existentialists point out, it is quite *important* that others to some degree value us. But it is our tendency to exaggerate the importance of others' acceptance that often causes unhealthy feelings about ourselves (Ellis, 1985).

Psychological Aspects of Personality

How, specifically, do people become psychologically disordered? According to REBT, they usually needlessly upset themselves as follows.

When individuals feel upset at point C, after experiencing an obnoxious occurrence at point A, they almost always convince themselves of irrational beliefs (B), such as; "I *can't stand* this (activating event)! It is *awful* that it exists! It *shouldn't* exist! I am a *worthless person* for not being able to get rid of it!" This set of beliefs is irrational because:

(a) People *can* stand noxious activating events, even though they may never like them.

(b) The events are hardly *awful* because *awful* is an essentially undefinable term, with surplus meaning and no empirical referent. By calling the noxious activating events *awful*, the disturbed individual means (1) they are highly inconvenient, and (2) *more than* inconvenient, disadvantageous, and unbeneficial. But what noxious stimuli can be, in point of fact, *more than* inconvenient, disadvantageous, and unbeneficial?

(c) By holding that the unfortunate happenings in their lives *should not* exist, people really contend that they have godly power and that whatever they *want* not to exist, *must* not. This hypothesis is, to say the least, highly dubious!

(d) By contending that they are *worthless persons* because they have not been able to ward off unfortunate activating events, people hold that they should be able to control the universe and that because they are not succeeding in doing what they cannot do, they are obviously worthless. (What drivel!)

The basic tenet of REBT is that emotional *upsets*, as distinguished from feelings of sorrow, regret, annoyance, and frustration, largely stem from irrational beliefs. These beliefs are irrational because they magically insist that something in the universe *should, ought, or must* be different from the way it is. Although these irrational beliefs are ostensibly connected with reality (the activating events at point A), they are magical ideas beyond the realm of empiricism. They generally take the form of the statement, "Because I *want* something, it is not only desirable or preferable that it exist, but it *absolutely should*, and it is awful when it doesn't!" No such proposition, obviously, can be substantiated. Yet, such propositions are devoutly held, every day, by literally billions of human beings. That is how incredibly disturbance-prone most people are!

Once people become emotionally upset—or, rather, upset themselves!—a peculiar thing frequently occurs. Most of the time, they know they feel anxious, depressed, or otherwise agitated, and also know their symptoms are undesirable and (in our culture) socially disapproved. For who approves or respects highly agitated or "crazy" people? They therefore make their emotional consequence (C) or symptom into another activating event (A) and create a secondary symptom (C_2) about this new A!

Thus, if you originally start with something like (A): "I did poorly on my job today." (B) "Isn't that horrible!", you may wind up with (C): feelings of anxiety, worthlessness, and depression. You may now start all over with (A_2): "I feel anxious and depressed, and worthless!" (B_2): "Isn't *that* horrible!" Now you end up with (C_2): even greater feelings of anxiety, worthlessness, and depression. In other words, once you become anxious, you frequently make yourself anxious about *being* anxious; once you become depressed, you make yourself depressed about *being* depressed; and so on. You now have two consequences or symptoms for the price of one, and you often go around and around, in a vicious cycle of (a) condemning yourself for doing poorly at some task, (b) feeling guilty or depressed because of this self-condemnation, (c) condemning yourself for your feelings of guilt and depression, (d) condemning yourself for condemning yourself, (e) condemning yourself for seeing that you condemn yourself and for still not stopping condemning yourself, (f) condemning yourself for going for psychotherapeutic help and still not getting better, (g) condemning yourself for being more disturbed than other individuals, (h) concluding that you are indubitably hopelessly disturbed and that nothing can be done about it; and so on, in an endless spiral.

No matter what your original self-condemnation is about—and it hardly matters what it was, the activating event (A) is often not that important—you eventually tend to end up with a chain of disturbed reactions only obliquely related to the original "traumatic events" of your life. That is why dynamic psychotherapies are often misleading—they overemphasize "traumatic events" rather than self-condemnatory attitudes *about* these events—and that is why these therapies fail to help with any secondary disturbance, such as being anxious about being anxious. Most major psychotherapies also concentrate either on A, the activating events, or on C, the emotional consequences, and rarely consider B, the belief system, which is the vital factor in creating self-disturbance.

Even assuming, moreover, that activating events and emotional consequences are important, as in post-traumatic stress disorder (PTSD), there is not too much we can do by concentrating our therapeutic attention on them. The activating events belong to the past. There is nothing that anyone can do to *change* the past.

As for clients' present feelings, the more we focus on them, the worse they are likely to feel. If we keep talking about their anxiety, getting clients to reexperience this feeling, they can become still more anxious. The best point to interrupt their disturbed process is usually to get them to focus on their anxiety-creating belief system—point B—because this is the main (though not the only) cause of their disturbance.

If, for example, a male client feels anxious during a therapy session and the therapist reassures him that there is nothing for him to be anxious about, he may achieve a palliative "solution" to his problem by thinking "I am afraid that I will act foolishly right here and now, and wouldn't that be awful! No, it really wouldn't be awful, because *this* therapist will accept me, anyway." He may thereby temporarily decrease his anxiety.

Or the therapist can concentrate on the activating events in the client's life, that are presumably making him anxious—by, for instance, showing him that his mother used to point out his deficiencies, that he was always afraid his teachers would criticize him for reciting poorly, that he is still afraid of speaking to authority figures who might disapprove of him, and that, *therefore*, because of all his prior and present fears, in situations A_1, A_2, $A_3 \ldots A_n$, he is *now* anxious with the therapist. Whereupon the client might convince himself, "Ah! Now I see that I am generally anxious when I am faced with authority figures. No wonder I am anxious even with my own therapist!" In which case, he might feel better and temporarily lose his anxiety.

It would be much better for the therapist to show this client that he was anxious as a child and is still anxious with authority figures because he has always believed, and still believes, that he *must* be approved, that it is *awful* when an authority figure disapproves of him.

Whereupon the anxious client would tend to (a) become diverted from concentrating on A (criticism by an authority figure) and from C (his feelings of anxiety) to a consideration of B (his irrational belief system). This diversion would help him become immediately nonanxious—for when he is focusing on "What am I telling myself (at B) to *make myself* anxious" he cannot focus upon the self-defeating, useless thought, "Wouldn't it be terrible if I said something stupid to my therapist and if even he disapproved of me!" (b) He would begin actively to dispute (at point D) his irrational beliefs, and not only could he then temporarily change them (by convincing himself, "It would be *unfortunate* if I said something stupid to my therapist and he disapproved of me, but it would hardly be *terrible* or *catastrophic!*"), but he would also tend to have a much weaker allegiance to these self-defeating beliefs the next time. So he would obtain, by the therapist's getting him to focus primarily on B rather than on A and C, curative and preventive, rather than palliative, results in connection with his anxiety.

This is the basic personality theory of RET: Humans often create their own emotional consequences. They appear to be born with a distinct proneness to do so, and they learn, through social conditioning, to exaggerate (rather than to minimize) that proneness. They nonetheless have considerable ability to understand what they are foolishly believing to cause their distress (because they have a unique talent for thinking about their thinking) and to train themselves to change their self-sabotaging beliefs (because they also have a unique capacity for self-discipline or self-reconditioning). If they *think* and *work* hard at understanding and contradicting their *musturbatory* belief systems, they can make amazing curative and preventive changes. And if they are helped to zero in on their crooked thinking and unhealthy emoting and behaving by a highly active-directive homework-assigning therapist, they are more likely to change their beliefs than if they mainly work with a dynamically oriented, client-centered, conventional existential, or classical behavior-modification-centered therapist.

Although REBT is mainly a theory of personality change, it is also a personality theory in its own right (Ellis, 1985, 1991c).

Variety of Concepts

Ellis largely agrees with Sigmund Freud that the pleasure principle (or short-range hedonism) tends to run most people's lives; with Karen Horney and Erich Fromm that cultural influences as well as early family influences tend to play a significant part in bolstering people's irrational thinking; with Alfred Adler that fictitious goals tend to order and to run human lives; with Knight Dunlap and Gordon Allport that when individuals begin to think and act in a certain manner, they find it very difficult to think or act differently, even when they want very much to do so; with Ivan Pavlov that humans' large cerebral cortices provide them with a secondary signaling system through which they often become cognitively conditioned; with Jerome Frank that people are exceptionally prone to the influence of suggestion; with Jean Piaget that active learning is much more effective than passive learning; with Anna Freud that people frequently refuse to acknowledge their mistakes and resort to defenses and rationalizations to cover up underlying feelings of shame and self-deprecation; and with Abraham Maslow and Carl Rogers that humans, however disturbed they may be, have great untapped growth forces.

On the other hand, REBT has serious differences with certain aspects of many popular personality theories:

1.   It opposes the Freudian concept that people have clear-cut libidinous instincts, which if thwarted must lead to emotional disturbances. It also objects to the view of William Glasser that all humans have *needs* to be approved and to succeed—and that if these are blocked, they cannot possibly accept themselves or be happy. REBT, instead, thinks in terms of strong human *desires*, which only become *needs* or *necessities* when people foolishly *define* them as such.

2.   REBT places the Oedipus complex as a relatively minor subheading under people's major irrational belief that they absolutely have to receive the approval of their parents (and others), that they *must not* fail (at lusting or almost anything else), and that when they are disapproved of and when they fail they are worthless. Most so-called sexual problems—such as sexual inadequacy, severe inhibition, and obsessive-compulsive behavior—partly result from people's irrational beliefs that they *need* approval, success, and immediate gratification.

3.   REBT holds that people's environment, particularly childhood parental environment, *reaffirms* but does not always *create* strong tendencies to think irrationally and to be disturbed. Parents and culture teach children standards and values, but they do not always teach them *musts* about these values. People *naturally* and *easily* add rigid commands to socially imbibed standards.

4.   REBT looks skeptically at anything mystical, devout, transpersonal, or magical, when these terms are used in the strict sense. It believes that reason itself is limited, ungodlike, and unabsolute (Ellis, 1962). It holds that humans may in some ways transcend themselves or experience altered states of consciousness—for example, hypnosis—that may enhance their ability to know themselves and the world and to solve some of their problems; but it does not believe that people can transcend their humanness and become superhuman. They can become more adept and competent, but they still remain *fallible* and in no way godly. RET holds that minimal disturbance goes with people's surrendering all pretensions to superhumanness and accepting their own and the world's limitations.

5.   REBT believes that no part of a human is to be reified into an entity called the unconscious, although it holds that people have many thoughts, feelings, and even acts of which they are unaware. These "unconscious" or tacit thoughts and feelings are, for the most part, slightly below the level of consciousness, are not often deeply repressed, and can usually be brought to consciousness by some brief, incisive probing. Thus, suppose that a wife is more angry at her husband than she is aware of, and that her anger is motivated by the unconscious grandiose thought, "After all I've done for him he *absolutely should be* having sex with me more frequently!" A rational emotive behavior therapist (who suspects that she has these unconscious feelings and thoughts) can usually induce her to (a) *hypothesize* that she is angry with her husband and look for some evidence with which to test that hypothesis and (b) *check* herself for grandiose thinking whenever she feels angry. In the majority of instances, without resorting to free association, dream analysis, analyzing the transference relationship, hypnosis, or other presumably "depth-centered" techniques for revealing unconscious thoughts and feelings, REBT practitioners can reveal these in short order—sometimes in a matter of minutes. They show the client her unconsciously held attitudes, beliefs, and values and, in addition, teach the client how to bring her self-defeating, hidden ideas to consciousness and to actively dispute them.

People often see how REBT differs significantly from psychoanalysis, Rogerianism, Gestalt therapy, and orthodox behavior therapy but have difficulty seeing how it differs from more closely related schools, such as Adler's Individual Psychology. REBT agrees with almost all of Adlerian theory but has a much more hardheaded and behavior-oriented practice (Ellis, 1985, 1988; Ellis & Dryden, 1987). It also minimizes most of the Adlerian emphasis on early childhood memories and the importance of birth order. But the *basic mistakes* that Adlerians emphasize are similar to the irrational beliefs of REBT.

REBT overlaps with Beck's cognitive therapy (CT) in several ways, but is also differs in significant ways: (a) It usually disputes clients' irrational beliefs more actively, directly, quickly, and forcefully than does CT. (b) It emphasizes absolutist musts more than CT and holds that most major irrationalities implicitly stem from dogmatic shoulds and musts. (c) It uses psychoeducational approaches—such as books, pamphlets, audiovisual cassettes, talks, and workshops—as intrinsic elements and stresses their use more than does CT. (d) It clearly distinguishes between healthy negative feelings (e.g., sadness and frustration) and unhealthy negative feelings (e.g., depression and hostility). (e) REBT emphasizes several emotive-evocative methods—such as shame-attacking exercises, rational-emotive imagery, and *strong* self-statements and self-dialogues—that CT ignores. (f) REBT favors in vivo desensitization, preferably done implosively, while CT does not. (g) REBT often uses penalties as well as reinforcements to help people do their homework (Ellis, 1985, 1988).

REBT is humanistic and to some degree existentialist. It first tries to help people minimize their emotional and behavioral disturbances, but it also encourages them to make themselves happier than they normally are and to strive for more self-actualization and human growth (Ellis, 1991a, 1992c). It is closer in some respects to Rogers's (1961) person-centered approach than to other therapies in that it mainly emphasizes people's giving themselves unconditional self-acceptance, no matter how well or badly they perform, just because they are human and alive (Ellis, 1973; Ellis & Harper, 1975; Hauck, 1992).

❖ PSYCHOTHERAPY

Theory of Psychotherapy

According to the theory of REBT, neurotic disturbance occurs when individuals *demand* that their wishes be satisfied, that they succeed and be approved, that others treat them fairly, and that the universe be more pleasant. But if people's demandingness (and not their desirousness) gets them into emotional trouble, they tend to alleviate their pain in both inelegant and elegant ways.

Distraction

Just as a whining child can be temporarily diverted by receiving a piece of candy, so can adult demanders be transitorily sidetracked by distraction. Thus, a therapist who sees someone who is afraid of being rejected (that is, one who *demands* that significant others accept him) can try to divert him into activities such as sports, aesthetic creation, a political cause, yoga exercises, meditation, or preoccupation with the events of his childhood. While the individual is so diverted, he will not have the time, or inclination, to demand acceptance by others and to make himself anxious. Distraction techniques are mainly palliative, given that distracted people are still underlyingly demanders and as soon as they are not diverted they will probably return to their childish dictating.

Satisfying Demands

If a client's insistences are always catered to, she will tend to feel better (but not necessarily get better). To arrange this kind of "solution," a therapist can give her love and approval, provide her with pleasurable sensations (for example, put her in an encounter group where she is hugged or massaged), teach her methods of having her demands met, or give her reassurance that she eventually will be gratified. Many clients will feel immensely better when given this kind of treatment, but may well have their demandingness reinforced rather than minimized.

Magic and Mysticism

A boy who demands may be assuaged by magic: by, for example, his parents saying that a fairy godmother will soon satisfy his demands. Similarly, adolescent and adult demanders can be led to believe (by a therapist or someone else) that their therapist is a kind of magician who will take away their troubles merely by listening to what bothers them. These magical solutions sometimes work beautifully by getting the true believer to feel better and to give up disturbed symptoms, but they rarely work for any length of time and frequently lead to eventual disillusionment.

Giving Up Demandingness

The most elegant solution to the problems resulting from irrational demandingness is to help individuals to become less demanding. As children mature they normally become less childish, less insistent that they must have their desires immediately gratified. REBT encourages clients to achieve minimal demandingness and maximum tolerance. REBT practitioners may, at times, use temporary "solutions," such as distraction, satisfying the client's "needs," and even (on rare occasions) magic. But they realize that these are low-level, inelegant, palliative solutions, mainly to be used with clients who refuse to accept a more elegant and permanent resolution. The therapist prefers to strive for the highest-order solution: minimization of musturbation, perfectionism, grandiosity, and intolerance.

In REBT, helping clients to minimize their absolutistic core philosophies is attempted by using cognitive, emotive, and behavioristic procedures.

1.   REBT cognitively attempts to show clients that giving up perfectionism can help them lead happier, less anxiety-ridden lives. It teaches them how to recognize their *shoulds, oughts,* and *musts*; how to separate rational (preferential) from irrational (absolutistic) beliefs; how to be logical and pragmatic about their own problems; and how to accept reality, even when it is pretty grim. REBT is oriented toward helping disturbed people philosophize more effectively and thereby uncreate the needless problems they have constructed. It not only employs a one-to-one Socratic-type dialogue between the client and the therapist, but it also, in group therapy, encourages other members of the group to discuss, explain, and reason with ineffectually thinking clients. It teaches logical and semantic precision—that a man's being rejected does not mean he will *always* be rejected and that a woman's failure does not mean she *cannot* succeed. It helps clients to keep asking themselves whether the worst things that could happen would really be as bad as they melodramatically fantasize they would be.

2.   REBT emotively employs various means of dramatizing preferences and musts so clients can clearly distinguish between the two. Thus, the therapist may employ *role-playing* to show clients how to adopt different ideas; *humor* to reduce disturbance-creating ideas to absurdity; *unconditional acceptance* to demonstrate that clients are acceptable, even with their unfortunate traits; and *strong disputing* to persuade people to give up some of their crazy thinking and replace it with more efficient notions. The therapist may also encourage clients, either in individual or group counseling, to take risks (for example,

telling another group member what they really think of him) that will prove to be really not that risky; to reveal themselves (for example, give the details of their sex problems); to convince themselves that others can accept them with their failings; and to get in touch with their "shameful" feelings (such as hostility) so they can zero in on the exact things they are telling themselves to create these feelings. Experiential exercises are used to help clients overcome denial of their feelings and then work at REBT's ABCDs (the D refers to disputation) to change their self-defeating emotions. The therapist may also use pleasure-giving techniques, not merely to satisfy clients' unreasonable demands for immediate gratification, but to show them they are capable of doing many pleasant acts that they think, wrongly, they *cannot* do, and that they can seek pleasure for its own sake, even though others may frown upon them for doing so.

3. *Behavior therapy* is employed in REBT not only to help clients to become habituated to more effective ways of performing, but also to help change their *cognitions*. Thus, their demandingness that they perform beautifully may be whittled away by their agreeing to do risk-taking assignments, such as asking a desired person for a date, deliberately failing at some task (for example, making a real attempt to speak badly in public), imagining themselves in failing situations, and throwing themselves into unusual activities that they consider especially dangerous. Clients' demandingness that others treat them fairly and that the world be kind may be challenged by the therapist's encouraging them to stay in poor circumstances and teach themselves, at least temporarily, to accept them; to take on hard tasks (such as enrolling in college); to imagine themselves having a rough time at something and not feeling terribly upset or having to "cop out" of it; to allow themselves to do a pleasant thing, such as go to a movie or see their friends, only after they have done unpleasant but desirable tasks, such as studying French or finishing a report for their boss; and so on.

REBT often employs operant conditioning to reinforce people's changing behavior (e.g., smoking or overeating) or to change irrational thinking (e.g., condemning themselves when they smoke or overeat).

REBT accepts that there are many kinds of psychological treatment and that most of them work to some degree. An elegant system of therapy includes (a) economy of time and effort, (b) rapid symptom reduction, (c) effectiveness with a large percentage of different kinds of clients, (d) depth of solution of the presenting problems, and (e) lastingness of the therapeutic results. Philosophically, REBT combats absoluteness and ruthlessly persists at undermining childish demandingness—the main elements of much neurotic disturbance (Ellis, 1962, 1991c).

Process of Psychotherapy

REBT helps clients acquire a more realistic, tolerant philosophy of life. Because some of its methods are similar to methods used by other therapists, they are not detailed in this chapter. Most of the space here is devoted to the cognitive-persuasive aspects of REBT, one of its most distinguishing characteristics.

REBT practitioners generally do not spend a great deal of time listening to the client's history, encouraging long tales of woe, sympathetically getting in tune with emotionalizing, or carefully and incisively reflecting feelings. They may at times use all these methods, but they usually keep them short because they consider most long-winded dialogues a form of indulgence therapy, in which the client may be helped to *feel* better but rarely to *get* better. Even when these methods work, they are often highly inefficient and side-tracking.

Similarly, the rational emotive behavior therapist makes little use of free association, dream analysis, interpretations of the transference relationship, explanations of the client's present symptoms in terms of past experiences, disclosure and analysis of the so-called Oedipus complex, and other "dynamically" directed interpretations or explanations. When these are employed at all, they are used to help clients see some of their basic irrational ideas.

Thus, if a male therapist notes that a female client rebels against him, just as she previously rebelled against her father during childhood, he will not interpret the present rebelliousness as stemming from the prior pattern, but will instead probably say something such as this:

> It looks like you frequently hated your father because he kept forcing you to follow certain rules you considered arbitrary and because you kept convincing yourself: "My father isn't being considerate of me and he *ought* to be! I'll get even with him!" I think you are now telling yourself approximately the same thing about me. But your angry rebelliousness against your father was senseless because (a) he was not a *total bastard* for perpetrating a bastardly act; (b) there was no reason why he *ought* to have been considerate of you (although there were several reasons why *it would have been preferable* if he had been); and (c) your getting angry at him and trying to "get even with him" would not, probably, encourage him to act more kindly, but actually to be more cruel.
>
> You consequently confused—as most children will—being displeased with your father's *behavior* with being "righteously" angry at *him*, and you needlessly *made yourself* upset about his real or imagined unfair treatment of you. In my case, too, you may be doing much the same thing. You may be taking the risks that I encourage you to take and insisting they are too onerous (when in point of fact, they are only onerous), and after assuming that I am wrong in suggesting them (which I indeed may be), you are condemning me for my supposedly wrong deeds. Moreover, you are quite possibly assuming that I am "wrong" and a "louse" for being wrong because I resemble, in some ways, your "wrong" and "lousy" father.
>
> But this is another illogical conclusion (that I resemble him in all ways) and an irrational premise (that I, like your father, am a *bad person* if I do a wrong act). So you are not only *inventing* a false connection between me and your father, but you are creating today, as you have done for many years now, a renewed *demand* that the world be an easy place for you and that everyone *ought* to treat you fairly. Now, how can you challenge these irrational premises and illogical deductions?

REBT practitioners often employ a fairly rapid-fire active-directive-persuasive-philosophic methodology. In most instances, they quickly pin clients down to a few basic dysfunctional beliefs. They challenge them to try to defend these ideas; show that they contain illogical premises that cannot be substantiated logically; analyze these ideas and actively dispute them; vigorously show why they cannot work and why they will almost inevitably lead to more disturbance; reduce these ideas to absurdity, sometimes in a humorous manner; explain how they can be replaced with more rational philosophies; and teach clients how to think scientifically, so they can observe, logically parse, and minimize any subsequent irrational ideas and illogical deductions that lead to self-defeating feelings and behaviors.

When working with certain clients who have suffered from extreme traumas, however, such as incest, rape, child abuse, or other violent situations, REBT practitioners may well be quite empathic and go more slowly before doing any vigorous disputing of clients' dysfunctional beliefs about these traumatic events or about anything else in their lives.

To show how REBT is sometimes, but hardly always, actively-directively done, here is a verbatim transcript of a session with a 25-year-old single woman who worked as the head of a computer programming section of her firm and who, without any traumatic or violent history, was very insecure and self-denigrating.

T-1: What would you want to start on first?

C-1: I don't know. I'm petrified at the moment!

T-2: You're petrified—of what?

C-2: Of you!

T-3: No, surely not of me—perhaps of yourself!

C-3: [Laughs nervously.]

T-4: Because of what I am going to do to you?

C-4: Right! You are threatening me, I guess.

T-5: But how? What am I doing? Obviously, I'm not going to take a knife and stab you. Now, in what way am I threatening you?

C-5: I guess I'm afraid, perhaps, of what I'm going to find out—about me.

T-6: Well, so let's suppose you find out something *dreadful* about you—that you're thinking foolishly or something. Now why would that be awful?

C-6: Because I, I guess I'm the most important thing to me at the moment.

T-7: No, I don't think that's the answer. It's, I believe, the opposite! You're really the *least* important thing to you. You are prepared to beat yourself over the head if I tell you that you're acting foolishly. If you were not a self-*blamer*, then you wouldn't care what I said. It would be important to you—but you'd just go around correcting it. But if I tell you something really negative about you, you're going to beat yourself mercilessly. Aren't you?

C-7: Yes, I generally do.

T-8: All right. So perhaps *that's* what you're really afraid of. You're not afraid of me. You're afraid of your own self-criticism.

C-8: [Sighs.] All right.

T-9: So why do you have to criticize yourself? Suppose I find you're the worst person I ever met? Let's just suppose that. All right, now *why* would you have to criticize yourself?

C-9: [Pause.] I'd have to. I don't know any other behavior pattern, I guess, in this point of time. I always do. I guess I think I'm just a shit.

T-10: Yeah. But that, that isn't so. If you don't know how to ski or swim, you could learn. You can also learn not to condemn yourself, no matter what you do.

C-10: I don't know.

T-11: Well, the answer is: You don't know how.

C-11: Perhaps.

T-12: I get the impression you're *saying,* "I *have* to berate myself if I do something wrong." Because isn't that where your depression comes from?

C-12: Yes, I guess so. [Silence.]

T-13: Now, what are you *mainly* putting yourself down for right now?

C-13: I don't seem quite able, in this point of time, to break it down very neatly. The form gave me a great deal of trouble. Because my tendency is to say *everything.* I want to change everything; I'm depressed about everything; etc.

T-14: Give me a couple of things, for example.

C-14: What I'm depressed about? I, uh, don't know that I have any purpose in life. I don't know what I—what I am. And I don't know in what direction I'm going.

T-15: Yeah, but that's—so you're saying, "I'm ignorant!" [Client nods.] Well, what's so awful about being ignorant? It's too bad you're ignorant. It would be nicer if you weren't—if you *had* a purpose and *knew* where you were going. But just let's suppose the worst: for the rest of your life you didn't have a purpose and you stayed this way. Let's suppose that. Now, why would *you* be so bad?

C-15: Because everyone *should* have a purpose!

T-16: Where did you get the *should?*

C-16: 'Cause it's what I believe in. [Silence.]

T-17: I know. But think about it for a minute. You're obviously a bright woman. Now, where did that *should* come from?

C-17: I, I don't know! I'm not thinking clearly at the moment. I'm too nervous! I'm sorry.

T-18: Well, but you *can* think clearly. Are you now saying, "Oh, it's hopeless! I can't think clearly. What a shit I am for not thinking clearly!" You see: you're blaming yourself for *that*.

[From C-18 to C-26 the client upsets herself about not reacting well to the session, but the therapist shows her this is not overly important and calms her down.]

C-27: I can't imagine existing, uh, or that there would be any reason for existing without a purpose!

T-28: No, but the vast majority of human beings don't have much purpose.

C-28: [Angrily.] All right, then, I should not feel bad about it.

T-29: No, no, no! Wait a minute, now. You just *jumped*. [Laughs.] You jumped from one extreme to another! You see, you said a sane sentence and an *insane* sentence. Now, if we could get you to separate the two—which you're perfectly able to do—you would solve the problem. What you really mean is "It *would be better* if I had a purpose. Because I'd be happier." Right?

C-29: Yes.

T-30: But then you magically jump to "Therefore I *should!*" Now do you see the difference between "It *would be better* if I had a purpose" and "I *should*, I *must*, I've *got to*"?

C-30: Yes, I do.

T-31: Well, what's the difference?

C-31: [Laughs.] I just said that to agree with you!

T-32: Yes! See, that won't be any good. We could go on that way forever, and you'll agree with me, and I'll say, "Oh, what a great woman! She agrees with me." And then you'll go out of here just as nutty as you were before!

C-32: [Laughs, this time with genuine appreciation and good humor.]

T-33: You're perfectly able, as I said, to think—to stop giving up. That's what you've done most of your life. That's why you're disturbed. Because you refuse to think. And let's go over it again: "It would be better if I had a purpose in life; if I weren't depressed, etc., etc. If I had a good, nice, enjoyable purpose." We could give reasons why it would be better. "It's fairly obvious why it would be better!" Now, why is that a magical statement, that "I *should* do what would be better"?

C-33: You mean, why do I feel that way?

T-34: No, No. It's a belief. You feel that way because you believe that way.

C-34: Yes.

T-35: If you believed you were a kangaroo, you'd be hopping around and you'd *feel* like a kangaroo. Whatever you *believe* you feel. Feelings come from your beliefs. Now, I'm temporarily forgetting about your feelings, because we really can't change feelings without changing beliefs. So I'm showing you; you have two beliefs—or two feelings, if you want to call them that. One, "It would be better if I had a purpose in life." Do you agree? [Client nods.] Now that's perfectly reasonable. That's quite true. We could prove it. Two, "Therefore, I *should* do what would be better." Now those are two different statements. They may seem the same, but they're vastly different. Now, the first one, as I said, is sane. Because we could prove it. It's related to reality. We can list the advantages of having a purpose—for almost anybody, not just for you.

C-35: [Calm now, and listening intently to T's explanation.] Uh-huh.

T-36: But the second one, "Therefore I *should* do what would be better," is crazy. Now, why is it crazy?

C-36: I can't accept it as a crazy statement.

T-37: Because who said you *should*?

C-37: I don't know where it all began! Somebody said it.

T-38: I know, but I say whoever said it was screwy!

C-38: [Laughs.] All right.

T-39: How could the world possibly have a *should*?

C-39: Well, it does.

T-40: But it *doesn't*! You see, that's what emotional disturbance is: believing in *shoulds, oughts, and musts* instead of *it would be betters*. That's exactly what makes people neurotic!

Suppose you said to yourself, "I wish I had a dollar in my pocket right now," and you had only ninety cents, how would feel?

C-40: Not particularly upset.

T-41: Yes, you'd be a little disappointed. *It would be better* to have a dollar. But now suppose you said, "I *should*, I *must* have a dollar in my pocket at all times," and you found you had only ninety cents. Now, how would you feel?

C-41: Then I would be terribly upset, following your line of reasoning.

T-42: But not because you had only the ninety cents.

C-42: Because thought I *should* have a dollar.

T-43: THAT'S RIGHT! The *should*. And what's more, let's just go one step further. Suppose you said, "I must have a dollar in my pocket at all times." And you found you had a dollar and ten cents. Now how would you feel?

C-43: Superb, I guess!

T-44: No—anxious!

C-44: [Laughs.] You mean I'd be guilty: "What was I doing with the extra money?"

T-45: No.

C-45: I'm sorry, I'm not following you. I—

T-46: Because you're not *thinking*! Think for a minute. Why, if you said "I *must* have a dollar, I *should* have a dollar," and you had a dollar and ten cents, would you still be anxious? *Anybody* would be. Now why would anybody be anxious if they were saying, "I've got to have a dollar!" and they found they had a dollar and ten cents?

C-46: Because it violated their *should*. It violated their rule of what they thought was right, I guess.

T-47: Well, not at the moment. But they could easily lose twenty cents.

C-47: Oh! Well.

T-48: Yeah! They'd still be anxious. You see, because *must* means, "At *all* times I must—"

C-48: Oh, I see what you mean! All right. I see what you mean. They could easily lose some of the money and would therefore feel insecure.

T-49: Yeah. Most anxiety comes from *musts*.

C-49: [Long silence.] Why do you create such an anxiety-ridden situation initially for someone?

T-50: I don't think I do. I see hundreds of people and you're one of the few who *makes* this so anxiety provoking for yourself. The others may do it mildly, but you're making it very anxiety provoking. Which just shows that you may carry *must* into *everything*, including this situation. Most people come in here very relieved. They finally got to talk to somebody who knows how to help them, and they're very happy that I stop the horseshit, and stop asking about their childhood, and don't talk about the weather, etc. And I get *right away* to what bothers them. I tell them in five minutes. I've just explained to you the secret of most emotional disturbance. If you really followed what I said, and used it, you'd never be disturbed about practically anything for the rest of your life!

C-50: Uh-huh

T-51: Because practically every time you're disturbed, you're changing *it would be better* to a *must*. That's all neurosis is! Very very simple. Now, why should I waste your time and not explain this—and talk abut irrelevant things?

C-51: Because perhaps I would have followed your explanation a little better if I hadn't been so threatened initially.

T-52: But then, if I pat you on the head and hold back, etc., then you'll think for the rest of your life you have to be patted on the head! You're a bright woman!

C-52: All right—

T-53: That's another *should*. "He *should* pat me on the head and take it slowly—*then* a shit like me can understand! But if he goes *fast* and makes me *think*, oh my God I'll make an error—and that is awful!" More horseshit! You don't have to believe that horseshit! You're perfectly able to follow what I say—if you stop worrying about "I *should* do perfectly well!" For that's what you're basically thinking, sitting there. Well, why *should* you do perfectly well? Suppose we had to go over it twenty times before you got it?

C-53: I don't *like* to appear stupid!

T-54: No. See. Now you're lying to yourself! Because you again said a sane thing—and then you added an insane thing. The sane thing was "I don't like to appear stupid, because *it's better to* appear bright." But then you immediately jumped over to the insane thing: "And it's *awful* if I appear stupid—"

C-54: [Laughs appreciatively, almost joyously.]

T-55: "—I *should* appear bright!" You see?

C-55: (With conviction.) Yes.

T-56: The same crap! It's always the same crap. Now if you would look at the crap— instead of "Oh, how stupid I am! He hates me! I think I'll kill myself!"—then you'd get better right away.

C-56: You've been listening! (Laughs.)

T-57: Listening to what?

C-57: (Laughs.) Those wild statements in my mind, like that, that I make.

T-58: That's right! Because I know that you have to make those statements—because I have a good *theory*. And according to my theory, people couldn't get upset *unless* they made those nutty statements to themselves.

C-58: I haven't the faintest idea why I've been so upset—

T-59: But you *do* have the faintest idea. I just told you!

C-59: All right, I know!

T-60: Why are you upset? Repeat it to me.

C-60: I'm upset because I know, I—the role that I envisioned myself being in when I walked in here and what I (Laughs, almost joyously.) and what I would do and should do—

T-61: Yeah?

C-61: And therefore you forced me to violate that. And I don't like it.

T-62: "And isn't it *awful* that I didn't come out greatly! If I had violated that *beautifully*, and I gave him the *right* answers immediately, and he beamed, and said, 'Boy, what a bright woman, this!' then it would have been all right."

C-62: (Laughing good-humoredly.) Certainly!

T-63: Horseshit! You would have been exactly as disturbed as you are now! It wouldn't have helped you a bit! In fact, you would have got nuttier! Because then you would have gone out of here with the same philosophy you came in here with: "That when I act well and people pat, uh, when they pat me on the head and say, 'What a great woman I am!' then everything is rosy!" It's a nutty philosophy! Because even if I loved you madly, the next person you talk to is likely to hate you. So I like brown eyes and he likes blue eyes or something. So you're then dead! Because you really think: "I've got to be *accepted*! I've got to act intelligently!" Well, why?

C-63: (Very soberly and reflectively.) True.

T-64: You see?

C-64: Yes.

T-65: Now, if you will learn that lesson, then you've had a very valuable session. Because you *don't* have to upset yourself. As I said before, if I thought you were the worst shit who ever existed, well, that's my *opinion*. And I'm entitled to it. But does it make you a turd?

C-65: (Reflective silence.)

T-66: *Does* it?

C-66: No.

T-67: *What* makes you a turd?

C-67: *Thinking* that you are.

T-68: That's right! Your *belief* that you are. That's the only thing that could ever do it. And you never have to believe that. See? You control your thinking. I control *my* thinking—*my* belief about you. But you don't have to be affected by that. You *always* control what you think. And you believe you don't. So let's get back to the depression. The depression, as I said before, stems from self-castigation. That's where it comes from. Now what are you castigating yourself for?

C-68: Because I can't live up to it—There's a basic conflict in what people appear to think I am and what I think I am.

T-69: Right.

C-69: And perhaps it's not fair to blame other people. Perhaps I thrust myself into a leader's role. But, anyway, my feeling right now is that all my life I've been forced to be something that I'm not, and the older I get the more difficult this *facade*, huh, this *appearance*, uh—that the veneer is becoming thinner and thinner and thinner, until I just can't do it any more.

T-70: Well, but really, yeah, I'm afraid you're a little wrong. Because oddly enough, almost the opposite is happening. You are thrust into this role. That's right: the role of something of a leader. Is that correct?

C-70: Yes.

T-71: And *they* think you're filling it.

C-71: Everyone usually does.

T-72: And it just so happens they're *right*.

C-72: But it's taking more and more out of me.

T-73: Because you're not doing something else. You see, you are fulfilling their expectations of you. Because, obviously, they wouldn't think you are a leader, they'd think you were nothing if you *were* acting like a nonleader. So you are filling their expectations. But you're not fulfilling your own idealistic and impractical expectations of leadership.

C-73: (Verging on tears.) No, I guess I'm not.

T-74: You see, that's the issue. So therefore you *are* doing OK by them—by your job, etc. But you're not being an angel, you're not being *perfect!* And you should be, to be a real *leader.* And therefore you're a *sham!* You see? Now, if you give up those nutty expectations of yourself and go back to their expectations, you're in no trouble at all. 'Cause obviously you're doing all right by them and *their* expectations.

C-74: Well, I haven't been. I had to, to give up one very successful situation. And, uh, when I left, they thought it was still successful. But I just couldn't go on—

T-75: "Because I must, I must *really* be a leader in *my* eyes, be pretty *perfect.*" You see, "If I satisfy the world, but I know I did badly, or less than I *should*, then I'm a slob! And they haven't found me out, so that makes me a *double* slob. Because I'm pretending to them to be a nonslob when I really am one!"

C-75: (Laughs in agreement, then grows sober.) True!

T-76: But it's all your silly *expectations.* It's not *them.* And oddly enough, you are—even with your *handicap*, which is depression, self-deprecation, etc.— you're doing remarkably well. Imagine what you might do *without* this nutty handicap! You see, you're satisfying them while you're spending most of your time and energy flagellating yourself. Imagine what you might do *without* the self-flagellation! Can you see that?

C-76: [Stopped in her self-blaming tracks, at least temporarily convinced, speaks very meaningfully.] Yes.

Mechanisms of Psychotherapy

From the foregoing partial protocol (which consumed about 15 minutes of the first session with the client), it can be seen that the therapist tries to do several things:

1. No matter what *feelings* the client brings out, the therapist tries to get back to her main irrational *ideas* that most probably lie behind these feelings—especially her ideas that it would be *awful* if someone, including him, disliked her.

2. The therapist does not hesitate to contradict the client, using evidence from the client's own life and from his knowledge of people in general.

3. He usually is a step *ahead* of her—tells her, for example, that she is a self-blamer before she has said that she is. Knowing, on the basis of REBT *theory*, that she has *shoulds*, *oughts*, and *musts* in her thinking if she becomes anxious, depressed, and guilty, he helps her to admit these *shoulds* and then disputes them (T-16, T-17).

4. He uses the strongest philosophic approach he can think of. "Suppose," he keeps saying to her, "the *worst* thing happened and you really did do badly and others hated you, would you *still* be so bad?" (T-15). He assumes if he can convince her that *none* of her behavior, no matter how execrable, denigrates *her*, he has helped her to make a *deep* attitudinal change.

5. He is not thrown by her distress (C-17), is hardly sympathetic about these feelings, but *uses* them to try to prove to her that, right now, she still believes in foolish ideas and thereby upsets herself. He does not dwell on her "transference" feelings. He interprets the *ideas* behind these feelings, shows her why they are self-defeating, and indicates why his acting sympathetically would probably reinforce instead of help change her demanding philosophy.

6. He is fairly stern with her but also shows full acceptance and demonstrates confidence in her abilities.

7. Instead of merely *telling* her that her ideas are irrational, he keeps trying to get her to see this for herself (T-36). He does, however, *explain* some relevant psychological processes, such as that her *feelings* largely come from her *thinking* (T-35, T-68).

8. He deliberately, on several occasions, uses strong language (T-18, T-50). This is done (a) to help loosen up the client, (b) to show that he, the therapist, is a down-to-earth human being, and (c) to give her an emotive jolt or shock, so his words may take a more dramatic effect. Note that in this case the client *first* called herself a "shit" (C-9).

9. Although hardly sympathetic to her ideas, he is really quite empathic. Rational-emotive therapists are usually attuned to the client's unexpressed concepts (her negative ideas about herself and the world) rather than to her superficial feelings (her perceptions that she is doing poorly or that others are abusing her).

10. The therapist keeps *checking* the client's ostensible understanding of what he is teaching her (T-65, 66, 67).

11. The therapist—as is common in early sessions of REBT—does most of the talking and explaining. He gives her plenty of opportunity to express herself, but uses her responses as take-off points for further teaching. He tries to make each "lecture" brief and trenchant and to relate it specifically to her problems and feelings. Also, at times he stops to let ideas sink in.

As can be seen from the first part of this initial REBT session, the client does not receive feelings of love and warmth from the therapist. Transference and countertransference spontaneously occur, but they are quickly analyzed, the philosophies behind them are revealed, and they tend to evaporate in the process. The client's deep feelings (shame, self-pity, weeping, anger) clearly exist, but the client is not given too much chance to revel in these feelings or to abreact strongly about them. As the therapist points out and attacks the ideologies that underlie these feelings, they swiftly change and are sometimes almost miraculously transformed into other, contradictory feelings (such as humor, joy, and reflective contemplation). The therapist's "coolness," philosophizing, and encouraging insistence that the client can feel something besides anxiety and depression, tends to help change her destructiveness into constructive feelings.

What the client does seem to experience, as the session proceeds, are (a) full acceptance of herself, in spite of her poor behavior, (b) renewed confidence that she can do certain things—e.g., think for herself, (c) the belief that it is her own perfectionistic *shoulds* that are upsetting her and not the attitudes of others (including the therapist); (d) reality testing, in her starting to see that even though she performs inefficiently (with the therapist and with some of the people she works with), she can still recover, try again, and probably do better in the future; and (e) reduction of some of her defenses in that she can stop blaming others (such as her therapist) for her anxiety and can start to admit that she is doing something herself to cause it.

In these 15 minutes the client is getting only *glimmerings* of these constructive thoughts and feelings. The REBT intent, however, is that she will *keep* getting insights — that is, *philosophic* rather than merely *psychodynamic* insights — into the self-causation of her disturbed symptoms; that she will use these insights to change some of her most enduring and deep-seated ways of thinking about herself, about others, and about the world; and that she will thereby eventually become ideationally, emotionally, and behaviorally less self-defeating. Unless she finally makes *attitudinal* (as well as symptom-reducing) change, although helped to some degree, she will still be far from the ideal REBT goal of making a basic personality change.

❖ APPLICATIONS

Problems

It is easier to state what kind of problems are *not* handled than the kind that *are* handled in REBT. Individuals who are out of contact with reality, in a highly manic state, seriously autistic or brain injured, and in the lower ranges of mental deficiency are not normally treated by REBT (or most other) practitioners. They are referred for medical treatment, for custodial or institutional care, or for behavior therapy along operant conditioning lines.

Most other individuals with difficulties are treated with REBT. These include (1) clients with maladjustment, moderate anxiety, or marital problems, (2) those with sexual difficulties, (3) run-of-the-mill "neurotics," (4) individuals with character disorders, (5) truants, juvenile delinquents, and adult criminals, (6) borderline personalities and others with personality disorders, (7) overt psychotics, including those with delusions and hallucinations, when they are somewhat in contact with reality, (8) individuals with higher-grade mental deficiency, and (9) clients with psychosomatic problems.

Although varying types of problems are treated with REBT, no claim is made that they are treated with equal effectiveness. As is the case with virtually all psychotherapies, the REBT approach is significantly more effective with mildly disturbed individuals and those who have a single major symptom (such as sexual inadequacy) than with seriously disordered clients (Ellis, 1962, 1985). This conforms to the hypotheses of REBT theory that the tendency toward emotional distress is largely inborn and not merely acquired, that individuals with serious aberrations are more innately predisposed to have rigid and crooked thinking than are those with lesser aberrations, and that consequently they are less likely to make major advances. Moreover, REBT emphasizes hard work at changing one's thinking and at doing homework activity assignments, and it is clinically observable that many of the most dramatically symptom-ridden individuals (such as those who are severely depressed) tend to do considerably less work and more shirking (including shirking at therapy) than those with milder symptoms. Nevertheless, seasoned REBT practitioners claim they get better results with a wide variety of clients than do therapists from other schools of psychological thought (Lyons & Woods, 1991); McGovern & Silverman, 1984; Silverman, McCarthy, & McGovern, 1992).

REBT is applicable for preventative purposes. Rational-emotive procedures are closely connected to the field of education and have enormous implications for emotional prophylaxis. A number of clinicians have shown how they can help prevent normal children from eventually becoming seriously disturbed. Evidence shows that when nondisturbed grade school pupils are given, along with regular elements of an academic education, a steady process of rational-emotive education, they can learn to understand themselves and others and to live more rationally and happily in this difficult world (Bernard & Joyce, 1993).

Evaluation

REBT has directly or indirectly inspired scores of experimenters to test its theories, and there now are hundreds of research studies that tend to validate its hypotheses (Ellis & Whiteley, 1979). More than 200 outcome studies have been published showing that REBT is effective in changing the thoughts, feelings, and behaviors of groups of individuals with various kinds of disturbances. These studies tend to show that REBT disputing usually works better than no therapy and is often more effective than other methods of psychotherapy (Lyons & Woods, 1991; McGovern & Silverman, 1984; Silverman, McCarthy, & McGovern, 1992).

In addition, scores of other outcome studies have been done by other cognitive therapists and their associates—particularly by Aaron Beck (1991) and his associates—that also support the clinical hypotheses of REBT. Finally, more than 400 other investigations have shown that the irrationality scales derived from Ellis's original list of irrational ideas significantly correlate with the diagnostic disorders with which these scales have been tested (Hollon & Beck, 1994; Woods, 1992).

Individual Evaluations

REBT therapists may use various diagnostic instruments and psychological tests, and they especially employ tests of irrationality, such as the Jones Irrational Beliefs Test, the Beck Depression Inventory, and the Dysfunctional Attitude Scale. Many of these tests have been shown to have considerable reliability and validity in controlled experiments.

Treatment

REBT employs virtually all forms of individual and group psychotherapy. Some of the main methods are described in this section.

Individual Therapy

Most clients with whom REBT is practiced are seen for *individual* sessions, usually on a once-a-week basis, for from 5 to 50 sessions. They generally begin their sessions by telling their most upsetting feelings or consequences (C) during the week. REBT therapists then discover what activating events (A) occurred before clients felt so badly and help them to see what rational beliefs and what irrational beliefs (B) they held in connection with the activating events. They teach clients to dispute (D) their irrational beliefs and often agree upon concrete homework activity assignments to help with this disputing. They then check up in the following session, sometimes with the help of an REBT Self-Help Report Form, to see how the clients have tried to use the REBT approach during the week. If clients work at REBT, they arrive at an Effective New Philosophy (E)—which they reach through *Effort* and *Exercise*.

In particular, REBT therapists try to show clients how to (1) minimize anxiety, guilt, and depression by fully accepting themselves as human beings, (2) alleviate their anger, hostility, and violence by becoming tolerant of other people, and (3) reduce their low frustration tolerance and inertia by learning to endure unpleasant reality when it is truly inevitable.

Group Therapy

REBT is particularly applicable to *group therapy*. Because group members are taught to apply REBT procedures to one another, they can help others learn the procedures and get practice (under the direct supervision of the group leader) in applying them. In group work, moreover, there is usually more opportunity for the members to agree upon homework assignments (some of which are to be carried out in the group itself), to get assertion training, to engage in role playing, to interact with other people, to take verbal and nonverbal risks, to learn by the experiences of others, to interact therapeutically and socially with each other in after-group sessions, and to have their behavior directly observed by the therapist and other group members (Ellis, 1992b).

Rational Encounter Marathons and Intensives

REBT has successfully used marathon encounter groups and large-scale one-day intensive workshops that include many verbal and nonverbal exercises, dramatic risk-taking procedures, evocative lectures, personal encounters, homework agreements, and other emotive and behavioral methods. Research studies have shown that these marathons and intensive workshops have beneficial, immediate, and lasting effects (Ellis & Dryden, 1987; Ellis, Sichel, Leaf, & Mass, 1989).

Brief Therapy

REBT is naturally designed for *brief therapy*. It is preferable that individuals with severe disturbances come to individual and/or group sessions for at least six months. But for individuals who are going to stay in therapy for only a short while, REBT can teach them, in from 1 to 10 sessions, the A-B-C method of understanding emotional problems, seeing their main philosophic source, and beginning to change fundamental disturbance-creating attitudes (Ellis, 1985, 1992a; Ellis & Dryden, 1987).

This is particularly true for the person who has a specific problem—such as hostility toward a boss or sexual inadequacy—and who is not too *generally* disturbed. Such an individual can, with the help of REBT, be almost completely "cured" in a few sessions. But even clients with long-standing difficulties may be significantly helped as a result of brief therapy.

Two special devices often employed in REBT can help speed the therapeutic process. The first is to tape the entire session. These recordings are then listened to, usually several times, by the clients in their own home, car, or office so they can more incisively see their problems and the rational-emotive way of handling them. Many clients who have difficulty in hearing what goes on during the face-to-face sessions (because they are too intent on talking themselves, are easily distractible, or are too anxious) are able to get more from listening to a recording of these sessions than from the original encounter.

Second, an REBT Self-Help Form is frequently used with clients to help teach them how to use the method when they encounter emotional problems between therapy sessions or after therapy has ended. This form is reproduced on the next two pages.

227
RATIONAL-EMOTIVE THERAPY

RET SELF-HELP FORM

Institute for Rational-Emotive Therapy
45 East 65th Street, New York, N.Y. 10021
(212) 535-0822

(A) ACTIVATING EVENTS, thoughts, or feelings that happened just before I felt emotionally disturbed or acted self-defeatingly: _____

_____

(C) CONSEQUENCE or CONDITION—disturbed feeling or self-defeating behavior—that I produced and would like to change: _____

_____

(B) BELIEFS—Irrational BELIEFS (IBs) leading to my CONSEQUENCE (emotional disturbance or self-defeating behavior). Circle all that apply to these ACTIVATING EVENTS (A).	**(D) DISPUTES** for each circled IRRATIONAL BELIEF. Examples: *"Why* MUST I do very well?" *"Where is it written* that I am a BAD PERSON?" *"Where is the evidence* that I MUST be approved or accepted?"	**(E) EFFECTIVE RATIONAL BELIEFS (RBs)** to replace my IRRATIONAL BELIEFS (IBs). *Examples: "I'd* PREFER *to do very well but I don't* HAVE TO." *"I am a* PERSON WHO *acted badly, not a BAD PERSON." "There is no evidence that I* HAVE TO *be approved, though I would* LIKE *to be."*
1. I MUST do well or very well!	....	....
2. I am a BAD OR WORTHLESS PERSON when I act weakly or stupidly.	....	....
3. I MUST be approved or accepted by people I find important!	....	....
4. I NEED to be loved by someone who matters to me a lot!	....	....
5. I am a BAD, UNLOVABLE PERSON if I get rejected.	....	....
6. People MUST treat me fairly and give me what I NEED!	....	....

(OVER)

228
ALBERT ELLIS

7. People MUST live up to my expectations or it is TERRIBLE!		
8. People who act immorally are undeserving, ROTTEN PEOPLE!		
9. I CAN'T STAND really bad things or very difficult people!		
10. My life MUST have few major hassles or troubles.		
11. It's AWFUL or HORRIBLE when major things don't go my way!		
12. I CAN'T STAND IT when life is really unfair!		
13. I NEED a good deal of immediate gratification and HAVE to feel miserable when I don't get it!		
Additional Irrational Beliefs:		

(F) FEELINGS and BEHAVIORS I experienced after arriving at my EFFECTIVE RATIONAL BELIEFS:

I WILL WORK HARD TO REPEAT MY EFFECTIVE RATIONAL BELIEFS FORCEFULLY TO MYSELF ON MANY OCCASIONS SO THAT I CAN MAKE MYSELF LESS DISTURBED NOW AND ACT LESS SELF-DEFEATINGLY IN THE FUTURE.

Marriage and Family Therapy

From its beginning, REBT has been used extensively in marriage and family counseling (Ellis, 1962; Ellis & Dryden, 1987; Ellis & Harper, 1975). Usually marital or love partners are seen together. REBT therapists listen to their complaints about each other, then try to show that even if the complaints are justified, being upset is not. Work is done with either or both participants to minimize anxiety, depression, guilt, and (especially) hostility. As they begin to learn and apply the REBT principles, they usually become much less disturbed, often within a few sessions, and then are much better able to minimize their incompatibilities and maximize their compatibilities. Sometimes, of course, they decide that they would be better off separated or divorced, but usually they decide to work at their problems to achieve a happier marital arrangement. They are frequently taught contracting, compromising, communication, and other relating skills. The therapist is concerned with each of them as individuals who can be helped emotionally, whether or not they decide to stay together. But the more they work at helping themselves, the better their relationship tends to become (Ellis, 1991b; Ellis, Sichel, Yeager, DiMattia, & DiGiuseppe, 1989).

In family therapy, REBT practitioners sometimes see all members of the same family together, see the children in one session and the parents in another, or see them all individually. Several joint sessions are usually held to observe the interactions among family members. Whether together or separately, parents are frequently shown how to accept their children and to stop condemning them, and children are similarly shown that they can accept their parents and their siblings. The general REBT principles of tolerance for oneself and for others are repeatedly taught. As is common in REBT procedures, bibliotherapy supplements counseling with REBT materials such as *A New Guide to Rational Living* (Ellis & Harper, 1975), *A Rational Counseling Primer* (Young, 1974), and *How to Stubbornly Refuse to Make Yourself Miserable About Anything—Yes, Anything!* (Ellis, 1988).

The *setting* of REBT sessions is much like that for other types of therapy. Most individual sessions take place in an office, but there may well be no desk between the therapist and the client, and REBT therapists tend to be informally dressed and to use down-to-earth language. Because they presumably have relatively few ego hang-ups, they tend to be more open, authentic, and less "professional" than the average therapist. The main special equipment used is a cassette tape recorder, with the client being encouraged to make a recording of the session to take home for replaying.

REBT therapists are highly active, give their own views without hesitation, usually answer direct questions about their personal lives, do a good deal of speaking, particularly during early sessions, and are quite energetic and often directive in group therapy. At the same time, they may engage in considerable explaining, interpreting, and "lecturing"; may be accepting but not overly warm to some clients; and may easily work with clients they personally do not like, as they are much more interested in helping them than in relating to them personally. Because they tend to have complete tolerance for all individuals, REBT therapists are often seen as warm and caring by their clients.

Resistance is usually handled by showing clients that they resist changing because they would like to find a magical, easy solution rather than work at changing themselves. Resistance is not usually interpreted as their particular feelings about the therapist. If a client tries to seduce a therapist, this is not usually explained in terms of "transference" but in terms of (a) needs for love, (b) normal attraction to a helpful person, and (c) the natural sex urges of two people who have intimate mental-emotional contact. If the therapist is attracted to the client, he or she usually admits the attraction, but explains why it is unethical to have sexual relations with a client (Ellis, 1985).

Client Problems

No matter what the presenting problem, REBT therapists do not become overly interested in it or nor devote too much time trying to induce the client to fully express it or the emotions surrounding it. Rather, they try to get the client to see and tackle the basic ideas or philosophies that underlie the problem. This is notably shown in the course of workshops for executives. In these workshops, the executives constantly bring up business, management, organizational, personal, and other problems. But they are shown that they usually have a problem about the problem and it is *this* problem that the rational-emotive method can solve more easily than the original, practical problem (Ellis, 1972).

The main exception to this rule is individuals who are so inhibited or defensive that they do not permit themselves to feel and who therefore may not even be aware of some of their underlying problems. Thus, the successful businessman who comes for psychological help only because his wife insists they have a poor relationship, and who claims that nothing really bothers him other than his wife's complaints, may have to be jolted out of his complacency by direct confrontation. REBT group therapy may be particularly helpful for such an individual, so that he finally expresses underlying anxieties and resentments and begins to acknowledge he has emotional problems.

Extreme emotionalism in the course of REBT sessions—such as crying, psychotic behavior, and violent expressions of suicidal or homicidal intent—are naturally difficult to handle. But therapists handle them by their own presumably rational philosophy of life and therapy, which includes these ideas: (a) Client outbursts make things difficult, but they are hardly *awful*, *terrible*, or *catastrophic*. (b) Behind each outburst is some irrational idea. Now, what is this idea? How can it be brought to the client's attention and what can be done to help change it? (c) No therapist can possibly help every client all the time. If this particular client cannot be helped and has to be referred elsewhere or lost to therapy, that is unfortunate. But it does not mean that the therapist is a failure.

REBT therapists usually handle profound depressions by showing clients, as quickly, directly, and vigorously as possible, that they are probably causing their depression by (a) blaming themselves for what they have done or not done, (b) castigating themselves for being depressed and inert, and (c) bemoaning their fate because of the hassles and harshness of environmental conditions. This self-condemnation is not only revealed but firmly disputed and, in the meantime, the therapist may give clients reassurance and support, may refer them for supplementary medication, may speak to their relatives or friends to enlist their aid, and may recommend temporary withdrawal from some activities. Through an immediate and direct disputing of clients' extreme self-deprecation and self-pity, the therapist often helps deeply depressed and suicidal people in a short period.

The most difficult clients are usually the chronic avoiders or shirkers who keep looking for magical solutions. These individuals are shown that no such magic exists; that if they do not want to work hard to get better, it is their privilege to keep suffering; and that they are not *terrible persons* for goofing off, but that they could live much more enjoyably if they worked at helping themselves. To help them get going, a form of people-involved therapy, such as group therapy, is frequently a method of choice. Results with unresponsive clients are still relatively poor in REBT (and virtually all other therapies), but persistence and vigor on the part of the therapist often overcome this kind of resistance eventually (Ellis, 1985).

❖ CASE EXAMPLE

This section is relatively brief because it concerns the 25-year-old computer programmer whose initial session was presented earlier in this chapter. Other case material on this client follows.

Background

Sara R. came from an orthodox Jewish family. Her mother died in childbirth when Sara was two years of age, so Sara was raised by a loving, but strict and somewhat remote father and a dominating paternal grandmother. She did well in school, but had few friends up to and through college. Although fairly attractive, she was always ashamed of her body, did little dating, and occupied herself mainly with her work. At the age of 25, she was head of a section in a data processing firm. She was highly sexed and masturbated several times a week, but she had intercourse with a male only once, when she was too drunk to know what she was doing. She had been overeating and overdrinking steadily since her college days. She had three years of fairly classical psychoanalysis, thought her analyst was "a very kind and helpful man," but got little or no help from the process. She was quite disillusioned about therapy as a result of this experience and came to see the present therapist only because the president of her company, who liked her a great deal, told her that he would no longer put up with her constant drinking and insisted that she come to see the writer.

Treatment

Treatment continued for six sessions along the same lines indicated in the transcript included previously in this chapter. This was followed by 24 weeks of REBT group therapy and one weekend of rational encounter.

Cognitively, the client was shown repeatedly that her central problem was that she devoutly believed she *had to be* almost perfect and that she *must not* be criticized in any major way by significant others. She was persistently taught, instead, to refrain from rating her *self* but only to measure her *performances*; to see that she could never be, except by arbitrary definition, a worm even if she never rid herself of her overeating, her compulsive drinking, and her foolish symptoms; to see that it was highly desirable but not necessary that she relate intimately to a man and win the approval of her peers and her bosses at work; and first to accept herself *with* her hostility and then to give up her childish *demands* on others that led her to be so hostile to them. Although she devoutly believed in the "fact" that she and others *should* be extremely efficient and follow strict disciplinary rules, and although she time and again resisted the therapist's and the group members' assaults against her moralistic *shoulds*, she was finally induced to replace them, in her vocabulary as well as in her internalized beliefs, with *it would be betters*. She claimed to have completely overthrown her original religious orthodoxy, but she was shown that she had merely replaced it with an inordinate demand for certainty in her personal life and in world affairs, and she was finally induced to give this up, too.

Emotively, Sara was fully accepted by the therapist *as a person*, even though he strongly assailed many of her *ideas* and sometimes humorously reduced them to absurdity. She was assertively confronted by some of the group members, who took her to task for condemning other members for their stupidities and their shirking, and she was helped to relate to these people in spite of their inadequacies. The therapist and some of the others in her group and in the marathon weekend of rational encounter in which she participated used vigorous, down-to-earth language with her, which she initially disliked but which she later began to use to some extent herself. When she went on a drinking bout for a few weeks and felt utterly depressed and hopeless, two group members brought out their own previous difficulties with alcohol and drugs and showed how they had managed to get through that almost impossible period of their lives. Another member gave her steady support through many phone calls and visits. At times when she clammed up or sulked, the therapist and other group members pushed her to open up and voice her real feelings. Then they went after her defenses and revealed her foolish ideas (especially the idea that she had to be terribly hurt if others rejected her) and showed how these could be uprooted. During the marathon, she was able, for the first time in her life, to let herself be really touched emotionally by a male who, up to that time, was a perfect stranger to her, and this showed her that she could afford to let down her long-held barriers to intimacy and let herself love.

Behaviorally, Sara was given homework assignments that included talking to attractive males in public places and thereby overcoming her fears of being rejected. She was shown how to stay on a long-term diet (which she had never done before) by only allowing herself rewarding experiences (such as listening to classical music) when she had first maintained her diet for a certain number of hours. Through the use of role-playing with the therapist and other group members, she was given training in being assertive with people at work and in her social life without being hostile (Ellis & Grieger, 1977, 1986).

Resolution

Sara progressed in several ways: (1) She stopped drinking completely, lost 25 pounds, and appeared to be maintaining both her sobriety and her weight loss. (2) She became considerably less condemnatory of both herself and others and began to make some close friends. (3) She had satisfactory sex relations with three different males and began to steadily date the second one of the three. (4) She only rarely made herself guilty or depressed, accepted herself with her failings, and began to focus much more on enjoying than on rating herself.

Follow up

Sara had REBT individual and group sessions for six months—and occasional follow-up sessions for the next year. She married her steady boyfriend about a year after she had originally begun treatment, having two premarital counseling sessions with him following their engagement. Two and one-half years after the close of therapy, she and her husband reported that everything was going well in their marriage, at her job, and in their social life. Her husband seemed particularly appreciative of the use she was making of REBT principles and noted that "she still works hard at what she learned with you and the group and, frankly, I think that she keeps improving, because of this work, all the time." She smilingly and enthusiastically agreed.

❖ SUMMARY

Rational emotive behavior therapy (REBT) is a comprehensive system of personality change that includes a large variety of cognitive, emotive, and behavior therapy methods. It is based on a clear-cut theory of emotional health and disturbance. The many techniques it employs are used in the light of that theory. Its major hypotheses also apply to childbearing, education, social and political affairs, the extension of people's intellectual-emotional frontiers, and the abetting of their unique potential for growth. REBT psychology is hardheaded, empirically oriented, rational, and nonmagical. It fosters the use of reason, science, and technology. It is humanistic, existentialist, and hedonistic. It makes growth and happiness the relevant core of a person's intrapersonal and interpersonal life.

REBT theory holds that people are biologically and culturally predisposed to choose, create, relate, and enjoy, but that they are also strongly predisposed to over-conform, be suggestible, hate, and foolishly block their enjoying. Although they have remarkable capacities to observe, reason, imaginatively enhance their experiencing, and transcend some of their own essential limitations, they also have an incredibly facile and easy propensity to ignore reality, misuse reason, and rigidly and intolerantly invent absolutist musts that frequently sabotage their health and happiness. In the course of their refusals to accept social reality, their continual *must*urbation, and their absorption in deifying and devil-ifying themselves and others, they frequently wind up with emotional disturbances.

More specifically, when noxious stimuli occur in people's lives at point A (the activating event), they usually observe these events fairly objectively and conclude, at point rB (their rational belief), that this event is unfortunate, inconvenient, and disadvantageous and that they wish it would change. They then appropriately feel, at point C (the consequence), sad, regretful, frustrated, or annoyed. These healthy negative feelings usually help them to try to do something about the noxious activating event to improve or change it. Their inborn and acquired hedonism and constructivism encourage them to have, in regard to noxious or unpleasant activating events (or activating experiences), thoughts ("I don't like this; let's see what I can do to change it") and feelings (sorrow and annoyance) that enable them to reorder their environment and to live more enjoyably.

Very often, however, when similar noxious activating events occur in people's lives, they observe these events intolerantly and grandiosely and conclude, at point iB (their irrational beliefs), that these events are awful, horrible, and catastrophic, that they *must* not exist, and that they absolutely cannot stand them. They then self-defeatingly feel the consequence, at point C, of worthlessness, guilt, anxiety, depression, rage, and inertia. Their disturbed feelings usually interfere with their doing something constructive about the noxious activating events, and they tend to condemn themselves for their unconstuctiveness and to experience more feelings of shame, inferiority, and hopelessness. Their inborn and acquired person-downing, antihumanistic, deifying and devil-ifying philosophy encourages them to have, in regard to noxious or unpleasant activating events, foolish thoughts ("How awful this is and I am! There's nothing I can do about it!") and dysfunctional feelings (hatred of themselves, of others, and of the world) that drive them to whine and rant and live less enjoyably.

REBT is a cognitive-emotive-behavioristic method of psychotherapy uniquely designed to enable people to observe, understand, and persistently dispute their irrational, grandiose, perfectionistic *shoulds*, *oughts*, and *musts*. It employs the logico-empirical method of science to encourage people to surrender magic, absolutes, and damnation; to acknowledge that nothing is sacred or all-important (although many things are exceptionally unpleasant and inconvenient); and to gradually teach themselves and to practice the philosophy of desiring rather than demanding and of working at changing what they can change and gracefully putting up with what they cannot (Bernard, 1991; Ellis & Dryden, 1987).

In conclusion, rational emotive behavior therapy is a method of personality change that quickly and efficiently helps people resist their tendencies to be too conforming, suggestible, and anhedonic. It actively and didactically, as well as emotively and behaviorally, shows people how to abet and enhance one side of their humanness while simultaneously changing and living more happily with (and not repressing or squelching) another side. It is thus realistic and practical as well as idealistic and future-oriented. It helps individuals more fully to actualize, experience, and enjoy the here and now, but it also espouses long-range hedonism, which includes planning for their own (and others') future. It is what its name implies: rational *and* emotive, realistic *and* visionary, empirical *and* humanistic. As, in all their complexity, are humans.

❖ ANNOTATED BIBLIOGRAPHY

Ellis, A., & Dryden, W. (1987). *The practice of rational-emotive therapy.* New York: Springer Publishing Company.

Presents the general theory and basic practice of rational emotive behavior therapy (REBT), with special chapters on how it is used in individual, couples, family, group, and sex therapy. Brings the original seminal book on REBT, *Reason and Emotion in Psychotherapy* (Ellis, 1962), up to date, and gives many details of its therapy procedures.

Ellis, A., & Harper, R. A. (1975). *A new guide to rational living.* North Hollywood, CA: Wilshire Books.

This completely revised and rewritten version of the REBT self-help classic is one of the most widely read self-help books ever published and the one most often recommended by cognitive-behavior therapists to their clients. It is a succinct, straightforward approach to REBT based on self-questioning and homework and shows how readers can help themselves with various emotional problems.

❖ CASE READINGS

Ard, B. N. (1971). The case of the black and silver masochist. In A. Ellis, *Growth through reason: Verbatim cases in rational-emotive therapy* (pp. 15–45). Hollywood: Wilshire Books. [Reprinted in D. Wedding & R. J. Corsini (1979). *Great cases in psychotherapy.* Itasca, IL: F. E. Peacock.]

Ard tackles the case of a 24-year-old schizophrenic woman who pays men to beat her with black and silver belts to assuage the guilt feelings that stem from her religious assumptions. By courageously disputing some of her religious and other irrational beliefs, the therapist makes real progress with an unusually disturbed woman who had not previously been helped by shock treatments or other forms of therapy.

Ellis, A. (1971). A twenty-three-year-old woman, guilty about not following her parents' rules. In A. Ellis, *Growth through reason: Verbatim cases in rational-emotive therapy* (pp. 223–286). Hollywood: Wilshire Books. [Reprinted in D. Wedding & R. J. Corsini (Eds.) (1995). *Case studies in psychotherapy.* Itasca, IL: F. E. Peacock.]

Ellis presents a verbatim protocol of the first, second, and fourth sessions with a woman who comes for help because she is self-punishing, impulsive and compulsive, afraid of males, has no goals in life, and is guilty about her relations with her parents. The therapist quickly zeroes in on her main problems and shows her that she need not feel guilty about doing what she wants to do in life, even if her parents keep upsetting themselves about her beliefs and actions.

Maultsby, M. C., Jr. (1971). A relapsed client with severe phobic reactions. In A. Ellis, *Growth through reason: Verbatim cases in rational-emotive therapy* (pp. 179–222). Hollywood: Wilshire Books.

Maultsby presents a verbatim first session and parts of subsequent sessions with a 24-year-old undergraduate student who had been previously hospitalized for a psychotic episode, who had 30 sessions of traditional psychotherapy, who reported significant improvement in most of his problems after 50 sessions of group rational emotive behavioral therapy, but who a year later reported that his gains were being whittled away, that he was becoming afraid of having a concussion and a consequent major loss of intelligence, that he again felt stupid in his schoolwork, and that he blamed many of his personal failings on an automobile accident. Maultsby deals with this relapsed client in an active-directive manner and in relatively few additional sessions helps the client get to the point where he no longer feels disturbed.

Ellis, A. (1977). Verbatim psychotherapy session with a procrastinator. In A. Ellis & W. J. Knaus, *Overcoming procrastination* (pp. 152–167). New York: New American Library.

Ellis presents a single verbatim session with a procrastinator who was failing to finish her doctoral thesis in sociology. He deals with her problems in a direct, no-nonsense manner typical of rational-emotive therapy, and as a result of a single session, she later reports she finished her thesis, although she had previously been procrastinating on it for a number of years.

❖ REFERENCES

Adler, A. (1931). *What life should mean to you*. New York: Blue Ribbon Books.

Adler, A. (1964). *Social interest: A challenge to mankind*. New York: Capricorn.

Beck, A. T. (1991). Cognitive therapy: A 30-year retrospective. *American Psychologist, 46*, 382–389.

Bernard, M. E. (Ed.). (1991). *Using rational-emotive therapy effectively: A practitioner's guide*. New York: Plenum.

Bernard, M. E., & Joyce, M. R. (1993). *Rational-emotive therapy with children and adolescents*. 2nd ed. New York: Wiley.

Bernard, M. E., & Wolfe, J. (Eds.) (1993). *The RET resource book for practitioners*. New York: Institute for Rational-Emotive Therapy.

Corsini, R. J. (1979). The betting technique in counseling and psychotherapy. *Individual Psychology, 16*, 5–11.

Ellis, A. (1962). *Reason and emotion in psychotherapy*. Secaucus, NJ: Citadel. Rev. ed., 1994. New York: Carol Publishing.

Ellis, A. (1972). *Executive leadership*. New York: Institute for Rational-Emotive Therapy.

Ellis, A. (1973). *Humanistic psychotherapy: The rational-emotive approach*. New York: McGraw Hill.

Ellis, A. (1975). The rational-emotive approach to sex therapy. *Counseling Psychologist, 5* (1), 14–22.

Ellis, A. (1976). The biological basis of human irrationality. *Journal of Individual Psychology, 32*, 145–168. Reprinted: New York: Institute for Rational-Emotive Therapy.

Ellis, A. (1985). *Overcoming re-resistance: Rational-emotive therapy with difficult clients*. New York: Springer.

Ellis, A. (1988). *How to stubbornly refuse to make yourself miserable about anything—yes, anything!* Secaucus, NJ: Lyle Stuart.

Ellis, A. (1991a). Achieving self-actualization. In A. Jones & R. Crandall (Eds.), *Handbook of self-actualization* (pp. 1–18). Corte Madera, CA: Select Press.

Ellis, A. (1991b). Rational-emotive family therapy. In A. M. Horne & J. L. Passmore (Eds.), *Family counseling and therapy*. 2nd edition (pp. 403–434). Itasca, IL: F. E. Peacock.

Ellis, A. (1991c). The revised ABCs of rational-emotive therapy. In J. Zeig (Ed.), *The evolution of psychotherapy: The second conference* (pp. 79–99). New York: Brunner/Mazel. Expanded version: *Journal of Rational-Emotive and Cognitive-Behavior Therapy, 9*, 139–172.

Ellis, A. (1992a). Brief therapy: The rational-emotive method. In S. H. Budman, M. F. Hoyt, & S. Friedman, *The first session in brief therapy* (pp. 36–58). New York: Guilford.

Ellis, A. (1992b). Group rational-emotive and cognitive-behavioral therapy. *International Journal of Group Psychotherapy, 42*, 63–80.

Ellis, A. (1992c). Rational-emotive approaches to peace. *Journal of Cognitive Psychotherapy, 6*, 79–104.

Ellis, A., & Dryden, W. (1987). *The practice of rational-emotive therapy*. New York: Springer.

Ellis, A., & Grieger, R. (Eds.). (1977). *Handbook of rational-emotive therapy. Vol. 1*. New York: Springer.

Ellis, A., & Grieger, R. (Eds.). (1986). *Handbook of rational-emotive therapy. Vol. 2*. New York: Springer.

Ellis, A., & Harper, R. A. (1975). *A new guide to rational living*. North Hollywood, CA: Wilshire Books.

Ellis, A., Sichel, J., Leaf, R. C., & Mass, R. (1989). Countering perfectionism in research on clinical practice. I: Surveying rationality changes after a single intensive RET intervention. *Journal of Rational-Emotive & Cognitive-Behavior Therapy, 7*, 197–218.

Ellis, A., Sichel, J., Yeager, R., DiMattia, D., & DiGiuseppe, R. (1989). *Rational-emotive couples therapy*. Des Moines, IA: Allyn & Bacon.

Ellis, A., & Whiteley, J. (1979). *Theoretical and empirical foundations of rational-emotive therapy*. Pacific Grove, CA: Brooks/Cole.

Hauck, P. A. (1992). *Overcoming the rating game: Beyond self-love—beyond self-esteem*. Louisville, KY: Westminster/John Knox.

Hollon, S. D., & Beck, A. T. (1994). Cognitive and cognitive-behavioral therapies. In A. E. Bergin & S. L. Garfield (Eds.), *Handbook of psychotherapy and behavior change* (pp. 428–466) 4th edition. New York: Wiley.

Landry, E. E. (1994). Disjunctive psychotherapies. In R. J. Corsini (Ed.), *Encyclopedia of psychology*. 2nd edition, pp. 426–428. New York: Wiley.

Lyons, L. C., & Woods, P. J. (1991). The efficacy of rational-emotive therapy: A quantitative review of the outcome research. *Clinical Psychology Review, 11*, 357–369.

McGovern, T. E., & Silverman, M. S. (1984). A review of outcome studies of rational-emotive therapy from 1977 to 1982. *Journal of Rational-Emotive Therapy, 2*(1), 7–18.

Rogers, C. R. (1961). *On becoming a person*. Boston: Houghton Mifflin.

Silverman, M. S., McCarthy, M., & McGovern, T. (1992). A review of outcome studies of rational-emotive therapy from 1982–1989. *Journal of Rational-Emotive and Cognitive-Behavior Therapy, 10*(3), 111–186.

Walen, S., DiGiuseppe, R., & Dryden, W. (1992). *A practitioner's guide to rational-emotive therapy*. New York: Oxford University Press.

Woods, P. J. (1992). A study of belief and nonbelief items from the Jones irrational beliefs test with implications for the theory of RET. *Journal of Rational-Emotive and Cognitive-Behavior Therapy, 10*, 41–52.

Young, H. S. (1974). *A rational counseling primer*. New York: Institute for Rational-Emotive Therapy.

Ivan Pavlov 1849–1936

B. F. Skinner 1904–1990

Albert Bandura

Joseph Wolpe

7 Behavior Therapy

G. Terence Wilson

❖ OVERVIEW

Behavior therapy is a relative newcomer on the psychotherapy scene. Not until the late 1950s did it emerge as a systematic approach to the assessment and treatment of psychological disorders. In its early stages, behavior therapy was defined as the application of modern learning theory to the treatment of clinical problems. The phrase *modern learning theory* referred to the principles and procedures of classical and operant conditioning. Behavior therapy was seen as the logical extension of behaviorism to complex forms of human activities.

Behavior therapy has undergone significant changes in both nature and scope, and it has been responsive to advances in experimental psychology and innovations in clinical practice. It has grown more complex and sophisticated. Behavior therapy can no longer be defined simply as the clinical application of classical and operant conditioning theory.

Behavior therapy today is marked by a diversity of views. It now comprises a broad range of heterogeneous procedures with different theoretical rationales and open debate about conceptual bases, methodological requirements, and evidence of efficacy. As behavior therapy expands, it increasingly overlaps with other psychotherapeutic approaches. Nevertheless, the basic concepts characteristic of the behavioral approach are clear and its commonalities with and differences from nonbehavioral therapeutic systems can be readily identified.

Basic Concepts

Three main approaches in contemporary behavior therapy include (a) *applied behavior analysis,* (b) *a neo-behavioristic mediational stimulus-response model, and* (c) *social-cognitive theory.* These three approaches differ in the extent to which they use cognitive concepts and procedures. At one end of this continuum is *applied behavior analysis,* which focuses exclusively on observable behavior and rejects all cognitive mediating processes. At the other end is *social-cognitive theory,* which relies heavily on cognitive theories.

Applied Behavior Analysis

This approach is a direct extension of Skinner's (1953) radical behaviorism. It relies on operant conditioning, the fundamental assumption being that behavior is a function of its consequences. Accordingly, treatment procedures are based on altering relationships between overt behaviors and their consequences. Applied behavior analysis makes use of reinforcement, punishment, extinction, stimulus control, and other procedures derived from laboratory research. Cognitive processes are considered private events and are not regarded as proper subjects of scientific analysis.

The Neobehavioristic Mediational Stimulus-Response Model

This approach features the application of the principles of classical conditioning, and it derives from the learning theories of Ivan Pavlov, E. R. Guthrie, Clark Hull, O. H. Mowrer, and N. E. Miller. Unlike the operant approach, the S-R model is mediational, with intervening variables and hypothetical constructs prominently featured. S-R theorists have been particularly interested in the study of anxiety; the techniques of systematic desensitization and flooding, both closely associated with this model, are directed toward the extinction of the underlying anxiety assumed to maintain phobic disorders. Private events, especially imagery, have been an integral part of this approach, including systematic desensitization. The rationale is that covert processes follow the laws of learning that govern overt behaviors.

Social-Cognitive Theory

The social-cognitive approach depends on the theory that behavior is based on three separate but interacting regulatory systems (Bandura, 1986). They are (a) external stimulus events, (b) external reinforcement, and (c) cognitive mediational processes.

In the social-cognitive approach, the influence of environmental events on behavior is largely determined by cognitive processes governing how environmental influences are perceived and how the individual interprets them. Psychological functioning, according to this view, involves a reciprocal interaction among three interlocking sets of influences: behavior, cognitive processes, and environmental factors. Bandura put it as follows:

> Personal and environmental factors do not function as independent determinants; rather, they determine each other. Nor can "persons" be considered causes independent of their behavior. It is largely through their actions that people produce the environmental conditions that affect their behavior in a reciprocal fashion. The experiences generated by behavior also partly determine what individuals think, expect, and can do, which in turn affect their subsequent behavior. (1977, p. 345)

In social-cognitive theory, the person is the agent of change. The theory emphasizes the human capacity for self-directed behavior change. Strongly influenced by the social-cognitive model, the clinical practice of behavior therapy has increasingly included cognitive methods, especially those described by Aaron Beck (see Chapter 8). A primary focus of both cognitive and behavioral techniques is to change the cognitive processes viewed as essential to therapeutic success. The basic assumption is that it is not so much experience itself, but rather the person's interpretation of that experience, that produces psychological disturbance. This position is also reflected in the work of Albert Ellis (see Chapter 6). Both cognitive and behavioral methods are used to modify faulty perceptions and interpretations of important life events. For these reasons it is now common to refer to "cognitive behavior therapy" (CBT) instead of "behavior therapy." As Jacobson (1987) has pointed out, "incorporation of cognitive theory and therapy into behavior therapy has been so total that it is difficult to find pure behavior therapists working with outpatients" (pp. 4–5). The term "behavior therapy" is used throughout this chapter, although it could just as easily be replaced with "CBT." Behavior therapy, in a broad sense, refers to practice based primarily on social-cognitive theory and encompassing a range of cognitive principles and procedures.

Common Characteristics

Although the three preceding behavior therapy approaches involve conceptual differences, behavior therapists subscribe to a common core of basic concepts. The two foundations of behavior therapy are (a) a psychological model of human behavior that differs fundamentally from the traditional psychodynamic model, and (b) a commitment to the scientific method.

The emphasis on a psychological model of abnormal behavior and the commitment to a scientific approach have the following consequences:

1.   Many types of abnormal behavior formerly regarded as illnesses or as signs and symptoms of illness are better construed as nonpathological "problems of living" (key examples include anxiety reactions, sexual and conduct disorders). This position is similar to that of Alfred Adler.

2.   Most abnormal behavior is assumed to be acquired and maintained in the same manner as normal behavior. It can be treated through the application of behavioral procedures.

3.   Behavioral assessment focuses on the current determinants of behavior rather than on the analysis of possible historical antecedents. Specificity is the hallmark of behavioral assessment and treatment, and it is assumed that the person is best understood and described by what the person does in a particular situation.

4.   Treatment requires a prior analysis of the problem into components or subparts. Procedures are then systematically targeted at specific components.

5.   Treatment strategies are individually tailored to different problems in different individuals.

6.   Understanding the origins of a psychological problem is not essential for producing behavior change. Conversely, success in changing a problem behavior does not imply knowledge about its etiology.

7.   Behavior therapy involves a commitment to the scientific approach. This includes an explicit, testable conceptual framework; treatment derived from or at least consistent with the content and method of experimental-clinical psychology; therapeutic techniques that have measurable outcomes and can be replicated; the experimental evaluation of treatment methods and concepts; and the emphasis on innovative research strategies that

allow rigorous evaluation of specific methods applied to particular problems instead of global assessment of ill-defined procedures applied to heterogeneous problems.

Other Systems

Behavior therapy has much in common with other psychological therapies, particularly those that tend to be brief and directive. In some cases, behavior therapy has "borrowed" concepts and methods from other systems. For example, behavioral marital therapy places great emphasis on communication skills (Jacobson & Margolin, 1979), an approach that was derived from the clinical tradition of client-centered therapy (Knudson, Gurman, & Kniskern, 1979).

Cognitive-behavioral treatment strategies have incorporated some of the concepts of Albert Ellis's rational emotive behavior therapy and especially Beck's cognitive therapy (Hawton, Salkovskis, Kirk, & Clark, 1989; O'Leary & Wilson, 1987). CBT is closer to Beck's cognitive therapy than Ellis's approach because Beck emphasizes the importance of behavioral procedures in correcting the dysfunctional beliefs assumed to cause emotional distress. Ellis's REBT, despite the later inclusion of *behavior* in the name, is mainly a semantic treatment in which the goal is to alter the person's basic philosophy of life through reason and logic. The overlap between BT and Beck's cognitive therapy is more extensive, especially in the treatment of unipolar depression and some anxiety disorders. Both systems include cognitive and behavioral components but may differ in how these components are combined and especially in their theories about mechanisms of therapeutic change (Hawton et al., 1989; Hollon & Beck, 1994).

In terms of clinical practice, behavior therapy and multimodal therapy are similar. The majority of the techniques that Arnold Lazarus (1981) lists as the most frequently used in multimodal therapy (see Chapter 11) are standard behavior therapy strategies. This is not surprising, given that Lazarus (1971) was one of the pioneers of clinical behavior therapy.

Therapists are guided in their formulations and treatment of different problems either by clearly stated principles or their personal experience and intuition. Behavior therapy represents an attempt to move beyond idiosyncratic practices and to base clinical practice on secure scientific foundations. This does not mean that clinical practice by behavior therapists is always based on solid empirical evidence. Behavior therapists, not unlike therapists from other approaches, have developed their own clinical lore, much of which is not based on experimental research. Lacking sufficient information and guidelines from research, behavior therapists often adopt a trial-and-error approach. Nonetheless, behavior therapy is clearly linked to a specifiable and testable conceptual framework.

Behavior therapy differs fundamentally from psychodynamic approaches to treatment. Based on a learning or educational model of human development, it rejects the psychoanalytic model, in which abnormal behavior is viewed as a symptom of underlying unconscious conflicts. Psychoanalytic therapy has difficulty explaining successes of behavior therapy that contradict basic concepts that psychoanalysts claim are crucial for therapeutic change. Some psychodynamic therapists state that behavioral treatments result in symptom substitution because behavioral treatment allegedly overlooks the "real" cause of the problem. Yet the evidence is clear that symptom substitution does not occur in successful behavior therapy (e.g., Sloane, Staples, Cristol, Yorkston, & Whipple, 1975).

Family and systems therapists assert that individuals can best be understood and treated by changing the interpersonal system within a family. Behavior therapy has increasingly emphasized the importance of including family members in treatment. However, behavior therapists reject the assumption that every problem requires a broad-scale intervention in the family system. The findings of outcome studies show that this is not always necessary (Mathews, Gelder, & Johnston, 1981). For example, not only does individual behavior therapy for agoraphobics produce long-term improvement in phobic avoidance, it often also results in increases in marital satisfaction and other aspects of interpersonal functioning (Marks, 1981). Data such as these discredit the claims of some family systems theorists.

Most forms of psychotherapy are limited to specific populations. Traditional psychoanalytic therapy, for instance, has focused predominantly on white, well-educated, socially and economically advantaged clients. Behavior therapy is more broadly applicable to the full range of psychological disorders than is traditional psychotherapy (Kazdin & Wilson, 1978). In the Sloane et al. (1975) study, for example, behavior therapy appeared to be more effective than traditional psychotherapy, particularly with the complex problems of severely disturbed patients. Areas of successful application of behavior therapy procedures are found in education, rehabilitation, and medicine (Franks, Wilson, Kendall, & Brownell, 1982; Kazdin, 1978b). Finally, behavior therapy is the preferred treatment for certain problems, such as phobic and obsessive-compulsive disorders, sexual dysfunction, and a number of childhood disorders.

Overall evaluation of the comparative efficacy of behavior therapy versus other psychotherapies is uncertain. Nevertheless, in no comparative outcome study to date has behavior therapy been shown to be less effective than any alternative form of psychotherapy (Kazdin & Wilson, 1978). The evidence, unsatisfactory as it is, indicates that behavior therapy is more effective than psychoanalytic and other verbal psychotherapies (see Hollon & Beck, 1994; O'Leary & Wilson, 1987).

✷ HISTORY

Precursors

Two historical events stand out as foundations for behavior therapy. The first was the rise of behaviorism in the early 1900s. The key figure in the United States was J. B. Watson, who criticized the subjectivity and mentalism of the psychology of the time and advocated behaviorism as the basis for the objective study of behavior. Watson's emphasis on the importance of environmental events, his rejection of covert aspects of the individual, and his claim that all behavior could be understood as a result of learning became the formal bases of behaviorism.

Watson's position has been widely rejected by behavior therapists, and more refined versions of behaviorism have been developed by theorists such as B. F. Skinner, whose radical behaviorism has had a significant impact not only on behavior therapy but also on psychology in general. Like Watson, Skinner insisted that overt behavior is the only acceptable subject of scientific investigation.

The second event was experimental research on the psychology of learning. In Russia, around the turn of the twentieth century, Ivan Pavlov, a Nobel Laureate in physiology, established the foundations of classical conditioning. About the same time in the United States, pioneering research on animal learning by E. L. Thorndike showed the influence of consequences (rewarding and punishing events) on behavior.

Research on conditioning and learning principles, conducted largely in the animal laboratory, became a dominant part of experimental psychology in the United States following World War II. Workers in this area, in the traditions of Pavlov and Skinner, were committed to the scientific analysis of behavior using the laboratory rat and pigeon as their prototypic subjects. Among the early applications of conditioning principles to the treatment of clinical problems were two particularly notable studies. In 1924, Mary Cover Jones described different behavioral procedures for overcoming children's fears. In 1938, O. Hobart Mowrer and E. Mowrer extended conditioning principles to the treatment of enuresis, now an effective and widely used approach (Ross, 1981). These isolated and sporadic efforts had scant impact on psychotherapy at the time partly because conditioning principles, demonstrated with animals, were rejected as too simplistic for treating complex human problems. Conditioning treatments were rejected as superficial, mechanistic, and naive. In addition, a schism existed between academic-experimental and clinical psychologists. The former were trained in scientific methods, with an emphasis on controlled experimentation and quantitative measurement. The latter concerned themselves with the "soft" side of psychology, including uncontrolled case studies, speculative hypotheses, and psychodynamic hypotheses. Some efforts were made to integrate conditioning principles with psychodynamic theories of abnormal behavior, but these formulations only obscured crucial differences between behavioral and psychodynamic approaches.

The advent of behavior therapy was marked by its challenge of the status quo through the presentation of a systematic and explicitly formulated clinical alternative that attempted to bridge the gap between the laboratory and the clinic.

Beginnings

The formal beginnings of behavior therapy can be traced to separate but related developments in the 1950s in three countries.

Joseph Wolpe (1958), in South Africa, presented procedural details and results of his application of learning principles to adult neurotic disorders. Wolpe introduced several therapeutic techniques based on Pavlov's conditioning principles, Hull's stimulus-response (S-R) learning theory, and his own experimental research on fear reduction in laboratory animals. Anxiety was regarded as the causal agent in all neurotic reactions. It was defined as a persistent response of the autonomic nervous system acquired through classical conditioning. Wolpe developed specific techniques designed to extinguish these conditioned autonomic reactions, including systematic desensitization, one of the most widely used methods of behavior therapy. A particularly controversial statement found in Wolpe's book was his claim that 90 percent of his patients were either "cured" or "markedly improved." Moreover, this unprecedented success rate was apparently accomplished within a few months, or even weeks. Wolpe influenced A. A. Lazarus and S. Rachman, both of whom became leading figures in the development of behavior therapy. Wolpe's conditioning techniques in therapy were consistent with similar proposals that had been put forward by Andrew Salter (1949) in New York.

Another landmark in the development of behavior therapy was the research and writings of Hans J. Eysenck and his students at the Institute of Psychiatry of London University. In a seminal paper published in 1959, Eysenck defined behavior therapy as the application of modern learning theory to the treatment of behavioral and emotional disorders. Eysenck emphasized the principles and procedures of Pavlov and Hull, as well as learning theorists such as Mowrer (1947) and Miller (1948). In Eysenck's formulation, behavior therapy was an applied science, the defining feature of which was that it was testable and falsifiable. In 1963 Eysenck and Rachman established the first journal devoted exclusively to behavior therapy—*Behaviour Research and Therapy*.

A third force in the emergence of behavior therapy was the publication in 1953 of Skinner's book *Science and Human Behavior*, in which he criticized psychodynamic concepts and reformulated psychotherapy in behavioral terms. The most important initial clinical application of operant conditioning was with children, work carried out under the direction of Sidney Bijou at the University of Washington. The broad application of operant conditioning to the whole range of psychiatric disorders reached full expression in the 1965 publication of Leonard Ullmann and Leonard Krasner's *Case Studies in Behavior Modification*. In 1968, the first issue of the *Journal of Applied Behavior Analysis* was published. This journal provided the premier outlet for research on the modification of socially significant problems through the use of operant conditioning.

Toward the end of the 1960s, the theoretical and research bases of behavior therapy began to expand. Increasingly, behavior therapists turned to social, personality, and developmental psychology as sources of innovative therapeutic strategies. Particularly noteworthy in this regard was Bandura's (1969) social learning theory, with its emphases on vicarious learning (modeling), symbolic processes, and self-regulatory mechanisms. The 1970s witnessed an increased emphasis on cognitive processes and procedures in behavior therapy, as noted in the preceding section.

The 1980s and 1990s have been marked by an even broader focus on developments in other areas of psychology. Particular attention has been paid to the role of affect in therapeutic change. The experimental analysis of the complex interactions among cognition, affect, and behavior is one of the more important areas of theory and research in contemporary behavior therapy. There is also increasing recognition of the importance of biological factors in many of the disorders commonly treated with behavioral methods (e.g., anxiety disorders and obesity). The study of biobehavioral interactions is an increasingly significant part of behavior therapy (O'Leary & Wilson, 1987). (See Kazdin [1978a] for a detailed history of behavior therapy.)

Current Status

Behavior therapy has established itself as a major form of psychological therapy. It has helped to transform graduate training in clinical psychology in the United States. Several doctoral training programs are predominantly behavioral in orientation, and most training programs in clinical psychology offer behavioral training. Counseling programs in schools of education and doctoral programs in schools of psychology have also been influenced by behavior therapy.

The Association for Advancement of Behavior Therapy (AABT) is the major behavior therapy organization in North America. It is a professional, interdisciplinary organization with over 3,000 members. AABT does not certify or license behavior therapists. It publishes a major journal, *Behavior Therapy*, produces a monthly newsletter, the *Behavior Therapist*, and holds annual conventions.

Behavior therapy is also well represented throughout Europe, particularly in Great Britain, the Netherlands, Germany, and Scandinavia. The umbrella organization in Europe is the European Association of Behaviour Therapy. The British Association of Behaviour Therapy alone has over 1,100 members and publishes *Behavioural Psychotherapy*, an interdisciplinary international journal for the helping professions. Behavior therapy is also a major treatment approach in Australia, represented by the Australian Behavior Modification Association.

The practice of behavior therapy is developing in Latin America, with active organizations in Bolivia, Chile, Columbia, Mexico, Peru, and Venezuela, among other countries. The federated association representing Central and South America is the Latin American Association for the Analysis and Modification of Behavior (ALOMOC).

The explosion of literature on behavior therapy has been dramatic. Numerous journals are devoted exclusively to behavior therapy, including the following: *Advances in Be-*

haviour Research and Therapy, Behaviour Research and Therapy, Behavior Therapy, Behavioural Psychotherapy, Behavior Modification, Journal of Behavior Therapy and Experimental Psychiatry, and *Journal of Applied Behavior Analysis*.

❖ PERSONALITY

Theory of Personality

There are specific theoretical differences within the broad framework of contemporary behavior therapy. These differences are most noticeable in the personality theories on which the respective approaches are based. For example, Eysenck (1967) has developed an elaborate trait theory of personality. Briefly, Eysenck classifies people on two major personality dimensions. The first, *introversion-extraversion*, refers to characteristics usually associated with the words *introverted* and *extraverted*. The second dimension is *neuroticism—emotional stability*, ranging from moody and touchy at one extreme to stable and even-tempered at the other. Eysenck believes these personality dimensions are genetically determined and that introverts are more responsive to conditioning procedures than extraverts. In general, however, personality theory appears to have had little impact on clinical behavior therapy, and most behavior therapists have rejected trait theories of personality.

Applied behavior analysis, derived directly from Skinner's radical behaviorism, restricts itself to the study of overt behavior and environmental conditions that presumably regulate behavior. Covert, unobservable elements, such as needs, drives, motives, traits, and conflicts, are disregarded. Skinner's analyses of behavior, for example, are couched in terms of conditioning processes, such as reinforcement, discrimination, and generalization.

Radical behaviorism has been criticized for losing sight of the importance of the person and for lacking a theory of personality. Humanistic psychologists believe applied behavior analysts treat people as though they were controlled only by external, situational forces. A solution to this clash between two extreme viewpoints is to recognize that the characteristics of the environment *interact* with the nature of the people in it. Both commonsense and experimental findings demonstrate the folly of ignoring either side of this crucial interaction. A social learning framework of personality development and change provides a detailed and sophisticated analysis of this interaction between person and situation (Bandura, 1969; Mischel, 1968, 1981).

Many people have debated whether the person or the situation is more important in predicting behavior. This question is unanswerable. The relative importance of individual differences and situations will depend on the situation selected, the type of behavior assessed, the particular individual differences sampled, and the purpose of the assessment (Mischel, 1973).

Evidence clearly shows that an individual's behavioral patterns are generally stable and consistent over time. However, the specificity of behavior in different situations poses a problem for trait theories of personality. The central assumption of such theories is that stable and generalized personality traits determine behavioral consistency in a wide variety of different situations. Yet, as Mischel (1968) has pointed out, the correlations between different measures of the same trait are usually very low, and there is little consistency in behavior patterns across different situations.

Psychodynamic conceptualizations of personality assume that the underlying personality structure is stable across situations. Overt behavior is of interest to psychodynamic theorists only to the extent that the behavior provides signs of deep-seated personality traits. Psychodynamic theorists believe that behavior cannot be taken at face value but must be interpreted symbolically because the personality's defense mechanisms disguise and distort the "real" motivations being expressed. However, "the accumulated findings give little support for the utility of clinical judgments.... Clinicians guided by concepts about underlying genotypic dispositions have not been able to predict behavior better than have the person's own direct self-report, simple indices of directly relevant past behavior, or demographic variables" (Mischel, 1973, p. 254).

Social-cognitive theory readily accounts for the discriminativeness of human behavior. A person would be predicted to act consistently in different situations only to the extent that similar behavior leads, or is expected to lead, to similar consequences. An illustration from Mischel will help clarify this key concept:

> Consider a woman who seems hostile and fiercely independent some of the time but passive, dependent, and feminine on other occasions. What is she really like? Which one of these two patterns reflects the woman that she really is? Is one pattern in the service of the other, or might both be in the service of a third motive? Must she be a really aggressive person with a facade of passivity—or is she a warm, passive-dependent woman with a surface defense of aggressiveness? Social learning theory suggests that it is possible for her to be all of these—a hostile, fiercely independent, passive, dependent, feminine, aggressive, warm person all in one. Of course, which of these she is at any particular moment would not be random and capricious; it would depend on discriminative stimuli—who she is with, when, how, and much, much more. But each of these aspects of herself may be a quite genuine and real aspect of her total being. (1976, p. 86)

The difference between the behavioral and psychodynamic approaches in explaining the development of abnormal behavior can be illustrated by Freud's case of Little Hans. This child developed a phobia for horses, which Freud attributed to castration anxiety and oedipal conflict. In their reinterpretation of this case, Wolpe and Rachman (1960) point out that Little Hans had recently experienced four incidents in which horses were associated with frightening events that could have created a classically conditioned phobic reaction. For example, Hans was terrified when he saw a horse that was pulling a loaded cart knocked down and apparently killed. From a psychodynamic viewpoint, the external stimuli (what Little Hans saw) had little effect on the phobia; the fear of horses per se was less significant than the underlying conflict. As Freud put it, "the anxiety originally had no reference to horses but was transposed onto them secondarily." This interpretation does not account for the discriminative pattern of the boy's reactions. For example, he was fearful of a single horse pulling a loaded cart (viewed by Freud as a symbol of pregnancy) but not of two horses, of large horses but not small ones, and of rapidly moving horse-drawn carts but not slowly moving ones. How is this pattern predicted by a global, internal construct such as an Oedipus conflict? In the accident that the boy witnessed, a single, large horse, moving rapidly, was believed to have been killed. A conditioning explanation emphasizes that specific stimulus elements elicit particular responses and therefore accounts plausibly for the discriminative fear responses of Little Hans.

Trait theories emphasize differences among people on dimensions selected by the clinician. For some purposes, such as gross screening (e.g., administering an MMPI to a client) or group comparisons, a trait approach is useful. But it does not aid the therapist in making treatment decisions about a particular individual. For example, consider the trait of introversion-extraversion. According to Eysenck's theory, particular treatments will have different effects on clients who vary along these dimensions. In a well-controlled study, Paul (1966) correlated performance on paper-and-pencil personality tests measuring extraversion, emotionality, and anxiety, among other traits, with the therapeutic success obtained by treating public speaking anxiety with systematic desensitization. His results revealed no relationship whatsoever between global personality measures and therapeutic outcome. This result is typical of other outcome studies.

Variety of Concepts

Learning Principles

The case of Little Hans illustrates the role of classical conditioning. When a previously neutral stimulus is paired with a frightening event (the unconditioned stimulus, or US), it can become a conditioned stimulus (CS) that elicits a conditioned response (CR) such as anxiety. Current analyses of classical conditioning have moved away from the once-popular notion that what was learned consisted of simple stimulus-response (S-R) bonds. Rather, people learn that there are correlational or contingent relationships between the CS and US. This learning defines the conditioning process. Classical conditioning is no longer seen as the simple pairing of a single CS with a single US. Instead, correlations between entire classes of stimulus events can be learned. People may be exposed to traumatic events (contiguity) but not develop phobic reactions unless a correlational or contingent relationship is formed between the situation and the traumatic event.

Operant conditioning emphasizes that behavior is a function of its environmental consequences. Behavior is strengthened by positive and negative reinforcement; it is weakened by punishment. *Positive reinforcement* refers to an increase in the frequency of a response followed by a favorable event. An example would be a teacher or parent praising a child for obtaining a good report card. *Negative reinforcement* refers to an increase in behavior as a result of avoiding or escaping from an aversive event that one would have expected to occur. For example, an agoraphobic, fearing loss of control and panic in a crowded shopping mall, will escape this aversive prospect by staying at home. This individual then experiences relief from anxiety by having avoided this panic and finds it increasingly difficult to leave the house.

In *punishment*, an aversive event is contingent on a response; the result is a decrease in the frequency of that response. If a child is criticized or punished by his parents for speaking up, he is likely to become an inhibited and unassertive adult.

Extinction refers to the cessation or removal of a response. For example, the family of an obsessive-compulsive client might be instructed to ignore requests for reassurance from the client that he has not done something wrong. The reinforcer that is no longer presented is inappropriate attention.

Discrimination learning occurs when a response is rewarded (or punished) in one situation but not in another. Behavior is then under specific *stimulus control*. This process is particularly important in explaining the flexibility of human behavior. For example, an obese client who goes on eating binges may show good food self-control under some circumstances but lose control in predictable situations (e.g., when alone and feeling frustrated or depressed). *Generalization* refers to the occurrence of behavior in situations other than that in which it was acquired. A therapist might help a client to become more assertive and expressive during treatment sessions. But the ultimate goal of therapy is to have the client act more assertively in real-life situations.

Social-cognitive theory recognizes both the importance of awareness in learning and the person's active cognitive appraisal of environmental events. Learning is facilitated when people are aware of the rules and contingencies governing the consequences of their actions. Reinforcement does not involve an automatic strengthening of behavior. Learning is a consequence of the informative and incentive functions of rewards. By observing the consequences of behavior, a person learns what action is appropriate in what situation. By symbolic representation of anticipated future outcomes of behavior, one generates the motivation to initiate and sustain current actions (Bandura, 1977). Often, people's expectations and hypotheses about what is happening to them may affect their behavior more than the objective reality.

The importance social-cognitive theory attaches to *vicarious learning* (*modeling*) is consistent with its emphasis on cognitive processes. In this form of learning, people acquire new knowledge and behavior by observing other people and events, without engaging in the behavior and without any direct consequences to themselves. Vicarious learning may occur when people watch what others do. The influence of vicarious learning on human behavior is pervasive, and this concept greatly expands the power of social-cognitive theory.

Person Variables

People do not passively interact with situations with empty heads or an absence of feelings. Rather, they actively attend to environmental stimuli, interpret them, encode them, and selectively remember them. Mischel (1973) has spelled out a series of *person variables* that explain the interchange between person and situation. These person variables are the products of each person's social experience and cognitive development that, in turn, determine how future experiences influence him or her. Briefly, they include the individual's *competencies* to construct diverse behaviors under appropriate conditions. In addition, there is the person's *categorization* of events and people, including the self. To understand how a person will perform in particular situations also requires attention to his or her *expectancies*, the *subjective values* of any expected outcomes, and the individual's *self-regulatory systems and plans*.

A full discussion of these person variables is beyond the scope of the present chapter, but some illustrative examples may be given. For example, consider the role of *personal constructs*. It is common in clinical practice to find clients who constantly "put themselves down," even though it is clear to the objective onlooker that they are competent and that they are distorting reality. In cases like these, behavior is mainly under the control of internal stimuli rather than environmental events. Different people might respond differently to the same objective stimulus situation, depending on how they interpret what is happening to them. Therapy concentrates on correcting such faulty cognitive perceptions. But the behavior therapist must also assess a client's cognitive and behavioral *competencies* to ascertain whether he or she really can respond in a particular way. A client may be depressed not because he misperceives the situation but because he actually lacks the appropriate skills to secure rewards. A case in point would be a shy, underassertive college freshman who is motivated to date but who realizes he does not have the social skills needed to establish relationships with women. Therapy would be geared to overcoming his behavioral deficit, helping the student acquire the requisite interpersonal skills.

Self-efficacy is assessed simply by asking a person to indicate the degree of confidence that he or she can do a particular task.

Such person variables differ from traits in that they do not assume broad cross-situational consistency but depend on specific contexts. Constructs such as generalized expectancies have not proved fruitful in predicting behavior. However, specific evaluations of individuals' efficacy expectations with respect to particular tasks are useful.

Applied behavior analysts reject cognitive mediating processes and have little use for person variables. They agree that the environment interacts with the person but contend that the role of the person is best explained in terms of *past history of reinforcement*. To illustrate the differences between the social-cognitive approach and the radical behaviorist position, imagine a client who is phobic about flying. This client typically becomes highly anxious when he hears the plane's landing gear retracting. A therapist with a social-cognitive view might attribute this anxiety reaction to the client's perception that something is wrong. The radical behaviorist would suggest that the client is reacting, not only to the present environment (the sudden noise), but also to stories he has heard in the past about engines falling off and planes crashing. This example makes it clear that radical behaviorism is not free from inferential reasoning. The question is not whether inferences will be made in trying to account for human behavior, but what sort of inference is the most useful. There is now evidence to demonstrate that taking person variables into account improves prediction about behavior and enhances therapeutic efficacy (O'Leary & Wilson, 1987).

❖ PSYCHOTHERAPY

Theory of Psychotherapy

Learning

Behavior therapy emphasizes corrective learning experiences in which clients acquire new coping skills, improve communication, or learn to break maladaptive habits and overcome self-defeating emotional conflicts. These corrective learning experiences involve broad changes in cognitive, affective, and behavioral functioning: they are not limited to modifications of narrow response patterns in overt behavior.

The learning that characterizes behavior therapy is carefully structured. Perhaps more than any other form of treatment, behavior therapy involves asking a patient to do something such as practice relaxation training, self-monitor daily caloric intake, engage in assertive acts, confront anxiety-eliciting situations, and refrain from carrying out compulsive rituals. The high degree to which behavior therapists emphasize the client's activities in the real world between therapy sessions is one of the distinctive features of the behavioral approach. However, behavior therapy is not a one-sided influence process by the therapist to effect changes in a client's beliefs and behavior. It involves both dynamic interaction between therapist and client and directed work on the part of the client. A crucial factor in all forms of therapy is the client's motivation, the willingness to cooperate in the arduous and challenging task of making significant changes in real-life behavior. Resistance to change and lack of motivation are common reasons for treatment failures in behavior therapy. Much of the art in therapy involves coping with these issues (Lazarus & Fay, 1982).

The Therapeutic Relationship

Behavior therapy demands skill, sensitivity, and clinical acumen. Brady underscores the importance of the therapeutic relationship as follows.

> There is no question that qualitative aspects of the therapist-patient relationship can greatly influence the course of therapy for good or bad. In general, if the patient's relationship to the therapist is characterized by belief in the therapist's competence (knowledge, sophistication, and training) and if the patient regards the therapist as an honest, trustworthy, and decent human being with good social and ethical values (in his own scheme of things), the patient is more apt to invest himself in the therapy. Equally important is the quality and tone of the relationship he has with the therapist. That is, if he feels trusting and warm toward the therapist, this generally will facilitate following the treatment regimen, will be associated with higher ex-

pectations of improvement, and other generally favorable factors. The feelings of the therapist toward the patient are also important. If the therapist feels that his patient is not a desirable person or a decent human being or simply does not like the patient for whatever reasons, he may not succeed in concealing these attitudes toward the patient, and in general they will have a deleterious effect. (1980, pp. 285–286)

A survey of behavior practitioners indicated that treatment frequently aims at improving the therapeutic relationship (Swan & MacDonald, 1978). O'Leary, Turkewitz, and Tafel (1973) found that virtually all parents whose children were treated at a child-guidance clinic rated their behavior therapists as understanding, warm, sincere, and interested. Similarly, in a study of marital therapy by Turkewitz and O'Leary (1981), clients' ratings of their behavior therapists were positive.

As opposed to the neutral and detached role that the psychoanalytically oriented therapist is taught to assume, the behavior therapist is directive and concerned—a problem solver and a coping model. In their comparative study of behavior therapy and psychoanalytically oriented psychotherapy, Staples, Sloane, Whipple, Cristol, and Yorkston concluded:

> Differences between behavior therapy and analytically-oriented psychotherapy …involved the basic patterns of interactions between patient and therapist and the type of relationship formed. Behavior therapy is not psychotherapy with special "scientific techniques" superimposed on the traditional therapeutic paradigm; rather, the two appear to represent quite different styles of treatment although they share common elements. (1975, p. 1521)

The behavior therapists in this study were rated as more directive, more open, more genuine, and more disclosing than their psychoanalytically oriented counterparts.

Both behavioral and psychodynamic treatments attempt to modify underlying causes of behavior. The difference is what proponents of each approach regard as causes. Behavior analysts look for current variables and conditions that control behavior. Some psychodynamic approaches (e.g., psychoanalysis) ask, "How did the client become this kind of person?" Others (e.g., Adlerian psychotherapy) ask, "What is this person trying to achieve?" Behavioral approaches ask, "What is causing this person to behave in this way right now, and what can we do right now to change that behavior?"

Ethical Issues

In behavior therapy the client is encouraged to participate actively. Consider, for example, the important issue of who determines the goals of therapy. Because it is fundamental to behavior therapy that the client should have the major say in setting treatment goals, it is important that the client is fully informed and consents to and participates in setting goals. A distinction is drawn between how behavior is to be changed—in which the therapist is presumably expert—and the objectives of therapy. The latter must ultimately be determined by the client. The client controls what; the therapist controls how. The major contribution of the therapist is to assist clients by helping them to generate alternative courses of action and to analyze the consequences of pursuing various goals. Because this process involves an expression of the therapist's own values, the therapist should identify them and explain how they might affect his or her analysis of therapeutic goals.

Selecting goals is far more complicated in the case of disturbed clients (such as institutionalized psychotics) who are unable to participate meaningfully in deciding treatment objectives. To ensure that treatment is in the client's best interests, it is important to monitor program goals and procedures through conferences with other professionals (Risley & Sheldon-Wildgen, 1982).

All forms of therapy involve social influence. The critical ethical question is whether therapists are aware of this influence. Behavior therapy entails an explicit recognition of the influence process and emphasizes specific, client-oriented behavioral objectives. Behavior therapists have formulated procedures to guarantee protection of human rights and personal dignity of all clients (Stolz, 1978; Wilson & O'Leary, 1980).

Process of Psychotherapy

Problem Identification and Assessment

The initial task of a behavior therapist is to identify and understand the client's presenting problem(s). The therapist seeks detailed information about the specific dimensions of problems, such as initial occurrence, severity, and frequency. What has the client done to cope with the problems? What does the client think about his or her problem and any previous therapeutic contacts? Obtaining answers to such searching questions is facilitated by a relationship of trust and mutual understanding. To achieve this, the therapist is attentive, trying to be objective and empathic. The therapist then proceeds to make a functional analysis of the client's problem, attempting to identify specific environmental and person variables that are thought to be maintaining maladaptive thoughts, feelings, or behavior. The emphasis on variables currently maintaining the problem does not mean that the client's past history is ignored. However, past experiences are important only to the degree that they directly contribute to the client's present distress.

Assessment Methods

In the behaviorally oriented interview the therapist seldom asks the client *why* questions; for example, "Why do you become anxious in crowded places?" Questions starting with *how, when, where,* and *what* are more useful. The therapist does not necessarily take everything the client says at face value and is constantly looking for inconsistencies, evasiveness, or apparent distortions. Nevertheless, the therapist relies heavily on clients' self-reports, particularly in assessing thoughts, fantasies, and feelings. Self-report has often proved to be a superior predictor of behavior as compared to clinicians' judgments or scores on personality tests (Mischel, 1981). Of course, therapists must ask the right questions if they are to get meaningful answers. Given the tendency of most people to describe themselves with broad personality labels, therapists may have to help clients to identify specific behavioral referents for global subjective impressions.

Guided Imagery

A useful method for assessing clients' reactions to particular situations is to have them symbolically recreate a problematic life situation. Instead of asking clients simply to talk about an event, the therapist has them imagine it actually happening to them. When clients have conjured up an image of a situation, they are then asked to verbalize any thoughts that come to mind, an especially useful way of uncovering the specific thoughts associated with particular events.

Role-playing

Another option is to ask clients to role-play a situation. This method lends itself to the assessment of interpersonal problems, with the therapist adopting the role of the person with whom the client reports problems. Role-playing provides the therapist with a sample of the problem behavior, albeit under somewhat artificial circumstances. If the therapist is assessing a client couple, the two partners are asked to discuss chosen issues that enable the therapist to observe first-hand the extent of their interpersonal skills and their ability to resolve conflict.

Physiological Recording

Technological progress in monitoring different psychophysiological reactions has made it possible to objectively measure a number of problems. Monitoring a client's sexual arousal in response to specific stimuli that cause changes in penile or vaginal blood flow (Rosen & Keefe, 1978) is an example of the use of physiological recording instruments in behavioral assessment and treatment strategies.

Self-Monitoring

Clients are typically instructed to keep detailed, daily records of particular events or psychological reactions. Obese clients, for example, are asked to self-monitor daily caloric intake, the degree to which they engage in planned physical activities, the conditions under which they eat, and so on. In this way it is possible to detect behavioral patterns in clients' lives functionally related to their problems.

Behavioral Observation

Assessment of overt problem behavior, ideally, is based on actual observation of the client's behavior in the natural environment. Accordingly, behavior therapists have developed sophisticated behavioral observation rating procedures. These procedures most often have been used with children and with hospitalized patients. Parents, teachers, nurses, and hospital aides have been trained as behavioral observers. Once these individuals have learned to observe behavior, they can be taught to make a behavioral analysis of a problem and then instructed to alter their own behavior to influence the problem behavior of another person.

Psychological Tests and Questionnaires

In general, behavior therapists do not use standardized psychodiagnostic tests. Tests such as the MMPI may be useful for providing an overall picture of the client's personality profile, but they do not yield the kind of information necessary for a functional analysis or for the development of therapeutic interventions. Projective tests are widely rejected because of a lack of acceptable evidence for their validity or utility (Mischel, 1968). Behavior therapists do use checklists and questionnaires, such as the Marks and Mathews Fear Questionnaire (1979), self-report scales of depression like the Beck Depression Inventory (Beck, Rush, Shaw & Emery, 1979). assertion inventories like the Rathus (1973) questionnaire, and paper-and-pencil measures of marital satisfaction such as the Locke and Wallace inventory of marital adjustment (1959). These assessment devices are not sufficient for carrying out a functional analysis of the determinants of a problem, but are useful in establishing the initial severity of the problem and charting therapeutic efficacy over the course of treatment.

Treatment Techniques

Behavior therapy offers a wide range of different treatment methods and attempts to tailor the principles of social-cognitive theory to each individual's unique problem. In selecting treatment techniques, the behavior therapist relies heavily on empirical evidence about the efficacy of that technique applied to the particular problem. In many cases the empirical evidence is unclear or largely nonexistent. Here the therapist is influenced by accepted clinical practice and the basic logic and philosophy of a social-cognitive approach to human behavior and its modification. In the process, the therapist must often use intuitive skill and clinical judgment to select appropriate treatment methods and determine the best time to implement specific techniques. Both science and art influence clinical practice, and the most effective therapists are aware of the advantages and limitations of each.

The following are some selective illustrations of the varied methods the typical behavior therapist is likely to employ in clinical practice.

Imagery-Based Techniques

In systematic desensitization, after isolating specific events that trigger unrealistic anxiety, the therapist constructs a stimulus hierarchy in which different situations that the client fears are ordered along a continuum from mildly stressful to very threatening. The client is instructed to imagine each event while he or she is deeply relaxed. Wolpe (1958) adapted Jacobson's (1938) method of progressive relaxation training as a means of producing a response incompatible with anxiety. Briefly, this consists of training clients to concentrate on systematically relaxing different muscle groups. When any item produces excessive anxiety, the client is instructed to cease visualizing the particular item and to restore feelings of relaxation. The item is then repeated, or the hierarchy adjusted, until the client can visualize the scene without experiencing anxiety. Only then does the therapist present the next item of the hierarchy. Real-life exposure, where possible, is even more powerful than using imagination and is the technique of choice for treating anxiety disorders. An example of exposure treatment for an agoraphobic client is described in the section on *treatment*.

Symbolically generated aversive reactions are used to treat problems including alcoholism and sexual disorders such as exhibitionism. In this procedure the client is asked to imaging aversive consequences associated with the problem behavior. An alcoholic might be asked to imagine experiencing nausea at the thought of a drink. As illustrated in the "Case Example," an exhibitionist might be asked to imagine being apprehended by the police. This method is often referred to as covert sensitization (Cautela, 1967). A hierarchy of scenes that reliably elicit the problem urge or behavior is developed, and each scene is systematically presented until the client gains control over the problem.

Cognitive Restructuring

The treatment techniques in this category are based on the assumption that emotional disorders result, at least in part, from dysfunctional thinking. The task of therapy is to alter this maladaptive thinking. Although there is some overlap with Ellis's REBT, the cognitive restructuring method most commonly used by behavior therapists is derived from Beck's cognitive therapy. An example of this method is illustrated in the following excerpt from a therapy session. Notice how the therapist prompts the patient to examine his dysfunctional assumptions and how behavioral tasks are used to help the patient to alter his assumptions:

> Patient: In the middle of a panic attack, I usually think I am going to faint or collapse....
> Therapist: Have you ever fainted in an attack?

P: No.

T: What is it then that makes you think you might faint?

P: I feel faint, and the feeling can be very strong.

T: So, to summarize, your evidence that you are going to faint is the fact that you feel faint?

P: Yes.

T: How can you then account for the fact that you have felt faint many hundreds of times and have not yet fainted?

P: So far, the attacks have always stopped just in time or I have managed to hold onto something to stop myself from collapsing.

T: Right. So one explanation of the fact that you have frequently felt faint, had the thought that you would faint, but have not actually fainted, is that you have always done something to save yourself just in time. However, an alternative explanation is that the feeling of faintness that you get in a panic attack will never lead to you collapsing, even if you don't control it.

P: Yes, I suppose.

T: In order to decide which of these two possibilities is correct, we need to know what has to happen to your body for you to actually faint. Do you know?

P: No.

T: Your blood pressure needs to drop. Do you know what happens to your blood pressure during a panic attack?

P: Well, my pulse is racing. I guess my blood pressure must be up.

T: That's right. In anxiety, heart rate and blood pressure tend to go together. So, you are actually less likely to faint when you are anxious than when you are not.

P: That's very interesting and helpful to know. However, if it's true, why do I feel so faint?

T: Your feeling of faintness is a sign that your body is reacting in a normal way to the perception of danger. Most of the bodily reactions you are experiencing when anxious were probably designed to deal with the threats experienced by primitive man, such as being approached by a hungry tiger. What would be the best thing to do in that situation?

P: Run away as fast as you can.

T: That's right. And in order to help you run, you need the maximum amount of energy in your muscles. This is achieved by sending more of your blood to your muscles and relatively less to the brain. This means that there is a small drop in oxygen to the brain and that is why you feel faint. However, this feeling is misleading because your overall blood pressure is up, not down.

P: That's very clear. So next time I feel faint, I can check out whether I am going to faint by taking my pulse. If it is normal, or quicker than normal, I know I won't faint. (Clark, 1989, pp. 76–77)

Assertiveness and Social Skills Training

Unassertive clients often fail to express their emotions or to stand up for their rights. They are often exploited by others, feel anxious in social situations, and lack self-esteem. In behavior rehearsal the therapist may model the appropriate assertive behavior and may ask the client to engage repeatedly in a graduated sequence of similar actions. Initially, the therapist focuses on expressive behavior (e.g., body posture, voice training, and eye contact). The therapist then encourages the client to carry out assertive actions in the real world to ensure generalization. Behavior therapy is frequently conducted in a group as well as on an individual basis (Upper & Ross, 1981). Behavior rehearsal for assertiveness training is well suited to group therapy, because group members can provide more varied sources of educational feedback and can also offer a diversified range of modeling influences.

The instructional, modeling, and feedback components of behavior rehearsal facilitate a broad range of communication competencies, including active listening, giving personal feedback, and building trust through self-disclosure. These communication principles, drawn from nonbehavioral approaches to counseling but integrated within a behavioral framework, are an important ingredient of behavioral marital therapy (Jacobson & Margolin, 1979).

Self-Control Procedures

Behavior therapists use a number of self-control procedures (Bandura, 1977; Kanfer, 1977). Fundamental to successful self-regulation of behavior is self-monitoring, which requires helping the client set goals or standards that guide behavior. In the treatment of obesity, for example, daily caloric goals are mutually selected. Behavioral research has identified certain properties of goals that increase the probability of successful self-control. For example, one should set highly specific, unambiguous, and short-term goals, such as consumption of no more than 1,200 calories each day. Compare this to the goal of "cutting back" on eating for the "next week." Failure to achieve such vague goals elicits negative self-evaluative reactions by clients, whereas successful accomplishment of goals produces self-reinforcement that increases the likelihood of maintaining the new behavior.

Self-instructional training, described above, is often used as a self-control method for coping with impulsivity, stress, excessive anger, and pain. Similarly, progressive relaxation training is widely applied as a self-control method for reducing different forms of stress, including insomnia, tension headaches, and hypertension (O'Leary & Wilson, 1987). Biofeedback methods used to treat a variety of psychophysiological disorders also fall under the category of self-control procedures (Yates, 1980).

Real-Life Performance-Based Techniques

The foregoing techniques are applied during treatment sessions, and most are routinely coupled with instructions to clients to complete homework assignments in their natural environment.

The diversity of behavioral treatment methods is seen in the application of operant conditioning principles in settings ranging from classrooms to institutions for the retarded and the mentally ill. An excellent illustration is the use of a *token economy*. The main elements of a token reinforcement program can be summarized as follows: (a) carefully specified and operationally defined target behaviors, (b) backup reinforcers, or (c) tokens that represent the backup reinforcers, and (d) rules of exchange that specify the number of tokens required to obtain backup reinforcers.

A token economy in a classroom might consist of the teacher, at regular intervals, making ratings indicating how well a student had behaved, both academically and socially. At the end of the day, good ratings could be exchanged for various small prizes. These procedures reduce disruptive social behavior in the classroom and can improve academic performance (O'Leary & O'Leary, 1977). In the case of psychiatric inpatients the staff might make tokens contingent upon improvements in self-care activities, reductions in belligerent acts, and cooperative problem-solving behavior (Kazdin, 1977). The behavior therapist designs the token economy and monitors its implementation and efficacy. The procedures themselves are implemented in real-life settings by teachers, parents, nurses, and psychiatric aides—whoever has most direct contact with the patient. Ensuring that these psychological assistants are well trained and supervised is the responsibility of the behavior therapist.

Length of Treatment

Much of behavior therapy is short-term treatment, but therapy lasting from 25 to 50 sessions is commonplace, and still longer treatment is not unusual. Therapy in excess of 100 sessions is relatively rare. There are no established guidelines for deciding on the length of therapy. The usual approach in clinical practice is to carry out a detailed behavioral assessment of a client's problem(s) and to embark upon interventions as rapidly as possible. Assessment is an ongoing process, as the consequences of initial treatment interventions are evaluated against therapeutic goals. Unless treatment time is explicitly limited from the start, the length of therapy and the scheduling of the treatment sessions are contingent upon the patient's progress.

Typically, a behavior therapist might contract with a patient to pursue a treatment plan for two to three months (approximately 8 to 12 sessions) and reevaluate progress at the end of this period. The relative absence of any discernible improvement is cause for the therapist to reevaluate whether he or she conceptualized the problem accurately, whether he or she is using the appropriate techniques or needs to switch tactics, whether there is some personal problem with him or her as the therapist, or whether a referral to another therapist or another form of treatment might be necessary.

In terminating a successful case, the behavior therapist usually avoids abruptness. A typical procedure is to lengthen gradually the time between successive therapy sessions, from weekly to fortnightly to monthly and so on. These concluding sessions may be shorter than earlier ones, with occasional telephone contact.

Mechanisms of Psychotherapy

Research on behavior therapy has demonstrated that particular treatment methods are effective and has identified what components of multifaceted treatment methods and programs are responsible for therapeutic success. For example, empirical evidence has established that the changes produced by token reinforcement programs are due to the learning principles of operant conditioning on which they are based (Kazdin, 1977).

Learning Processes

Ayllon and Azrin (1965) described a pioneering token reinforcement program with predominantly schizophrenic patients on a psychiatric hospital ward. The target behaviors in this investigation were self-care and improved capacity for productive work. Rewards were made contingent on improvement in these two areas. Following a period during which the job assignments of all 44 patients on the entire ward were rewarded contingently (phase A), tokens were administered on a noncontingent basis (phase B). In phase B, patients were given tokens each day regardless of their performance, which broke the contingency between reinforcer and response. This ensured that the amount of social interaction between the attendants and ward staff who administered the tokens and the patients remained unchanged. Any deterioration in performance was then directly attributable to the precise functional relationship between behavior and reinforcement.

Phase C marked a return to contingent reinforcement as in phase A. The results showed that "free" reinforcement (phase B) was totally ineffective. Similarly, the complete withdrawal of all tokens resulted in performance decreasing to less than one-fourth the rate at which it had previously been maintained by contingently rewarding the patients with tokens.

No single, monolithic theory encompasses the diverse methods and applications of the different behavior therapies. Although operant conditioning principles explain the efficacy of a broad range of behavioral procedures, they do not account for the success of a number of other methods. Classical conditioning and different cognitive processes all play a part in determining the effects of the various cognitive behavioral treatment methods described in this chapter. In many cases, the mechanisms responsible for the therapeutic success of a method remain unclear. Consider exposure treatment for phobic and obsessive-compulsive disorders. The effectiveness of this method has been well established, but its explanation is still a matter of some controversy. Originally, the explanation was based on Mowrer's (1947) two-factor theory of learning, according to which repeated exposure to anxiety-eliciting situations, as in systematic desensitization, resulted in the extinction of the classically conditioned anxiety that mediates phobic avoidance behavior. However, recent research (Bandura, 1986) casts doubt on the validity of this explanation.

Cognitive Mechanisms

In terms of social-cognitive theory, exposure leads not to the extinction of any underlying anxiety drive state, but rather to modification of the client's expectations of self-efficacy (Bandura, 1982). Self-efficacy refers to clients' beliefs that they can cope with formerly feared situations. For efficacy expectations to change, the client must make a self-attribution of behavioral change. For example, it is not uncommon for an agoraphobic client to approach situations she has avoided without increases in self-efficacy or reductions in fear. The explanation seems to be that some clients do not credit themselves for the behavioral change. The agoraphobic might say that she was "lucky" that she did not have a panic attack or that she just happened to have one of those rare "good days." The therapist must be prepared to help the client use cognitive methods to attribute changes to herself so that her sense of personal efficacy increases.

Initial studies with phobic subjects have generally provided empirical support for self-efficacy theory, although the findings are mixed. Experiments by Bandura and his associates have shown that efficacy expectations accurately predicted reductions in phobic avoidance regardless of whether they were created by real-life exposure or symbolic modeling, covert modeling, or systematic desensitization. Moreover, measures of personal efficacy predicted differences in coping behavior by different individuals receiving the same treatment and even specific performance by subjects in different tasks. Consistent with the theory, participant modeling, a performance-based treatment, produced greater increases in level and strength of efficacy expectations and in related behavior change (Bandura, 1986).

❖ APPLICATIONS

Problems

Behavior therapy can be used to treat a full range of psychological disorders in different populations (Kazdin & Wilson, 1978). It also has broad applicability to problems in education, medicine, and community living. The following are selected examples of problems for which behavior therapy is an effective treatment.

Anxiety Disorders

Several well-controlled studies have established that behavior therapy is an effective form of treatment for anxiety disorders. Simple phobias are successfully eliminated within a short number of sessions by using guided exposure treatment in which patients are helped to gradually approach and confront the phobic objects or situations they fear and avoid.

Even more importantly, behavior therapy is the treatment of choice for more complex and debilitating disorders such as panic disorder, generalized anxiety disorder, and obsessive-compulsive disorder (Barlow & Cerny, 1988).

Consider the treatment of panic disorder. Effective treatment typically combines both behavioral and cognitive components. Studies by David Barlow and his colleagues have evaluated the effects of a panic control treatment (PCT) that includes both behavioral and cognitive components. PCT was more effective than a wait list control condition (in which patients were assessed but their treatment delayed) or relaxation training alone. A two-year follow-up showed that 81 percent of patients treated with PCT were panic-free (Craske, Brown, & Barlow, 1991). At Oxford University in England, David Clark and his colleagues tested the effects of a treatment that focused mainly on changing panic patients' catastrophic interpretation of bodily sensations. This cognitive-behavioral treatment proved to be superior to pharmacological therapy with imipramine, often assumed to be the therapy of choice for panic disorder. At the end of treatment, 90 percent of patients treated with cognitive-behavior therapy were panic-free, compared with only 55 percent of patients treated with imipramine. Patients treated with cognitive-behavioral therapy maintained their improvement over a one-year follow-up, whereas patients treated with imipramine tended to relapse when the drug was discontinued (Clark et al., 1994).

Unipolar Depression

In addition to Beck's pioneering work (see Chapter 8), two other forms of cognitive behavioral treatment have been used successfully to treat unipolar depression. One, developed by Peter Lewinsohn, combines many of the cognitive strategies of Beck's approach with a more traditional behavioral emphasis on increasing the range of patients' positive reinforcers. It has been shown to be effective in overcoming depression in adolescents (Lewinsohn, Clarke, Hops, & Andrews, 1990). The other is a form of behavioral marital therapy. The goal in this treatment is to modify the interpersonal influences on unipolar depression by reducing marital conflict and facilitating increased feelings of closeness and open sharing of thoughts and feelings (O'Leary & Beach, 1990). This treatment seems especially effective with depressed women who also have marital problems.

Sexual Disorders

Behavior therapy is an effective and widely used treatment for male and female sexual problems, such as erectile disorder, premature ejaculation, orgasmic dysfunction, and vaginismus. Perhaps the best known form of behavioral treatment for sexual dysfunction in both heterosexual and homosexual men and women is Masters and Johnson's (1970, 1979) two-week rapid therapy program. These pioneers of research on sexuality and its disorders reported a treatment success rate of roughly 80 percent. Subsequent sex therapists have made more modest claims.

Simple sexual problems, uncomplicated by other personal or interpersonal difficulties, are relatively easy to treat. Women can become orgasmic, and males overcome premature ejaculation using self-help manuals with minimal instruction from a therapist. Clinical experience, nevertheless, shows that relationship problems tend to complicate sex therapy and hinder its success. This is additionally significant if, as sex therapists widely believe, the population seeking sex therapy today is more likely to have fundamental relationship problems than the patients treated in the early 1970s. Successful therapy for these more complex cases may take months or even years.

A variety of other sexual disorders such as exhibitionism, transvestism, and sado-masochism are commonly treated with different cognitive-behavioral methods.

Interpersonal and Marital Problems

Social skills training and assertiveness training are used to treat a broad range of interpersonal problems, from limited social-behavioral repertoires to social anxiety. Behavioral marital therapy is a relatively recent development, the central focus of which is helping partners to learn more positive and productive means of achieving desired behavioral changes in one another (Jacobson & Margolin, 1979). As in the case of anxiety and sexual disorders, specialized behavior marital therapy clinics are now in operation. Behavior therapy has shown clear promise as an effective and efficient treatment for marital problems, but comprehensive investigations of severely distressed couples, with longer follow-ups, are necessary before definitive conclusions can be reached.

Chronic Mental Patients

Behavior therapy is not useful in treating acute psychotic reactions, and most behavior therapists favor pharmacotherapy as the treatment of choice for schizophrenic disorders. Yet behavioral programs are clearly indicated for treating the chronically mentally ill. Paul and Lentz (1977) studied chronic mental patients, all of whom were diagnosed as process schizophrenic and were of low socioeconomic status. These patients had been confined to a mental hospital for an average of 17 years, and had been treated previously with drugs and other methods without success. Approximately 90 percent were taking medication at the onset of the study. Their level of self-care was too low and the severity of their bizarre behavior too great to permit community placement. According to Paul and Lentz, these subjects were " the most severely debilitated chronically institutionalized adults ever subjected to systematic study" (p. v.). In the most detailed, comprehensive, and well-controlled evaluation of the treatment of chronic mental hospital patients ever conducted, Paul and Lentz produced a wealth of objective data, including evidence of cost effectiveness, showing that behavioral procedures (predominantly a sophisticated token reinforcement program) are the treatment of choice.

Childhood Disorders

Children have been treated from the earliest days of behavior therapy. Treatment programs have addressed problems ranging from circumscribed habit disorders in children to multiple responses of children who suffer all-encompassing excesses, deficits, or bizarre behavior patterns. These problems include conduct disorders, aggression, and delinquency. Hyperactivity is widely treated by behavioral methods, such as token reinforcement programs. The documented success of the behavioral approach, particularly in improving the academic performance of these children, suggests that it can sometimes be used as an alternative to drug treatment (O'Leary, 1980).

Autism is a particularly severe early childhood disorder with a very poor prognosis. Traditional psychological and medical treatments have proved ineffective. Behavioral methods, however, have achieved notable success. Lovaas (1987) has recently reported that intensive, long-term behavioral treatment of autistic children resulted in 47 percent achieving normal intellectual and educational functioning. Another 40 percent were mildly retarded and assigned to special classes for the language delayed. Of a control group of autistic children, only 2 percent achieved normal functioning. These findings are the most positive ever obtained with autistic children and illustrate the efficacy of behavioral methods with serious childhood disorders.

Childhood psychoses have also been treated with behavioral techniques. Self-stimulatory and self-destructive behavior such as biting and head banging have been eliminated with aversive procedures. Positive behaviors have been developed to improve language and speech, play, social interaction and responsiveness, and basic academic skills (O'Leary & Carr, 1982).

One of the most effectively treated childhood problems has been enuresis. The bell-and-pad method has produced improvement rates greater that 80 percent in many reports. Toileting accidents have been effectively altered with other behavioral procedures (Ross, 1981).

Behavioral Medicine

Behavioral medicine has been defined as the "interdisciplinary field concerned with the development and integration of behavioral and biomedical science knowledge and techniques relevant to health and illness and application of this knowledge and these techniques to prevention, diagnosis, treatment and rehabilitation" (Schwartz & Weiss, 1978, p. 250). Behavior therapy has helped to catalyze the rapid growth of this field.

Prevention and Treatment of Cardiovascular Disease

Specific behavior patterns appear to increase the risk of needless or premature cardiovascular disease. Modification of these behavior patterns is likely to produce significant reductions in cardiovascular disease. Among the risk factors that have been the target of behavioral treatment programs are cigarette smoking, obesity, lack of exercise, stress, hypertension, and excessive alcohol consumption. Substance abuse is typically treated with a combination of the self-control procedures. Stress and hypertension have been successfully treated using methods such as relaxation training. Behavior intervention methods have been applied not only to identified clients in both individual and group therapy sessions, but also to essentially healthy individuals in the workplace and the community in programs designed to prevent cardiovascular disease.

Other Applications

Behavioral techniques have been successfully applied to such diverse health-related problems as tension headaches, different forms of pain, eating disorders such as anorexia nervosa and bulimia nervosa, asthma, epilepsy, sleep disorders, nausea reactions in cancer patients (resulting from radiation therapy), and children's fears about being hospitalized and undergoing surgery (Melamed & Siegel, 1980). Finally, cognitive-behavioral principles show promise in increasing compliance with medical treatments.

Evaluation

Evaluation of therapy outcome must be guided by the question "*What* treatment, by *whom*, is most effective for *this* individual with *that* specific problem and under *which* set of circumstances?" (Paul, 1967, p. 111). "On what measures" and "at what cost" round off this appeal to specificity of therapy outcome evaluation.

What Treatment Methods?

Behavior therapy consists of a broad range of different techniques, some of which are differentially effective for different problems. Hence, it is difficult to evaluate some global entity called "behavior therapy." Instead, evaluation must be directed at specific methods applied to particular problems.

What Measures Should Be Used to Evaluate Therapy Outcome?

A major contribution of behavior therapy to the evaluation of therapy outcome has been the development of a wide range of measurement strategies for the assessment and modification of various disorders. Examples include behavioral measures of phobic avoidance and compulsive rituals, coding systems for direct behavioral observation of diverse behaviors across different situations, and psychophysiological systems for anxiety and sexual disorders. Adequate assessment of treatment outcome will necessarily require multiple objective and subjective measures. In the treatment of anxiety-related disorders, for example, it is now clear that measures of three response systems—avoidance behavior, physiological arousal, and self-report—are necessary. The correlations among these systems are often low. Thus, by simply measuring one dimension, one might miss important changes in the other two. Moreover, there is evidence that these response systems may change at different speeds and be differentially reactive to different treatment methods.

Treatment at What Cost?

Behavior therapy is cost-effective. Paul and Lentz (1977) found that their behavioral treatment program was less expensive than either of the two alternative approaches with which it was compared: milieu therapy and traditional psychiatric care typical of state hospitals in the United States. This benefit, added to the significantly greater efficacy of the behavioral program, makes it the cost-effective choice. In England, Marks (1981) and his colleagues improved on the cost-effectiveness of the behavioral treatment of agoraphobics and obsessive-compulsives by using nurses as therapists instead of more highly trained clinical psychologists and psychiatrists. No falloff in efficacy was observed.

Evaluating Therapy Outcomes

Behavior therapists have developed various research strategies for evaluating therapy outcome. Single-case experimental designs are particularly important because they enable cause-effect relationships to be drawn between treatments and outcome in the individual case. The ABA, or reversal, design was illustrated in the Ayllon and Azrin study previously described. In the multiple-baseline design, different responses are continuously measured. Treatment is then applied successively to each response. If the desired behavior changes maximally only when treated, then a cause-effect relationship can be inferred. Single-case experimental designs can be used to study individual clinical problems that are unsuitable for group designs. Limitations of single-subject methodology include the inability to examine the interaction of subject variables with specific treatment effects and difficulty in generalizing findings to other cases. Laboratory-based studies permit the evaluation of specific techniques applied to particular problems under tightly controlled conditions; for example, evaluating fear reduction methods with snake-phobic subjects (Bandura, 1986). The advantages of this methodology include the use of multiple objective measures of outcome, the selection of homogeneous subject samples and therapists, and the freedom to assign subjects to experimental and control groups. Limitations include the possibility that findings with only mildly disturbed subjects might not be generalizable to more severely disturbed clients.

The treatment package strategy evaluates the effect of a multifaceted treatment program. If the package proves to be successful, its effective components are analyzed in subsequent research. One way of doing this is to use the dismantling strategy, in which components of the treatment package are systematically eliminated and the associated decrement in treatment outcome is measured.

The comparative research strategy is directed toward determining whether some therapeutic techniques are superior to others. Comparative studies are appropriate after specific techniques have been shown to be effective in single-subject or laboratory-based research and the parameters that maximize their efficacy are known. Different group designs require different control groups, depending on the research question addressed. The no-treatment control group controls for the possible therapeutic effects of assessment of outcome, maturation, and other changes in clients' behavior that occur independently of formal treatment. Attention-placebo control groups are used to parcel out the contribution to treatment effects of factors that are common to all forms of therapy. These factors include the relationship between therapist and client, expectations of therapeutic progress, and suggestion.

Treatment

Some clinical details of a cognitive-behavioral approach to therapy may be illustrated by the treatment of agoraphobia, a complex anxiety disorder. Initially, the therapist carries out a careful assessment of the nature of the problem and the variables that seem to be maintaining it. Subsequent treatment may vary, but it is probable that some form of real-life exposure will be a central part of therapy. Together, therapist and client work out a hierarchy of increasingly fear-eliciting situations that the client has been avoiding. Repeated and systematic exposure to these situations occurs until avoidance is eliminated and fear is decreased.

The therapist is careful to distinguish systematic exposure from the unsystematic and ill-considered attempts clients have typically made to enter feared situations too quickly. Preparation for each exposure experience involves anticipating the inevitable fearful reactions and teaching clients appropriate coping skills. This includes recognizing and accepting feelings of fear, identifying cognitive distortions that elicit or exacerbate fear, and counteracting cognitive distortions.

The therapist might accompany the client during real-life exposure sessions, providing encouragement, support, and social reinforcement. Although empathic, the therapist remains firm about the necessity for systematic exposure. Once the client enters the feared situation it is important for the client not to leave until his or her anxiety has decreased.

Following exposure, therapist and client analyze what happened. This provides the therapist an opportunity to see how the client interprets his or her experience and to uncover any faulty cognitive processing. For example, agoraphobics tend to discount positive accomplishments, do not always attribute success experiences to their own coping ability, and therefore do not develop greater self-efficacy.

Clients are given specific instructions about exposure homework assignments between therapy sessions and are asked to keep detailed daily records of what they attempted, how they felt, and what problems they encountered. These self-recordings are reviewed by the therapist at the beginning of each session. In addition to providing the therapist with information on clients' progress (or lack of progress), these daily records facilitate the process of changing clients' cognitive sets about their problems. By directing their attention to the records of their own experience, the therapist helps clients to gain a more objective and balanced view of their problems and progress.

Homework assignments typically require the active cooperation of the client's spouse (or some other family member). The therapist invites the spouse to one or more therapy sessions to assess his or her willingness and ability to provide the necessary support and to explain what is required. Mathews et al. (1981) have developed treatment manuals for both the client and the spouse in which they detail each step of real-life exposure treatment and describe mutual responsibilities. In many cases, these manuals can greatly reduce the number of sessions the couple spends with the therapist.

It is common for clients to fail to complete homework assignments. There are several possible reasons for lack of compliance, ranging from poorly chosen homework assignments to resistance to change. Another possibility is that the spouse is uncooperative or tries to sabotage therapy. One of the advantages of including the spouse in treatment is that this resistance to progress is rapidly uncovered and can be directly addressed in the therapy sessions.

To supplement real-life exposure, some clients need assertiveness training, whereas others need to acquire ways of coping with suppressed anger. Before terminating successful treatment, the therapist works on relapse prevention training with clients. Briefly, clients are told that it is possible that they might experience an unexpected return of some fear at unpredictable points in the future. Using imagery to project ahead to such a recurrence of fear, clients learn to cope with their feelings by reinstituting previously successful coping responses. They are reassured that these feelings are quite normal and time-limited and do not necessarily signal a relapse. Clients learn that it is primarily the way they interpret these feelings that determines whether or not they experience a relapse. Specifically, the therapist tries to inoculate them against such anxiety-inducing cognitive errors as catastrophizing or selective focus on an isolated anxiety symptom.

❖ CASE EXAMPLE[1]

Mr. B was a 35-year-old man, married, with two sons aged eight and five, from a successful, middle-class family. He was a persistent exhibitionist whose pattern over the past 20 years had been to expose his genitals to unsuspecting adult women as often as five or six times a week. Fifteen years of intermittent psychoanalytic treatment, several hospitalizations at psychiatric institutions in the United States, and a six-year prison sentence for his deviant sexual behavior had failed to help Mr. B change his apparently uncontrollable behavior. He was currently under grand jury indictment for exposing himself to an adult woman in the presence of a group of young children. There was every prospect that he would receive a life sentence in view of his repeated offenses and numerous failures to show improvement. At least one psychiatrist had diagnosed him as untreatable and had advocated lifelong incarceration. Shortly before Mr. B came to trial, his psychoanalyst referred him to a behavior therapist as a last resort.

Mr. B was hospitalized and treated on a daily basis for six weeks, receiving a total of about 50 hours of therapy. After spending some time to develop a trusting personal relationship so that Mr. B would feel comfortable in disclosing intimate details about his problems, the therapist conducted a series of intensive interviews to ferret out the specific environmental circumstances and psychological factors that were maintaining Mr. B's de-

---

[1]This case example, with minor modifications, is taken from G. T. Wilson and K. D. O'Leary, *Principles of Behavior Therapy* (Englewood Cliffs, NJ: Prentice-Hall, 1980). Reprinted with permission.

viant behavior. With Mr. B's permission, his parents and wife were also interviewed to obtain more information and to corroborate aspects of his own description of the development and present status of the problem. To obtain a sample of his actual exhibitionist behavior, a situation was arranged in a hospital office that closely resembled the conditions under which Mr. B would normally expose himself in real life. Two attractive female professional colleagues of the therapist were seated in a simulated doctor's waiting room, reading magazines, and the patient was instructed to enter, sit across from them, and expose himself. Despite the artificial setting, he proceeded to expose himself, became highly aroused, and nearly masturbated to orgasm. This entire sequence was videotaped, and objective measures of his response to this scene as well as to various other adult sexual stimuli were obtained by recording the degree of penile erection he showed while observing the videotape and selected other erotic films.

A detailed picture was developed of the sequence of internal and external stimuli and responses that preceded his acts of exposure. For example, a woman standing alone at a bus stop as he drove past in his car often triggered a pattern of thoughts and images that caused him to circle the block and eventually expose himself. Alternatively, the anger he experienced after a heated argument with his father would also elicit the urge to expose himself. The more Mr. B thought about exposing himself, the more obsessed he became with a particular woman and her anticipated reactions. Because he tuned out everything except his immediate feelings and intentions, he became oblivious to the consequences of his actions. His behavior was out of control. Mr. B hoped that his victim would express some form of approval, either by smiling or making some sexual comment. Although this did happen occasionally, most women ignored him, and some called the police.

Mr. B believed he would be passively "conditioned" through therapy so that his problem would disappear. The therapist systematically disabused him of this notion by explaining that success could be achieved only with his active cooperation in all phases of the treatment program. He was told that there was no automatic "cure" for his problem, but that he could learn new behavioral self-control strategies, which, if practiced conscientiously and applied at the right time, would enable him to avoid further deviant behavior.

As in most complex clinical cases, treatment was multifaceted. Mr. B's own belief about his problem was that he was suddenly seized by a desire, which he could not consciously control, and that his subsequent actions were "involuntary." Analysis of the sequence of events that always preceded exposure altered Mr. B's expectation that he was unable to control his behavior. He was shown how he himself was instrumental in transforming a relatively weak initial urge into an overpowering compulsion to expose because he attended to inappropriate thoughts and feelings and engaged in behaviors that increased, rather than decreased, the temptation. It was explained that the time to break this behavioral chain and to implement the self-control strategies was at the beginning, when the urge was weakest. In order to do this, he would have to learn to be aware of his thoughts, feelings, and behavior and to recognize the early danger signals.

Specific tension states had often precipitated exposure. Accordingly, Mr. B was trained to reduce this tension with progressive relaxation. Instead of exposing himself, he learned to relax, an activity incompatible with exposure behavior. Assertion training was used to help Mr. B cope constructively with feelings of anger and to express them appropriately. Using role-playing, the therapist modeled an appropriate reaction and then provided Mr. B with reinforcing feedback as he rehearsed more effective ways of responding to anger-inducing events. In covert modeling, Mr. B was taught to imagine himself in a range of situations that customarily resulted in exposure and to see himself engaging in alternative responses to exposure; for example, relaxing away tension, expressing anger appropriately, reminding himself of the consequences of being caught, or simply walking away from a tempting situation.

Aversion conditioning was used to decrease the positive appeal of exposure. During repeated presentations of the videotape of his exposure scene, on an unpredictable schedule, a loud, subjectively aversive police siren was blared over earphones. Whereas Mr. B initially found watching the videotape pleasurable and sexually arousing, he progressively lost all sexual interest in it. He reported that he experienced marked difficulty in concentrating on the scene because he began to anticipate the disruptive—and given his personal social learning history, understandably frightening—police siren in connection with thoughts of exposure. The siren was also paired systematically with a range of fantasies of different situations in which he would expose himself. In addition to the siren, Mr. B learned how to associate self-administered aversive cognitive events with deviant thoughts or images. For example, imagery of an aversive event, such as being apprehended by the police, was coupled with thoughts of exposure. Periodically, Mr. B's sexual arousal to the videotape was assessed directly by measuring penile erection to provide an evaluation of his progress.

Following every session with the therapist, Mr. B was given specific homework assignments. These included monitoring and recording any urges to expose himself in order to ensure awareness about any signs of reverting back to old habits. Other assignments involved (a) practicing relaxation exercises and recording the degree to which the relaxation was associated with reduced tension; (b) rehearsing the association of aversive imagery with fantasies of exposure and recording the intensity of the aversive imagery and the clarity of the exposure fantasies on 10-point rating scales; and (c) engaging in assertive behavior, where appropriate, during interactions with other patients and staff on his assigned ward. Direct observation of his interpersonal behavior on the hospital ward provided an index of his utilization of assertive behavior.

Finally, after speaking with the therapist about cooperation and apparent progress in the treatment program, Mr. B's wife agreed to several joint therapy sessions that used behavioral methods for improving marital communication and interaction. Although the behavioral assessment had indicated that Mr. B's exhibitionist behavior was not directly caused by an unhappy marriage or lack of sexual satisfaction from his wife, the therapist believed improvement in these spheres of functioning would help consolidate and support Mr. B's self-control.

On leaving the hospital at the end of treatment, Mr. B continued to self-monitor thoughts or feelings about exposing himself, relax systematically, assert himself, and rehearse the pairing of aversive imagery with thoughts of exposure. Every week he mailed these records to the therapist, a procedure designed to generalize treatment-produced improvement to the real world and to maintain self-control over time. Another facet of this maintenance strategy was a series of booster sessions scheduled approximately four months after therapy in which he returned to the hospital for a week of intensive treatment along the same lines as described above.

In large part owing to the therapist's strong recommendation, the court gave Mr. B a suspended sentence. A five-year follow-up showed that Mr. B had refrained from any exhibitionism, had experienced very few such desires, and felt confident in his newly found ability to control his behavior.

❖ SUMMARY

Behavior therapy is still developing. The future will witness continued development and change in its theoretical foundations, research bases, and practical applications. As the theoretical bases of behavior therapy are broadened, there will be renewed interest in identifying commonalities among different therapies and in bringing about a rapprochement between behavior therapy and other forms of psychotherapy (Goldfried, 1980).

The whole system of health care delivery in the United States is constantly under scrutiny in an effort to contain soaring financial costs while providing benefits to the large numbers of currently uninsured people. The extent to which mental health care will be included in a radically revised health care system remains to be seen. Nevertheless, there is general agreement that the practice of psychotherapy will undergo fundamental changes in the decade of the 1990s. A survey of 75 expert psychotherapists, embracing eclectic, behavioral, cognitive, psychodynamic, humanistic, and family systems practitioners, yielded some sobering findings (Norcross, Alford, & DeMichele, 1992). Overwhelmingly, these experts predicted that psychotherapy in the future will consist primarily of directive, present-centered, problem-focused, and brief treatments. This shift to brief therapy will be necessary to reduce costs. The most favored theoretical orientations were eclectic, cognitive, and systemic.

These predicted trends fit well with the practice of behavior therapy. Indeed, the ten interventions predicted to increase most in the future included several standard cognitive-behavioral methods, such as homework assignments, cognitive restructuring, and real-life exposure. The experts, including those of a psychodynamic orientation, also predicted that the use of historically oriented, long-term treatment such as psychoanalysis would decline.

❖ ANNOTATED BIBLIOGRAPHY

Franks, C. M., Wilson, G. T., Kendall, P., & Brownell, K. D. *Annual review of behavior therapy: Theory and practice.* New York: Guilford Press.

The latest volume in this annual review series begun in 1973 offers broad coverage of virtually all aspects of theory, research, and application in behavior therapy, with critical commentary by the authors. This series provides perhaps the most up-to-date and comprehensive overview of the field on a year-to-year basis.

Goldstein, A., & Foa, E. (Eds.) (1980). *Handbook of behavioral interventions: A clinical guide.* New York: Wiley.

This edited volume presents chapters of specific behavioral techniques applied to anxiety and sexual disorders. By remaining close to the clinical data, including the generous use of transcripts from individual therapy sessions, the authors provide a flavor of the clinical practice of behavior therapy.

Kazdin, A. E. (19080). *Behavior modification in applied settings (Rev. Ed.).* Homewood, IL: Dorsey.

A clearly written, comprehensive review of primarily operant-conditioning principles and procedures in behavior modification, this book focuses on application of learning principles in applied settings (e.g., classrooms and institutions for the retarded and psychiatric patients).

O'Leary, K. D., & Wilson, G. T. (1987). *Behavior therapy. Application and outcome (2nd ed.).* Englewood Cliffs, NJ: Prentice-Hall.

This book presents detailed description and evaluation of cognitive-behavior treatment of a wide range of childhood and adult disorders. Aside from traditional psychiatric disorders (e.g., anxiety, addictive, and schizophrenic disorders), areas covered include interpersonal and marital problems, behavioral medicine and preventive health care, and various educational and clinical problems in children.

Rhoades, L. J. (1981). *Treating and assessing the chronically ill: The pioneering research of Gordon L. Paul.* Rockville, MD: U.S. Department of Health and Human Services.

One of the *Science Reports* series published by the National Institute of Mental Health, this publication explains significant achievements in mental health services and is directed at the general scientific, academic, and professional communities. A clearly written, nontechnical summary account of the detailed Paul and Lentz (1977) book, it describes the treatment procedures and important findings of the most thorough study of chronic mental hospital patients ever conducted.

❖ CASE READINGS

Barlow, D. H., & Cerny, J. A. (1988). *Psychological treatment of panic*. New York: Guilford Press.

Chapter 8 of this treatment manual provides a detailed description of the cognitive-behavioral treatment of a patient with panic disorder.

Melamed, B., & Siegel, L. (1975). Self-directed in vivo treatment of an obsessive-compulsive checking ritual. *Journal of Behavior Therapy and Experimental Psychiatry*, 6, 31–35.

This case illustrates the application of exposure and response prevention, among other techniques, in the treatment of compulsions. The case also describes the detailed, ongoing assessment of treatment progress characteristic of behavior therapy.

Novaco, R. (1977). Stress inoculation: A cognitive therapy for anger and its application to a case of depression. *Journal of Consulting and Clinical Psychology*, 45, 600–608.

This case illustrates the use of cognitive techniques within behavior therapy. It also shows how cognitive-behavioral methods are used to treat problems of anger, which, together with anxiety and depression, are the most common emotions encountered by clinicians.

Wilson, G. T., & Pike, K. (1993). Eating disorders. In D. H. Barlow (Ed.), *Clinical handbook of psychological disorders* (2nd ed.). New York: Guilford Press.

This chapter provides an in-depth illustration of the treatment of a female patient with bulimia nervosa, an eating disorder that is common among college-aged and young adult women.

Wolf, M. M., Risley, T., & Mees, H. (1965). Application of operant conditioning procedures to the behavior problems of an autistic child. In L. P. Ullmann & L. Krasner (Eds.), *Case studies in behavior modification* (pp. 138–145). New York: Holt, Rinehart and Winston.

This classic case study illustrates the application of operant principles and procedures to the treatment of an autistic child. The assessment and treatment approach described here provides a model for the use of behavioral methods with a wide range of problems among the developmentally disabled.

Wolpe, J. (1991). Some complex cases. *The practice of behavior therapy* (4th ed.). New York: Pergamon. [Reprinted in D. Wedding and R. J. Corsini (Eds.) (1995). *Case studies in psychotherapy*. Itasca, IL: F. E. Peacock.]

This case study describes the way one of the founders of behavior therapy treated a 31-year-old man who presented with symptoms of anxiety and an obsession about his wife's premarital loss of virginity.

❖ REFERENCES

Ayllon, T., & Azrin, N. H. (1965). The measurement and reinforcement of behavior of psychotics. *Journal of the Experimental Analysis of Behavior*, 8, 357–383.

Bandura, A. (1969). *Principles of behavior modification*. New York: Holt, Rinehart and Winston.

Bandura, A. (1977). *Social learning theory*. Englewood Cliffs, N.J.: Prentice-Hall.

Bandura, A. (1982). Self-efficacy mechanism in human agency. *American Psychologist*, 37, 122–147.

Bandura, A. (1986). Social foundations of thought and action: A *social cognitive theory*. Englewood Cliffs, NJ: Prentice-Hall.

Barlow, D. H., & Cerny, J. A. (1988). *Psychological treatment of panic*. New York: Guilford Press.

Beck, A. T., Rush, A. J., Shaw, B. F., & Emery, G. (1979). *Cognitive therapy of depression*. New York: Guilford Press.

Brady, J. P. (1980). In M. Goldfried (Ed.). Some views on effective principles of psychotherapy. *Cognitive Therapy and Research*, 4, 271–306.

Cautela, J. (1967). Covert sensitization. *Psychological Reports*, 20, 459–468.

Clarke, D. M. (1989). Anxiety states. In K. Hawton, P. M. Salkovskis, J. Kirk, & D. M. Clark (Eds.), *Cognitive behaviour therapy for psychiatric problems* (pp. 52–96). New York: Oxford Medical Publications.

Clark, D. M., Salkovskis, P. M., Hackmann, A., Middleton, H., & Gelder, M. (1994). *A comparison of cognitive therapy, applied relaxation and imipramine in the treatment of panic disorder*. British Journal of Psychiatry, 164, 759–769.

Craske, M. G , Brown, T. A., & Barlow, D. H. (1991). Behavioral treatment of panic disorder: A two-year follow-up. *Behavior Therapy*, 22, 289–304.

Eysenck, H. J. (1959). Learning theory and behavior therapy. *British Journal of Medical Science*, 105, 61–75.

Eysenck, H. J. (1967). *The biological basis of personality*. Springfield, IL: Charles C. Thomas.

Franks, C. M., Wilson, G. T., Kendall, P., & Brownell, K. (1982). *Annual review of behavior therapy: Theory and practice (Vol. 8)*. New York: Guilford Press.

Goldfried, M. R. (1980). Toward the delineation of therapeutic change principles. *American Psychologist*, 35, 991–999.

Hawton, K., Salkovskis, P. M., Kirk, J.,& Clark, D. M. (Eds.) (1989). *Cognitive behaviour therapy for psychiatric problems*. Oxford University Press.

Hollon, S. D., & Beck, A. (1994). Cognitive and cognitive-behavioral therapies. In S. L. Garfield & A. E. Bergin (Eds.), *Handbook of psychotherapy and behavior change: An empirical analysis* (4th ed.). New York: Wiley.

Hollon, S. D., DeRubeis, R. J., Evans, M. D., Wiemmer, M. J., Garvey, M. J., Grove, W. M., & Tuason, V. B. (1992). Cognitive therapy and pharmacotherapy for depression: Singly and in combination. *Archives of General Psychiatry, 49*, 774–781.

Jacobson, E. (1938). *Progressive relaxation*. Chicago: University of Chicago Press.

Jacobson, N. S. (Ed.) (1987). *Psychotherapists in clinical practice: Cognitive and behavioral perspectives*. New York: Guilford Press.

Jacobson, N., & Margolin, G. (1979). *Marital therapy*. New York: Brunner/Mazel.

Jones, M. C. (1924). The elimination of children's fears. *Journal of Experimental Psychology, 7*, 382–390.

Kanfer, F. H. (1977). The many faces of self-control, or behavior modification changes its focus. In R. B. Stuart (Ed.), *Behavioral self-management*. New York: Brunner/Mazel.

Kazdin, A. E. (1977). *The token economy*. New York: Plenum.

Kazdin, A. E. (1978a). The application of operant techniques in treatment, rehabilitation, and education. In S. L. Garfield & A. E. Bergin (Eds.). *Handbook of psychotherapy and behavior change* (2nd ed.). (pp. 549–590). New York: Wiley.

Kazdin, A. E. (1978b). *History of behavior modification*. Baltimore, MD: University Park Press.

Kazdin, A. E., & Wilson, G. T. (1978). *Evaluation of behavior therapy: Issues, evidence and research strategies*. Cambridge, MA: Ballinger.

Knudson, R. M., Gurman, A. S., & Kniskern, D. P. (1979). Behavioral marriage therapy: A treatment in transition. In C. M. Franks & G. T. Wilson (Eds.), *Annual review of behavior therapy. Theory and practice* (Vol. 7). (pp. 543–574). New York: Brunner/Mazel.

Lazarus, A. A. (1971). *Behavior therapy and beyond*. New York: McGraw-Hill.

Lazarus, A. A. (1981). *The practice of multimodal therapy*. New York: McGraw-Hill.

Lazarus, A. A., & Fay, A. (1982). Resistance or rationalization? A cognitive-behavioral perspective. In P. L. Wachtel (Ed.), *Resistance: Psychodynamic and behavioral approaches*. (pp. 94–107). New York: Plenum.

Lewinsohn, P. M., Clarke, G. N., Hops, H., & Andrews, J. (1990). Cognitive-behavioral treatment for depressed adolescents. *Behavior Therapy, 21*, 385–401.

Locke, H. J., & Wallace, K. M. (1959). Short marital adjustment and prediction tests: Their reliability and validity. *Marriage and Family Living, 21*, 251–255.

Lovaas, O. I. (1987). Behavioral treatment and normal educational and intellectual functioning in young autistic children. *Journal of Consulting and Clinical Psychology, 55*, 3–9.

Marks, I. M. (1981). *Cure and care of the neuroses*. New York: Wiley.

Marks, I., & Mathews, A. (1979). Brief standard self-rating for phobic patients. *Behaviour Research and Therapy, 17*, 263–267.

Masters, W., & Johnson, V. (1970). *Human sexual inadequacy*. Boston: Little, Brown.

Masters, W., & Johnson, V. (1979). *Homosexuality in perspective*. Boston: Little, Brown.

Mathews, A. M., Gelder, M. G., & Johnston, D. W. (1981). *Agoraphobia: Nature and treatment*. New York: Guilford.

Melamed, B., & Siegel, L. (1980). *Behavioral medicine*. New York: Springer.

Miller, N. E. (1948). Studies of fear as an acquirable drive. I. Fear as motivation and fear reduction as reinforcement in the learning of new responses. *Journal of Experimental Psychology, 38*, 89–101.

Mischel, W. (1968). *Personality and assessment*. New York: Wiley.

Mischel, W. (1973). Toward a cognitive social learning reconceptualization of personality. *Psychological Review, 80*, 252–283.

Mischel, W. (1976). *Introduction to personality*. New York: Holt, Rinehart and Winston.

Mischel, W. (1981). A cognitive social learning approach to assessment. In T. V. Merluzzi, C. R. Glass, & M. Genest (Eds.). *Cognitive assessment*. (pp. 479–500). New York: Guilford Press.

Mowrer, O. H. (1947). On the dual nature of learning—A reinterpretation of "conditioning" and "problem solving." *Harvard Educational Review, 17*, 102–148.

Mowrer, O. H., & Mowrer, E. (1938). Enuresis: A method for its study and treatment. *American Journal of Orthopsychiatry, 4*, 436–459.

Norcross, J. C., Alford, B. A., & DeMichele, J. T. (1992). The future of psychotherapy: Delphi data and concluding observations. *Psychotherapy, 29*, 150–158.

O'Leary, K. D. (1980). Pills or skills for hyperactive children. *Journal of Applied Behavior Analysis, 13*, 191–204.

O'Leary, K. D., & Beach, S. R. H. (1990). Marital therapy: A viable treatment for depression. *American Journal of Psychiatry, 147*, 183–186.

O'Leary, K. D., & Carr, E. G. (1982). Childhood disorders. In G. T. Wilson & C. M. Franks (Eds.). *Contemporary behavior therapy: Conceptual and empirical foundations*. (pp. 495–496). New York: Guilford.

O'Leary, K. D., & O'Leary, S. G. (1977). *Classroom management*. New York: Pergamon Press.

O'Leary, K. D., Turkewitz, H., & Tafel, S. (1973). Parent and therapist evaluation of behavior therapy in a child psychological clinic. *Journal of Consulting and Clinical Psychology, 41*, 289–293.

O'Leary, K. D., & Wilson, G. T. (1987). *Behavior therapy: Application and outcome (2nd ed.).* Englewood Cliffs, NJ: Prentice-Hall.

Paul, G. L. (1966). *Insight versus desensitization in psychotherapy.* Stanford: Stanford University Press.

Paul, G. L. (1967). Outcome research in psychotherapy. *Journal of Consulting Psychology, 31,* 109–188.

Paul, G. L., & Lentz, R. J. (1977). *Psychological treatment of chronic mental patients.* Cambridge, MA: Harvard University Press.

Rathus, S. A. (1973). A 30-item schedule for assessing assertive behavior. *Behavior Therapy, 4,* 398–406.

Risley, T., & Sheldon-Wildgen, J. (1982). Invited peer review: The AABT experience. *Professional Psychology, 13,* 125–131.

Rosen, R. C., & Keefe, F. J. (1978). The measurement of human penile tumescence. *Psychophysiology, 15,* 366–376.

Ross, A. (1981). *Child behavior therapy.* New York: Wiley.

Salter, A. (1949). *Conditioned reflex therapy.* New York: Farrar, Straus.

Schwartz, G. E., & Weiss, S. M. (1978). Behavioral medicine revisited: An amended definition. *Journal of Behavioral Medicine, 1,* 249–252.

Skinner, B. F. (1953). *Science and human behavior.* New York: Macmillan.

Sloane, R. B., Staples, F. R., Cristol, A. H., Yorkston, J. J., & Whipple, K. (1975). *Psychotherapy versus behavior therapy.* Cambridge, MA: Harvard University Press.

Staples, F. R., Sloane, R. B., Whipple, K., Cristol, A. H., & Yorkston, N. (1975). Differences between behavior therapists and psychotherapists. *Archives of General Psychiatry, 32,* 1517–1522.

Stolz, S. G. (1978). *Ethical issues in behavior modification.* San Francisco: Jossey-Bass.

Swan, G. E., & MacDonald, M. D. (1978). Behavior therapy in practice: A national survey of behavior therapists. *Behavior Therapy, 9,* 799–807.

Turkewitz, H., & O'Leary, K. D. (1981). A comparative outcome study of behavioral marital and communication therapy. *Journal of Marital and Family Therapy, 7,* 159–169.

Ullmann, L. P., & Krasner, L. (1965). *Case studies in behavior modification.* New York: Holt, Rinehart and Winston.

Upper, D., & Ross, S. M. (Eds.) (1981). *Behavioral group therapy.* Champaign, IL: Research Press.

Wilson, G. T., & O'Leary, K. D. (1980). *Principles of behavior therapy.* Englewood Cliffs, NJ: Prentice-Hall.

Wolpe, J. (1958). *Psychotherapy by reciprocal inhibition.* Stanford: Stanford University Press.

Wolpe, J., & Rachman, S. (1960). Psychoanalytic evidence: A critique based on Freud's case of Little Hans. *Journal of Nervous and Mental Disorders, 131,* 135–145.

Yates, A. J. (1980). *Biofeedback and the modification of behavior.* New York: Plenum.

Aaron T. Beck

8 Cognitive Therapy

Aaron T. Beck and
Marjorie E. Weishaar

❖ OVERVIEW

Cognitive therapy is based on a theory of personality which maintains that how one thinks largely deter mines how one feels and behaves. The therapy is a collaborative process of empirical investigation, reality testing, and problem solving between therapist and patient. The patient's maladaptive interpretations and conclusions are treated as testable hypotheses. Behavioral experiments and verbal procedures are used to examine alternative interpretations and to generate contradictory evidence that supports more adaptive beliefs and leads to therapeutic change.

Basic Concepts

Cognitive therapy can be thought of as a theory, a system of strategies, and a series of techniques. The theory is based on the idea that the processing of information is crucial for the survival of any organism. If we did not have a functional apparatus for taking in relevant information from the environment, synthesizing it, and formulating a plan of action on the basis of this synthesis, we would soon die or be killed.

In various psychopathological conditions, such as anxiety disorders, depressive disorders, mania, paranoid states, obsessive-compulsive neurosis, and others, a systematic bias is introduced into processing of information. A specific bias plays a central role in the symptomatology of the various psychological disturbances. Thus, an individual whose thinking selectively synthesizes themes of loss or defeat is likely to be depressed. Similarly, in anxiety there is a systematic shift toward selectively interpreting themes of danger, in paranoid conditions the dominant shift is toward indiscriminate attribution of abuse or interference, and in mania the shift is toward exaggerated interpretations of personal gain.

Contributing to these shifts are certain specific attitudes that predispose people under the influence of certain life situations to start interpreting their experiences in this biased way. For example, a person may have an attitude that any minor loss represents a major deprivation and may thus react catastrophically to even the smallest losses. A person who feels vulnerable to sudden death may, after exposure to a life-threatening episode, begin to interpret normal body sensations as signs of impending death and experience a panic attack.

Strategies

The overall strategies of cognitive therapy involve primarily a collaborative enterprise between the patient and the therapist to explore dysfunctional interpretations and try to modify them. This *collaborative empiricism* views the patient as a practical scientist who lives by interpreting stimuli but who has been temporarily thwarted by his or her own information-gathering and integrating apparatus (cf. Kelly, 1955).

The second strategy, *guided discovery*, is directed toward discovering what threads run through the patient's present misperceptions and beliefs and linking them to analogous experiences in the past. Thus, the therapist and patient collaboratively weave a tapestry that tells the story of the development of the patient's disorder.

The therapy attempts to improve reality testing through continuous evaluation of personal conclusions. The immediate goal is to shift the information-processing apparatus to a more "neutral" condition so that events will be evaluated in a more balanced way.

The cognitive shift that occurs may be pictured as analogous to a computer program. Each disorder has a separate, specific program. The program dictates the kind of data admitted, decides the way data are integrated, and determines the resultant behavior. In anxiety disorder, for instance, a "survival program" has been activated: one selectively attends to "danger signals" and blocks out "safety signals." The resulting behavior will be consistent with how one integrates this information, dictating that one will overreact to relatively minor stimuli as though they are major threats, responding with avoidance or escape.

The program activated is responsible for the *cognitive shift* in information processing. The normal program of orderly selecting and interpreting data is dislocated by the anxiety program, panic program, depressive program, or some other program. When this occurs, the individual experiences the typical symptoms of anxiety, depression, or panic. The strategies and techniques of cognitive therapy are designed to deactivate such maladaptive programs, to shift the cognitive apparatus to a more neutral position. This shift to normal is accomplished by systematically checking and reversing misinterpretations. Corrective information is "fed back" into the system and catalyzes a readjustment.

Techniques

Techniques used in cognitive therapy are designed to shift information processing to a more functional position and to modify basic beliefs that promote misinterpretation. A variety of techniques may be used consistent with the cognitive model. The purely cognitive techniques focus on the patient's misinterpretations and provide a mechanism for testing them, exploring their logical (or illogical) basis, and correcting them if they fail an empirical or logical test. In addition, the patient's imagery is used as a pictorial representation of his or her cognitive distortions. Imagery is subjected to the same type of evaluation and modification as cognitions.

Basic beliefs are explored in a somewhat similar manner and are tested for their accuracy and adaptiveness. The patient who discovers these beliefs are not accurate is encouraged to try out a different set of beliefs to determine if the new beliefs are more accurate and functional.

Other Systems

Procedures used in cognitive therapy, such as identifying common themes in a patient's emotional reactions, narratives, and imagery, are similar to the *psychoanalytic method*. However, in cognitive therapy the common thread is a meaning readily accessible to conscious interpretation, whereas in psychoanalysis the meaning is unconscious (or repressed) and must be inferred.

Both psychodynamic psychotherapy and cognitive therapy assume that behavior can be influenced by beliefs of which one is not immediately aware. However, cognitive therapy maintains that the thoughts contributing to a patient's distress are not deeply buried in the unconscious. Moreover, the cognitive therapist does not regard the patient's self-report as a screen for more deeply concealed ideas. Cognitive therapy focuses on the linkages among symptoms, conscious beliefs, and current experiences. Psychoanalytic approaches are oriented toward repressed childhood memories and motivational constructs, such as libidinal needs and infantile sexuality.

Cognitive therapy is highly structured and short-term, lasting from 12 to 16 weeks. The therapist is actively engaged in collaboration with the patient. Psychoanalytic therapy is long-term and relatively unstructured. The analyst is largely passive. Cognitive therapy attempts to shift biased information processing through the application of logic to dysfunctional ideas and the use of behavioral experiments to test dysfunctional beliefs. Psychoanalysts rely on free association and depth interpretations to penetrate the encapsulated unconscious residue of unresolved childhood conflicts.

Cognitive therapy and *rational emotive behavior therapy* (REBT) share emphases on the primary importance of cognition in psychological dysfunction, seeing the task of therapy as changing maladaptive assumptions and the stance of the therapist as active and directive. There are some differences, nevertheless, between these two approaches.

Cognitive therapy, using an information-processing model, is directed towards modifying the "cognitive shift" by addressing biased selection of information and distorted interpretations. The shift to normal cognitive processing is accomplished by testing the erroneous inferences that result from biased processing. Continual disconfirmation of cognitive errors, working as a feedback system, gradually restores more adaptive functioning. However, the dysfunctional beliefs that contributed to the unbalanced cognitive processing in the first place also require further testing and invalidation.

REBT theory states that a distressed individual has irrational beliefs that contribute to irrational thoughts and that by modifying these through confrontation, they will disappear and the disorder will clear up. The cognitive therapist, operating from an inductive model, helps the patient translate interpretations and beliefs into hypotheses, which are then subjected to empirical testing. An REBT therapist is more inclined to use a deductive model to point out irrational beliefs. The cognitive therapist eschews the word "irrational" in favor of "dysfunctional" because problematic beliefs are nonadaptive rather than irrational. They contribute to psychological disorders because they interfere with normal cognitive processing, not because they are irrational.

A profound difference between these two approaches is that cognitive therapy maintains that each disorder has its own typical cognitive content. The *cognitive profiles* of depression, anxiety, and panic disorder are significantly different and require substantially different approaches. REBT, on the other hand, assumes that all psychopathology has a similar set of underlying irrational beliefs.

The cognitive therapy model emphasizes the impact of cognitive deficits in psychopathology. Some clients experience problems because their cognitive deficits do not let them foresee delayed or long-range negative consequences. Others have trouble with concentration, directed thinking, or recall. These difficulties occur in severe anxiety, depression, and panic attacks. Cognitive deficits produce perceptual errors as well as faulty interpretations. Further, inadequate cognitive processing may interfere with use of coping abilities or techniques and with interpersonal problem solving, as occurs in suicidal people.

Finally, REBT views patients' beliefs as philosophically incongruent with reality. Meichenbaum (1977) criticizes this perspective, stating that non-patients have irrational beliefs as well, but are able to cope with them. Cognitive therapy teaches patients to *self-correct* faulty cognitive processing and to bolster assumptions that allow them to cope. Thus, REBT views the problem as philosophical; cognitive therapy views it as functional.

Cognitive therapy shares many similarities with some forms of *behavior therapy* but is quite different from others. Within behavior therapy are numerous approaches that vary in their emphasis on cognitive processes. At one end of the behavioral spectrum is applied behavioral analysis, an approach that ignores "internal events," such as interpretations and inferences, as much as possible. As one moves in the other direction, cognitive mediating processes are given increasing attention until one arrives at a variety of cognitive-behavioral approaches. At this point, the distinction between the purely cognitive and the distinctly behavioral becomes unclear.

Cognitive therapy and behavior therapy share some features: they are empirical, present-centered, problem-oriented, and require explicit identification of problems and the situations in which they occur as well as the consequences resulting from them. In contrast to radical behaviorism, cognitive therapy applies the same kind of functional analysis to internal experiences—to thoughts, attitudes, and images. Cognitions, like behaviors, can be modified by active collaboration through behavioral experiments that foster new learning. Also, in contrast to behavioral approaches based on simple conditioning paradigms, cognitive therapy sees individuals as active participants in their environments, judging and evaluating stimuli, interpreting events and sensations, and judging their own responses.

Studies of some behavioral techniques, such as exposure methods for the treatment of phobias, demonstrate that cognitive and behavioral changes work together. For example, in agoraphobia, cognitive improvement has been concomitant with behavioral improvement (Williams & Rappoport, 1983). Simple exposure to agoraphobic situations while verbalizing negative automatic thoughts may lead to improvement on cognitive measures (Gournay, 1986). Bandura (1977) has demonstrated that one of the most effective ways to change cognitions is to change performance. In real-life exposure, patients confront not only the threatening situations, but also their personal expectations of danger and their assumed inability to cope with their reactions. Because the experience itself is processed cognitively, exposure can be considered a cognitive procedure.

Cognitive therapy maintains that a comprehensive approach to the treatment of anxiety and other disorders includes targeting anxiety-provoking thoughts and images. Work with depressed patients (Beck, Rush, Shaw, & Emery, 1979) demonstrates that desired cognitive changes do not necessarily follow from changes in behavior. For this reason, it is vital to know the patient's expectations, interpretations, and reactions to events. Cognitive change must be demonstrated, not assumed.

Cognitive therapy has some similarities with *multimodal therapy* (MMT), a cognitive-behavioral approach to psychotherapy. Both approaches are empirically based, thoughts and images are assessed and are targets of intervention, and functional analyses are done of problem behaviors. Yet, cognitive therapy differs from MMT in several ways. Cognitive therapy stresses the primacy of cognition; it uses thoughts and images as the entry to the system of behavior, affect, relationships, and biology. Multimodal therapy gives equal coverage to all modalities. Further, the specific cognitive profile for each disorder guides the cognitive therapist in the selection of techniques and tactics. The multimodal therapist, in contrast, is required to approach each case without a superordinate theory to help organize the mass of available data.

Multimodal therapy does not maintain that borrowed techniques be theoretically uniform. In contrast, cognitive therapy uses techniques consistent with the cognitive theory of emotional disorders. Finally, while MMT claims to address many areas of the patient's functioning, Kwee & Lazarus (1986) state that only in the assessment phase is MMT "multi." In actual practice, treatment is usually bimodal or unimodal.

❖ HISTORY

Precursors

Cognitive therapy's theoretical underpinnings are derived from three main sources: (1) the phenomenological approach to psychology, (2) structural theory and depth psychology, and (3) cognitive psychology. The phenomenological approach posits that the individual's view of self and the personal world are central to behavior. This concept was originally founded in Greek Stoic philosophy and can be seen in Immanuel Kant's (1798) emphasis on conscious subjective experience. This approach is also evident in the writings of Adler (1936), Alexander (1950), Horney (1950), and Sullivan (1953).

The second major influence was the structural theory and depth psychology of Kant and Freud, particularly Freud's concept of the hierarchical structuring of cognition into primary and secondary processes.

Finally, more modern developments in cognitive psychology have had an impact. George Kelly (1955) is credited with being the first among contemporaries to describe the cognitive model through his use of "personal constructs" and his emphasis on the role of beliefs in behavior change. Cognitive theories of emotion, such as those of Magda Arnold (1960) and Richard Lazarus (1984), which give primacy to cognition in emotional and behavioral change, have also contributed to cognitive therapy.

Beginnings

Cognitive therapy began in the early 1960s as the result of Aaron Beck's research on depression (Beck, 1963, 1964, 1967). Trained in psychoanalysis, Beck attempted to validate Freud's theory of depression as having at its core "anger turned on the self." To substantiate this formulation, Beck made clinical observations of depressed patients and investigated their treatment under traditional psychoanalysis. Rather than finding retroflected anger in their thoughts and dreams, Beck observed a negative bias in their cognitive processing. With continued clinical observations and experimental testing, Beck developed his theory of emotional disorders and a cognitive model of depression.

The work of Albert Ellis (1962) gave major impetus to the development of cognitive-behavior therapies. Both Ellis and Beck believed that people can consciously adopt reason, and both viewed the patient's underlying assumptions as targets of intervention. Similarly, they both rejected their analytic training and replaced passive listening with active, direct dialogues with patients. While Ellis confronted and persuaded patients that the philosophies they lived by were unrealistic, Beck "turned the client into a colleague who researches verifiable reality" (Wessler, 1986, p. 5).

The work of a number of contemporary behaviorists influenced the development of cognitive therapy. Bandura's (1977) concepts of expectancy of reinforcement, self and outcome efficacies, the interaction between person and environment, modeling, and vicarious learning catalyzed a shift in behavior therapy toward the cognitive domain. Mahoney's (1974) early work on the cognitive control of behavior and his continuing theoretical contributions also influenced cognitive therapy. Along with cognitive therapy and rational-emotive therapy, Meichenbaum's (1977) cognitive-behavior modification is recognized as one of the three major self-control therapies (Mahoney & Arnkoff, 1978). Meichenbaum's combination of cognitive modification and skills training in a coping skills paradigm is particularly useful in treating anxiety, anger, and stress.

Current Status

Research: Cognitive Model and Outcome Studies

The cognitive model of depression postulates three specific concepts (Beck, 1967; Beck et al., 1979): (1) the cognitive triad, (2) schemas, and (3) cognitive errors. Subsequent research provided empirical support for this model and demonstrated the efficacy of cognitive therapy in the treatment of unipolar depression. These results are summarized by Dobson (1989) and by Haaga, Dyck, and Ernst (1991). For example, an unpublished study by Don Ernst (1987) indicated that 86 of 99 studies supported specific hypotheses of the cognitive model of depression and 30 of 34 studies supported hypotheses of bias in information processing.

Studies from seven independent centers have compared the efficacy of cognitive therapy to antidepressant medication, a treatment of established efficacy. Comparisons of cognitive therapy alone to drugs alone have found cognitive therapy to be superior (Blackburn, Bishop, Glen, Whalley, & Christie, 1981; Dunn, 1979; Maldonado, 1982; Rush, Beck, Kovacs, and Hollon, 1977) or equal to antidepressant medication (Blackburn, Eunson & Bishop, 1986; Hollon, Evans, & DeRubeis, 1983; Murphy, Simons, Wetzel, & Lustman, 1983; Simons, Murphy, Levine, & Wetzel, 1986; Hollon, DeRubeis, Evans, Wiemer, Garvey, Grove, & Tuason, 1992).

Six studies compared drugs alone to the combination of cognitive therapy and medication. Four showed superiority of the combination (Blackburn et al., 1981; Blackburn et al., 1986; Maldonado, 1982; Teasdale, Fennell, Hibbert, & Amies, 1984), and two showed drugs alone to be equivalent to the combined treatment (Murphy et al., 1983; Simons et al., 1986).

A multi-site study of the treatment of depression conducted by the National Institute of Mental Health compared pharmacotherapy with two short-term psychotherapies: interpersonal therapy and cognitive therapy. At the time of termination from treatment, both psychological treatments were as effective as medication in the treatment of moderately depressed persons. In the case of severely depressed persons, both antidepressant medication and interpersonal therapy were significantly more effective than the placebo condition, whereas cognitive therapy was not (Elkin, Shea, Watkins, Imber, Sotsky, Collins,

Glass, Pilkonis, Leber, Docherty, Fiester, & Perloff, 1989). However, site differences in the study were significant. At one of the three study sites, cognitive therapy was very successful in treating severely depressed patients. Moreover, long-term follow-up results indicate that patients receiving cognitive therapy had the lowest relapse rates at the one-year point (Shea, Elkin, Imber, Sotsky, Watkins, Collins, Pilkonis, Beckham, Glass, Dolan, & Perloff, 1992).

Other follow-up studies, observing patients for three months to two years after treatment, indicate that cognitive therapy has greater long-term effects than drug therapy (Blackburn et al., 1986; Hollon et al., 1983; Kovacs, Rush, Beck, & Hollon, 1981; Maldonado, 1982; Simons et al., 1986; Evans, Hollon, DeRubeis, Piasecki, Grove, Garvey, & Tuason, 1992). Thus, cognitive therapy has demonstrated efficacy alone and in combination with standard drug treatment. Of special significance is the evidence of greater sustained improvement over time with cognitive therapy.

Suicide Research

Beck has developed key theoretical concepts regarding suicide and its prevention. Chief among his findings about suicide risk is the notion of hopelessness. Longitudinal studies of both inpatients and outpatients who had suicidal ideation have found that a cut-off score of nine or more on the Beck Hopelessness Scale is predictive of eventual suicide (Beck, Brown, Berchick, Stewart, & Steer, 1990; Beck, Steer, Kovacs, & Garrison, 1985). Hopelessness as a predictor of eventual suicide has been confirmed in subsequent studies.

Assessment Scales

Beck's work has generated a number of assessment scales for depression and suicidality, most notably the Beck Depression Inventory (Beck, Ward, Mendelson, Mock, & Erbaugh, 1961), the Scale for Suicide Ideation (Beck, Kovacs, & Weissman, 1979), the Suicide Intent Scale (Beck, Schuyler, & Herman, 1974), and the Hopelessness Scale (Beck, Weissman, Lester, & Trexler, 1974). The Beck Depression Inventory is the best known of these. It has been used in hundreds of outcome studies and is routinely employed by psychologists, physicians, and social workers to monitor depression in their patients and clients.

Training

The Center for Cognitive Therapy at the University of Pennsylvania, affiliated with the University of Pennsylvania Medical School, provides outpatient services and trains pre- and postdoctoral psychologists and psychiatric residents in cognitive therapy. The center is also a research institute, integrating clinical observations with empirical findings to develop theory. Each year, visiting scholars from diverse areas of the world participate in the research and clinical activities of the center, learning about cognitive therapy and then training therapists in their home sites. They also exchange information on the theory and practice of cognitive therapy.

There are currently 10 other training centers for cognitive therapy in the United States. Research and treatment efforts in cognitive therapy are being conducted in a number of universities and hospitals in the United States and Europe. The *International Cognitive Therapy Newsletter* began in 1985 for the exchange of information among cognitive therapists. Therapists from five continents participate in the newsletter network.

Cognitive therapists routinely contribute to behavior therapy journals as well as to psychiatric journals. The primary journals devoted to research in cognitive therapy are *Cognitive Therapy and Research* and the *Journal of Cognitive Psychotherapy: An International Quarterly*. Cognitive therapy is represented at the annual meetings of the American Psychological Association, the American Psychiatric Association, the American Orthopsychiatric Association, the Phobia Society of America, and others. It is a major force in the Association for the Advancement of Behavior Therapy. As of 1993, there had been four world congresses of the International Association of Cognitive Therapy, in the United States, Sweden, England, and Canada. Because of its efficacy as a short-term form of psychotherapy, cognitive therapy is achieving wider use in settings that must demonstrate cost-effectiveness or that require short-term contact with patients. It has applications in both inpatient and outpatient settings.

Many talented researchers and innovative therapists have contributed to the development of cognitive therapy. Controlled outcome studies comparing cognitive therapy with other forms of treatment are conducted with anxiety disorders, panic, drug abuse, anorexia and bulimia, geriatric depression, acute depression, and dysphoric disorder. Beck's students and associates do research on the nature and treatment of depression, anxiety, loneliness, marital conflict, eating disorders, agoraphobia, pain, and personality disorders.

As cognitive therapy has interacted with behavior therapy and other disciplines, new theories of cognitive processing have emerged, represented in the writings of Mahoney (1980) and Guidano and Liotti (1983), who combined the cognitive model with such fields as evolutionary epistemology and the philosophy of science to propose a theory of individual knowledge.

❖ PERSONALITY

Theory of Personality

Cognitive therapy emphasizes the role of cognitive processing in emotion and behavior. An individual's emotional and behavioral responses to a situation are largely determined by how that individual perceives, interprets, and assigns meaning to that event.

Cognitive therapy views personality as shaped by the interaction between innate disposition and environment (Beck, Freeman, & Associates, 1990). Personality attributes are seen as reflecting basic schemas or interpersonal "strategies" developed in response to the environment.

Cognitive therapy sees psychological distress as being "caused" by a number of factors. While people may have biochemical predispositions to illness, they respond to specific stressors because of their learning history. The phenomena of psychopathology (but not necessarily the cause) are on the same continuum as normal emotional reactions, but they are manifested in exaggerated and persistent ways. In depression, for example, sadness and loss of interest are intensified and prolonged, in mania there is heightened investment in self-aggrandizement, and in anxiety there is an extreme sense of vulnerability and danger.

Individuals experience psychological distress when they perceive a situation as threatening their vital interests. At such times, their perceptions and interpretations of events are highly selective, egocentric, and rigid. This results in a functional impairment of normal cognitive activity. There is a decreased ability to turn off idiosyncratic thinking, to concentrate, recall, or reason. Corrective functions, which allow reality testing and refinement of global conceptualizations, are attenuated.

Cognitive Vulnerability

Each individual has a set of idiosyncratic vulnerabilities and sensitivities that predispose him or her to psychological distress. These vulnerabilities appear related to personality structure. Personality is shaped by *schemas*, cognitive structures that consist of the individual's fundamental beliefs and assumptions, which develop early in life from personal experiences and identification with significant others. These concepts are reinforced by further learning experiences and, in turn, influence the formation of other beliefs, values, and attitudes.

Schemas may be adaptive or dysfunctional. They may be general or specific in nature. A person may even have competing schemas. Schemas are enduring cognitive structures, latent during nonstressful periods, that become active when triggered by specific stimuli, stressors, or circumstances.

The basic nature of schemas can be unraveled by observing people whose cognitive structures are least accessible to exploration through introspection, such as patients with borderline personality disorder (Pretzer, 1983, 1990; Young, 1983). This disorder is characterized by intensity of emotion and reactivity to events, abrupt shifts in mood, impulsive and counter-productive behavior, and unstable relationships. Dichotomous (black-white) thinking (particularly seeing self or others as *all good* or *all bad*) and subjective reasoning (equating feelings with facts) are dominant cognitive distortions.

Pretzer (Beck, Freeman, & Associates, 1990) has identified three basic beliefs common to many individuals with borderline personality disorder: (1) "The world is dangerous and malevolent," (2) "I am powerless and vulnerable," and (3) "I am inherently unacceptable." The combination of these beliefs and the tendency toward all-or-nothing thinking leads to extreme emotional and behavioral responses, including vacillations between autonomy and dependence. With such beliefs, the individual's delicate emotional balance is easily upset, especially by perceived abandonment by others. Other disorders may similarly be characterized by core beliefs that are similar but less strong or rigid.

Another ubiquitous belief has been labeled *conditional assumption*. Such assumptions or attitudes begin with an *if*. Two examples, frequently found in depression-prone patients, are "If I don't succeed at everything I do, nobody will respect me" and "If a person doesn't like me, it means I'm unlovable." Such individuals may function fairly well until they experience a series of defeats or rejections. At this point, they begin to believe that nobody respects them or that they are unlovable. In most cases, such beliefs can be dispelled in brief therapy—however, if they constitute core beliefs, more protracted treatment is necessary.

Dimensions of Personality

The idea that certain clusters of personality attributes or cognitive structures are related to certain types of emotional response has been studied by Beck, Epstein, and Harrison (1983), who found two major personality dimensions relevant to depression and possibly other disorders: social dependence (sociotropy) and autonomy. Beck's research revealed that dependent individuals became depressed following disruption of relationships. Autonomous people became depressed after defeat or failure to attain a desired goal. The sociotropic dimension is organized around closeness, nurturance, and dependency; the autonomous dimension around independence, goal setting, self-determination, and self-imposed obligations.

Research has also established that while "pure" cases of sociotropy and autonomy do exist, most people display features of each, depending on the situation. Thus, sociotropy and autonomy are modes of behavior, not fixed personality structures. This position stands in marked contrast with psychodynamic theories of personality, which postulate fixed personality dimensions.

Thus, cognitive therapy views personality as reflecting the individual's cognitive organization and structure, which are both biologically and socially influenced. Within the constraints of one's neuroanatomy and biochemistry, personal learning experiences help determine how one develops and responds.

Variety of Concepts

Cognitive therapy emphasizes the individual's learning history, including the influence of significant life events, in the development of psychological disturbance. It is not a reductionistic model but recognizes that psychological distress is usually the result of many interacting factors.

Cognitive therapy's emphasis on the individual's learning history endorses social learning theory and the importance of reinforcement. The social learning perspective requires a thorough examination of the individual's developmental history and his or her own idiosyncratic meanings and interpretations of events. Cognitive therapy emphasizes the idiographic nature of cognition, for the same event may have very different meanings for two individuals.

The conceptualization of personality as reflective of schemas and underlying assumptions also relates to social learning theory. The way a person structures experience is based on consequences of past behavior, vicarious learning from significant others, and expectations about the future.

Theory of Causality

Psychological distress is ultimately caused by many innate, biological, developmental, and environmental factors interacting with one another, and so there is no single "cause" of psychopathology. Depression, for instance, is characterized by predisposing factors such as hereditary susceptibility, diseases that cause persistent neuro-chemical abnormalities, developmental traumas leading to specific cognitive vulnerabilities, inadequate personal experiences that fail to provide appropriate coping skills, and counterproductive cognitive patterns, such as unrealistic goals, assumptions, or imperatives. Physical disease, severe and acute stress, and chronic stress are also precipitating factors.

Cognitive Distortions

Systematic errors in reasoning called *cognitive distortions* are evident during psychological distress (Beck, 1967). These include:

Arbitrary inference: Drawing a specific conclusion without supporting evidence or even in the face of contradictory evidence. An example of this is the working mother who concludes after a particularly busy day, "I'm a terrible mother."

Selective abstraction: Conceptualizing a situation on the basis of a detail taken out of context, ignoring other information. An example is a man who becomes jealous upon seeing his girlfriend tilt her head towards another man to hear him better at a noisy party.

Overgeneralization: Abstracting a general rule from one or a few isolated incidents and applying it too broadly and to unrelated situations. After a discouraging date, a woman concluded, "All men are alike. I'll always be rejected."

Magnification and minimization: Seeing something as far more significant or less significant than it actually is. A student catastrophized, "If I appear the least bit nervous in class it will mean disaster." Another person, rather than facing the fact that his mother is terminally ill, decides that she will soon recover from her "cold."

Personalization: Attributing external events to oneself without evidence supporting a causal connection. A man waved to an acquaintance across a busy street. After not getting a greeting in return, he concluded, "I must have done something to offend him."

Dichotomous thinking: Categorizing experiences in one of two extremes; for example, as complete success or total failure. A doctoral candidate stated, "Unless I write the best exam they've ever seen, I'm a failure as a student."

Systematic Bias in Psychological Disorders

A bias in information processing is a characteristic of most psychological disorders. This bias is generally applied to "external" information, such as communications or threats, and may start operating at early stages of information processing. The bias may be extended to misinterpretation of internal "messages" received within the body, as in panic attacks, hysteria, anorexia nervosa, and hypochondriasis. The kind of bias found in typical disorders is described in Table 8.1.

Cognitive Model of Depression

A *cognitive triad* characterizes depression (Beck, 1967). The depressed individual has a negative view of the self, the world, and the future, and perceives the self as inadequate, deserted, and worthless. A negative view is apparent in beliefs that enormous demands exist and that immense barriers block access to goals. The world seems devoid of pleasure or gratification. The depressed person's view of the future is pessimistic, reflecting the belief that current troubles will not improve. This hopelessness may lead to suicidal ideation.

Motivational, behavioral, and physical symptoms of depression stem from these cognitive patterns. *Paralysis of will* is created by the belief that one lacks the ability to cope or control an event's outcome. Consequently, there is a reluctance to commit oneself to a goal. Suicidal wishes often reflect a desire to escape from unbearable problems.

The increased dependency often observed in depressed patients reflects the view of self as incompetent, an overestimation of the difficulty of normal life tasks, the expectation of failure, and the desire for someone more capable to take over. Indecisiveness similarly reflects the belief that one is incapable of making correct decisions. The physical symptoms of depression—low energy, fatigue, and inertia—are also related to negative expectations. Work with depressed patients indicates that initiating activity actually reduces inertia and fatigue. Moreover, refuting negative expectations and demonstrating motor ability play important roles in recovery.

TABLE 8.1 ◈ The Cognitive Profile of Neurotic Disorders

Disorder	*Systematic Bias in Processing Information*
Depression	Negative view of self, experience, and future
Hypomania	Inflated view of self and future
Anxiety disorder	Sense of physical or psychological danger
Panic disorder	Catastrophic interpretation of bodily/mental experiences
Phobia	Sense of danger in specific, avoidable situations
Paranoid state	Attribution of bias to others
Hysteria	Concept of motor or sensory abnormality
Obsession	Repeated warning or doubts about safety
Compulsion	Rituals to ward off perceived threat
Suicidal behavior	Hopelessness and deficiencies in problem solving
Anorexia nervosa	Fear of being fat
Hypochondriasis	Attribution of serious medical disorder

Cognitive Model of Anxiety Disorders

Anxiety disorders are conceptualized as excessive functioning or malfunctioning of normal survival mechanisms. Thus, the basic mechanisms for coping with threat are the same for both normal and anxious people: physiological responses prepare the body for escape or self-defense. The same physiological responses occur in the face of psychosocial threats as in the case of physical dangers. The anxious person's perception of danger is either based on false assumptions or excessive, while the normal response is based on a more accurate assessment of risk and the magnitude of danger. In addition, normal individuals can correct their misperceptions using logic and evidence. Anxious individuals have difficulty recognizing cues of safety and other evidence that would reduce the threat of danger. Thus, in cases of anxiety, cognitive content revolves around themes of danger, and the individual tends to maximize the likelihood of harm and minimize his or her ability to cope.

Mania

The manic patient's biased thinking is the reverse of the depressive's. Such individuals selectively perceive significant gains in each life experience, blocking out negative experiences or reinterpreting them as positive, and unrealistically expecting favorable results from various enterprises. Exaggerated concepts of abilities, worth, and accomplishments lead to feelings of euphoria. The continued stimulation from inflated self-evaluations and overly optimistic expectations provide vast sources of energy and drive the manic individual into continuous goal-directed activity.

Panic Disorder

Patients with panic disorder are prone to regard any unexplained symptom or sensation as a sign of some impending catastrophe. Their cognitive processing system focuses their attention on bodily or psychological experiences and shapes these sources of internal information into a belief of impending disaster. Each patient has a specific "equation." For one, distress in the chest or stomach equals heart attack; for another, shortness of breath means the cessation of all breathing; and for another, lightheadedness is a sign of imminent unconsciousness.

Some patients regard a sudden surge of anger as a sign that they will lose control and injure somebody. Others interpret a mental lapse, momentary confusion, or mild disorientation as a sign they are losing their mind. A crucial characteristic of people having panic attacks is the conclusion that vital systems (cardiovascular, respiratory, or central nervous system) will collapse. Because of their fear, they tend to be overly vigilant towards internal sensations and thus detect and magnify sensations that pass unnoticed in other people.

Patients with panic disorder show a specific *cognitive deficit*—an inability to view their symptoms and catastrophic interpretations realistically.

Agoraphobia

Patients who have had one or more panic attacks in a particular situation tend to avoid that situation. For example, people who have had panic attacks in supermarkets will avoid going there. If they push themselves to go, they become increasingly vigilant toward their sensations and begin to anticipate having another panic attack.

The anticipation of such an attack triggers a variety of autonomic symptoms that are then misinterpreted as signs of an impending disaster (e.g., heart attack, loss of consciousness, suffocation), which can lead to a full-blown panic attack. Patients with a panic disorder that goes untreated frequently develop agoraphobia. They may eventually become housebound or so restricted in their activities that they cannot travel far from home and require a companion to venture any distance.

Phobia

In phobias, there is anticipation of physical or psychological harm in specific situations. As long as the patients can avoid these situations, they do not feel threatened and may be relatively comfortable. When they enter into these situations, they experience the typical subjective and physiological symptoms of severe anxiety. As a result of this unpleasant reaction, their tendency to avoid the situation in the future is reinforced.

In *evaluation phobias*, there is fear of disparagement or failure in social situations, examinations, and public speaking. The behavioral and physiological reactions to the potential "danger" (rejection, devaluation, failure) may interfere with the patient's functioning to the degree that these responses can produce just what the patient fears will happen.

Paranoid States

The paranoid individual is biased toward attributing prejudice to others. The paranoid persists in assuming that other people are deliberately abusive, interfering, or critical. In contrast to depressed patients, who believe that supposed insults or rejections are justified, paranoid patients persevere in thinking others treat them unjustly.

Unlike depressed patients, paranoid patients do not experience low self-esteem. They are more concerned with the *injustice* of the presumed attacks, thwarting, or intrusions than with the actual loss, and they rail against the presumed prejudice and malicious intent of others.

Obsessions and Compulsions

Patients with obsessions introduce uncertainty into the appraisal of situations that most people would consider safe. The uncertainty is generally attached to circumstances that are potentially unsafe and is manifested by continual doubts—even though there is no evidence of danger.

Obsessives continually doubt whether they have performed an act necessary for safety (for example, turning off a gas oven or locking the door at night). They may fear contamination by germs, and no amount of reassurance can alleviate the fear. A key characteristic of obsessives is this *sense of responsibility* and the belief that they are accountable for having taken an action—or having failed to take an action—that could harm them or their family.

Compulsions are attempts to reduce excessive doubts by performing rituals designed to neutralize the anticipated disaster. A hand-washing compulsion, for instance, is based on the patients' belief that they have not removed all the dirt or contaminants from parts of their body. Some patients regard dirt as a source of danger, either as a cause of physical disease or as a source of offensive, unpleasant odors, and they are compelled to remove this source of physical or social danger.

Suicidal Behavior

The cognitive processing in suicidal individuals has two features. First, there is a high degree of hopelessness. The greater the hopelessness, the more the likelihood of suicide increases (Beck, Steer, Kovacs, & Garrison, 1985). A second feature is a cognitive deficit—a difficulty in solving problems. Although the hopelessness accentuates poor problem solving and vice versa, the difficulties in coping with life situations can, by themselves, contribute to the suicidal potential.

Anorexia Nervosa

Anorexia nervosa and bulimia represent a constellation of maladaptive beliefs that revolve around one central assumption: "My body weight and shape determine my worth and/or my social acceptability." Centered around this assumption are such beliefs as "I will look ugly if I gain much more weight," "The only thing in my life that I can control is my weight," and "If I don't starve myself, I will let go completely and become enormous."

Anorexics show typical distortions in information processing. They misinterpret symptoms of fullness after meals as signs they are getting fat. And they misperceive their image in a mirror or photograph as being much fatter than it actually is.

❖ PSYCHOTHERAPY

Theory of Psychotherapy

The goals of cognitive therapy are to correct faulty information processing and to help patients modify assumptions that maintain maladaptive behaviors and emotions. Cognitive and behavioral methods are used to challenge dysfunctional beliefs and to promote more realistic adaptive thinking. Cognitive therapy initially addresses symptom relief, but its ultimate goal is to remove systematic biases in thinking.

Cognitive therapy fosters change in patients' beliefs by treating beliefs as testable hypotheses to be examined through behavioral experiments jointly agreed upon by patient and therapist. The cognitive therapist does not tell the client that the beliefs are irrational or wrong or that the beliefs of the therapist should be adopted. Instead, the therapist asks questions to elicit the meaning, function, usefulness, and consequences of the patient's beliefs. The patient ultimately decides whether to reject, modify, or maintain all personal beliefs, being well aware of their emotional and behavioral consequences.

Cognitive therapy is not the substitution of positive beliefs for negative ones. It is based in reality, not in wishful thinking. Similarly, cognitive therapy does not maintain that people's problems are imaginary. Patients may have serious social, financial, or health problems as well as functional deficits. In addition to real problems, however, they have biased views of themselves, their situations, and their resources that limit their range of responses and prevent them from generating solutions.

Cognitive change can promote behavioral change by allowing the patient to take risks. In turn, experience in applying new behaviors can validate the new perspective. Emotions can be moderated by enlarging perspectives to include alternative interpretations of events. Emotions play a role in cognitive change, for learning is enhanced when emotions are triggered. Thus, the cognitive, behavioral, and emotional channels interact in therapeutic change, but cognitive therapy emphasizes the primacy of cognition in promoting and maintaining therapeutic change.

Cognitive change occurs at several levels: voluntary thoughts, continuous or automatic thoughts, and assumptions. According to the cognitive model, cognitions are organized in a hierarchy, with each level differing from the next in its accessibility and stability. The most accessible and least stable cognitions are voluntary thoughts. At the next level are automatic thoughts, which come to mind spontaneously when triggered by circumstances. They are the thoughts that intercede between an event or stimulus and the individual's emotional and behavioral reactions.

An example of an automatic thought is "Everyone will see I'm nervous," experienced by a socially anxious person before going to a party. Automatic thoughts are accompanied by emotions and at the time they are experienced seem plausible, are highly salient, and are internally consistent with individual logic. They are given credibility without ever being challenged. Though automatic thoughts are more stable and less accessible than voluntary thoughts, patients can be taught to recognize and monitor them. Cognitive distortions are evident in automatic thoughts.

Automatic thoughts are generated from underlying assumptions. For example, the belief "I am responsible for other people's happiness" produces numerous negative automatic thoughts in people who perceive themselves as causing distress to others. Assumptions shape perceptions into cognitions, determine goals, and provide interpretations and meanings to events. They may be quite stable and outside the patient's awareness.

Core beliefs are called *schemas*. Therapy aims at identifying these assumptions and counteracting their effects. If the assumptions themselves can be changed, the patient is less vulnerable to future distress.

The Therapeutic Relationship

The therapeutic relationship is collaborative. The therapist assesses sources of distress and dysfunction and helps the patient clarify goals. In cases of severe depression or anxiety, patients may need the therapist to take a directive role. In other instances, patients may take the lead in determining goals for therapy. As part of the collaboration, the patient provides the thoughts, images, and beliefs that occur in various situations as well as the emotions and behaviors that accompany the thoughts. The patient also shares responsibility by helping to set the agenda for each session and by doing homework between sessions. Homework helps therapy to proceed more quickly and gives the patient an opportunity to practice newly learned skills and perspectives.

The therapist functions as a guide who helps the patient understand how beliefs and attitudes influence affect and behavior. The therapist is also a catalyst who promotes corrective experiences that lead to cognitive change and skills acquisition. Thus, cognitive therapy employs a learning model of psychotherapy. The therapist has expertise in examining and modifying beliefs and behavior but does not adopt the role of a passive expert.

Cognitive therapists actively pursue the patient's point of view. By using warmth, accurate empathy, and genuineness (see Rogers, 1951), the cognitive therapist appreciates the patient's personal world view. However, these qualities alone are not sufficient for therapeutic change. The cognitive therapist specifies problems, focuses on important areas, and teaches specific cognitive and behavioral techniques.

Along with having good interpersonal skills, cognitive therapists are flexible. They are sensitive to the patient's level of comfort and use self-disclosure judiciously. They provide supportive contact, when necessary, and operate within the goals and agenda of the cognitive approach. Flexibility in the use of therapeutic techniques depends on the targeted symptoms. For example, the inertia of depression responds best to behavioral interventions, while the suicidal ideation and pessimism of depression respond best to cognitive techniques. A good cognitive therapist does not use techniques arbitrarily or mechanically, but with sound rationale and skill, and with an understanding of each individual's needs.

To maintain collaboration, the therapist elicits feedback from the patient, usually at the end of each session. Feedback focuses on what the patient found helpful or not helpful, whether the patient has concerns about the therapist, and whether the patient has questions. The therapist may summarize the session or ask the patient to do so. Another way the therapist encourages collaboration is by providing the patient with a rationale for each procedure used. This demystifies the therapy process, increases patients' participation, and reinforces a learning paradigm in which patients gradually assume more responsibility for therapeutic change.

Definitions

Three fundamental concepts in cognitive therapy are *collaborative empiricism*, *Socratic dialogue*, and *guided discovery*.

Collaborative empiricism.   The therapeutic relationship is collaborative and requires jointly determining the goals for treatment, eliciting and providing feedback, thereby demystifying how therapeutic change occurs. The therapist and patient become co-investigators, examining the evidence to support or reject the patient's cognitions. As in scientific inquiry, interpretations or assumptions are treated as testable hypotheses.

Empirical evidence is used to determine whether particular cognitions serve any useful purpose. Prior conclusions are subjected to logical analysis. Biased thinking is exposed as the patient becomes aware of alternative sources of information. This process is conducted as a partnership between patient and therapist, with either taking a more active role as needed.

Socratic dialogue.   Questioning is a major therapeutic device in cognitive therapy (Beck & Young, 1985) and Socratic dialogue is the preferred method. The therapist carefully designs a series of questions to promote new learning. The purposes of the therapist's questions are generally to (1) clarify or define problems, (2) assist in the identification of thoughts, images, and assumptions, (3) examine the meanings of events for the patient, and (4) assess the consequences of maintaining maladaptive thoughts and behaviors.

Socratic dialogue implies that the patient arrives at logical conclusions based on the questions posed by the therapist. Questions are not used to "trap" patients, lead them to inevitable conclusions, or attack them. Questions enable the therapist to understand the patient's point of view and are posed with sensitivity so that patients may look at their assumptions objectively and nondefensively.

Beck and Young describe how questions change throughout the course of therapy:

> In the beginning of therapy, questions are employed to obtain a full and detailed picture of the patient's particular difficulties. They are used to obtain background and diagnostic data; to evaluate the patient's stress tolerance, capacity for introspection, coping methods and so on; to obtain information about the patient's external situation and interpersonal context; and to modify vague complaints by working with the patient to arrive at specific target problems to work on.
>
> As therapy progresses, the therapist uses questioning to explore approaches to problems, to help the patient weigh advantages and disadvantages of possible solutions, to examine the consequences of staying with particular maladaptive behaviors, to elicit automatic thoughts, and to demonstrate maladaptive assumptions and their consequences. In short, the therapist uses questioning in most cognitive therapeutic techniques. (1985, p. 223)

Guided discovery   Through guided discovery the patient modifies maladaptive beliefs and assumptions. The therapist serves as a "guide" who elucidates problem behaviors and errors in logic by designing new experiences (*behavioral experiments*) that lead to the acquisition of new skills and perspectives. Guided discovery implies that the therapist does not exhort or cajole the patient to adopt a new set of beliefs. Rather, the therapist encourages the patient's use of information, facts, and probabilities to obtain a realistic perspective.

Process of Psychotherapy

Initial Sessions

The goals of the first interview are to initiate a relationship with the patient, to elicit essential information, and to produce symptom relief. Building a relationship with the patient may begin with questions about feelings and thoughts about beginning therapy. Discussing the patient's expectations helps put the patient at ease, provides information to the therapist regarding the patient's expectations, and presents an opportunity to demonstrate the relationship between cognition and affect (Beck, Rush, et al., 1979). The therapist also uses the initial sessions to socialize the patient to cognitive therapy, establish a collaborative framework, and deal with any misconceptions about therapy. The types of information the therapist seeks in the initial session regard diagnosis, past history, present life situation, psychological problems, attitudes about treatment, and motivation for treatment.

Problem definition and symptom relief begin in the first session. Although problem definition and background may take several sessions, it is often critical to focus on a very specific problem and provide rapid relief in the first session. For example, a suicidal patient needs direct intervention to undermine hopelessness immediately. Symptom relief can come from several sources: specific problem solving, clarifying vague or general complaints into workable goals, or gaining objectivity about a disorder (e.g., that a patient's symptoms represent anxiety, and nothing worse, or that difficulty concentrating is a symptom of depression and not a sign of brain disease).

Problem definition entails both functional and cognitive analyses of the problem. A functional analysis identifies elements of the problem: how it is manifested; situations in which it occurs; its frequency, intensity, and duration; and its consequences. A cognitive analysis of the problem identifies the thoughts and images a person has when emotion is triggered. It also includes investigation of the extent to which the person feels in control of thoughts and images, what the person imagines will happen in a distressing situation, and the probability of such an outcome actually occurring.

In the early sessions, the cognitive therapist plays a more active role than does the patient. The therapist gathers information, conceptualizes the patient's problems, socializes the patient to cognitive therapy, and actively intervenes to provide symptom relief. The patient is assigned homework beginning at the first session.

Homework, at this early stage, is usually directed at recognizing the connections between affect and behavior. Some patients might be asked to record their automatic thoughts when distressed. Others might practice recognizing thoughts by counting them, as they occur, on a wrist counter. Thus, the patient is trained from the outset to self-monitor thoughts and behaviors. In later sessions, the patient plays an increasingly active role in determining homework, and assignments focus on testing very specific assumptions.

During the initial sessions, a problem list is generated. A problem list may include specific symptoms, behaviors, or pervasive problems. These problems are assigned priorities as targets for intervention. Priorities are based on the relative magnitude of distress, the likelihood of making progress, the severity of symptoms, and the pervasiveness of a particular theme or topic.

If the therapist can help the patient solve a problem early in treatment, this success can motivate the patient to make further changes. As each problem is approached, the therapist chooses the appropriate cognitive or behavioral technique to apply and provides the patient with a rationale for the technique. Throughout therapy, the therapist elicits the patient's reactions to various techniques to ascertain whether they are being applied correctly, whether they are successful, and how they can be incorporated into homework or practical experience outside the session.

Middle and Later Sessions

As cognitive therapy proceeds, the emphasis shifts from the patient's symptoms to the patient's patterns of thinking. The connections among thoughts, emotions, and behavior are chiefly demonstrated through the examination of automatic thoughts. Once the patient can challenge thoughts that interfere with functioning, he or she can consider the underlying assumptions that generate such thoughts.

There is usually a greater emphasis on cognitive rather than behavioral techniques in later sessions, which focus on complex problems that involve several dysfunctional thoughts. Often these thoughts are more amenable to logical analysis than to behavioral experimentation. For example, the prophecy "I'll never get what I want in life" is not easily tested. However, one can question the logic of this generalization and look at the advantages and disadvantages of maintaining it as a belief.

Often such assumptions outside the patient's awareness are discovered as themes of automatic thoughts. By observing automatic thoughts over time and across situations, assumptions appear or can be inferred. Once these assumptions and their power have been recognized, therapy aims at modifying them by examining their validity, adaptiveness, and utility for the patient.

In later sessions, the patient assumes more responsibility for identifying problems and solutions and for creating homework assignments. The therapist takes on the role of advisor rather than teacher as the patient becomes more able to use cognitive techniques to solve problems. The frequency of sessions decreases as the patient becomes more self-sufficient. Therapy is terminated when goals have been reached and the patient feels able to practice his or her new skills and perspectives.

Ending Treatment

Length of treatment depends primarily on the severity of the client's problems. The usual length for unipolar depression is 15 to 25 sessions at weekly intervals (Beck, Rush, et al., 1979). Moderately to severely depressed patients usually require sessions twice a week for 4 to 5 weeks and then require weekly sessions for 10 to 15 weeks. Most cases of anxiety are treated within a comparable period of time.

Some patients find it extremely difficult to tolerate the anxiety involved in giving up old ways of thinking. For them, therapy may last for several months. Still others experience early symptom relief and leave therapy early. In these cases, little structural change has occurred and problems are likely to recur.

From the outset, the therapist and patient share the expectation that therapy is time-limited. Because cognitive therapy is present-centered and time-limited, there tend to be fewer problems with termination than in longer forms of therapy. As the patient develops self-reliance, therapy sessions become less frequent.

Termination is planned for, even in the first session as the rationale for cognitive therapy is presented. Patients are told that a goal of the therapy is for them to learn to be their own therapists. The problem list makes explicit what is to be accomplished in treatment. Behavioral observation, self-monitoring, self-report, and sometimes questionnaires (e.g., the Beck Depression Inventory), measure progress towards the goals on the problem list. Feedback from the patient aids the therapist in designing experiences to foster cognitive change.

Some patients have concerns about relapse or about functioning autonomously. Some of these concerns include cognitive distortions, such as dichotomous thinking ("I'm either sick or 100 percent cured") or negative prediction ("I'll get depressed again and won't be able to help myself"). It may be necessary to review the goal of therapy: to teach the patient ways to handle problems more effectively, not to produce a "cure" or restructure core personality (Beck, Rush, et al., 1979). Education about psychological disorders, such as the possibility of recurrent depression, is done throughout treatment so that the patient has a realistic perspective on prognosis.

During the usual course of therapy, the patient experiences both successes and setbacks. Such problems give the patient the opportunity to practice new skills. As termination approaches, the patient can be reminded that setbacks are normal and have been handled before. The therapist might ask the patient to describe how prior specific problems were handled during treatment. Therapists can also use cognitive rehearsal prior to termination by having patients imagine future difficulties and report how they would deal with them.

Termination is usually followed by one to two booster sessions, usually one and two months after termination. Such sessions consolidate gains and assist the patient in employing new skills.

Mechanisms of Psychotherapy

Several common denominators cut across effective treatments. Three mechanisms of change common to all successful forms of psychotherapy are (1) a comprehensible framework, (2) the patient's emotional engagement in the problem situation, and (3) reality testing in that situation.

Cognitive therapy maintains that the modification of dysfunctional assumptions leads to effective cognitive, emotional, and behavioral change. Patients change by recognizing automatic thoughts, questioning the evidence used to support them, and modifying cognitions. Next, the patient behaves in ways congruent with new, more adaptive ways of thinking.

Change can occur only if the patient experiences a problematic situation as a real threat. According to cognitive therapy, thoughts underlie emotions, and with *affective arousal*, thoughts become accessible and modifiable. One mechanism of change, then, centers on making accessible those cognitive constellations that produced the maladaptive behavior or symptomatology. This mechanism is analogous to what psychoanalysts call "making the unconscious conscious."

Simply arousing emotions and the accompanying cognitions is not sufficient to cause lasting change. People express emotion, sometimes explosively, throughout their lives without benefit. However, the therapeutic milieu allows the patient to simultaneously experience emotional arousal and reality testing. For a variety of psychotherapies, what is therapeutic is the patient's ability to be engaged in a problem situation and yet respond to it objectively. In terms of cognitive therapy, this means to experience the cognitions and to test them within the therapeutic framework.

❖ APPLICATIONS

Problems

Cognitive therapy is a present-centered, directive, active, problem-oriented approach best suited for cases in which problems can be delineated and cognitive distortions are apparent. It is not designed for "personal growth" or exploration, nor necessarily as a way to understand one's past. It has wide-ranging applications to a variety of clinical problems. While originally used in individual psychotherapy, it is now used with couples, families, and groups as well. It can be applied alone or in conjunction with pharmacotherapy in inpatient and outpatient settings.

Cognitive therapy is widely recognized as an effective treatment for unipolar depression. Beck, Rush, Shaw, and Emery (1979, p. 27) list criteria for using cognitive therapy alone or in combination with medication. It is the treatment of choice in cases in which the patient refuses medication, prefers a psychological treatment, has unacceptable side effects to antidepressant medication, has a medical condition that precludes the use of antidepressants, or has proven to be refractory to adequate trials of antidepressants.

Cognitive therapy is not recommended as the exclusive treatment in cases of bipolar affective disorder or psychotic depression. It is also not used alone for the treatment of other psychoses, such as schizophrenia. While some patients with anxiety may begin treatment on medication, cognitive therapy teaches them to function without relying on medication.

Cognitive therapy produces the best results with patients who have adequate reality testing (i.e., no hallucinations or delusions), good concentration, and sufficient memory functions. It is ideally suited to patients who can focus on their automatic thoughts, accept the therapist-patient roles, are willing to tolerate anxiety in order to do experiments, can alter assumptions permanently, will take responsibility for their problems, and are willing to postpone gratification in order to complete therapy. Although these ideals are not always met, this therapy can proceed with some adjustment of outcome expectations and flexibility of structure. For example, therapy may not permanently alter schemas but may improve the patient's daily functioning.

Cognitive therapy works best with psychologically sophisticated patients. Lower-social-class and psychologically naive patients can also benefit after appropriate preparation for therapy. As long as the patient can recognize the relationships among thoughts, feelings, and behavior and takes some responsibility for self-help, cognitive therapy can be beneficial.

Evaluation

Therapists

Therapists who are beginning training at the Center for Cognitive Therapy are evaluated prior to training through live observation and videotaped role-playing. A confederate plays the role of the patient, and raters, using the Competency Checklist for Cognitive Therapists (Young & Beck, 1980), observe the roleplay through a one way mirror as the session is videotaped. At the end of a year's training, another roleplay interview is done and the therapist's progress is assessed. The Competency Checklist for Cognitive Therapists is divided into three parts. Part One, General Interview Procedures, assesses collaboration and mutual understanding. Part Two evaluates the use of specific cognitive and behavioral techniques. Part Three assesses the personal and professional characteristics of the therapist.

Therapists in training are supervised by experienced therapists. Supervision consists of weekly meetings during which trainees and supervisors review videotapes, audiotapes, or notes of cases in progress.

Patients

Patients' presenting problems are evaluated by clinical interviews and psychological tests. The intake interview at the Center for Cognitive Therapy is part of a three-hour protocol during which patients also complete psychological tests and questionnaires. The clinical interview contributes to a diagnosis and provides a thorough description of the background factors contributing to the patient's distress. Current level of functioning, prominent symptoms, and expectations for therapy are also explored.

The psychological tests most frequently used are the Beck Depression Inventory (BDI) (Beck et al., 1961), the Scale for Suicide Ideation (SSI) (Beck et al., 1979), the Anxiety Checklist (Beck, 1978), the Young Loneliness Inventory (Young, 1979), and the Dysfunctional Attitudes Scale (Weissman, 1979). These self-report inventories increase the efficiency of therapy by quickly providing the therapist with information that would otherwise have to be elicited in interview. Questionnaires like the BDI and the SSI may also alert a therapist to suicidal risk. These questionnaires are not projective tests and their purposes are obvious to the patient. Cognitive therapists do not generally use standard personality tests but may use the Sociotropy and Autonomy Scale (Beck, Epstein & Harrison, 1983) to determine how best to work with the patient's style of interaction.

Progress in Therapy

Progress evaluation depends on the goals of therapy. In general, relief from symptoms is indicated by changes in scores on standardized inventories such as the BDI, changes in behavior as indicated through self-monitoring and observation by others, and changes in thinking as evident in such measures as the Daily Record of Dysfunctional Thoughts. Because patients have weekly homework designed for their particular goals, progress can be assessed by the outcome of the homework assignments. Progress in therapy is apparent in the relative ease with which a patient challenges automatic thoughts, the decrease in frequency of maladaptive cognitions and behaviors, the increase in ability to generate solutions to problems, and improved mood.

If there are problems in the progress of therapy, several factors must be considered: the patient may have dysfunctional beliefs about therapy or the therapist; the therapist may lack rapport or may have failed to provide a rationale for a procedure; as assignment may be too difficult for the patient or the patient may have higher-order anxieties; or there may be a lack of consensus on the aims and goals of therapy (see Beck, Rush, et al., 1979, and Golden, 1983). Feedback during each session is designed to clarify misunderstandings and increase collaboration, thereby reducing the likelihood of problems in the progress of therapy.

Treatment

Cognitive therapy consists of highly specific learning experiences designed to teach patients (1) to monitor their negative, automatic thoughts (cognitions), (2) to recognize the connections between cognition, affect, and behavior, (3) to examine the evidence for and against distorted automatic thoughts, (4) to substitute more reality-oriented interpretations for these biased cognitions, and (5) to learn to identify and alter the beliefs that predispose them to distort their experiences (Beck, Rush, et al., 1979).

Both cognitive and behavioral techniques are used in cognitive therapy to reach these goals. The technique used at any given time depends on the patient's level of functioning and the particular symptoms and problems presented.

Cognitive Techniques

Verbal techniques are used to elicit the patient's automatic thoughts, analyze the logic behind the thoughts, identify maladaptive assumptions, and examine the validity of those assumptions. Automatic thoughts are elicited by questioning the patient about those thoughts that occur during upsetting situations. If the patient has difficulty recalling thoughts, imagery or role-playing can be used. Automatic thoughts are most accurately reported when they occur in real-life situations. Such "hot" cognitions are accessible, powerful, and habitual. The patient is taught to recognize and identify thoughts and to record them when upset.

Cognitive therapists do not interpret patients' automatic thoughts, but explore their meanings, particularly when a patient reports fairly neutral thoughts yet displays strong emotions. In such cases, the therapist asks what those thoughts mean to the patient. For example, after an initial visit, an anxious patient called his therapist in great distress. He had just read an article about drug treatments for anxiety. His automatic thought was, "Drug therapy is helpful for anxiety." The meaning he ascribed to this was, "Cognitive therapy can't possibly help me. I am doomed to failure again."

Automatic thoughts are tested by direct evidence or by logical analysis. Evidence can be derived from past and present circumstances, but true to scientific inquiry, it must be as close to the facts as possible. Data can also be gathered in behavioral experiments. For example, if a man believes he cannot conduct a conversation, he might try to initiate brief exchanges with three people. The empirical nature of behavioral experiments allows patients to think in a more objective way.

Examination of the patient's thoughts can also lead to cognitive change. Questioning may uncover logical inconsistencies, contradictions, and other errors in thinking. Identifying and labeling cognitive distortions is in itself helpful, for patients then have specific errors to correct.

Maladaptive assumptions are usually much less accessible to patients than are automatic thoughts. While some patients are able to articulate their assumptions, most find it difficult. Assumptions appear as themes in automatic thoughts. The therapist may ask the patient to abstract rules underlying specific thoughts. The therapist might also make assumptions from these data and present these assumptions to the patient for verification. A patient who had trouble identifying her assumptions broke into tears upon reading an assumption inferred by her therapist, an indication of the salience of that assumption. Patients always have the right to disagree with the therapist and find more accurate statements of their beliefs.

Once an assumption has been identified, it is open to modification. This can occur in several ways: by asking the patient if the assumption seems reasonable, by having the patient generate reasons for and against maintaining the assumption, and by presenting evidence contrary to the assumption. While a particular assumption may seem reasonable in a specific situation, it may appear dysfunctional when universally applied. For example, being highly productive at work is generally reasonable. To be highly productive during recreational time may be unreasonable. A physician who believed he should work to his top capacity throughout his career may not have considered the prospect of early burnout. Thus, what may have made him successful in the short run could lead to problems in the long run. Specific cognitive techniques include decatastrophizing, reattribution, redefining, and decentering.

Decatastrophizing, also known as the "what if" technique (Beck and Emery, 1979), helps patients prepare for feared consequences. This is helpful in decreasing avoidance, particularly when combined with coping plans (Beck and Emery, 1985). If anticipated consequences are likely to happen, these techniques help to identify problem-solving strategies. Decatastrophizing is often used with a time-projection technique to widen the range of information and broaden the patient's time perspective.

Reattribution techniques test automatic thoughts and assumptions by considering alternative causes of events. This is especially helpful when patients personalize or perceive themselves as the cause of events. It is unreasonable to conclude, in the absence of evidence, that another person or single factor is the sole cause of an event. Reattribution techniques encourage reality testing and appropriate assignment of responsibility by requiring examination of all the factors that impinge on a situation.

Redefining is a way to mobilize a patient who believes a problem to be beyond personal control. Burns (1985) recommends that lonely people who think, "Nobody pays any attention to me," redefine the problem as, "I need to reach out to other people and be caring." Redefining a problem may include making it more concrete and specific and stating it in terms of the patient's own behavior.

Decentering is used primarily in treating anxious patients who wrongly believe they are the focus of everyone's attention. After examining the logic behind why others would stare at them and be able to read their minds, behavioral experiments are designed to test these particular beliefs. For example, one student who was reluctant to speak in class believed his classmates watched him constantly and noticed his anxiety. By observing them instead of focusing on his own discomfort, he saw some students taking notes, some looking at the professor, and some daydreaming. He concluded his classmates had other concerns.

The cognitive domain comprises thoughts and images. For some patients, pictorial images are more accessible and easier to report than thoughts. This is often the case with anxious patients. Ninety percent of anxious patients in one study reported visual images before and during episodes of anxiety (Beck, Laude, and Bohnert, 1974). Gathering information about imagery, then, is another way to understand conceptual systems. Spontaneous images provide data on the patient's perceptions and interpretations of events. Other specific imaginal procedures used to modify distorted cognitions are discussed by Beck and Emery (1979, 1985).

Behavioral Techniques

Cognitive therapy uses behavioral techniques to modify automatic thoughts and assumptions. It employs behavioral experiments designed to challenge specific maladaptive beliefs and promote new learning. In a behavioral experiment, for example, a patient may predict an outcome based on personal automatic thoughts, carry out the agreed-upon behavior, and then evaluate the evidence in light of the new experience.

Behavioral techniques are also used to expand patients' response repertories (skills training), to relax them (progressive relaxation) or make them active (activity scheduling), to prepare them for avoided situations (behavioral rehearsal), or to expose them to feared stimuli (exposure therapy). Because behavioral techniques are used to foster cognitive change, it is crucial to know the patient's perceptions, thoughts, and conclusions after each behavioral experiment.

Homework gives patients the opportunity to apply cognitive principles between sessions. Typical homework assignments focus on self-observation and self-monitoring, structuring time effectively, and implementing procedures for dealing with concrete situations. Self-monitoring is applied to the patient's automatic thoughts and reactions in various situations. New skills, such as challenging automatic thoughts, are also practiced as homework.

Hypothesis testing has both cognitive and behavioral components. In framing a "hypothesis" it is necessary to make it specific and concrete. A resident who insisted, "I am not a good doctor," was asked to list what was needed to arrive at that conclusion. The therapist contributed other criteria as well, for the physician had overlooked such factors as rapport with patients and the ability to make decisions under pressure. The resident then monitored his behavior and sought feedback from colleagues and supervisors to test his hypothesis, coming to the conclusion, "I am a good doctor after all."

Exposure therapy serves to provide data on the thoughts, images, physiological symptoms and self-reported level of tension experienced by the anxious patient. Specific thoughts and images can be examined for distortions, and specific coping skills can be taught. By dealing directly with a patient's idiosyncratic thoughts, cognitive therapy is able to focus on that patient's particular needs. Patients learn that their predictions are not always accurate and they then have data to challenge anxious thoughts in the future.

Behavioral rehearsal and *roleplaying* are used to practice skills or techniques that are later applied in real life. Modeling is also used in skills training. Often role-playing is videotaped so that an objective source of information is available with which to evaluate performance.

Diversion techniques, which are used to reduce strong emotions and to decrease negative thinking, include physical activity, social contact, work, play, and visual imagery.

Activity scheduling provides structure and encourages involvement. By rating the degree of mastery and pleasure (using a scale of 0 to 10) experienced during each activity of the day, several goals are accomplished: patients who believe their depression is at a constant level see mood fluctuations; those who believe they cannot accomplish or enjoy anything are contradicted by the evidence; and those who believe they are inactive because of an inherent defect are shown that activity involves some planning and is reinforcing in itself.

Graded task assignment calls for the patient to initiate an activity at a nonthreatening level while the therapist gradually increases the difficulty of assigned tasks. For example, someone who has difficulty socializing might begin interacting with one other person or a small group of acquaintances, or might socialize with people for just a brief period of time. Step-by-step, the patient comes to increase the time spent with others.

Cognitive therapists work in a variety of settings. Patients are referred by physicians, schools and universities, and other therapists who believe that cognitive therapy would be especially helpful to a patient. Many patients are self-referred. The Center for Cognitive Therapy maintains an international referral list of therapists.

Cognitive therapists generally adhere to 45-minute sessions. Because of the structure of cognitive therapy, much can be accomplished in this time. Patients are frequently asked to complete questionnaires, such as the Beck Depression Inventory, prior to the start of each session. Most sessions take place in the therapist's office. However, real-life work with anxious patients occurs outside the therapist's office. A therapist might travel on public transportation with an agoraphobic, go to a pet store with a rodent phobic, or fly in an airplane with someone afraid of flying.

Confidentiality is always maintained, and the therapist obtains informed consent for audiotaping and videotaping. Such recording is used in skills training or as a way to present evidence contradicting the patient's assumptions. For example, a patient who believes she looks nervous whenever she converses might be videotaped in conversation to test her assumption. Her appearance on camera may convince her that her assumption was in error or help her to identify specific behaviors to improve. Occasionally, patients take home audiotaped sessions to review content material between sessions.

Sessions are usually conducted on a weekly basis, with severely disturbed patients seen more frequently in the initial sessions. Cognitive therapists give their patients their home phone numbers in case of emergency.

Whenever possible, and with the patient's permission, significant others, such as friends and family members, are included in a therapy session to review the treatment goals and to explore ways in which the significant others might be helpful. This is especially important when family members misunderstand the nature of the illness, are overly solicitous, or are behaving in counterproductive ways. Significant others can be of great assistance in therapy, helping to sustain behavioral improvements by encouraging homework and assisting the patient with reality testing.

Problems may arise in the practice of cognitive therapy. For example, patients may misunderstand what the therapist says, resulting in anger, dissatisfaction, or hopelessness. When the therapist perceives such a reaction, he or she elicits the patient's thoughts, as with any other automatic thoughts. Together the therapist and client look for alternative interpretations. The therapist who has made an error accepts responsibility and corrects the mistake.

Problems sometimes result from unrealistic expectations about how quickly behaviors should change, from the incorrect or inflexible application of a technique, or from lack of attention to central issues. Problems in therapy require that the therapist attend to his or her own automatic thoughts and look for distortions in logic that create strong affect or prevent adequate problem solving.

Beck et al. (1979) provide guidelines for working with difficult patients and those who have histories of unsuccessful therapy: (1) avoid stereotyping the patient as *being* the problem rather than *having* the problem; (2) remain optimistic; (3) identify and deal with your own dysfunctional cognitions; (4) remain focused on the task instead of blaming the patient; and (5) maintain a problem-solving attitude. By following these guidelines, the therapist is able to be more resourceful with difficult patients. The therapist also can serve as a model for the patient, demonstrating that frustration does not automatically lead to anger and despair.

❖ CASE EXAMPLE

This case example of the course of treatment for an anxious patient illustrates the use of both behavioral and cognitive techniques.

Presenting Problem

The patient was a 21-year-old male college student who complained of sleep onset insomnia and frequent awakenings, halting speech and stuttering, shakiness, feelings of nervousness, dizziness, and worrying. His sleep difficulties were particularly acute prior to exams or athletic competitions. He explained his speech problems as due to his search for the "perfect word."

The patient was raised in a family that valued competition. As the eldest child, he was expected to win all the contests. His parents were determined that their children should surpass them in achievements and successes. They so strongly identified with the patient's achievements that he believed, "My success is their success."

The patient was taught to compete with other children outside the family as well. His father reminded him, "Never let anyone get the best of you." As a consequence of viewing others as adversaries, he developed few friends. Feeling lonely, he tried desperately to attract friends by becoming a prankster and by telling lies to enhance his image and make his family appear more attractive. Although he had acquaintances in college, he had few friends, for he was unable to self-disclose, fearing that others would discover he was not all that he would like to be.

Early Sessions

After gathering initial data regarding diagnosis, context, and history, the therapist attempted to define how the patient's cognitions contributed to his distress.

> *Therapist:* What types of situations are most upsetting to you?
> *Patient:* When I do poorly in sports, particularly swimming. I'm on the swim team. Also, if I make a mistake, even when I play cards with my roommates. I feel really upset if I get rejected by a girl.
> *Therapist:* What thoughts go through your mind, let's say, when you don't do so well at swimming?
> *Patient:* I think people think much less of me if I'm not on top, a winner.
> *Therapist:* And how about if you make a mistake playing cards?
> *Patient:* I doubt my own intelligence.

Therapist: And if a girl rejects you?

Patient: It means I'm not special. I lose value as a person.

Therapist: Do you see any connections here, among these thoughts?

Patient: Well, I guess my mood depends on what other people think of me. But that's important. I don't want to be lonely.

Therapist: What would that mean to you, to be lonely?

Patient: It would mean there's something wrong with me, that I'm a loser.

At this point, the therapist began to hypothesize about the patient's organizing beliefs: that his worth is determined by others, that he is unattractive because there is something inherently wrong with him, that he is a loser. The therapist looked for evidence to support the centrality of these beliefs and remained open to other possibilities.

The therapist assisted the patient in generating a list of goals to work on in therapy that included (1) decreasing perfectionism, (2) decreasing anxiety symptoms, (3) decreasing sleep difficulties, (4) increasing closeness in friendships, and (5) developing his own values apart from those of his parents. The first problem addressed was anxiety. An upcoming exam was chosen as a target situation. This student typically studied far beyond what was necessary, went to bed worried, finally fell asleep, woke during the night thinking about details or possible consequences of his performance, and went to exams exhausted. To reduce ruminations about his performance, the therapist asked him to name the advantages of dwelling on thoughts of the exam.

Patient: Well, if I don't think about the exam all the time I might forget something. If I think about the exam constantly, I think I'll do better. I'll be more prepared.

Therapist: Have you ever gone into a situation less "prepared"?

Patient: Not an exam, but once I was in a big swim meet and the night before I went out with friends and didn't think about it. I came home, went to sleep, got up, and swam.

Therapist: And how did it work out?

Patient: Fine. I felt great and swam pretty well.

Therapist: Based on that experience, do you think there's any reason to try to worry less about your performance?

Patient: I guess so. It didn't hurt me not to worry. Actually, worrying can be pretty distracting. I end up focusing more on how I'm doing than what I'm doing.

The patient came up with his own rationale for decreasing his ruminations. He was then ready to consider giving up his maladaptive behavior and risk trying something new. The therapist taught the patient progressive relaxation and the patient began to use physical exercise as a way to relieve anxiety.

The patient was also instructed in how cognitions affect behavior and mood. Picking up on the patient's statement that worries can be distracting, the therapist proceeded:

Therapist: You mentioned that when you worry about your exams you feel anxious. What I'd like you to do now is imagine lying in your bed the night before an exam.

Patient: Okay, I can picture it.

Therapist: Imagine that you are thinking about the exam and you decide that you haven't done enough to prepare.

Patient: Yeah, OK.

Therapist: How are you feeling?

Patient: I'm feeling nervous. My heart is beginning to race. I think I need to get up and study some more.

Therapist: Good. When you think you're not prepared, you get anxious and want to get up out of bed. Now, I want you to imagine that you are in bed the night before the exam. You have prepared in your usual way and are ready. You remind yourself of what you have done. You think that you are prepared and know the material.

Patient: OK. Now I feel confident.
Therapist: Can you see how your thoughts affect your feelings of anxiety?

The patient was instructed to record automatic thoughts, recognize cognitive distortions, and respond to them. For homework, he was asked to record his automatic thoughts if he had trouble falling asleep before an exam. One automatic thought he had while lying in bed was, "I should be thinking about the exam." His response was, "Thinking about the exam is not going to make a difference at this point. I did study." Another thought was, "I must go to sleep now! I must get eight hours of sleep!" His response was, "I have left leeway, so I have time. Sleep is not so crucial that I have to worry about it." He was able to shift his thinking to a positive image of himself floating in clear blue water.

By observing his automatic thoughts across a variety of situations—academic, athletic, and social—the patient identified dichotomous thinking (e.g., "I'm either a winner or a loser") as a frequent cognitive distortion. Perceiving the consequences of his behavior as either totally good or completely bad resulted in major shifts in mood. Two techniques that helped with his dichotomous thinking were reframing the problem and building a continuum between his dichotomous categories.

Here the problem is reframed:

Therapist: Can you think of reasons for someone not to respond to you other than because you're a loser?
Patient: No. Unless I really convince them I'm great, they won't be attracted.
Therapist: How would you convince them of that?
Patient: To tell you the truth, I'd exaggerate what I've done. I'd lie about my grade point average or tell someone I placed first in a race.
Therapist: How does that work out?
Patient: Actually, not too well. I get uncomfortable and they get confused by my stories. Sometimes they don't seem to care. Other times they walk away after I've been talking a lot about myself.
Therapist: So in some cases, they don't respond to you when you focus the conversation on yourself.
Patient: Right.
Therapist: Does this have anything to do with whether you're a winner or a loser?
Patient: No, they don't even know who I am deep down. They're just turned off because I talk too much.
Therapist: Right. It sounds like they're responding to your conversational style.

The therapist reframed the problem from a situation in which something was inherently wrong with the patient to one characterized by a problem of social skills. Moreover, the theme "I am a loser" appeared so powerful to the patient that he labeled it as his "main belief." This assumption was traced historically to the constant criticism from his parents for mistakes and perceived shortcomings. By reviewing his history, he was able to see that his lies prevented people from getting closer, reinforcing his belief that they didn't want to be close. In addition, he believed that his parents made him whatever success he was and that no achievement was his alone. This had made him angry and lacking in self-confidence.

Later Sessions

As therapy progressed, the patient's homework increasingly focused on social interaction. He practiced initiating conversations and asking questions in order to learn more about other people. He also practiced "biting his tongue" instead of telling small lies about himself. He monitored people's reactions to him and saw that they were varied, but generally positive. By listening to others, he found that he admired people who could openly admit shortcomings and joke about their mistakes. This experience helped him understand that it was useless to categorize people, including himself, as winners and losers.

In later sessions, the patient described his belief that his behavior reflected on his parents and vice versa. He said, "If they look good, it says something about me and if I look good, they get the credit." One assignment required him to list the ways in which he was different from his parents. He remarked, "Realizing that my parents and I are separate made me realize I could stop telling lies." Recognizing how he was different from his parents freed him from their absolute standards and allowed him to be less self-conscious when interacting with others.

Subsequently, the patient was able to pursue interests and hobbies that had nothing to do with achievement. He was able to set moderate and realistic goals for schoolwork, and he began to date.

❖ SUMMARY

Although a relative newcomer to the field of psychotherapy, cognitive therapy has enjoyed an enormous increase in popularity. Borrowing some of its concepts from psychodynamic therapy and a number of techniques from behavior therapy and client-oriented psychotherapy, cognitive therapy consists of a broad theoretical structure of personality and psychopathology, a set of well-defined therapeutic strategies, and a wide variety of therapeutic techniques. Similar in many ways to rational emotive therapy, which preceded but developed in parallel to cognitive therapy, this new system of psychotherapy has acquired strong empirical support for its theoretical foundations. A number of outcome studies have demonstrated its efficacy, especially in the treatment of depression. The related theoretical formulations of depression have been supported by over 100 empirical studies. Other concepts, such as the cognitive triad in depression, the concept of specific cognitive profiles for specific disorders, cognitive processing, and the relationship of hopelessness to suicide, have also received strong support.

Outcome studies have investigated cognitive therapy with major depressive disorders, generalized anxiety disorder, dysthymic disorder, drug abuse, alcoholism, panic disorder, anorexia, and bulimia. In addition, cognitive therapy has been applied successfully to the treatment of obsessive-compulsive disorder, hypochondriasis, and various personality disorders. In conjunction with psychotropic medication, it has been used for the treatment of delusional disorders and manic-depressive disorder.

Much of the popularity of cognitive therapy is attributable to strong empirical support for its theoretical framework and the large number of outcome studies with clinical populations. In addition, there is no doubt that the zeitgeist represented by the "cognitive revolution" has made the field of psychotherapy more receptive to this new therapy. A further attractive feature of cognitive therapy is the fact that it is not only testable, but is readily teachable. The various therapeutic strategies and techniques have been described and defined in such a way that one year's training is usually sufficient for a psychotherapist to attain a reasonable level of competence as a cognitive therapist.

Although cognitive therapy focuses on understanding the patient's problems and applying appropriate techniques, it also attends to the nonspecific therapeutic characteristics of the therapist. Consequently, the basic qualities of empathy, acceptance, and personal regard are highly valued.

Because therapy is not conducted in a vacuum, cognitive therapists pay close attention to patients' interpersonal relations and confront patients continuously with problems they may be avoiding. Further, therapeutic change can only take place when patients are emotionally engaged with their problems. Therefore, the experience of emotion during therapy is a crucial feature. The patient's reactions to the therapist, and vice versa, are also important. Excessive and distorted responses to the therapist are elicited and evaluated just like any other type of ideational material. In the presence of the therapist, patients learn to correct their misconceptions, which were often derived from early experiences.

Cognitive therapy may offer an opportunity for a rapprochement between psychodynamic therapy and behavior therapy. In many ways it provides a common ground for these two disciplines. At the present time, the number of cognitive therapists within the behavior therapy movement is growing. In fact, many behavior therapists view themselves as cognitive-behavior therapists.

Looking to the future, it is anticipated that there will be a gradual expansion of the boundaries of the theoretical background of cognitive therapy that will encompass or penetrate the fields of cognitive psychology and social psychology. There is already an enormous amount of interest in social psychology, which provides the theoretical background of cognitive therapy.

In an era of cost containment, this short-term approach will prove to be increasingly attractive to third-party payers as well as to patients. Future empirical studies of its processes and effectiveness will undoubtedly be conducted to determine whether cognitive therapy can fulfill its promise.

❧ ANNOTATED BIBLIOGRAPHY

Beck, A. T., & Emery, G. (1985. *Anxiety disorders and phobias; A cognitive perspective*. New York: Basic Books.

The first half of this book, written by Beck, presents the cognitive theory and model of anxiety disorders, including agoraphobia and panic. The second half of the book, by Emery, is devoted to clinical techniques used with anxious patients.

Freeman, A., Simon, K. M., Beutler, L. E., & Arkowitz, H. (Eds.) (1989). *Comprehensive handbook of cognitive therapy*. New York: Plenum.

This volume offers a review of the great range of clinical applications of cognitive therapy, including depression, anxiety, obesity, anorexia, chronic pain, marital therapy, and sex therapy. It also contains chapters on using cognitive therapy with various populations (e. g., women, children, inpatients) and chapters exploring the relationship between cognitive therapy and other modalities (e.g., psychodynamic, experiential, and Piagetian).

Weishaar, M. E. (1993). *Aaron T. Beck*. London: Sage Publications, Ltd.

This book presents a biography of Aaron Beck, and includes chapters on the theoretical and practical contributions of cognitive therapy to psychotherapy, as well as criticisms of cognitive theory and therapy, rebuttals to the criticisms, and a review of the overall contributions of Beck's cognitive therapy to psychotherapy and counseling.

❧ CASE READINGS

Abrams, J. L. (1983). Cognitive-behavioral strategies to induce and enhance a collaborative set in distressed couples. In A. Freeman (Ed.), *Cognitive therapy with couples and groups* (pp. 125–155). New York: Plenum.

Two cases of married couples demonstrate the importance of including cognitive interventions with traditional behavioral approaches to marital therapy. The dysfunctional attitudes and expectations that these couples bring to their marriages are explored.

Beck, A. T., Rush, J., Shaw, B., & Emery, G. (1979). Interview with a depressed and suicidal patient. In *Cognitive therapy of depression* (pp. 225–243). New York: Guilford Press. [Reprinted in D. Wedding & R. J. Corsini (Eds.) (1995). *Case studies in psychotherapy*. Itasca, IL: F. E. Peacock.]

This interview with a suicidal patient features an outline of the types of assessments and interventions made by cognitive therapists in an initial session. Substantial change occurs in one session, as demonstrated in the verbatim transcript of the interview.

Beck, A. T., & Young, J. E. (1985). Cognitive therapy of depression. In D. Barlow (Ed.), *Clinical handbook of psychological disorders: A step-by-step treatment manual* (pp. 206–244). New York: Guilford Press.

This case of a depressed young woman demonstrates how a therapist elicits and challenges maladaptive thoughts and assumptions throughout the course of treatment.

Young, J. E. (1981). Cognitive therapy and loneliness. In G. Emery, S. Hollon, & R. C. Bedrosian (Eds.), *New directions in cognitive therapy.* (pp. 139–159). New York: Guilford Press.

The treatment of a lonely college student demonstrates both the cognitive and the behavioral techniques that are used to help the patient initiate and deepen relationships.

❖ REFERENCES

Adler, A. (1936). The neurotic's picture of the world. *International Journal of Individual Psychology, 2,* 3–10.

Alexander, F. (1950). *Psychosomatic medicine: Its principles and applications.* New York: Norton.

Arnold, M. (1960). *Emotion and personality* (Vol. 1). New York: Columbia University Press.

Bandura, A. (1977). *Social learning theory.* Englewood Cliffs, NJ: Prentice Hall.

Beck, A. T. (1963). Thinking and depression. 1. Idiosyncratic content and cognitive distortions. *Archives of General Psychiatry, 9,* 324–333.

Beck, A. T. (1964). Thinking and depression. 2. Theory and therapy. *Archives of General Psychiatry, 10,* 561–571.

Beck, A. T. (1967). *Depression: Clinical, experimental, and theoretical aspects.* New York: Hoeber. (Republished as *Depression: Causes and treatment.* Philadelphia: University of Pennsylvania Press, 1972.)

Beck, A. T. (1978). *Anxiety checklist.* Philadelphia: Center for Cognitive Therapy.

Beck, A. T., Brown, G., Berchick, R. J., Stewart, B. L., & Steer, R. A. (1990). Relationship between hopelessness and ultimate suicide: A replication with psychiatric outpatients. *American Journal of Psychiatry, 147*(2), 190–195.

Beck, A. T., & Emery, G. (1979). *Cognitive therapy of anxiety and phobic disorders.* Philadelphia: Center for Cognitive Therapy.

Beck, A. T., & Emery, G. (1985). *Anxiety disorders and phobias: A cognitive perspective.* New York: Basic Books.

Beck, A. T., Epstein, N., & Harrison, R. (1983). Cognitions, attitudes and personality dimensions in depression. *British Journal of Cognitive Psychotherapy, 1* (1), 1–16.

Beck, A. T., Freeman, A., & Associates. (1990). *Cognitive therapy of personality disorders.* New York: Plenum.

Beck, A. T., Kovacs, M., & Weissman, A. (1979). Assessment of suicidal intention: The scale for suicidal ideation. *Journal of Consulting and Clinical Psychology, 47,* 343–352.

Beck, A. T., Laude, R., & Bohnert, M. (1974). Ideational components of anxiety neurosis. *Archives of General Psychiatry, 31,* 319–325.

Beck, A. T., Rush, A. J., Shaw, B. F., & Emery, G. (1979). *Cognitive therapy of depression.* New York: Guilford Press.

Beck, A. T., Schuyler, D., & Herman, I. (1974). Development of the suicidal intent scales. In A. T. Beck, H. L. P. Resnik, & D. J. Lettieri (Eds.), *The prediction of suicide* (pp. 45–56). Bowie, MD: Charles Press.

Beck, A. T., Steer, R. A., Kovacs, M., & Garrison, B. (1985). Hopelessness and eventual suicide: A 10-year study of patients hospitalized with suicidal ideation. *American Journal of Psychiatry, 412,* 559–563.

Beck, A. T., Ward, C. H., Mendelson, M., Mock, J. E., & Erbaugh, J. K. (1961). An inventory for measuring depression. *Archives of General Psychiatry, 4,* 561–571.

Beck, A. T., Weissman, A., Lester, D., & Trexler, L. (1974). The measurement of pessimism: The hopelessness scale. *Journal of Consulting and Clinical Psychology, 42,* 861–865.

Beck, A. T., & Young, J. E. (1985). Cognitive therapy of depression. In D. Barlow (Ed.), *Clinical handbook of psychological disorders: A step-by-step treatment manual* (pp. 206–244). New York: Guilford Press.

Blackburn, I. M., Bishop, S., Glen, A. I. M., Whalley, L. J., & Christie, J. E. (1981). The efficacy of cognitive therapy in depression: A treatment trial using cognitive therapy and pharmacotherapy, each alone and in combination. *British Journal of Psychiatry, 139,* 181–189.

Blackburn, I. M., Eunson, K. M., & Bishop, S. (1986). A two-year naturalistic follow-up of depressed patients treated with cognitive therapy, pharmacotherapy, and a combination of both. Unpublished manuscript. Royal Edinburgh Hospital, Scotland.

Burns, D. D. (1985). *Intimate connections.* New York: Morrow.

Dobson, K. S. (1989). A meta-analysis of the efficacy of cognitive therapy for depression. *Journal of Consulting and Clinical Psychology, 57* (3), 414–419.

Dunn, R. J. (1979). Cognitive modification with de-pression-prone psychiatric patients. *Cognitive Therapy and Research, 3,* 307–317.

Elkin, I., Shea, M. T., Watkins, J. T., Imber, S., Sotsky, S. M., Collins, J. F., Glass, D. R., Pilkonis, P. A., Leber, W. R., Docherty, J. P., Fiester, S. J., & Perloff, M. B. (1989). National Institute of Mental Health treatment of depression collaborative research program: General effectiveness of treatments. *Archives of General Psychiatry, 46,* 971–983.

Ellis, A. (1962). *Reason and emotion in psychotherapy.* New York: Lyle Stuart.

Ernst, D. (1987). *A review of systematic studies of the cognitive model of depression.* Unpublished manuscript. Center for Cognitive Therapy, Philadelphia, PA.

Evans, M. D., Hollon, S. D., DeRubeis, R. J., Piasecki, J. M., Grove, W. M., Garvey, M. J., & Tuason, V. B. (1992). Differential relapse following cognitive therapy and pharmacotherapy for depression. *Archives of General Psychiatry, 49,* 802–808.

Golden, W. L. (1983). Resistance in cognitive-behavior therapy. *British Journal of Cognitive Psychotherapy, 1* (2), 33–42.

Gournay, K. (1986). *Cognitive change during the behavioral treatment of agoraphobia.* Paper presented at Congress of European Association for Behavior Therapy, Lucerne, Switzerland.

Guidano, V. P., & Liotti, G. (1983). *Cognitive processes and emotional disorders.* New York: Guilford Press.

Haaga, D. A. F., Dyck, M. J., & Ernst, D. (1991). Empirical status of cognitive theory of depression. *Psychological Bulletin, 110* (2), 215–236.

Hollon, S. D., DeRubeis, R. J., Evans, M. D., Wiemer, M. J., Garvey, M. J., Grove, W. M., & Tuason, V. B. (1992). Cognitive therapy and pharmacotherapy for depression: Singly and in combination. *Archives of General Psychiatry, 49,* 774–781.

Hollon, S. D., Evans, M. D., & DeRubeis, R. (1983). *The cognitive-pharmacotherapy project: Study design, outcome, and clinical follow-up.* Paper presented at the World Congress of Behavior Therapy, Washington, DC.

Horney, K. (1950). *Neurosis and human growth: The struggle toward self-realization.* New York: Norton.

Kant, I. (1798). *The classification of mental disorders.* Konigsberg, Germany: Nicolovius.

Kelly, G. (1955). *The psychology of personal constructs.* New York: Norton.

Kovacs, M., Rush, A. J., Beck, A. T., & Hollon, S. D. (1981). Depressed outpatients treated with cognitive therapy or pharmacotherapy. *Archives of General Psychiatry, 38,* 33–39.

Kwee, M. G. T., & Lazarus, A. A. (1986). Multimodal therapy: The cognitive-behavioral tradition and beyond. In W. Dryden & W. Golden (Eds.), *Cognitive-behavioral approaches to psychotherapy* (pp. 320–355). London: Harper & Row.

Lazarus, R. (1984). On the primacy of cognition. *American Psychologist, 39* 124–129.

Mahoney, M. J. (1974). *Cognition and behavior modification.* Cambridge, MA: Ballinger.

Mahoney, M. J. (1980). Psychotherapy and the structure of personal revolutions. In M. J. Mahoney (Ed.), *Psychotherapy process* (pp. 157–180). New York: Plenum.

Mahoney, M. J., & Arnkoff, D. (1978). Cognitive and self-control therapies. In S. L. Garfield & A. E. Bergin (Eds.), *Handbook of psychotherapy and behavior change: An empirical analysis* (pp. 689–722). New York: Wiley.

Maldonado, A. (1982). Terapía de conducta y depresión: Un análisis experimental de los modelos conductal y cognitivo (Cognitive and behavioral therapy for depression. Its efficacy and interaction with pharmacological treatment). *Revista de psicología general y aplicada, 37* (1), 31–56.

Meichenbaum, D. (1977). *Cognitive-behavior modification: An integrative approach,* New York: Plenum.

Murphy, G. E., Simons, A. D., Wetzel, R. D., & Lustman, P. J. (1983). Cognitive therapy and pharmacotherapy: Singly and together in the treatment of depression. *Archives of General Psychiatry, 41,* 33–41.

Pretzer, J. L. (1983). *Borderline-personality disorder: Too complex for cognitive therapy?* Paper presented at the annual meeting of the American Psychological Association, Anaheim, CA.

Pretzer, J. L. (1990). Borderline personality disorder. In A. T. Beck, A. Freeman, & Associates. *Cognitive therapy of personality disorders* (pp. 176–207). New York: Guilford Press.

Rogers, C. (1951). *Client-centered therapy.* Boston: Houghton Mifflin.

Rush, A. J., Beck, A. T., Kovacs, M., & Hollon, S. (1977). Comparative efficacy of cognitive therapy and imipramine in the treatment of depressed outpatients. *Cognitive Therapy and Research, 1,* 17–37.

Shea, M. T., Elkin, I., Imber, S., Sotsky, S., Watkins, J. T., Collins, J. F., Pilkonis, P. A., Beckham, E., Glass, D. R., Dolan, R. T., & Perloff, M. B. (1992). Course of depressive symptoms over follow-up: Findings from the National Institute of Mental Health treatment of depression collaborative research program. *Archives of General Psychiatry, 49,* 782–787.

Simons, A. D., Murphy, G. E., Levine, J. L., & Wetzel, R. D. (1986). Cognitive therapy and pharmacotherapy: Sustained improvement over one year. *Archives of General Psychiatry, 43,* 43–48.

Sullivan, H. S. (1953). *The interpersonal theory of psychiatry.* New York: Norton.

Teasdale, J. D., Fennell, M. J. V., Hibbert, G. A., & Amies, P. L. (1984). Cognitive therapy for major depressive disorder in primary care. *British Journal of Psychiatry, 144,* 400–406.

Weissman, A. (1979). *The dysfunctional attitudes scale.* Philadelphia: Center for Cognitive Therapy.

Wessler, R. L. (1986). Conceptualizing cognitions in the cognitive-behavioral therapies. In W. Dryden & W. Golden (Eds.), *Cognitive-behavioural ap-*

proaches to psychotherapy (pp. 1–30). London: Harper & Row.

Williams, S. L., & Rappoport, A. (1983). Cognitive treatment in the natural environment for agoraphobics. *Behavior Therapy, 14,* 299–313.

Young, J. E. (1979). *An instrument for measuring loneliness.* Paper presented at the annual meeting of the American Psychological Association, New York.

Young, J. E. (1983). *Borderline personality: Cognitive theory and treatment.* Paper presented at the annual meeting of the American Psychological Association, Anaheim, CA.

Young, J. E., & Beck, A. T. (1980). *Development of an instrument for rating cognitive therapy: The Cognitive Therapy Rating Scale.* Philadelphia, PA: University of Pennsylvania.

Rollo May (1909–1994)

Irvin Yalom

9   Existential Psychotherapy

Rollo May and
Irvin Yalom

❖ OVERVIEW

Existential psychotherapy arose spontaneously in the minds and works of a number of psychologists and psychiatrists in Europe in the 1940s and 1950s who were concerned with finding a way of understanding human beings that was more reliable and more basic than the then-current psychotherapies. The "existential orientation in psychiatry," wrote Ludwig Binswanger, "arose from dissatisfaction with the prevailing efforts to gain scientific understanding in psychiatry" (1956, p. 144). These existential therapists believed drives in Freudian psychology, conditioning in behaviorism, and archetypes in Jungianism all had their own significance. But where was the actual, *immediate person* to whom these things were happening? Are we seeing patients as they really are, or are we simply seeing a projection of our theories *about* them?

These therapists were keenly aware that we are living in an age of transition, when almost every human being feels alienated from fellow humans, threatened by nuclear war and economic upsets, perplexed by the radical changes in marriage and almost all other mores in our culture—in short, almost everyone is beset by anxiety.

Existential psychotherapy is not a specific technical approach that presents a new set of rules for therapy. It asks deep questions about the nature of the human being and the nature of anxiety, despair, grief, loneliness, isolation, and anomie. It also deals centrally with the questions of creativity and love. Out of the understanding of the meaning of these human experiences, existential psychotherapists have devised methods of therapy that do not fall into the common error of distorting human beings in the very effort of trying to help them.

Basic Concepts

The "I-Am" Experience

The realization of one's being—"I am now living and I could take my life"—can have a salutary effect on a patient. "The idea of suicide has saved many lives," said Nietzsche. The human being will be victimized by circumstances and other people until he or she is able to realize, "I am the one living, experiencing. I choose my own being."

It is not easy to define *being* because in our society we often subordinate the sense of being to our economic status or the external type of life that we lead. A person is known (and knows self) not as a being or a self, but as a ticket seller in the subway, a grocer, a professor, a vice president of AT&T, or as whatever his or her economic function may be. This loss of the sense of being is related to mass collectivist trends and widespread conformist tendencies in our culture. The French existentialist Gabriel Marcel (May, Angel & Ellenberger, 1958, p. 40), makes this trenchant challenge: "Indeed I wonder if a psychoanalytic method, deeper and more discerning than any that has been evolved until now, would not reveal the morbid effects of the repression of this sense [of being] and of the ignoring of this need."

Existential therapy endeavors to be this "deeper and more discerning" type of therapy.

A patient, the daughter of a prostitute, had been an illegitimate child and had been brought up by relatives. She said:

> I remember walking that day under the elevated tracks in a slum area, feeling the thought, *I am an illegitimate child*. I recall the sweat pouring forth in my anguish in trying to accept that fact. Then I understood what it must feel like to accept "I am a Negro in the midst of privileged whites," or "I am blind in the midst of people who see." Later on that night I woke up and it came to me this way, "I accept the fact that I am an illegitimate child." But "I am not a child anymore." So it is "I am illegitimate." That is not so either. "I was born illegitimate." Then what is left? What is left is this, "I Am." This act of contact and acceptance with "I am," once gotten hold of, gave me the experience "Since I Am, I have the right to be." (May et al., 1958)

This "I-Am" experience is not in itself a solution to an individual's problems. It is, rather, the *precondition* for the solution. The patient in the preceding example spent some two years thereafter working through specific psychological problems, which she was able to do on the basis of her experience of being.

This experience of being points also to the experience of *not being*, or nothingness. Nonbeing is illustrated in the threat of death, or destructive hostility, severe incapacitating anxiety, or critical sickness. The threat of nonbeing is present in greater or lesser intensity at all times. When we cross the street while looking both ways to guard against being struck by an automobile, when someone makes a remark that disparages us, or when we go into an examination ill-prepared—all of these represent the threat of nonbeing.

The "I-Am" experience, or the experience of being, is known in existential therapy as an *ontological* experience. This word comes from two Greek words, *ontis* meaning "to be" and *logical* meaning "the science of." Thus it is the "science of being." The term *ontological* is valuable in existential psychotherapy.

Normal and Neurotic Anxiety

Existential therapists define anxiety more broadly than other psychotherapeutic groups. *Anxiety arises from our personal need to survive, to preserve our being, and to assert our being.* Anxiety shows itself physically in faster beating of the heart, rising blood pressure, preparation of the skeletal muscles for fighting or fleeing, and a sense of apprehension. Rollo May defines anxiety as "the threat to our existence or to values we identify with our existence" (1977, p. 205).

Anxiety is more basic than fear. In psychotherapy, one of our aims is to help the patient confront anxiety as fully as possible, thus reducing anxiety to fears, which are then objective and can be dealt with. But the main therapeutic function is to help the patient confront the normal anxiety that is an unavoidable part of the human condition.

Normal anxiety has three characteristics. First, it is proportionate to the situation confronted. Second, normal anxiety does not require repression: we can come to terms with it, as we come to terms with the fact that we all face eventual death. Third, such anxiety can be used creatively, as a stimulus to help identify and confront the dilemma out of which the anxiety arose.

Neurotic anxiety, on the other hand, is not appropriate to the situation. For example, parents may be so anxious that their child will be hit by a car that they never let the child leave the house. Second, it is repressed, in the way most of us repress the fear of nuclear war. Third, neurotic anxiety is destructive, not constructive. Neurotic anxiety tends to paralyze the individual rather than stimulate creativity.

The function of therapy is *not* to do away with all anxiety. No person could survive completely without anxiety. Mental health is living as much as possible without *neurotic* anxiety, but *with* the ability to tolerate the unavoidable existential anxiety of living.

Guilt and Guilt Feelings

The experience of guilt has special meaning for the existential therapist. Guilt can, like anxiety, take both normal and neurotic forms. Neurotic guilt feelings (generally called *guilt*) often arise out of fantasized transgressions. Other forms of guilt, which we call *normal guilt*, sensitize us to the ethical aspects of our behavior.

Still another form is guilt toward ourselves for failure to live up to our potentialities, for "forgetting being" as Medard Boss puts it. The attitude toward such guilt in existential therapy is well illustrated in a case Medard Boss (1957b) cites of a severe obsessive-compulsive whom he treated. This patient, a physician suffering from hand-washing compulsions, had gone through both Freudian and Jungian analyses. He had had for some time a recurrent dream involving church steeples, interpreted in the Freudian analysis in terms of phallic symbols and in the Jungian in terms of religious archetypal symbols. The patient could discuss these interpretations intelligently and at length, but his neurotic compulsive behavior, after temporary abeyance, continued, as crippling as ever. During the first months of his analysis with Boss, the patient reported a recurrent dream in which he would approach a lavatory door that would always be locked. Boss confined himself only to asking each time why the door needed to be locked. Finally the patient had a dream in which he opened the door and found himself inside a church. He was waist deep in feces and was tugged by a rope wrapped around his waist and leading up to the bell tower. The patient was suspended in such tension that he thought he would be pulled to pieces. He then went through a psychotic episode of four days, after which the analysis continued with an eventual successful outcome.

Boss (1957b) points out that the patient was guilty because he had locked up some essential potentialities in himself. *Therefore* he had guilt feelings. "If you lock up potentialities, you are guilty…(or indebted to)…what is given you in your origin, in your 'core.' In this…condition of being indebted and being guilty are founded all guilt feelings." This patient had locked up both the bodily and the spiritual possibilities of his experience. The patient had previously accepted the libido and archetype explanations and knew them all too well; but that is a good way, says Boss, to escape the whole thing. Because the patient did not accept and take into his existence these two aspects, he was guilty, indebted to himself. This was the origin of his neurosis and psychosis.

The Three Forms of World

Another basic concept in existential psychotherapy is called being-in-the-world. We must understand the phenomenological world in which the patient exists and participates.

A person's world cannot be comprehended by describing the environment, no matter how complex the description. The environment is only one mode of world. The biologist J. von Uexküll argues that one is justified in assuming as many environments as there are animals. "There is not one space and time only," he goes on to say, "but as many spaces and times as there are subjects" (von Uexküll, cited in May et al., 1958). How much more is it true that the human being also has his or her own world? This confronts us with no easy problem: for we cannot describe world in purely objective terms, nor is world to be limited to our subjective, imaginative participation in the structure around us.

The human world is the structure of meaningful relationships in which a person exists and in the design of which he or she participates. That is, the same past or present circumstances can mean very different things to different people. Thus, one's world includes the past events that condition one's existence and all the vast variety of deterministic influences that operate upon one. But it is these *as one relates to them*, as one is aware of them, molds, and constantly reforms them. For to be aware of one's world means at the same time to be designing it, *constituting* one's world.

From the point of view of existential psychotherapy, there are three modes of world. The first is *Umwelt*, meaning "world around," the biological world, the environment. The second is *Mitwelt*, literally the "with-world," the world of one's fellow human beings. The third is *Eigenwelt*, the "own-world," the relationship to one's self.

Umwelt is the world of objects about us, the natural world. All organisms have an *Umwelt*. For animals and human beings the *Umwelt* includes biological needs, drives, instincts. It is the world of natural law and natural cycles, of sleep and awakeness, of being born and dying, of desire and relief, the world of finiteness and biological determinism to which each of us must in some way adjust. Existential analysts accept the reality of the natural world. "The natural law is as valid as ever," as Kierkegaard put it.

The *Eigenwelt*, or "own-world," has been least adequately dealt with or understood in modern psychology and depth-psychology. Own-world presupposes self-awareness and self-relatedness and is uniquely present in human beings. It is a grasping of what something in the world personally means to the individual observer. D.T. Suzuki has remarked that in Eastern languages, such as Japanese, adjectives always include the implication of "for-me-ness." That is to say, "This flower is beautiful" means "For me, this flower is beautiful."

One implication of this analysis of the modes of being-in-the-world is that it gives us a basis for understanding love. The human experience of love obviously cannot be adequately described within the confines of *Umwelt*. We can never accurately speak of human beings as "sexual objects," because once a person is a sexual object, we are not talking about a person anymore. The interpersonal schools of personality theory have dealt with love as an interpersonal relationship. Without an adequate concept of *Umwelt*, love becomes empty of vitality, and without *Eigenwelt*, it lacks power and the capacity to fructify itself. The importance of *Eigenwelt* was stressed by Friedrich Nietzsche and Søren Kierkegaard, who continually insisted that to love presupposes that one must already have become the "true individual," the "Solitary One," the one who "has comprehended the deep secret that also in loving another person one must be sufficient unto oneself."

The Significance of Time

Existential psychotherapists are struck by the fact that the most profound human experiences, such an anxiety, depression, and joy, occur more in the dimension of time than in space.

Existential therapists agree with Henri Bergson that "time is the heart of existence" and that our error in the modern day has been to think of ourselves primarily in terms of space, as though we were objects that could be located like substances at this spot or that. By this distortion we lost our genuine existential relation with ourselves, and indeed also with other persons around us. As a consequence of this overemphasis on spatial thinking, says Bergson, "the moments when we grasp ourselves are rare, and consequently we are seldom free" (Bergson, cited in May et al., 1958, p. 56).

But in the with-world, the mode of personal relations and love, we can see particularly that quantitative time has much less to do with the significance of an occurrence. The nature or degree of one's love, for example, can never be measured by the number of years one has known the loved one. It is true, of course, that clock time has much to do with *Mitwelt*. We are referring rather to the inner meaning of the events. "No clock strikes for the happy one," says a German proverb. Indeed, the most significant events in a person's psychological existence are likely to be precisely the ones which are "immediate," breaking through the usual steady progression of time, like a sudden insight or a view of beauty that one sees in an instant, but which may remain in one's memory for days and months.

Finally, the *Eigenwelt*, the world of self-relatedness, self-awareness, and insight into the meaning of an event for one's self, has practically nothing whatever to do with clock time. The essence of self-awareness and insight is that they are there—instantaneous and immediate—and the moment of awareness has its significance for all time. One can see this easily by noting what happens in oneself at the instant of an insight. The instant occurs with suddenness; it is born whole, so to speak. One will discover that, though meditating on an insight for an hour or so may reveal many of its further implications, the insight is not clearer—and disconcertingly enough, often not as clear—at the end of the hour as it was at the beginning.

Whether or not a patient can even recall the significant events of the past depends upon his or her decision with regard to the future. Every therapist knows that patients may bring up past memories ad nauseam without any memory ever moving them, the whole recital being flat, inconsequential, and tedious. From an existential point of view, the problem is not that these patients endured impoverished pasts; it is rather that they cannot or do not commit themselves to the present and future. Their past does not become alive because nothing matters enough to them in the future. Some hope and commitment to work toward changing something in the immediate future, be it overcoming anxiety or other painful symptoms or integrating the self for further creativity, are necessary before a patient's uncovering of the past will have reality.

Our Human Capacity to Transcend the Immediate Situation

If we are to understand a given person as existing, dynamic, at every moment becoming, we cannot avoid the dimension of transcendence. Existing involves a continual emerging, in the sense of emergent evolution, a transcending of one's past and present in order to reach the future. Thus *transcendere*—literally "to climb over and beyond"—describes what every human being is engaged in doing every moment when not seriously ill or temporarily blocked by despair or anxiety. One can, of course, see emergent evolution in all life processes. Nietzsche has his old Zarathustra proclaim, "And this secret spake Life herself to me. 'Behold' said she, 'I am that which must ever surpass itself'" (cited in May et al., 1958, p. 72).

The neurobiological base for this capacity is classically described by Kurt Goldstein (cited in May et al., 1958, p. 72). He found that brain-injured patients—chiefly soldiers with portions of the frontal cortex shot away—had specifically lost the ability to abstract, to think in terms of the possible. They were tied to any immediate concrete situation in which they happened to be. When their closets happened to be in disarray, they were thrown into profound anxiety and disordered behavior. They exhibited compulsive orderliness—which is a way of holding oneself at every moment rigidly to the concrete situation. When asked to write their names on a sheet of paper, they would typically write in the very corner, any venture out from the specific boundaries of the edges of the paper representing too great a threat. Goldstein held that the distinctive capacity of the normal human being is precisely this capacity to abstract, to use symbols, to orient oneself beyond the immediate limits of the given time and space, to think in terms of "the possible." The injured, or "ill," patients were characterized by loss of range of possibility. Their world space was shrunk, their time curtailed, and they suffered a consequent radical loss of freedom.

We human beings possess the ability to transcend time and space by transporting ourselves back 2,000 years to ancient Greece, and we can watch the drama of Oedipus being performed in ancient Athens. We can instantaneously transport ourselves to the future, conceiving what life will be like in, say, the year 2500. These forms of transcendence are part and parcel of human consciousness. This capacity is exemplified in the human being's unique capacity to think and talk in symbols. Thus, to make promises presupposes conscious self-relatedness and is a very different thing from simple conditioned social behavior, acting in terms of the requirements of the group or herd or hive. Jean-Paul Sartre writes that dishonesty is a uniquely human form of behavior. "The lie is a behavior of transcendence," because to lie we must at the same moment know we are departing from the truth.

This capacity to transcend the immediate situation is not a "faculty." It is, rather, given in the ontological nature of being human. To abstract, to objectivate, are evidences of it, but as Martin Heidegger puts it, "transcendence does not consist of objectivation, but objectivation presupposes transcendence" (cited in May et al., 1958, p. 75). The fact that human beings can be self-related gives them the capacity to objectify their world, to think and talk in symbols. This is Kierkegaard's point when he reminds us that to understand the self we must see clearly that "imagination is not one faculty on a par with others, but, if one would so speak, it is the faculty for all faculties. What feeling, knowledge, or will a man has depends upon what imagination he has, that is to say, upon how these things are reflected. Imagination is the possibility of all reflection, and the intensity of this medium is the possibility of the intensity of the self" (Kierkegaard, 1954, p. 163).

Other Systems

Behaviorism

First we shall consider the differences between existential theory and the theory of *behaviorism*. This radical distinction can be seen when we note the chasm between abstract truth and existential reality.

Kenneth W. Spence (1956), a leader of one wing of behavior theory, wrote: "The question of whether any particular realm of behavior phenomena is more real or closer to real life and hence should be given priority in investigation does not, or at least should not, arise for the psychologist as scientist." That is to say, it does not primarily matter whether what is being studied is real or not.

What realms, then, should be selected for study? Spence gives priority to phenomena that lend themselves "to the degrees of control and analysis necessary for the formulation of abstract laws." Nowhere has this point been put more clearly than by Spence — what can be reduced to abstract laws is selected, and whether what is studied has *reality* or not is irrelevant to this goal. Many an impressive system in psychology has been erected, with abstraction piled high upon abstraction until an admirable and imposing structure is built. The only trouble is that the edifice has often been separated from reality in its very foundations.

Psychiatrists and psychologists in the existential psychotherapy movement insist that it is necessary and possible to have a science that studies human beings in their reality.

Orthodox Freudianism

Ludwig Binswanger and some other existential therapists differed from Freud in several important respects, including rejection of the concept of the patient propelled by instincts and drives. As Sartre put it, Freudians have lost the human being *to whom* these things happen.

The existentialists also question the view of the unconscious as a reservoir of tendencies, desires, and drives from which the motivation for behavior arises. This "cellar" view of the unconscious leads patients in therapy to avoid responsibility for their actions by such phrases as, "My unconscious did it, not I." Existentialists always insist that the patient in therapy accept responsibility by asking such questions as, "Whose unconscious is it?"

The differences between existentialism and Freudianism are also seen in the modes of the world. The genius and the value of Freud's work lie in uncovering the mode of instincts, drives, contingency, and biological determinism. But traditional Freudianism has only a shadowy concept of the interrelation of persons as subjects.

The Interpersonal School of Psychotherapy

A consideration of the three modes of world discloses the differences between existential therapy and the interpersonal school. Interpersonal schools do have a theoretical basis for dealing directly with *Mitwelt*. Though they should not be considered identical, *Mitwelt* and interpersonal theory have a great deal in common. The danger of this point, however, is that if *Eigenwelt*, one's own-world, is omitted, interpersonal relations tend to become hollow and sterile. H.S. Sullivan argued against the concept of individual personality and went to great efforts to define the self in terms of "reflected appraisal" and social categories—that is, the roles the person plays in the interpersonal world. Theoretically, this suffers from considerable logical inconsistency and indeed goes directly against other contributions of Sullivan. Practically, it tends to make the self a mirror of the group around one, to empty the self of vitality and originality, and to reduce the interpersonal world to mere "social relations." It opens the way to a tendency directly opposed to the goals of Sullivan and other interpersonal thinkers: namely, social conformity.

Jungian Psychology

There are similarities between Jungian and existential therapy. But the main criticism existentialists make is that Jungians too quickly avoid the immediate existential crises of patients by leaping into theory. This is illustrated in Medard Boss's case related in the section "Guilt and Guilt Feelings." A patient who was afraid to go out of the house alone was analyzed by a Jungian therapist for six years, in the course of which the therapist interpreted several dreams as indicating that "God is speaking to you." The patient was flattered, but still couldn't go out of the house alone. She later was enabled to get over her crippling neurosis by an existential therapist who insisted that she could overcome her problem only if she actively *wanted* to, which was a way of insisting that she, not God, needed to take responsibility for her problem.

Client-Centered Approach

The difference between existentialism and Rogerian therapy is seen in statements made by Rollo May when he was acting as a judge of client-centered therapy in the client-centered experiment at the University of Wisconsin. Twelve outside experts were sent tapes of the therapy to judge. Rollo May (1982) as one of the outside experts, reported that he often felt that there were not two distinct people in the room. When the therapist only reflects the patient's words, there transpires "only an amorphous kind of identity rather than two subjects interacting in *a world in which both participate, and in which love and hate, trust and doubt, conflicts and dependence, come out and can be understood and assimilated"* (p. 16). May was concerned that the therapist's overidentification with the patient could "take away the patient's opportunity to experience himself as a subject in his own right or to take a stand against the therapist, to experience being in an interpersonal world" (p. 16).

In spite of the fact that client-centered therapists, both individually and collectively, have advocated openness and freedom in the therapeutic relationship, the outside judges concluded that "the therapist's rigid and controlling nature closed him off to many of his own as well as to the patient's experiences" (p. 16)

One of the Rogerian therapists, after experience as an independent therapist, wrote this criticism:

> I used the early concept of the client-centered therapist to bolster the inhibition of my anger, my aggression, etc. I got some feedback at that time that it was difficult for people, because I was so nice, to tell me things that were not nice, and that it was hard for people to get angry at me. (Raskin, 1978, p. 367)

In other words, client-centered therapy is not fully existential in that it does not confront the patient directly and firmly.

❖ HISTORY

Precursors

There are two streams in the history of human thought. One is of *essences*, seen most clearly in Plato's belief that there are perfect forms of everything and that things such as a specific chair are imperfect copies. These essences are clearest if we imagine mathematics: a perfect circle and a perfect square exist in heaven, of which our human circles and squares are imperfect copies. This requires an abstraction that leaves the *existence* of the individual thing out of the picture. A proposition can be true without being real. Perhaps just because this approach has worked in certain areas of science, we tend to forget that it omits *the living individual.*

But there is another stream of thought coming down through history: namely, *existence.* This viewpoint holds that truth depends upon the existing person, existing in a given situation (world) at that *time.* Hence the term *existential.* This is what Sartre meant in his famous statement, "Existence precedes essence." The human being's awareness (i.e., his existence) precedes everything he has to say about the world around him.

Down through history, the existential tradition is exemplified by many thinkers. These include Augustine, who held that "Truth dwells in the inner man"; Duns Scotus, who argued against Thomas Aquinas's rational essences and insisted that human *will* must be taken as basic to any statement; and Blaise Pascal, as in his famous statement, "The heart has its reasons which reason knows nothing of."

There remains in our day the chasm between truth and reality. And the crucial question that confronts us in psychology is precisely this chasm between what is abstractly true and what is existentially real for the given living person.

Beginnings

Kierkegaard, Nietzsche, and those existentialists who followed them foresaw this growing split between truth and reality in Western culture, and they opposed the delusion that reality can be comprehended in an abstracted, detached way. Though they protested vehemently against arid intellectualism, they were by no means simple activists, nor were they antirational. Anti-intellectualism and other movements that make thinking subordinate to feeling must not be confused with existentialism. Either alternative—making a human being entirely subject or object—results in *losing the living, existing person.* Kierkegaard and the existential thinkers appealed to a reality underling *both* subjectivity and objectivity. We must not only study a person's experience as such, they held, but even more, we must study the one who is doing the experiencing.

It is by no means accidental that the greatest existentialists in the nineteenth century, Kierkegaard and Nietzsche, happen also to be among the most remarkable psychologists of all time. A contemporary leader of existential philosophy, Karl Jaspers, originally a psychiatrist, wrote a notable text on psychopathology. When one reads Kierkegaard's profound analyses of anxiety and despair or Nietzsche's amazingly acute insights into the dynamics of resentment and the guilt and hostility that accompany repressed emotional powers, it is difficult to realize that one is reading works written 75 and 100 years ago and not a contemporary psychological analysis.

Existential therapists are centrally concerned with rediscovering the living person amid the dehumanization of modern culture, and in order to do this they engage in depth psychological analysis. Their concern is not with isolated psychological reactions in themselves but rather with the psychological being of the living person doing the experiencing. They use psychological terms with an ontological meaning.

Existential therapy sprang up spontaneously in different parts of Europe and among different schools, and has a diverse body of researchers and creative thinkers. There were psychiatrists—Eugene Minkowski in Paris, Erwin Straus in Germany and then in America, V.E. von Gebsattel in Germany—who represent chiefly the first, phenomenological stage of this movement. Ludwig Binswanger, A. Storch, Medard Boss, G. Bally, Roland Kuhn in Switzerland, and J. II. Van Den Berg and F. J. Buytendijk in Holland represented the second, or existential, stage.

Current Status

Existential psychotherapy was introduced to the United States in 1958 with the publication of *Existence: A New Dimension in Psychiatry and Psychology*, edited by Rollo May, Ernest Angel, and Henri Ellenberger. The main presentation and summary of existential therapy was in the first two chapters, written by May: "The Origins of the Existential Movement in Psychology" and "Contributions of Existential Psychology." The remainder of the book is made up of essays and case studies by Henri Ellenberger, Eugene Minkowski, Erwin Straus, V. E. von Gebsattel, Ludwig Binswanger, and Ronald Kuhn. The first comprehensive textbook in existential psychiatry was by Irvin Yalom (1981) and entitled *Existential Psychotherapy*.

The spirit of existential psychotherapy has never supported the formation of specific institutes because it deals with the *presuppositions underlying therapy of any kind*. Its concern was with concepts about human beings and not with specific techniques. This leads to the dilemma that existential therapy has been quite influential, but there are very few adequate training courses in this kind of therapy simply because it is not a specific training in technique.

The founders of the existential movement always stated that specific training in techniques of therapy could be obtained at any number of schools of therapy, and that the student was responsible for molding his or her own presuppositions in existential form.

Rollo May, an existentialist before he knew the word, found that the existing person was the important consideration, and not a theory *about* this person. He had argued in his Ph.D. dissertation, published under the title *The Meaning of Anxiety* in 1950, for a concept of normal anxiety as the basis for a theory of human beings. He had already, before his training in the William Alanson White Institute, experienced the futility of going to analysis five times a week for two years. He was trained as a psychoanalyst in the William Alanson White Institute, the neo-Freudian institute in New York, and was already a practicing analyst when he read in the early 1950s about existential therapies in Europe. He felt these new concepts in existential psychology were the ones he needed but had never been able to formulate.

The founders of existential psychotherapy believe that its contributions will be absorbed into other schools. Fritz Perls, in the foreword of *Gestalt Therapy Verbatim* (1969), states quite accurately that Gestalt therapy is a form of existential psychotherapy. Therapists trained in different schools can legitimately call themselves existential if their assumptions are similar to those described in this chapter. Irvin Yalom was trained in the neo-Freudian tradition. Even such an erstwhile behavior therapist as Arnold Lazarus uses some existential presuppositions in his multimodal psychotherapy. All of this is possible because existential psychotherapy is a way of conceiving the human being. It goes deeper than the other forms of psychotherapy to emphasize the assumptions underlying all systems of psychotherapy.

Major works include May's *The Meaning of Anxiety* (1977), *Man's Search for Himself* (1953), and *Existential Psychology* (1961). Others are James Bugental's *The Search for Existential Identity* (1976), Medard Boss's *The Analysis of Dreams* (1957a) and *Psychoanalysis and Daseinanalysis* (1982), and Viktor Frankl's *Man's Search for Meaning* (1963). Helmut Kaiser has written valuably on existential therapy in his *Effective Psychotherapy* (1965). Leslie Farber (1966, 1976), Avery Weisman (1965), and Lester Havens (1974) have also contributed significantly to the existential literature.

❖ PERSONALITY

Theory of Personality

Existential psychotherapy is a form of *dynamic psychotherapy* that posits a dynamic model of personality structure. *Dynamic* is a commonly used term in psychology and psychotherapy. We often, for example, speak of the patient's "psychodynamics," or a "dynamic" approach to therapy. *Dynamic* has both lay and technical meanings, and it is necessary to be precise about its meaning in the context of personality theory. In its lay meaning *dynamic* has the connotation of vitality.

The technical meaning of *dynamic* relevant to personality theory refers to the concept of *force*. Its use in personality theory was first invoked by Freud, who viewed the personality as a system consisting of forces in conflict with one another. The result of this conflict is the constellation of emotions and behavior (both adaptive and pathological) that constitute personality. Furthermore (and this is an essential part of the definition), these forces in conflict *exist at different levels of awareness*. Indeed, some of the forces are entirely out of awareness and exist on an unconscious plane.

Thus, when we speak of the "psychodynamics" of an individual, we refer to that individual's conflicting, conscious and unconscious forces, motives, and fears. "Dynamic psychotherapy" is psychotherapy based upon this dynamic model of personality structure.

There are many dynamic models of personality. To differentiate these various models and to define the existential model of personality structure, we must ask: What is the *content* of the internal, conscious, and unconscious struggle? Force, motives, and fears conflict with one another within the personality. But which forces? Which motives? Which fears?

The existential view of the internal struggle can be made clearer by contrasting it with two other common dynamic views of personality: the Freudian model and the interpersonal (neo-Freudian) model.

The Freudian Model of Psychodynamics

The Freudian model posits that the individual is governed by innate instinctual forces that inexorably unfurl throughout the psychosexual developmental cycle. Freud postulated conflicts on several fronts: dual instincts collide with one another (ego instincts versus libido instincts in Freud's first theory or, in the second theory, Eros versus Thanatos); the instincts also collide with the demands of the environment, and later the instincts collide with the superego (the internalized environment).

We can summarize the nature of the conflict in the Freudian dynamic model by stating that an instinctually driven being is at war with a world that prevents the satisfaction of these innate aggressive and sexual drives.

The Interpersonal (Neo-Freudian) Model of Psychodynamics

In the interpersonal model of personality the individual is not instinct-guided and pre-programmed, but is instead almost entirely shaped by the cultural and interpersonal environment. The child desperately requires acceptance and approval by important survival figures. But the child also has an inner press toward growth, mastery, and autonomy, and these tendencies are not always compatible with the demands of significant adults in the child's life. If the child is unlucky enough to have parents who are too caught up in their own neurotic struggles to provide the child security *and* encourage the child's autonomous development, then a conflict develops between the child's need for security and natural growth inclinations. In such a struggle, growth is always compromised for the sake of security.

Existential Psychodynamics

The existential model of personality rests on a different view of inner conflict. It postulates that the basic conflict is not with suppressed instinctual drives or with the significant adults in the individual's early life; instead the conflict is between the individual and the "givens" of existence.

What are these "givens"? The reflective individual can discover them without a great deal of effort. If we "bracket" the outside world, if we put aside the everyday concerns with which we ordinarily fill our lives and reflect deeply upon our situation in the world, then we must confront certain "ultimate concerns" that are an inescapable part of the human being's existence in the world.

Yalom (1981) identifies four ultimate concerns that have considerable relevance for psychotherapy: *death, freedom, isolation,* and *meaninglessness.* The individual's confrontation with each of these constitutes the content of the inner conflict from the existential frame of reference.

Death.   Death is the most obvious ultimate concern. It is apparent to all that death will come and that there is no escape. It is a terrible truth, and at the deepest levels we respond to it with mortal terror. "Everything," as Spinoza states, "wishes to persist in its own being" (1954, p. 6). From the existential point of view a core inner conflict is between awareness of inevitable death and the simultaneous wish to continue to live.

Death plays a major role in one's internal experience. It haunts the individual as nothing else. It rumbles continuously under the membrane of life. The child at an early age is pervasively concerned with death, and one of the child's major developmental tasks is to deal with the terror of obliteration.

To cope with this terror, we erect defenses against death awareness. These defenses are denial-based; they shape character structure and, if maladaptive, result in clinical maladjustment. Psychopathology, to a very great extent, is the result of failed death transcendence; that is, symptoms and maladaptive character structure have their origin in the individual terror of death.

Freedom.   Ordinarily we do not think of freedom as a source of anxiety. Quite the contrary, freedom is generally viewed as an unequivocally positive concept. The history of Western civilization is punctuated by a yearning and striving toward freedom. Yet freedom in the existential frame of reference has a technical meaning—one that is riveted to dread.

In the existential frame of reference, freedom means that, contrary to everyday experience, the human being does not enter and ultimately exit from a structured universe with a coherent, grand design. Freedom refers to the fact that the human being is responsible for and the author of his or her own world, own life design, own choices and actions. The human being, as Sartre puts it, is "condemned to freedom" (1956, p. 631). Rollo May (1981) holds that freedom, in order to be authentic, requires the individual to confront the limits of his or her destiny.

The existential position that the human being constitutes a personal world has been germinating for a long time in philosophic thought. The heart of Kant's revolution in philosophy was his postulate that human consciousness, the nature of the human being's mental structures, provides the external form of reality. Kant stated that even space "is not something objective and real but something subjective and ideal; it is, as it were, a schema issuing by a constant law from the nature of the mind for the coordinating of all outer sensa" (1954, p. 308).

This existential view of freedom has terrifying implications. If it is true that we create our own selves and our own world, then it also means that there is no ground beneath us: there is only an abyss, a void, nothingness.

An important internal dynamic conflict emanates from our confrontation with freedom: conflict issues from our awareness of freedom and groundlessness on the one hand and, on the other hand, our deep need and wish for ground and structure.

The concept of freedom encompasses many themes that have profound implications for psychotherapy. The most apparent is *responsibility*. Individuals differ enormously in the degree of responsibility they are willing to accept for their life situation and in their modes of denying responsibility. For example, some individuals displace responsibility for their situation onto other people, onto life circumstances, onto bosses and spouses, and, when they enter treatment, they transfer responsibility for their therapy to their psychotherapist. Other individuals deny responsibility by experiencing themselves as "innocent victims" who suffer from external events (and remain unaware that they themselves have set these events into motion). Still others shuck responsibility by temporarily being "out of their minds"—they enter a temporary irrational state in which they are not accountable even to themselves for their behavior.

Another aspect of freedom is *willing*. To be aware of responsibility for one's situation is to enter the vestibule of action or, in a therapy situation, of change. Willing represents the passage from responsibility to action. Willing, as May (1969) points out, consists first of wishing and then of deciding. Many individuals have enormous difficulties in experiencing or expressing a wish. Wishing is closely aligned to feeling, and affect-blocked individuals cannot act spontaneously because they cannot feel and thus cannot wish. *Impulsivity* avoids wishing by failing to discriminate among wishes. Instead, individuals act impulsively and promptly on all wishes. *Compulsivity*, another disorder of wishing, is characterized by individuals not pro-acting, but instead being driven by ego-alien inner demands that often run counter to their consciously held desires.

Once an individual fully experiences a wish, he or she is faced with decision. Many individuals can be extremely clear about what they wish but still not be able to decide or to choose. Often they experience a decisional panic; they may attempt to delegate the decision to someone else, or they act in such a way that the decision is made for them by circumstances that they, unconsciously, have brought to pass.

Isolation.   A third ultimate concern is isolation. It is important to differentiate *existential isolation* from other types of isolation. *Interpersonal isolation* refers to the gulf that exists between oneself and other people—a gulf that results from deficient social skills and psychopathology in the sphere of intimacy. *Intrapersonal isolation*, a term first introduced by Freud, refers to the fact that we are isolated from parts of ourselves. Enclaves of self (of experience, affect, desire) are dissociated out of awareness, and the goal of psychotherapy is to help the individual reclaim these split-off parts of self.

Existential isolation cuts beneath other forms of isolation. No matter how closely we relate to another individual, there remains a final unbridgeable gap. Each of us enters existence alone and must depart from it alone. Each individual in the dawn of consciousness created a primary self (*transcendental ego*) by permitting consciousness to curl back upon itself and to differentiate a self from the remainder of the world. Only after that does the individual, now "self-conscious," begin to constitute other selves. Beneath this act, as Mijuskovic (1979) notes, there is a fundamental loneliness; the individual cannot escape the knowledge that (1) he constitutes others and (2) he can never fully share his consciousness with others.

There is no stronger reminder of existential isolation than a confrontation with death. The individual who faces death invariably becomes acutely aware of isolation.

The third dynamic conflict is between the awareness of our fundamental isolation and the wish to be protected, to merge and to be part of a larger whole.

Fear of existential isolation (and the defenses against it) underlie a great deal of interpersonal psychopathology. This dynamic offers a powerful, parsimonious explanatory system for understanding many miscarried interpersonal relationships in which one *uses* another for some function rather than *relates* to the other out of caring for that person's being.

Although no relationship can eliminate isolation, it can be shared with another in such a way that the pain of isolation is assuaged. If one acknowledges one's isolated situation in existence and confronts it with resoluteness, one will be able to turn lovingly toward others. If, on the other hand, one is overcome with dread in the face of isolation, one will not be able to turn toward others but instead will use others as a shield against isolation. In such instances relationships will be out-of-joint miscarriages and distortions of what might have been authentic relationships.

Some individuals (and this is particularly true of individuals with a borderline personality disturbance) experience panic when they are alone that emanates from a dissolution of ego boundaries. These individuals begin to doubt their own existence and believe that they exist only in the presence of another, that they exist only so long as they are responded to or are thought about by another individual.

Many attempt to deal with isolation through fusion: they soften their ego boundaries and become part of another individual. They avoid personal growth and the sense of isolation that accompanies growth. Fusion underlies the experience of being in love. The wonderful thing about romantic love is that the lonely "I" disappears into the "we." Others may fuse with a group, a cause, a country, a project. To be like everyone else—to conform in dress, speech, and customs, to have no thoughts or feelings that are different—saves one from the isolation of the lonely self.

Compulsive sexuality is also a common response to terrifying isolation. Promiscuous sexual coupling offers a powerful but temporary respite for the lonely individual. It is temporary because it is only a caricature of a relationship. The sexually compulsive individual does not relate to the whole being of the other but relates only to the part of that individual that meets his or her need. Sexually compulsive individuals do not know their partners; they show and see only those parts that facilitate seduction and the sexual act.

Meaninglessness.   The fourth ultimate concern is meaninglessness. If each person must die, and if each person constitutes his or her own world, and if each is alone in an indifferent universe, then what possible meaning can life have? Why do we live? How shall we live? If there is no preordained design in life, then we must construct our own meaning in life. The fundamental question then becomes, "Is it possible that a self-created life meaning is sturdy enough to bear one's life?"

The human being appears to require meaning. Our perceptual neuropsychological organization is such that we instantaneously pattern random stimuli. We organize them automatically into figure and ground. When confronted with a broken circle, we automatically perceive it as complete. When any situation or set of stimuli defies patterning, we experience dysphoria, which persists until we fit the situation into a recognizable pattern. In the same way individuals organize random stimuli so too do they face existential situations: in an unpatterned world an individual is acutely unsettled and searches for a pattern, an explanation, a meaning of existence.

A sense of meaning of life is necessary for still another reason: from a meaning schema we generate a hierarchy of values. Values provide us with a blueprint for life conduct; values tell us not only *why* we live but *how* to live.

The fourth internal conflict stems from this dilemma: *How does a being who requires meaning find meaning in a universe that has no meaning?*

Variety of Concepts

The content of the internal conflict from the existential frame of reference consists of ultimate concerns and the conscious and unconscious fears and motives spawned by them. The dynamic existential approach retains Freud's basic dynamic *structure* but has a radically different *content*. The old Freudian formula of

$$\text{DRIVE} \rightarrow \text{ANXIETY} \rightarrow \text{DEFENSE MECHANISM}$$

is replaced in the existential system by

$$\text{AWARENESS OF ULTIMATE CONCERN} \rightarrow \text{ANXIETY} \rightarrow$$
$$\text{DEFENSE MECHANISM}[1]$$

Both psychoanalysis and the existential system place anxiety at the center of the dynamic structure. Anxiety fuels psychopathology: conscious and unconscious psychic operations (i.e., defense mechanisms) are generated to deal with anxiety. These psychic operations constitute psychopathology: they provide safety, but they also restrict growth.

An important difference is that Freud's sequence begins with drive, whereas an existential framework begins with awareness. The existential frame of reference views the individual primarily as fearful and suffering rather than as driven.

To an existential therapist, anxiety springs from confrontation with death, groundlessness (freedom), isolation, and meaninglessness. The individual uses two types of defense mechanisms to cope with anxiety. The first, the conventional mechanisms of defense, thoroughly described by Sigmund Freud, Anna Freud, and Harry Stack Sullivan, defend the individual against anxiety regardless of source. The second are specific defenses that serve to cope with specific primary existential fears.

---

[1]To Freud, anxiety is a signal of danger (i.e., if instinctual drives are permitted expression, the organism becomes endangered; either the ego is overwhelmed or retaliation by the environment is inevitable). The defense mechanisms restrict direct expression of drives but provide indirect expression—that is, in displaced, sublimated, or symbolic form.

For example, consider the individual's defense mechanism for dealing with the anxiety emerging from awareness of death. Yalom (1981, p. 115) describes two major, specific intrapsychic defenses: an irrational belief in personal "specialness" and an irrational belief in the existence of an "ultimate rescuer." These defenses resemble delusions in that they are fixed, false beliefs. However, they are not delusions in the clinical sense, but are universally held irrational beliefs.

Specialness

Individuals have deep, powerful beliefs in personal inviolability, invulnerability, and immortality. Although, at a rational level, we recognize the foolishness of these beliefs, nonetheless, at a deeply unconscious level, we believe that the ordinary laws of biology do not apply to us.

If this defense is weak or absent, then the individual manifests one of a number of clinical syndromes: for example, the narcissistic character, the compulsive workaholic consumed by a search for glory, the self-aggrandizing, paranoid individual. The crisis in the lives of these individuals occurs when their belief system is shattered and a sense of unprotected ordinariness intrudes. They frequently seek therapy when the defense of specialness is no longer able to ward off anxiety— for example, at times of severe illness or at the interruption of what had always appeared to be an eternal, upward spiral.

The Belief in the Existence of an Ultimate Rescuer

The other major mechanism of defense that serves to block death awareness is our belief in a personal omnipotent servant who eternally guards and protects our welfare, who may let us get to the edge of the abyss but who will always bring us back. A hypertrophy of this particular defense mechanism results in a character structure displaying passivity, dependency, and obsequiousness. Often such individuals dedicate their lives to locating and appeasing an ultimate rescuer. In Silvano Arieti's terms, they live for the "dominant other" (1977, p. 864)—a life ideology that precedes and prepares the ground for clinical depression. These individuals may adapt well to life while basking in the presence of the dominant other, but they decompensate and experience extraordinary distress at the loss of this dominant other.

Another major difference between the existential dynamic approach and other dynamic approaches lies in temporal orientation. The existential therapist works in the present tense. The individual is to be understood and helped to understand himself from the perspective of a here-and-now *cross-section*, not from the perspective of a historical *longitudinal section*. Consider the use of the word *deep*. Freud defines *deep* as "early," and so the deepest conflict meant the earliest conflict in the individual's life. Freud's psychodynamics are developmentally based. *Fundamental* and *primary* are to be grasped chronologically: each is synonymous with "first." Thus, the fundamental sources of anxiety, for example, are considered to be the earliest calamities: separation and castration.

From the existential perspective, *deep* means the most fundamental concerns facing the individual at that moment. The past (i.e., one's memory of the past) is important only insofar as it is part of one's current existence and has contributed to one's current mode of facing ultimate concerns. The immediate, currently existing ground beneath all other ground is important from the existential perspective. Thus, the existential conception of personality is in the awareness of the depths of one's immediate experiences. Existential therapy does not attempt to excavate and understand the past; instead it is directed toward the future's becoming the present and explores the past only as it throws light on the present. The therapist must continually keep in mind that we create our past and that our present mode of existence dictates what we choose to remember of the past.

❖ PSYCHOTHERAPY

Theory of Psychotherapy

A substantial proportion of practicing psychotherapists consider themselves existentially (or "humanistically") oriented. Yet few, if any, have received any systematic training in existential therapy. One can be reasonably certain of this because there are few comprehensive training programs in existential therapy. Although many excellent books illuminate some aspect of the existential frame of reference (Becker, 1973; Bugental, 1956; Koestenbaum, 1978; May, 1953, 1977; May et al., 1958), Yalom's book (1981) is the first to present a systematic, comprehensive view of the existential therapeutic approach.

Existential therapy is *not* a comprehensive psychotherapeutic system; it is a frame of reference—a paradigm by which one views and understands a patient's suffering in a particular manner.

Existential therapists begin with presuppositions about the sources of a patient's anguish and view the patient in human rather than behavioral or mechanistic terms. They may employ any of a large variety of techniques used in other approaches insofar as they are consistent with basic existential presuppositions and a human, authentic therapist-patient encounter.

The vast majority of experienced therapists, regardless of adherence to some particular ideological school, employ many existential insights and approaches. All competent therapists realize, for example, that an apprehension of one's finiteness can often catalyze a major inner shift of perspective, that it is the relationship that heals, that patients are tormented by choice, that a therapist must catalyze a patient's "will" to act, and that the majority of patients are bedeviled by a lack of meaning in their lives.

It is also true that the therapist's belief system determines the type of clinical data which he or she encounters. Therapists subtly or unconsciously cue patients to provide them with certain material. Jungian patients have Jungian dreams. Freudian patients discover themes of castration, anxiety, and penis envy. The therapist's perceptual system is affected by her ideological system. She "tunes in" to the material that she wishes to obtain. So too with the existential approach. If the therapist tunes her mental apparatus to the right channel, it is astounding how frequently patients discuss concerns emanating from existential conflicts.

The basic approach in existential therapy is strategically similar to other dynamic therapies. The therapist assumes that the patient experiences anxiety which issues from some existential conflict that is at least partially unconscious. The patient handles anxiety by a number of ineffective, maladaptive defense mechanisms that may provide temporary respite from anxiety but ultimately so cripple the individual's ability to live fully and creatively that these defenses merely result in still further secondary anxiety. The therapist assists the patient to embark on a course of self-investigation in which the goals are to understand the unconscious conflict, to identify the maladaptive defense mechanisms, to discover their destructive influence, to diminish secondary anxiety by correcting these heretofore restrictive modes of dealing with self and others, and to develop other ways of coping with primary anxiety.

Although the basic strategy in existential therapy is similar to other dynamic therapies, the content is radically different. In many respects, the process differs as well; the existential therapist's different mode of understanding the patient's basic dilemma results in many differences in the strategy of psychotherapy. For example, because the existential view of personality structure emphasizes the depth of experience at any given moment, the existential therapist does not spend a great deal of time helping the patient to recover the past. The existential therapist strives for an understanding of the patient's *current* life situation and *current* enveloping unconscious fears. The existential therapist believes, as do other dynamic therapists, that the nature of the therapist-client relationship is fundamental in good psychotherapeutic work. However, the accent is not upon transference but instead upon the relationship as fundamentally important in itself.

Process of Psychotherapy

Each of the ultimate human concerns (death, freedom, isolation, and meaninglessness) has implications for the process of therapy. Let us examine the practical, therapeutic implications of the ultimate concern of freedom. A major component of freedom is *responsibility*—a concept that deeply influences the existential therapist's therapeutic approach.

Sartre equates responsibility to authorship: to be responsible means to be the author of one's own life design. The existential therapist continually focuses upon each patient's responsibility for his or her own distress. Bad genes or bad luck do not cause a patient to be lonely or chronically abused or neglected by others. Until patients realize that they are responsible for their own conditions, there is little motivation to change.

The therapist must identify methods and instances of responsibility avoidance and then make these known to the patient. Therapists may use a wide variety of techniques to focus the patient's attention on responsibility. Many therapists interrupt the patient whenever they hear the patient avoiding responsibility. When patients say they "can't" do something, the therapist immediately comments, "You mean you 'won't' do it." As long as one believes in "can't," one remains unaware of one's active contribution to one's situation. Such therapists encourage patients to *own* their feelings and statements and actions. If a patient comments that he did something "unconsciously," the therapist might inquire, "Whose unconscious is it?" The general principle is obvious: whenever the patient laments about his or her life situation, the therapist inquires how the patient created that situation.

Often it is helpful to keep the patient's initial complaints in mind and then, at appropriate points in therapy, juxtapose these initial complaints with the patient's in therapy behavior. For example, consider a patient who sought therapy because of feelings of isolation and loneliness. During the course of therapy the patient expressed at great length his sense of superiority and his scorn and disdain of others. These attitudes were rigidly maintained; the patient manifested great resistance to examining, much less changing, these opinions. The therapist helped this patient to understand his responsibility for his personal predicament by reminding the patient, whenever he discussed his scorn of others, "And you are lonely."

Responsibility is one component of freedom. Earlier we described another, *willing*, which may be further subdivided into *wishing* and *deciding*. Consider the role of *wishing*. How often does the therapist participate with a patient in some such sequence as this:

"What shall I do? What shall I do?"

"What is it that stops you from doing what you want to do?"

"But I don't *know* what I want to do! If I knew that, I wouldn't need to see you!"

These patients actually know what they should do, ought to do, or must do, but they do not experience what they *want* to do. Many therapists, in working with patients who have a profound incapacity to wish, have shared May's inclination to shout "Don't you ever *want* anything?" (1969, p. 165). These patients have enormous social difficulties because they have no opinions, no inclinations, and no desires of their own.

Often the inability to wish is imbedded in a more global disorder—the inability to feel. In many cases, the bulk of psychotherapy consists of helping patients to dissolve their affect blocks. This therapy is slow and grinding. Above all, the therapist must persevere and, time after time, must continue to press the patient with, "What do you feel?" "What do you want?" Repeatedly the therapist will need to explore the source and nature of the block and of the stifled feelings behind it.

The inability to feel and to wish is a pervasive characterological trait, and considerable time and therapeutic perseverance are required to effect enduring change.

There are other modes of avoiding wishing in addition to blocking of affect. Some individuals avoid wishing by not discriminating among wishes, by acting impulsively on all wishes. In such instances, the therapist must help the patient to make some internal discrimination among wishes and assign priorities to each. The patient must learn that two wishes which are mutually exclusive demand that one be relinquished. If, for example, a meaningful, loving relationship is a wish, then a host of conflicting interpersonal wishes—such as the wish for conquest or power or seduction or subjugation—must be denied.

Decision is the bridge between wishing and action. Some patients, even though they are able to wish, are still unable to act because they cannot *decide*. One of the more common reasons that deciding is difficult is that every yes involves a no. Renunciation invariably accompanies decision, and a decision requires a relinquishment of other options—often options that may never come again. There are other patients who cannot decide because a major decision makes them more aware of the degree to which they constitute their own lives. Thus, a major, irreversible decision is a boundary situation in the same way that awareness of death may be a boundary situation.

The therapist must help patients make choices. The therapist must help patients recognize that they themselves, not the therapist, must generate and choose among options. In helping patients to communicate effectively, therapists teach that one must *own* one's feelings. It is equally important that one owns one's decisions. Some patients are panicked by the various implications of each decision. The "what ifs" torment them. *What if I leave my job and can't find another? What if I leave my children alone and they get hurt?* It is often useful to ask the patient to consider the entire scenario of each "what if" in turn, to fantasize it happening with all the possible ramifications, and then to experience and analyze emerging feelings.

A general posture toward decision making is to assume that the therapist's task is not to *create* will but instead to *disencumber* it. The therapist cannot flick the decision switch or inspirit the patient with resoluteness. But the therapist can influence the factors that influence willing. After all, no one has a congenital inability to decide. Decision making is blocked by obstacles, and it is the therapist's task to help move obstacles. Once that is done, the individual will naturally move into a more autonomous position in just the way, Karen Horney (1950) put it, an acorn develops into an oak tree.

The therapist must help patients understand that decisions are unavoidable. One makes decisions all the time and often conceals from oneself the fact that one is deciding. It is important to help patients understand the inevitability of decisions and to identify how they make decisions. Many patients decide *passively* by, for example, letting another person decide for them. They may terminate an unsatisfactory relationship by unconsciously acting in such a way that the partner makes the decision to leave. In such instances the final outcome is achieved, but the patient may be left with many negative repercussions. The patient's sense of powerlessness is merely reinforced and he continues to experience himself as one to whom things happen rather than as the author of his own life situation. The *way* one makes a decision is often as important as the content of the decision. An active decision reinforces the individual's active acceptance of his own power and resources.

Mechanisms of Psychotherapy

We can best understand the mechanisms of the existential approach by considering the therapeutic leverage inherent in some of the ultimate concerns.

Death and Psychotherapy

There are two distinct ways in which the concept of death plays an important role in psychotherapy. First, an increased awareness of one's finiteness stemming from a personal confrontation with death may cause a radical shift in life perspective and lead to personal change. Second, the concept that death is a primary source of anxiety has many important implications for therapy.

Death as a Boundary Situation.   A *boundary situation* is a type of urgent experience that propels the individual into a confrontation with an existential situation. The most powerful boundary situation is confrontation with one's personal death. Such a confrontation has the power to provide a massive shift in the way one lives in the world. Some patients report that they learn simply that "existence cannot be postponed." They no longer postpone living until some time in the future; they realize that one can really live only in the present. The neurotic individual rarely lives in the present but is either continuously obsessed with events from the past or fearful of anticipated events in the future.

A confrontation with a boundary situation persuades individuals to count their blessings, to become aware of their natural surroundings: the elemental facts of life, changing seasons, seeing, listening, touching, and loving. Ordinarily what we *can* experience is diminished by petty concerns, by thoughts of what we cannot do or what we lack, or by threats to our prestige.

Many terminally ill patients, when reporting personal growth emanating from their confrontation with death, have lamented, "What a tragedy that we had to wait till now, till our bodies were riddled with cancer, to learn these truths." This is an exceedingly important message for therapists. The therapist can obtain considerable leverage to help "everyday" patients (i.e., patients who are not physically ill) increase their awareness of death earlier in their life cycle. With this aim in mind, some therapists have employed structured exercises to confront the individual with personal death. Some group leaders begin a brief group experience by asking members to write their own epitaph or obituary, or they provide guided fantasies in which group members imagine their own death and funeral.

Many existential therapists do not believe that artificially introduced death confrontations are necessary or advisable. Instead they attempt to help the patient recognize the signs of mortality that are part of the fabric of everyday life. If the therapist and the patient are "tuned-in," there is considerable evidence of death anxiety in every psychotherapy. Every patient suffers losses through death of parents, friends, and associates. Dreams are haunted with death anxiety. Every nightmare is a dream of raw death anxiety. Everywhere around us are reminders of aging: our bones begin to creak, senile plaques appear on our skin, we go to reunions and note with dismay how everyone *else* has aged. Our children grow up. The cycle of life envelops us.

An important opportunity for confrontation with death arises when patients experience the death of someone close to them. The traditional literature on grief primarily focuses on two aspects of grief work: loss and the resolution of ambivalence that so strongly accentuates the dysphoria of grief. But a third dimension must be considered: the death of someone close to us confronts us with our own death.

Often grief has a very different tone, depending upon the individual's relationship with the person who has died. The loss of a parent confronts us with our vulnerability: if our parents could not save themselves, who will save us? When parents die, nothing remains between ourselves and the grave. At the moment of our parents' death, we ourselves constitute the barrier between our children and their death.

The death of a spouse often evokes the fear of existential isolation. The loss of the significant other increases our awareness that, try as hard as we can to go through the world two by two, there is nonetheless a basic aloneness we must bear. Yalom reports a patient's dream the night after learning that his wife had inoperable cancer.

> I was living in my old house in _____ [a house that had been in the family for three generations]. A Frankenstein monster was chasing me through the house. I was terrified. The house was deteriorating, decaying. The tiles were crumbling and the roof leaking. Water leaked all over my mother. [His mother had died six months ago.] I fought with him. I had a choice of weapons. One had a curved blade with a handle, like a scythe. I slashed him and tossed him off the roof. He lay stretched out on the pavement below. But he got up and once again started chasing me through the house. (1981, p. 168)

The patient's first association to this dream was "I know I've got a hundred thousand miles on me." Obviously his wife's impending death reminded him that his life and his body (symbolized in the dream by the deteriorating house) were also finite. As a child this patient was often haunted by the monster who returned in this nightmare.

Children try many methods of dealing with death anxiety. One of the most common is the personification of death—imagining death as some finite creature: a monster, a sandman, a bogeyman, and so on. This is very frightening to children but nonetheless far less frightening than the truth—that they carry the spores of their own death within them. If death is "out there" in some physical form, then possibly it may be eluded, tricked, or pacified.

Milestones provide another opportunity for the therapist to focus the patient on existential facts of life. Even simple milestones, such as birthdays and anniversaries, are useful levers. These signs of passage are often capable of eliciting pain (consequently, we often deal with such milestones by reaction formation, in the form of a joyous celebration).

Major life events, such as a threat to one's career, a severe illness, retirement, commitment to a relationship and separation from a relationship, are important boundary situations and offer opportunities for an increased awareness of death anxiety. Often these experiences are painful, and therapists feel compelled to focus entirely on pain alleviation. In so doing, however, they miss rich opportunities for deep therapeutic work that reveal themselves at those moments.

Death as a Primary Source of Anxiety.   The fear of death constitutes a primary fount of anxiety: it is present early in life, it is instrumental in shaping character structure, and it continues throughout life to generate anxiety that results in manifest distress and the erection of psychological defenses. However, it is important to keep in mind that death anxiety exists at the very deepest levels of being, is heavily repressed, and is rarely experienced in its full sense. Often death anxiety per se is not easily visible in the clinical picture. There are patients, however, who are suffused with overt death anxiety at the very onset of therapy. There are often life situations in which the patient has such a rush of death anxiety that the therapist cannot evade the issue. In long-term, intensive therapy, explicit death anxiety is always to be found and must be considered in the therapeutic work.

In the existential framework, anxiety is so riveted to existence that it has a different connotation from the way anxiety is regarded in other frames of reference. The existential therapist hopes to alleviate crippling levels of anxiety but not to eliminate it. Life cannot be lived (nor can death be faced) without anxiety. The therapist's task, as May reminds us (1977, p. 374), is to reduce anxiety to tolerable levels and then to use the anxiety constructively.

It is important to keep in mind that, even though death anxiety may not explicitly enter the therapeutic dialogue, a theory of anxiety based on death awareness may provide therapists with a frame of reference that greatly enhances their effectiveness. Therapists, as well as patients, seek to order events into some coherent sequence. Once that is done, the therapist begins to experience a sense of control and mastery that allows organization of clinical material. The therapist's self-confidence and sense of mastery will help patients develop trust and confidence in the therapy process.

The therapist's belief system provides a certain consistency. It permits the therapist to know what to explore so that the patient does not become confused.

The therapist may, with subtlety and good timing, make comments that at an unspoken level click with the patient's unconscious and allow the patient to feel understood.

Existential Isolation and Psychotherapy

Patients discover in therapy that interpersonal relationships may temper isolation but cannot eliminate it. Patients who grow in psychotherapy learn not only the rewards of intimacy but also its limits: they learn what they *cannot* get from others. An important step in treatment consists of helping patients address existential isolation directly. Those who lack sufficient experiences of closeness and true relatedness in their lives are particularly incapable of tolerating isolation. Otto Will[2] made the point that adolescents from loving, supportive families are able to grow away from their families with relative ease and to tolerate the separation and loneliness of young adulthood. On the other hand those who grow up in tormented, highly conflicted families find it extremely difficult to leave the family. The more disturbed the family, the harder it is for children to leave—they are ill equipped to separate and therefore cling to the family for shelter against isolation and anxiety.

Many patients have enormous difficulty spending time alone. Consequently they construct their lives in such a way that they eliminate alone time. One of the major problems that ensues from this is the desperation with which they seek certain kinds of relationships and use others to avoid some of the pain accompanying isolation. The therapist must find a way to help the patient confront isolation in a dosage and with a support system suited to that patient. Some therapists, at an advanced stage of therapy, advise periods of self-enforced isolation during which the patient is asked to monitor and record thoughts and feelings.

Meaninglessness and Psychotherapy

To deal effectively with meaninglessness, therapists must first increase their sensitivity to the topic, listen differently, and become aware of the importance of meaning in the lives of individuals. For some patients the issue of meaninglessness is profound and pervasive. Carl Jung once estimated that over 30 percent of his patients sought therapy because of a sense of personal meaninglessness (1966, p. 83).

---

[2] Oral communication. Child psychiatry grand rounds. Stanford University, Department of Psychiatry, 1978.

The therapist must be attuned to the overall focus and direction of the patient's life. Is the patient reaching beyond himself or herself? Or is he or she entirely immersed in the daily routine of staying alive? Yalom (1981) reported that his therapy was rarely successful unless he was able to help patients focus on something beyond these pursuits. Simply by increasing their sensitivity to these issues, the therapist can help them focus on values outside themselves. Therapists, for example, can begin to wonder about the patient's belief systems, inquire deeply into the loving of another, ask about long-range hopes and goals, and explore creative interests and pursuits.

Viktor Frankl, who placed great emphasis on the importance of meaninglessness in contemporary psychopathology, stated that "happiness cannot be pursued, it can only ensue" (1969, p. 165).

The more we deliberately search for self-satisfaction, the more it eludes us, whereas the more we fulfill some self-transcendent meaning, the more happiness will ensue.

Therapists must find a way to help such patients develop curiosity and concern for others. The therapy group is especially well suited for this endeavor: the pattern in which self-absorbed, narcissistic patients take without giving often becomes highly evident in the therapy group. In such instances therapists may attempt to increase an individual's ability and inclination to empathize with others by requesting, periodically, that patients guess how others are feeling at various junctures of the group.

But the major solution to the problem of meaninglessness is engagement. Wholehearted engagement in any of the infinite array of life's activities enhances the possibility of one's patterning the events of one's life in some coherent fashion. To find a home, to care about other individuals, about ideas or projects, to search, to create, to build—all forms of engagement are twice rewarding: they are intrinsically enriching, and they alleviate the dysphoria that stems from being bombarded with the unassembled brute data of existence.

The therapist must approach engagement with the same attitudinal set used with wishing. The desire to engage life is always there with the patient, and therefore the therapist's activity should be directed toward the removal of obstacles in the patient's way. The therapist begins to explore what prevents the patient from loving another individual. Why is there so little satisfaction from his or her relationships with others? Why is there so little satisfaction from work? What blocks the patient from finding work commensurate with his or her talents and interests or finding some pleasurable aspects of current work? Why has the patient neglected creative or religious or self-transcendent strivings?

❖ APPLICATIONS

Problems

The clinical setting often determines the applicability of the existential approach. In each course of therapy, the therapist must consider the goals appropriate to the clinical setting. To take one example, in an acute inpatient setting where the patient will be hospitalized for approximately one to two weeks, the goal of therapy is crisis intervention. The therapist hopes to alleviate symptoms and to restore the patient to a precrisis level of functioning. Deeper, more ambitious goals are unrealistic and inappropriate to that situation.

In situations where patients desire not only symptomatic relief but also hope to attain greater personal growth, the existential approach is generally useful. A thorough existential approach with ambitious goals is most appropriate in long-term therapy, but even in briefer approaches some aspect of the existential mode (e.g., an emphasis on responsibility, deciding, an authentic therapist-patient encounter, grief work, and so on) is often incorporated into the therapy.

An existential approach to therapy is appropriate with patients who confront some boundary situation—that is, a confrontation with death, the facing of some important irreversible decision, a sudden thrust into isolation, milestones that mark passages from one life era into another. But therapy need not be limited to these explicit existential crises. In every course of therapy, there is abundant evidence of patients' anguish stemming from existential conflicts. The availability of such data is entirely a function of the therapist's attitudinal set and perceptivity. The decision to work on these levels should be a joint patient-therapist decision.

Evaluation

Psychotherapy evaluation is always a difficult task. The more focused and specific the approach and the goals, the easier it is to measure outcome. Symptomatic relief or behavioral change may be quantified with reasonable precision. But more ambitious therapies, which seek to affect deeper layers of the individual's mode of being in the world, defy quantification. These problems of evaluation are illustrated by the following vignettes reported by Yalom (1981, p. 336).

A 46-year-old mother accompanied the youngest of her four children to the airport, from which he departed for college. She had spent the last 26 years rearing her children and longing for this day. No more impositions, no more incessantly living for others, no more cooking dinners and picking up clothes. Finally she was free.

Yet as she said good-bye she unexpectedly began sobbing loudly, and on the way home from the airport a deep shudder passed through her body. "It is only natural," she thought. It was only the sadness of saying good-bye to someone she loved very much. But it was much more than that, and the shudder soon turned into raw anxiety. The therapist whom she consulted identified it as a common problem: the empty-nest syndrome. Of course she was anxious. How could it be otherwise? For years she had based her self-esteem on her performance as a mother and suddenly she found no way to validate herself. The whole routine and structure of her life had been altered. Gradually, with the help of Valium, supportive psychotherapy, an assertiveness training group, several adult education courses, a lover or two, and a part-time volunteer job, the shudder shrunk to a tremble and then vanished. She returned to her premorbid level of comfort and adaptation.

This patient happened to be part of a psychotherapy research project and there were outcome measures of her psychotherapy. Her treatment results could be described as excellent on each of the measures used—symptom checklists, target problem evaluation, self-esteem. Obviously she had made considerable improvement. Yet, despite this, it is entirely possible to consider this case as one of missed therapeutic opportunities.

Consider another patient in almost precisely the same life situation. In the treatment of this second patient the therapist, who was existentially oriented, attempted to nurse the shudder rather than to anesthetize it. This patient experienced what Kierkegaard called "creative anxiety." The therapist and the patient allowed the anxiety to lead them into important areas for investigation. True, the patient suffered from the empty-nest syndrome; she had problems of self-esteem; she loved her child but also envied him for the chances in life she had never had; and, of course, she felt guilty because of these "ignoble" sentiments.

The therapist did not simply allow her to find ways to help her fill her time but plunged into an exploration of the *meaning* of the fear of the empty next. She had always desired freedom but now seemed terrified of it. Why?

A dream illuminated the meaning of the shudder. The dream consisted simply of herself holding in her hand a 35-mm photographic slide of her son juggling and tumbling. The slide was peculiar, however, in that it showed movement; she saw her son in a multitude of positions all at the same time. In the analysis of the dream her associations revolved around the theme of time. The slide captured and framed time and movement. It kept everything alive but made everything stand still. It froze life. "Time moves on," she said, "and there's no way I can stop it. I didn't want John to grow up…whether I like it or not time moves on. It moves on for John and it moves on for me as well."

This dream brought her own finiteness into clear focus and, rather than rush to fill time with various distractions, she learned to appreciate time in richer ways than previously. She moved into the realm that Heidegger described as authentic being: she wondered not so much at the *way* things are but *that* things are. Although one could argue that therapy helped the second patient more than the first, it would not be possible to demonstrate this conclusion on any standard outcome measures. In fact, the second patient probably continued to experience more anxiety than the first did; but anxiety is a part of existence and no individual who continues to grow and create will ever be free of it.

Treatment

Existential therapy has it primary applications in an individual therapy setting. However, various existential themes and insights may be successfully applied in a variety of other settings including group therapy, family therapy, couples therapy, and so forth.

The concept of responsibility has particularly widespread applicability. It is a keystone of the group therapeutic process. Group therapy is primarily based on interpersonal therapy; the group therapeutic format is an ideal arena to examine and correct maladaptive interpersonal modes of behavior. However, the theme of responsibility underlies much interpersonal work. Consider, for example, the following sequence through which group therapists, explicitly or implicitly, attempt to guide their patients:

1. *Patients learn how their behavior is viewed by others* (Through feedback from other group members, patients learn to see themselves through others' eyes.)

2. *Patients learn how their behavior makes others feel.* (Members share their personal affective responses to one another.)

3. *Patients learn how their behavior creates the opinions others have of them.* (By sharing here-and-now feelings, members learn that, as a result of their behavior, others develop certain opinions and views of them.)

4. *Patients learn how their behavior influences their opinions of themselves.* (The information gathered in the first three steps leads to the patient formulating certain kinds of self-evaluations.)

Each of these four steps begins with the patients' own behavior, which underscores their role in shaping interpersonal relations. The end point of this sequence is that group members begin to understand that they are responsible for how others treat them and for the way in which they regard themselves.

This is one of the most fascinating aspects of group therapy: all members are "born" simultaneously. Each starts out on an equal footing. Each gradually scoops out and shapes a particular life space in the group. Thus, each person is responsible for the interpersonal position he scoops out for himself in the group (and in life). The therapeutic work in the group then not only allows individuals to change their way of relating to one another but also brings home to them in a powerful way the extent to which they have created their own life predicament—clearly an existential therapeutic mechanism.

Often the therapist uses his or her own feelings to identify the patient's contribution to his or her life predicament. For example, a depressed 48-year-old woman complained bitterly about the way her children treated her: they dismissed her opinions, were impatient with her, and, when some serious issue was at stake, addressed their comments to their father. When the therapist tuned in to his feelings about this patient, he became aware of a whining quality in her voice that tempted *him* not to take her seriously and to regard her somewhat as a child. He shared his feelings with the patient, and it proved enormously useful to her. She became aware of her childlike behavior in many areas and began to realize that her children treated her precisely as she "asked" to be treated.

Not infrequently, therapists must treat patients who are panicked by a decisional crisis. Yalom (1981) describes one therapeutic approach in such a situation. The therapist's basic strategy consisted of helping the patient uncover and appreciate the existential implications of the decision. The patient was a 66-year-old widow who sought therapy because of her anguish about a decision to sell a summer home. The house required constant attention to gardening, maintenance, and protection, and seemed a considerable burden to a frail elderly woman in poor health. Finances affected the decision as well, and she asked many financial and realty consultants to assist her in making the decision.

The therapist and the patient explored many factors involved in the decision and then gradually began to explore more deeply. Soon a number of painful issues emerged. For example, her husband had died a year ago and she mourned him yet. The house was still rich with his presence, and drawers and closets brimmed with his personal effects. A decision to sell the house also required a decision to come to terms with the fact that her husband would never return. She considered her house as her "drawing card" and harbored serious doubts whether anyone would visit her without the enticement of her lovely estate. Thus, a decision to sell the house meant testing the loyalty of her friends and risking loneliness and isolation. Yet another reason centered on the great tragedy of her life—her childlessness. She had always envisioned the estate passing on to her children and to her children's children. The decision to sell the house thus was a decision to acknowledge the failure of her major symbolic immortality project. The therapist used the house-selling decision as a springboard to these deeper issues and eventually helped the patient mourn her husband, herself, and her unborn children.

Once the deeper meanings of a decision are worked through, the decision generally glides easily into place, and after approximately a dozen sessions the patient effortlessly made the decision to sell the house.

Existentially oriented therapists strive toward honest, mutually open relationships with their patients. The patient-therapist relationship helps the patient clarify other relationships. Patients almost invariably distort some aspect of their relationship to the therapist. The therapist, drawing from self-knowledge and experience of how others view him or her, is able to help the patient distinguish distortion from reality.

The experience of an intimate encounter with a therapist has implications that extend beyond relationships with other people. For one thing, the therapist is generally someone whom the patient particularly respects. But even more important, the therapist is someone, often the only one, who *really* knows the patient. To tell someone else all one's darkest secrets and still to be fully accepted by that person is enormously affirmative.

Existential thinkers such as Erich Fromm, Abraham Maslow, and Martin Buber all stress that true caring for another means to care about the other's growth and to want to bring something to life in the other. Buber uses the term *unfolding*, which he suggests should be the way of the educator and the therapist: one uncovers what was there all along. The term *unfolding* has rich connotations and stands in sharp contrast to the goals of other therapeutic systems. One helps the patient unfold by *meeting*, by existential communication. The therapist is, in Sequin's terms, a "possibilitator" (1965, p. 123).

Perhaps the most important concept of all in describing the patient-therapist relationship is what Rollo May et al. term *presence* (1958, p. 80). The therapist must be present with the patient, must strive for an authentic encounter with the patient.

❖ CASE EXAMPLE

A *Simple Case of Divorce*

A 50-year-old scientist, whom we will call David, had been married for 27 years and had recently decided to separate from his wife. He applied for therapy because of the degree of anxiety he was experiencing in anticipation of confronting his wife with his decision.

The situation was in many ways a typical midlife scenario. The patient has two children; the younger had just graduated from college. In David's mind the children had always been the main element binding him and his wife together. Now that the children were self-supporting and fully adult, David felt there was no reasonable point in continuing the marriage. He reported that he had been dissatisfied with his marriage for many years and on three previous occasions separated from his wife, but, after only a few days, became anxious and returned, crestfallen, to his home. Bad as the marriage was, David concluded that it was less unsatisfactory than the loneliness of being single.

The reason for his dissatisfaction with his marriage was primarily boredom. He met his wife when he was 17, a time when he had been extremely insecure, especially in his relationships with women. She was the first woman who had ever expressed interest in him. David (as well as his wife) came from a blue-collar family. He was exceptionally intellectually gifted and was the first member of his family to attend college. He won a scholarship to an Ivy League school, obtained two graduate degrees, and embarked upon an outstanding academic research career. His wife was not gifted intellectually, chose not to go to college, and during the early years of their marriage worked to support David in graduate school.

For most of their married life his wife immersed herself in the task of caring for the children while David ferociously pursued his professional career. He had always experienced his relationship to his wife as empty and had always felt bored with her company. In his view she had an extremely mediocre mind and was so restricted characterologically that he found it constraining to be alone with her and embarrassing to share her with friends. He experienced himself as continually changing and growing, whereas his wife, in his opinion, had become increasingly rigid and unreceptive to new ideas.

The prototypic scenario of the male in midlife crisis seeking a divorce was made complete by the presence of the "other woman"—an intelligent, vivacious, attractive woman 15 years younger than himself.

David's therapy was long and complex, and several existential themes emerged during the course of therapy.

Responsibility was an important issue in his decision to leave his wife. First, there is the moral sense of responsibility. After all, his wife gave birth to and raised his children and had supported him through graduate school. He and his wife were at an age where he was far more "marketable" than she; that is, he had significantly higher earning power and was biologically able to father children. What moral responsibility, then, did he have to his wife?

David had a high moral sense and would, for the rest of his life, torment himself with this question. It had to be explored in therapy, and, consequently, the therapist confronted him explicitly with the issue of moral responsibility during David's decision-making process. The most effective mode of dealing with this anticipatory dysphoria was to leave no stone unturned in his effort to improve and, thus, to save the marriage.

The therapist helped David examine the question of his responsibility for the failure of the marriage. To what degree was he responsible for his wife's mode of being with him? For example, the therapist noted that he himself felt somewhat intimidated by David's quick, facile mind: the therapist also was aware of a concern about being criticized or judged by David. How judgmental was David? Was it not possible that he squelched his wife, that he might have helped his wife to develop greater flexibility, spontaneity, and self-awareness?

The therapist also helped David explore another major issue. Was he displacing onto the marriage dissatisfaction that belonged elsewhere in his life? A dream pointed the way toward some important dynamics:

I had a problem with liquefication of earth near my pool. John [a friend who was dying from cancer] sinks into the ground. It was like quicksand. I used a giant power auger to drill down into the quicksand. I expect to find some kind of void under the ground but instead I found a concrete slab five to six feet down. On the slab I found a receipt of money someone had paid me for $501. I was very anxious in the dream about that receipt since it was greater than it should have been.

One of the major themes of this dream had to do with death and aging. First, there was the theme of his friend who had cancer. David attempted to find his friend by using a giant auger. In the dream, David experienced a great sense of mastery and power during the drilling. The symbol of the auger seemed clearly phallic and initiated a profitable exploration of sexuality—David had always been sexually driven, and the dream illuminated how he used sex (and especially sex with a young woman) as a mode of gaining mastery over aging and death. Finally, he is surprised to find a concrete slab (which elicited associations of morgues, tombs, and tombstones).

He was intrigued by the numerical figures in the dream (the slab was "five to six feet" down and the receipt was for precisely $501). In his associations David made the interesting observation that he was 50 years old and the night of the dream was his 51st birthday. Though he did not consciously dwell on his age, the dream made it clear that at an unconscious level he had considerable concern about being over 50. Along with the slab that was between five and six feet deep and the receipt that was just over $500, there was his considerable concern in the dream about the amount cited in the receipt being too great. On a conscious level he denied his aging.

If David's major distress stemmed from his growing awareness of his aging and diminishment, then a precipitous separation from his wife might have represented an attempt to solve the wrong problem. Consequently, the therapist helped David plunge into a thorough exploration of his feelings about his aging and his mortality. The therapist's view was that only by fully dealing with these issues would he be more able to ascertain the true extent of the marital difficulties. The therapist and David explored these issues over several months. He attempted to deal more honestly with his wife than before, and soon he and his wife made arrangements to see a marital therapist for several months.

After these steps were taken, David and his wife decided that there was nothing salvageable in the marriage and they separated. The months following his separation were exceedingly difficult. The therapist provided support during this time but did not try to help David eliminate his anxiety; instead, he attempted to help David use his anxiety in a constructive fashion. David's inclination was to rush into an immediate second marriage, whereas the therapist persistently urged him to look at the fear of isolation that on each previous separation had sent him back to his wife. It was important now to be certain that fear did not propel him into an immediate second marriage.

David found it difficult to heed this advice because he felt so much in love with the new woman in his life. The state of being "in love" is one of the great experiences in life. In therapy, however, being in love raises many problems; the pull of romantic love is so great that it engulfs even the most well-directed therapeutic endeavors. David found his new partner to be the ideal woman, no other woman existed for him, and he attempted to spend all his time with her. When with her he experienced a state of continual bliss: all aspects of the lonely "I" vanished, leaving only a very blissful state of "we-ness."

What finally made it possible for David to work in therapy was that his new friend became somewhat frightened by the power of his embrace. Only then was he willing to look at his extreme fear of being alone and his reflex desire to merge with a woman. Gradually he became desensitized to being alone. He observed his feelings, kept a journal of them, and worked hard on them in therapy. He noted, for example, that Sundays were the very worst time. He had an extremely demanding professional schedule and had no difficulties during the week. Sundays were times of extreme anxiety. He became aware that part of that anxiety was that he had to take care of himself on Sunday. If he wanted to do something, he himself had to schedule the activity. He could no longer rely on that being done for him by his wife. He discovered that an important function of ritual in culture and the heavy scheduling in his own life was to conceal the void, the total lack of structure beneath him.

These observations led him, in therapy, to face his need to be cared for and shielded. The fears of isolation and freedom buffeted him for several months, but gradually he learned how to be alone in the world and what it meant to be responsible for his own being. In short, he learned how to be his own mother and father—always a major therapeutic objective of psychotherapy.

❖ SUMMARY

Existential psychotherapy perceives the patient as an existing, immediate person, not as a composite of drives, archetypes, or conditioning. Instinctual drives and history are obviously present, but they come into existential therapy only as parts of the living, struggling, feeling, thinking human being in unique conflicts and with hopes, fears, and relationships. Existential therapy emphasizes that normal anxiety and guilt are present in all of life and that only the neurotic forms of these need to be changed in therapy. The person can be freed from neurotic anxiety and guilt only as he or she recognizes normal anxiety and guilt at the same time.

The original criticism of existential therapy as "too philosophical" has lessened as people recognize that all effective psychotherapy has philosophical implications.

Existential therapy is concerned with the "I Am" (being) experience, the culture (world) in which a patient lives, the significance of time, and the aspect of consciousness called transcendence.

Karl Jaspers put his finger on the harmfulness of a therapist's lack of presence and of its importance: "What we are missing! What opportunities of understanding we let pass by because at a single, decisive moment we were, with all our knowledge, lacking in the simple virtue of a *full human presence!*" It is this presence that existential therapy seeks to cultivate.

The central aim of the founders of existential psychotherapy was that its emphases would influence therapy of all schools. That this has been occurring is quite clear.

The depth of existential ideas is shown in what is called the existential neurosis. This refers to the condition of the person who feels life is meaningless.

Existential therapy always sees the patient in the center of his or her own culture. Most people's problems are now loneliness, isolation, and alienation.

Our present age is one of disintegration of cultural and historical mores, of love and marriage, the family, the inherited religions, and so forth. This disintegration is the reason psychotherapy of all sorts has burgeoned in the twentieth century; people cried for help for their multitudinous problems. Thus, the existential emphasis on different aspects of the world (environment, social world, and subjective world) will, in all likelihood, become increasingly important. It is predicted that the existential approach in therapy will then become more widely used.

❖ ANNOTATED BIBLIOGRAPHY

May, R. (1977). *The meaning of anxiety* (Rev. Ed.). New York: Norton. (First edition published in 1950.)

A discussion of the prevalence of anxiety in the twentieth century and its roots in philosophy, biology, psychology, and modern culture, this is the first book written in America on the central theme of anxiety and the third book in history on this topic. The others were written by Sigmund Freud and Søren Kierkegaard. *The Meaning of Anxiety* was the first firm presentation of anxiety as a normal as well as a neurotic condition, and it argues that normal anxiety has constructive uses in human survival and human creativity.

Yalom, I. D. (1980). *Existential psychotherapy.* New York: Basic Books.

This volume offers a comprehensive clinical overview of the field of existential psychotherapy. A major task of the book is to build a bridge between theory and clinical application. It posits that psychopathology issues from the individual's confrontation with the ultimate concerns of death, freedom, isolation, and meaninglessness and explores the implications of each ultimate concern for the practice of psychotherapy.

Yalom, I. D. (1989). *Love's Executioner and other tales of psychotherapy.* New York: Basic Books.

This collection of stories is based on cases of existential therapy and gives an intimate view of the clinical application of existential therapeutic principles and techniques.

Yalom, I. D. (1991) *When Nietzsche wept.* New York: Basic Books.

This teaching novel examines a thought experiment: What might have happened if Nietzsche had turned his attention to the invention of a psychotherapy based on his own published philosophical insights?

❖ CASE READINGS

Binswanger, L. (1958). The case of Ellen West. In R. May, E. Angel, & H. Ellenberger (Eds.), *Existence: A new dimension in psychology and psychiatry* (pp. 237–364). New York: Basic Books.

This is a classic case of considerable historical importance. It should be read by all serious students of psychotherapy.

Holt, H. (1966). The case of Father M: A segment of an existential analysis. *Journal of Existentialism,* 6, 369–495. [Also in Wedding, D., & Corsini, R. J. (Eds.). (1979). *Great cases in psychotherapy.* Itasca, IL: F. E. Peacock.]

This is a well-written case study that offers insight into the manner in which an existential analysis might unfold.

May, R. (1973). Black and impotent: The life of Mercedes. In *Power and innocence* (pp. 81–97). New York: Norton. [Reprinted in Wedding, D., & Corsini, R. J. (Eds.) (1995). *Case studies in psychotherapy.* Itasca, IL: F. E. Peacock.]

This brief case history illustrates the existential treatment by Rollo May of a young black woman dealing with core issues of power and self-esteem. This case provides an excellent example of many of the fundamental points made in the current chapter.

❖ REFERENCES

Arieti, S. (1977). Psychotherapy of severe depression. *American Journal of Psychiatry, 134,* 864–868.

Becker, E. (1973). *Denial of death.* New York: Free Press.

Binswanger, L. (1956). Existential analysis and psychotherapy. In E. Fromm-Reichmann and J. L. Moreno (Eds.), *Progress in psychotherapy* (pp. 144–168). New York: Grune & Stratton.

Boss, M. (1957a). *The analysis of dreams.* London: Rider & Co.

Boss, M. (1957b). *Psychoanalyse und daseinsanalytik.* Bern & Stuttgart: Verlag Hans Huber.

Boss, M. (1982). *Psychoanalysis and daseinalysis.* New York: Simon & Schuster.

Bugental, J. (1956). *The search for authenticity.* New York: Holt, Rinehart and Winston.

Bugental, J. (1976). *The search for existential identity.* San Francisco: Jossey-Bass.

Farber, L. (1966). *The ways of the will: Essays toward a psychology and psychopathology of will.* New York: Basic Books.

Farber, L. (1976). *Lying, despair, jealousy, envy, sex, suicide, drugs, and the good life.* New York: Basic Books.

Frankl, V. (1963). *Man's search for meaning: An introduction to logotherapy.* New York: Pocket Books.

Frankl, V. (1969). *Will to meaning.* New York: World Publishing.

Havens, L. (1974). The existential use of the self. *American Journal of Psychiatry, 131.*

Horney, K. (1950). *Neurosis and human growth.* New York: Norton.

Jung, C. G. (1966). *Collected works: The practice of psychotherapy* (Vol. 16). New York: Pantheon, Bollingen Series.

Kaiser, H. (1965). *Effective psychotherapy.* New York: Free Press.

Kant, I. (1954). *The encyclopedia of philosophy* (Vol. 4). P. Edwards (Ed.). New York: Macmillan and Free Press.

Kierkegaard, S. (1954). *Fear and trembling and the sickness unto death.* Garden City, NY: Doubleday.

Koestenbaum, P. (1978). *The new image of man.* Westport, CT: Greenwood Press.

May, R. (1953). *Man's search for himself.* New York: Norton.

May, R. (1961). *Existential psychology.* New York: Random House.

May, R. (1969). *Love and will.* New York: Norton.

May, R. (1977). *The meaning of anxiety* (Rev. Ed.). New York: Norton.

May, R. (1981). *Freedom and destiny.* New York: Norton.

May, R. (1982). The problem of evil: An open letter to Carl Rogers. *Journal of Humanistic Psychology, 3,* 16.

May, R., Angel, E., & Ellenberger, H. (Eds.) (1958). *Existence: A new dimension in psychiatry and psychology.* New York: Basic Books.

Mijuskovic, B. (1979). *Loneliness in philosophy, psychology and literature.* The Netherlands: Van Gorcum.

Perls, F. (1969). *Gestalt therapy verbatim.* Moab, UT: Real People Press.

Raskin, N. (1978). Becoming—A therapist, a person, a partner, and a parent. *Psychotherapy: Theory, Research and Practice, 4,* 15.

Sartre, J. P. (1956). *Being and nothingness.* New York: Philosophical Library.

Sequin, C. (1965). *Love and psychotherapy.* New York: Libar Publishers.

Spence, K. (1956). *Behavior therapy and conditioning.* New Haven, CT: Yale University.

Spinoza, B. (1954). Cited by M. De Unamuno in *The tragic sense of life* (E. Flitch, Trans). New York: Dover.

Weisman, A. (1965). *Existential core of psychoanalysis: Reality sense and responsibility.* Boston: Little, Brown.

Yalom, I. (1981). *Existential psychotherapy.* New York: Basic Books.

William Glasser

10 Reality Therapy

William Glasser and
Robert E. Wubbolding

Reality therapy is a method of counseling and psychotherapy developed originally by William Glasser, a psychiatrist.

Control theory, which serves as the basis of reality therapy, regards human beings as motivated to survive and to fulfill four basic psychological human needs: *belonging, power, fun,* and *freedom.* Human behavior is seen as based on choices.

Reality therapy helps people examine their wants and needs, evaluate behaviors, and make plans for fulfilling needs. It is mostly free of obscure psychological terminology, which leads to the misconception that it is easy to put into practice. Nevertheless, it is a practical method that can be used by therapists, counselors, teachers, parents, and others.

❖ OVERVIEW

Basic Concepts

The purposes of undergoing psychotherapy are generally to gain insight, to see connections, and to reach a higher level of self-awareness. The primary goal of reality therapy is neither insight nor resolution of unconscious conflicts. Rather, the desired outcome is behavioral change resulting in greater need satisfaction. People enter psychotherapy because they feel that something has gone wrong in their lives. The reality therapist believes such people are not fulfilling their needs effectively, and thus they feel discomfort, anxiety, depression, guilt, fear, or shame. Others act negatively or develop psychosomatic symptoms. If they are comfortable with their behavior, but others believe they have problems, they are often coerced into therapy. Often such a person does not want to change, at least in the beginning of the therapy process. Yet, through the skillful use of reality therapy, it is possible to help a person evaluate whether behavioral change is desirable and possible and whether adjusting to the demands of the "real world" would be appropriate and satisfying. If clients decide that change is beneficial to them, they are helped to make better choices designed to maintain or increase their need fulfillment.

Reality therapy is based on control theory, a system of brain functioning (Powers, 1973). Glasser (1981, 1985) adapted this theory to the clinical setting and formulated it in a way that makes it useful to therapists, counselors, and others. Control theory states that the human brain functions like a thermostat that seeks to regulate its own behavior (much like a furnace or air conditioner) in order to change the world around it. Adding to the highly theoretical work of William Powers (1973), Glasser saw the human being as motivated by five internal forces. These human needs are innate, not learned; general, not specific; and universal, not limited to any specific race or culture. All behavior is aimed at fulfilling the four psychological needs of belonging, power, fun (or enjoyment), and freedom, as well as the physical need for survival. Effective satisfaction of these needs results in a sense of control that other theories refer to as self-actualization, self-fulfillment, or becoming a fully functioning person.

All sensate creatures, from primitive life forms to human beings, have a need to stay alive and to reproduce. Many behaviors are related to this need, such as the inner functioning of the organism. The working of the autonomic nervous system, as it controls the motor functions of the heart, glands, digestion, and all other internal organs, attempts to maintain life and satisfy the need for survival. Generally labelled the "old brain," it keeps our body machinery functioning.

Psychological needs are located in the cerebral cortex, or "new brain." The cerebral cortex functions for the most part at the level of awareness and regulates our voluntary behaviors as well as some routine behaviors such as walking. Creatures high on the evolutionary scale attempt to congregate and have a need for belonging. Because of this need, they learn to cooperate and function as a unit, finding belonging in families, schools, jobs, social clubs, and religious organizations. One of the goals of psychotherapy is to help clients fulfill this basic human drive.

Furthermore, human beings seek power in the form of achievement, competence and accomplishment. The need for power does not imply the exploitation of another person. And although power prompts human beings to compete, it is not true that when someone fulfills a need for power, someone else must lose power. Satisfying the need for power involves accomplishment or achievement. Another goal of psychotherapy is to assist clients to fulfill their needs for power without diminishing anyone else's right to do the same.

Human beings also have a need for fun or enjoyment. Infants seek out comfort. Children spend a major part of their time having fun. Effective fulfillment of this need results in the opposite of boredom, apathy, and depression. Aristotle defined a human being as a creature who is "risible," that is, one that can laugh. The word "fun" as used here does not mean "silliness." Rather, it refers to enjoyment or pleasure. Consequently, one of the goals of reality therapy is to help people fulfill the need for fun or enjoyment within reason and without infringing on the right of others to meet this same need.

The last psychological need is freedom, independence, or autonomy. The need for independence implies that if human beings are to function in a fully human manner, they must have the opportunity to make choices and to act on their own, without unreasonable restraints. Thus, another goal of reality therapy is to help clients find need-satisfying options for realizing autonomy.

As human beings interact with their environment, some parts of the external world satisfy the four psychological needs, while other parts do not. Consequently, each person assembles a mental file of wants. These are specific images of people, activities, objects, events, or situations that are need-fulfilling. Because they are appealing, they are said to have high quality. The conglomerate of these "wants" is the world a person would like to live in. The phrase "quality world" aptly describes the collection of wants related to the five needs. Each of these quality images or wants is specific. They are sometimes referred to as "pictures" and the conglomerate as "the mental picture album" (Glasser, 1985).

When a person perceives that he or she is getting what is desired from the external world, the five needs are satisfied. But when there is a difference between what is desired and the input one receives by way of the perceptual system, the person is motivated to generate a choice, a behavior in the external world. Therefore, behavior serves to close the gap between what a person wants and what a person has at a given moment.

The behavior generated is always composed of four elements: actions, thinking, feeling, and physiology (digestion, breathing, circulation, and so on). Total behavior is teleological or purposeful, designed to maneuver the external world so that wants and needs are met.

The input desired from the world enters the brain first through the sensory system and then through two filters: the total knowledge filter, by which the perception is first recognized, and the valuing filter, by which the person makes a positive or negative judgment about the perception. The thousands of perceptions stored in the mind are kept in the perceived world or what is sometimes called the "all we know world." When a desired perception (want) is compared with a current perception of what a person has, behavior is generated. Thus, the output and the input constitute a loop. Behavior is generated toward the world for the purpose of gaining a specific input or perception.

A simple example illustrates the output-input loop of control theory. Leslie walks to the kitchen and takes a drink of water. This ordinary event, like more complicated behaviors, can be seen in the context of needs, wants, perceptions, and behaviors. Leslie has a need for survival, based on the experience of thirst. The need leads to a drive that prompts Leslie to quench her thirst. She compares her present condition of thirst with her want for comfort. Thus, her mental scale is out of balance. Because of this internal motivation, she chooses a total behavior: walking to the kitchen to get a glass of water. Her behavior is described as "total" because it contains four basic psychological elements: *action* (walking, *thinking* (internal self-talk: "I want a drink"), *feeling* (the satisfaction of quenching her thirst), and *physiological behavior* (swallowing). Having completed this effective total behavior, her perception of what she has matches what she wants and she is now in equilibrium or homeostasis.

Because the theory and practice of reality therapy are based on conscious behavior, wants, needs, and perceptions of human beings, they are applicable in virtually every setting. People marry and form intimate relationships to fulfill their need for belonging. But often, after a while, conflict arises over the need for power. In an age of equality between genders, wants and behaviors related to the power need become more evident and pronounced. In relationship therapy, each person is asked to examine his or her own wants, behavior, and perceptions, evaluate them, and make more effective plans.

Other Systems

Reality therapy has been compared to the rational emotive behavior therapy of Albert Ellis. While there is some overlap between the two theories, there are also significant differences. Reality therapy and rational emotive behavior therapy share the principle that outside forces do not cause stress, depression, anxiety, or any other disturbance. They over-lap in their belief that the current life of the client is paramount and endless scrutinizing of past experience is useless. Reality therapists, however, emphasize that behavior is a *choice*. Just as ineffective, harmful behaviors can be selected to satisfy a specific want re-lated to a need, so too, effective alternative behaviors can be chosen in the future. The re-ality therapist emphasizes choice as a means to more effective living, rather than requiring a change in thinking as a prerequisite. Thinking is seen as only one component of the behavioral totality.

A significant difference between the two systems is the emphasis on human needs as sources of human behavior. Human beings attempt to fulfill their needs from moment to moment and never fulfill them completely. Rational emotive behavior therapy is based on the principle that we are human because we can think and that when human beings are disturbed, they are not thinking rationally. Reality therapy, on the other hand, states that thinking is a behavior generated from within, accompanied by actions, feelings, and phys-iological changes. This "total behavior," of which thinking is only one part, has a clear purpose—to fulfill the five needs.

Reality therapy, based on control therapy, is very different from the operant condi-tioning of B. F. Skinner and the classical psychoanalytic approach of Sigmund Freud. From the perspective of the reality therapist, operant conditioning (and, to some extent, other behaviorist theories) neglects the inner control of clients and may even deny the existence of human needs. Albert Bandura allows for cognitive processes, but human needs are not an important part of social learning theory or the mediation model of be-haviorism. However, effective techniques such as systematic desensitization and flooding can be used by the reality therapist, because the client gains a sense of control over his or her symptoms and is able to relinquish them when the results of surrendering the symp-tom become more need-satisfying than retaining it.

The cognitive behaviorism of Donald Meichenbaum and others is similar to reality therapy in that it embraces thinking and actions as important components of change. Yet change in any component of the behavioral system, in the view of reality therapy, requires a searching self-inventory or self-evaluation and the realization that one's current way of life is not effective. Thus, clients receiving treatment in reality therapy genuinely restruc-ture their thinking by changing their judgment about aspects of their lives.

Reality therapy rejects many of the basic assumptions of psychoanalysis and the psychoanalytic method. Because reality therapy sees behavior as a person's best attempt to fulfill current human needs, it rejects the "reactive terminology" that disturbances are due to outside forces or past events. Thus, anxiety, phobias, and even psychoses are believed to be the result of unmet needs and wants. Even though some limited discussion of past ex-periences is acceptable, the reality therapist encourages clients to discuss what they can control—their current actions, thinking, and feelings.

It is important to note that because current behaviors are seen as choices, it does not follow that better choices are readily available to the client. Quite the contrary is true. A client, raised in a dysfunctional family, will respond to that environment. This may be the only choice available at the time and thus represents the client's best attempt to fulfill wants and needs. The therapist's role is to help the client develop more satisfying choices. If clients could easily make other choices, they would not need therapists.

William Glasser has acknowledged similarities between reality therapy and Adlerian therapy (Evans, 1982). There are many areas of agreement and many ways in which the two theories are quite different. Harold Mosak (1989) stated that Adlerian therapy changes the questions, "How do heredity and environment shape the individual?" to "How does the individual use heredity and environment?" (p. 77). Reality therapy is in complete agreement with this question and extends it to "How can an individual make better choices to fulfill the five needs without infringing on the rights of others who also seek to fulfill their wants and needs?" Adlerians study the family constellation and emphasize early experience. In contrast, birth order is unimportant to the reality therapist. The current wants, perceptions, and behaviors of the client vis à vis the other family members are of paramount importance, irrespective of how they were developed in the past. The emphasis for the reality therapist is on the "here and now."

The reality therapist helps the client to see how he or she is fulfilling the five human needs, one of which is power. This is similar to the Adlerian view of the person seeking significance. Even as children we seek to excel, to gain recognition, and to be competent. These efforts fulfill the need for power or achievement, as seen in reality therapy.

In the process of therapy, there are also some differences between reality therapy and other systems. Reality therapists see dreams as behaviors, but they are of little therapeutic value because they can't be controlled. In addition, the insight gained in reality therapy is not simply that there is some underlying dynamic causing a particular behavior, but more profound and far-reaching realizations such as "I am responsible," "I can make a change," "I cannot change others," "My current behavior is not helping me," and so on.

On a superficial level, reality therapy appears to be at odds with person-centered therapy. Reality therapists emphasize action, questions, and a therapist-led approach. Carl Rogers stressed feelings, reflective listening, and a client-initiated agenda. In reality therapy, an attempt is made to take the lead and actively encourage specific changes. Though it is not heavy-handed or coercive, it is markedly different from the style of a person-centered therapist who follows the lead of clients and is more inclined to wait for clients to decide to change. Thus, while it is true that therapy sessions conducted by a reality therapist would be very different from those conducted by a person-centered therapist, on a more profound level there is a common bedrock. Common beliefs include the essential goodness of human nature, the personal responsibility of human beings, the purposefulness of behavior, and the importance of trust and authenticity.

In general, reality therapy is most similar to those systems of therapy that see the client as inner-directed. Systems emphasizing the influence of parents, environment, past experience, and the unconscious, all of which minimize the present ability of the client to change, are most unlike reality therapy.

❖ HISTORY

Precursors

William Glasser created reality therapy based on his experience with clients. Almost all of his training, however, came from conventional psychoanalysis. As the concepts of reality therapy emerged, Glasser rebelled against his formal training and noticed that many of his teachers did not practice what they taught. As they demonstrated by their interactions with patients, he noticed that what seemed to work was not what was said to work. What was actually done in effective therapy was often much closer to what later became reality therapy.

One of his few nonanalytical teachers, G. L. Harrington, encouraged Glasser to put his ideas into practice and to discuss his thoughts. Harrington became Glasser's mentor and helped him to formalize reality therapy in the early 1960s. Harrington was influenced by Helmuth Kaiser, a psychoanalyst who had worked with Harrington in the 1950s at the Menninger Clinic, and who also had begun to turn away from conventional analysis.

Beginnings

Reality therapy began when Glasser became dissatisfied with psychoanalytic psychiatry as taught at the Veterans Administration Brentwood Hospital and at the University of California at Los Angeles. What disturbed him most was endless ruminations about how the patient's behavior was "caused" by others in the patient's family or by a "harsh" world. The patient was generally seen as a victim of forces beyond his or her control, and the role of the analyst was to give the patient insight into his or her unconscious so he or she could regroup and cope. Even when patients gained insight after insight and when transferences were worked through, the patients stayed the same or even became worse, taking less responsibility for what they did.

On his own, Glasser began to focus on the present and to try to get patients to realize that they were responsible for what they did, they had to change themselves, and they could not count on others to change or help them, no matter how much insight they gained. For example, one woman had been attending the clinic for three years and had spent most of that time blaming her nervousness and depression on her now-dead grandfather. Glasser told her that he would see her only if she would never again mention her grandfather. She was shocked and responded, "If I don't talk about my grandfather, what will I talk about?" Glasser told her to talk about what she was doing now in her life to solve her problems, because her grandfather was dead and no longer had anything to do with her life. In a few short months, even with this early crude version of reality therapy, the woman stopped depressing and anxietying (control theory behavior terms) and started doing many things to fulfill her needs. She had taken control of her own life. For three years traditional therapy had deprived her of the chance to help herself.

Donald O'Donnell (1987) described how Glasser explained his unorthodox move to his residency consultant, G. L. Harrington. Instead of reprimanding Glasser, Harrington shook his hand and said, "Join the club." This started a seven-year relationship during which Harrington continued to consult with Glasser and helped him formulate the ideas that became reality therapy.

In 1965, Glasser became a consultant to the Ventura School, a California Youth Authority institution for delinquent girls, where the young women had all been told that they were emotionally disturbed and were not responsible for their lawbreaking. The people who ran the school were upset by this view and supported Glasser in his attempt to introduce the beginnings of reality therapy into this and other Youth Authority institutions.

Current Status

At present, reality therapy is recognized as an effective therapeutic modality with many applications. For example, an unpublished document of the Department of Defense used at a 1981 conference on drug abuse in the armed forces stated that over 90% of the more than 200 armed forces clinics that treat drug and alcohol abuse use reality therapy as their preferred therapeutic approach.

The Institute for Control Theory, Reality Therapy, and Quality Management in Los Angeles, founded in 1968, promotes the teaching of reality therapy applied to psychotherapy, counseling, schools, agencies, and management. A certification process was gradually developed, and in 1975 the first certificates were given for the practice of reality therapy.

The title Reality Therapy Certified (RTC) is given to persons completing an 18-month training program. This program consists of workshops, supervised practice, video and audio taping, small group practice, feedback, and other experiences.

The Institute for Reality Therapy administers the certification process. In 1988, Glasser asked Robert E. Wubbolding to become the first director of training for the Institute. In this capacity, Wubbolding monitors the certification process and the faculty training programs.

Much of the work of practitioners of reality therapy extends beyond the world of psychotherapy. In 1968, Glasser wrote *Schools Without Failure*, in which he asserted that when children are unable to control their world successfully (i.e., succeed in school), it hurts so much that they often stop trying to learn. At the present time, the Institute for Reality Therapy and its instructors teach the concepts in Glasser's *The Quality School* (1990b) to schools in the United States and elsewhere. In this groundbreaking work, Glasser applied the ideas of W. Edwards Deming (1982) to education. The major problem underlying the educational system is not the disruption of the students, poorly paid teachers, unused computers, lack of community involvement, or dozens of other problems. Rather, these problems are symptoms of the simple but overlooked fact that Americans have settled on mediocre work, behavior and efforts on the part of students. If the nation is indeed at risk, it is because of lack of quality education. Glasser believes that control theory and reality therapy, if taught properly, can enhance the quality of performance in schools. In a quality school, everyone has been trained to use the principles of Deming and Glasser. Schools interested in these principles have formed a consortium numbering well over 200 schools as of 1995.

Still, reality therapy remains the counseling and therapy tool that it was from the very beginning. It is taught in many countries besides the U.S. and Canada, and the Institute has ties to Japan, Korea, Ireland, Norway, the United Kingdom, Australia, New Zealand, Hong Kong, Singapore, and the former Yugoslavia.

Since the publication of Glasser's *Stations of the Mind* (1981) and *Control Theory* (1985), thousands of persons have heard about control theory and its delivery system, reality therapy. Moreover, Glasser has reconceptualized the essentials of reality therapy under two general categories: environment and procedures (1990a). Robert Wubbolding (1992) has extended these ideas by describing them as a cycle of therapy and the WDEP system (Wants, Doing, Evaluation, and Planning). Robert Cockrum (1989) stated, "William Glasser has never been content to allow his theories to be taught or used without constant scrutiny, addition and sometimes even major changes."

In 1981, *The Journal of Reality Therapy* was launched, edited by Lawrence Litwack. Since that time, more than 200 essays, articles, and research studies have been published on the applications of reality therapy.

As of 1994, nearly 4500 people had completed the reality therapy certification process worldwide, with the numbers increasing each year. Reality therapy has seen a slow but steady increase in acceptance as a viable and respected psychotherapy theory and educational system.

❖ PERSONALITY

Theory of Personality

Reality therapy, based on control theory, views the human brain as a system that seeks to manipulate the external world, and explains the development of human personality as an attempt to fulfill five innate drives: belonging, power, fun or enjoyment, freedom, and physical survival. From the cradle to the grave we generate behaviors, and through experimentation we find them need-satisfying or need-threatening. As these behaviors influence the external world, we learn that other persons, events, objects, and situations are either need-satisfying, need-threatening, or neutral.

Choice and Discovery

Reality therapy teaches that human beings choose behaviors. When choices are made, people discover that the result attained is desirable or undesirable. They thus discover whether their behaviors are effective or ineffective in satisfying their needs. They also discover whether particular aspects of the external world are pleasurable (need-satisfying), painful (not need-satisfying), or neutral.

Infants "choose" the only behavior available to them when they attempt to fulfill their physiological needs related to survival, specifically comfort and hunger. As children grow, they discover that other behaviors are available. They see other people smiling, talking, walking, reaching, touching, and playing and then choose some of these behaviors at appropriate developmental and maturational points as more effective ways to fulfill their needs.

Personality Development and Identity

Glasser (1972, 1985) has described two general types of human personality. These are explained primarily in terms of how individuals see themselves and secondarily in terms of how others see them. All persons generate behaviors to fulfill human needs. As people attempt to accomplish various developmental tasks, they either succeed or fail. When they habitually fail to fulfill their needs effectively, they develop a failure identity (Glasser, 1972, 1985) characterized by ineffective or out-of-control behaviors.

Failure Identity, Less Effective Life Direction

Three stages of regression are characterized by identifiable total behaviors.

Stage 1: Giving up.   This occurs when a person is unable to fulfill his or her needs effectively. Thus, when a student fails to develop effective behaviors, he or she may decide that the only choice is giving up.

Stage 2: Choosing negative symptoms.   The "giving up" stage of failure is often a prelude to additional failure and further ineffective behaviors such as (a) anti-social actions, (b) negative thinking, (c) negative feelings such as depression, and (d) negative physiological conditions, such as psychosomatic disorders.

These negative symptoms, although ineffective, are still the clients' best efforts at a given moment to fulfill their needs. The role of the reality therapist is to help clients choose other actions, thoughts, and feelings. This occurs after helping them define their Wants, describe what they are Doing (total behavior), Evaluate their behaviors, and Plan for a better future *(the WDEP system).*

Stage 3: Negative addictions.   Some persons regress beyond negative symptoms and perceive even more ineffective behaviors as need-satisfying. These behaviors produce, at least in their early stages, an illusion of immediate need satisfaction. They can provide a "high" that includes a short-term sense of belonging, power, fun, and freedom. Alcohol, drugs, gambling, food, even an addiction to work can all provide a person with a distorted and momentary sense of popularity, power, excitement, or liberation from stress and pain.

Success Identity, More Effective Life Direction

Just as the human personality can be characterized by a sense of failure, an ineffective or destructive life direction, and out-of-control behaviors, so too the personality can develop in the opposite direction and achieve health and success. An individual growing in this direction possesses a willingness as well as a repertoire of skills for meeting the five needs of belonging, power, fun, freedom, and survival in positive ways. Glasser (1972) describes this kind of person as having a success identity. Wubbolding (1988) has completed a positive developmental model that is the mirror image of the failure identity as characterized by giving up and negative symptoms. These positive stages are described below.

Stage 1: "I want to change, and I want to grow."   The desire to fulfill human needs effectively without infringing on the rights of others represents the first stage in the development of a healthy personality.

Stage 2: Positive symptoms.   The second stage in the development of success identity and an effective life direction is the mirror image of negative symptoms. These positive symptoms include (a) altruistic actions, (b) effective thinking, such as "I can" or "I am a valuable person," (c) positive feelings, such as self-confidence, enthusiasm, and trust, and (d) effective behaviors, such as a healthy diet and exercise.

Stage 3: Positive addictions.   Relatively few people are able to reach a state of "positive addiction." This condition, the opposite of the negative addiction described above, is the result of explicit, life-enhancing choices. Although other activities can create mental states that approach the positive addiction state, Glasser (1976) found two activities especially helpful in achieving the conditions necessary for positive addiction: meditation and noncompetitive exercise. These two behaviors involve all the following conditions of a positively addicting activity.

1. The activity occurs regularly, such as running on an almost daily basis for a limited amount of time, usually 45 to 60 minutes.
2. An altered state of consciousness or natural "high" accompanies the activity for short periods of time.
3. The activity requires little concentration. On the contrary, the mind is freed from the responsibility of attending to procedures, rules, and even ideas.
4. Cessation of the activity is painful or uncomfortable.

Even though few people reach the positively addicted state, many enhance their personal growth by activities that share some of the qualities of pure positive addiction. Such activities include travel, reading, walking, and other habitual enjoyment-related behaviors.

In the view of reality therapists, endless discussions of diagnosis, past history, and external uncontrollable events are not effective in achieving desired changes. While such discussions are interesting to the therapist and necessary at times, they precede the *most* effective use of reality therapy, which consists of building on already existing effective behaviors by eliciting a commitment to change, defining what is realistically attainable, helping the client conduct a searching and detailed self-evaluation, and making specific plans for life enrichment as represented by the stages of growth.

Variety of Concepts

Reality therapy is a logical, common-sense system. It requires that the therapist have a sense of direction and a knowledge of the components of a healthy personality. It is not a system by which change automatically occurs if the therapist labels a problem, helps the client gain insight, or analyzes the past. It is similar to the work of an artist who, following some basic principles, uses creativity to produce a unique work of art.

Language

In formulating the principles of reality therapy, a conscious decision was made to use easily understood words. The use of simple words such as *belonging, power, fun, freedom, choices, wants,* and *plans,* is not an accident. The happy result of this effort has been to introduce basic concepts of mental health to new audiences. Yet this demystification and relative understandability of the concepts is a two-edged sword, and the principles of reality therapy are more difficult to practice than to understand.

Psychopathology

Reality therapy recognizes the importance of diagnosis but views psychopathology in terms of behaviors rather than static conditions. Thus, people do not exist in an immutable *place* when they are depressed. Rather, clients are said to be "depress-ing," "anxiety-ing," "guilt-ing," "phobic-ing," "compuls-ing" "headach-ing" and "sick-ing" themselves. *To reframe such phenomena from conditions to behaviors is to see them as more controllable.* Alternatives can be sought. Clients are not passive victims of these oppressive problems, but are generators of behaviors. Nevertheless, they are not blamed or criticized for their behavior, as they can generate only the behaviors that are available to them. The reality therapist, using the WDEP (Wants, Doing, Evaluation, Planning) system, assists them to develop better, more need-satisfying behaviors.

Multicultural Applications

Most psychotherapies originated in the western hemisphere, many of them in North America. Reality therapy began as an American theory applied to the many cultures of the United States and Canada. It is now taught, studied, or practiced in varying degrees in many countries. Because of its application to many other cultures, the practice and teaching of reality therapy needs to be adjusted when people's values, wants, and manner of expression are quite different and usually more indirect than in North America. On the surface, reality therapy is a very direct method, yet it needs to be used more indirectly in "indirect cultures."

   In some cultures in the Pacific Rim, for example, psychotherapists are seen not as partners but as authority figures. Maintaining a delicate balance between practicing and teaching the theory accurately and authentically, on one hand, and adapting it to "other" cultures requires sensitivity to the culture as well as knowledge of the social, economic, historical, political, and psychological processes of the individual culture. For example, in helping an American student evaluate her own behavior, the therapist might emphasize questions such as, "Is what you are doing helping or hurting *you?*" "Do your current actions have a reasonable chance of getting you what you want?" In counseling a Chinese youth in Singapore, it would be appropriate to ask similar questions, but more emphasis should be placed on questions such as, "What does your family think about your actions?" "Do they approve or disapprove?" "Do your actions bring shame or honor to your parents?"

Reality therapy requires specific skills and procedures, as summarized in the WDEP system. Nevertheless, these should be seen as flexible and adaptable to the style and personality of the user as well as the experience, manner of expression, thought patterns (total behavior), and specific wants of members of various cultures.

❖ PSYCHOTHERAPY

Theory of Psychotherapy

Based on the principle that human beings are born with at least five generic needs already discussed, reality therapy provides a structure for helping clients more effectively satisfy their needs for belonging, achievement, fun or enjoyment, independence or freedom, and survival. Thus, the overall goal of the practitioner is more effective need satisfaction by the client.

Purposeful Behavior

Behavior is the mechanism used to fulfill human needs. Marcus Aurelius, perhaps the first control theorist, stated, "Nature has an aim in everything." We all act as sculptors molding the clay of our own behaviors in an attempt to shape the world around us to match the image of what we want. The age-old vaudeville joke is quite true—the chicken *does* cross the road to get to the other side. Likewise, the human behaviors of acting, thinking, feeling, and even "physiologic-ing" serve a purpose, have an aim, and are teleological. Their purpose is to fulfill human needs.

Behavior as Choice

One of the most empowering aspects of reality therapy is experienced by clients when the reality therapist repeatedly speaks of "choice." While the word is not used with an identical meaning for all behaviors, it is useful to discuss with clients the degree of choice that they perceive available to them. And though they cannot instantly choose to make radical changes in their feelings or thoughts, they can make small, incremental changes in their behavior. Over a period of time, these changes result in changes in feelings, thinking, and, at times, even physiological or health-related behaviors. Consequently, reality therapists totally reject the notion that human beings are victims of external stimuli or conditioning that allow little or no choice.

Emphasis on Present

Since choice is a "here and now" phenomenon, the therapist emphasizes current and recent life-style behaviors. It is true that our personal history is important and interesting, and our current life and our direction for the future are the sum of all that we have experienced. Still, as Glasser frequently points out in his lecturers, we do not need to find the nail that caused the tire of a car to lose its air. Past behavior should be discussed only as it impacts on present choices or future behavior.

Role of Therapist

Whether to lead the client (for example, by asking questions) or to follow (for example, letting the client speak without interruption) is an individual decision of the therapist and will vary across settings and situations. The use of reality therapy with a grieving person is quite different from its use with an habitual drunkard who denies being an alcoholic and blames others for his problems. In the former situation, the therapist would listen supportively and gently help the client take better charge of need-satisfying actions. In the latter situation, the therapist might be somewhat confrontive, feeding back specific behaviors and asking for dozens of self-evaluations.

But no matter what the setting, the practitioner creates an environment that is firm, friendly, and conducive to change. Sometimes this is accomplished quickly, but more often it is the result of *continued* effort. A system of therapeutic interventions, in which the client sees the therapist as a need-satisfying person, is built upon this foundation, and these basic principles comprise the essence of the practice of reality therapy (Wubbolding, 1991a).

Environment

The atmosphere in the counseling relationship is one of firmness and friendliness. The ideal relationship is a partnership in which both client and therapist struggle to find more effective behavioral patterns for the client. Therapists use many skills in this endeavor, some of which are common to other therapeutic methods, e.g., attending behaviors such as eye contact, verbal following, an ongoing awareness of nonverbal behaviors, valuing the client, creating a sense of hope for a better future, appropriate use of self-disclosure, using metaphors presented by the client, and working within the boundaries of professional ethics.

These skills, while not exhaustive, illustrate how the counseling relationship is enhanced in reality therapy. Setting the atmosphere is an ongoing process that continues throughout the relationship. Utilizing such procedures enhances the environment, and the distinction between environment and procedures is not absolute since each interacts with the other.

Process of Psychotherapy

Procedures

There are clearly identifiable interventions that constitute the essence of reality therapy. Glasser (1990a) said, "the art of counseling is to weave these components together in ways that lead clients to evaluate their lives and decide to move in more effective directions." Wubbolding (1991a, 1992) has formulated these components into the **WDEP system**, with each letter representing a cluster of skills and techniques for assisting clients to take better control of their own lives and thereby fulfill their needs in ways satisfying to them and to society.

W: Ask clients what they *want*. By skillful and persistent questioning, the therapist helps clients formulate, clarify, delineate, and prioritize the elements (desires) contained in their quality world of mental pictures. All human beings have specific wants related to each of their needs. Some wants are clear and non-negotiable, such as the desire for air.

Others are weak whims, such as selecting a specific pair of socks from a drawer. All are related to the five sources of human motivation, the needs for belonging, power, fun, freedom, and survival.

By means of questioning, therapists help clients describe what they want from themselves, from the world around them, from the therapy process, from parents, children, spouse, job, friends, associates, religion, and from any institution that impinges upon their lives. The clients are also asked to describe what they are getting and what they are not getting from each of these relationships.

The W refers not only to wants, but also perceptions. More specifically, the perceived locus of control (*the perceived source of control over one's behavior*) is discussed. The reality therapist, believing there is a high correlation between a perceived external locus of control and ineffective behaviors, helps clients ascertain how much control over their behavior they think they have now and have had in the past. Thus, one of the goals of therapy is to help clients perceive some inner control and realize that they can increase it by consciously getting the feeling that they are in charge and then changing their behavior.

D: Ask clients *what they are doing* and *their overall direction*. "Where are your current choices taking you?" "Are you headed in a direction where you want to be in a month, a year, two years from now?" "Will you describe the direction you are going without making a judgment about it?" These global questions are an attempt to help clients increase their awareness of what their choices look like "from a distance." By describing their overall destination, clients become ready to evaluate and change their thinking and behavior.

E: Ask clients to conduct a searching *self-evaluation*. Glasser (1990a, 1990b) has described self-evaluation as the core of reality therapy. Wubbolding (1990) sees it as the keystone in the arch of procedures. It holds the other elements together, and if it is removed, the arch crumbles.

The many forms of self-evaluation include the following:

1. *Evaluation of wants as realistic.* Clients are asked to evaluate the attainability of their wants.

2. *Evaluation of wants as genuinely beneficial.* All wants are related to needs and thus appear to be need-satisfying and genuinely helpful to the client. Still, many people have desires which, upon further examination, are found not to be truly advantageous to their welfare. Consequently, clients are asked to evaluate wants in terms of their short- and long-range impact on themselves, on others, and on their environment.

3. *Evaluation of behavioral direction.* Clients are asked to examine whether their overall life journey is headed toward a desirable destination.

4. *Evaluation of specific actions.* The most commonly used form of evaluation is a judgment made about the effectiveness of specific actions. The student is asked, "Did your procrastination help you study for the test?" On the other hand, a parent might be asked "What impact did lecturing your child about school three times a day have on him? Did it help? What did it do to you and to the family?" A husband and wife could be evaluated with inquiries such as, "If you don't talk to each other, or avoid each other as you said you did yesterday, will you get what you said you want—a happier marriage?"

5. *Evaluation of perception.* After helping clients describe their perceptions of the current situation, especially their perceived locus of control, the reality therapist asks clients to decide if the way they see the world is genuinely the best for them. "Is it true that you

really have no control, that you are completely incapable of making the situation better?" "By doing just enough to slide by, are you achieving the highest quality behavior you are capable of?" "If you haven't caused any of the trouble you've experienced, is there any way you could make the situation worse?" Most clients enjoy telling the therapist that they could indeed choose to worsen their plight. With such paradoxical questioning, they come to realize that if they can make life more miserable, they have more control than they at first thought, and can thus improve their condition.

6.   *Evaluation of the plan of action.* One of the hoped-for outcomes of therapy sessions is the formulation and execution of action plans. Clients are asked questions such as, "If you follow through on your plans, how will your life be better? How will you be living a more need-satisfying life? What specifically will you have, in terms of inner need satisfaction, that you don't have now?" Also, the plan is evaluated using the criteria of an effective plan, to be described later.

7.   *Professional self-evaluation.* Part of this procedure is the inner self-evaluation of the therapist including such questions as: "How am I facilitating my own professional growth? Do I work within the boundaries of my limitations? How committed am I to my profession and to this particular client? Am I aware of the special ethical applications of reality therapy? Is the quality of my service to the public the highest it can be? How can I improve it?"

The therapist's continual self-inspection is a cornerstone of the effective use of reality therapy. If therapists are to be skilled in helping others confront their own wants, actions, thoughts, feelings, and motivational level, it follows that therapists must be willing to engage in the same process.

The goals of reality therapy are behavioral changes, personal growth, improved and enhanced life-style, better decision making, remediation of personal deficits and, in the language of control theory, the more effective satisfaction of the human needs of belonging, power, fun, and freedom. Human beings will make changes after they decide that a change would be advantageous. Thus, reality therapists are relentless in their efforts to help clients conduct explicit self-evaluations of each component of their control systems.

P: Ask clients to make *Plans* to more effectively fulfill their needs. When clients make plans and follow through, they are taking charge of their lives by redirecting their energy. The therapist facilitates plan formulation by teaching clients that successful plans have several characteristics. The plan should have SAMIC characteristics—i.e., it should be Simple, Attainable, Measurable, Immediate, and Committed to.

The most effective plans are those originating with the client. When clients answer the question, "What is your plan?" with a detailed strategy for change, they are clearly taking better charge of their life and its direction. Still, many clients, especially in the initial stages of counseling, are unable to formulate such plans. Consequently, the reality therapist often assists actively in helping clients make plans.

The procedures used in the effective practice of reality therapy have wide application to virtually every type of client, and their use is limited only by the creativity of the practitioner. Because behavior is seen more as ineffective than pathological, the therapist spends a minimal amount of time discussing problems and a maximum amount of time exploring better ways to fulfill needs. Even a psychotic person exhibits some effective behavior. This behavior receives the attention and interest of the therapist. Every attempt is made to build on it and to expand it, while helping the client self-evaluate both less effective and more helpful behaviors. The same can be said of other applications. Drug abuse, depression, low self-esteem, acting-out behaviors, and the entire catalogue of out-of-control behaviors can be discussed to some degree. But the procedures that are most helpful and most efficiently used are those that encourage clients to search out a positive lifestyle characterized by a wide range of habitual choices that are satisfactory to clients, to their families, and to society at large.

A typical first session of therapy is summarized below. It is assumed that ethical issues have been discussed as well as the therapist's credentials, informed consent, confidentiality and its limitations, and the rights and responsibilities of both client and therapist. In this dialogue, only the components of reality therapy are presented and the professional issues common to any therapy (such as rapport-building dialogue) are omitted.

Louis, age 39, unemployed for eight months, has been looking unsuccessfully for a job at the middle managerial level. His wife is employed, and they have two children, a twelve-year-old boy and a ten-year-old girl. On the telephone, Louis previously stated that he was still angry at his previous employer and depressed about not finding work. Family problems include long-standing tension between him and his wife, Sally.

> T: Louis, we've talked about the professional details and you said you understand them. You also gave me a summary of your situation on the phone. What do you want to accomplish as a result of therapy?
>
> L: I think if I found a job everything would be fine.
>
> T: You indicated on the phone that the "no job" situation is a major factor. What else is bothering you?
>
> L: I'm still angry at the company for letting me go. It just wasn't justified.
>
> T: What else is going on with you?
>
> L: I've searched for a job and gone to the out-placement firm. But not finding a job is getting me down. This just adds to the other problems.
>
> T: You hinted at other problems on the phone. Do you want to describe them?
>
> L: My wife and I haven't gotten along for a long time, probably three or four years. And it's had an effect on the children. They seem to be nervous, have low grades, and bicker more than most kids.
>
> T: So you have a number of issues to deal with: job, feeling better, and a happier family life?
>
> L: You describe them a little differently than I did.
>
> T: Oh, how?
>
> L: I'm not sure.
>
> T: Like framing them as goals to reach rather than merely as problems to overcome?
>
> L: Yes, that's it.
>
> T: As you hear them described in that way, what thoughts go through your mind?
>
> L: I've never thought of these problems as goals. I've thought of them as standing in the way of reaching my goals.
>
> T: From working with people, I've found that if they can think of their problems in a different way, the problems become more manageable.
>
> L: It's hard to think that way.
>
> T: Yes, it is and it won't happen merely because we agree that it is a good idea. But let me ask you this: Has thinking about your situation the way you've thought about it been helping you or holding you back?
>
> L: It's definitely held me back. I've been shackled by these problems.
>
> T: I like how you said that…"shackled." Let me try to understand that more. "Shackled." What does that mean?
>
> L: I've been imprisoned by this mess.
>
> T: Wait, that's a new idea. "Shackled" and in "prison." Even if you broke the bonds you would still have a wall to climb. Is that accurate?

L: Right! I'm feeling trapped, cornered.

T: So, if you chose to see your situation differently, would it help or hurt?

L: It couldn't hurt.

T: And it might help?

L: Yes, But that's not the main problem. The problem is no job, wife and kids.

T: Yet, for an instant, when you thought about your problem differently, how did you feel? Better or worse?

L: I guess just a tiny bit better.

T: That's interesting. Would you like to take that microsecond of change and extend it to minutes, hours, days, weeks, and even a lifetime?

L: That's why I'm here.

T: And that's why I'm here…To help you make it happen.

L: Do you think it can happen?

T: I believe it can. And I'm saying that, not as a wishful thought, but as evidenced by the microsecond we spoke of. There is already some solid proof. What do you think this tells you about the "shackles" and your "prison?"

L: That I can get rid of the mess I'm in.

T: Exactly, I agree. Now I want to ask you about something else. How hard is it to simply say, "I'll change how I think about my situation?"

L: Well, I don't think it is very easy.

T: I agree. It will be necessary to change your thoughts. You can sit around and think about a job all day, and I doubt if a job will find you. Thinking about it is good and helpful, but not enough. You need more specific choices.

L: I'm an action sort of person. So, I'm not averse to doing something.

T: So, tell me what you chose to do yesterday about these issues, or as you used to call them your "problems," "shackles," and "prison cell," "swamp," "quagmire," and "solitary confinement?"

L: Did I say all that? The situation is not really that bad.

T: Oh, so there's more hope than it seemed at first?

L: Do you think there is hope?

T: No doubt about it in my mind. I suppose I was exaggerating when I used all those labels.

L: (Smiling wryly.) I got your point.

T: It's good you can smile, even for a moment. So we've had two bits of data showing that you can feel better!

L: You do look for even the slightest success!

T: Yes, any successful choice is a step in the right direction. What's the saying? "A journey of a thousand miles is begun with one step."

L: I've taken two steps.

T: Actually, you've taken more. You also came here. That is a major step. You took action.

L: Yeah!

T: Now, let's talk about what happened yesterday. Describe your actions, starting in the morning.

L: I got up about 10:00 a.m., looked through the paper, ate breakfast, watched TV, and loafed most of the day.

T: Could you be more specific by describing in detail exactly what you chose to do? What precisely did you do?

L: (Client elaborates on how he spent his time from 10:00 a.m. until bedtime at 10:00 p.m. For the most part, he was passive and did nothing towards accomplishing any of his goals.)

T: Now, I'm going to ask you what might, at first, seem to be a simple and obvious series of questions. Are you ready?

L: Yes.

T: Did the way you spent your day yesterday help you or hurt you?

L: It hurt. But in the afternoon I did do some things around the house that had to be done.

T: And so what impact did the entire day have on your overall direction?

L: My wife was glad I did a few things.
T: So, doing things *for* her helps?
L: Yes.
T: So, that part was slightly helpful regarding the relationship with Sally?
L: Yes.
T: Did the rest of the day take you where you wanted to go?
L: No, it was a waste.
T: And if you continue to go in this direction, where will you be in six months or a year?
L: Nowhere.
T: Will you feel better or worse?
L: Worse.
T: What effect will it have on your marriage and on how you feel?
L: Everything will be worse.
T: Now, Louis, what do you want to come away with today from this session?
L: A way to get out of this swamp.
T: I believe you can. But one more question. How hard do you want to work at turning your life around?
L: I would like to do it!
T: Is that a "maybe" or an "I will"?
L: "I will."
T: So what will you do differently tonight? What will you choose to do that is different from what you would have done if we had not had this conversation?
L: (Client formulates a realistically attainable plan that helps him to move in a positive direction.)

The above dialogue illustrates various components of reality therapy: asking what the client wants and eliciting the client's summary description of actions, thinking, and feelings with emphasis on the actions, the client's self-evaluation and a minor plan. However, the main goal of the first session is deeper. If the procedures are used properly, the client gains a sense of hope. By using the WDEP system the client learns, as a side effect, that his life can improve and that he need not be locked in a psychological prison permanently. This underlying message of hope is the primary goal of the first therapy session.

Mechanisms of Psychotherapy

Reality therapy can help clients change because it is based on how people live from moment to moment. From the viewpoint of reality therapy, humans have more control over their actions, thinking, and feelings than they have been led to believe through the popular culture and certainly more than is reflected in some of the more traditional theories of psychology. Some of the more important components of change include the following.

More Effective Control and Need Fulfillment

When clients become aware of their general needs, they realize that everything they do, think, feel, and even their physiological functioning is an attempt to fulfill these needs. When they identify their sources of motivation, i.e., what they want related to their needs, their behavioral system is activated. They feel liberated and empowered when they make more effective choices. They no longer are imprisoned or victimized by the past. Consequently, a major part of reality therapy is helping clients develop, extend, clarify, examine, and verbally describe their specific wants related to belonging, power, fun and freedom.

Appropriate Environment

As with many theories of psychotherapy, the use of reality therapy includes the establishment of a friendly and safe atmosphere. A prerequisite to change in therapy is trust in the therapist. Through acceptance by the therapist, clients come to believe that they can speak without fear and tell their story without being criticized or blamed. Feeling appreciated, they are more willing to look deeper at the effectiveness of their specific behaviors as well as their overall life direction.

Client Self-Evaluation

All change, great and small, is preceded by the client's judgment that life is not as it could be and that a better, more rewarding future is possible. Explicit choice of more effective behaviors leading to improvement in relationships, career, and leisure can be attained only after explicit evaluation of current wants, behaviors, and perceptions.

In summary, change is facilitated by the effective use of reality therapy to establish an environment characterized by trust. This safe atmosphere allows clients to incorporate the therapist into their quality worlds and to see him or her as reliable, helpful and competent. Following this, the skillful use of the WDEP system helps clients choose more need-satisfying behaviors.

❖ APPLICATIONS

Problems

Reality therapy has been applied as a psychotherapy instrument, a personal growth program, a tool for managing or coaching employees, a classroom strategy, and an educational reform philosophy/strategy. It has been applied successfully to severe mental conditions such as bipolar disorder, catatonia, and depression. It has been used in marriage therapy and with suicide ideation and threats, family issues such as caring for elderly parents, identity issues, and school achievement (N. Glasser, 1980). Other areas in which reality therapy has been used successfully include child abuse, adolescent rebellion, incest survival, bereavement, parental relations, and eating disorders (N. Glasser, 1989), self-help (Good, 1987), mental health (Garner, 1983), and recovery programs (Reuss, 1985).

Reality therapy was based on outcome research from its very beginning. Glasser (1965) described the treatment of long-term hospitalized psychotic patients in the Veterans Administration Neuropsychiatric Hospital in Los Angeles, including 210 patients whose "problems were categorized into paranoid schizophrenia, catatonic schizophrenia, hebephrenic schizophrenia...and undifferentiated schizophrenia" (p. 131). These patients hallucinated, were delusional, and spent most of their time passively sitting and waiting. The average stay in the hospital for the 210 men was fifteen years. Two years after the reality therapy program was initiated, 100 of the 210 had been released.

Other studies have shown an increase in self-esteem, a reduction in court referrals (Shea, 1973), and improvement in classroom behavior (Hart-Hester, Heuchert, & Whittier, 1989). Yarish (1985) noted significant differences in clients' perceived locus of control as a result of their treatment with reality therapy. Other studies have shown positive results with addicted clients (Honeyman, 1990). Parish, a leading researcher on the effects of reality therapy on undergraduate students and teachers, has repeatedly shown its beneficial effects (Parish, 1988, 1991). Still other studies have shown positive effects with graduate students (Peterson, Woodward, & Kissko, 1991), and in residential youth programs (Bratter, Bratter, Maxym, Radda, & Steiner, 1993).

For many decades, the governments of the world have been dealing with local, national, regional, and international crises. The conventional method for resolving internecine conflict has often involved a gladiatorial style of stimulus-response psychology. Like many public and private schools, nations often function on the supposition that fear is a source of motivation and can produce international harmony if it is sufficiently exploited.

On the contrary, as seen from the point of view of reality therapy, fear is not an effective motivator. When human needs are threatened, suspicious defensive thinking as well as aggressive actions occur. If diplomats were to learn control theory and use the principles of reality therapy, they would have a systematic structure for dealing with each other and might realize that both individuals and nations are motivated to fulfill their needs for belonging, power, fun, freedom, and survival. When these needs are unfulfilled or even attacked, nations often take hostile, destructive courses of action. But if a community of nations could work together to establish an appropriate environment, as a therapist attempts to do, it is more likely that its members will make responsible choices. It is clear that many national leaders operate on a blind stimulus-response philosophy, believing the only way to fulfill their needs is to deny others access to their respective needs fulfillment.

Evaluation

An increasing amount of research evidence validates the effectiveness of reality therapy. It is useful to examine several forms of evaluation. First, compelling evidence for the efficacy of reality therapy lies in the large numbers of professional people who seek credentialling in this field. During 1994, over 500 persons completed the 18-month program to become certified as reality therapists. Certification requires a major commitment of personal time and resources, and the decision to get training is most often made after using some of the ideas learned through self-study or short training sessions. These people come from many of the helping disciplines: teaching, social work, counseling, psychotherapy, corrections, management, and others.

Evidence from case studies illustrates the applicability and effectiveness of reality therapy. Tollefson (1980) described the case of Henry, who had spent 17 years in mental hospitals. A heavy drinker and member of a chemically dependent family, Henry was arrested and first hospitalized for antisocial, hostile, and threatening behavior shortly after high school. He continued to deteriorate, becoming aggressive and impulsive. Abusiveness and lack of cooperation continued to plague him and those around him. Tollefson stated, "He also became untidy" (p. 237), urinated into his own mouth, and became infected playing with his feces. He remained in this condition and even became worse, "hostile, suspicious, regressed, autistic, disoriented, untidy, and sloppy in appearance" (p. 238). When other patients began to harm him in minor ways he withdrew into a corner of the ward, "…coming out only to steal coffee or cigarettes" (p. 238). Anyone approaching his corner was greeted with bellowing, curses, and threats.

The therapist spent many months attempting to establish a relationship by speaking only briefly to Henry. As the therapist continued to ask simple questions, Henry gradually began to answer briefly. Over a period of time, Henry began leaving his corner for brief conversations with the therapist. As success began to be more evident, the therapist used reality therapy procedures more explicitly, asking questions about whether the way Henry had acted on the ward was helping him. At first, he would put his head between his legs and answer, "No." Eventually, as he was able to conduct more and more self-evaluations of both positive and negative behaviors, he would come into the therapist's office, sit in a chair and formulate plans. In spite of occasional regressions, progress continued. The therapist then insisted that Henry talk normally, rather than in a "crazy" way. Henry gradually began to interact with other patients and made off-ward trips that enhanced his self-perceptions (self-esteem, power, achievement). Eventually he was able to go to the commissary, the library, and the gym without incident. This was need-satisfying to him, and because of his strength and size (six feet five inches), gratifying to the other patients and staff. The therapist was finally transferred, but Tollefson said, "at the time I left the ward, Henry was still functioning well, using his plan and continuing to raise his self-esteem and take more responsibility for his own behavior" (p. 20). Later, Henry wrote a letter to his mother for the first time in ten years.

The case illustrates the use of reality therapy with an extremely disturbed person. It is clear, however, that the system is quite applicable to clients more widely encountered by practitioners.

Honeyman (1990) investigated the effects of reality therapy group treatment on addicts. The self-perceptions of clients were inventoried upon admission to treatment and at the second week, fourth week, and sixth week. Among the significant changes in the clients' perceptions of themselves were the following:

1. Increased self-esteem as a result of coming to sense their own power.
2. Heightened awareness that they were taking more responsibility for their behavior.
3. Deeper conviction that they were unable to control their drinking.
4. Learning to relate to others in altruistic ways rather than exploitive ways.
5. Greater awareness of addict-identity.
6. Realization of the importance of a "higher power."

Honeyman concluded, "As a measure of concurrent validity, the Minnesota Multiphasic Personality Inventory (MMPI) profiles of the 24 clients…[showed] a general reduction in [negative] symptom behavior indicating that clients are in more control of their lives at the time of discharge" (p. 58).

The above data constitute an attempt to get beyond the necessary but highly intellectualized findings of many scientific studies that claim to be based on "hard data." One of the most striking anecdotes regarding the effectiveness of the WDEP system of reality therapy procedures came to Wubbolding in a conversation with a woman who attended, for the second time, a presentation he had made. She stated that by asking her 19-year-old daughter and her husband to evaluate their arguing while traveling in a car to a vacation spot, she was able to have eight hours of pleasant driving. She remarked, "I want to learn more about any system that can do that for me."

Treatment

Reality therapy has been used in virtually every kind of setting, from private practice to prisons. In private practice it is usually short-term, but in institutions where residents are confined for years, it is used as long as clients are required to be in the program or until their rehabilitation is sufficient to allow them to be returned to society. Moreover, the system is applied with individuals, groups, and families.

Individual Therapy

Most clients who voluntarily enter reality therapy receive treatment on a one-to-one basis. As in any therapy, the therapist discusses professional details including the procedures used in treatment. Clients are then asked to tell their story. They often describe their upset feelings and how they are stressed about something that has happened to them, how society is unfair, how they want their external worlds to change. Some already have a sense of inner control and wish to change their own behavior. They admit they are depressed, angry, shamed, or guilty and wish to find better choices. Involuntary clients, on the other hand, are sometimes resistant, hostile, withdrawn, or passive.

The therapist attempts to make psychological contact using skills fundamental to most therapies: active listening, reflection, clarification, and many other processes useful in establishing a desirable therapeutic environment. Allowing clients to tell their story as they see it helps the therapist determine the perceived locus of control of the client, i.e., how much responsibility the client has taken for past behavior and how much responsibility he or she can realistically take for immediate future choices. Having determined the perceived locus of control by patiently listening to the client's perception of his or her story, the therapist helps the client set goals for the therapy by asking what he or she wants to have happen as a result of the relationship. More specifically, it is useful to ask what the person wants to gain from the individual session. The impact of this question can hardly be overestimated. The implicit message is that some change can be made immediately and that there is hope. For the upset, depressed person living in psychological darkness, even a glimmer of daylight is greeted with astonishment.

Focusing on the current behavior of the client, rather than on past history or the onslaughts from the client's external world, helps clients become aware of their actions—the component of their behavior over which they have most control. Depending on the style of the therapist, they are asked intermittently to make judgments on their wants. Are they realistic? Are they beneficial wants, or would having their wants met be harmful to them? Are their overall behavior and their specific actions helping them? They are then asked to make plans that fulfill the characteristics of effective planning. Simple planning sheets are frequently used. In private practice, optimal termination occurs through a joint decision by therapist and client based on whether the client has been able to adopt more effective need-fulfilling behaviors in his or her life.

Group Therapy

Reality therapy is especially applicable to groups. After ice-breaking activities during which people psychologically connect with the therapist and with each other, genuine reality therapy begins.

Wubbolding (1991b) has shown how reality therapy is integrated into the stages of groups (Corey, 1994). At every stage of group development, the needs of the clients should be addressed, though it is not possible for all needs consistently to be met to the same degree. The need for belonging is met in the initial stage in that everyone feels included in the group. The therapist asks what people want from the group. Total behavior is also explored: life direction, specific actions, ineffective and effective self-talk, feelings, and even physiological behaviors. In the next transitional stage of group development, the power need is addressed when anxiety, conflict, and resistance surface. In the third stage, the working phase of group development, belonging is addressed when the group members come to believe that others in the group can be of some help to them. Power or achievement is evident when participants begin to want to change. The leader helps them decide how hard they want to work at changing their behavior. In the consolidation and termination stage, further planning helps to address fun and belonging needs. Discussion of progress touches on the need for freedom or autonomy. Final closure of the group can come about in many ways, depending on the decisions of the group members.

Marriage and Family Therapy

Reality therapy, based on control theory which explains how the human brain functions, is a preeminent tool for marriage and family therapy. It can also be integrated into systems theory and adds a practical structure and delivery system.

Wubbolding (1988) has described how reality therapy is applied to family therapy. The goals of reality-therapy-based family therapy include the following:

1. *Gain at least a modicum of need fulfillment.* As in all applications, the therapist helps family members fulfill their psychological needs without infringing on the rights of other family members.

2. *Change levels of perception.* Family members are helped to become less judgmental toward each other.

3. *Use "quality time."* Time spent together in a non-critical way, doing activities that are enjoyable, builds a storehouse of positive perceptions that serve as a basis for the healthy interactions required for future problem solving and for negotiating decisions.

4. *Change behavior.* The most visible goal is to help family members change how they act toward each other, both in the therapy session and in the ongoing life of the family.

Because human beings are control systems, i.e., they function as creatures who choose behaviors to satisfy their needs, it is important that the use of reality therapy in family counseling ensures that each member and the family as a unit examine what is desirable, how they are attempting to function as a family, and the effectiveness of their individual total behaviors and the family's total behavior. Only when these preliminary components are present can action planning be successful.

❖ CASE EXAMPLE

Fay, 28, single, has completed two years of college. She works as a buyer for a large department store. She has a history of transitory relationships with men who become interested in her to the point of proposing marriage. She finds them attractive, but when "they get too close" she turns away from them. Although she wants to get married, her friends tell her she is too demanding as well as fearful of intimacy. Approximately one year ago, she was attacked on a street while on an out-of-town business trip. Though not raped, she was jostled, knocked to the ground, her purse taken, and her jewelry seized. After the attack, she experienced an increased fear of journeying out at night even to shopping malls and turned down numerous dates from attractive and eligible men. Her parents, who lived in another city, and her friends urged her to seek psychological therapy.

The therapist reviewed the professional details regarding informed consent, rights and responsibilities of both client and therapist, nature and limitations of confidentiality, possible benefits of therapy, credentials, and fees. A summary of reality therapy was presented, and both client and therapist signed two written statements indicating that the client understood the issues. Fay received one copy, and another was put in her file.

T: Fay, now that we've discussed the professional details, including the fact that I'll be asking you a lot of questions, I'd like to begin by asking you a very important one. Is there anything that you don't want me to ask you about? Anything I should stay away from?

F: No, I don't think so. I'm a little nervous, but I'll let you know if you ask about such topics.

T: OK. Tell me what your parents and friends said when they urged you to come here.

F: They said that because of the mugging a year ago, I am acting strange, keeping to myself, not wanting to be around them. Kind of withdrawing.

T: How do you see it?

F: They're right. What they say is true, but they don't know the whole story. I'm much more afraid than I let on to them. When I have to be out at night, I'm afraid of every shadow. They also don't know something that haunts me even now after about 18 years.

T: Do you want to tell me?

F: I've been wanting to get rid of this burden for a long time. But it's hard to say it out loud.

T: Do you want to get it out suddenly or gradually?

F: I might as well say it right now. When I was ten years old, I was abused by a friend of a neighbor. He was visiting his friend and I went into the neighbor's house which I did regularly, but this time he was there alone and he touched me sexually, rubbing my genital area.

T: Did he rape you?

F: No, it wasn't that bad, but the thoughts have remained with me all these years.

T: In other words, this is not a past event, it is still very present in your mind and you even have some of the same creepy feelings about it?

F: Yes. I still feel guilty and ashamed.

T: I'm not sure you will believe this just yet, but I'd like to assure you, that absolutely, positively, without doubt you were not to blame.

F: I know that, but I'm not yet convinced as much as I need to be. I've read a lot about this problem and it could be that I'm having trouble with men because of it.

T: Is that what you tell yourself? "I can't relate to men because of this past experience."

F: Yes. When I drop some guy that thought goes through my mind.

T: Does it help you to indulge that kind of thinking?

F: What do you mean?

T: Does it really help you to tell yourself that you can't relate to men as you want to because of events that are past and therefore beyond your control?

F: No, but I can't help it.

T: Until today you couldn't. But I would like to help you rid yourself of this pain — if you want to work on it.

F: I want so much to get rid of this pain. It's like carrying around a weight on my shoulders.

T: I like how you describe it. Maybe you could leave part of the weight here.

F: I'd like to leave it all here today!

T: How realistic is it to drop this weight all at once?

F: Well, I guess not very realistic.

T: How do you feel at this very moment now that you've talked about it?

F: Oh, I feel relieved that I said it out loud.

T: So, already you've tasted relief, dropped part of the weight. Maybe you can work hard so as to drop the rest of it. After all, you have taken two major steps to turn your life around.

F: I have? What are they?

T: You came here. That's a major step. How long have you been thinking about getting help?

F: Years. Maybe three or four.

T: So you took the big step. Congratulations! You also talked about this. And you've disclosed the details to me so quickly. That's unusual.

F: Well, it's on my mind. And I learned that many people have had even worse experiences.

T: I just thought of a third strength.

F: What is that?

T: You seem to be willing to work at feeling better.

F: Yes, I am, indeed.

T: OK. We'll come back to that point. But I'd like to ask you some other questions. Besides leaving behind some or all of the weight on your back, what else do you want to accomplish through therapy?

F: I'm afraid to go out at night and I'm having problems with relationships.

T: Are these the goals you would like to work on? Feeling comfortable wherever you are and more satisfying relationships with men?

F: Yes, they are.

T: Can you state what you want from this counseling in positive terms rather than in terms only of what you want to overcome?

F: I think you just did. But I'll try to do it myself. I want to feel free of a weighty burden, go out at night, and get married.

T: Get married! You've gone beyond what I expected as a goal. That's terrific!

F: I might as well aim high.

T: OK, we have three goals and you've stated that you actually felt better about the abuse, at least for a few minutes. You know, the thought just occurred to me that when you *did* something about the situation, you had some slight relief. That's so interesting.

F: Why does that seem so intriguing to you?

T: Because there's a lesson in there.

F: I think I know it. When I take action, things get better. (Smiling broadly).

T: Right.

F: I read the summary of reality therapy.

T: (Smiling). You're absolutely right. Action leads to change in how you think, what you think, how you feel and even your physiology. By the way do you have any chronic aches and pains?

F: No, but I have nights when I don't sleep very much.

T: That doesn't surprise me in the least. All these things go together. And when you change what you're doing, the thoughts will change, your feelings will be better, and I believe you'll sleep more soundly. Now how do you want to proceed? There are two roads. One involves spending a lot of time rehashing the past. Or we could move to the part of your life over which you have control.

F: Well, I guess I better emphasize what's going on now.

T: That sounds good to me. If you feel the need, you can talk about past events any time. Talking can always provide momentary relief.

F: That's good to know.

T: Now before we end, I have one more question. How hard do you want to work at turning things around?

F: I'd sure like to turn things around.

T: Does that mean you'll give it a try or will you really do it?

F: I'll do my best. Do you think there's hope?

T: Absolutely…on one condition…

F: What is that?

T: That you are willing to work at it.

F: I said I would.

T: And you said you would do your best. But let me ask you this. If you were on a plane and the pilot announced over the loudspeaker, "I'll do my best to land the plane," would you feel confident?

F: I see what you mean. I need to say that I'll give it my all.

T: I think you are truly motivated to make some changes.

In this initial session, the therapist helped the client decide what she wanted from therapy. He helped her reframe the problems as positive wants, helped her to briefly examine her current thinking, and helped her self-evaluate its effectiveness. The level of commitment was also identified. Throughout the dialogue, he put responsibility on her to decide direction and topics for discussion while suggesting that he could best help her if she was willing to talk about behaviors that are controllable. Finally, he helped her determine her level of commitment for working at the problem. At the end, he intentionally avoided pushing for a plan, as it seemed necessary to spend more time on the D (doing) and E (evaluation), rather than W (wants) and P (planning) of the WDEP system.

Problem.   Fay's problem is not what appears obvious at first glance. Although the problem is indeed connected to the traumatic events of her past, the underlying problem is the unmet need for belonging and a gradual lessening of her ability to fulfill the power need. She is not enjoying her life and feels trapped. Even her survival need is frustrated, as evidenced by her lack of sleep and perhaps by other symptoms not yet brought to the surface. To help her fulfill her needs, it is necessary to define precisely her wants and the degree of energy she expects to exert to satisfy her wants. She is directing her life toward ineffective behaviors when she avoids desirable relations with men and when she chooses "fearing" behaviors such as staying indoors.

Treatment.   The WDEP system, based on establishing a friendly, empathic, and hopeful environment, was used to help Fay take more control of her life. The therapist helped her identify attainable wants: letting go of pain and achieving closer relationships, marriage, and freedom from fear.

In later sessions Fay examined her specific behaviors relative to dating relationships and going out of her home in the evening and at other times. She was continually asked to make self-evaluations as to the effectiveness of specific actions. Even though she was already uncomfortable and pained by her present choices, she was asked, "Did it help?" "Did it hurt?" "What was the relationship between what you did and your want for a close relationship with a man?"

Her enthusiastic commitment to change remained, but at times, she showed resistance to success. Paradoxical interventions were used that resulted in lowering her resistance. Resistance is always an attempt to control.

The following exchange took place one month later:

T: Fay, I'd like to ask you about something you mentioned last week. You said that you could not follow through on the plan about looking men in the eye for a few seconds when you passed them on the street or at work when you walked through the store. You said that it was not something you felt comfortable doing.

F: It was not easy. I didn't really want to do it.

T: What impact will not taking these steps have on you?

F: I know, I know. It won't help. But it's more uncomfortable than I thought.

T: Well, maybe we rushed into that plan too soon. It seems you're not ready for that. But it is still a step forward because we both know that we need to work on other things first. Could I make another suggestion?

F: Yes, I'll try anything!

T: This week, will you make a definite effort to avoid men's eyes, even men you feel comfortable around such as the friends who encouraged you to come here, or your colleagues at work? (This is an example of paradoxical intention.)

F: Yes, I could do that. It sounds stupid, but fairly easy.

T: I'd like to ask you what will seem like a strange question. What are other choices you could make to worsen your situation? How could you really make your life miserable?

F: That's a weird question.

T: Yes, I have a lot of them. Could you answer it, just for fun?

F: Well, I could quit my job. I could refuse to date any guy. I could sit around my condo even when I feel like going out.

T: You could turn your back when you talk to men, especially your boss at work or a person you date who you like.

F: Yes, that would really mess me up! (laughs heartily).

T: It's good you can laugh.

F: Well, it is a bit silly not to look at strangers.

T: But it's the best you can do now and what's the difference if you look away?

F: It's just a quirk.

T: What's wrong with quirks? Could you indulge your quirk for a week or so?

F: It might be hard to do that for a week.

T: Well, give it your best shot.

F: OK, no eye contact with strangers.

The therapist prescribed paradoxical situations, and Fay agreed even though she said such tasks were difficult. She rebelled against the therapist because by her subsequent real-world behaviors she looked at strangers and reported that to force herself to avoid their eyes took too much effort and thought. In reality, by rebelling against the therapist, she was doing exactly what he wanted her to do—looking at strangers. She could then use this behavior to show how much control she had in that she had rebelled against the authority of the therapist, showing her strength and actually doing what she had feared doing—looking a stranger in the eye.

Resolution.   Fay gained better control of her life and was seen by the therapist for about six months. More effective need satisfaction was evident in her own self-evaluation. She said that she felt better and was able to have long periods when she was not bothered by thinking about the abusive incident. When she experienced mild guilt and shame, she simply told herself that this was part of her life experience and that it would be less of a weight in the future. This self-acceptance lessened the intensity of the flashback.

Looking at men soon became no problem, and she was able to sustain satisfying social relationships with men. She was dating several men when therapy terminated, but she was not interested in marrying any of them. Though she still felt appropriate fear at times when away from home, she took necessary precautions. Excessive fears overtook her occasionally, but did not stop her from performing the tasks necessary to function as an independent professional woman.

Follow-up.   A phone call a year later revealed that she had continued to make progress and had become seriously interested in a man. She was fearful, but was considering marrying him and so was delaying a decision. She noted that this new experience indicated immense progress. She stated that occasionally she "gave in to the fear" of going out, but that she was functioning as a "normal human being." Her parents were quite pleased that she was not permanently scarred by the street attack. She stated that she had summoned the courage to tell them about the abuse she had experienced as a child and her parents were furious. Telling them was a good idea, she said, as she thought it unwise to keep such a secret from them any longer.

❖ SUMMARY

Reality therapy is a comprehensive system of treatment that can be used by any person who deals with others: psychotherapists, counselors, teachers, corrections officers, youth workers, group leaders, parents, business managers and supervisors, administrators, and many others. It is comprehensive because it is based on the way all human beings relate to each other and to the world around them in a free and conscious way. Because of its down-to-earth nature, it is taught to persons whose professional allegiance is to help at any level.

Because it is based on universal human needs, it is a multicultural approach that allows for the indirectness of some cultures as well as the direct, assertive behavior of North Americans. It can be adjusted to work with clients from indirect cultures and does not require that "other" cultures adjust to it.

Its uncomplicated language makes reality therapy appear to be simpler than it is. To incorporate the system into professional behavior requires time, practice, and effort. In its thirty years of use, reality therapy has undergone major changes. Not only has it been applied to virtually every kind of interaction, but it has acquired a theoretical base and will probably undergo changes in the future. The expression of the procedures as a WDEP system puts flesh and blood on the theory and renders it accessible to people at nearly every level of society.

Therapies that survive in the future will need to be based on solid theory as well as proven effectiveness. Long-term psychotherapy systems have lost much of their popularity and with the growth of managed care are becoming accessible only to the rich. Those systems that will flourish will provide measurable outcomes in relatively few sessions and be applicable to people from all socioeconomic levels of society. These systems must be taught and used by persons other than psychotherapists: teachers, group workers, drop-in center employees, and so on. Reality therapy offers a results-centered approach that can be learned by people who deliver mental health services in virtually any setting.

❖ ANNOTATED BIBLIOGRAPHY

Glasser, N. (Ed.). (1989). *Control theory in the practice of reality therapy.* New York: HarperCollins.

Control theory is integrated with reality therapy in this book of cases. Applications are made to child abuse, grieving, prison, aging, depression, and eating disorders. This book is a useful guide for learning how the theory is used with a variety of issues.

Glasser, W. (1965). *Reality therapy.* New York: HarperCollins.

This book marked the beginning of reality therapy. It explains the basic principles of reality therapy and its early development in the language used at that time. While there have been many extensions of theory and practice, the book remains a classic. It describes how reality therapy was used in a mental hospital and a correctional setting, detailing the astonishing results.

Glasser, W. (1985). *Control theory.* New York: HarperCollins.

Adapting the work of William Powers (1973) to the clinical setting, Glasser explains how the human brain functions as a control system attempting to regulate its own behavior so as to mold the world around it, its environment, in order to gain a desired perception. He describes how human behavior is "total" and states that in thera-py feelings, actions, and thinking should be treated as a unit. This book is required reading for anyone seeking to understand the psychological basis for the practice of reality therapy.

Glasser, W. (1990). *The quality school.* New York: HarperCollins.

W. Edwards Deming is credited with the renewal of Japanese industry since World War II. His fourteen points on quality are now known worldwide and practiced by excellent companies in many countries. Glasser has applied the concept of quality to education by describing the remedy for an educational system that fails to educate many of its students. In this book, he describes how quality educational experiences can be created by combining the principles of Deming with control theory and reality therapy.

Wubbolding, R. E. (1988). *Using reality therapy.* New York: HarperCollins.

Practicality and usefulness are the themes of this book. The author integrates theory with practice by describing specific applications of reality therapy. The Cycle of Therapy is a design for teaching and using reality therapy that can be applied in virtually any setting. Wubbolding describes specifically how the use of paradox is integrated into reality therapy and presents ethical guidelines for its use. The book is intended as a supplemental text for courses in theories of counseling and for anyone wishing to learn specifically how to get started using reality therapy.

Wubbolding, R. E. (1991). *Understanding reality therapy*. New York: HarperCollins.

One hundred twenty metaphors, anecdotes, analogies, and similes are presented as concrete ways to understand control theory and reality therapy. Rather than starting with abstract principles, the author begins with literary examples, scenarios, and stories from everyday life to illustrate central ideas of reality therapy. This book makes the theory of reality therapy come alive.

❖ CASE READINGS

Good, E. P. (1980). Be my friend. In N. Glasser (Ed.), *What are you doing* [pp. 18–33]. New York: HarperCollins.

Rebecca, a young woman, lived with her mother. She had seen other therapists and was quite unhappy with her progress. She felt confused about her future, had no friends, and did not know how to support herself. She also felt uncomfortable about the effects of her prescription drugs. Because of her lack of skills necessary to function as an independent adult, the therapist discussed the "reality" issues and taught her socialization skills such as how to shop for clothes and how to look for friends. A year later she was on the dean's list at college and reported success in all her activities.

Tollefson, W. B. (1980). Coming out of a corner. In N. Glasser (Ed.), *What are you doing?* New York: HarperCollins. [Reprinted in D. Wedding & R. J. Corsini (Eds.) (1995). *Case studies in psychotherapy*. Itasca: F. E. Peacock.]

This case demonstrates the use of reality therapy to treat a severely regressed psychotic patient on a back ward of a mental hospital.

Wubbolding, R. (1980). Teenage loneliness. In N. Glasser (Ed.), *What are you doing?* [pp. 120–129]. New York: HarperCollins.

A suicidal young man describes how he isolated himself by spending his weekends depressed and sitting alone in his bedroom for the entire weekend. The therapist helped him to define his wants, examine his actions, and make short-range plans for keeping his drapes open and eventually asking women for dates. He is thus gradually led to choose specific, effective actions, thereby bringing about permanent changes in his ability to fulfill his needs.

❖ REFERENCES

Bratter, B., Bratter, T., Maxym, C., Radda, H., & Steiner, K. (1993). The John Dewey Academy: A residential quality school for self-destructive adolescents who have superior intellectual and intuitive potential. *Journal of Reality Therapy, 9*, 42–53.

Cockrum, J. R. (1989). Reality therapy: Interviews with Dr. William Glasser. *Psychology, 26*, 1, 13–16.

Corey, G. (1994). *Theory and practice of group counseling*. Pacific Grove, CA: Brooks/Cole.

Deming, W. F. (1982). *Out of the crisis*. Cambridge, MA: MIT.

Evans, D. B. (1982). What are you doing? An interview with William Glasser. *Personnel & Guidance Journal, 60*, 460–65.

Garner, A. (1983). Living with mental patients. *Journal of Reality Therapy, 2*, 27–31.

Glasser, N. (Ed.). (1980). *What are you doing?* New York, NY: HarperCollins.

Glasser, N. (Ed.). (1989) *Control theory in the practice of reality therapy*. New York, NY: HarperCollins.

Glasser, W. (1965). *Reality therapy*. New York, NY: HarperCollins.

Glasser, W. (1968). *Schools without failure*. New York, NY: HarperCollins.

Glasser, W. (1972). *Identity society*. New York, NY: HarperCollins.

Glasser, W. (1976). *Positive addiction*. New York, NY: HarperCollins.

Glasser, W. (1981). *Stations of the mind*. New York, NY: HarperCollins.

Glasser, W. (1985). *Control theory*. New York, NY: HarperCollins.

Glasser, W. (1990a). A diagram of the brain as a control system (chart). Los Angeles, CA: Institute for Reality Therapy.

Glasser, W. (1990b). *The quality school*. New York, NY: HarperCollins.

Good, E. P. (1987). *In pursuit of happiness*. Chapel Hill, NC: New View Publications.

Hart-Hester, S., Heuchert, C., & Whittier, K. (1989). The effects of teaching reality therapy techniques to elementary students to help change behaviors. *Journal of Reality Therapy, 8*, 13–18.

Honeyman, A. (1990). Perceptual changes in addicts as a consequence of reality therapy based on group treatment. *Journal of Reality Therapy, 9*, 53–59.

Mosak, H. H. (1994). Adlerian psychology. In R. J. Corsini & D. Wedding, *Current psychotherapies.* Itasca, IL: F. E. Peacock.

O'Donnell, D. J. (1987). History of the growth of the Institute for Reality Therapy. *Journal of Reality Therapy, 8*, 2–8.

Parish, T. (1988). Helping teachers take more effective control. *Journal of Reality Therapy, 8*, 41–43.

Parish, T. (1991). Helping students take control via an interactive voice communications system. *Journal of Reality Therapy, 11*, 38–40.

Peterson, A., Woodward, G., & Kissko, R. (1991). A comparison of basic week students and introduction to counseling graduate students on four basic need factors. *Journal of Reality Therapy, 9*, 31–37.

Powers, W. (1973). *Behavior: The control of perception.* New York, NY: Aldine Press.

Reuss, N. (1985). Alternatives to cocaining. *Journal of Reality Therapy, 4*, 8–11.

Shea, G. (1973). The effects of reality-therapy-oriented group counseling with delinquent, behavior-disordered students. *Dissertation Abstracts International, 34*, 4889–4890.

Tollefson, W. (1980). Coming out of the corner. In *What are you doing?* New York, NY: HarperCollins.

Wubbolding, R. (1988). *Using reality therapy.* New York, NY: HarperCollins.

Wubbolding, R. (1990). Evaluation: The cornerstone in the practice of reality therapy. *Omar Psychology Practitioner Series, 2*, 6–27.

Wubbolding, R. (1991a). *Understanding reality therapy.* New York, NY: HarperCollins.

Wubbolding, R. (1991b). *Using reality therapy in group counseling* (videotape). Cincinnati, OH: Center for Reality Therapy.

Wubbolding, R. (1992). *Reality therapy training manual.* Cincinnati, OH: Center for Reality Therapy.

Yarish, P. (1985). Reality therapy and locus of control of juvenile offenders. *Journal of Reality Therapy, 6*, 3–10.

Arnold A. Lazarus

11 Multimodal Therapy

Arnold A. Lazarus

❖ OVERVIEW

Multimodal therapy is a systematic and comprehensive psychotherapeutic approach developed by Arnold Lazarus, a clinical psychologist. While respecting the assumption that clinical practice should adhere firmly to the principles, procedures, and findings of psychology as an experimental science, the multimodal orientation transcends the behavioral tradition by adding unique assessment procedures and by dealing in great depth and detail with sensory, imagery, cognitive, and interpersonal factors and their interactive effects. A basic premise is that patients are usually troubled by a multitude of specific problems that should be dealt with by a similar multitude of specific treatments. A multimodal assessment examines each area of a person's BASIC I.D.:

B = Behavior

A = Affect

S = Sensation

I = Imagery

C = Cognition

I = Interpersonal relationships

D = Drugs/Biology

It provides an operational way of answering the questions, What works? For whom? Under which conditions?

Basic Concepts

Multimodal therapy is personalized and individualistic. Scrutiny for individual exceptions to general rules and principles characterizes the search for appropriate interventions for each person. Clinical effectiveness is predicated on the therapist's flexibility, versatility, and technical eclecticism. The technical eclectic uses procedures drawn from different sources without necessarily subscribing to the theories or disciplines that spawned them (Lazarus, 1992). The upshot is a consistent, systematic, and testable set of beliefs and assumptions about human beings and their problems, and an armamentarium of effective therapeutic strategies for remedying their afflictions.

While remaining technically eclectic, multimodal therapy rests primarily on the theoretical base of *social learning theory* (Bandura, 1969, 1977, 1986) while also drawing from *general system theory* (Bertalanffy, 1974; Buckley, 1967) and *group and communications theory* (Watzlawick, Weakland & Fisch, 1974). These diverse theories blend harmoniously into a congruent framework.

Most of our experiences comprise moving, feeling, sensing, imagining, thinking, and relating to one another. In the final analysis, we are biochemical-neurophysiological entities. Human life and conduct are products of ongoing *b*ehaviors, *a*ffective processes, *s*ensations, *i*mages, *c*ognitions, *i*nterpersonal relationships, and *b*iological functions. BASIC I.B. is derived from the first letters of each of these modalities, but by referring to the biological modality as "Drugs/Biology" (because one of the most common biological interventions is the use of psychotropic medication), we have the acronym BASIC I.D. It is crucial to remember that D stands not only for drugs, medication, or pharmacological intervention, but also includes nutrition, hygiene, exercise, and all basic physiological and pathological inputs.

The BASIC I.D. is presumed to comprise human temperament and personality, and it is assumed that everything from anger, disappointment, disgust, greed, fear, grief, awe, contempt, and boredom to love, hope, faith, ecstasy, optimism, and joy can be explained by examining components and interactions within a person's BASIC I.D. It is also essential to recognize and include factors that fall outside the BASIC I.D., such as sociocultural, political, and other macro-environmental events. While external realities are not part of temperament and personality, "psychopathology and society are inextricably bound together" (Nathan & Harris, 1980, p. xvii). There are obviously crucial differences in adaptive interpersonal styles between people raised and living in New York and New Guinea, but regardless of an individual's background, detailed descriptions of salient behaviors, affective responses, sensory reactions, images, cognitions, interpersonal dealings, and biological propensities will provide the principal ingredients of his or her psychological makeup. To appreciate further the interactions among the various modalities—for example, how certain behaviors influence and are influenced by affects, sensations, images, cognitions, and significant relationships—is to know a great deal about individuals and their social networks.

While multimodal theory (MMT) draws heavily from several systems (especially behavior therapy, rational-emotive therapy, and cognitive therapy), six distinctive features set MMT apart from all other approaches:

1. The specific and comprehensive attention given to the entire BASIC I.D.
2. The use of *second-order* BASIC I.D. assessments
3. The use of *modality profiles*
4. The use of *structural profiles*

5. Deliberate *bridging* procedures
6. *Tracking* the modality firing order

Each of these features will be discussed in this chapter.

The term *bespoke therapy*, which has been used to describe the multimodal orientation (see Zilbergeld, 1982), aptly conveys the custom-made, personalistic emphasis. The form, style, and cadence of therapy are fitted, whenever possible, to each client's perceived requirements. The basic question is, *Who or what is best for this particular individual?* Some clients respond best to therapists who are warm and empathic; others do better with more distant and formal relationships. Quiet, passive, reflective listeners are especially suited to some clients; others want therapists who are active, directive, and bluntly outspoken. The same client may respond favorably to various therapeutic styles at different times. How is the therapist to gauge whether pensive reflection is more likely to succeed than direct disputation? The answer can be found largely by noting the client's implicit and explicit expectations and by observing the impact of applying various tactics (cf., Howard, Nance & Myers, 1987). Even effective therapists will make mistakes in gauging clients' expectations and in tactics applied, but capable therapists, on noticing these errors, will usually make adjustments to change the course of therapy. The choice of a particular therapeutic style and the selection of techniques are not capricious affairs. After drawing up a detailed modality profile (a chart depicting excesses and deficits across the client's BASIC I.D.), the multimodal therapist resorts to two main procedures—bridging and tracking.

Bridging

Bridging refers to a procedure in which the therapist deliberately tunes into the client's preferred modality before branching off into other dimensions that seem likely to be more productive. For example, instead of challenging a client or even pointing out that he or she tends to eschew the expression of feelings by erecting intellectual barriers, we find it better first to enter into the client's domain and then gently lead him or her into other (potentially more meaningful) channels. Here is an example:

> *Client:* I think that Molly resorts to what I call a three-down maneuver when we disagree about virtually anything. In other words, I am not placed in a one-down position, but I am seen as the lowest man on the totem pole.
> *Therapist:* How does that make you feel?
> *Client:* I realize why she does it. It is exactly what her mother does to her father, and Molly is very much like her mother in many ways.
> *Therapist:* [Going along with client's cognitive leanings.] So Molly has imitated her mother and uses her tactics. What are some of the other things she does that remind you of her mother?
> *Client:* Well, there are a couple of things that come to mind immediately. First...[Client intellectualizes about the alleged similarities between Molly and her mother.]
> *Therapist:* [Bridging] When you think about all these ties that Molly has to her mother and the way she puts you down, are you aware of any feelings or sensations in your body?
> *Client:* Right now I've got a knot in my stomach.
> *Therapist:* Can you concentrate fully on that stomach tension? Can you focus on that knot?
> *Client:* It feels like a vise is gripping it.
> *Therapist:* Do you feel tension anywhere else in your body?
> *Client:* My jaws feel tight.
> *Therapist:* Will you concentrate on the tension in your jaws and your stomach and tell me what feelings or mental pictures come to mind?
> *Client:* I feel sad. I think it gets down to the fact that I am afraid that my relationship with Molly will be a carbon copy of her parents' marriage.
> *Therapist:* Let's hear more about your fears and your feelings of sadness.

The therapist wanted to move into affective areas right from the start but instead went along with the client's apparent desire to dwell on cognitive components. Shortly thereafter, when the therapist again inquired about affective and sensory responses, the client was willing to reveal his sensations and then to verbalize his feelings. Failure to tune into the client's presenting modality often leads to feelings of alienation—the client feels misunderstood or may conclude that the therapist does not speak his or her language. Thus, multimodal therapists *start where the client is* and then bridge into more productive areas of discourse.

Tracking

Tracking refers to a careful examination of the "firing order" of the different modalities. For example, some clients tend to generate negative emotions by dwelling first on sensations (S) (e.g., a slight dizziness accompanied by mild heart palpitations), to which they attach negative cognitions (C) (e.g., ideas of illness and death), immediately followed by aversive images (I) (e.g., pictures of hospitals and catastrophic disease), culminating in maladaptive behavior (B) (e.g., unnecessary avoidance or extreme withdrawal). Other people tend to experience a different firing order. Rather than a sensory-cognitive-imagery-behavioral sequence as just outlined, they may display a CISB pattern (cognitive-imagery-sensory-behavior), an I.BSCA order (interpersonal-behavior-sensory-cognitive-affective), or any other combination. An example of an I.BSCA firing order can be seen at a social gathering where a man insults one of his friends (I.) and walks out of the room (B). He starts feeling hot and shaky and develops a severe tension headache (S). He then regrets having acted aggressively and impulsively, but starts rationalizing his conduct (C). Nonetheless, he concludes that he is a stupid and unbalanced person. Soon he begins to feel depressed (A).

In studying panic disorders, Margraf, Ehlers, and Roth (1986) identified positive feedback loops in which unpleasant body sensations are followed by "catastrophizing cognitions," resulting in full-blown panic attacks. Clark (1986) also discusses trigger stimuli (excitement, anger), followed by bodily sensations (dizziness, breathlessness), followed by cognitive appraisals, culminating in a panic attack.

Firing orders are not fixed tendencies. A person may generate negative affect through a particular sequence on some occasions and follow a different pattern at other times. Different emotions may follow distinct firing orders. Thus, a client, when anxious, found that a CISB sequence was operative, but when depressed, an IBLS order was established. Most people, however, report a reasonably stable proclivity toward a particular firing order much of the time. By tracking the precise sequence of events that results in the affective disturbance, the therapist enables the client to gain insight into the antecedent events and also enables him or her to intercede appropriately. The therapist may elect to track the I.BSCA order more closely. Thus, questions might be asked to determine what thoughts or feelings had led the client to insult his friend in the first place, thereby uncovering additional antecedent factors. Such precise information permits intervention at any of several entry points in the sequence.

Tracking also enables one to select the most appropriate intervention techniques. An agoraphobic woman complained of panic and anxiety. Medication helped to control her outbreaks of panic, but when she exposed herself to feared situations (such as shopping in a supermarket), she nevertheless experienced considerable anxiety. When asked to take particular note of how these anxious feelings arose, she observed a cognitive-imagery-sensory-affective sequence (CISA). First, she tended to *think* about the probability of becoming anxious, and this, in turn, led to other negative self-statements such as, "What if I pass out?" "What if I start feeling weak and dizzy?" Soon, she formed mental *images* of these unpleasant events—in her mind's eye she would see herself hyperventilating and fainting. As these thoughts and images grew stronger, she would notice a *sensation* of lightheadedness, and her palms would sweat. She would immediately feel tense and anxious.

Following her firing order, she was first given *self-instructional training* (Meichenbaum, 1977) in which her irrational, self-defeating thoughts were replaced with self-statements that tend to mitigate anxiety. ("I will handle the situation." "I will remain in control." "I will stay cool, calm, and collected.") Next, she was taught *coping imagery* (Lazarus, 1978, 1982), which involves picturing oneself coping, vividly imagining oneself remaining calm and in control. In the sensory modality, she was taught slow abdominal breathing and differential muscle relaxation. While shopping in the supermarket, she was to follow a specified sequence—first to use positive self-instructions, then to add positive mental imagery, and then to employ breathing while deliberating relaxing those muscles she was not using at the time.

If the client had reported a different firing order, say sensory-imagery-cognitive-affect (SICA), she would have been advised to commence with slow abdominal breathing and differential relaxation and follow with coping images. The positive self-statements would have been her third line of defense. Our clinical observations suggest that when one selects techniques that follow the client's habitual sequence, the positive impact is greater than if one follows any other order. If a client who follows, say, a CSI sequence is treated first with sensory procedures, followed by imagery techniques, and then with cognitive methods (i.e., an SIC treatment order) the results are less impressive than outcomes that adhere to the client's firing order.

Other Systems

All systems of psychotherapy, and most therapists, advocate a stance of respect and regard for clients or patients. Therapists generally serve as facilitators who provide direct or indirect guidance. It is widely agreed that it is often necessary to alter clients' self-perceptions as well as the ways in which they perceive the world. These and many other commonalities can be delineated, but upon close scrutiny, these similarities between systems are more specious than real.

For example, both multimodal therapy and psychoanalysis regard "conflict resolution" as necessary for successful treatment outcomes. Upon closer scrutiny, these phenotypical similarities reflect genotypical differences. The meaning of "conflict," its origins, functions, effects, and overall impact, as well as the best ways of dealing with or resolving conflicts, are all quite different according to psychoanalytic and multimodal tenets (Lazarus, 1989). It is a serious error to emphasize insignificant similarities at the expense of significant differences.

There are hundreds of different schools of psychological thought and practice (e.g., Corsini, 1981; Herink, 1980). When examining the claims and counterclaims of their proponents, one discerns a number of trends or clusters. Some advocate particular techniques or procedures and tout them as virtual panaceas. Thus, one finds relaxation pundits, meditation gurus, scream advocates, and promulgators of megavitamins, hypnosis, psychodrama, rebirthing, or other unimodal interventions. These one-track procedures are the antithesis of multimodal therapy, which views human disquietude as multilayered and multileveled and calls for the correction of deviant behaviors, unpleasant feelings, negative sensations, intrusive images, irrational beliefs, stressful relationships, and physiological difficulties. Yet multimodal therapy is equally opposed to those theoretical eclectics who endeavor to unite the morass of competing systems, models, vocabularies, and personal idiosyncrasies into a unified whole, thus ending up with an agglomerate of incompatible and contradictory notions (which might be called *multimuddle therapy*).

Each system can be evaluated on the extent to which it assesses and treats—or ignores—each modality of the BASIC I.D. For example, Gestalt therapy tends to neglect the cognitive domain in favor of "gut reactions." Cognitive-behavior therapy does not delve thoroughly into sensory and imagery modalities, nor are behavior therapists sufficiently sensitive to interpersonal factors or unexpressed emotions. Beck's cognitive therapy places heavy emphasis on dysfunctional thoughts and on reparative behaviors but pays insufficient attention to specific sensory components, the rich array of imagery procedures, and the client's interpersonal networks. (See Zilbergeld & Lazarus, 1988, for a detailed account of the synergistic properties of mental imagery and muscular relaxation.) The polar opposite of the multimodal approach is the person-centered approach that offers the therapist's genuineness, empathy, and unpossessive caring to all clients and regards these conditions as necessary and sufficient for therapeutic growth and change. The multimodal position emphasizes that people have diverse needs and expectancies, come from different molds, and require a wide range of stylistic, tactical, and strategic maneuvers from the therapist. No amount of empathy, genuineness, or unpossessive caring is likely to fill the gaps left by impoverished learning histories (behavioral and attitudinal deficits). These require teaching, coaching, training, modeling, shaping, and directing.

When a multimodal therapist is consulted by a client who requires a genuine, empathic, unpossessive listener, nothing prevents the multimodalist from adopting a Rogerian stance. Multimodal therapists constantly ask, "What works, for whom, and under which particular circumstances?" Thus, they take care *not* to attempt to fit the client to a predetermined treatment. With most practitioners, the client seems to get only what the therapist practices—which may not necessarily be what is best for the client. In multimodal therapy, there is a deliberate attempt to determine precisely what type of relationship or what type of interactive posture each client will respond to. The multimodal orientation emphasizes therapeutic flexibility and versatility above all else. There is no unitary way to approach people's problems. To exude empathy and warmth to a client who prefers distant, formal, businesslike interactions is likely to impede treatment. In some cases, instead of attempting to match the client to the therapy and therapist, the multimodal therapist may prescribe *no therapy*. For example, we were consulted by a middle-aged woman who had been seeing therapists on and off for years. She complained of vague anxiety, depression, tension, and general dissatisfaction with her life. After conducting a BASIC I.D. assessment we gave the following advice: "Use the money that you would have spent on therapy to have someone clean your house, have your hair done, and take tennis lessons. You will still have some money left over to meet friends for coffee or a snack. Be sure to engage in these activities on four different days each week, and after doing this for two months, please call and let us know if you are enjoying life more, if you feel less tense, less anxious and less depressed." This no-treatment prescription resulted in a distinct amelioration of her problems.

Many therapists express the need for flexibility. Thus, Haley (1976) stated, "A skillful therapist will approach each new person with the idea that a unique procedure might be necessary for this particular person and social situation" (p. 10). Nevertheless, he then goes on to say, "Today it is assumed that to begin therapy by interviewing one person is to begin with a handicap" (p. 10). Haley then stresses that "at every stage of the interview *all* family members should be involved in the action, and particularly during the greeting stage" (p. 15). We have seen clients at Multimodal Therapy Institutes who were upset by family therapists' insistence that significant others had to be present at initial meetings. After working with these individuals and gaining their trust and confidence, we were then able to get them to bring family members into the treatment (if and when indicated). The multimodal therapist will shift the focus of attention back and forth from the individual and his or her personal responses to the individual in his or her social settings.

Multimodal clinicians may draw on Haley's strategic therapy, Beck's cognitive therapy, Skinner's operant conditioning, or any other school without being locked into that system. Whereas Beck employs a Socratic method of asking questions, multimodal therapists are apt to employ a directive stance because it exemplifies the psychoeducational thrust of MMT. For a detailed discussion of the differences between rational emotive behavior therapy and multimodal therapy, see Lazarus (1988).

Were an observer to watch a multimodal therapist in action, he or she might observe the therapist behaving in a rather cold and austere manner with one client on a particular day, but in a warm and effusive mode with the same client at a different time. Yet another client might be exposed to a question-and-answer session. The next one might be treated in a directive, demanding manner, whereas a different client would receive a soft, warm, and accepting mode. Multimodal therapists constantly adjust to the client in terms of that mode of interaction most likely to achieve the desired aims of the therapy.

Zilbergeld summarized the multimodal position succinctly and accurately:

> The aim of MMT is to come up with the best methods for each client rather than force all clients to fit the same therapy....Three depressed clients might be given very different treatments depending on their therapists' assessments and the methods they prefer....The only goal is helping clients make desired changes as rapidly as possible. (1982, p. 85)

Given that the BASIC I.D. is presumed to represent the pillars of human temperament and personality, any system that glosses over any of these seven dimensions is bound to be incomplete. The reader should have no difficulty, when reading the other chapters in this book, in determining which systems deal *explicitly* with maladaptive behaviors + affective disorders + negative sensations + intrusive images + faulty cognitions + interpersonal difficulties + biological factors. It seems to us that most systems are based on unimodal, bimodal, or at best, trimodal conceptions of human functioning—stressing affect, behavior, and cognition.

❖ HISTORY

Precursors

Hippocrates (c. 400 B.C.) was aware that human personality is multilayered. He underscored the need for eliciting a complete life history of all patients and he recognized the importance of relationship factors in therapy. Galen in the second century and Swiss psychiatrist Paul Dubois in the nineteenth century foreshadowed many of the best tactics advocated by multimodal therapists. One may also note many similarities between present-day multimodal conceptions and more recent writings. Thus, in 1874, Franz Brentano's *Psychologie vom Empirischen Standpunkte* underscored the importance of acts (including ideation), together with feeling states and "sensory judgments." There is considerable overlap between multimodal eclecticism and the theory of functionalism put forth by William James (1890). W. H. Burnham's *The Normal Mind* (1924) was decidedly "multimodal" in its scope.

The direct precursors date back to the 1950s, when Lazarus was a student at the University of the Witwatersrand in Johannesburg, South Africa, where the psychotherapeutic climate was predominantly Freudian and Rogerian. There were some followers of Melanie Klein, Harry Stack Sullivan, and Carl Jung. Two behavioristic faculty members—C. A. L. Warffemius and Alma Hannon—underscored the internal inconsistencies in psychoanalytic theory and emphasized the untestable nature of most Freudian postulates. The contributions of James Taylor of the University of Cape Town and visiting lectures by Joseph Wolpe, a medical practitioner who was applying "conditioning methods" to his patients, led to the formation of a coterie of "neobehaviorists." The members of this group embraced animal analogues, extrapolated from infrahuman to human levels of functioning, and focused heavily on classical conditioning paradigms.

It became apparent to these individuals that performance-based methods were usually better than purely verbal and cognitive approaches at effecting change. Whereas the psychotherapeutic establishment viewed behavior as the outward manifestation of psychic processes, the neobehaviorists stressed that behavior per se is often clinically significant. It became clear that people could acquire insight or alter significant beliefs and still engage in self-destructive behavior. Yet, after behaving differently, it was evident that people were inclined to feel and think differently. (Unfortunately, most professionals still view overt behavior as the tip of the iceberg, as symptomatic of an underlying disease, as symbolic of unconscious complexes.)

To legitimize behavioral intervention as an essential part of effective clinical practice, Lazarus (1958) introduced the terms *behavior therapy* and *behavior therapist* into the scientific and professional literature. The observation and quantification of significant actions became established as a starting point for effective clinical interventions. Coupled with a search for relevant antecedents as well as maintaining variables, the focus on maladaptive behaviors and their remediation resulted in positive outcomes. But when follow-up studies revealed a disappointingly high relapse rate for people who were exposed to behavioral methods alone, it became necessary to employ techniques that were considered outside the boundaries of traditional behavior therapy (Lazarus, 1971, 1989).

Beginnings

In 1965 Lazarus wrote a paper on the need to treat alcoholism from a multi-dimensional perspective. The following components were involved:

1. Medical care to return the patient to physical well-being

2. Aversion therapy and anxiety-relief conditioning to mitigate the patient's uncontrolled drinking

3. A thorough assessment to identify "specific stimulus antecedents of anxiety" in the patient's environment

4. The use of additional techniques, including systematic desensitization, assertiveness training, behavior rehearsal, and hypnosis

5. The development of a cooperative relationship with the patient's spouse

This was foreshadowed by Lazarus's earlier (1956) statement that "the emphasis in psychological rehabilitation must be on a *synthesis* which would embrace a diverse range of effective therapeutic techniques, as well as innumerable adjunctive measures, to form part of a wide and all-embracing re-educative programme." (p. 710)

These earlier publications reveal a definite penchant for broad-based, or comprehensive, psychotherapeutic procedures. By 1966 Lazarus had become suspicious of what he subsequently termed *narrow band behavior therapy* and published "Broad-Spectrum Behavior Therapy and the Treatment of Agoraphobia" (Lazarus, 1966). This article not only challenged narrow stimulus-response formulations, but also elaborated on the notion that dyadic transactions, or interpersonal systems, are an integral part of the genesis and maintenance of agoraphobia. The durability of narrow-band behavior therapy was seriously questioned, and in *Behavior Therapy and Beyond* (Lazarus, 1971), a "broad-spectrum" approach was advocated. The work of Salter (1949) and Ellis (1962) had an enduring impact on underscoring the crucial significance of emotional freedom and rational thinking as integral elements of the broad-spectrum therapy.

While A. A. Lazarus was gathering outcome and follow-up data, a number of questions arose repeatedly. When do behavior therapy techniques suffice? What sorts of people with what types of problems seem to require more than behavior therapy? When the clinician steps outside the bounds of behavior therapy, which effective nonbehavioral methods are best incorporated into what types of specific treatment programs for which particular problems, under what set of circumstances, and with which individuals (cf., Paul, 1967)? The careful scrutiny of case notes revealed that positive results were obtained by individuals with situational crises, circumscribed phobias, specific adjustment problems, transient or relatively mild sexual inadequacies, stress and tension-related difficulties, and some psychobiological disorders. Enduring benefits seemed to accrue to those who needed support over a trying period or reassurance about difficult life decisions and to those who lacked assertiveness and other social skills. Less impressive results were obtained with obsessive-compulsive individuals (despite the use of flooding and response prevention procedures), in cases with self-destructive tendencies, with addicts (be they addicted to drugs, food, or alcohol), and with highly anxious individuals who were prone to panic attacks.

The search for additional systematic interventions led to an awareness that cognitive restructuring often called for more than the correction of misconceptions or the straightforward alteration of negative self-talk. For example, when intrusive images conjure up a gloomy and troubled future, no amount of rational self-talk seems to alter the depressive affect—it is necessary to change the negative imagery itself. Thus, a wide range of specific imagery techniques was added to the clinical armamentarium—goal rehearsal, time projection, coping imagery, and many others (see Lazarus, 1978, 1982). Similarly, people with sensory complaints (e.g., tension headaches, muscle spasms, bruxism) required specific sensory techniques (e.g., deep muscle relaxation, biofeedback, muscle-toning exercises) in addition to behavioral change, cognitive shifts, affective expression, and attention to other aspects of functioning. It seemed important to separate affect from sensation as well as imagery from cognition. The importance of overt behavior was well documented in the writings and practices of behavior therapists, but they seemed to gloss over crucial interpersonal factors. A comprehensive appraisal of human interactions called for an examination of Behavior, Affect, Sensation, Imagery, Cognition, and Interpersonal relationships (the first letters of which form the acronym BASIC I.). To ignore the physical-medical aspects would obviously bypass the fundamental realities of the neurophysiological-biochemical elements that contribute to human personality and temperament. Hence the D. modality was added to the BASIC I. (It should be emphasized again that the D. stands for Drugs/Biology and represents far more than an awareness that some people require medication.)

While multimodal therapy is essentially behavioral, it has evolved into an approach that employs additional (extrabehavioral) assessment and treatment procedures and strategies. Kwee, in a critical review of multimodal therapy, concludes that "whether or not multimodal therapy can be classified as behavior therapy is less important than the method itself" (1981, p. 65).

Current Status

Since the appearance of multimodal therapy as a distinctive orientation (Lazarus, 1973), a considerable number of clinicians have been using the BASIC I.D. framework. The first book on multimodal procedures had 11 contributors (Lazarus, 1976). One issue of the *Journal of Humanistic Education and Development* (1985, Volume 23) and two issues of *Elementary School Guidance and Counseling* (Volume 13, 1978, and Volume 16, 1982) were devoted to multimodal approaches. Nieves (1978) has provided a multimodal self-assessment procedure dealing with self-control systems for minority college students and (1978a) has described a multimodal self-help program for college achievement. Detailed accounts of multimodal assessment and therapy have been presented in several textbooks (Anchor, 1991; Dryden, 1992; Dryden & Golden, 1986; Jacobson, 1987; Leiblum & Rosen, 1988; Norcross, 1986; Norcross & Goldfried, 1992). Numerous articles in professional journals have focused on the BASIC I.D. format. Books, articles, and chapters on multimodal therapy have been written or translated into several languages—German, Italian, Portuguese, Spanish, and Dutch. In Holland, Kwee (1978, 1979, 1981, 1984, 1990; Kwee & Roborgh, 1987) has been most prolific. There are, at present, seven books on multimodal therapy (Brunell & Young, 1982; Keat, 1979, 1990; Lazarus, 1976, 1981, 1985, 1989). Multimodal therapy has been applied in such diverse environments as mental hospitals, residential facilities, day hospitals, and other complete care systems (e.g., Brunell & Young, 1982; O'Keefe & Castaldo, 1981a; Roberts et al., 1980).

Training in multimodal therapy has been a formal aspect of the clinical doctoral program at Rutgers University since 1972, and a number of former students teach multimodal therapy at various universities and centers throughout the United States. Several unpublished doctoral dissertations have focused on specific aspects of the approach. (e.g., Aigen, 1980; Ferrise, 1978; Herman, 1992; Landes, 1988; Lawler, 1985; Mann, 1985; Olson, 1979; Rosenblad, 1985). There are several additional doctoral dissertations in progress, including a study on multimodal relapse prevention planning for chemical addictions.

There are, as of 1995, two major multimodal therapy institutes in the United States, and six smaller centers. A multimodal therapy center has recently opened in London, England.

❖ PERSONALITY

Theory of Personality

Traditionally, American psychologists have tended to be environmentalists, but as geneticists have shed more light on the impact of DNA on various behaviors, the crucial relevance of our genetic heritage has grudgingly been brought back into the picture. It seems foolhardy to deny the biological substrate or the physiological basis of temperament and personality.

At the physiological level, the concept of *thresholds* is most compelling. While psychological interventions can undoubtedly modify various thresholds, the genetic diathesis will usually prevail in the final analysis. Thus, a person with an extremely low pain-tolerance threshold may, through hypnosis and other psychological means, be brought to a level of withstanding pain at somewhat higher intensities, but a penchant for overreacting to pain stimuli will nevertheless remain omnipresent. The person whose autonomic nervous system is *stable* will have a different "personality" from someone with *labile* autonomic reactions. The latter are anxiety-prone and are apt to become pathologically anxious under stressful conditions (Tyrer, 1982).

People tend to favor some BASIC I.D. modalities over others. Thus, we may speak of a "sensory reactor," an "imagery reactor," or a "cognitive reactor." This does not imply that a person will always favor or react in a given modality but that over time, a tendency

---

FIGURE 11.1 ❖ Rating Scales

---

1. *Behavior:* How active are you? How much of a doer are you? Do you like to keep busy?
$$\text{Rating:} \quad 6 \ 5 \ 4 \ 3 \ 2 \ 1 \ 0$$

2. *Affect:* How emotional are you? How deeply do you feel things? Are you inclined to impassioned or soul-stirring inner reactions?
$$\text{Rating:} \quad 6 \ 5 \ 4 \ 3 \ 2 \ 1 \ 0$$

3. *Sensation:* How much do you focus on the pleasures and pains derived from your senses? How tuned in are you to your bodily sensations—to sex, food, music, art?
$$\text{Rating:} \quad 6 \ 5 \ 4 \ 3 \ 2 \ 1 \ 0$$

4. *Imagery:* Do you have a vivid imagination? Do you engage in fantasy and daydreaming? Do you think in pictures?
$$\text{Rating:} \quad 6 \ 5 \ 4 \ 3 \ 2 \ 1 \ 0$$

5. *Cognition:* How much of a thinker are you? Do you like to analyze things, make plans, reason things through?
$$\text{Rating:} \quad 6 \ 5 \ 4 \ 3 \ 2 \ 1 \ 0$$

6. *Interpersonal:* How much of a social being are you? How important are other people to you? Do you gravitate to people? Do you desire intimacy with others?
$$\text{Rating:} \quad 6 \ 5 \ 4 \ 3 \ 2 \ 1 \ 0$$

7. *Drugs/Biology:* Are you healthy and health conscious? Do you take good care of your body and physical health? Do you avoid overeating, ingestion of unnecessary drugs, excessive amounts of alcohol, and exposure to other substances that may be harmful?
$$\text{Rating:} \quad 6 \ 5 \ 4 \ 3 \ 2 \ 1 \ 0$$

---

to value certain response patterns can be noted. Thus, when a person's most highly valued representational system is visual, he or she is inclined to respond to the world and organize it in terms of mental images.

A person with a high frustration tolerance but a low pain tolerance, someone who is extremely active and whose mental imagery is penetratingly clear, is bound to have a very different "personality" from someone who succumbs easily to frustration, who is at best moderately active, deeply analytical (cognitive), and incapable of forming more than fleeting visual images. *Structural profiles*[1] may readily be drawn up from the following instructions: "Here are seven rating scales that pertain to various tendencies that people have. Using a scale of 0 to 6 (6 is high—it characterizes you, or you rely on it greatly; 0 means that it does not describe you, or you rarely rely on it) please rate yourself in each of the seven areas." (See Figure 11.1.)

These subjective ratings are easily depicted on a graph. A 35-item Structured Profile Inventory has been developed, factor-analyzed, and tested for validity and reliability (see Herman, 1993, 1993a; Landes, 1991; Lazarus, 1989).

In couples' therapy, it can prove illuminating for partners to compare their structural profiles and also to anticipate what ratings their mates will give them in each modality (see Lazarus, 1989). Despite the arbitrary and subjective nature of these ratings, useful clinical information is often derived. When the therapist asks the client about the meaning and relevance of each rating, important insights are often gained. In addition, structural profiles may be obtained for specific areas of functioning. For example, in the realm of sexuality, the degree of activity, emotionality, sensuality, imagery, or fantasy may be rated on

---

[1] These differ from "modality profiles" that list problems and proposed treatments across the BASIC I.D.

separate scales, together with questions about how highly valued sexual participation is, its specific interpersonal importance, and the rater's overall biological adequacy.

How, when, where, and why are certain behaviors, outlooks, ideas, fantasies, and interpersonal patterns acquired?

Association plays a key role in all learning processes. Events that occur simultaneously or in close succession are more likely to be connected. Two stimuli that occur frequently in temporal proximity are likely to become associated. An association may be said to exist when responses evoked by one stimulus are similar to those provoked by another stimulus. Without becoming embroiled in the controversies and intricacies of learning theory or classical and operant conditioning, it is clear that a good deal of human thoughts, feelings, and behaviors are due to conditioning. Many aversions appear to result from classical conditioning. A client stated: "After undergoing surgery a few years ago, I experienced postoperative nausea for two days, during which time the man in the next bed kept playing a recording of Beethoven's Moonlight Sonata. Now every time I hear any part of that composition, I feel sick to my stomach!"

Operant conditioning is based on the observation that behavior is frequently a function of its consequences. Another client stated, "I now realize that my headaches were in large part due to the fact that the only time my husband showed me any real caring was when I was in pain."

In therapy, one endeavors to overcome classically conditioned problems by introducing new associations. Difficulties engendered by operant conditioning call for a reorganization of consequential behaviors.

How else do we acquire the habits that make up our personalities? If we had to rely solely on conditioning for all our responses, errors made during the acquisition phase of various skills would prove hazardous. It would probably prove fatal to rely on trial and error or successive approximation methods when learning to swim or to drive a car. In mastering these tasks and many complex occupational and social requirements, success often depends on imitation, observational learning, and identification (Bandura, 1969, 1977, 1986). Human personality (if not survival) is strongly determined by our ability to acquire new responses by watching someone else perform an activity and then doing it ourselves.

To Reiterate

Our personalities stem from the interplay among our genetic endowment, our physical environment, and our social learning history. The basic social learning triad—classical (respondent) conditioning, operant (instrumental) conditioning, and modeling and vicarious processes—does not account for the fact that people are capable of overriding the best-laid plans of contiguity, reinforcements, and example by their idiosyncratic perceptions. People do not respond to their real environment but rather to their perceived environment. This includes the personalistic use of language, expectancies, selective attention, goals, and performance standards as well as the impact of numerous values, attitudes, and beliefs. As Bandura's (1986) principle of reciprocal determinism underscores, people do not react automatically to external stimuli. Their thoughts will determine which stimuli are noticed, how they are noticed, how much they are valued, and how long they are remembered.

This brief outline has not addressed the specific ways in which mental and emotional disorders arise. The main learning factors are our conditioned associations (respondent and operant responses) and the models with whom we identified and whom we imitated—deliberately or inadvertently. During the course of exposure to these inputs, we may have acquired conflicting information, faulty cognitions, and a variety of inhibitions and needless defenses.

Emotional problems and disorders also arise from inadequate or insufficient learning. Here the problems do not arise from conflicts, traumatic events, or false ideas. Rather, gaps in people's repertoires—they were never given necessary information and essential coping processes—make them ill-equipped to deal with societal demands.

The multimodal view emphasizes that most clients suffer from conflicts, the aftermaths of unfortunate experiences, and various deficits in their social and personal repertoires. Hence, unimodal remedies are bound to leave significant areas untouched.

Variety of Concepts

What concepts are necessary for a full understanding of human personality? Can we do without instincts, racial unconscious, oedipal desires, archetypes, organ inferiority, psychic energy, the soul, and scores of other notions that are employed to account for the intricacies of human interaction? Psychotherapists could communicate their ideas with greater precision if they used everyday language instead of esoteric jargon. It could be argued that certain technical terms are useful for rapid and shorthand communication, but couldn't we keep these to the bare minimum? Moreover, if we heed Occam's razor (which holds that explanatory principles should not be needlessly multiplied), we can avoid much of the psychobabble that has risen in psychotherapy (Rosen, 1977).

In accounting for the structure and content of human personality, the previous section underscored the role of the biological substrate and the impact of learning (classical and operant conditioning, modeling, vicarious processes, and private events—thoughts, feelings, images, and sensations). Given that much of our learning is neither conscious nor deliberate (Shevrin & Dickman, 1980), is it not essential to include the unconscious in our compendium of basic concepts? Unfortunately, the unconscious has become a reified entity, and we prefer the term nonconscious processes. This merely acknowledges (1) that people have different degrees and levels of self-awareness, and (2) that despite a lack of awareness or conscious comprehension, unrecognized (subliminal) stimuli can nevertheless influence conscious thoughts, feelings, and behaviors. This completely bypasses the psychoanalytic notions of the unconscious, with its topographical boundaries, putative complexes, and intrapsychic functions, all tied into the intricate mosaic of elaborate inferences about state, stage, and trait theories of personality development.

Similarly, psychodynamic theory views the defense mechanisms as perceptual, attitudinal, or attentional shifts that aid the ego in neutralizing overbearing id impulses. In the multimodal orientation these convoluted theories are not necessary to account for the fact that people are capable of truncating their awareness, beguiling themselves, mislabeling their feelings, and losing touch with themselves (and others) in various ways. We are apt to defend against or avoid pain, discomfort, or negative emotions such as anxiety, depression, guilt and shame. The term *defensive reactions* avoids the surplus meanings that psychodynamic theory attaches to the mechanisms of defense. Empirically, it is clear that one may overintellectualize and rationalize. While attempting to reduce dissonance, we may deny the obvious or falsely attribute our own feelings to others (projection). We can readily displace our aggressions onto other people, animals, or things.

The addition of *nonconscious processes* and *defensive reactions* to our assemblage of basic concepts should not be misconstrued as falling into the quagmire of Freudian constructs. But it is impossible to have a comprehensive understanding of human personality without admitting that people are capable of disowning, denying, and projecting numerous thoughts, feelings, wishes, and impulses. Furthermore, it has been demonstrated time and again that during altered states of consciousness one may have access to memories and skills not amenable to conscious recall. In acknowledging and accounting for these important reactions, it is not necessary to resort to psychoanalytic hypotheses.

Multimodal therapy is not a conglomeration of psychoanalysis, behavior therapy, and many other systems. While effective techniques may be drawn from many available sources, one need not subscribe to any of their underlying theories.

As we enter the interpersonal modality and examine various complex interactions, communication breaks down (literally and figuratively) unless we add another explanatory concept. People not only communicate, they also metacommunicate (i.e., communicate about their communications). Effective communication requires one to step back, as it were, and examine the content and process of patterns of communication in ongoing relationships.

❖ PSYCHOTHERAPY

Theory of Psychotherapy

A fundamental premise of the multimodal approach is that clients are usually troubled by specific problems that should be dealt with through specific treatments. Multimodal therapy is different from systems that cluster presenting problems into ill-defined constructs and then employ one or two treatment procedures. The basic assumption of the multimodal approach is that durability of results is a function of the amount of effort expended by client and therapist across the seven dimensions of personality (BASIC I.D.). The more adaptive and coping responses clients learn in therapy, the less likely they are to relapse. Lasting change at the very least seems to depend upon combinations of techniques, strategies, and modalities. This outlook vitiates the search for a panacea—a single therapeutic modality.

Multimodal therapy overlaps cognitive behavior therapy and rational-emotive therapy in many important respects. They have several major points in common, including the following:

1. Most problems are presumed to arise from deficient or faulty social learning processes.

2. The therapist-client relationship is more that of a trainer and trainee than a doctor treating a sick patient.

3. Transfer of learning (generalization) from therapy to the client's everyday environment is not considered automatic but is deliberately fostered by means of homework assignments.

4. Labels such as diagnostic categories are operational definitions based on overt behavior.

There are important differences between MMT and other cognitive and behavioral orientations. MMT goes beyond the lip service often paid to tailoring treatment procedures to different problems in different people. The goodness of fit in terms of clients' expectancies, therapist-client compatibility, matching, and the selection of techniques is examined in great detail by multimodal therapists. Moreover, the scope of assessment and specific information obtained when examining sensory, imagery, cognitive, and interpersonal factors, and their interactive effects, goes beyond the confines of the usual stimulus and functional analyses conducted by some therapists.

Another assumption is that without new experiences there can be no change. In multimodal therapy clients are inspired and encouraged to do different things and to do things differently. Therapeutic change usually follows methods that are performance based. Purely cognitive or verbal methods are often less effective. Yet before certain clients can take effective action, they require help in eliminating barriers in their interpersonal domain, in their sensory reactions, mental images, and cognitive processing. Indeed, from the multimodal perspective, some of the most important insights are gained when clients develop an awareness and understanding of content areas and interactive relationships within their BASIC I.D. patterns. As one client put it:

> I never realized what an impact my mother and her older sister had on my life—how I let them shape my attitudes, how I treated my husband and children the way they treated my father, my uncle, my cousins, and me. Now I see that I even copied their aches and pains.... When I get a mental image I see their faces and hear their words.... Now I'm rewriting my BASIC I.D. the way I want to be. I'm tuning into my thoughts, my feelings, my images.... If I catch myself thinking the way they think, I crowd out their ideas with my ideas, and then I picture myself coping. I see myself succeeding. This has ended my tensions, my headaches, and all the neurotic cop-outs.

MMT disagrees with those who believe that as long as the client-therapist relationship is good, techniques are of little concern. Certainly, it is necessary for the therapist to be respected by clients and to be trusted enough for them to confide personal and emotionally significant material. Without the attainment of rapport, there will be little inclination for people to disclose distressing, embarrassing, and anxiety-provoking information. Woody stressed that an effective therapist "must be more than a 'nice guy' who can exude prescribed interpersonal conditions—he must have an armamentarium of scientifically derived skills and techniques to supplement his effective interpersonal relations" (1971, p. 8). In keeping with the pluralistic philosophy of the multimodal tradition, we see the client-therapist relationship on a continuum extending from a rather formal, businesslike investment at the one end to a close-knit, dependent bonding at the other. In multimodal therapy, the client-therapist relationship is examined or discussed only when there is reason to suspect that it is impeding therapeutic progress. When therapy is proceeding well, why waste time analyzing the interpersonal feelings between the client and therapist? (See Lazarus, 1981.)

Multimodal therapy is predicated on the assumption that the more disturbed the client is, the greater the specific excesses and deficits will be throughout the BASIC I.D. The model employed may be viewed as based on actualization and self-determination rather than on pathology. Everyone can benefit from a change in behavior that eliminates unwanted or surplus reactions while increasing the frequency, intensity, and duration of creative, fulfilling responses. Likewise, the control or elimination of unpleasant emotions and the augmentation of positive feelings are worthy goals.

In the sensory modality, it is eminently worthwhile to extinguish negative sensations and to derive more pleasure and meaning from each of our five basic senses. Our mental imagery—those mental pictures that ultimately coalesce in a series of self-images—has a direct impact on the tone and cadence of our actions and feelings. Thus, we would do well to focus heavily on various coping images and try to keep them overridingly positive. Faulty assumptions, misconceptions, and irrational cognitions clearly undermine effective living. They are best replaced with as many reality-oriented, factual, and rational assumptions as can be mustered. Everyone would do well to cultivate the specific skills and prosocial interactions that produce good, close, and rewarding inter-personal relationships.

Process of Psychotherapy

Multimodal therapy places primary emphasis on the uniqueness of each person. Hence, there is no typical treatment format. When tuning into the expectancies and demand characteristics of one client, the therapist may adopt a passive-reflective stance. At other times, or with someone else, the same therapist may be extremely active, directive, and confrontative. Bearing in mind the fundamental question of who or what is best for this individual, the first issue is whether the therapist will work with the client or refer him or her to someone else. If clients display grossly bizarre or inappropriate behaviors, delusions, thought disorders, and other signs of "psychosis," nonmedical therapists refer them to a psychiatrist or a psychiatric facility. Similarly, evidence of strong homicidal or suicidal tendencies often requires medical and custodial intervention.

In general, the initial interview focuses on presenting complaints and their main precipitants. Antecedent events are carefully assessed, as are those factors that appear to be maintaining the client's maladaptive behaviors. One endeavors to ascertain what the client wishes to derive from therapy. It is also useful to elucidate the client's strengths and positive attributes. Overriding each of these specific details is the question of adequate client-therapist compatibility. The therapist also tries to determine whether there are any clear indications or contraindications for the adoption of particular therapeutic styles (e.g., directive or nondirective postures).

The initial meeting may be with an individual, a couple, or a family. To put the client(s) at ease, a therapist may begin the first session with small talk, noting formal details, such as name, address, phone numbers, marital status, and occupation. This gives the client an opportunity to adjust to the environment of the consulting room, to experience a verbal interchange, and to be primed for the detailed inquiry that soon follows. After taking down formal details, the therapist may simply say, "What seems to be troubling you?" As various complaints are mentioned, the therapist pays particular attention to which modality of the BASIC I.D. they apply to, and two additional interlocking factors are carefully noted: (1) What has led to the current situation? and (2) Who or what is maintaining it?

In multimodal therapy, it is not uncommon for specific interventions to be made during the initial interview. One does not wait until the full assessment procedures are completed before commencing to alleviate distress, to correct misconceptions, or to redefine the presenting complaint. Here is an example from the initial interview with a 38-year-old man:

Therapist: What seems to be troubling you?
Client: Well, according to my wife, I'm a premature ejaculator.
Therapist: Exactly what does that mean?
Client: I was married before for 10 years. I got married because she was pregnant, but we really never should have gotten together because we just were too different and never got along. I met my present wife about a year ago, and we've been married almost three months. She's a psychiatric social worker.
Therapist: Just how rapidly do you ejaculate? Do you last 2 seconds, 30 seconds, 60 seconds?
Client: Well, I can go for about um, 10 vigorous thrusts. If I go slower, I can last longer, I've tried adding numbers in my head, pinching my thigh, thinking of work, wearing two condoms…
Therapist: Do these things help?

Client: To some extent, but it sure takes most of the pleasure away.

Therapist: have you ever ejaculated before entering your wife, or immediately after penetration?

Client: No. Like I said, if I do it vigorously, I come on the stroke of 10. [Laughs.]

Therapist: At which point you turn into a pumpkin.

Client: I become a jerk. My wife says I need help, so here I am!

Therapist: Is your pattern the same with other women? For example, were you the same with your first wife?

Client: Pretty much, but it never seemed to bother her or any of the others. If I wait 15 or 20 minutes and do it a second time, I can last almost indefinitely.

Therapist: Even with vigorous movements?

Client: That's right, If I feel myself getting too excited, I just stop for a few moments and then I can keep going.

Therapist: Well, from what you've told me, you are not a "premature ejaculator." You come fairly rapidly the first time, but after a rest pause you have excellent control. Do you usually want intercourse a second time, or after the first orgasm are you fully satisfied and maybe drop off to sleep?

Client: Let's put it this way. If the woman remains interested, I'm always willing and ready to give it a second go round. But I'm really happy to hear you say that I'm not a sexual cripple.

Therapist: Have you ever masturbated before having sex with your wife so that you will last longer right from the start of intercourse?

Client: Yes, but my wife says I shouldn't have to resort to that.

Therapist: If I may put it bluntly, I think your wife has several false ideas and you are a victim of her irrational shoulds.

Client: Her what?

Therapist: Shoulds. That you should do this and shouldn't do that. That this is a must. That everything is black or white.

Client: That's her all right! You've hit the nail on the head.

Therapist: I have the feeling that you take all this crap, that you allow yourself to be labeled, put down, and led by the nose. And my guess is that you endured a different type of abuse from your first wife until you reached a breaking point and got a divorce.

Client: I've always put women on a pedestal.

Therapist: What does that imply? That you treat woman as your superiors, that you look up to them, that you do not see men and women as equal but different?

Client: [±30 second silence.] I can't really say for sure. I know this sounds awfully Freudian, but my mother has always been sort of scary. [He appears to be deep in thought.]

Therapist: Well, if I can sum up my impressions, it seems to me that your problem is not premature ejaculation but lack of assertiveness, plus some subtle attitudes and values that are tied into this whole perception. What do you think?

Client: I think you're right. I know you're right. A long time ago one of my buddies—he's a psychologist with Bell Labs—said I seem to be attracted to castrating bitches. You seem to be saying the same thing.

Therapist: Well, I wouldn't put it that way. Frankly, my guess is that you bring out the worst in women by the way you react to them. At any rate, I feel you and I have a few things to sort out, and maybe a bit later, you and your wife might meet with me so that we can perhaps establish better communication and upgrade your marriage.

[As the multimodal assessment continued, several additional inadequacies were brought to light that called for extensive attention to behavioral, cognitive, imagery, and interpersonal domains. The wife, a woman apparently riddled with many problems of her own, elected to see a female therapist and refused marital therapy. After about 15 months the couple met with the therapist for an evaluation session, and both claimed that individually and maritally, things were decidedly better.]

At the end of the initial interview, the usual adult outpatient is given a Multimodal

Life History Inventory (Lazarus & Lazarus, 1991), a 15-page printed booklet that asks crucial questions about antecedent events, ongoing problems, and maintaining factors. The answers are divided into BASIC I.D. categories. The client is asked to bring the completed questionnaire to the second session. (Obviously, young children and many mental hospital patients are incapable of filling out questionnaires. Keat [1979, 1990] has addressed the multimodal treatment of children, and Brunell and Young [1982] have provided a multimodal handbook for mental hospitals.)

By the start of the third session, the therapist usually has gleaned sufficient information from the first two meetings and the life history inventory to construct a preliminary modality profile (i.e., a list of specific problems in each area of the client's BASIC I.D.). Typically, the client is invited to scrutinize the profile and to comment upon or modify specific items. Client and therapist then discuss strategies and techniques, and a general treatment plan is instituted.

A 33-year-old client with the presenting complaint of "depression" agreed that the following modality profile summed up her main problems:

Behavior:	Withdrawal, avoidance, inactivity
Affect:	Depression, guilt, self-recrimination
Sensation:	Heavy, sluggish, enervated
Imagery:	Death images, visions of family rejection
Cognition:	Monologue about past failures, self-statements about personal worthlessness
Interpersonal:	Unassertive, passive
Drugs/Biologicals:	After having taken an antidepressant for three months, the client was given a new medication by her physician about four weeks ago.

The interview with the client went as follows:

Therapist: Is there anything else we should add to the list?

Client: I don't know. The medicine helps me sleep better and I'm eating more, but I still don't feel any better.

Therapist: Well, three things stand out. First, regardless of how you feel, we've got to get you to do more things, to get out, to stop hiding from the world.

Client: [Shakes her head.]

Therapist: It's tough but necessary. The two other things are your negative images and all that nonsense you tell yourself about being utterly worthless. That needs to be changed.

Client: [On the verge of tears.] My brother was right. He said to me, "You're nothing!" God, how that hurt. I always heard that from my father. Us girls were nothing. But I looked up to my brother, and coming from him... [Cries.]

Therapist: It seems that you desperately want approval from your father, your brother, perhaps all the men in the world before you will feel adequate. Can you close your eyes and picture saying to your father and to your brother, "I don't need your approval!"

Client: I wish I could say that and mean it.

Therapist: Shall we try some role-playing? I'll be your brother. "You're nothing! You are just a complete zero!" Now will you challenge that?

[Role-playing, with considerable role reversal, in which the therapist modeled assertive answers, ensued for about 20 minutes.]

Client: I can say the right words, but the wrong feelings are still there.

Therapist: As long as you start with the right words and use them in the right places and to the relevant people, the feelings will soon start to change.

* * * * *

Client: I just have these awful ideas about death. I dream about being at funerals, or getting lost in a cemetery.... And my mind often goes back to my cousin's death, and how my brother cried for him, all these horrible thoughts.

Therapist: Let's deal with that, but first, I'd like to review the treatment plan. First, I want to be sure that you will increase your activity level, go out and do things. I want you to keep notes of the things you do, of the activities you wanted to avoid but did not avoid. Second, I want to be sure that you will express your feelings and not be passive, especially with your husband and your brother. No matter how miserable you feel, can you promise me that you will do these two things this week?

Client: I'll try.

Therapist: Promise me you'll do it.

Client: [Cries.]

Therapist: If I'm coming on too strong, tell me to back off.

Client: I realize it's for my own good.

Therapist: So can I count on you?

Client: I'll do my best

Therapist: Good. Now let's delve into those death images. Why don't we start with your dream about being lost in the cemetery? Close your eyes. Settle back and relax. You're in your dream, lost in the cemetery. Tell me what happens.

Client:[±30 second pause.] I feel awfully afraid. The ground is soggy as if it just rained. I see the tombstones but I can't make out the names.... There's someone else there. [Pause.] I'm frightened. [Pause.] I've seen him before, but his features are indistinct, he's too far from me to make out who it is.

Therapist: You have binoculars or a zoom lens. Look through the eyepiece. Who is it?

Client: It's.... no it's not. It looked like my cousin for a moment. He went away.

Therapist: Let's bring your cousin into the dream so that he can talk to you. Can you bring him into the picture?

Client: [Pause.] Peculiar! He's dressed like a funeral director in a black suit.

[Over several sessions, guided imagery was used to conjure up encounters with several of her deceased relatives—her cousin, maternal grandmother, and several paternal aunts and uncles. A theme emerged. She had been close to all of her deceased relatives for the first 12 to 20 years of her life and had what Gestalt therapists call unfinished business with each of them. Imaginary dialogues ensued with each one in turn. The therapist encouraged her to assume an assertive position throughout, which seemed to serve an important function. Problems in the other BASIC I.D. areas received equal attention. She was constantly encouraged to increase her activity level and to express her feelings, and her cognitive errors were corrected by emphasizing their irrational underpinnings.]

When treatment impasses arise, it is often helpful to introduce a second-order BASIC I.D. assessment. This consists of subjecting a problematic item on the initial modality profile to more detailed inquiry in terms of behavior, affect, sensation, imagery, cognition, interpersonal factors, and drugs or biological considerations. For example, the aforementioned woman remained extremely resistant to implementing assertive behaviors. While she acknowledged feeling less depressed and stated that her images and cognitions were more positive and rational, she remained interpersonally passive and unassertive. When asked for her BASIC I.D. associations to the concept of assertiveness, the following emerged:

Behavior:	Attacking
Affect:	Angry
Sensation:	Tension
Imagery:	Bombs bursting
Cognition:	Get even
Interpersonal:	Hurting
Drugs/Biologicals:	High blood pressure

She had been told, and paid lip service to understanding, the essential differences between assertion and aggression. Nevertheless, the second-order BASIC I.D. indicated that in her mind, an assertive response was tantamount to a vicious attack. This alerted the therapist to model, explain, rehearse, and define assertive behaviors in much greater detail.

With a different depressed individual, the treatment, while addressing all BASIC I.D. problem areas, might be quite dissimilar (Fay & Lazarus, 1981; Lazarus, 1992a).

Mechanisms of Psychotherapy

Consonant with the pluralistic outlook of the multimodal tradition, different mechanisms are responsible for positive change in different people. Thus, for some, the mere non-judgmental acceptance of a highly respected outsider is sufficient to offset faulty attitudes and behaviors. For others, the main mechanism is largely didactic—they have learned, through discussions with the therapist, more effective ways of processing information, of responding to significant others, of coping with the exigencies of life.

Some of the main mechanisms and ingredients of psychotherapeutic change and the modalities to which they apply are described below.

Behavior

Extinction (e.g., by applying methods such as massed practice, response prevention, and flooding). *Counterconditioning* (e.g., in using incompatible response techniques such as graded exposure and desensitization). *Positive reinforcement, negative reinforcement, and punishment* (e.g., when using operant procedures such as token economies, contingent praise, time-out, and aversion therapy).

Affect

Abreaction (e.g., when reliving and recounting painful emotions, usually in the presence of a supportive, trusted ally). *Owning and accepting feelings* (e.g., when therapy permits the client to acknowledge affect-laden materials that were nonconscious).

Sensation

Tension release (e.g., through biofeedback, relaxation, or physical exercise). *Sensory pleasuring* (e.g., the acquisition of positive tactile sensations during sexual retraining).

Imagery

Changes in self-image (e.g., when success in any modality is sustained). *Coping images* (e.g., when able to picture self-control or self-achievement in situations where these images previously had been impossible to evoke).

Cognition

Cognitive restructuring (e.g., changes in dichotomous reasoning, self-downing, overgeneralization, categorical imperatives, non sequiturs, and excessive desires for approval). *Awareness* (e.g., understanding antecedents and their relation to ongoing behaviors, appreciation of how specific firing orders culminate in various affective reactions).

Interpersonal

Modeling (e.g., the therapist as role model or through selective self-disclosure and deliberate modeling as during role-reversal exercises). *Dispersing unhealthy collusions* (e.g., changing counterproductive alliances). *Paradoxical maneuvers* (e.g., when countering double-binding responses). *Nonjudgmental acceptance* (e.g., when clients realize that in therapy they are offered considerations not usually available in most social relationships).

Drugs/Biologicals

In addition to medical examinations and interventions when warranted, the implementation of better exercise and nutrition, substance abuse cessation, or psychotropic medication is sometimes essential—particularly in the treatment of schizophrenia, affective disorders, and some anxiety states.

In the broadest terms, psychological problems may be due to *learning* and/or *lesions*. The latter falls into the D modality; learning is exemplified by the BASIC I. Full understanding of the exact mechanisms of change in any modality is yet to be achieved. Indeed, even in the D modality, while new knowledge about receptor sites, neurotransmitters, biological markers, and other biochemical parameters have emerged, much remains unknown. Perusal of the psychotropic drugs listed in the *Physician's Desk Reference* reveals that most of the descriptions under "Clinical Pharmacology" state that "The mechanism of action of…is not definitely known." In the psychological sphere, the exact and precise "mechanisms of action" are even less well elucidated.

❖ APPLICATIONS

Problems

The multimodal orientation has implications for both prevention and treatment. Its purview extends from individuals, couples, families, and groups to broader community and organizational settings. Thus, some multimodal therapists have special expertise in dealing with children (Keat, 1979, 1990), applying these methods in classroom settings (Gerler, 1979), in a child care agency (O'Keefe & Castaldo, 1980), in parent training (Judah, 1978), in mental retardation (Pearl & Guarnaccia, 1976), in management (O'Keefe & Castaldo, 1981), and in institutional settings (Roberts, Jackson & Phelps, 1980). Brunell and Young's (1982) *Multimodal Handbook for a Mental Hospital* shows the versatility of this framework in a variety of inpatient problem areas. The multimodal framework was even shown to have relevance when dealing with a community disaster (Sank, 1979), and when confronted by a nondisclosing black client (Ridley, 1984). Ponterotto & Zander (1984) have applied the approach to counselor supervision, Greenburg (1982) found multimodal methods especially helpful in counselor education, Edwards and Kleine (1986) used it as a model for working with gifted adolescents, and Ponterotto found it "a culturally sensitive and relevant therapeutic framework for nonminority and minority counselors working with clients of Mexican-American heritage" (1987, p. 308). Eimer (1988) described the application of multimodal assessment and therapy to the patient with chronic pain. Brunell (1990) devised multimodal strategies for overcoming the "strenuous lethargy" of depression.

Two distinct questions may be posed regarding the types of individuals and the variety of problems that may be dealt with: (1) Who can be helped by a multimodal practitioner? and (2) Who can be helped by multimodal therapy?

Multimodal therapists are drawn from the full range of health service providers. Psychiatrists, psychologists, social workers, psychiatric nurses, pastoral counselors, and other mental health workers each have members within their disciplines who employ multimodal methods. The therapist's professional background and personal qualities will equip him or her with special skills, talents, and knowledge to handle certain problems and particular individuals, and to function in specific settings. Thus, some multimodal therapists are highly skilled at using biofeedback, others have a strong background in behavioral medicine, and some are especially gifted and clinically adept with substance-abuse disorders, sexual offenders, school-related problems, and so forth. A multimodal psychiatrist, when prescribing medication to control psychotic behaviors (addressing the D modality), is not practicing multimodal therapy. However, when the psychotic symptoms are in remission, a multimodal psychiatrist will systematically deal with the other six modalities (the BASIC I.). When specific clients require services that lie outside the realm of the given multimodal therapist's compass of skills, referral to an individual or agency better equipped to deal with the situation is a standard procedure.

Multimodal practitioners constantly inquire, *Who or what is best for this individual (or couple, or family, or group)?* Referral to appropriate personnel is considered a most important technique. Thus, if the therapist is not equipped to manage the client's problems, the multimodal practitioner will not continue seeing the client. Nor is it sufficient for a multimodal therapist simply to inform the client that he or she needs to see someone with skills that the therapist does not possess—it is the clinician's duty to try to make a referral.

All therapists encounter clients who require long-term supportive therapy—the development of a stable relationship with a caring person. A well-trained multimodal therapist will do more than offer concern and empathy. Within the context of a supportive therapeutic relationship, specific attention to critical BASIC I.D. excesses and deficits can transform a holding pattern into a framework where constructive learning takes place. Thus, when the mesh and artistry between client and therapist are such that thorough coverage of the BASIC I.D. is accomplished, successful outcomes are obtained even with psychotic individuals, substance abusers, and depressed persons who have failed to respond to years of drug therapy and other medical interventions. Nevertheless, it is obviously easier to achieve noteworthy gains with clients whose excesses and deficits across the BASIC I.D. are not especially rigid, encrusted, or pervasive.

Colleagues at the various Multimodal Therapy Institutes report consistent positive outcomes and follow-ups with marriage and family problems, sexual difficulties, childhood disorders, inadequate social skills, smoking, stress-related difficulties, fears and phobias, anxiety states, psychosomatic complains and depression. Some colleagues report positive results with certain obsessive-compulsive problems.

Evaluation

In multimodal therapy, the evaluation of treatment outcomes is usually straightforward. Since modality profiles (i.e., lists of specific excesses and deficits throughout the client's BASIC I.D.) are routinely constructed, ongoing treatment evaluations are an integral part of the client-therapist interaction. Thus, instead of assuming that some ill-defined entity such as "emotional maturity" has evolved, the multimodal therapist specifies particular gains and achievements in each modality:

Behavior:	Less withdrawn; less compulsive; more outspoken
Affect:	More warm, less hostile; less depressed
Sensation:	Enjoys more pleasures; less tense, more relaxed
Imagery:	Fewer nightmares; better self-image

Cognition: Less self-downing; more positive self-statements
Interpersonal: Goes out on dates; expresses wishes and desires
Drugs/Biologicals: Has stopped smoking; sleeps well; exercises regularly

Structural profiles, before and after multimodal therapy, tend to reflect only minor changes in most instances; that is, doers are still doers and thinkers are still thinkers. People who are active, tuned into sensory pleasures, imaginative, and social before therapy will usually show the same tendencies after therapy. If a high score on the interpersonal scale reflected an overly dependent penchant, this may decrease a few points after therapy. Conversely, if a low score on the interpersonal scale before treatment was a function of shyness and withdrawal, the post-therapeutic score will usually show an increase of several points. Depressed people are inclined to show the greatest pre- and post-treatment differences. While depressed, they usually show a low activity level, few or no feelings apart from sadness, a conspicuous absence of sensory pleasures, and decreased social participation. They may rate themselves fairly high on imagery and cognition because of visions of doom, loneliness, illness, and failure, and because of high self-blame and pervasive ideas of self-worthlessness (Fay & Lazarus, 1981). When therapy is successful for those with depression, structural profiles tend to depict significant changes in terms of greater activity, sensory joys, and social participation (Lazarus, 1992a).

In evaluating marital therapy, the use of a 12-item marital satisfaction questionnaire (Lazarus, 1989) has been useful. The questionnaire pinpoints important areas of personal and familial distress, and quantitative changes in this pencil-and-paper test usually reflect significant improvements in marital happiness. Herman (1991) showed that the Marital Satisfaction Questionnaire has high levels of validity and reliability.

A three-year follow-up evaluation of 20 complex cases who had completed a course of multimodal therapy (e.g., people suffering from obsessive-compulsive rituals, extreme agoraphobia, pervasive anxiety and panic, depression, alcohol addiction, or enmeshed family and marital problems) showed that 14 maintained their gains or had made additional progress without further therapy; 2 felt the need for medication from time to time, and 3 other cases had failed to maintain their initial gains.

Over the past twelve years, treatment goals were achieved with more than 75 percent of the people who consulted us. Follow-ups reveal a relapse rate of less than 5 percent.

Kwee (1984) conducted a controlled outcome study using multimodal therapy with 44 obsessive-compulsive patients and 40 phobic individuals in a general psychiatric hospital. Ninety percent of these patients had previously undergone treatment without success, and 70 percent had suffered from their disorders for more than four years. Various process measures were administered at intake, on admission, after 12 weeks, at discharge, and at follow-up nine months later. The follow-up data showed that 64 percent of the obsessive-compulsive individuals remained significantly improved. Among the phobic individuals, 55 percent had maintained or had proceeded beyond their treatment gains.

Treatment

The average duration of a complete course of multimodal therapy is approximately 50 hours (about a year of therapy at weekly intervals). Brief multimodal therapy can be accomplished in 10 to 12 sessions (Lazarus, 1989a; Lazarus & Fay, 1990). Acutely disturbed people or those with special problems may require more frequent sessions, but once a week is often the best frequency to give people sufficient time to do the recommended homework. Fewer than 30 percent of the clients seen at the various Multimodal Therapy Institutes seem to require, or are willing to undergo, as much as 50 hours of therapy. While some clients may require extended support and trust building and therefore remain in therapy for several years, the majority favor short-term therapy (15 to 20 sessions). Multimodal therapy also lends itself well to crisis intervention. When clients learn to monitor each area of the BASIC I.D., self-management seems to be enhanced (Eskapa, 1992).

Various MMT treatment formats have been applied. Outpatient individual psychotherapy is perhaps most frequently used, although when the interpersonal modality becomes the focus of attention, spouses and other family members are usually seen as well. Thus, what often starts out as one-to-one psychotherapy may shift to couples therapy or family therapy, or the client may be invited to join a group. These decisions are based on the therapist's assessment of who or what appears most likely to benefit the client, and their implementation depends on the concurrence of the client and the willingness of significant others to participate. Thus, the multimodal therapist treats individuals, couples, families, and groups.

Regardless of the specific treatment format, multimodal therapy encompasses (1) specification of goals and problems, (2) specification of treatment techniques to achieve these goals and remedy these problems, and (3) systematic measurement of the relative success of these techniques. In essence, this boils down to eliminating distressing and unwanted responses throughout the BASIC I.D. and also overcoming deficits that exist in any of these modalities.

It is worth reiterating the main procedural sequences followed in multimodal therapy.

1. Information from the initial interviews and the life history inventory results in a modality profile (i.e., a systematic list of problems and proposed treatments in each area of the client's BASIC I.D.).

2. The therapist, usually in concert with the client, selects specific strategies to deal with each problem area. If treatment impasses arise, a second-order BASIC I.D. is carried out (i.e., the unresponsive problem is reexamined in each of the seven modalities).

3. Generalized complaints, such as anxiety and panic attacks, are usually dissected into modality firing orders. Appropriate techniques are selected to deal with each distressing element in turn.

In multimodal therapy, attention to what is traditionally called transference and countertransference phenomena takes place only when there is reason to suspect that therapeutic progress will thereby ensue. Sometimes treatment impasses are caused by specific client-therapist interactions that need to be addressed, but when therapy is proceeding well, why bother to examine the therapeutic relationship?

In multimodal marriage therapy, the couple is usually seen together for the initial interview, and the main presenting complaints are discussed. Each partner is given the life history inventory to take home and fill out independently. An individual session is then arranged with each one for the purpose of examining the completed questionnaire and constructing an initial modality profile. Thereafter, the treatment processes are tailored to the individuals and their unique dyadic requirements (see Brunell, 1985; Lazarus, 1989, pp. 165–186).

Participants in multimodal groups construct their own modality profiles, which serve as a blueprint for the specific gains they wish to derive. Groups can be particularly helpful in dispelling various myths (consensual validation tends to carry more weight than the views of one person, even if that person is a highly respected authority). When interpersonal deficiencies are present, group therapy can provide a more accurate training milieu. Groups lend the opportunity for vicarious or observational learning and offer a rich variety of modeling opportunities. Role-playing, behavior rehearsal, and other enactments are enhanced by psychodramatic nuances that groups provide. Lonely and isolated individuals particularly tend to benefit from group therapy, especially when the group provides a springboard for the development of friendships. Extremely hostile, paranoid, deluded, or severely depressed individuals are excluded from multimodal groups because they are usually too disruptive. Similarly, people who are locked into pervasive obsessive-compulsive rituals have responded poorly in multimodal groups. These people are better treated individually or, preferably, in marital or family contexts.

The use of standardized tests is not a usual procedure, but certain problems may necessitate their application. Intelligence tests (especially with children) may augment the appreciation of specific cognitive abilities and deficits. Neuropsychological assessment may shed light on matters of organicity, and tests of aptitude and special abilities may also be used to good effect with certain clients. The most frequently used test is a structured, interactive, projective procedure called the *deserted island fantasy technique* (Lazarus, 1971, 1989). In essence, the client is asked to describe what might transpire if he or she were on a deserted island for six months in the company of a congenial person unknown to the client. As clients describe their fantasies about their island sojourn, the therapist is usually able to discern several important facets. The presence or absence of the ordinary give-and-take of personal interaction emerges quite clearly. Some clients are unable to picture themselves suspending their hostility, aggression, or depression. One easily detects those instances where people are especially afraid of close contact. Evidence of autistic thinking may emerge. Direct questions concerning the evolution of friendship on the island can provide important clues about the way in which the therapeutic relationship should be structured. Many additional insights tend to be gained. An entire chapter has been devoted elsewhere (Lazarus, 1989) to this technique.

The application of multimodal therapy to inpatient settings is beyond the scope of this chapter. The interested reader is referred to the book edited by Brunell and Young (1982), which contains information about designing, planning, and implementing multimodal treatment programs with hospitalized psychiatric patients.

While the majority of sessions are held in the therapist's office, the flexibility of multimodal procedures leaves open a variety of other settings. In dealing with certain clients who do not show some improvement in a short period of time, Fay and Lazarus (1982) emphasized that it may be helpful to shift the locus of therapy outside the office, such as outdoor walking sessions or a session in the park, or, under certain circumstances, a home visit by the therapist. The use of ancillary personnel is also often found to facilitate extensive in vivo work. Thus, nurses, psychiatric aides, teachers, parents, and other paraprofessional volunteers may expedite desensitization, provide reinforcement of adaptive responses, and other helpful modeling experiences.

Relationships

In keeping with individuals' needs and expectancies, multimodal therapists see relationships with clients on a continuum. Some clients thrive when the relationship is formal, rather distant, and businesslike. At the other extreme, some clients require close, warm, and empathic bonding. The multimodal therapist is not likely to foster dependent, romantic, or other deep attachments because much of the therapy remains task-oriented.

It is widely held that people enter therapy with implicit (if not explicit) expectations and that the effectiveness of therapy is often linked with these expectations. If the therapist's personality and approach are very much at variance with the client's image of an effective practitioner, a therapeutic impasse is likely to result. This, however, should not be construed as a passive and inevitable process. Clients' expectations can be modified by the therapist. Many clients, for instance, expect the therapist to "cure them" and seem unprepared to take responsibility for the treatment process and outcome. In these instances, considerable therapeutic skill and artistry may be required to elicit the client's active cooperation. The most elegant outcomes often depend on a reasonable degree of congruence between the client's BASIC I.D. and the therapist's BASIC I.D. (Herman, 1991a). When inappropriate matching results in an absence of rapport, it is often advisable to effect referral to a more compatible resource instead of insisting that the client-therapist difficulties can or should be worked through.

Multimodal therapists make extensive use of bibliotherapy. When a book is recommended, the readings are discussed during the session so that the therapist can ascertain the book's impact and clarify any ambiguities. Similarly, audiotherapy (the use of cassette recordings) is also a most useful therapeutic adjunct.

❖ CASE EXAMPLE

Background

A 33-year-old woman was afraid of becoming pregnant. She was hypochondriacal and suffered from several somatic symptoms—headaches, chest pains, and gastro-intestinal distress. A medical evaluation disclosed no organic pathology. She also suffered from premenstrual tension—becoming irritable, bloated and anxious.

She had majored in mathematics at college and was working as a computer programmer. Her husband, a successful company president, had expressed a strong desire for children over the previous three years. "For the first five or six years of our marriage, neither of us wanted to have kids, but when Bill became very successful at work he wanted to start a family. That's when I realized that pregnancy, childbirth, and the whole scene terrified me."

For the past two and a half years she had been in therapy with a psychologist. "We explored my relationship with my mother, my father, my brother, and we also looked into my general home atmosphere....We spoke a lot about attachment and separation....it was very interesting." The client realized that what was interesting was not necessarily effective, and after reading a newspaper article, she consulted a behavior therapist who unsuccessfully attempted to desensitize her fears of pregnancy. "I think he hypnotized me and I was to see myself going through the whole pregnancy, including the labor and delivery." She acknowledged having fewer negative anticipations, but her overall clinical status remained essentially unchanged. Her brother advised her to try multimodal therapy because his senior partner's wife had mentioned that their son and daughter had both benefitted from multimodal therapy after failing with other treatment approaches.

Main Problem Areas

The foregoing information was obtained during the initial interview. The life history inventory (Lazarus & Lazarus, 1991) was completed and returned before her second visit. The following modality profile was drawn up:

Behavior:	Excessive cigarette smoking; insufficient exercise
Affect:	Anger/resentment/hostility (seldom directly expressed); fear (of pregnancy)

Sensation:	Headaches; palpitations; stomach pains; tremors; chest pains; menstrual pain
Imagery:	Death images; not coping; failing
Cognition:	Perfectionistic; false romantic ideas; overconcerned about parental approval
Interpersonal:	Resorts to passive-aggressive tactics (spiteful), especially with husband
Drugs/Biologicals:	May require medical intervention for menstrual dysfunction

During the second session, the modality profile was discussed, and the client indicated that her most distressing problems were numerous sensory discomforts that she feared were symptoms of organic disease (despite reassurances from physicians). Exploration of her death images resulted in graphic pictures of her succumbing to a heart attack. Thus, "fears heart attack" was added to her profile under *Affect*.

Treatment

It became clear immediately that the client's modality firing order almost invariably followed an SICA sequence (Sensation-Imagery-Cognition-Affect). First, she would observe sensory discomforts, whereupon she would dwell on them, thereby intensifying untoward pains and bodily tensions. Unpleasant and frightening images would then become intrusive. For example, she would recall vivid scenes of her maternal grandmother suffering a fatal heart attack when the client was 15 years old. Her negative imagery would lead her to label herself organically ill. "Instead of ignoring it and going about my business, I start thinking of all the things that could be wrong with me." Her unpleasant images and negative cognition culminated in severe bouts of anxiety. In keeping with her modality firing order, the following treatments were applied:

1. Biofeedback was administered by means of an EMG apparatus attached to her frontalis muscles. She was given relaxation training cassettes for home use.

2. Associated imagery was employed. She was asked to relax, close her eyes, and picture her grandmother's heart attack. When the image was vivid and clear, she was asked to focus on any other images that emerged. As each image was attended to, a pattern began to take shape. She appeared to have overidentified with her grandmother, but on an accelerated time frame. Thus, many of her physical complaints and infirmities paralleled those that her grandmother had suffered and finally succumbed to in her late 70s. Time projection was employed wherein she imagined herself going forward in time, remaining free from organic disease until she reached her late 70s. She was advised to practice the time projection exercise at least twice daily for 5 to 10 minutes each time.

3. Positive self-statements were implemented. "If I do take after my granny, I too will enjoy good health until I'm about 75. So I'll start worrying 40 years from now." These positive self-statements were to be practiced in conjunction with the time projection images.

The foregoing procedures were administered in two sessions. She arrived for her next session feeling "weepy and depressed" although she was not premenstrual. Exploration of her feelings was unproductive and it seemed appropriate to carry out the deserted island fantasy. Five distinct themes emerged:

1. She would inevitably be disappointed with her island companion: "I just know that I would feel let down."

2. She felt that someone would have to be in charge. (Strong, overcompetitive tendencies became evident.)

3.   Boredom would lead her to engage in compulsive projects.

4.   She would withhold information from her island companion—she would not disclose all relevant aspects of her life. (This led the therapist to speculate about important matters that were being kept from him.)

5.   She would never initiate any acts of affection but would always wait for the companion to do so. (She attributed her inhibitions in this area to her father, who showed affection "only when he was good and ready." She claimed that, as a young child, she learned that spontaneous acts of affection had punitive consequences when her father happened to be in a bad mood.)

The relevance of her island fantasies to ongoing life situations was clear-cut. She felt let down by her husband, who was less affectionate, less nurturing, than she desired. She was inclined to compete with him and tried, unsuccessfully, to take charge of his life. She never initiated sex or engaged in acts of spontaneous affection, although she craved greater warmth and caring. She frequently felt a childlike rage toward her husband, much of which was expressed in passive-aggressive and essentially indirect ways. Yet she felt a desire to achieve a close and loving relationship with him. Further clarification of her wishes indicated that her reluctance to have children was not due to phobic anxiety about the childbirth process. "I think my real hang-up is that kids will take Bill away from me even further than he is already." She had come to realize that before feeling able to make an emotional investment in a child, she would have to feel more secure within herself and in the marriage.

Therapy then focused on assertiveness training with special attention to (1) the direct expression of anger and resentment (instead of indirect, spiteful, manipulative responses), and (2) making requests, particularly asking for attention and affection. Role-playing and coping imagery (in which she pictured herself withstanding rejection and behaving rationally) were helpful facilitators of overt action.

Approximately two and a half months after her initial consultation (eight sessions), some progress was evident. Her gains across the BASIC I.D. were as follows:

B: She had stopped smoking.

A: She expressed feelings more openly and more frequently

S: She reported feeling more relaxed and was less bothered with physical discomforts

I: She was obtaining clear coping images of herself living a long and healthy life

C: She was somewhat less perfectionistic

I: She was taking emotional risks with her husband (e.g., asking for his affection)

D: She had seen her physician again and this time had agreed to take medication for her menstrual difficulties.

A week later, the client mentioned that the physician had prescribed a diuretic to be taken five or six days prior to menstruation together with oxazepam (15 mg twice a day). On the first day of menstruation she was to take zomepirac sodium tablets for pain, as needed. (This combination of drugs proved highly effective.)

At the start of the ninth session she suggested going for a walk instead of meeting inside the office. "I feel like talking today," she said, "I'm not in the mood for hypnosis, or imagery, or stuff like that. The Herrontown Woods are less than five minutes away. Can we spend about half an hour on one of the trails?" Whereas traditional therapists would probably be disinclined to leave the professional confines of their offices, multimodal therapists tend to be more flexible in such matters. Initially, client and therapist admired the scenery, and then the client asked the therapist for his views on extramarital relationships. Was this a proposition? The therapist very much doubted it. He explained that he had no fixed rules, that he was neither blindly for nor universally opposed to extramarital sex. The client then revealed that she had been having an affair for the past year and a half. She had taken courses in computer science and had become sexually involved with her instructor, with whom she enjoyed "coffee and sex" once a week. She derived a good deal of flattery and attention from this clandestine relationship. The therapist inquired if this was having an adverse impact on her marriage, whereupon she insisted that one had nothing to do with the other. The therapist's insinuation that her affair was perhaps partly based on her wish to get even with her husband for his lack of emotional support and nurturance met with denial. She appeared eager to drop the subject. The topic switched to her use of coping imagery. Additional material from the deserted island fantasy test was also discussed.

At this juncture, therapy sessions were scheduled every two weeks, so that she had time to practice her imagery exercises and other homework assignments. She continued to make progress for a month and then began having palpitations, chest pains, and tension headaches. After some evasive comments, she admitted having stopped using the relaxation cassettes, the time projection images, and the cognitive self-statements, and she had also reverted to her unassertive (but aggressive) stance vis-à-vis her husband. The following dialogue ensued:

Client: If you're mad at me and want to yell at me, I won't blame you. Go ahead,

Therapist: It's your life. You've got the tools to make it better. I can't force you to use them. Do you want me to yell at you? What good will that do?

Client: You're angry with me. I can tell.

Therapist: It sounds like you want me to get angry with you. What's happening? Did you decide to have a relapse in order to spite me? Is this some kind of test to see if I care? Or are you annoyed with me and you don't want to give me the satisfaction of having helped you?

Client: I've never seen you like this. You sound like Bill.

Therapist: That's a good observation. I feel you set me up the way you tend to set him up. It seems like some kind of test. But whatever is going on, it is not direct, honest, frank, or positive.

Client: Okay. I'll do the relaxation and all the rest of it.

Therapist: Not for my sake, I hope. Stop looking for my approval, or your father's approval, or anybody's approval. Do what's best for you.

Client: Arguing with you is like arguing with Bill. I can't win. You're both too smart, too well educated. You both think very fast on your feet.

Therapist: It's interesting that you feel we are arguing, and I am intrigued by the way you have bracketed me with your husband.

Client: I think I've always felt that Bill is too good for me. He is intellectually superior, his earning power is astronomical compared to mine.

Therapist: This brings us back to your overcompetitive feelings and it also shows me something else that was not apparent—you have a terrible self-concept.

Client: It took you this long to realize that?

Therapist: I never appreciated its full extent. We really need to do something to raise your self-esteem. [Pause.] I wonder if it would be a good idea one of these days for me to meet with you and Bill.

Client: What for?

Therapist: To upgrade the marriage.

Client: I would prefer you to meet with Bill alone so that you can get to know him first before seeing us together.

There were no further setbacks. In each dimension of her BASIC I.D. the client diligently addressed the relevant issues and carried out the prescribed exercises. Therapy reverted to weekly sessions and dwelled heavily on the false cognition that led to her self-ab-negation. The husband was seen only once. The therapist impressed upon him that the client desired a much more intense level of intimacy and emotional support and reassurance. The husband was under the false impression that his wife's disinclination to have children was due to her own career aspirations. A brief discussion cleared up this misconception. The therapist explained the client's competitive reactions as a cover-up for her feelings of insecurity and advised the husband to perceive them as cries for love and support from him.

Eight months after the initial interview, therapy was discontinued by mutual consent. The client casually mentioned that she had terminated her affair.

Resolution and Follow-Up

About four weeks after therapy had ended, the client called to say that she was pregnant and felt "very pleased" about it. During the brief telephone conversation the client added that she felt "infinitely more relaxed and self-confident" and said, "I'm so assertive these days that I even put my father in his place."

Approximately a year later she called for an appointment. Her baby boy was about four months old and she was delighted with motherhood. She had maintained all of her gains and added that since the birth of her son, her menstrual pains had cleared up, although she still took oxazepam a few days before her period. The reason she had made the appointment was to discuss the pros and cons of returning to work. As a result of the session, she decided to take a year's leave of absence and to take evening courses to maintain viability in the job market and ward off boredom.

❖ SUMMARY

Multimodal therapy is a comprehensive, systematic, and holistic approach to psychotherapy that seeks to effect durable change in an efficient and humane way. It is an open system in which the principle of technical eclecticism encourages the constant introduction of new techniques and the refinement or elimination of existing ones, but never in a random or shotgun manner. The major emphasis is on flexibility. There are virtues in using not only a variety of techniques but even a variety of therapists. The client always comes first, even if it means referring him or her to someone else. Multimodal therapists subscribe to no dogma other than the principles of theoretical parsimony and therapeutic effectiveness.

Assessments and interventions are structured around seven modalities summarized by the acronym BASIC I.D. (*b*ehavior, *a*ffect, *s*ensation, *i*magery, *c*ognition, *i*nterpersonal relationships, and *d*rugs/biological factors). This framework allows the therapist to take into account the uniqueness of each individual and to tailor treatment accordingly. The emphasis is constantly on who or what is best for this individual (couple, family, or group). By assessing significant deficits and excesses across the client's BASIC I.D., thorough coverage of diverse interactive problems is facilitated.

The therapist's role and the cadence of client-therapist interaction differ from person to person and even from session to session. Some clients respond best to somewhat austere, formal, businesslike transactions; others require gentle, tender, supportive encouragement. Two specific procedures that seem to enhance treatment effects are *bridging* and *tracking*. (Bridging is a procedure in which the therapist deliberately tunes into the client's preferred modality before branching off into other dimensions that seem likely to be more productive. Tracking is a careful examination of the firing order of the different modalities.)

The BASIC I.D. framework facilitates the roles of artistry and science in clinical intervention. For example, a recursive application of the BASIC I.D. to itself (a second-order assessment) often helps to shed new diagnostic light and helps to overcome some seemingly recalcitrant problems. A graphic representation of the BASIC I.D. in terms of a *structural profile* is most illuminating in couples therapy. Examination of each specific modality and its interactive effect on the other six readily enables the therapist to shift the focus of attention between the individual and his or her parts to the person in his or her social setting.

In general, the trend in current psychotherapy is toward multidimensional, multidisciplinary, and multifaceted interventions. Rigid adherents to particular schools seem to be receding into a minority. Multiform and multifactorial assessment and treatment procedures have become widespread. The multimodal (BASIC I.D.) framework permits the clinician to identify idiosyncratic variables and thereby not fit clients to preconceived treatments. It also offers an operational means for speaking the client's language. Apart from its heuristic virtues, the multimodal structure readily permits an examination of its own efficacy. While all multimodal therapists are eclectic, all eclectic therapists are not multimodal therapists.

❖ ANNOTATED BIBLIOGRAPHY

Brunell, L. F., & Young, W. T. (Eds.) (1982). *Multimodal handbook for a mental hospital.* New York: Springer.

This book is a practical guide to the use of multimodal therapy in mental hospitals, residential facilities, day hospitals, and other complete care centers. The book includes comprehensive details on goals and procedures for various treatment modules, from art and occupational therapy to social and problem skills training. Discussions focus on essential phases of patient assessment, program design, treatment, and evaluation of patient progress and the hospital system. Specific chapters transcend clinical, case-oriented considerations and address large-scale applications of multimodal procedures. The eight authors have pointed the way to more efficient and effective therapeutic interventions with people who are often given little more than custodial care.

Keat, D. B. (1990). *Child multimodal therapy.* Norwood, NJ: Ablex Publishing Corporation.

The artistry and technical repertoire of an effective child-therapist involves special skills that are not required by a clinician who is gifted with adults. To reach certain children, the therapist must be equipped with numerous techniques, including games, stories, and songs, and have a flair for communicating in special ways. This book shows how an imaginative clinician applies the BASIC I.D. to many problems and disorders of children.

Dryden, W. (1991). *A dialogue with Arnold Lazarus: "It depends."* Philadelphia: Open Universities Press.

The introduction and eight chapters in this book are the outcome of an intensive series of interviews conducted by Professor Dryden. It provides a clear picture of the origins of the multimodal concept and the factors that led to its refinement. The book covers the range from theories to practical applications, training, and supervision, and it has a particularly interesting chapter on "Dos and don'ts and sacred cows."

Lazarus, A. A. (1989). *The practice of multimodal therapy.* Baltimore: John Hopkins University Press.

This book is pragmatic and focuses on the common clinical situations confronting most psychotherapists. It spells out exactly how to conduct a thorough and comprehensive assessment. An attempt is made to integrate knowledge from diverse orientations into a coherent approach. The book is essentially a condensation of the author's own experience, the recorded experience of others, and scientific data. Transcripts from actual sessions and vignettes of typical transactions provide rich clinical material. The book also contains a glossary of 37 separate therapeutic techniques.

❖ CASE READINGS

Breunlin, D. C. (1980). Multimodal behavioral treatment of a child's eliminative disturbance. *Psychotherapy: Theory, Research and Practice*, 17, 17–23.

This case shows how even with highly targeted treatment goals, a multimodal approach can prove most advantageous.

Keat, D. B. (1976). Multimodal therapy with children: Two case histories. In A. A. Lazarus (Ed.), *Multimodal behavior therapy* (pp. 116–132). New York: Springer.

When working with children, the multimodal framework offers a comprehensive and systematic context, but special expertise is required above and beyond the BASIC I.D.

Lazarus, A. A. (Ed.) (1985). *Casebook of multimodal therapy*. New York: Guilford.

This book describes 14 different case studies in a variety of settings and situations.

Lazarus, A. A., Hasson, C., & Glat, M. (1991). Multimodal therapy. In K. N. Anchor (Ed.),

Handbook of medical psychotherapy (pp. 123–140). Toronto: Hogrefe & Huber.

This chapter provides a clear-cut example of the multimodal assessment and treatment of a case of panic, anxiety, and social phobia, and a marital therapy case compounded by depression.

Lazarus, A. A. (1994). The case of George. In D. Wedding and R. J. Corsini (Eds.), *Case studies in psychotherapy*. Itasca, IL: F. E. Peacock.

This case shows multimodal therapy in action and illustrates the treatment of a client who had been unresponsive to many different types of treatment.

Popler, K. (1977). Agoraphobia: Indications for the application of the multimodal conceptualization. *The Journal of Nervous and Mental Disease*, 164, 97–101.

One of several cases that demonstrates how multimodal assessment is crucial if treatment outcomes are to be long lasting.

❖ REFERENCES

Aigen, B. P. (1980). The BASIC I.D. obsessive-compulsive profile. Doctoral dissertation, Graduate School of Applied and Professional Psychology, Rutgers University.

Anchor, K. N. (Ed.) (1991). *Handbook of medical psychotherapy*. Toronto: Hogrefe & Huber.

Bandler, R. , & Grinder, J. (1976). *The structure of magic: A book about communication and change* (Vol. 2). Palo Alto, CA: Science and Behavior Books.

Bandura, A. (1969). *Principles of behavior modification*. New York: Holt, Rinehart and Winston.

Bandura, A. (1977). *Social learning theory*. Englewood Cliffs, NJ: Prentice-Hall.

Bandura, A. (1978). The self-system in reciprocal determinism. *American Psychologist*, 33, 344–358.

Bandura, A. (1986). *Social foundations of thought and action: A social cognitive theory*. Englewood Cliffs, NJ: Prentice-Hall.

Bertalanffy, L. von (1974). General systems theory and psychiatry. In S. Arieti (Ed.)., *American handbook of psychiatry* (Vol. 1) (pp. 1095–1117). New York: Basic Books.

Brentano, F. (1972). *Psychology from an empirical standpoint*. New York: Humanities Press. (Originally published in 1874.)

Brunell, L. F. (1985). Multimodal marital therapy. In D. C. Goldberg (Ed.), *Contemporary marriage* (pp. 354–373). Homewood, IL: Dorsey.

Brunell, L. F. (1990). Multimodal treatment of depression: A strategy to break through the "strenuous lethargy" of depression. *Psychotherapy in Private Practice*, 8, 13–22.

Brunell, L. F., & Young, W. T. (Eds.) (1982). *Multimodal handbook for a mental hospital*. New York: Springer.

Buckley, W. (1967). *Modern systems research for the behavioral scientist*. Chicago: Aldine.

Burnham, W. H. (1924). *The normal mind*. New York: Appleton.

Clark, D. M. (1986). A cognitive approach to panic. *Behaviour Research and Therapy*, 24, 461–470.

Corsini, R. J. (Ed.) (1981). *Handbook of innovative psychotherapies*. New York: Wiley.

Dryden, W. (Ed.) (1992). *Integrative and eclectic therapy*. Philadelphia: Open University Press.

Dryden, W., & Golden, W. (Eds.) (1986). *Cognitive behavioral approaches to psychotherapy*. London: Harper & Row.

Edwards, S. S., & Kleine, P. A. (1986). Multimodal consultation: A model for working with gifted adolescents. *Journal of Counseling and Development*, 64, 598–601.

Eimer, B. N. (1988). The chronic pain patient: Multimodal assessment and psychotherapy. *Medical Psychotherapy*, 1, 23–40.

Ellis, A. (1962). *Reason and emotion in psychotherapy*. New York: Lyle Stuart.

Eskapa, R. (1992). Multimodal therapy. In W. Dryden (Ed.), *Integrative and eclectic therapy* (pp. 109–129). Philadelphia: Open University Press.

Fay, A., & Lazarus, A. A. (1981). Multimodal therapy and the problems of depression. In J. F. Clarkin & H. Glazer (Eds.), *Depression: Behavioral and directive treatment strategies* (pp. 169–178). New York: Garland Press.

Fay, A., & Lazarus, A. A. (1982). Psychoanalytic resistance and behavioral nonresponsiveness: A dialectical impasse. In P. L. Wachtel (Ed.), *Resistance: Psychodynamic and behavioral approaches* (pp. 115–132). New York: Plenum.

Ferrise, F. R. (1978). The BASIC I.D. in clinical assessment. Doctoral dissertation, Graduate School of Applied and Professional Psychology, Rutgers University.

Gerler, E. R. (1979). Preventing the delusion of uniqueness: Multimodal education in mainstreamed classrooms. *The Elementary School Journal, 80,* 35–40.

Greenburg, S. L. (1982). Using the multimodal approach as a framework for eclectic counselor education. *Counselor Education and Supervision, 22,* 132–137.

Haley, J. (1976). *Problem solving therapy.* San Francisco: Jossey-Bass.

Herink, R. (1980). *The psychotherapy handbook.* New York: Meridian.

Herman, S. M. (1991). A psychometric evaluation of the Marital Satisfaction Questionnaire: A demonstration of reliability and validity. *Psychotherapy in Private Practice, 9,* 85–94.

Herman, S. M. (1991a). Client-therapist similarity on the Multimodal Structural Profile Inventory as predictive of psychotherapy outcome. *Psychotherapy Bulletin, 26,* 26–27.

Herman, S. M. (1992). Client-therapist similarity on the Multimodal Structural Profile Inventory as predictive of psychotherapy outcome. Doctoral dissertation, Department of Psychology, Rutgers University.

Herman, S. M. (1993). Predicting psychotherapists' treatment theories by Multimodal Structural Profile Inventory responses: An exploratory study. *Psychotherapy in Private Practice, 11* (in press).

Herman, S. M. (1993a). A demonstration of the validity of the Multimodal Structural Profile Inventory through a correlation with the Vocational Preference Inventory. *Psychotherapy in Private Practice, 11,* 71–80.

Howard, G. S., Nance, D. W., & Myers, P. (1987). *Adaptive counseling and therapy: A systematic approach to selecting effective treatments.* San Francisco: Jossey-Bass.

Jacobson, N. S. (1987). *Psychotherapists in clinical practice: Cognitive and behavioral perspectives.* New York: Guilford.

James, W. (1890). *Principles of psychology.* New York: Macmillan.

Judah, R. D. (1978). Multimodal parent training. *Elementary School Guidance and Counseling, 13,* 46–54.

Keat, D. B. (1979). *Multimodal therapy with children.* New York: Pergamon Press.

Keat, D. B. (1990). *Child multimodal therapy.* Norwood, NJ: Ablex Publishing.

Kwee, M. G. T. (1978). Gedragstherapie en neurotische depressie. In J. W. Orlemans, W. Brinkman, W. P. Haaijam & E. J. Zwaan (Ed). *Handboek voor gedragstherapie* (pp. 182–202). Deventer: Van Loghum.

Kwee, M. G. T. (1979). Over de ontwikkeling van een multimodale strategie van assessment en therapie. *Tijdschrift voor Psychotherapie, 5,* 172–188.

Kwee, M. G. T. (1981). Towards the clinical art and science of multimodal psychotherapy. *Current Psychological Reviews, 1,* 55–68.

Kwee, M. G. T. (1984). *Klinische multimodale gedragstherapie.* Lisse, Holland: Swets and Zeitlinger.

Kwee, M. G. T. (1990). *Denken und doen in psychotherapie.* Den Haag: East-West Publications.

Kwee, M. G. T., & Roborgh, M. (1987). *Multimodale therapie: Praktijk, theorie, en onderzoek.* Lisse, Holland: Swets and Zeitlinger.

Landes, A. A. (1988). Assessment of the reliability and validity of the Multimodal Structural Profile Inventory. Doctoral dissertation, Graduate School of Applied & Professional Psychology, Rutgers University.

Landes, A. A. (1991) Development of the Structural Profile Inventory. *Psychotherapy in Private Practice, 9,* 123–141.

Lawler, B. B. (1985). An interrater reliability study of the BASIC I.D. (multimodal assessment). Doctoral dissertation, Graduate School of Applied and Professional Psychology, Rutgers University.

Lazarus, A. A. (1956). A psychological approach to alcoholism. *South African Medical Journal, 30,* 707–710.

Lazarus, A. A. (1958). New methods in psychotherapy: A case study. *South African Medical Journal, 32,* 660–664.

Lazarus, A. A. (1965). Towards the understanding and effective treatment of alcoholism. *South African Medical Journal, 39,* 736–741.

Lazarus, A. A. (1966). Broad spectrum behavior therapy and the treatment of agoraphobia. *Behaviour Research and Therapy, 4,* 95–97.

Lazarus, A. A. (1971). *Behavior therapy and beyond.* New York: McGraw-Hill.

Lazarus, A. A. (1973). Multimodal behavior therapy: Treating the BASIC I.D. *Journal of Nervous and Mental Disease, 156,* 404–411.

Lazarus, A. A. (1976). *Multimodal behavior therapy.* New York: Springer.

Lazarus, A. A. (1978). *In the mind's eye: The power of imagery for personal enrichment.* New York: Rawson. (Reprinted 1984, Guilford.)

Lazarus, A. A. (1981). *The practice of multimodal therapy.* New York: McGraw-Hill. (Updated paperback edition, 1989, Johns Hopkins University Press.)

Lazarus, A. A. (1982). *Personal enrichment through imagery*. New York: BMA Audiocassettes.

Lazarus, A. A. (Ed.) (1985). *Casebook of multimodal therapy*. New York: Guilford.

Lazarus, A. A. (1988). The practice of rational-emotive therapy. In M. E. Bernard & R. DiGiuseppe (Eds.), *Inside rational-emotive therapy*. New York: Academic Press.

Lazarus, A. A. (1989). *The practice of multimodal therapy*. (Updated edition). Baltimore: Johns Hopkins University Press.

Lazarus, A. A. (1989a). Brief psychotherapy: The multimodal model. *Psychology, 26*, 6–10.

Lazarus, A. A. (1992). Multimodal therapy: Technical eclecticism with minimal integration. In J. C. Norcross & M. R. Goldfried (Eds.), *Handbook of psychotherapy integration* (pp. 231–263). New York: Basic Books.

Lazarus, A. A. (1992a). The multimodal approach to the treatment of minor depression. *American Journal of Psychotherapy, 46*, 50–57.

Lazarus, A. A., & Fay, A. (1990). Brief psychotherapy: Tautology or oxymoron? In J. K. Zeig, & S. Gilligan, (Eds.), *Brief therapy: Myths, methods & metaphors* (pp. 36–51). New York: Brunner/Mazel.

Lazarus, A. A., & Lazarus, C. N. (1991). Multimodal life history inventory. Champaign, IL: Research Press

Leiblum, S. R., & Rosen, R. C., (Eds.) (1988). *Sexual desire disorders*. New York: Guilford Press.

Mann, J. P. (1985). A study of the interrater agreement of therapists using the BASIC I.D. profile as an assessment tool. Doctoral dissertation, Department of Psychology, Western Kentucky University.

Margraf, J., Ehlers, A., & Roth, W. T. (1986). Panic attacks: Theoretical models and empirical evidence. In I. Hand & H. U. Wittchen (Eds.), *Panic and phobias*. Berlin: Springer-Verlag.

Meichenbaum, D. (1977). *Cognitive behavior modification*. New York: Plenum.

Nathan, P. E., & Harris, S. L. (1980). *Psychopathology and society* (2nd Ed.) New York: McGraw-Hill.

Nieves, L. (1978). *The minority college student experience: A case for the use of self-control*. Princeton, NJ: Educational Testing Service.

Nieves, L. (1978a). *College achievement through self-help*. Princeton, NJ: Educational Testing Service.

Norcross, J. C. (1986). *Handbook of eclectic psychotherapy*. New York: Brunner/Mazel.

Norcross, J. C., & Goldfried, M. R. (Eds.) (1992). *Handbook of psychotherapy integration*. New York: Basic Books.

O'Keefe, E. J.,& Castaldo, C. (1980). A multimodal approach to treatment in a child care agency. *Psychological Reports, 47*, 250.

O'Keefe, E. J.,& Castaldo, C. (1981). Multimodal management: A systematic and holistic approach for the 80s. *Proceedings of the Marist College Symposium on Local Government Productivity*. Poughkeepsie, NY.

O'Keefe, E. J., & Castaldo, C. (1981a). A multimodal approach to treatment in a child care agency. *Child Care Quarterly, 10*, 103–112.

Olson, S. C. (1979). A multimodal treatment of obesity using Lazarus' BASIC I.D. Doctoral dissertation, Department of Psychology, University of South Dakota.

Paul, G. L. (1967). Strategy of outcome research in psychotherapy. *Journal of Consulting Psychology, 31*, 109–118.

Pearl, C., & Guarnaccia, V. (1976). Multimodal therapy and mental retardation. In A. A. Lazarus (Ed.), *Multimodal behavior therapy* (pp. 189–204). New York: Springer.

Ponterotto, J. G. (1987). Counseling Mexican-Americans: A multimodal approach. *Journal of Counseling and Development, 65*, 308–312.

Ponterotto, J. G., & Zander, T.A. (1984). A multimodal approach to counselor supervision. *Counselor Education and Supervision, 24*, 40–50.

Rabkin, R. (1977). *Strategic psychotherapy*. New York: Basic Books.

Ridley, C. R. (1984). Clinical treatment of the nondisclosing black client: A therapeutic paradox. *American Psychologist, 39*, 1234–1244.

Roberts, T. K., Jackson, L. J., & Phelps, R. (1980). Lazarus' multimodal therapy model applied in an institutional setting. *Professional Psychology, 11*, 150–156.

Rosen, R. D. (1977). *Psychobubble*, New York: Atheneum.

Rosenblad, L. V. (1985). A multimodal assessment of perception and communication in distressed and nondistressed married couples. Doctoral dissertation, Department of Psychology, Rutgers University.

Salter, A. (1949). *Conditioned reflex therapy*. New York: Farrar, Strauss.

Sank, L. I. (1979). Community disasters: Primary prevention and treatment in a health maintenance organization. *American Psychologist, 34*, 334–338.

Shevrin, H., & Dickman, S. (1980). The psychological unconscious: A necessary assumption for all psychological theory? *American Psychologist, 35*, 421–434.

Tyrer, P. J. (1982). Anxiety states. In E. S. Paykel (Ed.), *Handbook of affective disorders*. New York: Guilford Press.

Watzlawick, P., Weakland, J., & Fisch, R. (1974). *Change: Principles of problem formation and problem resolution*. New York: Norton.

Woody, R. H. (1971). *Psychobehavioral counseling and therapy: Integrating behavioral and insight techniques*. New York: Appleton-Century-Crofts.

Zilbergeld, B. (1982). Bespoke therapy. *Psychology Today, 16*, 85–86.

Zilbergeld, B., & Lazarus, A. A. (1988). *Mind Power: Getting what you want through mental training*. New York: Ivy Books.

**Murray Bowen
1913–1990**

**Nathan Ackerman
1908–1971**

Salvador Minuchin

Carl Whitaker

12 Family Therapy

*Irene Goldenberg and
Herbert Goldenberg*

Family therapy is both a theory and a treatment method. It offers a way to view clinical problems within the context of a family's transactional patterns. Family therapy also represents a form of intervention in which members of a family are assisted to identify and change problematic, maladaptive, self-defeating, repetitive relationship patterns. Unlike individually focused therapies, in family therapy the *identified patient* (the family member considered to be the problem in the family) is viewed as a symptom bearer, expressing the family's disequilibrium or current dysfunction. The family system itself is the primary unit of treatment and not the identified patient. Helping families change leads to improved functioning of individuals as well as families.

❖ OVERVIEW

Basic Concepts

When a single attitude, philosophy, point of view, procedure or methodology dominates scientific thinking (known as a *paradigm*), solutions to problems are sought within the perspectives of that school of thought. If serious problems arise that do not appear to be explained by the prevailing paradigm, however, efforts are made to expand or replace the existing system. Once the old belief system changes, perspectives shift and previous events may take on entirely new meanings. The resulting transition to a new paradigm, according to Kuhn (1970), is a scientific revolution.

In the field of psychotherapy, such a dramatic shift in perspective occurred in the mid-1950s as some clinicians, dissatisfied with slow progress when working with individual patients, or frustrated when change in their patients was often undermined by other family members, began to look at the family as the locus of pathology. Breaking away from the traditional concern and investigation of individual personality characteristics and behavior patterns, they adopted a new perspective—a family frame of reference—that provided a new way of conceptualizing human problems, especially the development of symptoms and their alleviation. As is the case with all paradigm shifts, this new viewpoint called for a new set of premises about the nature of psychopathology and stimulated a series of new family-focused methods for collecting data and understanding individual functioning.

When the unit of analysis is the individual, clinical theories inevitably look to internal events, psychic organization, and the patient's intrapsychic problems to explain that person's problems. Based on a heritage dating back to Freud, such efforts turn to the reconstruction of the past to seek out root causes of current difficulties, producing hypotheses or explanations for *why* something happened to this person. With the conceptual leap to a family framework, attention is directed to the family context in which individual behavior occurs, to behavioral sequences between individuals, to *what* is now taking place and *how* each participant influences and in turn is influenced by other family members.

This view of reciprocal causality provides an opportunity to observe repetitive ways in which family members interact and to use such data to initiate therapeutic interventions. Family therapists therefore direct their attention to the dysfunctional or impaired family unit rather than to a symptomatic person, who is only one part of that family system and by his or her behavior is seen as expressing the family's dysfunction.

The Family as a System

By adopting a relationship frame of reference, family therapists pay simultaneous attention to the family's *structure* (how it arranges, organizes, and maintains itself at a particular cross-section of time), and also its *processes* (the way it evolves, adapts, or changes over time). They view the family as an ongoing, living system, a complexly organized, durable, causal network of related parts that together constitute an entity larger than the simple sum of its individual members.

A system, according to Buckley (1967), involves a "complex of elements or components directly or indirectly related in a causal network such that each component is related to at least some other parts in a more or less stable way within a particular period of time" (p. 41). This broad view directs attention to the relationship between interacting parts within a larger context, emphasizing the system's unity and organizational hierarchy.

Several key concepts are central to understanding how systems operate. *Organization* and *wholeness* are especially important. Systems are composed of units that stand in some consistent relationship to one another, and thus we can infer that they are organized around those relationships. In a similar way, units or elements, once combined, produce an entity—a whole—that is greater than the sum of its parts. A change in one part causes a change in the other parts and thus in the entire system. If this is indeed the case, argue systems theorists, then adequate understanding of a system requires study of the whole, rather than separate examination of each part. No element within the system can ever be understood in isolation, since elements never function separately. The implications for understanding family functioning are clear: a family is a system in which members organize into a group, forming a whole that transcends the sum of its individual parts.

The original interest in viewing a family as a system stems in part from the work of Gregory Bateson, an anthropologist who led an early study in which he and his colleagues hypothesized that schizophrenia might be the result of pathological family interaction (Bateson, Jackson, Haley, & Weakland, 1956). Although not a family therapist himself, Bateson (1972) deserves special credit for first seeing how a family might operate as a *cybernetic system*. That is, he helped focus attention on the flow of information and the back-and-forth communication patterns that exist within families. Rather than study the content of what transpires, family therapists were directed to attend to family processes, the interactive patterns among family members that define a family's functioning as a unit.

A Cybernetic Epistemology

A number of significant shifts in clinical outlook occur with the adoption of a cybernetic epistemology. For example, the locus of pathology changes from the identified patient to the social context, and the interaction between individuals is analyzed rather than the troubled person. Instead of assuming that one individual causes another's behavior ("You started it. I just reacted to what you did."), family therapists believe both participants are caught up in a circular interaction, a chain reaction that feeds back on itself, because each family member has defined the situation differently. Each argues that the other person is the cause; both are correct, but it is pointless to search for a starting point in any conflict between people, because a complex, repetitive interaction is occurring, not a simple, linear, cause-and-effect situation with a clear beginning and end.

The simple, nonreciprocal view that one event leads to another, in stimulus-response fashion, represents *linear causality*. Family therapists prefer to think in terms of *circular causality*: reciprocal actions occur within a relationship network by means of a network of interacting loops. From this perspective, any cause is seen as an effect of a previous cause, and in turn becomes the cause of a later event. Thus, the attitudes and behavior of system members, as in a family, are tied to one another in powerful, durable, reciprocal ways, and in a never-ending cycle.

Cybernetics, a Greek word for steersman, was coined by mathematician Norbert Wiener (1948) to describe regulatory systems that operate by means of *feedback loops*. The most familiar example of such a mechanism is the thermostat in a home heating system; set to a desired temperature, the furnace will turn on when the heat drops below that setting, and it will shut off when the desired temperature is reached. The system is balanced around a set point, and relies on information fed back into it about the temperature of the room. Thus, it maintains a dynamic equilibrium and undertakes operations to restore that equilibrium whenever the balance is upset or threatened.

So, too, with a family. When a crisis or other disruption occurs, family members try to maintain or regain a stable environment—family *homeostasis*—by activating family-learned mechanisms to decrease the stress and restore internal balance.

Families rely on the exchange of information—a word, a look, a gesture, or a glance that acts as a feedback mechanism, signaling that disequilibrium has been created and that some corrective steps are needed to help the relationship return to its previous balanced state. In effect, information about a system's output is fed back into its input, to alter, correct, or govern the system's functioning. *Negative feedback* has an attenuating effect, restoring equilibrium, while *positive feedback* leads to further change by accelerating the deviation. In negative feedback, a couple may exchange information during a quarrel that says, in effect, "It is time to pull back or we will regret it later." In positive feedback, the escalation may reach dangerous, runaway proportions; the quarreling couple may escalate an argument to the point when neither one cares about the consequences.

Subsystems and Boundaries

Following largely from the work of Minuchin (1974), family therapists view families as comprising a number of coexisting subsystems, in which members group together to carry out certain family functions or processes. Subsystems are organized components within the overall system, and may be determined by generation, sex, or family function. Each family member is likely to belong to several subsystems at the same time. A wife may also be a mother, daughter, younger sister, and so on, thus entering into different complementary relationships with other members at various times and playing different roles in each. In certain dysfunctional situations, families may split into separate camps: males opposed to females, parents against children, father and daughter in conflict with mother and son.

While family members may engage in temporary alliances, three key subsystems will always endure: the spousal, parental, and sibling subsystems (Minuchin, Rosman, & Baker, 1978). The first is especially important to the family: any dysfunction in the spousal subsystem is bound to reverberate throughout the family, resulting in the scapegoating of children or co-opting them into alliances with one parent against the other. Effective spousal subsystems provide security and teach children about commitment by presenting a positive model of marital interaction. The parental subsystem, when effective, provides child care, nurturance, guidance, limit setting, and discipline; problems here frequently take the form of intergenerational conflicts with adolescents, often reflecting underlying family disharmony and instability. Sibling subsystems help members learn to negotiate, cooperate, compete, and eventually attach to others.

Boundaries are invisible lines that separate a system, a subsystem, or an individual from outside surroundings. In effect, they protect the system's integrity, distinguishing between those considered to be insiders and those viewed as outsiders. Boundaries within a family vary from being rigid (overly restrictive, permitting little contact with one another) to being diffuse (overly blurred, so that roles are interchangeable and members are overinvolved in each other's lives). Thus, the clarity of the boundary and its permeability between subsystems are more important than the subsystem's membership. Excessively rigid boundaries characterize *disengaged families* in which members feel isolated from one another, while diffuse boundaries identify *enmeshed families* in which members are intertwined in one another's lives.

Boundaries between the family and the outside world need to be sufficiently clear to allow information to flow to and from the environment. In systems terms, the more flexible the boundaries, the better the information flow; the family is open to new experiences, is able to alter and discard unworkable or obsolete interactive patterns, and is operating as an *open system*. When boundaries are not easily crossed, the family is insular, not open to what is happening around it, suspicious of the outside world, and is said to be operating as a *closed system*. In reality, no family system is either completely open or completely closed, but exists along a continuum.

Other Systems

Differences between family therapy and other therapeutic approaches are less clear-cut than in the past, as systems ideas have permeated other forms of psychotherapy. While therapists may focus on the individual patient, many have begun to view that person's problems within a broader context, of which the family is inevitably a part, and have adapted family systems methods to individual psychotherapy (Wachtel & Wachtel, 1986). For example, *object relations theory*, a recent development within psychoanalysis, has emphasized the search for satisfactory "objects" (persons) in our lives, beginning in infancy.

Practitioners of psychoanalytic object relations family therapy such as Scharff & Scharff (1987) attempt to uncover faulty parent-child patterns from the past that patients impose on current family relationships. In general, as classically practiced, psychoanalysis remains committed to searching the past to uncover those unconscious conflicts believed to be the underlying causes of patients' current symptoms. Family therapy deals with current problems, views them as more interpersonal than intrapsychic, and uses a family forum procedure to help eliminate troubling individual symptoms and improve overall family functioning.

Conceptually, Adlerian psychotherapy is compatible with family therapy formulations. Far less reliant on biological or instinctual constructs than psychoanalysis, Adlerian theory emphasizes the social context of behavior, the embeddedness of the individual in his or her interpersonal relationships, and the importance of present circumstances and future goals, rather than unresolved issues from childhood. Both Adlerian psychotherapy and family therapy take a holistic view of the person and emphasize intent and conscious choices. Adler's efforts to establish a child guidance movement, as well as his concern with improving parenting practices, reflect his interest beyond the individual to family functioning. However, the individual focus of his therapeutic efforts fails to change the dysfunctional family relationships that underlie individual problems.

The person-centered approach developed by Carl Rogers is concerned with the client's here-and-now issues, is growth-oriented, and is applicable to helping families move in the direction of self-actualization. Its humanistic outlook is particularly appealing to experiential family therapists such as Virginia Satir (1972) and Carl Whitaker (Whitaker & Bumberry, 1988), who believe families are stunted in their growth and will find solutions if provided with a growth-facilitating therapeutic experience. Experiential family therapists are usually more directive than Rogerians, and in some cases (Satir) act as teachers to help families open up their communication processes.

Existential psychotherapies are phenomenological in nature, emphasizing awareness and the here-and-now of the client's existence. Considered by most family therapists to be too concerned with the organized wholeness of the single person, this viewpoint nevertheless has found a home among some family therapists, such as Walter Kempler (1981), who argues that people define themselves and their relationships with one another through their current choices and decisions and what they choose to become in the future, rather than through their reflections on the past.

Behavioral family therapists traditionally take a more linear view of causality regarding family interactions than do most systems theory advocates. A child's tantrums, for example, are viewed by behaviorists as maintained and reinforced by parental responses that act as reinforcements. Systems theorists view the tantrum as an interaction, including an exchange of feedback information, occurring within a family system. However, some leading behaviorists (Patterson, 1975; Stuart, 1980) have moved in the direction of viewing the family as a social system whose members exercise mutual control over one another's social reinforcement schedules.

Rational emotive behavior therapy's view that problems stem from maladaptive thought processes and require cognitive restructuring seems too individually oriented and too cognitive for most family therapists. However, a movement within the family therapy field called *constructivism* (White, 1989) shifts attention from action to the meaning people give their experiences. Somewhat akin to REBT, therapy from a constructivist viewpoint attempts to help families understand and change some of the burdensome assumptions they have made about their lives, and in effect develop alternative "stories" about themselves.

❖ HISTORY

Precursors

Freud, Adler, Sullivan

Family therapy can trace its ancestry to efforts begun early in this century, led largely by Sigmund Freud, to discover intervention procedures for uncovering and mitigating symptomatic behavior in neurotic individuals. However, while Freud acknowledged in theory the often powerful impact of individual fantasy and family conflict and alliances (e.g., Oedipus conflict) on the development of such symptoms, he steered clear of involving the family in treatment, choosing instead to help the symptomatic person resolve personal or intrapsychic conflicts.

Adler went further than Freud in emphasizing the family context for neurotic behavior, stressing the importance of the family constellation (e.g., birth order, sibling rivalry) on individual personality formation. He drew attention to the central role of the family in the formative years, contending that family interactive patterns provide the key for understanding a person's current relationships both within and outside the family.

Harry Stack Sullivan, beginning in the 1920s, adopted an interpersonal relations view in working with hospitalized schizophrenics. Sullivan (1953) argued that people were the product of their "relatively enduring patterns of recurrent interpersonal situations" (p. 10). While not working directly with families, Sullivan speculated on the role family played in the transitional period of adolescence, thought to be the typical time for the onset of schizophrenia. Sullivan's influence on Don Jackson and Murray Bowen, two pioneers in family therapy who trained under Sullivan, as well as on his colleague Frieda Fromm-Reichmann, is apparent both in their adoption of Sullivan's early notion of redundant family interactive patterns and in their active therapeutic interventions with families.

General Systems Theory

Beginning in the 1940s, Ludwig von Bertalanffy (1968) and others began to develop a comprehensive theoretical model embracing all living systems. General systems theory challenged the traditional reductionistic view in science that complex phenomena could be understood by carefully breaking them down into a series of less complex cause-and-effect reactions, then analyzing in linear fashion how A causes B, B causes C, and so forth. Instead, this new theory argued for a systems focus, in which the interrelations between parts assume far greater significance: A may cause B, but B affects A, which in turn affects B, and so on in a circular causality. General systems theory ideas can be seen in such family systems concepts as circular causality and symptoms in one family member, a part of the overall family system, signaling family dysfunction rather than individual psychopathology.

Group Therapy

John Bell (1961) developed a therapeutic approach called *family group therapy*, applying some of the social psychological theories of small group behavior to the natural group that is the family. Adopting group therapy's holistic outlook, family therapists involve entire families in the therapeutic process, believing that kinship groups are more real situations and provide a greater opportunity for powerful and longer lasting systems changes as a result of family-level interventions.

Beginnings

Research on Schizophrenia

A number of researchers, working independently, began in the 1950s to zero in on schizophrenia as a possible area where family influences might be related to the development of psychotic symptoms. Taking a linear viewpoint at first, seeking causes of the schizophrenic condition in early family child-rearing practices, the researchers ultimately branched out into a broader systems point of view. Early efforts by the following are particularly noteworthy: Bateson's group in Palo Alto, Theodore Lidz's project at Yale, and the efforts at the National Institute of Mental Health of Murray Bowen and Lyman Wynne. The idea of seeing family members together for therapeutic purposes came later, as a result of research discoveries and subsequent theorizing.

A landmark paper by Bateson, Jackson, Haley, & Weakland (1956) speculated that *double-bind* communication patterns within a family may account for the onset of schizophrenia in one of its members. Double-bind situations exist when an individual, usually a child, habitually receives contradictory messages from the same important person, typically a parent (verbally, "I'm interested in what you are telling me" but nonverbally by gesture or glance signaling "Go away, you are bothering me, I don't care about you."), who forbids comment on the contradiction. Compelled to respond, but doomed to failure whatever the response, the child becomes confused and ultimately withdraws after repeated exposure to such incongruent messages, unable to understand the true meaning of his or others' communications.

Lidz and his colleagues (Lidz, Cornelison, Fleck, & Terry, 1957) hypothesized that schizophrenics did not receive the necessary nurturance as children and thus failed to achieve autonomy as adults. According to this premise, a parent's (most likely the mother's) own arrested development was responsible, especially because that person was likely to be part of a conflict-ridden marriage, providing poor role models for children. These researchers distinguished two patterns of chronic marital discord common in schizophrenic families. In one, labelled *marital skew*, extreme domination by one emotionally disturbed partner is accepted by the other, who implies to the children that the situation is normal. In the *marital schism* scenario, parents undermine their spouses, threats of divorce are common, and each parent vies for the loyalty and affection of the children.

Bowen was especially interested in the symbiotic mother-child bonds that he hypothesized might lead to schizophrenia. Hospitalizing entire families on the research wards for months at a time in order to observe ongoing family interactions, Bowen (1960) broadened his outlook, observing emotional intensity throughout these families. As a result, he moved from his previous psychoanalytic viewpoint to one that emphasized reciprocal functioning, in what he labelled the *family emotional system*.

Lyman Wynne, who succeeded Bowen at NIMH, turned his attention to the blurred, ambiguous, confused communication patterns he and his associates found in families with schizophrenic members (Wynne, Ryckoff, Day, & Hirsch, 1958). Wynne coined the term *pseudomutuality* to describe a false sense of family closeness in which the family gives the appearance of taking part in a mutual, open, and understanding relationship without really doing so. The members of these families have poorly developed personal identities and doubt their ability to accurately derive meaning from personal experiences outside the family, preferring to remain within the safe and familiar family system with its enclosed boundaries.

Psychodynamics of Family Life

Trained in psychoanalytic work with children, Nathan Ackerman nevertheless saw the value of treating entire families as a unit in assessing and treating dysfunctional families. In his landmark book, *The Psychodynamics of Family Life*, often considered the first text to define the new field, Ackerman (1958) argued for family sessions aimed at untangling interlocking pathologies, thus endorsing the systems view that problems of any one family member cannot be understood apart from those of all other members.

By working therapeutically with non-schizophrenic families, Ackerman demonstrated the applicability of family therapy to less disturbed patients. By 1962, he in New York and Don Jackson on the West Coast founded the first journal in the field, *Family Process*, with Jay Haley as editor, enabling researchers and practitioners to exchange ideas and identify with the growing field of family therapy.

Delinquent Families

One project combining theory and practice was led by Salvador Minuchin (Minuchin, Montalvo, Guerney, Rosman, & Schumer, 1967) at the Wiltwyck School for Boys in upper New York State, a residential setting for delinquent youngsters from urban slums. Recognizing the limitations of traditional methods for reaching these boys and their families, generally from poor, underorganized, fatherless homes, Minuchin developed a number of brief, action-oriented therapeutic procedures aimed at helping reorganize unstable family structures.

Current Status

Six theoretical viewpoints and corresponding approaches to family therapy can be identified, according to Goldenberg & Goldenberg (1991):

Object Relations Family Therapy

The psychodynamic view is currently best expressed by object relations family therapists (Framo, 1982; Scharff & Scharff, 1987), who contend that the need for a satisfying relationship with some "object" (i.e., another person) is the fundamental motive of life. From the object relations perspective, we bring introjects—memories of loss or unfulfillment from childhood—into current dealings with others, seeking satisfaction but sometimes "contaminating" family relations in the process. Thus, they argue, people unconsciously relate to one another in the present based largely on expectations formed during childhood. Treatment is aimed at helping members become aware of those unresolved objects from their families of origin, increasing their understanding of the interlocking pathologies that have blocked both individual development and fulfillment from family relationships.

Experiential Family Therapy

Experiential family therapists such as Satir and Whitaker believe troubled families need a "growth experience" derived from an intimate interpersonal experience with an involved therapist. By being real or authentic themselves, and often self-disclosing, experiential therapists contend that families can learn to be more honest, more expressive of their feelings and needs, and better able to use their potential for self-awareness to achieve personal and interpersonal growth.

For Virginia Satir, building self-esteem and learning to communicate adequately and openly were essential therapeutic goals. Calling his approach symbolic-experiential family therapy, Carl Whitaker gives voice to his own impulses and fantasies and depathologizes human experiences, as he helps family members probe their own covert world of symbolic meanings, freeing them to activate their innate growth processes.

Bowenian Family Therapy

Murray Bowen offered a transgenerational view of family systems, arguing that family members are tied in thinking, feeling, and behavior to the family system, and thus individual problems arise and are maintained by relationship connections with fellow members. Those persons with the strongest affective connections (or *fusion*) with the family are most vulnerable to personal emotional reactions to family stress. The degree to which an individualized, separate sense of self independent from the family (or *differentiation of self*) occurs is correlated with the ability to resist being overwhelmed by emotional reactivity in the family; the greater the differentiation, the less likely the individual is to experience personal dysfunction.

Bowen (1978) believed that the child most vulnerable to dysfunction is the one most easily drawn into family conflict. He maintained that the most attached child will have the lowest level of differentiation, will be the least mature and thus have the hardest time separating from the family, and will likely select as a marital partner someone who is also poorly differentiated in his or her family. The least differentiated of their offspring will marry someone equally undifferentiated, and so forth. In this formulation, problems are passed along to succeeding generations by a multigenerational transmission process. Bowen maintained that schizophrenia may result after several generations of increased fusion and vulnerability.

Structural Family Therapy

Minuchin's (1974) structural view focuses on how families are organized and what rules govern their transactions. He pays particular attention to family rules, roles, alignments, and coalitions, as well as the boundaries and subsystems that make up the overall family system. Symptoms are viewed as conflict defusers, diverting attention from more basic family conflicts. Therapeutically, structuralists challenge rigid, repetitive transactions within a family, helping to "unfreeze" them to allow family reorganization.

Strategic Family Therapy

This approach involves designing novel strategies for eliminating undesired behavior. Strategists such as Jay Haley (1976) are not too interested in providing insight to family members, preferring assignment of tasks to get families to change those aspects of the system that maintain the problematic behavior. Sometimes indirect tasks, in the form of *paradoxical interventions*, are employed to force clients to abandon symptoms. Therapists at the Mental Research Institute in Palo Alto believe families develop unworkable "solutions" to problems that become problems themselves. Consequently, they have evolved a set of brief therapy procedures employing various forms of paradox, aimed at changing undesired family interactive patterns (Watzlawick, Weakland, & Fisch, 1974).

In Milan, Italy, Mara Selvini-Palazzoli and her colleagues (Selvini-Palazzoli, Boscolo, Cecchin, & Prata, 1978) have developed *systemic family therapy*, a variation of strategic family therapy that has found its greatest success with psychotic and anorectic patients. Selvini-Palazzoli (1986) believes behavioral symptoms in families represent "dirty games" in which parents and symptomatic children engage in power struggles, the children using their symptoms to try to defeat one parent for the sake of the other.

Behavioral Family Therapy

Those family therapists with a strict behavioral perspective contend that maladaptive or problematic behavior will be reduced or eliminated when the contingencies of reinforcement for that behavior are altered. Both operant and classical conditioning principles are employed. Advocates of a social learning approach, such as Bandura (1977), assert that complex behavior patterns are not learned exclusively by direct reinforcement, but often vicariously by observing the rewards and punishments received by others for various kinds of behavior.

❖ PERSONALITY

Family therapists as a group do not subscribe to a single, unified theory of personality, although all view individual development as embedded in the context of family life. Expanding on Sullivan's (1953) emphasis on the role of interpersonal relationships in personality development, family therapists believe behavior is the product of one's relationships with others. Symptomatic conduct in any individual family member is a response to that person's current situation, although it may have its roots in past experiences within the family.

Theories of Personality

Clinicians who adopt a family systems outlook have varying theoretical bases. Individual personality is not overlooked, but rather is recast as a unit of a larger system, such as the family. Nevertheless, family therapists remain aware that no matter how much individual behavior is related to and dependent upon the behavior of others in the family system, individual family members remain flesh-and blood persons with unique experiences, private hopes, ambitions, outlooks, expectations, and potentials (Nichols, 1987). Most family therapists try to remain focused on family interaction without losing sight of the singularity of the individual. The ultimate goal is to benefit all the persons who make up the family.

How a therapist views personality development depends largely on that person's initial theoretical framework. In keeping with their psychoanalytic roots, object relations theorists (Scharff & Scharff, 1987) investigate individual "object-loss" growing up, believing that if one's relational needs are unmet by parents, the child will internalize both the characteristics of the lost object and the accompanying anger and resentment over the loss. The resulting unresolved unconscious conflict develops into frustration and self-defeating habits in the adult. In a related but less pathologically oriented version, called *contextual family therapy*, Boszormenyi-Nagy (1987) argues that individuals grow up with family legacies, obligations, and entitlements, which they play out in adult life. Understanding each member's sense of loyalty, trust, and responsibility is undertaken in therapy to balance the ledger of entitlement and indebtedness within a family.

Behaviorally oriented family therapists believe all behavior, normal and abnormal, is learned as a result of a process involving the acquisition of knowledge, information, experiences, and habits. Classical conditioning, operant conditioning, and modeling concepts are used to explain how personality is learned. Following the early lead of B.F. Skinner, some strict behaviorists question whether an inner personality exists, maintaining that what we refer to as "personality" is nothing more than the sum of the environmental experiences in one's life. Rejecting explanations that infer the development of internal traits, they search instead for relationships between observable behavior and observable variations in the person's environment. In their view, situations determine behavior. That is, rather than attempt to reconstruct how certain personality traits developed, they attend to current situations in which the behavior is reinforced. These therapists are less interested in presumed internal processes or personality characteristics that cause the current behavior, preferring to direct their efforts to analyzing how undesired habits are supported by current contingencies within the family and how they can be extinguished and replaced by new learning.

Those therapists who adopt a more cognitive orientation believe people do develop personality traits, and that their behavior is based at least in part on those traits and not simply in response to situations. These family therapists contend that certain types of cognitions are learned, become ingrained as traits, and mediate a person's behavior. Perceptions of events, attitudes, beliefs, expectations of outcomes, and attributions are examples of such cognitions. Especially when negative or rigid, these cognitions can contribute to negative behavior exchanges within a family. Intervention is an attempt to change maladaptive cognitions.

Many family therapists view personality from a *family life cycle* perspective. This developmental outlook notes that certain predictable marker events or phases (marriage, birth of first child, children leaving home, and so on) occur in all families, regardless of structure or composition, compelling each family to deal in some manner with these events. Because there is an ever-changing family context in which individual members grow up, there are many chances for maladaptive responses. Situational family crises (such as the death of a parent during childhood, or the birth of a handicapped child) and certain key transition points are periods of special vulnerability.

Both continuity and change characterize family systems as they progress through the life cycle. Ordinarily, such changes are gradual and the family is able to reorganize as a system and adapt successfully. Certain discontinuous changes, however, may be disruptive, transforming a family system so that it will never return to its previous way of functioning. Divorce, becoming part of a stepfamily, serious financial reverses, and chronic illness in a family member are examples of sudden, disruptive changes that cause upheaval and disequilibrium in the family system. Symptoms in family members are especially likely to appear during these critical periods of change, as the family struggles to reorganize while negotiating the transition. Family therapists may seize the crisis period as an opportunity to help families develop higher levels of functioning.

Variety of Concepts

Family Rules

A family is a rule-governed system in which the interactions of its members follow organized, established patterns. Growing up in a family, members all learn what is expected or permitted in family transactions. Parents, children, relatives, males, females, older and younger siblings all have prescribed rules for the boundaries of permissible behavior, which may not be verbalized but which are understood by all. Such rules regulate and help stabilize the family system.

Family therapists are especially interested in persistent, repetitive behavioral sequences that characterize much of everyday family life, because of what these patterns reveal about the family's typical interactive patterns. Labeled the *redundancy principle*, the concept describes a family's usually restricted range of options for dealing with one another. Attending to a family's rules represents an interactive way of understanding behavior, rather than attributing that individual behavior to some inferred inner set of motives. Don Jackson (1965), an early observer of family behavioral patterns, believed that family dysfunction was due to a family's lack of rules for accommodating to changing conditions.

Family Paradigms

All families develop paradigms about the world (i.e., make enduring assumptions that are shared by family members). Studying families in a laboratory situation in which they were given problems to solve as a family, Reiss (1981) found that the various ways different families perceived the laboratory setting and developed strategies for coping with the situation were telling. For example, families with schizophrenic adolescents frequently perceived danger and threat, while those with delinquent adolescents viewed the task as an occasion to demonstrate distance and independence from one another. By way of contrast, families with normal adolescents viewed such tasks as an opportunity to explore and master the challenging situation together.

Based on these and related findings, Reiss (1981) suggested that families develop family paradigms (ways of perceiving, interpreting, and interacting with their social world) in one of three ways. *Consensus-sensitive* families are composed of enmeshed members who see the world as chaotic and confusing, so that they must maintain agreement in all matters in order to protect themselves from danger. *Interpersonal-distance-sensitive* families are made up of disengaged members who strive for autonomy from one another, believing that closeness represents a display of weakness. *Environmentally sensitive* families typically operate as open systems and are apt to be most problem-free. They see the world as knowable and orderly, with each member expected to contribute to its understanding and mastery.

Pseudomutuality and Pseudohostility

One result of Wynne's NIMH studies of families with schizophrenic members (Wynne, Ryckoff, Day, & Hirsch, 1958) was his observation of their recurrent fragmented and irrational style of communication. He discovered an unreal quality about how they expressed both positive and negative emotion to one another, a process he labeled *pseudomutuality*. Wynne reported that members in these families were absorbed with fitting together, at the expense of developing their separate identities. Rather than encourage a balance between separateness and togetherness, as occurs in well-functioning families, members in Wynne's group seemed concerned with the latter only, apparently dreading expressions of individuality as a threat to the family as a whole. By presenting a facade of togetherness, they learned to maintain a homeostatic balance, but at the expense of not allowing either disagreements or expressions of affection. The tactic kept them from dealing with any underlying conflict, and at the same time the surface togetherness prevented them from experiencing deeper intimacy with one another.

Wynne's research also identified *pseudohostility*, a similar collusion in which apparent quarreling or bickering between family members is in reality merely a superficial tactic for avoiding deeper and more genuine feelings. Members may appear alienated and split from one another, and may even appear intense, but the turmoil is merely a way of maintaining a connection without becoming either deeply affectionate or deeply hostile to one another. Like pseudomutuality, it represents a distorted way of communicating and fosters irrational thinking about relationships.

Mystification

Another masking effort to obscure the real nature of family conflict and thus maintain the status quo is called *mystification*. First described by R. D. Laing (1965) in analyzing the family's role in a child's development of psychopathology, the concept refers to parental efforts to distort a child's experience by denying what the child believes is occurring. Instead of telling the child, "It's your bedtime," or explaining that they are tired and want to be left alone, parents say "You must be tired. Go to bed." In effect, they have distorted what the child is experiencing ("I'm not tired"), especially if they add that they know better than the child what he or she is feeling.

Mystification, then, refers to the fact that some families deal with conflict by befuddling, obscuring, or masking whatever is going on between members. This device does not deter conflict but rather clouds the meaning of conflict and is called into play when a family member threatens the status quo, perhaps by expressing feelings. A husband who says, in response to his wife's query about why he appears angry, "I'm not angry. Where do you dream up these things?" when he actually *is* angry, is attempting to mystify her. His apparent intent to avoid conflict and return matters to their previous balance only leads to greater conflict within her, because if she believes him then she feels she must be "crazy" to imagine his anger, and if she trusts her own senses, then she must deal with a deteriorating marital relationship. Mystification contradicts one person's perceptions, and in extreme or repeated cases leads that person to question his or her grip on reality.

Scapegoating

Within some families, a particular individual is held responsible for whatever goes wrong with the family. *Scapegoating* directed at a particular child often has the effect of redirecting parental conflict, making it unnecessary for the family to look at the impaired father/mother relationship, something that would be far more threatening to the family. By conveniently picking out a scapegoat who becomes the identified patient, other family members can avoid dealing with one another or probing more deeply into what is really taking place.

Scapegoated family members are themselves often active participants in the family scapegoating process. Not only do they assume the role assigned them, but they may become so entrenched in that role that they are unable to act otherwise. Particularly in dysfunctional families, individuals may be repeatedly labeled as the "bad child"—incorrigible, destructive, unmanageable, troublesome—and they proceed to act accordingly. Scapegoated children are inducted into specific family roles, which over time become fixed and serve as the basis for chronic behavioral disturbance. Because the family retains a vested interest in maintaining the scapegoated person in that role, blaming all their problems on one member, changes in family interactive patterns must occur before scapegoating will cease. Otherwise, the scapegoated person, usually symptomatic, will continue to carry the pathology for the family.

❖ PSYCHOTHERAPY

Theory of Psychotherapy

There is no single theory of psychotherapy for family therapists, although all would probably agree with the following basic premises:

1. People are products of their social connections, and attempts to help them must take family relationships into account.

2. Symptomatic behavior in an individual arises from a context of relationships, and interventions to help that person are most effective when those faulty interactive patterns are altered.

3. Individual symptoms are maintained externally in current family system transactions.

4. Conjoint sessions in which the family is the therapeutic unit and the focus is on family interaction are more effective in producing change than attempts to uncover intrapsychic problems in individuals by therapy via individual sessions

5. Assessing family subsystems and the permeability of boundaries within the family and between the family and the outside world offers important clues regarding family organization and susceptibility to change.

6. Traditional psychiatric diagnostic labels based upon individual psychopathology fail to provide an understanding of family dysfunctions and tend to pathologize individuals.

7. The goal of family therapy is to change maladaptive or dysfunctional family interactive patterns.

Systems thinking most often provides the underpinnings for therapeutic interventions with the family. By viewing causality in circular rather than linear terms, the focus is on family transactional patterns, especially redundant maladaptive patterns that help maintain symptomatic behavior. By emphasizing family interrelationships over individual needs and drives, explanations shift from a *monadic* (based on the characteristics of a single person) to a *dyadic* (based on a two-person interaction) or *triadic* (based on interactions between three or more persons) model.

In a monadic outlook, a husband fails to pay attention to his wife because he is a cold and uncaring person. Adopting a dyadic mode, people are viewed in terms of their interlocking relationships and impact on one another. Here the therapist looks beyond the separate individuals who make up the couple, focusing instead on how these two individuals organize their lives together, and, more specifically, how each helps define the other. From a dyadic viewpoint, a husband's indifference arouses his wife's emotional pursuit, and she demands attention. Her insistence arouses the fear of intimacy that led to his withdrawal to begin with, and he retreats further. She becomes more insistent, he increasingly less available as their conflict escalates. A family therapist helping such a couple will direct attention to their interactive effect, thus making the dyad (and not each participant) the unit of treatment. Seeing the couple conjointly rather than separately underscores the therapist's view that the problem arises from both partners, and that both are responsible for finding solutions.

In a triadic model, the family therapist assumes the symptoms or presenting problems result from the dyad's inability to resolve the conflict, resulting in other family members being drawn into the conflict. A pre-teenage son who frustrates his father by refusing to do his homework and thus is performing badly at school may be doing so in alliance with his mother against his father, indirectly expressing her resentment at her husband's authoritarian behavior. The couple's original dyadic conflict has become a triadic one in which multiple interactions occur. To merely develop a behavioral plan or contract for the boy to receive money or special television privileges for school assignments completed would miss the complex family interaction involved. Family therapists would look at the overall impact of the symptomatic behavior in context; the youngster may or may not be included in the entire treatment, which certainly would deal with the unspoken and unresolved husband/wife conflicts and the recruitment of their child to express or act out their tensions.

In the example just presented, the child's symptom (the school problem) maintains the family homeostasis but obscures the underlying and unexpressed set of family conflicts. Symptoms often serve a function in maintaining family homeostasis; in this case, attention to the school problem keeps the parents from quarreling with each other and upsetting the family balance. If the school problem did not at some level sustain the family organization, it would not be maintained. Thus, the systems-oriented therapist might wonder: (1) Is the family member expressing feelings through symptoms that the other members are denying or not permitting themselves to experience? and (2) What would happen to other family members if the identified patient were to become symptom-free? (Wachtel & Wachtel, 1986). Symptoms thus have a protective function or are stabilizing devices used in families. Although they may not do so consciously, families usually are invested in the maintenance of the symptom for homeostatic purposes.

While the idea of the symptom's purpose in helping maintain family stability has been a mainstay of family therapy theory, critics argue that it suggests families need a "sick" member and are willing to sacrifice that person for the sake of family well-being. *Constructionists* such as White (1989) reject the notion that a child's problems necessarily reflect more serious underlying family conflict. In White's view, families may be oppressed rather than protected by the symptomatic behavior. White's efforts are directed at getting all family members to unite in gaining control of their lives from the oppressive set of symptoms.

Family therapists usually are active participants with families and concentrate on current family functioning. They attempt to help members achieve lasting changes in the functioning of the family system, not merely superficial changes that will allow the system to return to its former tenuous balance. Watzlawick, Weakland, & Fisch (1974) distinguish between *first-order changes* (changes within the system that do not alter the organization of the system itself) and *second-order changes* (fundamental changes in a system's organization and function). The former refers to specific differences that take place within the system, while the latter involves rule changes in the system, in effect changing the system itself.

For example, the following is a first-order change: The Ryan parents were concerned with the repeated school absences of their son Billy, and in an attempt to correct his behavior they told him that any time they learned he was truant from school he would be "grounded" the following Saturday.

The following is a second-order change: The Ryan parents were concerned with the repeated school absences of their son Billy. After consulting with a family therapist for several sessions, they realized that by struggling with Billy, they only encouraged his rebelliousness and thus were involved in sustaining the truant behavior. They also came to recognize that Billy's relationship with the school was truly his own, and that they should back off from intruding. Attempting to change the rules and pull themselves out of the struggle, they told Billy that from now on whether or not he went to school was between him and the school, and that henceforth he would be responsible for his education.

As in these examples, a problematic family on their own may try first-order changes by attempting to impose what appear to be logical solutions to their problems. Assuming the problem to be monadic—the result of Billy's rebelliousness—they are employing negative feedback, attempting to do the opposite of what has been occurring. The family actually may make some changes in behavior for a brief period, but they are still governed by the same rules, the cease fire is not likely to hold, and Billy will probably return to his school absences sooner or later.

Second-order changes, based on positive feedback, call for a change in the way the family organizes itself. Here the rules of the game must change, viewpoints must be altered, old situations seen in a new light, providing a revised context in which new behavior patterns may emerge. Most people attempt to solve everyday problems by attempting first-order changes and repeating the same solutions in a self-perpetuating cycle, which only makes things worse. Especially with seriously troubled families, fundamental second-order changes in the system are necessary, so that the family members can give different meanings to old feelings and old experiences.

Process of Psychotherapy

The Initial Contact

Family therapy begins when the client asks for help. One family member, or a coalition of members, begins the process by seeking help outside the family, thus acknowledging that a problem exists and that the family has been unsuccessful in its attempts to resolve it by themselves. While the caller is assessing whether the right person has been contacted, the therapist is forming tentative hypotheses about the family. How self-aware is the caller? What sort of impression is he or she trying to make? What other members are involved? Are they all willing to attend the initial session?

Initial contact, whether in person or by telephone, provides an opportunity for a mini-evaluation, and also represents the therapist's first opportunity to enter into the family system. If the therapist is careful not to get entangled into taking sides, or become engulfed by family anxiety, or become excessively sympathetic or angry with any member based on what the caller is reporting, then he or she can establish the "rules of the game" for further family sessions.

The Initial Session

The family therapist usually opts for as many family members as possible to attend the first session. Entering the room, members are encouraged to sit where they wish; their chosen seating arrangement (mother and child close together, father sitting apart) offers the therapist an early clue about possible family alliances and coalitions. Welcoming each member separately as equally important participants, the therapist becomes aware that some members may need extra support and encouragement to participate.

Each person's view of the problem must be heard, as well as the first-order solutions the family has attempted. Observing family interactive patterns, particularly repetitive behavioral sequences that occur around a problem, the therapist tentatively begins to redefine the identified patient's symptoms as a family problem in which each member has a stake. Together, therapist and family explore whether they wish to continue working together and who will attend; if they choose to discontinue, outside referrals to other therapists are in order. If they agree to stay, treatment goals are defined.

Engaging the Family

Beginning with the initial session, the therapist tries to build a working alliance with the family, accommodating to their transactional style, assimilating their language patterns and manner of affective expression. The therapist tries to create an atmosphere where each member feels supported and safe to voice previously unexpressed or unexplored problems. By "joining" them, the therapist is letting them know they are understood and cared about, and that in such a safe climate they can begin to confront divisive family issues.

Assessing Family Functioning

As is the case with all forms of psychotherapy, family therapy involves some form of assessment, formal or informal, as the clinician attempts to learn more about the family in order to make more informed treatment decisions. Early on, the therapist tries to determine: (1) Is treatment for the entire family called for? (2) Who are the appropriate family members with whom to work? (3) What underlying interactive patterns fuel the family disturbance and lead to symptoms in one or more of its members? and (4) What specific interventions will most effectively help this family? In later sessions, the therapist continues to revise hypotheses, basing subsequent interventions on assessments of the success of previous attempts to alter dysfunctional repetitive family patterns.

Behavioral family therapists are apt to make a careful, systematic behavioral analysis of the family's maladaptive behavioral patterns, often using questionnaires, pinpointing precisely which behaviors need to be altered and which events typically precede and follow that behavioral sequence. What exactly does the family mean by their child's "temper tantrums"? How often do they occur, under what circumstances, how long do they last, what specific reactions does each family member have, and what antecedent and subsequent events are associated with the outburst? The behavioral family therapist tries to gauge the extent of the problem, the environmental cues that trigger the behavior, and the behaviors of various family members that maintain the problem. The assessment, continuously updated, helps the therapist plan interventions to reduce undesired or problematic behaviors.

Experiential family therapists such as Virginia Satir spend less time on a formal family history. They work more in the here-and-now, helping families examine current interactive patterns with little regard for historical antecedents. Assessment is an informal, ongoing process indistinguishable from the therapeutic process itself. Such therapists attempt to provide families with an experience, using themselves as models to explore their own feelings and give voice to their own impulses. Carl Whitaker, an experiential therapist, insists on controlling the structure of the therapy at the start of treatment, making certain that the family is not successful in imposing its own definition of the upcoming therapeutic relationship and how it should proceed. Later, he believes, the family members must be encouraged to take responsibility for changing the nature of their relationships.

Many family therapists agree with Salvador Minuchin (1974) that they get a better sense of how families function by interacting with them over a period of time than from any formal assessment process. Therapists observe how subsystems carry out family tasks, how alliances and coalitions operate within the family, how flexible are family rules in the face of changing conditions, how permeable are the boundaries within the family and between the family and the outside world. These observations help family therapists modify and discard hypotheses and adjust intervention strategies based upon refined appraisals of family functioning.

History-Taking

Consistent with their theoretical leanings, object relations family therapists such as Scharff & Scharff contend that an examination of family history is essential to understanding current family functioning. Because they believe people carry attachments of their parental introjects (memories from childhood) into their current relationships, these therapists are especially interested in such matters as how and why marital partners chose each other. That choice is seen as seeking to rediscover, through the other person, the lost aspects of primary object attachments that had split off earlier in life. Similarly, contextual family therapists (Boszormenyi-Nagy, 1987) examine with their patients those interconnections from the past that bind families together, in an effort to help them discover new ways of making fresh inputs into stagnant relationships.

Bowen (1978) began with a set of evaluation interviews aimed at clarifying the history of the presenting problem, especially trying to understand how the symptoms affect family functioning. He tried to assess the family's pattern of emotional functioning as well as the intensity of the emotional process of the symptomatic person. What is this family's relationship system like? How well differentiated are the various members? What are the current sources of stress, and how adaptive is the family?

Because Bowen believed dysfunction may result from family fusion extending back over generations, he probed for signs of poor differentiation from families of origin. To aid in the process, Bowen constructed a family *genogram*, a schematic diagram in the form of a family tree, usually including at least three generations, to trace recurring family behavior patterns. Hypotheses developed from the genogram, such as fusion/differentiation issues or emotional cutoffs from family, are used to better understand the underlying emotional processes connecting generations. Careful not to become drawn into the family's emotional system, Bowen used this information to coach family members to modify their relationships and especially to differentiate themselves from their families of origin.

Satir (1972) attempted to get families to think about the relevant concepts that formed the basis of their developing relationships by compiling a family life chronology for each family member. More than simply gathering historical facts, this represented an effort to help people understand how family ideology, values, and commitments had emerged in the family and impacted current family functioning. Later, she used the therapeutic technique of family reconstruction, guiding family members back through stages of their lives in an attempt to discover and unlock dysfunctional patterns from the past.

Structural and strategic family therapists pay less attention to family or individual histories, preferring to focus on the current family organization, coalitions, hierarchies, and so on. They are concerned with developing ways to change ongoing dysfunctional family patterns, and typically show less concern for how these patterns historically emerged.

Facilitating Change

Family therapists use a number of therapeutic techniques to alter family functioning. Among these are the following:

1. Reframing.   This technique involves relabeling problematic behavior by putting it into a new, more positive perspective that emphasizes its good intention. (To an adolescent angry because he believes his mother is invading his privacy: "Your mother is concerned about your welfare and hasn't yet found the best way to help.") Labeling her as wishing to do well for her son, rather than agreeing with his perception that she does not trust him, alters the context in which he perceives her behavior, thus inviting new responses from him to the same behavior.

Reframing changes the meaning attributed to a behavior without changing the "facts" of the behavior itself. Strategic family therapists are most apt to use this technique, because it allows them to help clients change the basis for their perceptions or interpretation of events. This altered perspective leads to a change in the family system, as the problematic behavior becomes understood in a new light. Reframing, then, is a method for bringing about second-order changes in the family system.

2. Therapeutic Double-Binds.   Another technique favored by strategic and systemic family therapists is putting the family in a *therapeutic double-bind* by directing families to continue to manifest their presenting symptoms: obsessive people are asked to think about their problem for a specific period of time each day; quarreling husbands and wives are instructed to indulge in and even exaggerate their fighting. By instructing family members to enact symptomatic behavior, the therapist is demanding that the presentation of the symptom, claimed to be "involuntary" and thus out of their control, be done voluntarily. Such paradoxical interventions are designed to evoke one of two reactions, either of which is sought by the therapist. If the patient complies, continuing to be symptomatic, there is the admission that the symptomatology is under voluntary control, not involuntary as claimed, and thus can be stopped. On the other hand, if the directive to continue the symptom is resisted, the symptom will be given up.

3. Enactment.   Most likely to be used by structural family therapists, *enactments* are role-playing efforts to bring the outside family conflict into the session, so that family members can demonstrate how they deal with it and the therapist can start to devise an intervention procedure for modifying their interaction and creating structural changes in the family. Encouraged by the therapist, the family members act out their dysfunctional transactions rather than talk about them. This allows the therapist an opportunity for direct observation of the process instead of relying on family members' reports of what occurs at home. Because of the immediacy of this approach, the therapist can intervene on the spot and witness the results of such interventions as they occur.

Helping "unfreeze" family members from repetitive family interactions that end in conflict, the therapist has a chance to guide them in modifying the interactions. By introducing alternative solutions calling for structural changes in the family, the therapist can help the family create options for new behavior sequences. Treating the family of an anorectic adolescent, Minuchin (Minuchin, Rosman, & Baker, 1978) might arrange to meet the family for the first session and bring in lunch, thus deliberately provoking an enactment around eating. Observing their struggles over their daughter's refusal to eat, Minuchin can demonstrate that the parental subsystem is not working effectively. If parents begin to cooperate with one another in making their daughter eat, they form a stronger union. At the same time, the daughter is relieved of the too-powerful and destructive position she has been maintaining. The enactment impels the family to look at the system they have created together and to literally change the dysfunctional behavior displayed in the session.

4. Family Sculpting.   Rather than put their feelings or attitudes toward one another into words, which may be difficult or threatening, family members each take a turn at being a "director," placing each of the other members in a physical arrangement in space. The result is often revealing of how the "director" perceives his or her place in the family and that person's perception of what is being done to whom, by whom, and in what manner.

Individual perceptions of family boundaries, alliances, roles, subsystems, and so on are typically revealed, even if the "director" cannot, or will not, verbalize such perceptions. The resulting graphic picture of individual views of family life provides active, nonverbal depictions for other members to grasp. Because of its nonintellectualized way of putting feelings into action, family sculpting is especially suited to the experiential approach of Satir.

5. *Circular Questioning.*   This technique is often used by systemic family therapists (Boscolo, Cecchin, Hoffman, & Penn, 1987) to focus attention on family connections rather than individual symptomatology. Each question posed to the family by the therapist addresses differences in perception by different members about the same events or relationships. By asking several members the same question regarding their attitudes toward those situations, the therapist is able to probe more deeply without being confrontational or interrogating the participants in the relationship. In this non-confrontational therapeutic situation, the family is able to examine the origin of the underlying conflict. Advocates of this technique believe questioning is a therapeutic process that allows the family to untangle family problems by changing the ways they view their shared difficulties.

Mechanisms of Psychotherapy

Family therapists generally take an active, problem-solving approach with families. Typically, they are more interested in dealing with current dysfunctional interactive issues within the family than in uncovering or helping resolve individual intrapsychic problems from the past. While past family transactional patterns may be explored, this is done to home in on ongoing behavioral sequences that need changing rather than to reconstruct the past.

Depending on their specific emphases, family therapists may try to help clients achieve one or more of the following changes:

1. *Structural Change.*   Having assessed the effectiveness of a family's organizational structure and its ongoing transactional patterns, family therapists may actively challenge rigid, repetitive patterns that handicap optimum functioning of family members. Minuchin, for example, assumes the family is experiencing sufficient stress to overload the system's adaptive mechanisms, a situation that may be temporary due to failure to modify family rules to cope successfully with the demands of transitions. Helping families modify unworkable patterns creates an opportunity to adopt new rules and achieve realignments, clearer boundaries, and more flexible family interactions. Through restructuring, the family is helped to get back on track, so that it will function more harmoniously and the growth potential of each member will be maximized.

2. *Behavioral Change.*   All family therapists try to help clients achieve desired behavioral changes, although they may go about it in differing ways. Strategic therapists focus treatment on the family's presenting problems: what they came in to have changed. Careful not to allow families to manipulate or subdue the therapist and therefore control the treatment, strategic therapy is highly directive, and practitioners devise strategies for alleviating the presenting problem rather than explore its roots or hidden meanings. Through directives such as paradoxical interventions, they try to force the symptom-bearer to abandon old dysfunctional behavior. Similarly, systemic therapists (the Milan approach of Selvini-Palazzoli and her colleagues) may assign tasks or rituals for the family to carry out between sessions. These typically are offered in paradoxical form and call for the perfor-

mance of a task that challenges an outdated or rigid family rule. Behavioral change follows from the emotional experience gained by the family through enactment of the directive.

3. Experiential Change. Therapists such as Satir, Whitaker, and Kempler believe families need to feel and experience what previously was locked up. Their efforts are directed at growth-producing transactions in which therapists act as models of open communication, willing to explore and disclose their own feelings. Satir is especially intent on helping families learn more effective ways of communicating with one another, teaching them to express what they are experiencing. Kempler also tries to help family members learn to ask for what they want from one another, thus facilitating self-exploration, risk-taking and spontaneity. Whitaker champions family members giving voice to underlying impulses and symbols. Because he sees all behavior as human experience and not as pathological, clients are challenged to establish new and more honest relationships, simultaneously maintaining healthy separation and personal autonomy.

4. Cognitive Change. Psychodynamically oriented family therapists are interested in providing client families with insight and understanding. Boszormeni-Nagy stresses intergenerational issues, particularly how relationship patterns are passed on from generation to generation, influencing current individual and family functioning. By gaining awareness of one's "family ledger," a multigenerational accounting system of who, psychologically speaking, owes what to whom, clients can examine and correct old unsettled or unredressed accounts. J. L. Framo also helps clients gain insight into introjects reprojected onto current family members to compensate for unsatisfactory early object relations. He has clients meet with members of their families of origin for several sessions to discover what issues from the past they may have projected onto current members, and also to have a corrective experience with parents and siblings.

❖ APPLICATIONS

Problems

Individual Problems

Therapists who adopt a family frame of reference attend primarily to client relationships. Even if they work with single individuals, they look for the context of problematic behavior in planning and executing their clinical interventions. So, for example, they might see a college student, far away from family, for individual sessions, but continue to view his or her problems within a larger context in which faulty relations with others have helped create and are still maintaining the presenting troublesome behavior. Should the parents arrive for a visit, they might join their child for a counseling session or two, to provide clues regarding relationship difficulties within the family system and assist in their amelioration.

Intergenerational Problems

Family therapists frequently deal with parent/child issues, such as adolescents in conflict with their parents. Minuchin's structural approach might be adopted to help families, particularly at transition points in the family life cycle, to adapt to changes and modify outdated rules. Here they are likely to try to strengthen the parental subsystem, more clearly define generational boundaries, and help the family carve out new and more flexible rules to account for changing conditions as adolescence is reached. To cite an increasingly common example, families in which the children are raised in this country by foreign-born parents often present intergenerational conflicts that reflect differing values and attitudes, requiring intervention at the family level if changes in the family system are to be achieved.

Marital Problems

Troubled marriages are common today, and many of the problems involving symptomatic behavior in a family member can be traced to efforts by the family to deal with parents in conflict. In addition to personal problems of one or both spouses that contribute to their unhappiness, certain key interpersonal difficulties are frequently present: ineffective communication patterns; sexual incompatibilities; anxiety over making or maintaining a long-term commitment; conflicts over money, in-laws, and children; physical abuse; or conflicts over power and control. These issues, repeated without resolution over a period of time, escalate the marital dissatisfaction of one or both partners, placing the marriage in jeopardy. Couples who enter therapy conjointly, before one or both conclude that the costs of staying together outweigh the benefits, may be better able to salvage their relationship than if either or both seek individual psychotherapy.

Evaluation

Family researchers are particularly interested in two aspects of family therapy: the therapeutic process itself (What mechanisms bring about client change?) and the efficacy of the procedure (How effective are the outcomes?). Usually referred to, respectively, as process research and outcome research, both are concerned with family therapy as a treatment modality rather than as a conceptual framework

Process Research

Still in its infancy because of the inherent difficulty of developing measuring instruments for the family as a whole, process research seeks to identify the specific conditions that facilitate or impede therapeutic change. Are there certain therapist characteristics, or perhaps family characteristics, that influence outcomes? What kinds of therapist relationships, communicative or empathic skills, or intervention techniques facilitate positive change? Can the presence or absence of well-defined therapeutic interactions help determine outcomes? If so, what precisely are those therapist/family interactions, and with what set of family problems is it best to use which set of techniques?

Process research therefore focuses attention on the interaction between the family and therapist, looking for what contributes to the process of change (Greenberg & Pinsof, 1986). Beyond what actually transpires within the session, information is also sought about out-of-session events occurring during the course of therapy. Experiences reported by the family members, as well as their accompanying thoughts and feelings, are given as much credence as their overt and observable behavior. All are considered to be part of the therapeutic process and to contribute to therapeutic movement.

Client self-reports and direct observations of behavior constitute the major sources of process research data. Of the two, direct observation appears to be more promising, particularly when it differentiates specific kinds of therapist interventions and measures their effectiveness. Efforts by Pinsof (1986) to devise a family therapist coding system to study the verbal behavior of therapists within sessions have been particularly noteworthy in linking specific interventions with specific therapeutic outcomes.

Outcome Research

Gordon Paul (1967, p. 111) posed the following challenge to individual therapy outcome researchers: "What therapy is most effective for what problems, treated by what therapists, according to what criteria, in what setting?" Outcome research in family therapy must deal with the same problems that hinder such research in individual therapy, with the additional burden of gauging and measuring the various interactions taking place within a large and complex unit (the family) that is in a continuous state of change. Some family members may change more than others, different members may change in different ways, and the researcher must take into account intrapsychic, relationship, communication, and ordinary group variables in measuring therapeutic effectiveness. Some family therapists (Colapinto, 1979; Keeney & Sprenkle, 1982) argue that traditional research methods measuring therapy outcomes are actually of little use in untangling the complexities of systemic phenomena or in establishing a causal connection between a method of treatment and its effect on a family.

Despite these objections, some well-designed outcome research has been conducted. Minuchin, Rosman & Baker (1978), using a struculalist approach with anorectic adolescents, conducted follow-ups 18 months and seven years after treatment, and reported 43 of the 50 patients (86%) recovered from both physical symptoms and their psychosocial manifestations. These figures compared favorably with results from individual therapy with anorectic youngsters. Other such single-group studies ("Does treatment X produce measurable positive changes in population Y?") such as Patterson's (1975) family behavioral approach with problematic childhood behaviors or Stanton & Todd's (1979) work with drug-addicted families, again using a structural approach, have proven to be effective.

In an overall review of family therapy outcomes, Gurman, Kniskern, & Pinsof (1986) found conjoint sessions for marital discord to be clearly more effective than individual efforts. According to the results of their exhaustive survey, family therapy was found to be more effective than individual therapy, even for problems that seem intrapsychic in nature, rather than interpersonal.

Treatment

The Family Therapy Perspective

Family therapy represents an outlook regarding the origin and maintenance of symptomatic or problematic behavior, as well as a form of clinical intervention directed at changing dysfunctional aspects of the family system. Adopting such an outlook, the entire family may be seen together, or various dyads, triads, or subsystems may be seen, depending on what aspects of the overall problem are being confronted by the therapist. Methods of treatment may vary, depending largely on the nature of the presenting problem, the therapist's theoretical outlook, and his or her personal style.

However, family therapy involves more than seeing distressed families as a unit or group. Simply gathering members together and continuing to treat the individuals separately, but in a group setting, fails to make the paradigm shift called for in treating relationships. Nor is it enough to perceive individual psychopathology as the therapist's central concern while acknowledging the importance of the family context in which such psychopathology developed. Rather, family therapy calls for viewing the amelioration of individual intrapsychic conflicts as secondary to improving overall family functioning.

To work in a family systems mode, the therapist must give up the passive, neutral, nonjudgmental stance developed with so much care in conventional individual psychotherapy. To effectively help change family functioning, the therapist must become involved in the family's interpersonal processes (without losing balance or independence); be supportive and nurturing at some points and challenging and demanding at others; attend to (but not overidentify with) members of different ages; and move swiftly in and out of emotional involvements without losing track of family interactions and transactional patterns (Goldenberg & Goldenberg, 1991).

Indications and Contraindications

Family therapy is not a panacea for all psychological disturbances but is a valuable option in a therapist's repertoire of interventions. However, it is clearly the treatment of choice for certain problems within the family. Wynne (1965) suggests that family therapy is particularly applicable to resolving relationship difficulties (e.g., parent/children; husband/wife), especially those to which all family members contribute, collusively or openly, consciously or unconsciously. Many family therapists go beyond Wynne's position, arguing that all psychological problems of individuals and of groups such as families ultimately are tied to system issues and thus amenable to intervention at the family level.

Under what circumstances is family therapy contraindicated? In some cases, it may be too late to reverse the forces of fragmentation, or perhaps too difficult to establish or maintain a therapeutic working relationship with the family because key members are unavailable or refuse to attend. Sometimes one seriously emotionally disturbed member may so dominate the family with malignant and destructive motives and behavior, or be so violent or abusive or filled with paranoid ideation, that working with the entire family becomes impossible, although some members of the family may continue to benefit from the family therapy perspective.

Length of Treatment

Family therapy may be brief or extended, depending on the nature and complexities of the problem, family resistance to its amelioration, and the goals of treatment. Changes that most benefit the entire family may not in every case be in the best interest of each family member, and some may cling to old and familiar ways of dealing with one another. In general, however, family therapy tends to be relatively short term compared to most individual therapy approaches. In some cases, as few as ten sessions may eliminate symptomatic behavior; others may require twenty sessions or more for symptoms to subside.

Strategic therapy quickly focuses on what problems require attention; the therapist then devises a plan of action to change the family's dysfunctional patterns in order to eliminate the presenting problem. Structural approaches tend to be brief, as the therapist joins the family, learns of its transactional patterns, and initiates changes in its structure leading to changes in behavior and symptom reduction in the identified patient. The object relations approach, on the other hand, consistent with its psychoanalytic foundations, tends to be longer and to deal with material from earlier in clients' lives.

Settings and Practitioners

Outpatient offices, school counselor settings, and inpatient hospital wards all provide places where family therapy may be carried out. No longer out of the mainstream of psychotherapy, where it dwelt in its earlier years, family therapy has been accepted by almost all psychotherapists. Marital therapy, now considered a part of the family therapy movement, has grown at an astonishing rate since the 1970s.

Psychiatrists, psychologists, social workers, marriage and family counselors, and pastoral counselors practice family therapy, although their training and emphases may be different. Three basic kinds of training settings exist today: degree-granting programs in family therapy, freestanding family therapy institutes, and university-affiliated programs.

Stages of Treatment

Most family therapists want to see the entire family for the initial session, since overall family transactional patterns are most apparent when all participants are together. (Young children, attending the first session, are usually not expected to attend subsequent meetings unless they are an integral part of the problem.) After establishing contact with each member present and assessing their suitability for family sessions, therapists interested in family history, such as Bowen, may begin to construct a family genogram. Others, like Haley, may proceed to negotiate with the family about precisely what problem they wish to eliminate. Minuchin's opening move is to "join the family" by adopting an egalitarian role within it, making suggestions rather than issuing orders. He accommodates to the family's style of communicating, assesses problems, and prepares a treatment plan.

The middle phase of family therapy is usually directed at helping the family members redefine the presenting problem or symptomatic behavior in the identified patient as a relationship problem to be viewed within the family context. Here the family becomes the "patient" and together they begin to recognize that all have contributed to the problem and all must participate in changing ingrained family patterns. If therapy is successful, families, guided by the therapist, typically begin to make relationship changes.

In the final stage of family therapy, families learn more effective coping skills and learn better ways to ask for what they want from one another. Although they are unlikely to leave problem-free, they have learned problem-solving techniques for resolving relationship issues together. Termination is easier in family therapy than in individual therapy because the family has developed an internal support system and has not become overdependent on an outsider, the therapist. The presenting complaint or symptom has usually disappeared, and it is time for disengagement.

❖ CASE EXAMPLE

Background

While the appearance of troublesome symptoms in a family member typically brings the concerned family to seek help, it is becoming increasingly common for couples or entire families to recognize they are having relationship problems that require amelioration at the family level. Sometimes therapy is seen as a preventive measure. For example, adults with children from previous marriages who are planning to marry may become concerned enough about the potential problems involved in forming a stepfamily that they will consult a family therapist before marriage.

Frank, 38, and Michelle, 36, about to marry within a week, referred themselves because they worried about whether they were prepared, or had prepared their children, sufficiently for stepfamily life. The therapist saw them for two sessions, largely devoted to discussing common problems they had anticipated along with suggestions for their amelioration. Neither Frank's two children, Ann, 13, and Lance, 12, nor Michelle's daughter, Jessica, 16, attended these sessions.

Michelle and Frank had known each other since childhood, although she later moved to a large city and he settled in a small rural community. Their families had been friends in the past, and Frank and Michelle had visited and corresponded with each other over the years. When they were both 22, before Frank went away to graduate school, a romance blossomed between Frank and Michelle and they agreed to meet again as soon as feasible. When her father died unexpectedly, Michelle wrote to Frank, and when he did not respond, she was hurt and angry. On the rebound, she married Alex, who turned out to be a drug user, verbally abusive to Michelle and chronically unemployed. They divorced after two years, and Michelle, now a single mother, began working to support herself and her daughter Jessica. Mother and daughter became unusually close in the twelve years before Michelle and Frank met again.

Frank also had been married. Several years after his two children were born, his wife developed cancer and lingered for five years before dying. The children, although looked after by neighbors, were alone much of the time, with Ann, Frank's older child, assuming the parenting role for her younger brother, Lance. When Frank met Michelle again, their unfinished romance was rekindled, and in a high state of emotional intensity they decided to marry.

Problem

Approximately three months after their marriage, Frank and Michelle contacted the therapist again, describing increasing tension between their children. Needing a safe place to be heard (apparently no one was talking to anyone else), the children, Ann and Lance (Frank's) and Jessica (Michelle's), eagerly agreed to attend family sessions. What emerged were a set of individual problems compounded by the stresses inherent in becoming an "instant family."

Frank, never able to earn much money and burdened by debts accumulated during his wife's long illness, was frustrated and guilty over his feeling that he was not an adequate provider for his family. Michelle was jealous over Frank's frequent business trips, in large part because she felt unattractive (the reason for her not marrying for twelve years). She feared Frank would find someone else and abandon her again, as she felt he had done earlier, at the time of her father's death. Highly stressed, she withdrew from her daughter Jessica for the first time. Losing her closeness to her mother, Jessica remained detached from her stepsiblings and became resentful of any attention Michelle paid to Frank. In an attempt to regain a sense of closeness, she turned to a surrogate family—a gang—and became a "tagger" at school (a graffiti writer involved in pre-gang activities). Ann and Lance, who had not had time or a place to grieve over the loss of their mother, found Michelle unwilling to take over mothering them. Ann became bossy, quarrelsome, and demanding; Lance at age 12 began to wet his bed.

In addition to these individual problems, they were having the usual stepfamily problems: stepsibling rivalries, difficulties of stepparents assuming parental roles, and boundary ambiguities.

Treatment

From a systems view, the family therapist is able to work with the entire family or see different combinations of people as needed. Everyone need not attend every session. However, retaining a consistent conceptual framework of the system is essential.

The therapist had "joined" the couple in the two initial sessions, and they felt comfortable returning after they married and were in trouble. While constructing a genogram, the therapist was careful to establish contact with each of the children, focusing attention whenever she could on their evolving relationships. Recognizing that parent-child attachments preceded the marriage relationship, she tried to help them as a group develop loyalties to the new family. Boundary issues were especially important, as they lived in a small house with little privacy, and the children often intruded on the parental dyad.

When seeing the couple together without the children present, the therapist tried to strengthen their parental subsystem by helping them to learn how to support one another and share child-rearing tasks. (Each had continued to take primary responsibility for his or her own offspring in the early months of the marriage.) Jealousy issues were discussed, and the therapist suggested they needed a "honeymoon" period that they had never had. With the therapist's encouragement, the children stayed with relatives while their parents spent time alone with each other.

After they returned for counseling, Frank's concerns over not being a better provider were discussed. He and Michelle considered alternate strategies for increasing his income and helping more around the house. Michelle, still working, felt less exhausted and thus better able to give more of herself to the children. Frank and Lance agreed to participate in a self-help behavioral program aimed at eliminating bedwetting, thus strengthening their closeness to one another. As Lance's problem subsided, the entire family felt relieved of the mess and smell associated with the bedwetting problem.

The therapist decided to see Ann by herself for two sessions, giving her the feeling she was special. Allowed to be a young girl in therapy, and temporarily relieved of her job as a parent to Lance, she became more agreeable and reached outside the family to make friends. She and Lance had one additional session (with their father) grieving over the loss of their mother. Michelle and Jessica needed two sessions together to work out their mother/daughter adolescent issues as well as Jessica's school problems.

Follow-Up

Approximately twenty-five sessions were held. At first the sessions were weekly, later biweekly, and then they were spread over three-month periods. By the end of a year, the family had become better integrated and more functional. Frank had been promoted at work, and the family had rented a larger house, easing the problems brought about by space limitations. Lance's bedwetting had stopped, and he and Ann felt closer to Michelle and Jessica. Ann, relieved of the burden of acting older than her years, enjoyed being an adolescent and became involved in school plays. Jessica still had some academic problems but had broken away from the gang and was preparing to go to a neighboring city to attend a junior college.

The family contacted the therapist five times over the next three years. Each time they were able to identify the dyad or triad stuck in a dysfunctional sequence for which they needed help, and each time a single session seemed to get them back on track.

❖ SUMMARY

Family therapy, beginning in the 1950s, turned attention away from individual intrapsychic problems and placed the locus of pathology on dysfunctional transactional patterns within a family. Within this new perspective, families are viewed as systems, with members operating within a relationship network and by means of feedback loops aimed at maintaining homeostasis. Growing out of research aimed at understanding communication patterns in the families of schizophrenics, the focus of family therapy later broadened to include therapeutic interventions with a variety of family problems. These therapeutic endeavors are directed at changing repetitive maladaptive or problematic sequences within the system.

Symptomatic behavior in the identified patient is viewed as signaling family disequilibrium. Symptoms arise from, and are maintained by, current, ongoing family transactions. Viewing causality in circular rather than linear terms, the family therapist focuses on repetitive behavioral sequences between members that are self-perpetuating and self-defeating. Therapeutic intervention may take a number of forms, including approaches assessing the impact of the past on current family functioning (object relations, contextual), those largely concerned with individual family member growth (experiential), those that focus on family structure and processes (structural) or transgenerational issues (Bowen), and those heavily influenced by behavioral perspectives (strategic, behavioral). All attend particularly to the context of people's lives in which dysfunction originates and can be ameliorated.

Interest in family systems theory and concomitant interventions will probably continue to grow in the coming years. The stress on families precipitated by the lack of models or strategies for dealing with divorce, remarriage, alternative lifestyles, or acculturation in immigrant families will likely increase demand for professional help at a family level.

Consumers and cost containment managers will utilize family therapy with even greater frequency in the future because it is a relatively short-term procedure, solution-oriented, dealing with real and immediate problems. Moreover, it feels accessible to families with relationship problems who don't wish to be perceived as pathological. Its preventive quality, helping people learn more effective communication and problem-solving skills to head off future crises, is attractive not only to families, but also to practitioners of family medicine, pediatrics, or other primary care physicians to whom troubled people turn. As the field develops in both its research and clinical endeavors, it will better identify specific techniques for treating different types of families at significant points in their life cycles.

❖ ANNOTATED BIBLIOGRAPHY

Boscolo, L., Cecchin, G., Hoffman, L., & Penn, P. (1987). *Milan systemic family therapy: Conversations in theory and practice*. New York: Basic Books.

This is a clearly elaborated book describing how the Milan Associates have utilized cybernetic theory to help families change behavior. Following an introduction to the theoretical foundation for the systemic view, transcripts of sessions are presented along with enlightening conversation by a team of participating and observing therapists clarifying how non-manipulative techniques such as circular questioning are used therapeutically to bring about changes in the family system.

Goldenberg, I., & Goldenberg, H. (1991). *Family therapy: An overview* (3rd ed.). Pacific Grove, CA: Brooks/Cole.

This text describes the major theories and the assessment and intervention techniques of family therapy. Systems theory and family life cycle issues are outlined, a historical discussion of the field's development is included, and research, training, and professional issues are considered.

Kerr, M. E., & Bowen, M. (1988). *Family evaluation: An approach based on Bowen theory*. New York: W. W. Norton.

An updated explication of Bowen's ideas is presented by a longtime associate of Bowen's together with comments by Bowen. Bowen's contribution to family systems theory is elaborated and presented in an integrated fashion. Proposals for assessing families based on Bowen's theory are offered and illustrated in short case examples.

Minuchin, S. (1974). *Families and family therapy*. Cambridge, MA: Harvard University Press.

This widely used and influential book by the major architect of structural family therapy offers the best description of the fundamental concepts for understanding family formation and organization. Written in a lively and compelling style, and featuring specific techniques for restructuring families, Minuchin's book offers numerous detailed accounts of his work with families.

❖ CASE READINGS

Family therapy trainers commonly make use of videotapes of master therapists demonstrating their techniques with real families, since tapes provide a richer and greater dimensional sense of the emotional intensity of family sessions than what is available from case readings alone. Tapes are available to rent or purchase from the Ackerman Institute in New York, the Philadelphia Child Guidance Center, the Boston Institute, the Georgetown University Family Center, the Family Institute of Washington, D.C., and many other training establishments.

Three texts deal largely with descriptions and analyses of family therapy from the vantage point of leading practitioners:

> Napier, A. Y., & Whitaker, C. A. (1978). *The family crucible*. New York: Harper & Row.

This text gives a full account of co-therapy with one family, including both parents, a suicidal, runaway, teenage daughter, an adolescent son, and a six-year-old daughter.

> Satir, V. M., & Baldwin, M. (1983). *Satir step by step: A guide to creative change in families*. Palo Alto, CA: Science and Behavior Books.

Using double columns, Satir presents a transcript of a session accompanied by an explanation for each intervention.

> Grove, D. R., & Haley, J. (1993). *Conversations on therapy: Popular problems and uncommon solutions*. New York: W. W. Norton.

Grove and Haley, apprentice and master therapist, offer a question-and-answer conversation regarding specific cases seen at the Family Therapy Institute of Washington, D.C., and together they devise strategies for intervening effectively in problematic situations.

Two well-received edited texts contain case descriptions offered by family therapists with a variety of viewpoints as listed below. Although both books are somewhat dated, they effectively convey what transpires as family therapists attempt to put theory into practice.

> Haley, J., & Hoffman, L. (Eds.). (1967). *Techniques of family therapy*. New York: Basic Books.

Particularly noteworthy in the Haley and Hoffman text are the transcripts and comments of initial interviews by five therapists, including Jackson, Satir, and Whitaker.

> Papp, P. (1983). The daughter who said no. *The process of change* (pp. 67–120). New York: Guilford. [Reprinted in D. Wedding & R. J. Corsini (Eds.) (1994). *Case studies in psychotherapy*. Itasca: F. E. Peacock.]

This is a classic case that illustrates the way a master family therapist treats a young woman with anorexia nervosa.

> Penn, P. (Ed.). (1977). *Family therapy: Case studies*. New York: Gardner Press.

In this set of case studies, twelve prominent therapists with differing viewpoints (including James Framo, Carl Whitaker, Harry Aponte of the Philadelphia Child Guidance Clinic, Richard Fisch of the Palo Alto Mental Research Institute, and Peggy Papp of the Ackerman Institute for Family Therapy) discuss their cases from beginning to end, carefully describing the therapeutic process they created and explaining the rationale for interventions.

❖ REFERENCES

Ackerman, N. W. (1958). *The psychodynamics of family life*. New York: Basic Books.

Bandura, A. (1977). *Social learning theory*. Englewood Cliffs, NJ: Prentice Hall.

Bateson, G. (1972). *Steps to an ecology of mind*. New York: E.P. Dutton.

Bateson, G., Jackson, D. D., Haley J., & Weakland, J. (1956). Towards a theory of schizophrenia. *Behavioral Science, 1*, 251–264.

Bell, J. E. (1961). *Family group therapy*. Public Health Monograph No. 64., Washington, DC: U.S. Government Printing Office.

von Bertalanffy, L. (1968). *General systems theory: Foundation, development, applications*. New York: Braziller.

Boscolo, L., Cecchin, G., Hoffman, L., & Penn, P. (1987). *Milan systemic family therapy: Conversations in theory and practice*. New York: Basic Books.

Boszormenyi-Nagy, I. (1987). *Foundations of contextual therapy: Collected papers of Ivan Boszormenyi-Nagy*. New York: Brunner/Mazel.

Bowen, M. (1960). A family concept of schizophrenia. In D. D. Jackson (Ed.), *The etiology of schizophrenia*. New York: Basic Books.

Bowen, M. (1978). *Family therapy in clinical practice*. New York: Jason Aronson.

Buckley, W. Q. (1967). *Sociology and modern systems theory*. Englewood Cliffs, NJ: Prentice-Hall.

Colapinto, J. (1979). The relative value of empirical evidence. *Family Process, 18*, 427–441.

Framo, J. L. (1982). *Explorations in marital and family therapy: Selected papers of James L. Framo.* New York: Springer.

Goldenberg, I., & Goldenberg, H. (1991). *Family therapy: An overview* (3rd ed.). Pacific Grove, CA: Brooks/Cole Publishing Co.

Greenberg, L. S., & Pinsof, W. M. (Eds.). (1986). *The psychotherapeutic process: A research handbook.* New York: Guilford Press.

Gurman, A. S., Kniskern, D. P., & Pinsof, W. M. (1986). Research on the process and outcome of marital and family therapy. In S. Garfield & A. Bergin (Eds.), *Handbook of psychotherapy and behavior change* (3rd ed.). New York: Guilford Press.

Haley, J. (1976). *Problem-solving therapy.* San Francisco: Jossey-Bass.

Jackson, D. D. (1965). Family rules: Marital quid pro quo. *Archives of General Psychiatry, 12,* 589–594.

Kenney, B. P., & Sprenkle, D. H. (1982). Ecosystemic foundations of family therapy: Critical implications for the aesthetics and pragmatics of family therapy. *Family Process, 21,* 1–19.

Kempler, W. (1981). *Experiential psychotherapy with families.* New York: Brunner/Mazel.

Kuhn, T. (1970). *The structure of scientific revolutions.* Chicago: The University of Chicago Press.

Laing, R. D. (1965). Mystification, confusion, and conflict. In I. Boszormenyi-Nagy & J. L. Framo (Eds.), *Intensive family therapy: Theoretical and practical aspects.* New York: Harper & Row.

Lidz, T., Cornelison, A., Fleck, S., & Terry, D. (1957). The intrafamilial environment of schizophrenic patients: II. Marital schism and marital skew. *American Journal of Psychiatry, 114,* 241–248.

Minuchin, S. (1974). *Families and family therapy.* Cambridge, MA: Harvard University Press.

Minuchin, S., Montalvo, B., Guerney, B. G., Jr., Rosman, B. L., & Schumer, F. (1967). *Families of the slums: An exploration of their structure and treatment.* New York: Basic Books.

Minuchin, S., Rosman, B. L., & Baker, L. (1978). *Psychosomatic families: Anorexia nervosa in context.* Cambridge, MA: Harvard University Press.

Nichols, M. P. (1987). *The self in the system: Expanding the limits of family therapy.* New York: Brunner/Mazel.

Patterson, G. R. (1975). *Families: Applications of social learning to family life* (rev. ed.). Champaign, IL: Research Press.

Paul, G. L. (1967). Outcome research in psychotherapy. *Journal of Consulting Psychology, 31,* 109–188.

Pinsof, W. M. (1986). The process of family therapy: The development of the Family Therapist Coding System. In L. S. Greenberg & W. M. Pinsof (Eds.), *The psychotherapeutic process: A research handbook.* New York: Guilford Press.

Reiss, D. (1981). *The family's construction of reality.* Cambridge, MA: Harvard University Press.

Satir, V. (1972). *Peoplemaking.* Palo Alto, CA: Science and Behavior Books.

Scharff, D. E., & Scharff, J. S. (1987). *Object relations family therapy.* Northvale, NJ: Jason Aronson.

Selvini-Palazzoli, M. (1986). Towards a general model of psychotic games. *Journal of Marital and Family Therapy, 12,* 339–349.

Selvini-Palazzoli, M., Boscolo, L., Cecchin, G. F., & Prata, G. (1978). *Paradox and counterparadox: A new model in the therapy of the family schizophrenic transaction.* New York: Jason Aronson.

Stanton, M. D., & Todd, T. C. (1979). Structural family therapy with drug addicts. In E. Kaufman & P. Kaufman (Eds.), *The family therapy of drug and alcohol abuse.* New York: Gardner Press.

Stuart, R. B. (1980). *Helping couples change: A social learning approach to marital therapy.* Champaign, IL: Research Press.

Sullivan, H. S. (1953). *The interpersonal theory of psychiatry.* New York: W. W. Norton.

Wachtel, E. F., & Wachtel, P. L. (1986). *Family dynamics in individual psychotherapy: A guide to clinical strategies.* New York: Guilford Press.

Watzlawick, P., Weakland, J. H., & Fisch, R. (1974). *Change: Principles of problem formation and problem resolution.* New York: W. W. Norton.

Whitaker, C. A., & Bumberry, W. M. (1988). *Dancing with a family: A symbolic-experiential approach.* New York: Brunner/Mazel.

White, M. (1989). *Selected papers.* Adelaide, Australia: Dulwich Centre Publications.

Wiener, N. (1948). Cybernetics. *Scientific American, 179* (5), 14–18.

Wynne, L. C. (1965). Some indications and contraindications for exploratory family therapy. In I. Boszormenyi-Nagy & J. L. Framo (Eds.), *Intensive family therapy: Theoretical and practical aspects.* New York: Harper & Row.

Wynne, L. C., Ryckoff, I. M., Day, J., & Hirsch, S. I. (1958). Pseudomutuality in the family relationships of schizophrenics. *Psychiatry, 21,* 205–220.

13 Three Other Approaches

Buddha, Afghanistan

A   Asian Psychotherapies

Roger Walsh

There is a growing recognition that Western psychologists may have underestimated the psychologies and therapies of other cultures. Certain Asian disciplines contain sophisticated therapies, and experimental studies have demonstrated their ability to induce psychological, physiological, and psychotherapeutic effects. An increasing number of Westerners, including mental health professionals, now use Asian therapies. Benefits include new perspectives on psychological functioning, potential, and pathology, as well as new approaches and techniques. In addition, the study of other cultures and practices often has the healthy effect of revealing unsuspected ethnocentric assumptions and limiting beliefs, thus leading to a broader view of human nature and therapy.

Psychotherapies address three major levels of health and development: pathological, existential, and transpersonal. As this book demonstrates, Western psychologists have devised sophisticated maps of pathologies and techniques for alleviating them. Recently Westerners have begun to focus more on existential issues—such as meaninglessness, isolation, and freedom—that all of us face simply by virtue of our existence as human beings. Existentialists frequently regard these issues as unresolvable and suggest that the best we can do is to endure them with courage and authenticity.

Transpersonal therapies agree with the prescription for courage and authenticity. However, they claim that these issues are also helped by a transformation of one's state of consciousness and sense of identity, such as can occur through meditation. Techniques such as meditation have traditionally been conceived of as religious but can now also be understood psychologically.

Asian psychologies focus primarily on existential and transpersonal levels and little on the pathological. They contain detailed maps of states of consciousness, developmental levels, and stages of enlightenment that extend beyond traditional Western psychological maps. Moreover, they claim to possess techniques for inducing these states and conditions. However, Asian psychologies lack the West's sophisticated understanding and detailed analyses of areas such as early development, psychodynamics, and psychopathology, and until recently had little to offer those suffering severe psychological disturbances.

The two classic families of Asian psychotherapies are meditation and yoga. *Meditation* refers to a family of practices that train attention in order to bring mental processes under greater voluntary control. This control is used to cultivate specific mental qualities, such as awareness, concentration, joy, love, and compassion. The aim of these practices is deep insight into the nature of mind, consciousness, and identity and the development of optimal states of psychological well-being and consciousness.

Yoga refers to a family of practices with the same aims as meditation. However, yogas are disciplines encompassing ethics, life-style, body postures, breath control, and intellectual study in addition to meditation. In the West the best known practices are the body postures of Hatha yoga, which have frequently been taken to be the totality of yoga. In fact, they comprise only one aspect of a far more comprehensive training.

It has sometimes been argued that these Asian practices cannot really be considered psychotherapies because the essence of psychotherapy, as defined in the West, is the helping interaction, yet much meditation and yoga practice can be done alone. This argument seems to ignore the wide range of relationships possible in both Western and Asian therapies.

On the Western side, one can find therapies in which the patient is completely dependent on the therapist. At the other extreme is self-therapy, which Freud used on himself in his attempt to gain self-understanding, an understandable venture since there were no other psychoanalysts available at that time. Some Western therapies, such as psychoanalysis, foster transference. Others, such as behavior modification, try to minimize it and to substitute an instructor-student relationship.

The spectrum of relationships is almost as broad for Asian therapies. Some foster transference, others minimize it; in some the relationship is primary, in others definitely secondary. However, instruction and assistance from a skilled helper is regarded as essential in all Asian practices, which are never entirely solitary. These considerations justify inclusion of Asian practices among those we call psychotherapy.

❖ HISTORY

Past History

The origins of meditation and yoga can be traced back for 3000 years. Until recently very little was known of these practices in the West, and what was known was frequently misunderstood and dismissed. As late as 1946 a well-known psychiatrist proclaimed meditation to be "an attempt at psychological and physical regression to the condition of intrauterine life…a sort of artificial schizophrenia" (Alexander et al., 1946). However, such views are now clearly untenable, and since the 1960s there has been an explosion of popular, professional, and research interest in meditation and yoga.

Current Status

Although meditation and yoga were originally employed in the East for work at existential and transpersonal levels, considerable clinical and research data suggest that these practices may also be effective for reducing pathology. Thus, while significant numbers of Westerners employ these techniques for their traditional benefits, others use them for more modest and immediate benefits, such as relaxation, stress management, or a heightened sense of psychological well-being, or for managing specific psychological or psychophysiological disorders.

Research Findings

Several hundred experimental studies of meditation and yoga indicate that these therapies are effective for a wide range of disorders. Many studies report that meditation reduces both generalized anxiety and specific phobias. Clinical research indicates that drug and alcohol use may be reduced in those who practice meditation. Hospitalized psychiatric patients may also benefit from daily meditation. (For reviews of these therapeutic applications, see Kwee [1990], Shapiro [1982], Shapiro & Walsh [1984], and West [1987].)

Psychophysiological benefits also occur. Meditation has been employed successfully for rehabilitation after heart attacks; to treat irregular heartbeat, bronchial asthma, and insomnia; to reduce high blood pressure; and to help with the management of chronic pain (Kabat-Zinn, 1990).

Positive effects have also been noted in healthy nonclinical populations. Several studies suggest that meditators change more than controls in the direction of enhanced confidence, self-esteem, sense of self-control, empathy, marital satisfaction, creativity, academic achievement, moral and cognitive development, and self-actualization (Alexander et al., 1991).

Perhaps the most startling finding is that meditation may enhance longevity. A geriatric population taught meditation not only scored better on objective tests of psychological functioning and subjective measures of well-being than did any of three matched control groups, but also had a significantly lower mortality rate (Alexander et al., 1989).

It is clear that meditation has therapeutic potential. However, some studies are flawed by methodological problems, and several studies suggest that meditation may be no more effective for clinical disorders such as anxiety or high blood pressure than are other self-regulation strategies, such as relaxation training and self-hypnosis. On the other hand, some subjects have reported meditation to be more meaningful, pleasurable, and relaxing than other strategies. Patients most likely to benefit from meditation for psychological or psychophysiological problems are probably those who are less severely disturbed and already possess a sense of self-control.

Therapists who practice meditation and yoga themselves may also experience benefits, including enhanced therapeutic effectiveness. Several studies have shown that meditation increases perceptual sensitivity as well as empathic sensitivity and accuracy. The deep insights that meditation provides seem to foster understanding of, and compassion for, the painful experiences of others. These effects may be particularly valuable because research suggests that traditional training programs in the health sciences do little to enhance empathy and may even reduce it (Lesh, 1970).

In Asia the current status of meditation and yoga remains unchanged: these techniques are practiced by tens of millions of people and are regarded as essential practices for advanced psychological and religious development. Their relationship to religious goals has become psychologically understandable in terms of altered states of consciousness. Research in this area has brought the startling recognition that parts of the world's great religions can be viewed as methods for inducing altered, and especially transcendent, states of consciousness (Wilber, 1981).

Behind the better known practices of many religions, one often finds a core of disciplines such as contemplation, meditation, and yoga. These practices are used to induce states of consciousness embodying desired qualities, such as emotions of love and compassion, states of peace and joy, reductions of greed and anger, and motives of generosity and service. Consequently, aspects of both Western and Eastern religious life, such as meditation and yoga, can now be understood in psychological terms. Research studies have begun to lend support to these ideas. In one study, for example, Rorschach tests of advanced meditators showed "no evidence of sexual or aggressive drive conflicts" (Brown & Engler, 1986).

The classic Asian practices of meditation and yoga are the most widely used of all therapies, with perhaps 100 million practitioners worldwide. Meditation has been more thoroughly researched than all therapies except behavioral therapies, and several good reviews of this research are now available (Kutz, Borysenko, & Benson, 1985; Shapiro, 1982; Shapiro & Walsh, 1984; West, 1987). Wilber, Engler, and Brown (1986) provide more technical analyses of the experiences and stages of meditation and yoga. Several reviews describe integrations of Asian and Western therapies, especially in the field of transpersonal psychology (Goleman, 1988; Vaughan, 1994; Walsh & Vaughan, 1993; Wilber, 1981). Reviews of Morita and Naikan therapies are also available (Ishiyama, 1986; Reynolds, 1981).

For those who wish to learn to meditate, helpful books include Benson (1976), Goldstein (1983), Kabat-Zinn (1993), LeShan (1975), and Ram Dass (1990). The classic yoga text is Patanjali's millennia-old *Yoga Sutras* (Shearer, 1989). Although some progress can be made alone, the guidance of a good instructor/teacher/therapist is extremely valuable. A list of meditation centers is available in Ram Dass (1990).

❖ THEORY

Asian therapies stem from and lead to views of human nature, mind, psychology, and consciousness that in some ways differ markedly from traditional Western assumptions. In this section we shall compare Asian models with the traditional Western paradigm, examine the mechanisms involved in producing the effects of meditation and yoga, and briefly survey Morita and Naikan therapies.

Asian Models

Consciousness

Around the turn of the century, William James remarked:

> Our normal waking consciousness…is but one special type of consciousness, whilst all about it, parted from it by the filmiest of screens, there lie potential forms of consciousness entirely different. We may go through life without suspecting their existence; but apply the requisite stimulus, and at a touch they are there in all their completeness…No account of the universe in its totality can be final which leaves these other forms of consciousness quite disregarded. (1958, p. 298)

Asian psychologies agree fully. They describe a broad spectrum of these states unrecognized by Western psychology and provide detailed descriptions and techniques for attaining them. Perceptual sensitivity and clarity, concentration, sense of identity, and emotional, cognitive, and perceptual processes all vary with states of consciousness in predictable ways.

Some states are functionally specific, while a few are said to be true higher states. *Functionally specific states* are those in which certain functions are improved while others are less effective. For example, yogic *samadhi* states marked by deep calm and concentration may be conducive to introspective exploration but not to social interaction. True *higher states* are defined as those that possess the capacities present in the usual condition, plus heightened or additional ones (Tart, 1986; Walsh & Vaughan, 1993).

If higher states of consciousness exist, then, contrary to the typical Western assumption, our usual state must be less than optimal. This is exactly the claim of the Asian psychologies, which describe our usual state as hypnotic or dreamlike. Trained observation reveals that our minds are usually filled with a continual flux of unrecognized thoughts, images, internal dialogues, and fantasies that distort and reduce awareness, resulting in unappreciated trance states (Tart, 1986). As in any hypnotic state, the trance and its attendant constriction of awareness may not be recognized.

At times all of us daydream and become lost in fantasy. Asian psychologies claim that these fantasies are significantly more pervasive, distorting, and befogging than we realize. Their extent and consequences remain unrecognized because, like psychological defense mechanisms, they are partially self-masking. The result is said to be *maya*: an unrecognized, encompassing, illusory distortion of perception and experience that remains unrecognized until we subject our perceptual-cognitive processes to direct, rigorous scrutiny, as in meditation.

Thus, the "normal" person is considered to be usually "asleep," "dreaming," or in a "consensus trance" (Tart, 1986). When a dream is especially painful or disruptive it becomes a nightmare and is recognized as psychopathology, but because the vast majority of the population dreams, the usual more subtle forms remain unrecognized. People who eradicate this dream are said to have "awakened," and this awakening, known as *liberation* or *enlightenment*, is the aim of Asian therapies.

To some extent these concepts are an extension rather than a denial of Western psychology and psychiatry. Research (Langer, 1988) has shown that we have less awareness of our own cognitive processes than we usually assume and that we suffer from a broad range of usually unrecognized cognitive-perceptual distortions and automaticities (unconscious automatic habits). Asian psychologies suggest that these distortions and automaticities can be reduced and awareness enhanced by meditative training, a claim now supported by studies of perceptual processing in advanced meditators (Brown & Engler, 1986; Brown, Forte & Dysart, 1984).

These claims do not have to be taken on faith. Those willing to undertake intensive training in observation of their own mental processes—such as in a week of intensive meditation—can easily test the claims for themselves. All Asian therapies recommend personal testing because any thorough understanding requires direct experience. Some previously skeptical behavioral scientists have been shocked into acknowledging the potency of these disciplines only after personal experience (e.g., Tart, 1986; Walsh, 1977).

Psychopathology

Ideal psychological health is considered tantamount to enlightenment in Asian psychology. Consequently, most Asian philosophers agree with Abraham Maslow (1968), who said, "What we call 'normal' in psychology is really a psychopathology of the average, so undramatic and so widely spread that we don't even notice it (p. 16)." The roots of this pathology, both individual and social, are said to include addiction (craving), aversion, and ignorance (unconsciousness and misunderstanding of one's mind and true nature).

Asian psychologies point out that addiction can occur not only to food and drugs, but to practically anything, including external possessions and internal emotions, beliefs, and self-images. Indeed, the Buddha claimed that all suffering is rooted in addiction. It is an interesting challenge to try to find examples of psychological pain in one's own life that do not reflect addiction.

The mirror image of addiction is aversion. Whereas with addiction, happiness is dependent on possessing something, with aversion it is dependent on avoiding it.

The mind ruled by addiction and aversion is said to be a slave to every situation and environment in which it finds itself, constantly involved in a never-ending search to get what it wants and avoid what it fears. Happiness is said to be dependent on, and limited to, those occasions when the world is lined up to match one's particular pattern of addictions and aversions. From this perspective, psychological pain is a feedback signal indicating the existence of addictions and aversions and the need to relinquish them. Asian psychologies consequently claim that psychological health and happiness are dependent not so much on the satisfaction of addictions and the avoidance of aversions as on reducing and becoming free of them.

Psychological Health

For Asian psychologies the ideal of health is enlightenment or liberation, rather than only adjustment to, or compromise with, psychodynamic givens. The means for attaining health include reduction of the pathogenic factors of addiction, aversion, and ignorance. However, mental health is also defined in positive terms. Consequently, Asian therapies cultivate and strengthen specific healthy qualities, such as mindfulness, love, compassion, concentration, and calm.

For people in whom these healthy qualities have been cultivated, and addiction and aversion reduced, compassion and selfless service are said to become major motives (Walsh & Shapiro, 1983). This Eastern claim for a correlation between psychological maturity and service parallels several Western concepts, such as Alfred Adler's social interest and Erik Erikson's generativity. Abraham Maslow (1967) claimed that "self-actualizing people are, without one single exception, involved in a cause outside their own skin." (p. 282).

Therapeutic Mechanisms

A large number of mechanisms are involved in producing the effects of meditation and yoga. In this section we will examine those proposed by both Western and Asian psychologies.

The first of these Western mechanisms is dehypnosis. When we observe our minds carefully we find that we spend considerable time lost in fantasies that seem real at the time. This can be regarded as a type of hypnosis. When we develop concentration and awareness, we can recognize these fantasies for what they are: only fantasies. For example, a meditator may shift from believing that he or she is scared to simply being aware of, and unaffected by, a fearful fantasy. If the process of becoming lost in fantasies is regarded as a form of hypnosis, then the meditation process of recognizing thoughts and fantasies for what they are may be seen as dehypnosis (Tart, 1986).

Other psychological mechanisms that have been used to explain the effects of meditation include relaxation, habituation and desensitization to formerly stressful stimuli, and the deconditioning of old habits. A variety of cognitive mechanisms may also be involved, including the expectation of positive benefits. Physiological explanations have included reduced metabolism and arousal, changes in hemispheric lateralization (a shift in the relative activity of the two cerebral hemispheres), and brain-wave changes and autonomic nervous system changes (West, 1987).

Several Asian psychologies contain models to explain how therapeutic effects are produced through meditation. One Buddhist model based on mental factors (qualities of mind) is particularly useful in making comparisons with Western psychotherapeutic practices. Seven of these factors, the so-called *seven factors of enlightenment*, are regarded as particularly important for health (Goldstein, 1983).

The first is *mindfulness*, a precise, conscious awareness of the stimulus being observed, which might be regarded as a refinement of the psychoanalytic observing ego. The remaining six mental factors are divided into two groups of three arousing qualities and three calming qualities. The three arousing factors are *effort* (energy, arousal), *investigation* (active exploration of experience), and *rapture* (delight in the awareness and exploration of experience). The three calming factors are *concentration* (the ability to maintain attention on a specific object), *calm* (tranquility and freedom from anxiety and agitation), and *equanimity* (the capacity to experience stimuli without disturbance).

Western therapists have emphasized the arousing factors of *effort* and *investigation*. Less appreciated is the idea that sensitivity and insight can be enhanced by a complementary development of *concentration, calm,* and *equanimity*. Optimal effects occur when all seven factors are cultivated in a balanced, mutually facilitating manner (Goldstein, 1983).

Facilitating psychological development is another mechanism now being explored in the West. Some Western developmental psychologists have argued for the existence of stages of cognitive, motivational, and moral development beyond conventional norms. Several theoretical and experimental studies now suggest that advanced meditators and yogis may attain these higher stages (Alexander et al., 1991; Wilber, 1981; Wilber et al., 1986).

Innovative Asian Psychotherapies: Morita and Naikan

Morita is a Japanese therapy designed for the treatment of anxiety, especially in patients characterized by anxious self-preoccupation, perfectionistic self-expectations, social phobia, and extreme dislike of their symptoms. Treatment consists of four components: *acceptance, reattribution, dereflection,* and *active engagement*. Patients are taught to accept and reinterpret their symptoms (what Western behaviorists call reattribution) not as signs of weakness and inadequacy, but rather as reflections of strong ideals. They are also taught to participate fully in life without waiting for their anxiety to dissipate. Through engagement, attention is directed away from the self (a process Victor Frankl calls dereflection) and, secondarily, anxiety is reduced. Morita therapy has produced a large literature that has significantly influenced Japanese psychotherapy, and good success rates have been reported (Ishiyama, 1986).

A second Japanese therapy, Naikan, is adapted from a more intensive Buddhist practice and consists simply of intensive reflection on past relationships. Clients reflect specifically on three things: what other people have done for them, what they have done for others, and the difficulties they have caused others. The aim is to foster recognition of human interdependence, of how much we have received from others, how much gratitude is due them, and how little we have demonstrated this gratitude. Along with a confrontation with guilt and unworthiness comes the recognition that one has been loved and appreciated in spite of weaknesses and failings. The result is usually an upwelling of gratitude and a desire to contribute more. Little formal research has been done on Naikan therapy, but case reports document success with a variety of neuroses and personality disorders, the most noteworthy being with convicts and alcoholics (Reynolds, 1981).

❖ METHODOLOGY

The intensity and degree of commitment required to use meditation or yoga for intensive exploration and growth are far greater than that required for their use as more modest self-regulation strategies. For an individual committed to deep self-transformation, meditation and yoga are best viewed as components of an encompassing shift in attitudes, thought, speech, and behavior aimed at the deepest possible transformation of mind, awareness, identity, life-style, and relationships. Meditative and yogic training are usually accompanied by shifts in life-style so that all one's behavior, overt and covert, facilitates the growth process.

The first shift is a commitment to ethical behavior. Asian therapies recommend refraining from lying, stealing, sexual misconduct, killing, and taking mind-clouding intoxicants. Traditionally this is said to lead to "purification," in which counterproductive motives and behavior are gradually winnowed away. In Western behavioral terms this would be seen as the extinction of disruptive habits by the prevention of undesired behavior.

Ethical behavior is not to be confused with externally imposed moralism with its right-wrong, good-bad perspective. No meditator can long remain unaware that unethical behavior is motivated by such states of mind as greed, anger, and aversion, that unethical behavior reinforces these states, and that they in turn disrupt the mind. The end result of unethical behavior is that the mind is left more agitated, anxious, and trapped. Ethicality is therefore seen not as something imposed from without, but as something sought from within for its direct benefits to self and others.

The cultivation of generosity and service to others is recommended as a way of reducing self-centeredness and egotistical desire. Practitioners may also be drawn to a life of voluntary simplicity. With deepening practice, meditators increasingly recognize the disrupting effects of greed and attachment and find themselves better able to generate positive feelings that formerly depended on external stimuli. Thus, they may experience less need to own the latest and biggest car, boat, or appliance, and instead, find greater pleasure in a deepening sensitivity to the moment-to-moment flow of experience, with each moment increasingly becoming a source of rich and multifaceted stimulation.

For most people, meditation and yoga are slow, cumulative processes, and beginners should be cautioned that there may be a period of weeks before the benefits of brief daily practice are clearly evident. Meditation and yoga are skills, and as with any skill, the initial phase is usually the least rewarding. However, perseverance brings increasing benefits.

Most people begin meditating with short sessions of 20 to 30 minutes, once or twice a day. Others begin with a retreat in which they engage in more or less continuous practice for a period of days or weeks under careful supervision. While it is possible to make some progress unaided, any deep practice is greatly facilitated by the guidance of a teacher-therapist.

Meditation practices can be subdivided into two main categories: concentration and awareness. Concentration meditations aim especially at developing the ability of the mind to focus attention without distraction on specific objects, such as the breath, an emotion, or sound. Awareness meditations, on the other hand, aim at exploring any experiences that occur.

In concentration meditation, one attempts to fix attention on a specific stimulus, such as one's breath. However, attention remains fixed for a remarkably short period, and the individual is soon lost in fantasy. When this is recognized, one's attention is brought back to the breath and maintained there until lost again. This rapidly results in a startling and disconcerting recognition: We have little control of attention. Most beginning meditators, including Western trained psychotherapists, are astonished to find how much of their lives and mental processes are unconscious and automatic.

It is worthwhile to try the following exercise to appreciate the power and extent of this automaticity. Set an alarm for a minimum of 10 minutes. Then take a comfortable seat, close your eyes, and turn your attention to the sensations of breathing in your abdomen. Try to concentrate on the sensations continuously as the abdominal wall rises and falls. Focus your attention carefully, precisely, and microscopically on the sensations that arise and pass away. Do not let your attention wander for a moment. If thoughts and feelings arise, let them remain, but continue to focus your awareness on the sensations of the breath.

While you continue to pay close attention to the sensations, start counting the breaths from 1 to 10, and after you reach 10, go back to 1 again. However, if you lose count or if your mind wanders from the sensations of your breath, even for an instant, go back to 1 and begin again. If you get distracted or lost in fantasy, just recognize what has happened and gently bring your mind back to your breathing and start counting once more. Continue this process until the alarm tells you to stop; then estimate how much of the time your were actually fully aware of the experience of breathing.

Most people will find that only a very small percentage of their time was spent fully aware of the sensations of breathing. With prolonged practice, concentration gradually improves and, as it does, a number of beneficial experiences begin to occur, such as calm, equanimity, and joy.

Although the practice of concentration can be useful and pleasurable, some Asian traditions view concentration more as a facilitator of awareness meditation than as an end in itself. Insight or awareness practices do not fix attention on a single object but rather allow the mind to explore whatever experiences arise. In doing this, the first level of insights that develop might be called psychodynamic, and the individual will recognize patterns of thought and behavior such as might be noticed in traditional psychotherapy. However, as meditation deepens, the significantly enhanced capacities of concentration, calm, and equanimity allow deep insights into the nature of mental processes. This level of insight brings an illumination of how the mind is constructed. One begins to see, for example, the way a single thought or desire may rise into awareness and modify emotion, perception, and muscle tension patterns. One therefore begins to develop insight into the fundamental nature and effects of such mental processes as thought, motivation, and perception.

With increasing practice the range and intensity of experiences continue to increase and eventually exceed anything experienced in daily life. Yet at the same time calm and equanimity also increase so that this greater range of experiences can be observed and allowed with less and less disturbance, defensiveness, or interference. The individual identifies more and more with the calm observer or witness of these experiences rather than with the experiences per se and, in doing so, experiences a deep sense of peace and freedom.

Occasionally some of these experiences may be disturbing—for example, the occurrence of anxiety, tension, anger, and changes in perception of self and reality (Walsh & Vaughan, 1993; Wilber et al., 1986). These may sometimes be quite intense. However, usually symptoms are short-lived and disappear spontaneously. Consultation with a therapist familiar with both Asian and Western therapies may be particularly helpful in such cases. In many instances these difficulties seem to represent a greater sensitivity to, and emergence of, previously repressed psychological memories and conflicts. Thus, the initial discomfort of experiencing them may be a necessary price for processing and discharging them.

These are the procedures common to most meditation and yoga practices. In addition, numerous yogic techniques are designed to elicit specific qualities and skills. The following two very brief descriptions of skills (which until recently Western psychologists usually considered impossible) merely hint at the remarkable range of practices and powers of mind that Asians have discovered in their 3000-year-long exploration of our inner universe.

The first is the cultivation of love, especially unconditional love, or *agape*. Once preliminary skills such as concentration and calm have been mastered, then specific emotions can be cultivated. For example, the mind can focus intensely on the image of a love object, and the resulting emotion can then be intensified and extended to encompass all people. This is very different from the common Western assumption that love is an emotion largely outside our control that can encompass only a very few people.

"Lucid dreaming," an actual sleep state in which subjects know they are dreaming, is a 1200-year-old Tibetan Buddhist yoga for training and exploring the mind. However, in the West, lucid dreaming was either ignored or dismissed as impossible until Stephen LaBerge (1985) demonstrated its existence and similarities to ancient Tibetan accounts. LaBerge's induction techniques are freely available so that now one can develop this ancient yogic skill and investigate the nature and powers of the mind, all in the comfort of bed.

❖ SUMMARY

Asian psychotherapies include a variety of techniques: the oldest and most widely used are meditation and yoga. Across centuries and cultures they have led to the highest levels of human development, and after 3000 years they remain the world's most widely used psychotherapeutic techniques. Today several million Westerners have joined tens of millions of Asians in these practices. However, in the West their most popular application has been for relaxation and stress management rather than for the deeper psychological insights and altered states of consciousness traditionally sought in the East.

Experimental research has clearly demonstrated psychological, physiological, and chemical effects of meditation and *yoga*, as well as significant psychotherapeutic benefits. However, it remains unclear whether these techniques are necessarily more effective for the management of clinical disorders than are techniques such as relaxation training and self-hypnosis.

Both research findings and ancient Asian claims challenge some fundamental assumptions and paradigms of Western psychology. For example, the Asian claim that our usual state of consciousness is less than optimal runs counter to our basic assumptions that our usual state is best. Similarly, Asian therapies suggest the existence of true higher states of consciousness and claim that these can be achieved through training. A growing network of concepts and data points to the validity of some of these claims. Clearly, Asian therapies have significant implications for both psychological theory and therapeutic application.

Asian psychotherapies may offer several advantages over other clinical interventions. First of all, meditation and yoga are inexpensive. The practitioner is independent of location and instruments and can practice as much or as little as desired. In fact, there may be relatively little need for professional time and energy once the basic practice has been established. There are also multiple applications, as these therapies are useful for certain clinical problems as well as for psychological growth. Both therapists and clients may find them beneficial. They can be a useful adjunct to more traditional therapies, are often very enjoyable, and casualties are rare. Of course, Asian tradition suggests that the ultimate test of any theory is experiential. Their response to questions about the validity and effectiveness of these disciplines remains the same today as it has been for millennia: "To see if this be true, look within your own mind."

❖ REFERENCES

Alexander, C., Langer, E., Newman, R., Chandler, H., and Davies, J. (1989). Transcendental meditation, mindfulness and longevity: An experimental study with the elderly. *Journal of Personality and Social Psychology, 57*, 950–964.

Alexander, C., Rainforth, M., and Gelderloos, P. (1991). Transcendental meditation, self actualization and psychological health: A conceptual overview and statistical meta-analysis. *Journal of Social Behavior and Personality, 6*, 189–247.

Alexander, F., French, T. M., & Bacon, C. L. (1946). *Psychoanalytic therapy: Principles and applications.* New York: Ronald Press.

Benson, H. (1976). *The relaxation response.* New York: Avon.

Brown, D., & Engler, J. (1986). The stages of mindfulness meditation: A validation study. Part II. Discussion. In K. Wilber, J. Engler & D. Brown (Eds.), *Transformations of consciousness: Conventional and contemplative perspectives on development* (pp. 191–218). Boston: New Science Library/Shambhala.

Brown, D., Forte, M., & Dysart, M. (1984). Visual sensitivity and mindfulness meditation. *Perceptual and Motor Skills, 58*, 775–784.

Goldstein, J. (1983). *The experience of insight.* Boston: Shambhala.

Goleman, D. (1988). *The meditative mind.* Los Angeles: J. Tarcher.

Ishiyama, F. (1986). Morita therapy. *Psychotherapy, 23*, 375–380.

James, W. (1958). *The varieties of religious experience.* New York: New American Library. (Originally published in 1902.)

Kabat-Zinn, J. (1990). *Full catastrophe living.* New York: Delacorte.

Kabat-Zinn, J. (1993) *Wherever you go, there you are.* New York: Hyperion.

Kutz, I., Borysenko, J., & Benson, H. (1985). Meditation and psychotherapy. *American Journal of Psychiatry, 142*, 1–8.

Kwee, M. (Ed.). (1990) *Psychotherapy, meditation and health.* London: East-West.

LaBerge, S. (1985). *Lucid dreaming.* Los Angeles: Tarcher.

LeShan, L. (1975). *How to meditate.* New York: Bantam Books.

Langer, E. (1988). Minding matters: The consequences of mindlessness/mindfulness. In L. Berkowitz (Ed.), *Advances in Experimental Social Psychology.* New York: Academic Press.

Lesh, T. (1970). Zen meditation and the development of empathy in counselors. *Journal of Humanistic Psychology, 10*, 39–74.

Maslow, A. (1967). Self actualization and beyond. In J. Bugental (Ed.), *Challenges of humanistic psychology* (pp. 279–286). New York: McGraw-Hill.

Maslow, A. (1968). *Toward a psychology of being (2nd ed.).* Princeton: Van Nostrand.

Ram Dass. (1990). *Journey of awakening: A meditator's guidebook.* New York: Doubleday.

Reynolds, D. (1981). Naikan psychotherapy. In R. J. Corsini (Ed.), *Handbook of innovative psychotherapies* (pp. 544–553). New York: John Wiley.

Shapiro, D. H. (1982). Overview: Clinical and physiological comparison of meditation with other self-control strategies. *American Journal of Psychiatry, 139*, 267–274.

Shapiro, D., & Walsh, R. (Eds.) (1984). *Meditation: Classic and contemporary perspectives.* New York: Aldine.

Shearer, P. (Trans.). (1989). *Effortless being: The Yoga sutras of Patanjali.* London: Unwin.

Tart, C. (1986). *Waking up: Overcoming the obstacles to human potential.* Boston: New Science Library/Shambhala.

Vaughan, F. (1994). *The inward arc.* Nevada City, CA: Blue Dolphin.

Walsh, R. (1977). Initial meditative experiences: Part I. *Journal of Transpersonal Psychology, 9*, 151–192.

Walsh, R., & Shapiro, D. H. (Eds.)(1983). *Beyond health and normality: Explorations of exceptional psychological wellbeing.* New York: Van Nostrand Reinhold.

Walsh, R. & Vaughan, F. (Eds.). (1993). *Paths beyond ego: The transpersonal vision.* Los Angeles: J. P. Tarcher.

West, M. (Ed.). (1987). *The psychology of meditation.* Oxford: Clarendon Press.

Wilber, K. (1981). *No boundary.* Boston: New Science Library/Shambhala.

Wilber, K., Engler, J., & Brown, D. (Eds.) (1986). *Transformations of consciousness: Conventional and contemplative perspectives on development.* Boston: New Science Library/Shambhala.

Jacob L. Moreno,
1889–1974

B   Psychodrama

Adam Blatner, M.D.

Psychodrama is a method of psychotherapy in which clients are helped to enact situations in individual, family, or group settings. Scenes from the past, present, or future, imagined or real, are given intensity and relevance by being portrayed as if they were occurring at the moment. Special techniques such as role reversal, the mirror, and the double serve to bring out unspoken feelings and half-denied attitudes. The role-playing process offers a wealth of diagnostic cues because habitual verbal defenses are circumvented. In the process of working out solutions to problems, clients have an opportunity to discover their capacity for creativity.

Although classical psychodrama is a powerful technique that should be conducted only by professionals specifically trained in the method, psychodramatic *methods* may be adapted for use in individual, family, or milieu therapy settings involving a wide range of problems and clients. Their use is compatible with a number of psychodynamic, cognitive, and behavioral approaches. Psychodrama is no panacea, sufficient unto itself—it works best in the hands of those who are well grounded in professional judgment, yet open to applying an eclectic methodology in treatment.

Psychodrama differs from drama therapy in that the former focuses on specific problems of individuals and the latter addresses the more general processes of spontaneity development and the evocation of self-awareness of people in groups (Emunah, 1994, Landy, 1993). Psychodramatists typically are general psychotherapists with "subspecialty" training,* and drama therapists usually have their primary background in the theatre, followed by specific training in its therapeutic modifications and applications (Emunah 1994; Landy, 1994). Both psychodrama and drama therapists share in the advantages of using a medium of aesthetic expression, and they, along with the other creative arts therapists, recognize that the vitality so engendered is a valuable agent of healing.

Role-playing, a direct outgrowth of psychodrama, has applications not only in psychotherapy (Corsini, 1966; Kipper, 1986), but also in education, management, and other settings. Often the terms are used interchangeably, but psychodrama usually refers to a more in-depth exploration of emotions and role-playing to the working out of an effective behavioral response.

The principles of psychodrama contribute significantly to the field of psychotherapy. They serve to remind mental health professionals of the potential for healing associated with creativity, spontaneity, physical action, excitement, mutuality, imagination, playfulness, flexibility, self-expression, and a willingness to expand one's vitality by including the powerful channels of poetry, dance, song, music, drama, and art. These rich resources for vitality represent innate connections to the best part of childhood, and are suffused with pleasure. These qualities become intrinsically rewarding, useful motivators in treatment. Most importantly, however, they enhance the sense of personal autonomy, identity, effectiveness, and hopefulness.

❖ HISTORY

Psychodrama was originated and developed by Jacob L. Moreno, M.D. (1889–1974). A fascinating and complex person, Moreno was also a major pioneer of group psychotherapy, social psychology, and improvisational theatre. Moreno, a psychiatrist, was also a philosopher whose vision of an integrated approach to social welfare and individual treatment has only recently found a receptive historical *Zeitgeist*. His early influences included the work of the philosophers Henri Bergson and Charles Sanders Peirce. Interested in replicating aspects of children's make-believe play, Moreno observed and tested action methods with groups of children in the parks of Vienna. The results of these experiences convinced him of the importance of spontaneity as a part of the creative and vitalizing processes of life.

Moreno attended the University of Vienna from 1907 to 1917, first as a student of philosophy, then medicine, the field in which he received his degree. Vienna during that time was engaged in a renaissance of the arts and sciences. Moreno fully entered into the intellectual ferment, and during this period he originated the "self-help" group, the beginnings of sociometry (a method in which groups can give feedback about their interpersonal preferences, and which came to be a part of modern sociology), and an early form of existentialism, emphasizing new concepts such as "here-and-now" and "en-

---

*For more information about psychodramatic training, certification, and professional literature, you can write to the following organizations:

American Society for Group Psychotherapy and Psychodrama (ASGPP), 6728 Old McLean Village Road, McLean, VA 22101

American Board of Examiners in Psychodrama, P.O. Box 15572, Washington, D.C. 20003-0572

Journal of Group Psychotherapy, Psychodrama, and Sociometry (comes with membership in ASGPP), c/o HELDREF Publishers, 1319 Eighteenth St. NW, Washington, D.C. 20036-1802 counter." He experimented with ways to restore and develop spontaneity and creativity in a variety of situations, and chose theatre as an appropriate context to promote these philosophical and psychological explorations (Marineau, 1989). For Moreno, however, the traditional theatre had become too decadent, burdened by a lack of spontaneity resulting from rehearsed productions and memorized scripts that reflected the separation of the creative act of the playwright from the "performance" of the actor.

While serving as a general practitioner in a suburb of Vienna in 1921, Moreno, along with a group of actors with similar ideals, began his experimental "Theatre of Spontaneity." He later dated this as the beginning of psychodrama, because over the next several years the therapeutic implications of improvisational drama became increasingly apparent to him. In his theatre, he reintroduced and developed the method of improvisation as a renewal of the field of drama. His goal was to help people rediscover the aesthetic implications of the events and adventures of their own lives. Finding that post-war Europe was not able to support his dream of a "therapeutic theatre," he decided to emigrate to America. Even though Moreno's work in subsequent years addressed more limited applications in treating mental illness, he never lost his dream of helping society develop more effective forms of practical democracy, interpersonal freedom, and interactive creativity.

In 1925 Moreno came to the United States, where he gradually began to develop active group methods. He introduced the term "group psychotherapy" at a meeting of the American Psychiatric Association in 1932. In 1936 he opened a sanitarium in Beacon, New York, about sixty miles north of New York City. In his experiments with interpersonal approaches to psychotherapy, he introduced co-therapy (implicit in the technique of the "auxiliary") as well as marital and family therapy, and he worked with the phenomenology of the patient, a form of existential psychotherapy (Compernolle, 1981). In 1942, he opened an institute in New York City and offered open sessions where many professionals visited and enriched their own conceptual frames of reference. That year he started the first professional organization devoted to group psychotherapy, the American Society for Group Psychotherapy and Psychodrama. During the 1950s Moreno promoted group psychotherapy in all its forms, including family therapy and the use of the therapeutic community. He was also instrumental in supporting innovations in the creative arts therapies and the applied social sciences. He organized international conferences and wrote prolifically (Fox, 1987).

In 1949, Moreno married Zerka Toeman, and both of them taught and traveled internationally. Zerka carried on Moreno's work after his death, and at the time of this writing, she is the foremost exponent of psychodrama. In addition, hundreds of other directors of psychodrama now work and teach throughout this country and around the world. During his lifetime, Moreno was the major author of scores of articles and books and the editor of several journals about psychodrama and its related approaches. Since 1970, other authors have published a number of important books, including Corsini (1966); Corsini, Shaw, & Blake (1961); Blatner (1973e, 1988a, 1988b); Greenberg (1974); Yablonsky (1975); Starr (1977); Goldman and Morrison (1984); Kipper (1986); Fuhlrodt (1990); Williams (1989, 1991); Holmes & Karp (1991); Holmes (1992); Kellermann (1992); Leveton (1992); and Holmes, Karp, & Watson (1994).

At present, psychodrama has become a significant part of a number of hospital treatment programs, though it remains on the periphery of traditional psychiatry and psychology in this country. Nevertheless, applications of psychodramatic methods are found in the work of therapists of every discipline. Psychodrama is often integrated with other therapeutic methods; examples are described in books by Leveton (1984) and Nicholas (1984). Active approaches in psychotherapy have become more acceptable, in part because the way was paved by psychodrama. For example, techniques such as the *action sociogram* have become a recognized part of family therapy (where it is called "family sculpture") (Blatner, 1994b). Many aspects of the human potential movement and the encounter group were foreshadowed by Moreno's earlier work, because these approaches also have applications in personal growth settings, and in a modified form (as sociodrama or role-playing) in schools and community organizations (Sternberg & Garcia, 1989). Psychodrama has become part of the mainstream of therapeutic process in a number of other countries, especially Sweden, Germany, Argentina, Brazil, New Zealand, Australia, and Japan.

❖ THEORY

J. L. Moreno was among the pioneers of *role theory*, which has become one of the major approaches within the social sciences. However, in contrast to its tendency to be used simply for descriptive purposes, Moreno emphasized its potential for encouraging creative change. Always thinking in terms of practical application, Moreno believed that roles should be continuously reevaluated, experimented with, and shifted around. In this sense, role theory becomes a heuristic, clinically relevant approach (Z. Moreno, 1987; Blatner, 1991a).

The very concept of *role* implies a separation between the actor and the performance. When people are able to thus disidentify themselves from those complexes of expectation, habit, and reciprocal communications that constitute their various roles, they begin to develop *role distance*. In clinical situations, role distance gives patients perspective and allows them to consider alternatives to the assumptions inherent in their situations. From this viewpoint, they are helped to redefine, expand, and renegotiate their expectations of themselves and others. In the sense of mental flexibility, psychodrama generates an essentially playful context, although serious and painful matters are often addressed. The result is a the development and strengthening of that part of the patient's psyche which observes, chooses, makes a working alliance with the therapist, individuates, connects with ideals and aspirations, and expresses what Roberto Assagioli and Otto Rank called the "will."

Role theory has other advantages. The metaphor of "role" is relatively easy to understand. The variety of roles that can be described include the broadest range of human experiences, encompassing spirituality, fantasy, dreams, art, and temperament. Role theory also serves as a general framework that can integrate many of the insights of other psychologies—for example, it grants that in some roles Jungian ideas may be more clinically illuminating, while in other roles, the concepts of Wilhelm Reich, A. T. Beck, or Murray Bowen may have more relevance.

A special advantage of role theory is that it is the most useful framework—and psychodrama the most useful method—for exploring the realm of *interpersonal phenomena*. This area reflects a level of complexity distinct in quality and dynamics from the psychology of individuals or of larger groups (Blatner, 1988b). Family systems theories come closest to addressing this dimension, but the interpersonal field also includes other social relationships (Blatner, 1994a). Relevant factors include how roles are distributed, how fixed they are, and people's freedom or ability to comment on their complexes of expectations, hidden rules, associated emotions, and so on. In other words, role theory makes a bridge between individual and social psychology.

A corollary of this psychosocial focus in psychodrama is the idea that role theory can be used to help people understand each other. Empathy is trainable when the concept of role is used as a "lens" for considering one aspect of another person's situation at a time. Gradually, using the technique of role reversal (discussed more fully below), patients can be helped to relinquish their tendencies toward egocentricity. Moreno meant his concept of "encounter" to include not only a more honest and direct level of dialogue, but also a willingness to appreciate the other's point of view. In this sense, psychodramatic methods are useful in developing what Alfred Adler considered the key to mental health, a quality he called "social interest" (Adler, 1930).

Psychodrama implicitly encourages an expansion of one's role repertoire: By shifting roles freely, and enjoying playing several roles on several levels simultaneously (such as the role of observing the process and the role involved in carrying out the task), a sense of vitality is added to therapy. The contribution of psychodrama to psychotherapy resides in its powerful methodology, which demonstrates that healing comes not only through re-conditioning, learning, or insight, but also through the sense of empowerment gained as patients discover their own capacity for creativity. Here, too, psychodrama serves as a methodology for implementing the insights of Otto Rank's approach to therapy (Lieberman, 1985). Furthermore, creative activities are self-reinforcing: The more people discover their ability to be creative, the more confidence they develop that they can make use of such sources of creativity in times of need.

Moreno discovered that the practical key to everyday creativity was *spontaneity*, and methods that foster spontaneity increase patients' progress in therapy. Spontaneity does not refer to mere impulsivity, but rather to a fresh and effective response to a challenging situation. It is the opposite of fixations, addictions, or habitual/compulsive patterns of thought. Many forms of individual and social psychopathology may be viewed as a loss of spontaneity, an unwillingness to think creatively.

The principle of *physical activity* offers several benefits in psychotherapy: (1) The kinesthetic cues aroused in movement and the freeing up of the breath and voice evoke a host of preverbal associations. (2) The sense of being active helps to counter the sense of helplessness and passivity, with their attendant feelings of guilt and shame, which tend to be associated with the demoralization found in psychiatric problems. (3) Reintroduction of the rich dimension of nonverbal communication in enactments can be worked with both diagnostically and therapeutically. (4) Physically moving from place to place on stage when taking different roles symbolically compartmentalizes the different facets of a problem and helps to reduce confusion.

The principle of *concretization* engages patients in specifying their problems in dramatic form. Vague abstractions, often used as subtle defenses, are converted into specific scenes. By re-anchoring patients in their experiences, the therapist and group are aided in understanding the problem and can engage in more effective help. What Alfred Adler called "the private fictions," those internalized mini-dramas of secret desires, fears, expectations, and symbolic triumphs, can be reevaluated in the externalization process of psychodrama. With the support of the therapist and the group, and the recognition in the present moment that old strategies are no longer adaptive, new approaches to the problem can be devised. The currently popular "object-relations" approach of psychoanalytic thought can be enhanced by enacting the internal drama of the fantasied dialogue, and the extreme elements of these psychodynamics can be modulated.

The development of channels for *sublimation* through the use of psychodrama helps patients begin to release their neurotic patterns by working out alternative ways of achieving satisfaction (Blatner, 1992). Psychodrama, in fostering self-expression of the voice, body, and imagination, allows for metaphorical resolution of internal conflicts. The creative arts therapies also provide effective treatment using this principle. The therapeutic dynamics of psychodrama provide a vehicle for healing by serving as play therapy for adults. The dramatic context provides the benefits of a fail-safe "laboratory," a supportive place for experimentation with new behaviors. The vividness of the method and its similarity in essence to the psychodynamics of play—the symbolic resolution of seemingly paradoxical elements—lend a sense of pleasure and reintroduce humor to the process (Blatner & Blatner, 1988). This element of "fun" is a powerful motivating factor, for it counters tendencies in psychotherapy to stay overly focused on the client's pain. Although an expression of concern is appropriate, too much can discourage hopefulness and extinguish resources for change.

Catharsis, a major factor in psychological healing, is a fundamental element in psychodrama. It involves a freeing of psychic energy that accompanies an expansion of consciousness (Blatner, 1985; Nichols & Efran, 1985). As the psyche includes previously disowned parts of itself, the energies previously exerted in the service of repression become available for more conscious utilization. In addition, there is a sense of relief in reuniting with an important part of the self that previously had been disowned.

Psychodrama aims not only at rediscovery of the various aspects of the self, but also at developing constructive ways for utilizing these dimensions. Referring to this principle, Moreno noted that every catharsis of abreaction should be followed by a catharsis of integration. (Therapies aimed simply at abreactive catharses may have been less effective because they lacked the component of developing healthy behaviors to replace unhealthy ones.) When people discover that they can be accepted by a group or find a meaningful role in the world, a catharsis of "belonging" occurs—which may also include spiritual or transpersonal experiences. The unique focus of psychodrama in encouraging the expansion of the self in a group setting creates an opportunity for synthesizing the needs for both individuation and belonging.

By demanding a holistic involvement from the therapist, psychodrama functions not only as a method for developing insight, but also as a method of experiential learning that facilitates personal growth for the therapist as well as the patient. Furthermore, psychodramatic techniques have applications in many non-therapeutic contexts and thereby also serve the goals of prevention and social development.

Terminology

Moreno described five basic elements in psychodrama: (1) the director; (2) the protagonist; (3) the auxiliary; (4) the stage; and (5) the audience.

The *director* (the therapist) orchestrates the enactment.

The *protagonist* (the client) is the focus of the psychodramatic exploration. Protagonists may play themselves, their mothers, several different parts of themselves, or even step outside the scene as observers. In all these shifts of role, the protagonist remains the focus of the director's and the group's concern. In subsequent group therapy sessions other clients might become the focus of attention; during their enactments they would become protagonists.

The *auxiliary* is anyone who helps the protagonist by playing a supporting role. The auxiliary (also called "auxiliary ego") may portray the protagonist's employer, sibling, a figure in a dream, or even an abstract entity, such as "the government." For example, assume the protagonist is in a scene with an employer, played by an auxiliary. If role reversal is used, the auxiliary then takes the role of the protagonist while the protagonist takes the role of employer. The auxiliary can also take the role of the "double" for the protagonist, a technique described more fully below.

The *stage* refers to a designated area for the enactment. It is usually beneficial to use a separate area rather than playing the scene in the midst of the group. Providing a separate locus of dramatic action serves to remind the protagonist that the events in the enactment are clearly different from verbal interchanges. Moreno designed and installed special stages at his own institutes, and some hospitals have created stages for psychodramatic work. Generally, enactments are conducted in an area cleared of chairs in a group therapy room.

The *audience* refers to the other people present besides the director, the protagonist, and auxiliaries. In psychodrama, the role of the audience shifts during the course of a session, with some members becoming auxiliaries and others becoming protagonists. Sometimes the audience plays an active role, giving feedback, encouraging, making sound effects, or calling out pertinent evocative phrases at the request of the director. (This technique is termed the "chorus.")

❖ METHODOLOGY

A typical psychodramatic instruction is "Don't tell us, show us." With this phrase, the patient is encouraged to plunge into the situation at a more intense and committed level of experience, acting "as if" instead of talking "about." "Show us what happened with your family." "Show us the conflict you're having within yourself." "Show us what you'd like to be doing in ten years." (These are, respectively, the techniques of *enactment, multiple parts of self,* and *future projection.*) Scenes from the past, present, or future may be set up, and this kind of concretizing of issues has the benefit of cutting through defensive tendencies toward vagueness and circumstantiality.

The key to authentic work in psychodrama is spontaneity, usually developed gradually by *warming up* through structured experiences. Warm-up techniques are used to generate group cohesion and involvement from the very beginning; in addition, they may be applied to help patients become sensitized to a particular issue (Blatner, 1991b). For example, nonverbal interactions, art therapy activities, sensory awareness methods, guided imagery, theatre games, and brief role-playing of situations that challenge the participants' spontaneity can give a shared experience and introduce material they can explore further.

Another principle is *encounter*, a dialogue in the present moment, having the patient speak directly to significant others in one's life (either in reality or with another person played by an auxiliary). Another form of encounter can occur between different parts of the protagonist's "self" (Watkins, 1986). Some patients' sense of confusion can be productively reframed as a conflict in which the different parts of themselves interrupt each other too much. Externalizing internal dialogues and separating the various voices can help clarify the issues involved. Sometimes a client can play both parts in an encounter; the technique of monodrama uses an empty chair as a locus of the imagined other.

One of the advantages of using an auxiliary is that another person's reactions tend to evoke more spontaneity from the protagonist. Also, the use of the auxiliary allows transferences to be directed at the original or more relevant figures in the patient's life—parents, spouses, teachers, previous therapists, and so on—played by the auxiliary—while the therapist becomes a mediator. The protagonist is able to explore more intense feelings in the heat of the spontaneous interaction. The auxiliary can employ the evocative medium of touch, expressed through a tug on the sleeve, a squeeze of the hand, or a hand on the shoulder. Additional auxiliaries may play roles of other figures in the scene, so there may be several people on the stage at a time.

In the technique of the *double*, an auxiliary plays the role of the protagonist's inner self, helping to express and clarify one's unspoken thoughts. The double usually plays a supportive role for the protagonist; however, once a sense of alliance is developed between the two, the director may coach the double to include some mild provocation or confrontation to facilitate the clarification process. The double technique offers a type of "interpretation" phrased in terms of "I" messages and in words consistent with the patient's "self-system." The protagonist is explicitly instructed to correct any of the double's statements that feel inaccurate. This creates a mutuality in which the double helps the protagonist express in an enactment what might never be spoken in the course of an ordinary exchange.

The "heart" of psychodrama is the technique of *role reversal*. It is an operationalized approach to the Golden Rule ("Do unto others as you would have them do unto you"), aimed at helping patients to develop empathy for others and to transcend tendencies toward egocentricity. There is value inherent in the expectation that a patient will learn and exercise this skill. In this technique, the protagonist is directed to change parts and take the role of the other person—the parent, employer, or friend. The art of this technique lies in the therapist-director's ability to gently warm up the protagonist to the experience of the other's role by interviewing the protagonist as if he or she were the other person.

This technique may be used to portray the behavior of the other person, with an emphasis being on verbal components such as voice tone, tempo, or intensity, and nonverbal elements such as posture, facial expression, or gesture. These can be revealing and cathartic if the client is able to vividly communicate to the group the impact of the other person's manner. At a deeper level, role reversal can be used to help patients understand the feelings or attitudes of the other people in their lives. The technique of role reversal has a number of applications, such as helping therapists in supervision to understand their patients, or as a way of teaching psychology and other subjects.

Another principle in psychodrama is the incorporation of *surplus reality*. The term refers to that dimension of psychological experience that transcends the boundaries of physical reality. Phenomenologically, people can have relationships with others who are deceased, children who have never been born, God, hallucinatory figures, religious personages, and so on. These are often as important in a patient's psychodynamics as relationships with living people. In psychodrama, encounters with these significant psychological figures can be externalized and enacted. In this sense, as Moreno noted, psychodrama is the "theatre of truth," because the full truth of a person often encompasses not only what has actually happened, but, equally importantly, what has never happened and perhaps could never happen in reality.

Surplus reality can be utilized in several ways: One example is the technique of *act fulfillment*, in which the protagonist is helped to experience a corrective emotional event. Many patients suffer from acute or chronic trauma that left them with residual feelings of powerlessness, shame, and a secret sense that "this is the way life has to be." Reenactment of the traumatic situation breaks through layers of denial, allowing for a catharsis of "owning" the experience; this may then be healed by replaying the scene with a more satisfactory conclusion. The victim of abuse, for example, is helped to protest, to become empowered to seek effective protection, and then, using the technique of "the reformed auxiliary," given a chance to create a more benign relationship with the aggressor.

Moreno used surplus reality as a vital resource in healing. He once said to Freud, "…You analyze people's dreams. I try to give them the courage to dream again." (Moreno, 1946). In this sense, psychodrama offers patients an opportunity to envision life with more faith, to reinvest emotionally in the future. (Patients are often demoralized and frequently repress their hopes for a pleasant future as much as they repress desires/thoughts in the present and the past.) Moreno developed the *future projection technique* as a way to encourage patients to become more explicit in their goal-setting. It involves portraying scenes that are hoped for or anticipated. A variation of this is *role training*, a type of behavioral rehearsal used to help a patient prepare for an event such as a date, an employment interview, or an encounter with a relative. Using coaching, modeling, videotape or verbal feedback, and other techniques, the patient is allowed to repeat the enactment until satisfactory options are developed.

There are many other techniques used in psychodrama, and all of them can be modified and adapted for use with diverse populations and in a variety of contexts. Basic goals of all psychodramatic approaches are to involve patients in their ability to imagine, think, and behave in an *as-if* context, and to engage in dramatic play as a resource for insight, behavioral practice, the expansion of consciousness, and healing.

❖ SUMMARY

Psychodramatic methods can be used to enhance the effectiveness of many other therapies, and the principles of psychodrama address a number of dimensions of human experience that are important factors in healing and personal growth. Historically, psychodrama was developed in the 1920s and 1930s by J. L. Moreno in conjunction with his pioneering activities in group psychotherapy and applied social psychology (i.e., sociometry). His techniques have been integrated into many of the more directive forms of therapy in the last several decades. Specific techniques such as role reversal, dialogues between parts of the self, act fulfillment, and role-playing could become valuable parts of any therapist's repertoire of skills.

Moreno's emphasis on creativity and spontaneity deserves to be considered as a major contribution to a holistic psychology. Indeed, his clinical orientation to role theory can serve as an integrative approach that may help to create an intellectual foundation for a more eclectic psychotherapy. Psychodramatic methods have a unique capacity to integrate many of the dualities of human experience—the rational and imaginative; reality-testing and emotions; action and reflection; future and past; playfulness and seriousness. Utilizing the fullest potential of the group and of interpersonal relationships, and the innate potential of activities that generate spontaneity as a source of creativity, therapists can use psychodramatic methods to help their patients become more integrated—that is, more healed by becoming more whole. Part of this healing is the inclusion of excitement, playfulness, creativity, and spontaneity, which add the quality of enjoyment to those aspects of therapy that involve an adventure of self-discovery and reconciliation. It was this insight that led Moreno to choose as his epitaph, "Here lies the man who brought laughter and joy back into psychiatry."

❖ REFERENCES

Adler, A. (1930). *The science of living*. London: Kegan Paul.

Blatner, A. (1985). The dynamics of catharsis. *Journal of Group Psychotherapy, Psychodrama, & Sociometry, 37* (4), 157–166.

Blatner, A. (1988a). *Acting-in: Practical applications of psychodramatic methods* (2nd ed.). New York: Springer. (First Edition, 1973, translated into Spanish, Japanese, Dutch, Swedish, Chinese. Third edition due by 1996.)

Blatner, A. (1988b). *Foundations of psychodrama: History, theory, and practice*. New York: Springer.

Blatner, A. (1991a). Role dynamics: An integrative theory of psychology. *Journal of Group Psychotherapy, Psychodrama, & Sociometry, 44* (1), 33–40.

Blatner, A. (1991b). Imaginative interviews: A psychodramatic warm-up for developing role-playing skills. *Journal of Group Psychotherapy, Psychodrama, & Sociometry, 44* (3), 115–120.

Blatner, A. (1992). Theoretical principles underlying creative arts therapies. *Journal of the Arts in Psychotherapy, 18* (4), 405–409.

Blatner, A. (1994a). Tele: The dynamics of interpersonal preference. In P. Holmes, M. Karp, & M. Watson (Eds.), *Psychodrama since Moreno*. London: Routledge.

Blatner, A. (1994b). Psychodramatic methods in family therapy. In C. Schaefer & L. Carey (Eds.), *Family play therapy*. Northvale, NJ: Jason Aronson.

Blatner, A., & Blatner, A. (1988). *The art of play: An adult's guide to reclaiming imagination and spontaneity*. New York: Human Sciences Press.

Compernolle, T. (1981). J. L. Moreno: An unrecognized pioneer of family therapy. *Family Process, 20*, 331–335.

Corsini, R. J. (1966). *Role playing in psychotherapy*. Chicago: Aldine.

Corsini, R. J., Shaw, M. E., Blake, R. R. (1961). Role playing in business and industry. Glencoe, IL: Free Press.

Emunah, R. (1994). *Acting for real: Drama therapy process and technique*. New York: Brunner/Mazel.

Fox, J. (Ed.). (1987). *The essential Moreno: Writings...by J. L. Moreno*. New York: Springer.

Fuhlrodt, R. L. (Ed.). (1990). *Psychodrama: Its application to ACOA and substance abuse treatment*. Rutherford, NJ: Perrin & Treggett.

Goldman, E. E., & Morrison, D. S. (1984). *Psychodrama: Experience and process*. Phoenix, AZ: Eldemar Corp.

Greenberg, I. A. (Ed.). (1974). *Psychodrama: Theory and therapy*. New York: Behavioral Publications.

Holmes, P. (1992). *The inner world outside: Object relations theory and psychodrama*. London & New York: Routledge.

Holmes, P. & Karp, M. (Eds.). (1991). *Psychodrama: Inspiration and technique*. London: Routledge.

Holmes, P., Karp, M., & Watson, M. (Eds.). (1994). *Psychodrama since Moreno: Innovations in theory and practice*. London & New York: Tavistock/Routledge.

Kellermann, P. F. (1992). *Focus on psychodrama: The therapeutic aspects of psychodrama*. London: Jessica Kingsley.

Kipper, D. A. (1986). *Psychotherapy through clinical role playing*. New York: Brunner/Mazel.

Landy, R. J. (1993). *Persona and performance*. New York: Guilford.

Landy, R. J. (1994). *Drama therapy: Concepts and practices*. Springfield, IL: Charles C. Thomas.

Leveton, E. (1984). *Adolescent crisis*. New York: Springer.

Leveton, E. (1992). *A clinician's guide to psychodrama*. New York: Springer.

Lieberman, E. J. (1985). *Acts of will: The life and work of Otto Rank*. New York: The Free Press.

Marineau, R. F. (1989). *Jacob Levi Moreno, 1889–1974. (A Biography)*. London: Routledge.

Moreno, J. L. (1946–1969). *Psychodrama (Vols. 1–3)*. Beacon, NY: Beacon House.

Moreno, Z. T. (1987). Psychodrama, role theory, and the concept of the social atom. In J. Zeig (Ed.), *The evolution of psychotherapy*. New York: Brunner/Mazel.

Nicholas, M. W. (1984). *Change in the context of group therapy*. New York: Brunner/Mazel.

Nichols, M. P. & Efran, J. S. (1985). Catharsis in psychotherapy: A new perspective. *Psychotherapy, 22*(1), 46–58.

Starr, A. (1977). *Psychodrama: Rehearsal for living*. Chicago: Nelson-Hall.

Sternberg, P., & Garcia, A. (1989). *Sociodrama: Who's in your shoes?* Westport, CT: Praeger.

Watkins, M. (1986). *Invisible guests: The development of imaginal dialogue*. Hillsdale, NJ: L. Erlbaum Assoc./The Analytic Press.

Williams, A. (1989). *The passionate technique: Strategic psychodrama with individuals, families, and groups*. London: Tavistock/Routledge.

Williams, A. (1991). *Forbidden agendas: Strategic action in groups*. London: Tavistock/Routledge.

Yablonsky, L. (1975). *Psychodrama: Resolving emotional problems through role-playing*. New York: Brunner/Mazel.

C   Bioenergetic Analysis

Alexander Lowen

Bioenergetic analysis is a method of psychotherapy that integrates work with the body into the analytic process. The process aims at helping people understand who they are and why they function as they do. True understanding means more than just acquiring an intellectual knowledge of one's background and motivations. It involves a deep awareness defined as a connection to the events of one's life and to the forces that impel one to action in the present. This connection is made by getting in touch with the body, which is the repository on one's life's experiences. One gets in touch with the body by feeling what goes on in it. This is accomplished in bioenergetic therapy by mobilizing the body through certain active techniques. However, being an analytic therapy, bioenergetic analysis uses most analytic techniques to help in this objective. Dream analysis, slips of the tongue, transference and its associated resistance, and character analysis are all important aspects of bioenergetic analysis.

Work with the body is based on the concept that the more energy a person has, the more alive he or she is, which is translated into more movement, feeling, and thinking. Energy produces movement, which creates feelings and leads to thinking. This formulation is depicted in Figure 13.1, shown on the next page, which illustrates the hierarchy of personality functions.

By improving a person's energy processes, all functions above the base are affected: spontaneous movement is increased, more feeling develops, and

FIGURE 13.1 ◈ Hierarchy of Personality Functions

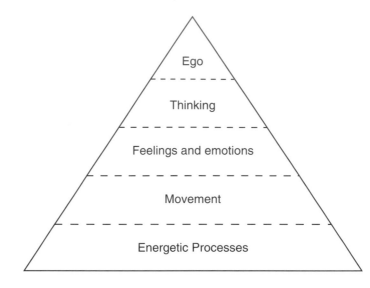

there is a corresponding gain in awareness and understanding. This is working from below. One can also affect all functions from above. Psychoanalysis, working from above, will affect all functions too, but one has a greater leverage working from below—i.e., from the body side. However, to limit the therapeutic program to working solely with the body or the mind is to handicap the process. Working with both body and mind is like walking on two legs, whereas an approach limited to the mind only (or the body only) is like hopping on one leg alone.

The way to modify energetic processes is through breathing and movement. Energy is produced in the body by the metabolism of food. In effect, food is burned in the body to produce energy, just as fuel is burned in an engine. This process requires oxygen. One can limit the amount of energy produced by decreasing either food (fuel) or oxygen. If one increases the amount of food without increasing the available oxygen, there is no increase of energy and the excess food becomes fat. If there is enough food, increasing oxygen immediately produces more energy. Body oxygen is increased by increasing the depth and fullness of respiration. Helping a person to breathe more deeply is one of the active techniques employed in bioenergetic analysis. However, this can pose a problem because increasing a person's energy leads directly to more movement and more feeling, and the feelings evoked may be painful or frightening (e.g., murderous rage).

One learns early in life that holding one's breath can suppress painful or frightening feelings. Restricting the depth of one's breathing reduces the intensity of all feeling. The mechanism for the diminution in breathing and the suppression of feeling is the blocking of spontaneous movement through muscular tension or rigidity. Thus, every chronically tense muscle in the body reflects an inner conflict between an impulse or feeling and the expression of that impulse or feeling. A tight jaw may hold back impulses to bite, and the person will be unaware of these impulses because the inhibition of the movement blocks the perception of the feeling. A tight throat may hold back impulses to cry or scream.

Tense shoulders represent the inhibition of impulses to reach out or strike out. A pelvis that is relatively immobile, due to unconscious tension in the muscles surrounding that structure, will decrease the strength of the sexual discharge. These tensions also act to reduce respiration. A tight throat reduces the amount of air flowing in and out of the lungs. A tight abdomen limits the depth of breathing at the same time that it reduces belly feelings: namely, belly crying, belly laughing, and sexuality. A rigid chest wall may cut off any awareness of the feeling of heartbreak, but at the same time it reduces the fullness of respiration.

Chronic muscular tension immobilizes the body, which reduces feeling by deadening the person. Aliveness is inversely proportional to rigidity. A dead person is a stiff; a stiff person is emotionally dead. In bioenergetic therapy one comes to sense personal rigidity and deadness and to get in touch with suppressed feelings through deeper breathing and movement. The ability to accept, integrate, and express these feelings appropriately requires considerable *talking* between therapist and client. About one-half of therapeutic time is spent in discussing problems, feelings, and behavior. In this respect bioenergetic analysis is like any other effective psychotherapy; it differs by adding another important dimension to the therapeutic process.

❧ HISTORY

Bioenergetic analysis was developed in 1953 as an offshoot of the work of Wilhelm Reich, which he called character-analytic-vegetotherapy. Reich, a psychoanalyst, was a member of the Vienna Psychoanalytic Society from 1921 to 1934.

Alexander Lowen was a patient of Reich in 1942. At that time Reich had incorporated working with the body into the analytic process. As an analyst Reich had observed that patients held their breath when they were resisting the full and free expression of their thoughts. Watching his patients as well as listening to them, he realized that there was functional identity between the way patients used their bodies and the way they used their minds. He recognized that a person's character is expressed physically and psychologically in identical terms. He stated that while there is an antithesis between body and mind, there is also a functional identity.

Reich emphasized the role of sexuality in the neuroses. He saw sexuality and the orgasm as the energy regulators of the body. The life process runs counter to the second law of thermodynamics in that it produces surplus energy—that is, more energy than the organism needs for its own survival. This excess energy is channeled into the sexual or reproductive process. Reich stated that the function of the orgasm was to discharge the excess energy of the organism. Theoretically, when all excess energy is discharged, there is no energy left for anxiety or other neurotic symptoms. This translates into the proposition that neurosis is inconsistent with full and complete orgastic responses. Unfortunately, it is the nature of neurosis to prevent such responses and so, in practice, one cannot cure neurosis by focusing solely upon sexuality. But this relationship between neurosis and sexuality is so direct that to the degree that neurotic attitudes are worked through, sexuality improves and orgasms become more complete and more satisfying. To the degree that sexuality improves, neurosis diminishes.

Reich conceptualized energy as a literal force operating at a physical level; in contrast, Freud's concept of libido was metaphysical and mental. Reich postulated that the energy operating in the living organism was a special energy, which he called *orgone energy* (from org-anism). Whether or not one agrees with Reich about this special energy, there is no doubt that a biological energy powers all living functions. Every neurotic character structure represents a reduction in an individual's energy level and a restriction upon the natural flow of that energy through the body.

Bioenergetic analysis is a true development of Reich's work that has enlarged and extended Reich's views. The need to separate from the Reichian movement grew out of the dogmatic position that his followers maintained. They believed that Reich had said the final word, and they made no allowance for change in theory or practice. In contrast, bioenergetic analysis introduced the following changes:

1. Pleasure was emphasized more than sexuality without denying the great importance of sexuality. The overall concept of pleasure includes sexual pleasure and fulfillment.

2. The introduction of the concept of grounding broadened Reich's approach to the body and the personality. In Reichian therapy the patient lies on a bed. In bioenergetic analysis many positions are used, especially standing, which allows one to get a better sense of one's legs and the ground that is one's basic support. How one stands can be analyzed, and one's ability to stand secure and firm can be developed through appropriate exercises.

3. Concomitant with grounding, physical exercises were developed that permitted patients to be active participants in the therapeutic program. Because many of these exercises can be done at home, the patient can be more independent of the therapist than in most other psychotherapies.

4. This emphasis upon the physical side of the therapy is not at the cost of analytic work. Bioenergetic analysis insists upon the thorough analytic working through of personality problems. The phenomena of transference and resistance are as important in bioenergetic analysis as they are in all psychoanalytic work.

Today, bioenergetic analysis is widely practiced in many countries. Located throughout the world are more than 40 centers that offer formal training programs to qualified professionals. These centers or local societies are affiliates of The International Institute for Bioenergetic Analysis, located in New York, which coordinates teaching, holds conferences, and publishes a clinical journal titled *Bioenergetic Analysis*.

❖ THEORY

A primary theoretical concept of bioenergetic analysis is Reich's concept of the unity and antithesis of all living processes. *Unity* refers to the fact that the organism functions as a whole. Every disturbance affects the total person. Thus, there can be no distinction between mental and physical illness, or between mental and physical pain. If a person has heart disease, the person is ill, not just the heart. Similarly, if a person suffers from anxiety, depression, a phobia, or a compulsion, the body is affected as well as the mind. A physical trauma affects the psyche just as a psychic trauma affects the body. The pain of a child's unfulfilled longing for its mother is not just a mental pain; it is physically structured in the tension and constriction of the throat and mouth as the areas of the body through which that longing would be expressed in a cry or in reaching out to suck or kiss. Evidence of this tension and constriction is proof of the early trauma and its persistence into the present.

The principle of unity also states that the whole body is affected by trauma. The unfulfilled longing of the child disturbs its breathing, its sense of security in its legs, and its self-confidence. Every trauma upsets the basic pulsatory movements of the body. These are the overall expansions and contractions of the organism (which on this level functions like a single cell) and the longitudinal wavelike movements that flow up and down through the body. This expansion and contraction can be clearly seen in the beating of the heart and the in-and-out movements of breathing. The longitudinal flow is seen in the peristaltic movements of the intestines, the sphincters, and the blood vessels. Pulsation is a quality of every cell in the body. When the pulsation is strong, life is strong. At death all pulsatory activity ceases. When pulsation is full and free, a person experiences a feeling of joy and pleasure in his or her body. Any disturbance of these natural pulsatory movements causes a loss of pleasurable feeling and, if intense, produces pain.

The quality of the body's pulsation is most manifest in its breathing, which combines the movements of expansion and contraction with those of the longitudinal wave. Breathing is not limited to the lungs, where the exchange of gases takes place with the outside air. Instead, the whole body participates in respiratory movements. Breathing in is accompanied by a wave that begins deep in the pelvis and moves upward to the mouth. In breathing out the wave is reversed. Given that breathing is disturbed in all emotional or neurotic problems, one can determine the existence of these problems from the nature of the respiratory disturbance. As a patient's problem clears up, breathing becomes easier and deeper. When breathing becomes totally free, the problem disappears.

The antithetical aspect of the living process is best reflected in the relation between mind and body. The unity between them doesn't alter the fact that each influences the other and on a superficial level there is a duality in human nature. Respecting this duality allows recognition that a person's conscious attitude has considerable influence on his or her total functioning. This allows the therapist to introduce *values* into any discussion of human behavior. Although one may be aware that a person's or a society's values are in part determined by unconscious forces, one must accept that they can to some degree be consciously altered in the interest of a better life. Making more energy available to the patient through bioenergetic work with the body facilitates these changes for the better.

Knowing that the body is the person (and that its form and movement reveal the personality and contain the history of the person) makes it possible for a bioenergetic therapist to make a tentative diagnosis of the character structure that defines an individual's habitual way of being.

According to bioenergetic analysis theory, there are five major types of character structure: schizoid, oral, narcissistic, masochistic, and rigid. These types are based on libidinal organization and ego development as manifested in the body. The following is an outline of these types:

1. The *schizoid* character structure is characterized by a tendency to split and dissociate. Thinking is split off from feeling. This is manifested on the body level by a lack of good connection between the head and trunk. In many of these individuals the neck is elongated; in others, the head is tilted away from the line of the body. With training this split can be easily recognized. This dissociation between head and body means that a person doesn't feel connected to his or her body. In a severe case, it may result in the phenomenon of depersonalization. In the schizoid personality one also sees a split between the upper and lower halves of the body, manifested by a severe contraction in the region of the waist or a lack of proportion and harmony between the two halves of the body. The schizoid personality is characterized by a fear of falling apart if one lets go, countered by the need to hold one's self together through tension in all the joint muscles.

2. The *oral* character structure stems from a deprivation of nurturing and support in early infancy and is associated with a fear of abandonment. Fear of abandonment is most manifest in thinness, lack of support in the legs and feet, and underdevelopment of the

musculature. The oral character has a strong tendency to be dependent, which can be denied through a pseudoindependence. The oral character holds on to self through strong tension in the shoulder girdle and in the legs to prevent falling, which would symbolize being left alone and abandoned.

3.   The *narcissistic* character structure is complex. It stems from an early childhood relationship in which the child was seduced by the parent into an intimacy that made the child feel special but in which the child was also used by the parent. Because the seduction was sexual, although not acted out, the child denies feeling as a way to prevent the danger of incest. From being special the child develops a sense of superiority and grandiosity. To be superior, the narcissistic person has to hold self above others. This is reflected in the body as an overdevelopment of the upper half and a relative weakness in the lower half. The narcissistic character structure holds self up through strong tensions in the legs and back.

4.   The *masochistic* character structure develops in a child who was nurtured but forced to be submissive to the parent. The masochist holds in all feelings through tension in the muscles that control the outlets at the upper and lower ends of the body. Masochistic attitudes are often associated with early toilet training—the need to hold in and the fear of letting out. On the body level, the masochist is heavy and muscularly overdeveloped, with the main tension in the flexor muscles, which results in a collapse of the body's erect posture.

5.   The *rigid* character structure, phallic-narcissistic in the man and hysterical in the woman, is characterized by a straight erect body with considerable pride. However, the erect posture is maintained through a rigidity of the back muscles that denotes an attitude of holding back. This holding back by the rigid character stems from early experiences of being humiliated by the parent of the opposite sex at the time in the oedipal period when the child felt a sexual interest in that parent.

Character types are neither pure nor individualistic. Many persons show a mixture of tendencies and belong to two or more types. In addition, no individual can be understood fully in terms of character type alone because it is only the framework for the clinical picture. As in working with a jigsaw puzzle, one starts with a border and slowly fills in all the pieces. The pieces of the clinical picture emerge as the person gets in touch with the body and, through it, with the experiences of life. Slowly the pieces are filled into the right places, and when nearly all are in, the picture emerges with unexpected clarity for both the patient and the therapist. Each insight, no matter how obtained, is a piece of the puzzle.

Seeing this picture clearly makes the character structure an objective reality for the patient and allows him or her to dissociate from it. At this point there is a major change in the personality, but this major change is also the culmination of many minor changes that have occurred as a result of the insights developed in the course of therapy. These changes are also related to increases in the person's energy level, in aliveness, and in feelings of pleasure.

One of the key elements in producing this change is the analysis and working through of the oedipal situation. Character structure becomes definitively set in that situation as a way of dealing with sexuality. Because character structure is a limitation upon being, it is also a limitation upon sexuality. In the course of working through the characterological issues, sexual feelings increase, with a corresponding increase in sexual pleasure.

No therapy is ever complete, and no one can be restored to a state of innocence. Therapy ends when an individual can take on personal responsibility for continued growth and when he or she has the necessary tools and techniques to promote that growth. Bioenergetics offers these tools through the special body exercises it teaches the patient.

❖ METHODOLOGY

Bioenergetic analysis adds an entirely new dimension to psychotherapy: namely, work with the body. The patient's bodily expression is studied to determine problems and conflicts in his or her personality. There is always an accord between what the body reveals and what the patient tells. Thus, if the patient complains about being depressed, that complaint can be related to the patient's depressed energy level and functioning. In a patient whose breathing is shallow, it can be shown that she is not allowing much feeling to be expressed. In a patient who complains of sexual problems, it can be shown that he has severe tension in the pelvis that reduces sexual potency. Most patients are not aware that their problems are manifested in their bodies until it is pointed out. Once this understanding is established, it becomes possible to work in a bioenergetic way with the patient.

There are four dimensions to bioenergetic analysis: (a) understanding and working with muscular tension, (b) analyzing associations, behavior, and transference, (c) understanding energy dynamics, and (d) focusing on the role of sexuality. All bioenergetic therapists are cognizant of these four dimensions, but their emphasis upon each varies according to their background and experience. Many focus strongly upon the psychological, with some attention to the body because it is the source of feeling. Others do more body work, largely aimed at the expression of feelings. However, all bioenergetic analysts note areas of contraction and tension, interpret the contraction, and then mobilize the body through breathing and movement to release the contraction. Each contraction is blocking a flow of excitation either upward into the head and eyes or downward into the pelvis, genitals, and legs. Pain is always involved in this blocking. On one level, the holding or the contraction is a maneuver to diminish pain, the pain of an unfulfilled longing or desire, the pain of a hurt or humiliation, or the pain of loss or frustration. The contraction diminishes the pain by reducing feeling and by numbing the person to the pain. One *deadens* the area. Releasing the holding is first experienced, therefore, as painful. The surge of an energetic force (blood) through a constricted area is painful. But after release has occurred it is experienced as pleasure. No one can achieve any significant characterological change without experiencing the pain of change. Normal growth is not painful, but therapy deals with distorted or blocked growth and development, and with removing obstacles to growth.

Although the primary focus in bioenergetic therapy is upon the body, it is a combined approach that works with both the body and the mind. The proportion of time spent on body work and analysis is approximately equal. In the initial interview, the therapist will spend the first half-hour listening to the patient's complaints and story, asking questions about the present situation and background, and studying facial expression, body attitude, and voice, all of which provide information about the patient's personality. Still more information can be obtained from a study of the form and motility of the body itself. How a person sits, stands, breathes, and moves all reveal problems and conflicts.

Once the relationship between the psychological and the physical is established, the patient knows that his or her body will have to change if personality is to change in a significant way. If the body is too rigid—that is, if one holds back feelings—the body will have to soften. If feelings are held in by muscular tensions that tend to compress the body and close the outlets, these tensions will have to be reduced to allow the expression of feeling. But changing the body in a significant way is a tremendous task. In almost all cases, positive but superficial changes occur rather quickly with bioenergetic therapy. The initial mobilization of the body through deeper breathing and bioenergetic exercises often evokes long-suppressed feelings. The patient may experience sadness, which can in turn lead to crying, or anger that can be expressed in hitting the bed. The patient may sense a degree of fear that was previously denied and may experience vibrations that provide new bodily sensations. This initial response to bioenergetic therapy is like the opening of a door to an exciting new world of feeling and being. It often produces welcome changes in behavior. At best it provides a foundation of understanding and trust for the more difficult task that lies ahead.

In working with the body, two principles are paramount:

1.   Any limitation of motility is both a result and a cause of emotional difficulties. Limitations arise as the result of unresolved infantile conflicts, but the persistence of the tension creates present-day emotional difficulties that clash with the demands of adult reality. Every physical rigidity interferes with and prevents a unitary response to situations.

2.   Any restriction of natural respiration is both the result and the cause of anxiety. Anxiety in childhood situations disturbs natural respiration. If the anxiety-producing situation persists and is prolonged, the disturbance of respiration becomes structured in thoracic and abdominal tension. The inability to breathe freely under emotional stress is the physiological basis for the experience of anxiety in such stressful situations.

Unity and coordination of physical responses depend upon the integration of the respiratory movements with the aggressive movements of the body. To the degree that respiration and motility are freed from the restrictions of chronic tensions, the physical functioning of the patient will improve. To that degree, contact with reality on the physical level will expand and deepen. But this will happen only if there is a concomitant and corresponding improvement in the patient's grasp of reality on the psychic and interpersonal levels. One should not be misled, however, by seeming improvements in a patient's functioning on the psychic and interpersonal levels that are not accompanied by an analogous improvement in physical functioning.

Through special movements and body positions, patients in bioenergetic therapy gain a deeper contact with their bodies and a better feeling for it. From this contact and feeling they begin to understand the relation between their present physical state and the experiences of infancy and childhood that created it. Clients learn that denial of the body is a rejection of a need for love; this denial is used to avoid hurt and disappointment. They learn to interpret rigidities as defenses against overwhelming rage and to sense that immobility stems from a deep-seated fear of aggression. Given the opportunity to express rage by pounding or kicking the couch, and given the chance to voice negativity, patients discover that they will not be abandoned or destroyed for expressing feelings. Through the acceptance of their bodies and feelings, individuals broaden contact with all other aspects of reality.

Because the body is the base of all reality functions, any increase in a person's contact with the body will produce a significant improvement in self-image (body image), interpersonal relationships, the quality of thinking and feeling, and enjoyment of life.

With this energetic understanding, one proceeds to interpret holding or contraction in terms of suppressed feelings. Because feeling has been suppressed, the patient is unaware of it. However, the nature of the holding (body language) identifies the feeling. Generally the feeling can be brought to consciousness by activating expressive movement.

For example, a jaw that is tightly held by tense muscles may hold back impulses to bite. Having a person bite on a towel can activate these impulses so that the suppressed desire to bite becomes conscious. A tightly contracted throat inhibits the expression of crying or screaming, but the person may not be conscious of this inhibition until he or she tries to cry or scream. Rigid shoulders may block impulses to strike out in anger. Often getting the person to hit the bed with his or her fists evokes a feeling of anger. Similarly, one can identify a lack of sexual aggressiveness in an individual from the immobility of the pelvis. However, the ability to read the language of the body is not easily or quickly acquired. Considerable training and experience are necessary to develop this skill to a high level of competence.

Interpreting different patterns of tension in separate body parts (mouth, eyes, shoulders, pelvis, feet, etc.) is much like reading words. Even if one can read words correctly, it doesn't follow that one can make sense of the words. To make full sense, words must be interpreted in the context of a sentence, a paragraph, and even a chapter. Each body has a unique expression that reveals the individual's personality and character. The character structure can be seen as a type that facilitates understanding and communication, but one can't do therapy with a type. Therapy deals with a very specific individual, and it is that specificity that one must understand from a reading of the body. The parts make sense in terms of the whole, but the whole cannot be determined from the parts. Only when we understand an individual in specific and holistic terms do we have a grasp of his or her problems, and only within that frame of reference does the work on the parts or segments become fully productive.

❖ SUMMARY

If therapy is a voyage of self-discovery, it should be conducted by a guide who has personally made this voyage. A therapist cannot help patients advance beyond the point where he or she has personally gone. However, too many therapists have failed to confront their character structure on a bodily level. This follows from the observation that they have not made any significant changes in their own body structure. Consequently, their knowledge of character structure is more theoretical than experiential. The result is that they count solely on awareness to modify personality. In fact, awareness and insight can do this to a limited degree and on a superficial level. However, insight is only a window through which one can see the reason for some aspect of behavior. Knowing the *why* of behavior does not strongly influence the *how* of behavior. To believe otherwise is to ignore the energetic factor.

Energetic considerations dictate that deep change involves continuous work at the breakthrough level. This is the level at which pain and fear are encountered. Fear stems from the fact that breakthrough often occurs together with breakdown. The old structure must crack and crumble so that a freer mode of being can develop. Successful therapists have experienced some of these breakdowns in their own growth and can attest to the pain and fear that accompany this process. One can appreciate the reluctance of many therapists to bring patients to the breakthrough point because they fear the possible breakdown that may occur. Yet this process, however painful, may be necessary if true therapeutic change is to occur.

Bioenergetic analysis, with its appreciation for the physical as well as the mental aspects of human experience, provides a theory for explaining human neuroses, a typology for classifying character structure, and a balanced therapy for treating patients with psychological problems. It builds on the work of Wilhelm Reich, but goes beyond Reich in both formulation of clinical issues and treatment techniques. It is analytical in nature but expands on traditional analytical methods by incorporating specific body and breathing exercises into the therapeutic hour. Body work suggests new directions for analytical therapy, and insights gained in analysis are used to formulate hypotheses to pursue in body work. Bioenergetic analysis uses these reciprocal and complementary sources of information to provide a comprehensive and balanced psychotherapy.

❖ REFERENCES

Lowen, A. (1958). *The language of the body*. New York: Macmillan.

Lowen, A. (1965). *Love and orgasm*. New York: Macmillan.

Lowen, A. (1967). *Betrayal of the body*. New York: Macmillan.

Lowen, A. (1970). *Pleasure: A creative approach to life*. New York: Penguin Books.

Lowen, A. (1972). *Depression and the body*. New York: Penguin Books.

Lowen, A. (1975). *Bioenergetics*. New York: Penguin Books.

Lowen, A. (1977). *The way to vibrant health*. New York: Harper & Row.

Lowen, A. (1980). *Fear of life*. New York: Macmillan.

Lowen, A. (1984). *Narcissism: Denial of the true self*. New York: Macmillan.

Lowen, A. (1990). *The spirituality of the body*. New York: Macmillan Publishing Company.

Reich, W. (1972). *Character analysis*. New York: Orgone Institute Press.

Reich, W. (1970). *The function of the orgasm*. New York: Farrar, Strauss.

14　Current Issues in Psychotherapy

Danny Wedding

❖ THE PROFESSIONS

During the eighteenth and nineteenth centuries, responsibility for people with emotional disorders and disorganized thinking gradually passed from clerics to physicians, and psychiatry became the dominant mental health profession. Since World War II, other groups have become influential. In 1994, about 35,000 psychiatrists were providing clinical services in the United States, in contrast to 44,000 psychologists, 50,000 state-regulated professional counselors[1], and around 100,000 clinical social workers[2]. The majority of these individuals practice technical eclecticism (described by Arnold Lazarus in Chapter 11) and use a variety of methods derived from many of the therapies described in *Current Psychotherapies*.

In recent years, psychologists and social workers have come closer to achieving the status of medical therapists, especially in the areas of insurance reimbursement, participation in federal health programs, and admission to psychoanalytic training. Psychologists also have gained hospital admitting privileges in

---

[1]Not all states formally regulate the practice of counseling. The American Mental Health Counselors' Association estimates that there are 67,000 practicing mental health counselors in the United States.

[2]These estimates were made by the American Psychiatric Association, the American Psychological Association, the National Board for Certified Counselors, and the National Association of Social Workers.

some states (Rosenblatt et al., 1992). Other groups that practice counseling or psychotherapy are making rapid strides toward achieving the privileges now available to psychologists and social workers.

Almost all states classify psychotherapy as a legitimate part of medical practice, without any requirement that its use be restricted to psychiatrists. In 1995, psychologists, psychiatric nurse practitioners, and social workers were licensed or certified in all 50 states, and professional counselors were licensed or certified in 38 states. A growing number of states also require marriage/family and substance abuse counselors to be licensed or certified. The growing importance of counseling as a primary mental health profession is reflected in its inclusion for the first time in 1992 in the health care human resource statistics compiled by the Center for Mental Health Services and the National Institute of Mental Health (Manderscheid & Sonnenschein, 1992).

Licensing is more meaningful than certification, since licensure restricts the practice of a profession, while certification restricts the use of a profession's name. These distinctions are difficult to apply to psychotherapy because it is virtually impossible to restrict the practice of a profession that includes such a wide range of activities. Certain professional activities may be state-regulated, however. Psychological testing may be restricted to psychologists, for example, while the authority to prescribe medication may be granted only to physicians, dentists, and some other health care practitioners such as advanced practice nurses, physicians' assistants, and podiatrists. Regulatory authority is usually invested in a state board appointed by the governor and composed of professionals and members of the public. Frequently, state boards will use reciprocity to license professionals who hold a license to practice in other states.

Licensing boards restrict the activities of unlicensed practitioners and rescind the licenses of those believed unfit to practice. Loss of a license may result from a felony conviction or from misrepresentation, unprofessional conduct, practicing beyond one's area of competence, abandoning patients, maintaining inadequate records, and breaching patients' confidentiality (Stromberg et al., 1988). In one study (Pope & Vasquez, 1991), the most frequent reasons for loss of license were dual relationships (including sexual intimacy), unprofessional conduct, conviction of a felony, failure to comply with a board order, improper billing practices, and incompetent practice. Other reasons include mental incompetence, falsification of Medicaid claims, fraud in application for license, misrepresentation of competence, and failure to report child abuse.

It is difficult to decide who should have the right to practice psychotherapy because there are no clear practice guidelines to define what is appropriate professional care for patients with mental and emotional disorders. A psychoanalyst and a behavior therapist may provide dramatically different treatment for an anxious patient, for example. Yet both will claim—and genuinely believe—that their mode of treatment is appropriate, and both will expect payment for their services. This problem is not limited to mental health; few clear guidelines exist for much of medical practice. The United States government has attempted to deal with this lack of uniform standards by establishing the Agency for Health Care Policy and Research (AHCPR). This agency has promulgated guidelines for the treatment of depression, and it plans to address other psychological problems in the future. The depression guidelines were rejected by the American Psychological Association, however, and future guidelines for mental health practice are likely to be just as controversial.

❖ ETHICAL ISSUES

Dual Relationships

John Schafer had been working hard to establish a private practice in social work. One of his clients was Keith Twiehaus, the Chief Executive Officer for a biotechnology company. One day in therapy, Mr. Twiehaus mentioned that he was worried about his decision to purchase Symatec, a promising but badly managed smaller company. The purchase was a sound business decision, and it was likely that Symatec stock would double in value as soon as word got out. The client was worried, however, because the purchase of the smaller company would eliminate the jobs of hundreds of Symatec's employees.

John devoted several therapy sessions to analyzing the options available to Mr. Twiehaus, who eventually decided his primary obligation was to his shareholders. In one of his therapy sessions he made a decision to go ahead and purchase Symatec. John slept fitfully that night, wondering if he could ethically buy Symatec stock. He was in a dual relationship, since Mr. Twiehaus had inadvertently become his investment advisor as well as his client.

It is often awkward for both the therapist and the client when interactions occur outside the psychotherapeutic relationship. Some relationships, such as those that include sexual or financial involvement, clearly violate the ethical codes of almost all professional organizations. Others, such as allowing a client to buy the therapist a cup of coffee after a chance meeting in a restaurant, appear to be quite harmless. Most decisions are not this straightforward, however, and deciding whether to accept a Christmas gift or flowers for the waiting room can become a vexing dilemma.

Social interaction with clients may be unavoidable, especially in rural areas, and contact with clients outside therapy will not necessarily impede therapeutic work if dual relationships are acknowledged and processed. A police officer who stops a speeding motorist who turns out to be his therapist, for example, may decide not to write a ticket, and the therapist may be grateful. However, is it important that both parties acknowledge the special features of their relationship and the unique nature of their encounter.

Psychotherapists Alfred Adler and Rudolf Dreikurs maintained that counseling and psychotherapy are essentially *educational*, and therefore therapeutic work with friends and even relatives is entirely appropriate. Other therapists argue that transference and countertransference are powerful responses that will inevitably influence therapy in every dual relationship; and consequently dual relationships should almost always be avoided.

Sexual Attraction to Clients

Nancy Tharp was a hospitalized patient diagnosed as a borderline personality after numerous suicide attempts. An attractive woman of 23, she had been assigned to a first-year psychiatry resident, Bill Wilson. The supervising psychiatrist felt it was important for Nancy to work with a male therapist because of her propensity to use her sexuality to manipulate men. Her prior history included childhood sexual abuse and a seemingly endless series of short, casual sexual relationships. She generally held men in contempt, and had never been able to sustain a relationship for more than a few months.

During the first therapy session, Nancy wore a short skirt and shifted positions in her chair indiscreetly. Dr. Wilson averted his eyes, but began to suspect that Nancy was using her sexuality to establish dominance in the relationship. He knew he probably should say something about his patient's immodesty, but he felt quite uncomfortable talking about sexual issues. He also believed her inappropriate behavior might be unconscious, and he wanted to avoid sexualizing the relationship. However, he felt manipulated each time he was forced to avert his gaze to avoid looking at his patient's panties. He realized he was both angry and sexually aroused, and he began having frequent sexual fantasies about Nancy.

It is not surprising that psychotherapy can result in sexual arousal and fantasies for both patients and therapists. Psychotherapy is a unique encounter in which the most intimate topics are discussed in a quiet and private setting, and the client is likely to be emotionally vulnerable. The feelings of intimacy and shared commitment that emerge during a therapeutic relationship are often strikingly similar to the emotions associated with the early stages of courtship.

After surveying 585 practicing psychologists, Pope, Keith-Spiegel, and Tabachnick (1986) reported that 95 percent of the men and 76 percent of the women therapists had been sexually attracted to clients. Sixty-three percent of the respondents felt guilty and confused by the attraction, and less than 10 percent felt their graduate training had prepared them to deal with the depth and intensity of their sexual feelings.

Sexual attraction for a client is common and usually quite harmless. However, some therapists cross ethical boundaries and become sexually involved with their patients. This can result in tremendous harm for both parties (Edelwich and Brodksy, 1991).

Pope and Bouhoutsos (1986) present ten common scenarios in which therapists cross professional boundaries and become sexually involved with their patients. These are listed in Table 14.1.

Professional associations have long recognized the potential for sexual exploitation in therapy. The Hippocratic oath includes the pledge to "abstain…from the seduction of

TABLE 14.1 ❧ Ten Common Scenarios

Scenario	Description
Role Trading	Therapist becomes the "patient," and the wants and needs of the therapist become the focus.
Sex Therapy	Therapist fraudulently presents therapist-patient sexual intimacy as a valid treatment for sexual or other kinds of problems.
As If…	Therapist treats positive transference as if it were not the result of the therapeutic situation.
Svengali	Therapist creates and exploits an exaggerated dependence on the part of the patient.
Drugs	Therapist uses cocaine, alcohol, or other drugs as part of the seduction.
Rape	Therapist uses physical force, threats, and/or intimidation.
True Love	Therapist uses rationalizations that attempt to disount the clinical/professional nature of the relationship with its attendant responsibilities.
It Just Got Out of Hand	Therapist fails to treat the emotional closeness that develops in therapy with sufficient attention, care, and respect.
Time Out	Therapist fails to acknowledge and take account of the fact that the therapeutic relationship does not cease to exist between scheduled sessions or outside the therapist's office.
Hold Me	Therapist exploits the patient's desire for nonerotic physical contact and possible confusion between erotic and nonerotic contact.

females or males, of freemen and slaves" (Braceland, 1969, p. 252). The American Psychological Association's ethical principles explicitly prohibit sexual involvement with current clients or acceptance of former lovers as patients. Psychologists are also advised to avoid sexual intimacy with former clients for at least two years after termination of therapy. Even then, the practice is discouraged, and psychologists bear the burden for proving that a sexual relationship with a former client is not exploitative. Similar injunctions against having sex with clients are found in the ethical principles of almost all mental health organizations. As noted by Edelwich and Brodsky (1991),

> The guidelines are clear. Although some doctors have been sleeping with their patients since the days of Hippocrates (and some teachers with their students since the days of Socrates), a consensus has developed with the helping professions (and the courts) that there is no place for sex or other forms of personal intimacy in a professional helping relationship with a vulnerable person. (p. xxi)

Despite these injunctions and the potential for serious harm to clients, a surprising number of therapists engage in sexual misconduct. Incidence rates are remarkably similar across professional groups, and rates of sexual involvement are always much higher for male therapists. Gartrell et al. (1989) surveyed 5,574 psychiatrists and found that 7 percent of the male respondents and 3 percent of the females admitted to having had sexual contact with a patient on at least one occasion. A third of those had had intercourse with more than one patient. Surveys of therapist-client intimacy among psychologists have produced incidence estimates that range from 4 to 12 percent for males and 1 to 3 percent for females (Brodsky, 1989). About 3 percent of male social workers surveyed—but none of the females—had been sexually involved with clients (Gechtman, 1989).

Four national studies have examined sexual intimacy between mental health educators (all psychologists) and their students. The data suggest that about 3 percent of male students and 16 percent of female students become sexually involved with professors or clinical supervisors (Pope, Levenson, & Schover, 1979). Despite this apparently widespread phenomenon, only 2 percent of respondents agreed that "sexual relations between students and their psychology teachers, administrators, or clinical supervisors can be beneficial to both parties" (Pope, Levenson, & Schover, 1979).

Third-Party Payers

Tom Jeffords, a counseling psychologist who limited his practice to marital therapy, had just completed his initial interview with Jim and Mary Daschle. The Daschles were an attractive and articulate couple who were hoping to salvage a strained marriage. Dr. Jeffords was encouraged by the couple's insight into their marital difficulties, and he thought he could help. He outlined a therapeutic plan, discussed his fees, and recommended that the Daschles return in a week. However, as he was walking the couple to the door, Mr. Daschle took him aside and remarked, "Look, Doctor, I think your fees are reasonable, but I simply can't afford them. I've got great insurance as long as you can give me or my wife a diagnosis my insurance company will accept. But if you can't do that for us, we can't come back." Dr. Jeffords had come across the problem before, and he was ready with his response. "Well, your wife's fairly discouraged because of all the marital problems, and she has low self-esteem and is having trouble sleeping. I suspect she's depressed, and that would qualify. Don't worry about it. We'll work something out."

Mental health providers have been frustrated by the myriad difficulties involved in working with dozens of insurance companies, and sometimes they have responded in ways that range from passive-aggressive to illegal. Some providers restrict their practices to clients who can pay for services "up front," and refuse to deal with insurance companies altogether. This solution restricts access for the poor. Other clinicians lower their rates or provide *pro bono* (free) care for poor clients rather than deal with the paperwork involved in submitting Medicaid claims.

Mental health providers occasionally manipulate the insurance system to serve their own needs. For example, some providers favor reimbursable diagnoses over those that don't get reimbursed, submit bills in the name of high status providers for services performed by lower status (and often nonreimbursable) providers, or bill for services that are reimbursable rather than for those procedures that are actually performed but not covered by insurance companies (e.g., biofeedback sessions may be billed under psychotherapy codes with the rationalization that some counseling occurs before and after each session). Finally, there are both overt and covert pressures to "stretch out" therapy with well-insured clients, to drop clients once their insurance benefits have run out, and to reduce services to indigent clients and those unlikely to pay their bills. New therapists can find themselves under considerable pressure, from both colleagues and clients, to accept dubious or illegal billing practices and to base treatment decisions on economic criteria.

❖ LEGAL ISSUES

Therapists often have multiple obligations that may overlap or conflict. Legal issues arise from competing responsibilities, such as those to clients, spouses, children, potential victims, and society.

Duty to Warn

Sarah Brown enjoyed her new job as a social worker in an inner city mental health clinic, but she was troubled by the fact that she knew one of her clients was HIV positive and yet continued to have unprotected sex. Sarah had given the client a diagnosis of antisocial personality, and it seemed to be justified. No amount of persuasion on her part could convince him that what he was doing was wrong. The client seemed to revel in the fact that he might be infecting his partners. Because his HIV status had been revealed in confidence, Sarah felt paralyzed by the need to balance her professional responsibility to her client against her responsibility to protect the public.

Deciding when to break a client's confidence is difficult. A past president of the American Psychological Association has taken the position that "psychologists may not break the confidentiality of a patient or client under any circumstances" (Siegel, 1979, p. 249). Of course, confidentiality is routinely broken when professionals consult with colleagues, participate in treatment team meetings, or provide diagnostic and treatment information to insurance companies. In these cases, sharing of information is assumed to be in the patient's best interest. In other situations, the needs of society may take precedence over one's obligations to a client, even when the client is harmed by disclosure.

Every therapist should be familiar with the case of *Tarasoff v. the Regents of the University of California*, in which the California Supreme Court held that a psychologist working in a university counseling center had a duty to break his client's confidence once the client declared his intent to murder his girlfriend. Furthermore, the psychologist, who had told the campus police that his client was dangerous and should be hospitalized, was found negligent in not attempting to notify the potential victim. In the words of the court, "…protective privilege ends where the public peril begins." In a related case, *Hedlund v. Superior Court of Orange County*, the court stated it was the therapist's duty to warn family members potentially at risk. This case extends the Tarasoff decision by explicitly stating that negligent failure to *diagnose* dangerousness is a basis for liability (Meyers, 1986).

Later cases involving the duty to warn include one in which a patient killed someone through reckless driving and another in which a client committed suicide by driving a car into a tree, also killing her daughter, who was a passenger (Beck, 1990).

Under the legal doctrine of *respondent superior* ("let the master respond"), supervisors of psychotherapy trainees may also be legally responsible for failure to warn. It is unlikely that once-a-week or once-a-month supervision of therapists is sufficient to absolve the supervisor of responsibility for tragic outcomes (Cohen, 1986).

Along with the duty to warn others of potential harm, all states have laws mandating immediate reporting of known or suspected cases of child abuse. In most states, reportable circumstances include physical abuse, sexual abuse, neglect, and mental or emotional maltreatment (Heyman, 1986). Therapists sometimes ignore these reporting requirements, which may appear to place an insurmountable obstacle between the therapist and a client seeking to control anger and abusive tendencies. Therapists who put client welfare ahead of public law do so at their own peril.

Privileged Communication

When a man angry about his ex-wife's decision to remarry held a busload of school children hostage at gunpoint, the police consulted a psychologist. After about fifteen hours of negotiation, the psychologist persuaded the man to turn himself in. Later, the psychologist testified in court that the gunman did not appear to be mentally ill when he held the children hostage. Much to his surprise, the psychologist was sued by the gunman some months later for violating doctor/patient confidentiality.

Privileged communication is a right *vested in the client,* and it can be waived only by the client. When a client waives the right to privileged communication, a therapist must testify as any other witness, and a therapist will be held in contempt of court for failure to do so (Knapp & VandeCreek, 1987).

The concept of privileged communication is an extension of the right to privacy established by the Fifth Amendment to the Constitution. Therapists have been granted by law the same right to privileged communication as that enjoyed by physicians and lawyers (Cohen, 1986).

Even the most superficial communication between a client and provider may be privileged. For example, a telephone call to a psychiatrist from a person seeking treatment was deemed confidential by the courts, even though the man who called did not know the psychiatrist and never became a patient at the state hospital where the psychiatrist worked (Knapp & VandeCreek, 1987).

Prediction of Dangerousness

Cynthia Townsend, a psychologist employed by a rural mental health clinic, was increasingly worried about Dave Mason, a rugged Appalachian "mountain man" who was coming in for weekly therapy. It had been difficult to establish rapport with Dave, but Cynthia was pleased they had established a meaningful therapeutic alliance and Dave was beginning to confide in her. In their last session, Dave admitted frequent sexual fantasies about children who played near his cabin. He denied any history of pedophilia and had not been abused as a child. Dave was confident he could control his fantasies, but he certainly looked dangerous, and Cynthia wondered about her moral and legal obligation to warn Dave's neighbors about his fantasy life.

Therapists routinely see patients who seem potentially dangerous. There is no evidence, however, that therapists have superior ability to predict violent behavior. In contrast, there is evidence that therapists *overpredict* violence, having accuracy rates somewhat lower than the average person (Stromberg et al., 1988). Although it is far more serious to make a false negative diagnosis of potential homicide than a false positive one, there are serious problems with curtailing the civil liberties of clients because of a small potential for dangerous behavior. Livermore, Malmquist, and Meehl (1968) have described this conundrum:

> Assume that one person out of a thousand would kill. Assume also an exceptionally accurate test is created which differentiates with 95% effectiveness those who will kill from those who will not. If 100,000 people were tested, out of the 100 who would kill, 95 would be isolated. Unfortunately, out of the 99,000 who would not kill, 4,995 people also would be isolated as potential killers. (p. 90)

Predicting violence is like predicting the weather—it is easier in the short term. Some short-term predictors that correlate positively with violence include male gender, youth, unemployment, or addiction to alcohol or drugs. A history of past violence is the most powerful predictor. Other variables associated with violence include low intelligence, impulsivity, paranoid ideation, and the stated desire to hurt or kill someone. Head injuries, being abused as a child, witnessing a family member abuse another, and a history of family psychosis are other predictors (Beck, 1990). Despite these relationships, it remains extraordinarily difficult for a therapist to predict which patients will become violent in stressful situations. Professional training in a mental health specialty appears to contribute little to this ability (Ziskin & Faust, 1988).

Informed Consent

Margaret McCulskey had grown increasingly despondent since her oldest daughter left for college. Now all three of her children were out on their own, and her husband was totally preoccupied with his work. She felt listless and bored and found little pleasure in her household routine. Hoping to gain some focus in her life, she sought counseling from a minister at the church she attended, a man recruited to provide pastoral counseling for the congregation. After three helpful sessions, she decided to return to college. Mrs. McCulskey was shocked when she received a bill from the church. She could easily afford to pay, but it seemed wrong that she had not been informed about the fee.

Clients are entitled to know about all matters that affect them. They deserve to know the likelihood of harm (physical or mental) that could result from treatment, the possibility of side effects, the probability of success for treatment, the limits of confidentiality, whether student counselors will be involved, and the likely duration and cost of treatment. Should the therapist doubt that he or she is the right person to treat the client, or that the proposed approach is the proper one, the therapist has an ethical obligation to inform the client and perhaps suggest alternative treatment by other providers. For example, while depressed patients often can be treated exclusively with psychotherapy (Rush & Hollon, 1991), antidepressant medication or electroconvulsive therapy may be the treatment of choice for some markedly depressed patients. Patients should be informed of the availability and efficacy of alternate treatments and providers.

One way to assure that clients understand the limits of confidentiality and their financial obligations is to have them sign a therapeutic contract before therapy begins. These contracts typically list clients' rights (e.g., terminating therapy at any time, reviewing their records, etc.) and specify conditions under which the therapist must reveal information without clients' permission (e.g., after a threat of harm to self or others, when the therapist is required to respond to a court subpoena, etc.). See Pinckney (1994) for an example of such a contract. This approach seems cold and mechanical to many therapists.

Others maintain the contract demonstrates respect for clients by making them active participants in treatment planning.

❖ SPECIAL POPULATIONS

Ethnic Minorities

Cindy Johnson, a graduate student in clinical psychology, was assigned to a juvenile court for a practicum. Cindy had been raised in an upper-class neighborhood, and her parents were affluent, professional people. She was unprepared for her first client, an angry fifteen-year-old African-American male, who asked "How you going to help me, lady? You don't know shit about me or my problems." With a sinking heart, Cindy realized he was right.

Cultural diversity poses difficulties for therapists uninformed about the cultural values of their clients, as well as therapists who respond to clients on the basis of cultural stereotypes. Striking the proper balance between cultural sensitivity and stereotyping requires clinical acumen as well as an understanding and appreciation of cultural differences.

A variety of resources can help clinicians relate to different cultural groups (see, for example, books by Baruth & Manning, 1991, and Ramirez, 1991). Reading selected books such as Amy Tan's *The Joy Luck Club* or *The Kitchen God's Wife* will also introduce clinicians to other cultures and values.

Specific strategies for conducting therapy with ethnic minorities include action-oriented and directive approaches for African-American clients, de-emphasizing the need for self-disclosure and reframing psychological problems as medical disorders with Hispanics, using highly structured therapy with Asian-Americans, and adopting an authoritative as opposed to an egalitarian role with Filipino Americans (Sue and Zane, 1987). Sue and Zane note that these approaches may be incompatible with the theoretical style or values of the clinician, and that they may ignore the broad range of individual differences within ethnic groups.

Ms. Kim, a 24 year-old second generation Korean American, lived at home with her parents. She initially sought counseling because she was depressed and unhappy with her lack of independence. Her father was angry about her plans to marry a non-Korean. Her therapist began assertion training and role-playing to prepare Ms. Kim to deal with her father. The counselor was disappointed when Ms Kim failed to keep her second appointment.

Problems occur when the cultural values of clients clash with those of therapists. For example, therapists may find it difficult to understand the parenting practices of clients who use strict corporal punishment to discipline their children, as is common in many Pacific Island countries. Similarly, therapists in the United States may find it difficult to work with clients from countries where women accept secondary societal roles. The values and beliefs of both therapists and clients are class- and culture-bound, and good therapists transfer cases to other therapists when conflicting cultural values interfere with therapy.

Working with Gay and Lesbian Clients

Jim Kellogg, who had retired at age 40 after being a policeman for twenty years, went back to school, received a master's degree in counseling, and obtained a position in a community mental health center. One of his first clients was Leo. Jim and Leo got along well and established good rapport in their early sessions. Jim was sympathetic with Leo's feelings of inferiority and his occasional panic attacks, and Leo felt comfortable with Jim, who played the role of a supportive, understanding, and caring older individual. The relationship changed in the fifth session, however, when Leo confided to Jim that he was a homosexual.

Jim and his fellow police officers had ridiculed homosexuals and expressed their disgust by using pejorative terms such as fags, homos, and dykes. Jim also belonged to a religious denomination that condemned homosexual behavior. He went to his supervisor and explained that he no longer wanted to work with Leo, and that in the future no "sexual deviates" should be assigned to him.

Almost all therapists will treat gay men and lesbians. In one survey of members of the American Psychological Association, 99 percent of psychotherapy providers reported they had seen at least one gay male or lesbian client in therapy, and the average respondent reported that 6 percent of their current clients were gay and 7 percent were lesbians (Garnets, Hancock, Cochran, Goodchilds, & Peplau, 1991). This survey produced numerous examples of biased, inadequate, or inappropriate practice. For example, one therapist commented to a lesbian client, "If you have a uterus, don't you think you should use it?"

A lesbian psychologist has described four ways in which homophobic therapists respond to lesbian clients. These include the "You're not a lesbian" response, in which the therapist dismisses the reality of the client's feelings; "the lecture," wherein the client's sexual feelings are described as pathological; the liberal response, in which the therapist simply treats the client's lesbianism as if it were no different from any other client's sexual orientation; and the inadequate response, characterized by the therapist's avoidance of the issue (Falco, 1991).

The American Psychiatric Association removed homosexuality from its official list of mental disorders in 1973. The American Psychological Association's Council of Representatives adopted the following resolution in 1974:

> Homosexuality, per se, implies no impairment in judgment, stability, reliability, or general social or vocational capabilities. Further, the American Psychological Association urges all mental health professionals to take the lead in removing the stigma of mental illness that has long been associated with homosexual orientations. (Conger, 1975)

Therapists who feel uncomfortable working with homosexual clients may need to learn more about gay and lesbian issues (see Garnets et al., 1991; Gonsiorek, 1988; Moses & Hawkins, 1982; Rothblum & Cole, 1989; Stein & Cohen, 1986). The article by Garnets et al. includes suggested readings for therapists and students who want to learn more about working with gay males, lesbians, and same-sex couples.

❖ PRESCRIPTION PRIVILEGES

A middle-aged man who had been in therapy for almost half his life was referred by his psychologist to a psychiatrist for medication management. The psychiatrist became intrigued with this case. He offered a number of different medications, but also delved into the patient's psychotherapeutic history. Dissatisfied with his psychologist, the patient began seeing the psychiatrist for therapy as well as for medication management. He described numerous therapeutic relationships in which he had first become deeply involved, gradually became angry and disappointed, and finally left those relationships. In pharmacotherapy, he went through a honeymoon period with each medication, then reported no effect. After a few months, he became angry and critical of the psychiatrist and left to find help elsewhere, repeating the same pattern. (Adapted from Beitman, 1991.)

One of the most divisive professional questions in mental health in the 1990s is whether non-medical mental health professionals should be trained to prescribe psychotropic medications. This issue is becoming especially important as health policy leaders look for new ways to contain escalating health care costs while attempting to expand coverage to traditionally underserved groups such as Native Americans, people living in rural areas or inner cities, and the seriously mentally ill. Consumer groups such as the Public Citizen Health Research Group and the National Alliance for the Mentally Ill (NAMI) have endorsed additional training and prescriptive authority for psychologists, physician assistants, and nurse practitioners to increase access to care for these underserved populations (Torrey, Erdman, Wolfe, & Flynn, 1990).

Opponents of prescription privileges for nonphysician practitioners argue that expansion of prescriptive authority will (a) blur the distinction between psychiatry and other mental health professions, and (b) potentially endanger the public because of failure to recognize medical risks and potential drug interactions (e. g., Coleman & Shellow, 1991). Studies by the U. S. Congress, however, suggest that nonphysicians are more cautious— and therefore safer—than physicians when prescribing medicine (Office of Technology Assessment, 1986). These comparisons are confounded by the fact that nonphysician therapists tend to prescribe from a formulary, use a smaller number of medications, and treat patients who are less seriously ill.

Fox, Schwelitz, and Barclay (1992) have proposed a psychopharmacology curriculum for professional psychologists. This training would produce *limited practice prescribers* with constraints similar to those found in dentistry, podiatry, or optometry. Limited practice providers would work independently and without physician oversight, their prescriptive authority would be limited, and they would be required to consult with physicians and other health professionals when treating clients whose problems lay outside their scope of practice. These providers would be differentiated from *physician extenders*, such as many nurses and all physicians' assistants, who work under direct physician supervision.

The value of prescriptive authority for nonphysician mental health practitioners is uncertain, its impact on mental health professions is unclear, and many practitioners find themselves disagreeing over this issue. However, it appears likely that many states will enact limited prescribing privileges for psychologists and other mental health professionals in order to hold down health care costs and expand access to care in underserved areas of the country.

Combining psychotherapy and pharmacotherapy may have important clinical ramifications. For example, medication may reduce symptoms to such an extent that patients become less motivated to work in therapy or even prematurely discontinue therapy. Other patients may regard medication as a crutch or an admission that they have failed to develop the necessary insight to work through their problems. On the positive side, drugs may facilitate psychotherapeutic work by improving cognitive functioning, enhancing memory, promoting abreaction, or contributing to a sense of confidence and enhanced optimism (Klerman, 1991). Beitman and Klerman (1991) discuss effective integration of pharmacotherapy and psychotherapy.

❖ THE FUTURE OF PSYCHOTHERAPY

Yalom (1975) has noted that it is difficult to distinguish between evanescent fads and genuine, durable trends in psychotherapy. It appears inevitable, however, that the field of psychotherapy will change dramatically in response to the social, political, and economic forces shaping clinical practice as we approach the twenty-first century.

Norcross, Alford, and DeMichele (1992) used a Delphi polling technique to assess the future of psychotherapy. This method requires each participant to respond twice: first anonymously and then after feedback from other respondents. The seventy-five experts polled included many prominent figures conducting research and writing about psychotherapy. These experts believed

> ...psychotherapy will become more directive, psychoeducational, present-centered, problem-focused, and briefer in the next decade. Concomitantly, aversive, relatively unstructured, historically oriented, and long-term approaches are predicted to decrease....self-help groups, social workers, and psychiatric nurses will proliferate....integrative, systemic, and cognitive persuasions will thrive....specialization and peer review will become vital activities and pharmacotherapy will expand at the expense of psychotherapy. (p. 155)

It is likely that practice guidelines and psychotherapy treatment manuals will be used more widely in the future. Practice guidelines define optimal treatments for specific problems as determined by expert committees (e.g., the Agency for Health Care Policy and Research has published practice guidelines for treating depressed patients). Therapy manuals operationally define good therapeutic practice, and some contain rating scales that can assess the quality of care provided by a therapist (Lambert & Ogles, 1988). Practice guidelines and treatment manuals are highly controversial, however. Some therapists feel they present contrived, "cookbook" psychotherapy; others believe guidelines are essential if policy-makers are to reach sound decisions about reimbursement by the government or insurance companies.

One fairly clear trend is the increasing feminization of psychotherapy. Clinical social work and psychiatric nursing have always been predominantly female professions, whereas psychologists and psychiatrists have been predominantly male. Gender patterns in the helping professions are changing, however, and more women are becoming psychologists and psychiatrists. In 1991, 42 percent of medical school applicants, 43 percent of psychiatry residents, and 48 percent of child psychiatry residents were women (Graduate Medical Education, 1992). Likewise, the percentage of doctoral degrees in clinical and counseling psychology awarded to women increased from 30 percent in 1974 to 56 percent in 1989 (Goodheart & Markham, 1992). This can be interpreted as evidence that both professions have succeeded in meeting affirmative action goals and eliminating gender bias from the admissions process; however, some reviewers suggest that increasing the numbers of women in psychotherapy and medicine in our sexist society will diminish the status of both professions.

Noting the decline of medical psychotherapy and the increasing political power of newer professional groups, the Group for the Advancement of Psychiatry has predicted that a new mental health profession—psychotherapy, with psychoanalysis as a subspecialty—will emerge from the current confusion regarding appropriate training (Rosenblatt et al., 1992).

It is fascinating to speculate about the future of psychotherapy. It is likely to be financed in dramatically different ways in the United States and will probably involve a wider range of providers. The legal, ethical, and professional dilemmas faced by therapists in the twenty-first century are likely to be similar to those encountered by today's therapists, however, and the core skills of therapists will continue to be those described in *Current Psychotherapies*.

❖ REFERENCES

Baruth, L. G., & Manning, M. L. (1991). *Multicultural counseling and psychotherapy: A lifespan perspective*. New York: Merrill.

Beck, J. C. (1990). *Confidentiality versus the duty to protect: Foreseeable harm in the practice of psychiatry*. Washington, DC: American Psychiatric Press.

Beitman, B. (1991). Medications during psychotherapy: Case studies of the reciprocal relationship between psychotherapy process and medication use. In B. Beitman & G. L. Klerman (Eds.), *Integrating pharmacotherapy and psychotherapy*. Washington, DC: American Psychiatric Press.

Beitman, B., & Klerman, G. L. (1991). *Integrating pharmacotherapy and psychotherapy.* Washington, DC: American Psychiatric Press.

Braceland, F. J. (1969). Historical perspectives of the ethical practice of psychiatry. *American Journal of Psychiatry, 126,* 230–237.

Brodsky, A. M. (1989). Sex between patient and therapist: Psychology's data and response. In G. O. Gabbard (Ed.), *Sexual exploitation in professional relationships* (pp. 15–25). Washington, DC: American Psychiatric Press.

Cohen, R. J. (1986). The professional liability of behavioral scientists: An overview. In L. Everstine and D. S. Everstine (Eds.), *Psychotherapy and the law* (pp. 251–265). Orlando: Grune & Stratton.

Coleman, P., & Shellow, R. A. (1991). Prescribing privileges for psychologists: Should only "medicine men" control the medicine cabinet? *The Journal of Psychiatry and Law, 18,* 269–318.

Conger, J. (1975). Proceedings of the American Psychological Association for the year 1974: Minutes of the annual meeting of Council of Representatives. *American Psychologist, 30,* 620–651.

Edelwich, J., & Brodsky, A. (1991). *Sexual dilemmas for the helping professional.* New York: Brunner/Mazel.

Ethical principles of psychologists and code of conduct. (1992). *American Psychologist, 47,* 1597–1611.

Falco, K. L. (1991). *Psychotherapy with lesbian clients: Theory into practice.* New York: Brunner/Mazel.

Fox, R. E., Schwelitz, F. D., & Barclay, A. G. (1992). A proposed curriculum for psychopharmacology training for professional psychologists. *Professional Psychology: Research and Practice, 23,* 216–219.

Garnets, L., Hancock, K. A., Cochran, S. D., Goodchilds, J., & Peplau, L. A. (1991). Issues in psychotherapy with lesbians and gay men. *American Psychologist, 46,* 964–972.

Gartrell, N., Herman, J., Olarte, S., Feldstein, M., & Localio, R. (1989). Prevalence of psychiatrist-patient sexual contact. In G. O. Gabbard (Ed.), *Sexual exploitation in professional relationships* (pp. 3–25). Washington, DC: American Psychiatric Press.

Gechtman, L. (1989). Sexual contact between social workers and their clients. In G. O. Gabbard (Ed.), *Sexual exploitation in professional relationships* (pp. 27–38). Washington, DC: American Psychiatric Press.

Gonsiorek, J. (1988). Current and future directions in gay/lesbian affirmative mental health practice. In M. Shernoff & W. Scott (Eds.), *The sourcebook on lesbian/gay affirmative health* (2nd ed., pp. 107–113). Washington, DC: National Lesbian-Gay Health Foundation.

Goodheart, C. D., & Markham, B. (1992). The feminization of psychology: Implications for psychotherapy. *Psychotherapy, 29,* 130–138.

Graduate Medical Education (Appendix II). (1992). *JAMA, 268,* 1170–1176.

Heyman, G. M. (1986). Mandated child abuse reporting and the confidentiality privilege. In L. Everstine and D. S. Everstine (Eds.), *Psychotherapy and the law* (pp. 145–155). Orlando: Grune & Stratton.

Klerman, G. L. (1991). Ideological conflicts in integrating pharmacotherapy and psychotherapy. In B. D. Beitman & G. L. Klerman (Eds.), *Integrating pharmacotherapy and psychotherapy* (pp. 3–20). Washington, DC: American Psychiatric Press.

Knapp, S., & VandeCreek, L. (1987). *Privileged communications in the mental health professions.* New York: Van Nostrand Reinhold.

Lambert, M. J., & Ogles, B. M. (1988). Psychotherapy treatment manuals: Problems and promise. *Journal of Integrative and Eclectic Psychotherapy, 7,* 187–204.

Livermore, J. M., Malmquist, C. P., & Meehl, P. E. (1968). On the justification for civil commitment. *University of Pennsylvania Law Review, 117,* 75–96.

Manderscheid, R. W., & Sonnenschein, M. A. (1992). *Mental health, United States, 1992* (DHHS Publication No. [SMA], 92 1942). Washington, DC: U.S. Government Printing Office.

Meyers, C. J. (1986). The legal perils of psychotherapeutic practice: The farther reaches of the duty to warn. In L. Everstine and D. S. Everstine (Eds.), *Psychotherapy and the law* (pp. 223–247). Orlando: Grune & Stratton.

Moses, A. E., & Hawkins, R. O. (1982). *Counseling lesbian women and gay men: A life issues approach.* St. Louis: Mosby.

Norcross, J. C., Alford, B. A., & DeMichele, J. T. (1992). The future of psychotherapy: Delphi data and concluding observations. *Psychotherapy, 29,* 150–158.

Office of Technology Assessment. (1986). *Nurse practitioners, physician assistants, and certified nurse-midwives: A policy analysis* (Health technology case study No. 37; OTA-HCS-37). Washington, DC: U.S. Government Printing Office.

Pinckney, N. (1994). Contracts for practicing psychologists. In R. J. Corsini (Ed.), *Encyclopedia of Psychology,* Vol. 4, pp. 544–546.

Pope, K. S., & Bouhoutsos, J. C. (1986). *Sexual intimacy between therapists and patients.* New York: Praeger.

Pope, K. S., Keith-Spiegel, P., & Tabachnick, G. G. (1986). Sexual attraction to clients: The human therapist and the (sometimes) inhuman training system. *American Psychologist, 41,* 147–158.

Pope, K. S., Levenson, H., & Schover, L. R. (1979). Sexual intimacy in psychology training: Results and implications of a national survey. *American Psychologist, 34,* 682–689.

Pope, K. S., & Vasquez, M. J. T. (1991). *Ethics in psychotherapy and counseling: A practical guide for psychologists*. San Francisco: Jossey-Bass.

Ramirez, M. (1991). *Psychotherapy and counseling with minorities: A cognitive approach to individual and cultural differences*. New York: Pergamon.

Rosenblatt, A. D., Adler, G., Bemporad, J. R., Feigelson, E. B., Michels, R., Morrison, A. P., & Offenkrantz, W. C. (1992). *Psychotherapy in the future*. Washington, DC: American Psychiatric Association.

Rothblum, E. D., & Cole, E. (Eds.). (1989). Lesbianism: Affirming non-traditional roles. *Women and Therapy*, 8 (Special Issue 1–2).

Rush, A. J., & Hollon, S. D. (1991). Depression. In B. D. Beitman & G. L. Klerman (Eds.), *Integrating pharmacotherapy and psychotherapy*. Washington, DC: American Psychiatric Press.

Siegel, M. (1979). Privacy, ethics, and confidentiality. *Professional Psychology, 10*, 249–258.

Stein, T., & Cohen, C. (Eds.). (1986). *Psychotherapy with lesbians and gay men*. New York: Plenum.

Stromberg, C. D., Haggarty, D. J., Leibenluft, R. F., McMillian, M. H., Mishkin, B., Rubin, B. L., & Trilling, H. R. (1988). *The psychologist's legal handbook*. Washington, DC: National Register of Health Service Providers.

Sue, S., & Zane, N. (1987). The role of culture and cultural techniques in psychotherapy. *American Psychologist, 42*, 37–45.

Torrey, E. F., Erdman, K., Wolfe, S. M., & Flynn, L. M. (1990). *Care of the seriously mentally ill: A rating of state programs* (3rd edition). Washington, DC: Public Citizen Health Research Group.

Yalom, I. D. (1975).*The theory and practice of group therapy* (2nd ed.). New York: Basic.

Ziskin, J., & Faust, D. (1988). *Coping with psychiatric and psychological testimony* (4th ed.). Marina del Rey, CA: Law and Psychology Press.

Glossary

The following abbreviations are used to indicate primary associations: (AD) Adlerian Psychotherapy; (AP) Analytical Psychotherapy; (AS) Asian Therapies; (BE) Bioenergetics: (BT) Behavior Therapy; (CT) Cognitive Therapy; (ET) Existential Therapy; (FT) Family Therapy; (MM) Multimodal Therapy; (PA) Psychoanalysis; (PC) Person Centered Therapy; (PD) Psychodrama; (RB) Rational Emotive Behavior Therapy; (RT) Reality Therapy.

Abreaction (PA). The reliving or recovery of painful, repressed emotional experiences in psychotherapy, accompanied by a discharge of affect or intense feelings. *See also* Catharsis.

Act Fulfillment (PD). Reenacting a traumatic situation correctively, producing more satisfactory results.

Active Imagination (AP). A form of reflection through which people activate and follow their imaginative reveries in a purposive way.

Activity Scheduling (CT, BT). Setting up routine activity in order to offset inertia.

Actualizing Tendency (PC). An innate human predisposition toward growth and fulfilling one's potential.

Agape. Unconditional love for humanity (literally, "love between friends").

Agoraphobia. An excessive fear of open spaces and/or leaving one's own home.

Anal Phase (PA). Freud's second phase of psychosexual development, extending roughly from 18 months to 3 years of age, in which most libidinal pleasure is derived from retaining and expelling feces.

Anima (AP). A feminine archetypal image that serves as a bridge to the unconscious in both men and women, but is most often expressed as the feminine part of a man. *See also* Animus.

Animus (AP). A masculine archetypal image that serves as a bridge to the unconscious in both men and women, but is most often expressed as the masculine part of a woman. *See also* Anima

Anorectic. A person engaging in self-starving behavior.

Antisuggestion (AD). *See* Paradoxical Interventions.

Antithesis (BT). The dual nature of mind and body; processes working in opposite directions.

Aphasia. An organic speech deficit involving difficulty understanding or using language.

Applied Behavior Analysis (BT). A form of behavior therapy, closely tied to Skinner's philosophy of radical behaviorism, that stresses observable behavior rather than private events and uses single-subject experimental design to determine the relationship between behavior and its antecedents and consequences.

Arbitrary Inference (CT). Drawing conclusions without supporting evidence or despite evidence to the contrary.

Archetype (AP). An innate universal pattern or organizing principle similar to an instinct. It has no specific form but can be seen through archetypal images observable in the common motifs present in myths, fairy tales, legends, and dreams across cultures and times. Examples include the Earth Mother, the Wise Old Man, the Hero's Quest, the Shadow, and the Trickster.

Assertion Training (BT). A treatment procedure designed to teach clients to openly and effectively express both positive and negative feelings.

Audience (PD). Any people present during an enactment other than the therapist, protagonist, and auxiliary.

Autoeroticism (PA). Obtaining gratification from self-stimulating a sensual area of the body.

Automatic Thought (CT). Personal notion or idea triggered by particular stimuli that lead to emotional response.

Autonomy. A personality dimension based on needs to be independent, to be self-determining, and to attain one's goals.

Auxiliary (PD). A person who aids the therapist or client in enacting a particular scene.

Awfulizing (RB). Seeing something inconvenient or obnoxious as awful, horrible, or terrible.

Basic Encounter (PC). One member of a group's responding with empathy to another member's being genuine and real.

BASIC I.D. (MM). An acronym that groups together the fundamental concerns of the multimodal therapist: Behaviors, Affective processes, Sensations, Images, Cognitions, Interpersonal Relations, and Drugs (i.e., biological functions).

Basic Mistake (AD). Myth used to organize and shape one's life. Examples include overgeneralizations, a desperate need for security, misperceptions of life's demands, denial of one's worth, and faulty values.

Behavioral Experiment (CT, RB). Testing distorted beliefs or fears scientifically in a real-life situation (e.g., having a shy person initiate a conversation to see what actually happens).

Behavioral Medicine (BT). Applying learning-theory techniques to prevent or treat physical problems (e.g., pain reduction, weight loss).

Behavioral Rehearsal (CT, BT, PD). Practicing an emotionally charged event and one's response to it prior to its actual occurrence.

Belonging (AD, BT, RT). An innate need, drive, and source of human behavior. It leads people to seek relationship and involvement with other human beings.

Boundary (FT). A barrier between parts of a system, as in a family in which rules establish who may participate and in what manner.

Bridging (MM). A procedure in which the therapist purposely tunes in to what the client wants to address, then gently channels the discussion into more productive areas.

Broad-Spectrum Behavior Therapy (MM). The treatment approach, based on learning theory, advocated by Arnold Lazarus prior to development of multimodal therapy.

Catastrophizing (RB, CT). Exaggerating the consequences of an unfortunate event.

Catharsis. The expression and discharge of repressed emotions; sometimes used as a synonym for *abreaction*.

Character Structure (BT). One's habitual way of being or common way of behaving; the five major types are *oral* (dependent, fearful of abandonment), *schizoid* (thought and emotion split off from one another), *narcissistic* (sense of superiority), *masochistic* (submissive, fearful of emotional expression), and *rigid* (unable to give, holding back).

Circular Causality (FT). The feedback model of a network of interacting loops that views any causal event as the effect of a prior cause, as in family interactions.

Classical Conditioning (BT). A form of learning in which existing responses are attached to new stimuli by pairing those stimuli with those that naturally elicit the response; also referred to as *respondent conditioning*.

Closed System (FT). A self-contained system that has impermeable boundaries and thus is resistant to new information and change.

Cognitive Behavior Modification (BT). A recent extension of behavior therapy that treats thoughts and cognition as behaviors amenable to behavioral procedures. Cognitive behavior modification is most closely associated with the work of Aaron Beck, Albert Ellis, and Donald Meichenbaum.

Cognitive Distortion (CT). Pervasive and systematic error in reasoning.

Cognitive Restructuring (AD, BT, RB). An active attempt to alter maladaptive thought patterns and replace them with more adaptive cognitions.

Cognitive Shift (CT). A systematic and biased interpretation of life experiences.

Cognitive Triad (CT). Negative views of the self, the world, and the future that characterize depression.

Cognitive Vulnerability (CT). Individual ways of thinking that predispose one to particular psychological distress.

Collaborative Empiricism (CT). A strategy of seeing the patient as a scientist capable of objective interpretation.

Collective Unconscious (AP). The part of the unconscious that is universal in humans, in contrast to the personal unconscious belonging to individual experiences. The contents of the collective unconscious come into consciousness through archetypal images or basic motifs common to all people. *See also* Personal Unconscious.

Complex (AP). An energy-filled cluster of emotions and ideas circling a specific subject. A complex has an archetypal core but expresses aspects of the personal unconscious. Jung's discovery and explanation of the complex lent validity to Freud's belief in the personal unconscious.

Conditional Assumption (CT). An erroneous "if-then" interpretation of events that leads to an erroneous conclusion (e.g., *"If one person dislikes me, then I* am not likable")

Congruence (PC). Agreement between the feelings and attitudes a therapist is experiencing and his or her professional demeanor; one of Rogers's necessary and sufficient conditions for therapeutic change. *See also* Genuineness.

Conjoint Session (FT). Psychotherapy in which two or more patients are treated together.

Consensus Trance (AS). View of the normal waking state as dreamlike, lacking real awareness.

Constructivism (FT). The view that emphasizes the subjective ways in which each individual creates a perception of reality.

Conviction. Conclusion based on personal experience and perceptions, usually biased because each person's perspective is unique.

Coping Imagery (MM). A technique that pairs relaxation with images of successful self-control in situations that previously elicited anxiety.

Counterconditioning (BT). Replacing a particular behavior by conditioning a new response incompatible with the maladaptive behavior. Counterconditioning is one of the explanations for the effectiveness of systematic desensitization.

Countertransference (PA, AP). The activation of unconscious wishes and fantasies on the part of the therapist toward the patient. It can either be elicited by and indicative of the patient's projections or come from the therapist's tendency to respond to patients as though they were significant others in the life, history, or fantasy of the therapist.

Courage. Willingness to take risks without being sure of the consequences; necessary for effective living.

Cybernetic Epistemology (FT). A framework for conceptualizing and analyzing what is being observed in terms of the flow of information through a system.

Cybernetic System (FT). The study of methods of feedback control within a system.

Decatastrophizing (CT, RB). A "what if" technique designed to explore actual, rather than feared, events and consequences.

Decentering (CT). Moving the supposed focus of attention away from oneself.

Decision (E). The bridge between wishing for something and taking action to see that it happens; often difficult to make because every "yes" choice means saying "no" to another possibility.

Defense Mechanism (PA). Method mobilized by the ego in response to its danger signal of anxiety as protection from inner and outer threat. Examples include repression, denial, and projection.

Dehypnosis (AS). Eliminating the assumption that fantasies are real, e.g., recognizing thoughts as thoughts rather than identifying with them

Dementia Praecox. An obsolete term for schizophrenia.

Denial (PA). A basic defense through which aspects of experienced reality are treated as if they did not exist; often directed against personal existential death anxieties.

Dereflection (AS). Directing one's attention away from the self.

Determinism. The assumption that every mental event is causally tied to earlier psychological experience.

Dialogue (ET). Genuine, equal, and honest communication between two people; the "I-Thou" relationship.

Dichotomous Thinking (CT, RB). Categorizing experiences or people in black-and-white or extreme terms only (e.g., all good vs. all bad), with no middle ground.

Differentiation of Self (FT). Psychological separation by a family member, increasing resistance to being overwhelmed by the emotional reactivity of the family.

Director (PD). The person who manages a psychodrama scene, usually the therapist.

Discriminative Stimulus (BT). A stimulus or set of stimuli signifying that reinforcement will (or will not) occur.

Disengaged Family (FT). A family whose members are psychologically isolated from one another because of overly rigid boundaries between the participants.

Disorientation. Inability to correctly identify time and place (e.g., dates and locations).

Double (PD). Playing someone else's inner self.

Double Bind (FT). Conflict created in a person who receives contradictory messages in an important relationship, but is forbidden to leave or comment on the discrepancy.

Drama Therapy (PD). Use of theater techniques to gain self-awareness or increase self-expression in groups.

Dual-Instinct Theory (PA). The notion that humans operate primarily in terms of pervasive and innate drives toward both love and aggression. *See also* Eros, Thanatos.

Dyadic (FT). Pertaining to a relationship between two persons.

Dynamics (PA). Interactions, usually conflicted, between one's basic drives or id and the ego's defenses. *See also* Psychodynamics.

Dysarthria. Speech deficit involving difficulty with the mechanical production of language.

Dysfunctional. Abnormal; impaired in the ability to cope with stress.

Early Recollection (AD). Salient memory of a single incident from childhood; used as a projective technique by Adlerian therapists.

Eclecticism. The practice of drawing from multiple and diverse sources in formulating client problems and devising treatment plans. Multimodal therapists are technical eclectics (e.g., they employ multiple methods without necessarily endorsing the theoretical positions from which they were derived.)

Ego (PA). The central controlling core of the personality mediating between the *id* (primitive, instinctive needs) and the *superego* (civilized, moralistic elements of the mind).

Eigenwelt (ET). One level of the way each individual relates to the world. *Eigenwelt* literally means "own world" and refers to the way each of us relates to self.

Electra Complex (PA). Erotic attraction of the female child for her father, with accompanying hostility for her mother; the female equivalent of the Oedipus complex. *See also* Oedipus Complex.

Elegant Solution (RB). Solution that helps clients make a profound philosophical change that goes beyond mere symptom removal.

Emotional Cognition (PA). The means by which, both consciously and unconsciously, we perceive and process emotionally charged information and meaning in the service of adaptation.

Emotive Techniques (RB). Therapy techniques that are vigorous, vivid, and dramatic.

Empathic Understanding (PC). The ability to appreciate a person's phenomenological position and to accompany the person's progress in therapy; one of the necessary conditions for therapeutic change.

Empathy (PC). Accurately and deeply feeling someone else's expressed emotions, concerns, or situation.

Enactment (PD). Showing (rather than verbalizing) an important life event.

Encounter (PD). Present dialogue between two persons, or two aspects of the same person, either in reality or with one part played by someone else.

Encounter Group. A small number of people who meet (sometimes only once, sometimes on a weekly basis for a specified time) to truly know and accept themselves and others.

Enmeshed Family (FT). Family in which individual members are overly involved in each other's lives, making individual autonomy impossible.

Environment (RT). The atmosphere of trust existing between client and therapist.

Equanimity (AS). The ability to experience any stimulus without disturbance.

Eros (PA). The life instinct, fueled by libidinal energy and opposed by Thanatos, the death instinct. *See also* Libido, Thanatos.

Ethicality (AS). Internally based emphasis on moral or principled behavior.

Existential Isolation (ET). Fundamental and inevitable separation of each individual from others and the world; can be reduced but not completely eliminated.

Existential Neurosis (ET). Feelings of emptiness, worthlessness, despair, and anxiety resulting from inauthenticity, abdication of responsibility, failure to make choices, and a lack of direction or purpose in life.

Existentialism (ET). A philosophical movement that stresses the importance of actual existence, one's responsibility for and determination of one's own psychological existence, authenticity in human relations, the primacy of the here and now, and the use of experience in the search for knowledge.

Experiential Family Therapist (FT). A therapist who reveals himself or herself as a real person and use that self in interacting with families.

Experiencing (PC). Sensing or awareness of self and the world, whether narrowly and rigidly or openly and flexibly. Experience is unique for each person.

Extinction (BT). In classical conditioning, the result of repeated presentation of a conditioned stimulus without the unconditioned stimulus and the resulting gradual diminution of the conditioned response. In operant conditioning, extinction (no response) occurs when reinforcement is withheld following performance of a previously reinforced response.

Facilitator. An individual who aids a group in going the direction they choose and accomplishing their chosen goals without doing harm to any member.

Factor of Enlightenment (AS). Seven mental qualities important for psychological well-being: mindfulness, effort, investigation, rapture, concentration, calm, and equanimity.

Family Constellation (AD). The number, sequencing, and characteristics of the members of a family. The family constellation is an important determinant of life style.

Family Sculpting (FT). A nonverbal technique to be used by individual family members for physically arranging other family members in space to represent the arranger's symbolic view of family relationships.

Feedback. The process by which a system makes adjustments in itself; can be positive (restoring a previous balance) or negative (destroying or preventing balance).

First-Order Change (FT). Change within a system that does not alter the basic organization of the system itself.

Formative Tendency (PC). An overall inclination toward greater order, complexity, and interrelatedness common to all nature, including human beings.

Free Association (PA). A basic technique of psychoanalysis in which analysands are asked to report, without structure or censure, whatever thoughts come to mind.

Freedom and Independence (RT). An innate need, drive and source of human behavior. It leads people to make choices and to function on their own without being excessively reliant on the approval of others.

Fun and Enjoyment (RT). An innate human need, drive, and source of behavior. It leads people to want to learn, to laugh, to relax, and to see humor.

Functionally Specific State (AS). State of consciousness in which particular abilities such as introspection are increased, while others are reduced.

Fusion (ET, FT). In existential therapy, the giving up of oneself to become part of another person or a group; a particular attempt to reduce one's sense of isolation. In family therapy, a blurring of boundaries between family members with the resultant loss of a separate sense of self by each member.

Future Projection (PD). Demonstration of what one sees going on in life at some specified time in the future.

Gemeinschaftsgefühl (AD). A combination of concern for others and appreciation of one's role in a larger social order; usually translated as "social interest."

Generalization (BT). The occurrence of behavior in situations that resemble but are different from the stimulus environment in which the behavior was learned.

Genital Stage (PA). The final stage in psychosexual development, also termed the oedipal phase, in which heterosexual relations are achieved. Its roots are formed at ages 5 to 6, and it is said to be the basis for the mature personality.

Genogram (FT). A schematic diagram of a family's relationship system, used to trace recurring family patterns over generations.

Genuineness (PC). The characteristic of being real and true to oneself; lack of pretense, social facade, or refusal to allow certain aspects of one's self into awareness.

Graded-Task Assignment (CT, BT). Starting with a simple activity and increasing the level of complexity or difficulty in a step-by-step fashion.

Grounding (BE). The use of many body positions, especially standing, to help patients get a better sense of their basic posture and support.

Hidden Agenda. The actual goal of an interaction between people (as in a game), which is different from what superficially appears to be the goal.

Higher State (AS). State of consciousness containing normal mental capacities plus additional, heightened ones.

Holism (AD). Studying individuals in their entirety, including how they proceed through life, rather than trying to separate out certain aspects or parts, such as studying the mind apart from the body.

Homeostasis. A balanced and steady state of equilibrium.

Homework (RB, BT). Specific activities to be done between therapy sessions.

Hot Cognition (CT). Powerful and highly meaningful idea that produces strong emotional reactions.

Hysteria. An early term for conversion reaction, a disorder in which psychological disturbance takes a physical form (e.g., paralysis in the absence of organic disturbance). Many of Freud's theories grew out of his experience in treating hysterical patients.

Id (PA). The reservoir of the biological, instinctual drives with innate and developmental components. (*See also* Ego, Superego.)

Identification (PA). A mental mechanism, used unconsciously in normal interactions and as a psychic defense, through which one person absorbs and takes on the traits, values, and defenses of another person.

Identified Patient (FT). The person who seeks treatment or for whom treatment is sought.

Imagery Reactor (MM). An individual who responds to the environment predominately in terms of images, usually auditory or visual.

Individual Psychology (AD). An approach to understanding human behavior that sees each person as a unique, whole entity who is constantly becoming rather than being, whose development can only be understood within a social context.

Individuation (AP). The process by which an individual becomes an indivisible and integrated whole person responsibly embodying his or her individual strengths and limitations.

Inferiority Complex (AD). An exaggeration of feelings of inadequacy and insecurity resulting in defensiveness and neurotic behavior. It is usually, but not always, abnormal.

Inferiority Feeling (AD). Seeing oneself as inadequate or incompetent in comparison with others, with one's ideal self, or with personal values; considered universal and normal. *Contrast with* Inferiority Complex.

Intensive Group (PC). A small number of people who come together for a brief but condensed period (e.g., a weekend) to engage in special interpersonal experiences that are designed to expand awareness of self and others.

Interlocking Pathologies (FT). Multiple forms of dysfunction within a family that are interdependent in the way they are expressed and maintained.

Interlocking Triangles (FT). Basic units of family relationships consisting of a series of three-person sets of interactions (e.g., father-mother-child; grandparent-parent-child).

Internal Frame of Reference (PC). A view or perception of both the world and self as seen by the individual, as distinguished from the viewpoint of an observer, psychotherapist, or other person.

Intrapsychic. Within the mind or psyche of the individual.

Introjection (PA). An unconscious process of identifying with other persons, real or imagined, by incorporating these attributes in oneself.

Irrational Belief (REBT). Unreasonable conviction that produces emotional upset (for example, insisting that the world should or must be different from what it actually is).

Latency Period (PA). A relatively inactive period of psychosexual development said to run between ages 6 and 11.

Leaning Tower of Pisa Approach (FT). A variation of paradoxical intention in which a therapist intentionally makes a problem worse until it falls of its own weight and is thereby resolved.

Libido (PA). The basic driving force of personality in Freud's system. It includes sexual energy but is not restricted to it.

Life-style (AD). One's characteristic way of living and pursuing long-term goals.

Life Tasks (AD). The basic challenges and obligations of life: society, work, and sex. Additional tasks of spiritual growth and self-identity are included by Rudolf Dreikurs and Harold Mosak.

Linear Causality (FT). The view that one event causes the other, not vice versa.

Locus-of-Evaluation (PC). The place of a judgment's origin, its source; whether the appraisal of an experience comes more from within the individual (internal) or from outside sources (external).

Logotherapy (ET). A therapeutic approach developed by Viktor Frankl emphasizing value and meaning as prerequisites for mental health and personal growth.

Lucid Dreaming (AS). A sleep state in which people know they are dreaming.

Magnification (CT). Exaggerating something's significance.

Marital Schism (FT). A disturbed family arrangement characterized by disharmony, undermining of the spouse, and frequent threats of divorce. *See also* Marital Skew.

Marital Skew. A disturbed family arrangement in which one person dominates to an extreme degree, and in which the marriage is maintained through the distortion of reality. *See also* Marital Schism.

Maya (AS). An illusory and encompassing distortion of one's perception and experience that is not recognized as such.

Mediational Stimulus-Response Model (BT). A behavioral model that posits internal events, such as thoughts and images, as links between perceiving a stimulus and making a response.

Meditation (AS). Practices designed to train attention and bring various mental processes under greater voluntary control.

Mindfulness (AS). Clear objective awareness of an ongoing experience.

Minimization (CT). Making an event far less important than it actually is.

Mirror (PD). A person who imitates a client's behavior and demeanor so that the client can more clearly see him- or herself in action.

Mitwelt (ET). The way in which each individual relates to the world, socially and through being with others; the age we live in, our age, our own times, the present generation, our contemporaries.

Modality Profile (MM). A specific list of problems and proposed treatments across the client's BASIC I.D.

Monadic (FT). Based on the characteristics or traits of a single person.

Monodrama (PD). One client's playing both parts in a scene by alternating between them.

Morita (AS). A Japanese therapy for treating anxiety by redirecting one's attention away from the self, including absolute rest and avoidance of distractions.

Motility (BE). Movement or activity; an essential principle in working with the body. Any limitation of movement both results from and causes emotional difficulties.

Multigenerational Transmission Process (FT). The passing on of psychological problems over generations as a result of immature persons marrying others with similar low levels of separateness from their families.

Multiple Parts of Self (PD). Physically acting out internal conflicts.

Multiple Psychotherapy (AD). A technique in which several therapists simultaneously treat a single patient.

Musturbation (RB). A term coined by Albert Ellis to characterize the behavior of clients who are absolutistic and inflexible in their thinking, maintaining that they must not fail, must be exceptional, must be successful, and so on.

Mystification (FT). The deliberate distortion of another person's experience by misinterpreting or mislabeling it.

Naikan (AS). Japanese therapy using intensive reflection on past relationships to increase social and interpersonal contributions.

Narcissism (PA). Self-absorption, self-concern, and self-love arising from psychic energy directed at the self; the term currently is used to include tension regulation, self-image, and self-esteem.

Negative Feedback (FT). The flow of output information back into a system to correct too great a deviation from normal and return the system to its steady state.

Negative Reinforcement (BT). Any behavior that increases the probability of a response by terminating or withdrawing an unpleasant stimulus. Negative reinforcement increases the likelihood of future occurrence of the behavior it follows.

Neurosis (PA). A term first used by Freud to include all but the most severe psychological syndromes; currently narrowly defined as an emotional disorder in which psychic functioning is relatively intact and contact with reality is sound.

Neurotic Anxiety (ET). A state of fear or apprehension out of proportion to an actual threat. Neurotic anxiety is destructive or paralyzing and cannot be used constructively. *Compare with* Normal Anxiety.

Normal Anxiety (ET). A sense of apprehension appropriate to a given threatening situation, which can be faced, dealt with, and used creatively. *Compare with* Neurotic Anxiety.

Object Relations Theory (PA, FT). The view that the basic human motive is the search for satisfying object (person) relationships.

Oedipus Complex (PA). Erotic attraction of the male child for his mother, accompanied by hostility toward the father. *See also* Electra Complex.

Ontological (ET). Concerned with the science of being or existence.

Open System (FT). A system with relatively permeable boundaries permitting the exchange of information with its environment.

Operant Conditioning (BT). A type of learning in which responses are modified by their consequences. Reinforcement increases the likelihood of future occurrences of the reinforced response; punishment and extinction decrease the likelihood of future occurrences of the responses they follow.

Oral Phase (PA). The earliest phase of psychosexual development, extending from birth to approximately 18 months, in which most libidinal gratification occurs through biting, sucking, and oral contact.

Organ Inferiority (AD). Perceived or actual congenital defects in organ systems believed by Alfred Adler to result in compensatory striving to overcome these deficits.

Organismic Valuing Process (PC). Making individual judgments or assessments of the desirability of an action or choice on the basis of one's own sensory evidence and life experience.

Orgone Energy (BE). A physical force that powers all human functions, including the psychological, proposed by Wilhelm Reich.

Overgeneralization (CT, RB). Constructing a general rule from isolated incidents and applying it too broadly.

Panacea. A remedy for all diseases and difficulties. A cure-all.

Paradigm (FT). A set of assumptions limiting an area to be investigated scientifically and specifying the methods used to collect and interpret the forthcoming data.

Paradoxical Intervention (FT). A therapeutic technique whereby the patient is directed to continue the symptomatic behavior; to conform is to admit voluntary control over the symptom; to rebel is to give up the symptom.

Persona (AP). A mask or way of appearing that is appropriate to a specific role or social setting. It both shields an individual and reveals suitable aspects of the personality, but is often at variance with the personality as a whole.

Personal Unconscious (AP). An individual unconscious layer of the personality containing undeveloped parts of the personality, repressed ideas, experiences, and emotions, and subliminal perceptions. *See also* Collective Unconscious.

Personalization (CT). Taking personal responsibility for negative events without supporting evidence of personal involvement.

Phallic Phase (PA). A psychosexual phase in boys of ages 3 to 5 in which penile experiences and fantasies of thrusting and exhibiting are predominant. The comparable phase in girls is termed the vaginal phase. *See also* Vaginal Phase.

Phenomenology (AD, ET). A method of exploration that primarily uses human experience as the source of data and attempts to include all human experience without bias (external observation, emotions, thoughts, and so on). Subjects are taught to distinguish between current experience and the biases brought to the situation. Phenomenology is the basic method of most existentialists.

Placebo. In medicine, placebos are inert substances given to patients in place of bona fide medications. In psychotherapy, placebos are most often sham treatment used in research to control for the nonspecific effects of attention.

Pleasure Principle (PA). The basic human tendency to avoid pain and seek pleasure, especially salient in the first years of life. *Contrast with* Reality Principle.

Positive Feedback (FT). The flow of output information back into the system in order to amplify deviation from a steady state, thus leading to instability and change.

Positive Reinforcement (BT). Any stimulus that follows a behavior and increases the likelihood of the occurrence of the behavior that it follows.

Power (RT). An innate need, drive and source of human behavior. It leads people to achieve and to accomplish tasks. Self-worth, self-esteem, and recognition are related to power.

Projection (PA, AP). Attributing to others unacceptable personal thoughts, feelings, or behaviors.

Projective Identification (PA). An interactional form of projection, used both normally and as a defense, through which one person places into another person his or her inner state and defenses.

Pseudohostility (FT). Superficial bickering that allows one to avoid dealing with deeper, more genuine, and more intimate feelings.

Pseudomutuality (FT). A facade of family harmony that gives the appearance of an open and satisfying relationship that does not truly exist.

Psychodynamics (PA). A term similar to dynamics, which refers to mental interactions and conflict, usually formulated in terms of ego, id, and superego. *See also* Dynamics.

Psychological Masquerade. Apparent psychological symptoms actually caused by physical or organic conditions.

Punishment (BT). An aversive event likely to terminate any behavior that it follows.

Rapture (AS). Delight in the awareness of experience.

Reality. An individual's private world, but more generally, a group of perceptions or "facts" with substantial consensus about their meaning.

Reality Principle (PA). The guiding principle of the ego, which permits postponement of gratification to meet the demands of the environment or secure greater pleasure at a later time. *Contrast with* Pleasure Principle.

Reattribution (CT). Assigning alternative causes to events; reinterpreting one's symptoms.

Redundancy Principle (FT). Repetitive behavioral sequences between participants, as within a family.

Reframing (FT). Relabeling behavior by putting it into a new, more positive perspective.

Regression (PA). Variously defined as an active or passive slipping back to more immature levels of defense or functioning, or seeking gratification from earlier phases of development.

Reinforcement (BT). The presentation of a reward or the removal of an aversive stimulus following a response. Reinforcement always increases the future probability of the reinforced response.

Repression (PA). A major defense mechanism in which distressing thoughts are barred from conscious expression.

Resistance (PA). Any obstacle, pathological or nonpathological, to the progress of an analysis or therapy, usually involving a modification of a ground rule of treatment and based on unconscious sources within both patient and analyst (i.e., interactionally determined).

Respiration (BE). Breathing; an essential principle in working with the body. Any restriction in breathing both results from and causes anxiety.

Respondent Conditioning (BT). *See* Classical Conditioning.

Role Distance (PD). An increase in objectivity about an event that comes from playing a part connected to or associated with it.

Role Reversal (PD). Playing the part of a person important in one's life in order to get a better perspective of that person.

Role Training (PD). Rehearsing an anticipated situation so that the response in real life will be appropriate.

Role-playing (PD). Acting the part of oneself or someone else under therapeutic guidance.

Samadhi (AS). Yogic state of consciousness marked by deep calm and concentration.

Scapegoating (FT). Casting a person in a role that unfairly exposes him or her to criticism, blame, or punishment.

Schema (CT). Strategy or way of thinking comprising core beliefs and basic assumptions about how the world operates.

Second-Order BASIC I.D. (MM). Focusing on a particular aspect of the BASIC I.D. to get more detailed information; useful for diagnosis and for breaking impasses in therapy.

Second-Order Change (FT). Fundamental change in a system's organization and function.

Selection Abstraction (CT). Basing a conclusion on a detail taken out of context and ignoring other information.

Self-Actualization. A basic human drive toward growth, completeness, and fulfillment.

Self-Concept. One's own definition of who one is, including one's attributes, emotions, abilities, character, faults, and so on.

Self-Instructional Training (BT). A technique, described most completely by Donald Meichenbaum, for replacing self-defeating thoughts with self-enhancing cognitions.

Self-Regard (PC). That aspect of the self-concept which develops from the esteem or respect accorded oneself.

Sensate Focus (BT). A series of exercises used in sex therapy and designed to reintroduce clients to receiving and giving sensual pleasure.

Sensory-Reactor (MM). An individual who interacts with the world primarily in terms of the five basic senses.

Shadow (AP). Unconscious, unaccepted, or unrecognized parts of the personality that are most often, but not always, negative. The shadow is that part of ourselves to which we are not sufficiently well related.

Social Interest (AD). The feeling of being part of a social whole; the need and willingness to contribute to the general social good. *See also* Gemeinschaftsgefühl.

Social Learning Theory (BT). A system that combines operant and classical conditioning with cognitive mediational processes (e.g., vicarious learning and symbolic activity) to account for the development, maintenance, and modification of behavior.

Sociometry (PD). A method in which groups give feedback about their interpersonal preferences (e.g., attraction or repulsion).

Sociotrophy (CT). A personality dimension characterized by dependency on interpersonal relationships and needs for closeness and nurturance.

Socratic Dialogue. A series of questions designed to arrive at logical answers to and conclusions about a hypothesis.

Splitting (PA). A primitive defense through which a person is divided into all-good and all-bad individuals, making it impossible to have a full and balanced picture of that person.

Stimulus Control (BT). Arranging the environment in such a way that a given response is either more likely or less likely to occur (e.g., buying only one pack of cigarettes per day in order to decrease the likelihood of smoking).

Strategic Intervention Therapy (FT). An approach to family therapy employing specific strategies, plans, and tactics to force changes in behavior.

Structural Profiles (MM). A quantitative assessment of the relative involvement of each of the elements of the BASIC I.D.

Structural Theory or Hypotheses (PA). Freud's second model of the mind. The model postulates three agencies of the mind—ego, superego, and id—each with conscious and unconscious components. *See also* Id, Ego, and Superego.

Structuralism (FT). An approach to family therapy, associated with Salvador Minuchin, that emphasizes the importance of the nuclear family and seeks to change pathological alliances and splits in the family.

Structuralist (FT). A therapist who emphasizes changing or realigning a family's organizational structure to improve its transactional patterns.

Stuck-Togetherness (FT). A situation observed in schizophrenic families in which roles and boundaries are blurred and no family member has an identity distinct from the family.

Subjective Reasoning (CT). Believing that feelings are the same as, or equivalent to, facts.

Subsystem (FT). An organized component within an overall system, such as a family.

Superego (PA). A structure of the mind, developed from innate tendencies and early parental interactions and identifications, that embraces moral and other standards and regulates psychic tensions, self-image, self-esteem, and drive-discharge. (*See also* Ego, Id.)

Surplus reality (PD). Psychological experiences involving other than physical reality (e.g., spiritual events, relationships with deceased people that still have an influence on individuals or groups.

Survival. An innate need, drive, and source of human behavior. It leads human beings to seek health, nutrition, and protection from physical danger.

Symbiosis (FT). A relationship in which two people, often a mother and her child, become so intertwined that it is impossible to find a boundary between them.

Symbolization (PC). A process of allowing a life event or experience into one's consciousness or awareness and interpreting it in terms of the self-concept; it may be straightforward, distorted, or prohibited altogether.

Synthesis. Making a whole from elements or parts; constructing the overall meaning of a situation from many different aspects of it.

System. A complete unit made up of interconnected and interdependent parts operating in a stable way over time.

Systematic Desensitization (BT). A step-by-step procedure for replacing anxiety with relaxation while gradually increasing exposure to an anxiety-producing situation or object.

Thanatos (PA). An instinct toward death and self-destruction, posited by Freud to oppose and balance Eros, the life instinct.

Third-Party Payer. Financial intermediary that controls the flow of money from clients to therapists. In therapy, third-party payers are usually insurance companies or government agencies (e.g., the Health Care Financing Administration).

Token Economy (BT). A program that provides people with short-term reinforcement for specific behaviors by allotting tokens (poker chips or points) that are accumulated and later exchanged for privileges or desired objects.

Topographic Theory (PA). Freud's first model of the mind in which access to awareness of contents and functions was the defining criterion. The model had interactional elements, but was eventually replaced by Freud's structural model. *See also* Unconscious Processes.

Tracking (MM). A careful examination of the firing order of the BASIC I.D. modalities to facilitate more effective sequencing of the treatment procedures.

Trait Theory (BT). The belief in stable and enduring personality characteristics.

Transference (PA, AP). The therapy situation in which the patient responds to the therapist as though he or she were a significant figure in the patient's past, usually a parent. *See also* Countertransference.

Triadic (FT). Pertaining to a relationship involving the interaction of three or more persons.

Trust (PC). Basic faith in oneself and others as being growth-directed and positively oriented.

Umwelt (ET). A way of relating to the world through its biological and physical aspects; one's relationship with nature and the surrounding world.

Unconditional Positive Regard (PC). A nonpossessive caring and acceptance of the client as a human being, irrespective of the therapist's own values. One of Rogers's necessary and sufficient conditions for therapeutic change.

Unconscious (PA, AP). A division of the psyche; the repository of psychological material of which the individual is unaware.

Unity (BE). Mind and body functioning as a whole, so that an imbalance in one area affects all other areas as well (e.g., physical illness affecting psychological well-being or anxiety affecting the body).

Vaginal Phase (PA). The phase in girls that corresponds to boys' phallic phase, ages 3 to 5, during which vaginal sensations and incorporative imagery predominate.

Vicarious Learning (BT). Learning through observation and imitation. Synonym: modeling.

Voluntary Simplicity (AS). Self-motivated choice to live more simply and to deemphasize material goods.

Warmth (PC). Positive and real feelings of acceptance toward another.

WDEP (RT). The formulation of reality therapy. Each letter stands for various procedures: W=Wants, D=Doing (behavior), E=Evaluation, and P=Planning.

Will to Power (AD). Individual striving for superiority and dominance in order to overcome feelings of inadequacy and inferiority.

Yoga (AS). Disciplines dealing with ethics, lifestyle, body postures, breath control, intellectual study, and meditation.

Zeitgeist. The spirit of the times; the prevailing cultural climate.

Name Index

Abraham, K., 25
Abrams, J. L., 258
Ackerman, N., 363
Adler, A., 12, 13, 17, 51, 52, 53, 54, 55,
    57, 58, 59, 60, 61, 62 63, 64,
    65, 66, 68, 69, 71, 73, 74, 75,
    76, 78, 81, 83, 88, 89, 95,
    96–97, 98, 101, 102, 131, 166,
    167, 170, 173, 174, 233, 360,
    361, 392, 403, 421
Adler, G., 420, 430
Adler, K., 81
Aigen, B. P., 331
Akiva, Rabbi, 53
Alexander, C., 389, 393
Alexander, F., 29, 66, 73, 87, 88, 166,
    167, 233, 388
Alford, B. A., 225, 429
Allport, G., 131, 173
Allred, G. H., 76
Amies, P. L., 234
Anchor, K. N., 331, 353
Angel, E., 263, 265, 266, 267, 271, 278,
    288, 291
Angers, W. P., 76
Angyal, A., 140
Ansbacher, H. L., 17, 52, 53, 55–56, 57,
    59, 64, 67, 77, 81, 89, 130, 131
Ansbacher, R. R., 17, 52, 55–56, 67, 81,
    89
Aquinas, T., 270
Ard, B. N., 195

Arieti, S., 277
Aristotle, 58, 294
Arkowitz, H., 258
Arlow, J. A., 15–47, 48
Arnkoff, D., 234
Assagioli, R., 402
Augustine, 270
Aurelius, M., 303
Axline, V. M., 152
Ayllon, T., 215, 220
Azrin, N. H., 215

Bach, G. R., 2
Bachofen, J., 99
Bacon, C. L., 388
Baker, L., 359, 374, 378
Baldwin, M., 384
Bally, G., 271
Bandura, A., 198, 203, 207, 214, 220,
    232, 234, 296, 323, 333, 365
Barclay, A. G., 429
Barlow, D. H., 217, 226
Barrett-Lennard, G. T., 135, 152
Baruthm L. G., 427
Bateson, G., 357–58, 362
Beach, F. A., 87
Beach, S. R. H., 217
Beck, A. T., 167, 175, 186, 199, 211,
    212, 217, 229–59, 327, 328, 402
Beck, J. C., 424, 426
Becker, E., 278
Beckham, E., 235

Subject Index